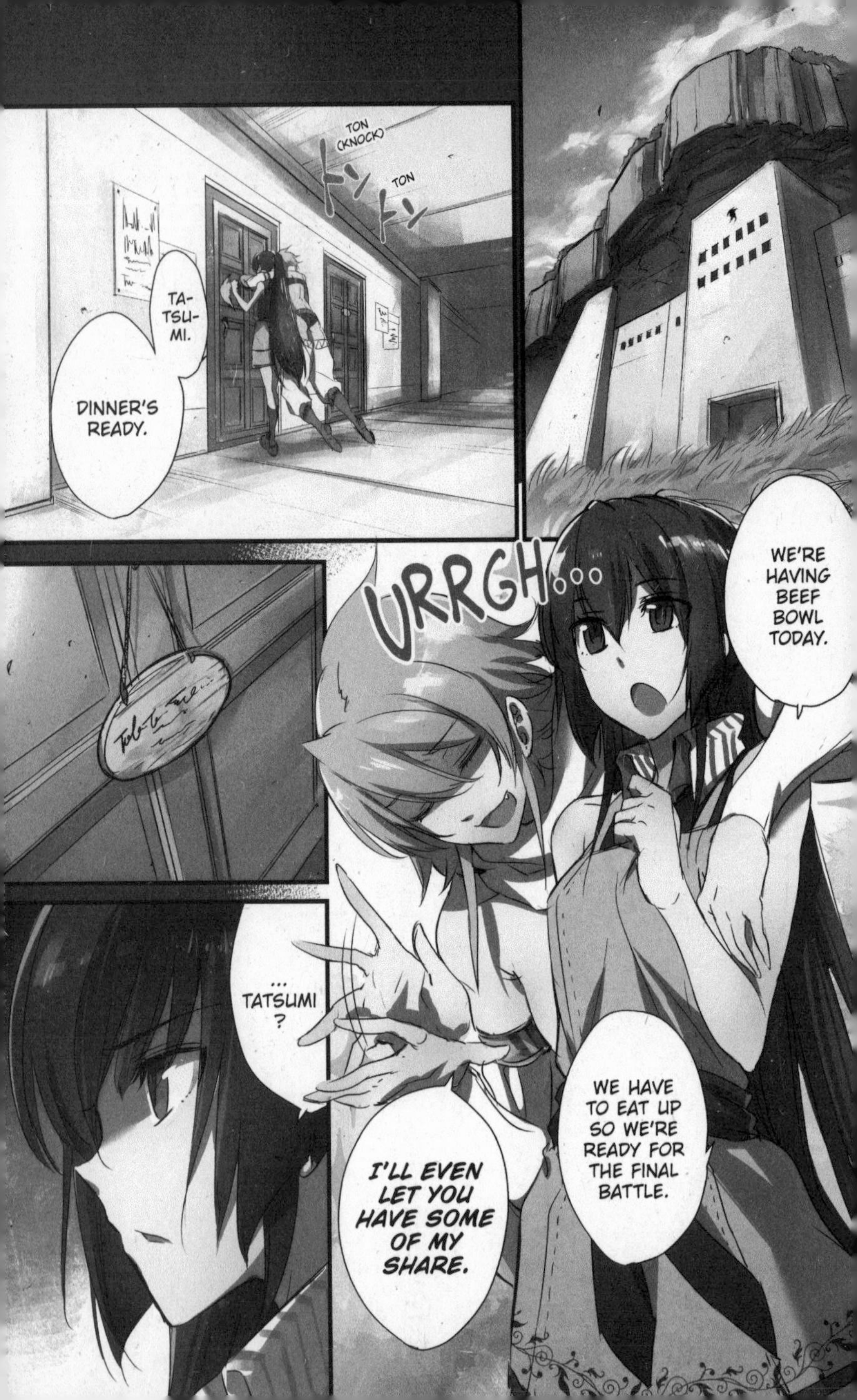

トン
TON (KNOCK)
トン
TON
TA-TSUMI.
DINNER'S READY.
WE'RE HAVING BEEF BOWL TODAY.
URRGH...
WE HAVE TO EAT UP SO WE'RE READY FOR THE FINAL BATTLE.
I'LL EVEN LET YOU HAVE SOME OF MY SHARE.
...TATSUMI?

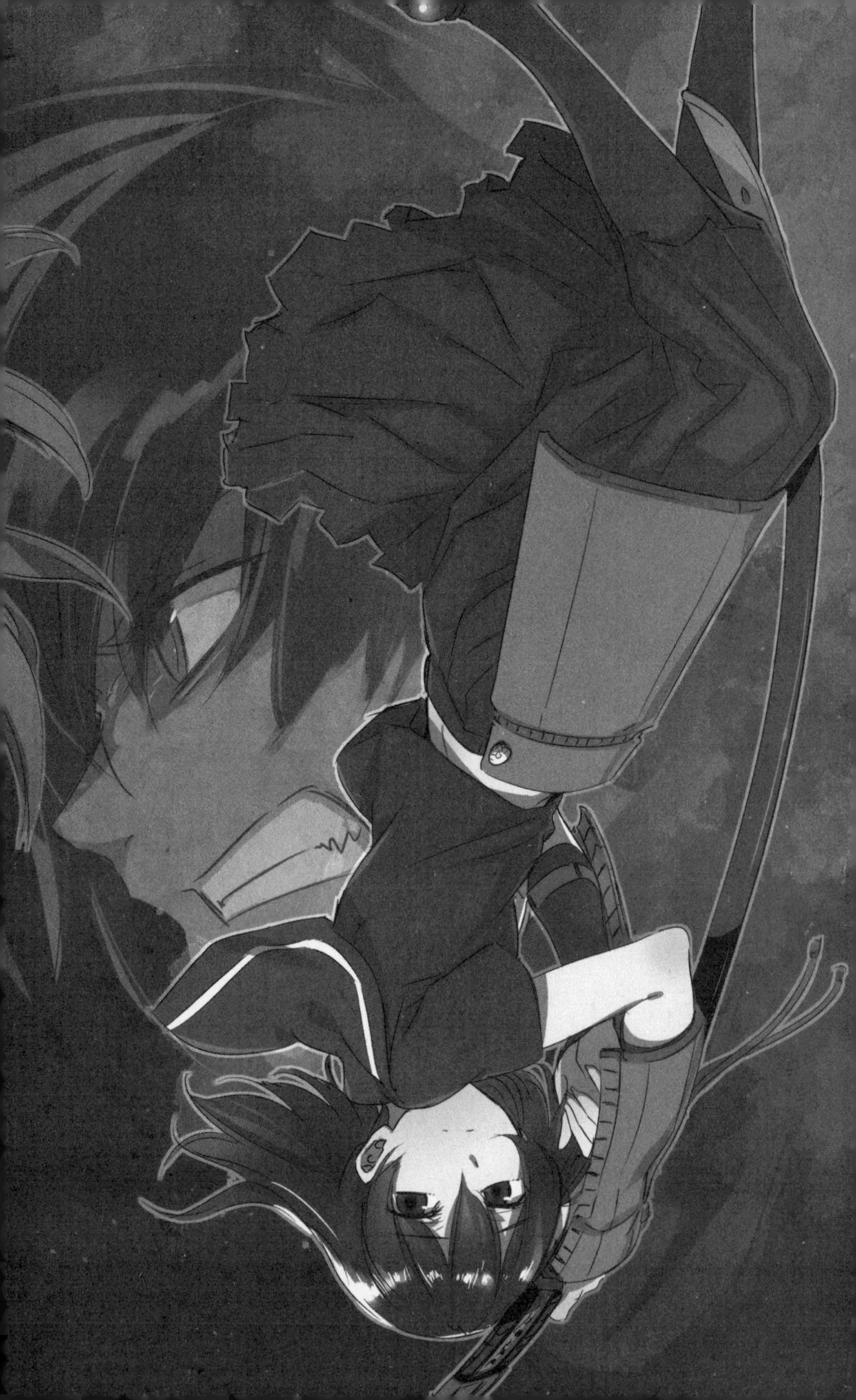

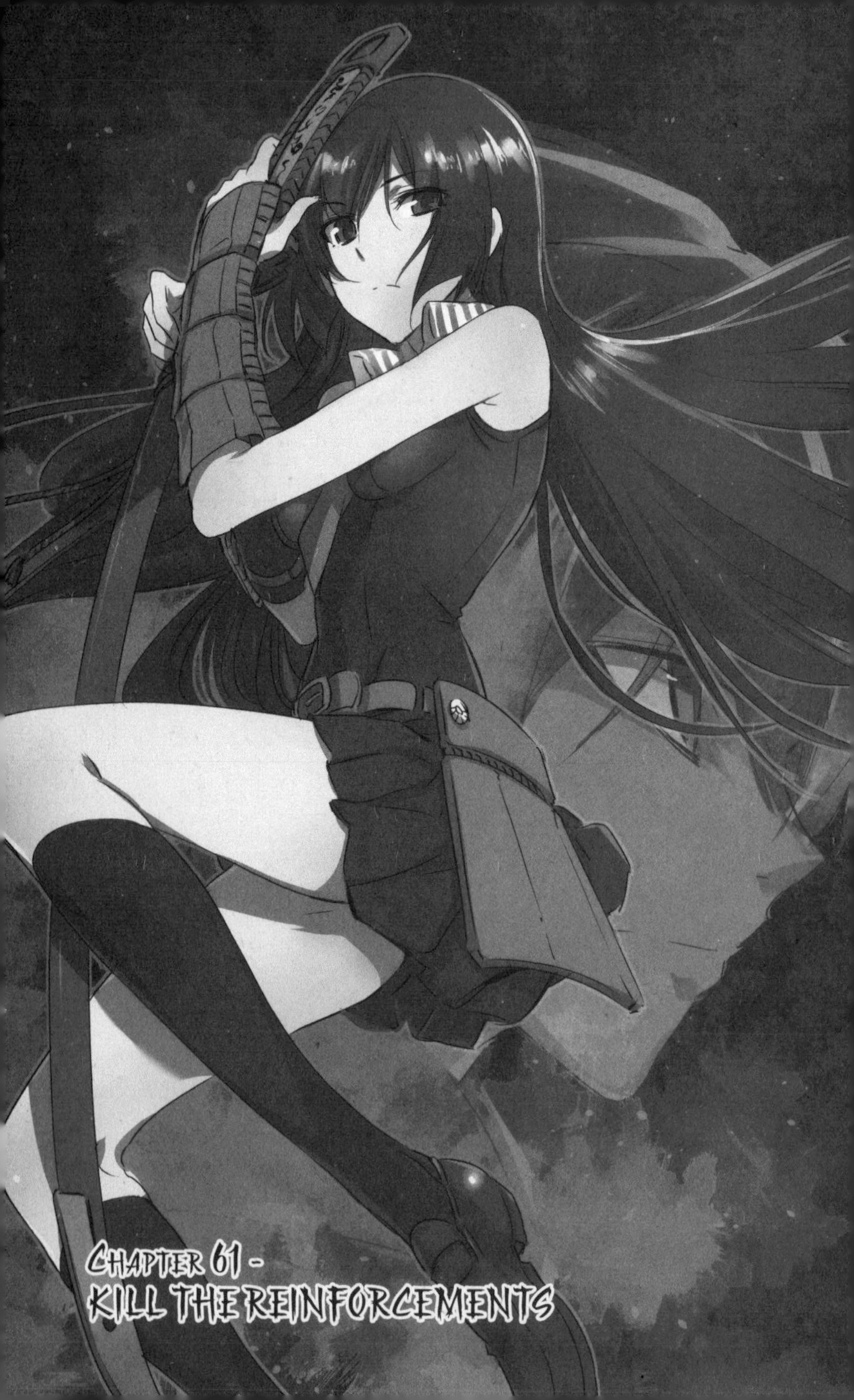
Chapter 61 -
Kill the Reinforcements

Akame ga KILL!

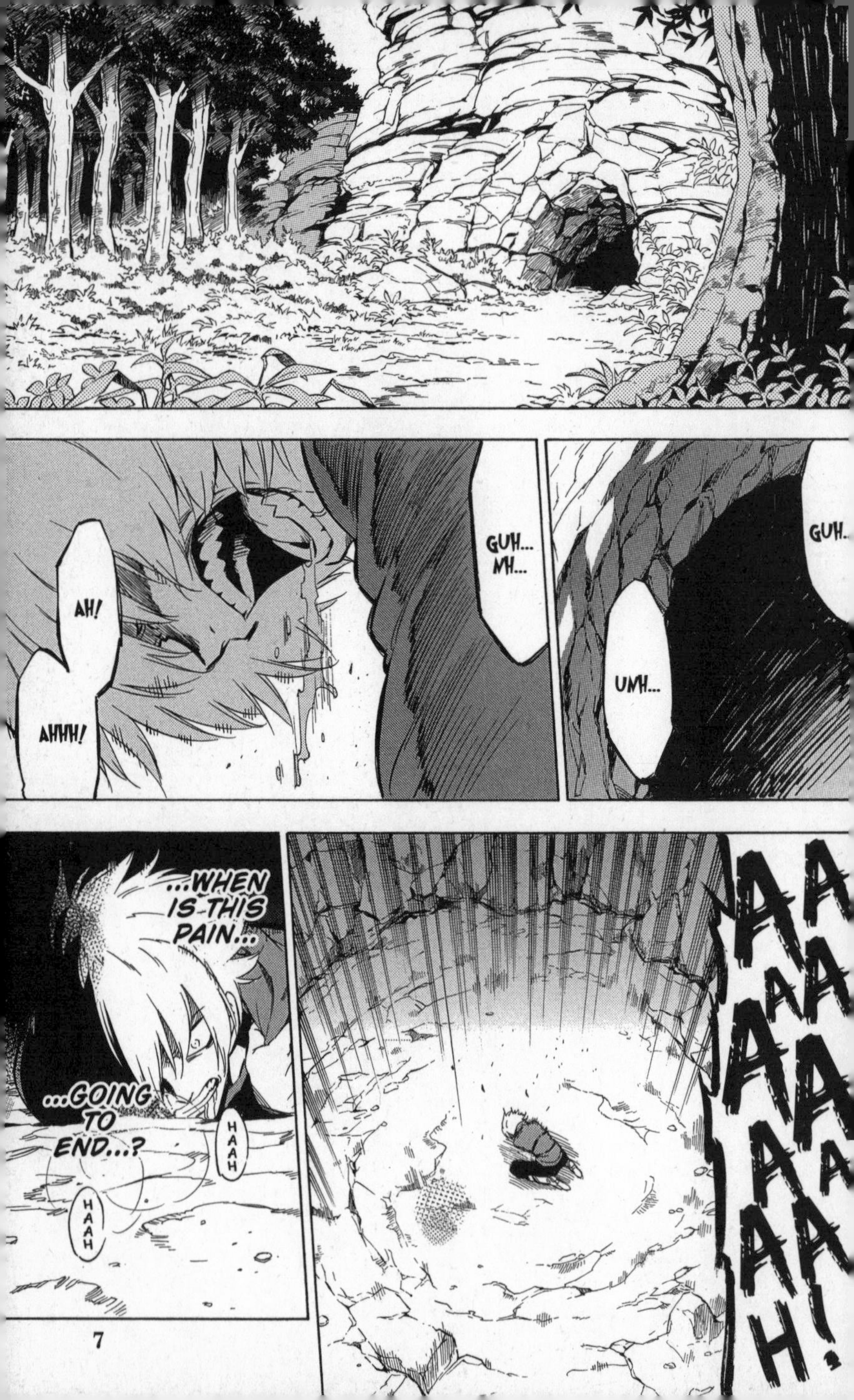
GUH...
UMH...
GUH... MH...
AH!
AHHH!
AAAAAAAAAAAAH!
...WHEN IS THIS PAIN...
...GOING TO END...?
HAAH
HAAH

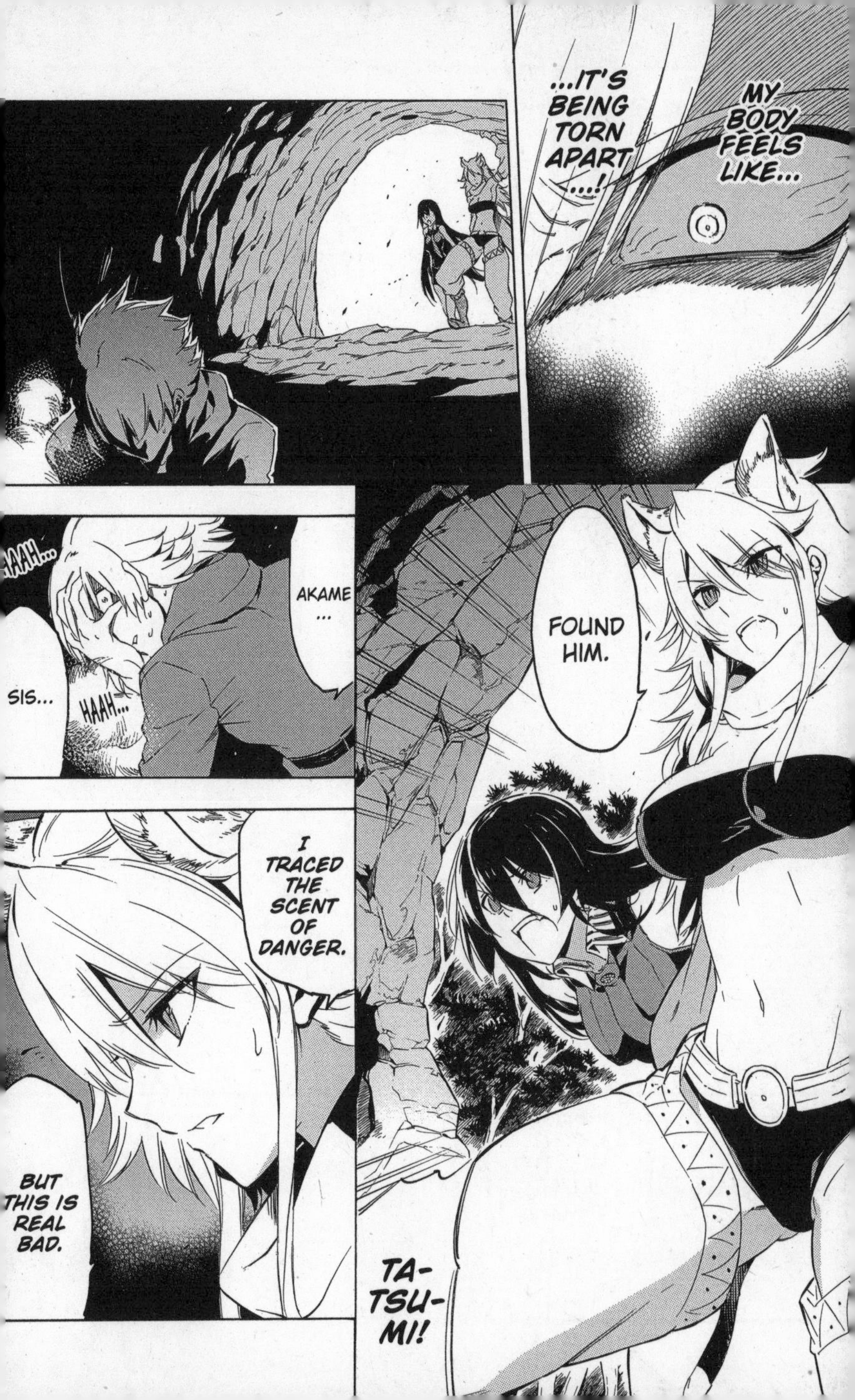
MY BODY FEELS LIKE...
...IT'S BEING TORN APART...!
FOUND HIM.
TA-TSU-MI!
AKAME...
HAAH...
SIS...
HAAH...
I TRACED THE SCENT OF DANGER.
BUT THIS IS REAL BAD.

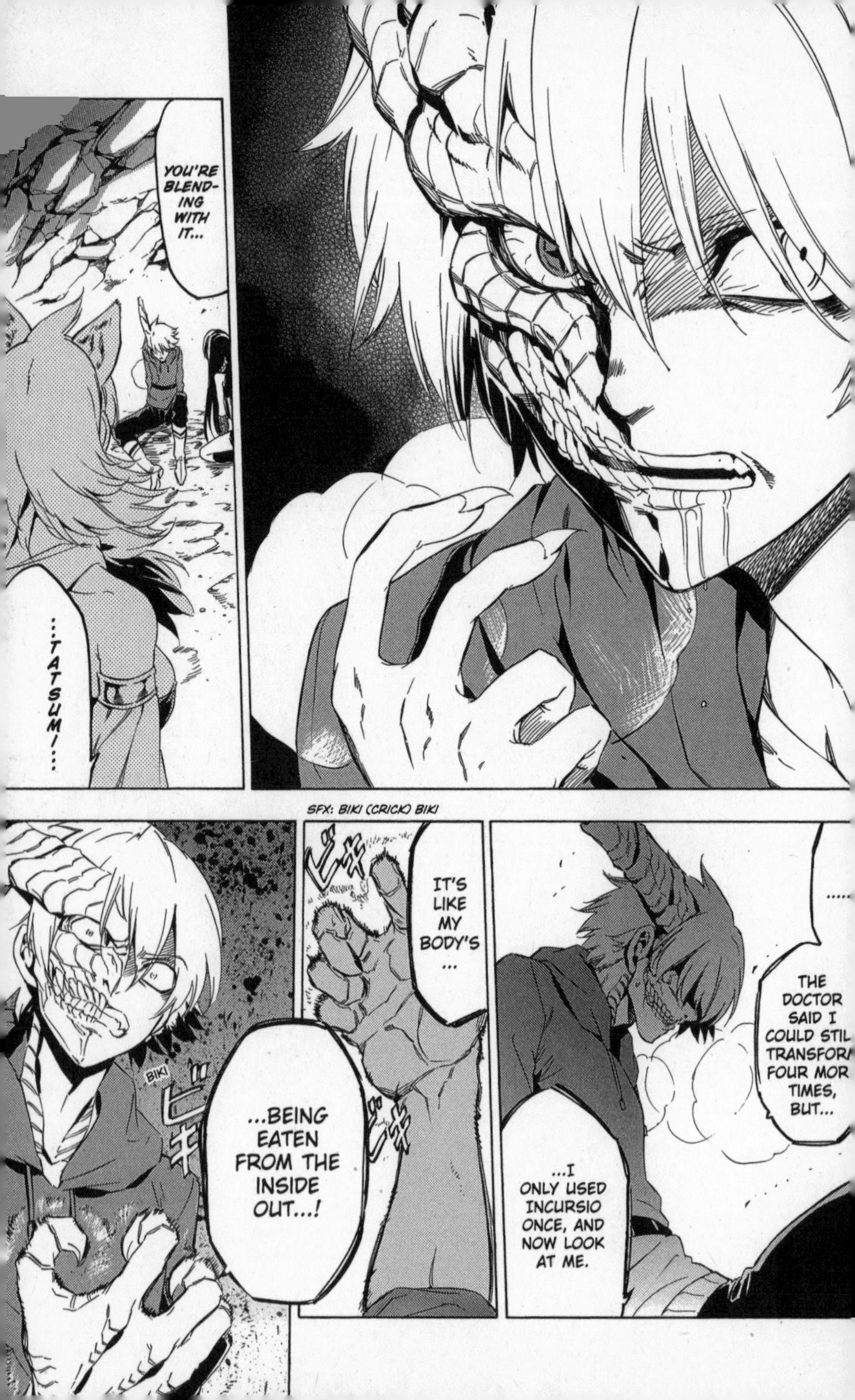
YOU'RE BLEND-ING WITH IT...
...TATSUMI...
SFX: BIKI (CRICK) BIKI
.....
THE DOCTOR SAID I COULD STIL TRANSFOR FOUR MOR TIMES, BUT...
...I ONLY USED INCURSIO ONCE, AND NOW LOOK AT ME.
IT'S LIKE MY BODY'S ...
...BEING EATEN FROM THE INSIDE OUT...!
BIKI

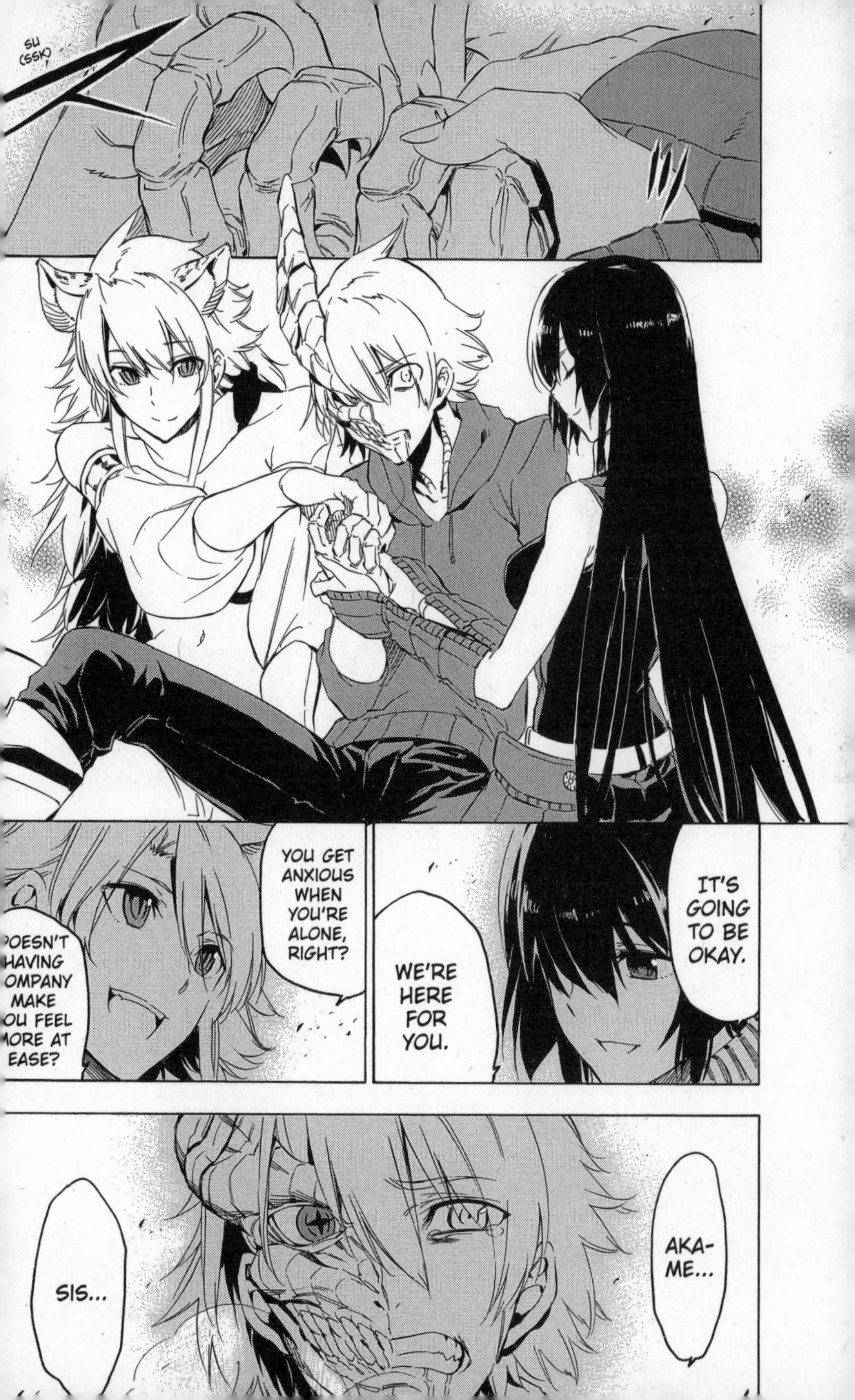
SU (SSK)
IT'S GOING TO BE OKAY.
WE'RE HERE FOR YOU.
YOU GET ANXIOUS WHEN YOU'RE ALONE, RIGHT?
OESN'T HAVING OMPANY MAKE OU FEEL ORE AT EASE?
AKA-ME...
SIS...

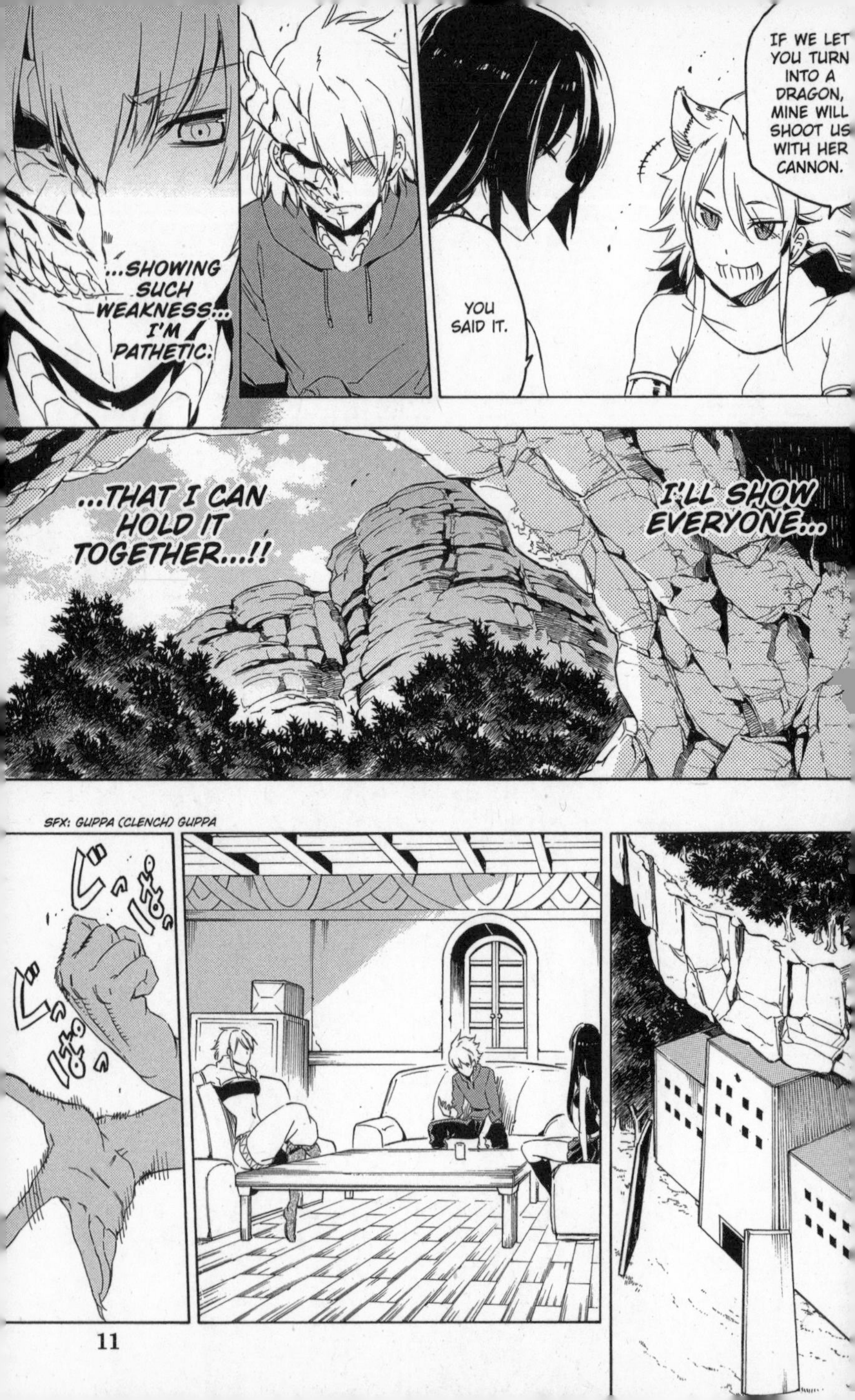
IF WE LET YOU TURN INTO A DRAGON, MINE WILL SHOOT US WITH HER CANNON.
YOU SAID IT.
...SHOWING SUCH WEAKNESS... I'M PATHETIC.
I'LL SHOW EVERYONE...
...THAT I CAN HOLD IT TOGETHER...!!
SFX: GUPPA (CLENCH) GUPPA

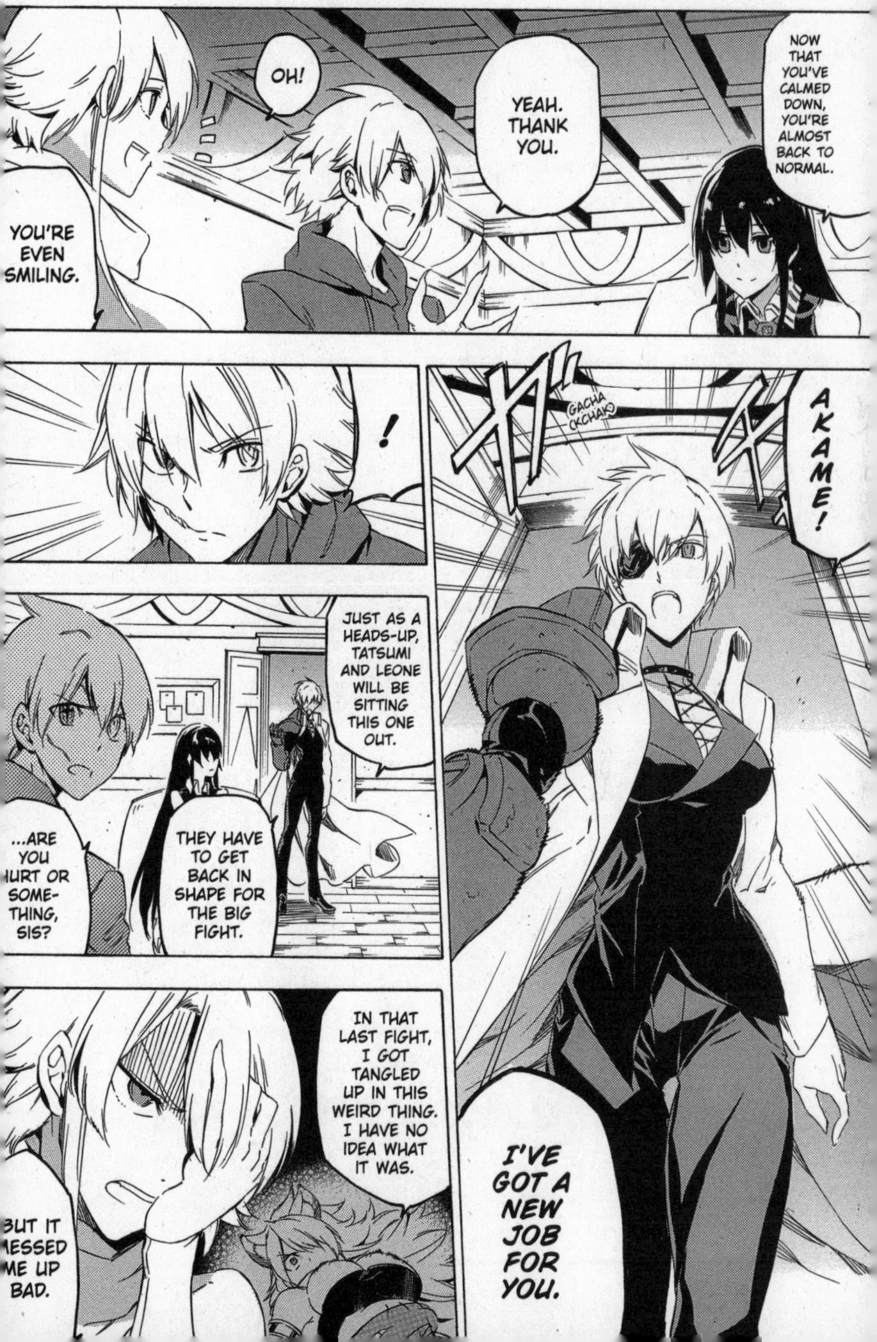
NOW THAT YOU'VE CALMED DOWN, YOU'RE ALMOST BACK TO NORMAL.
YEAH. THANK YOU.
OH!
YOU'RE EVEN SMILING.
GACHA (KCHAK)
AKAME!
I'VE GOT A NEW JOB FOR YOU.
!
JUST AS A HEADS-UP, TATSUMI AND LEONE WILL BE SITTING THIS ONE OUT.
THEY HAVE TO GET BACK IN SHAPE FOR THE BIG FIGHT.
...ARE YOU HURT OR SOME-THING, SIS?
IN THAT LAST FIGHT, I GOT TANGLED UP IN THIS WEIRD THING. I HAVE NO IDEA WHAT IT WAS.
BUT IT MESSED ME UP BAD.

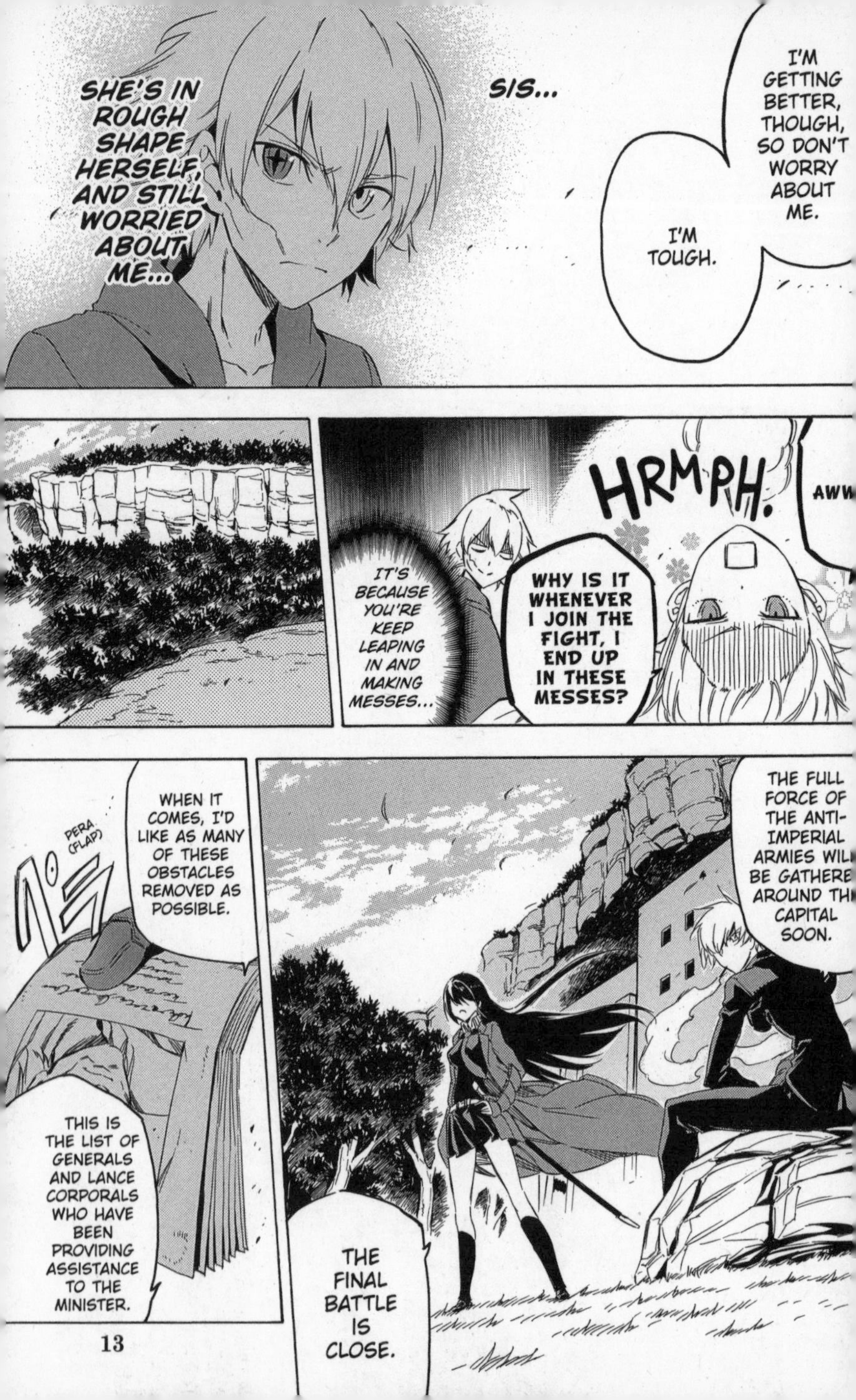
I'M GETTING BETTER, THOUGH, SO DON'T WORRY ABOUT ME.
I'M TOUGH.
SIS...
SHE'S IN ROUGH SHAPE HERSELF, AND STILL WORRIED ABOUT ME...
AWW
HRMPH.
WHY IS IT WHENEVER I JOIN THE FIGHT, I END UP IN THESE MESSES?
IT'S BECAUSE YOU'RE KEEP LEAPING IN AND MAKING MESSES...
THE FULL FORCE OF THE ANTI-IMPERIAL ARMIES WIL BE GATHERE AROUND TH CAPITAL SOON.
THE FINAL BATTLE IS CLOSE.
WHEN IT COMES, I'D LIKE AS MANY OF THESE OBSTACLES REMOVED AS POSSIBLE.
PERA (FLAP)
THIS IS THE LIST OF GENERALS AND LANCE CORPORALS WHO HAVE BEEN PROVIDING ASSISTANCE TO THE MINISTER.

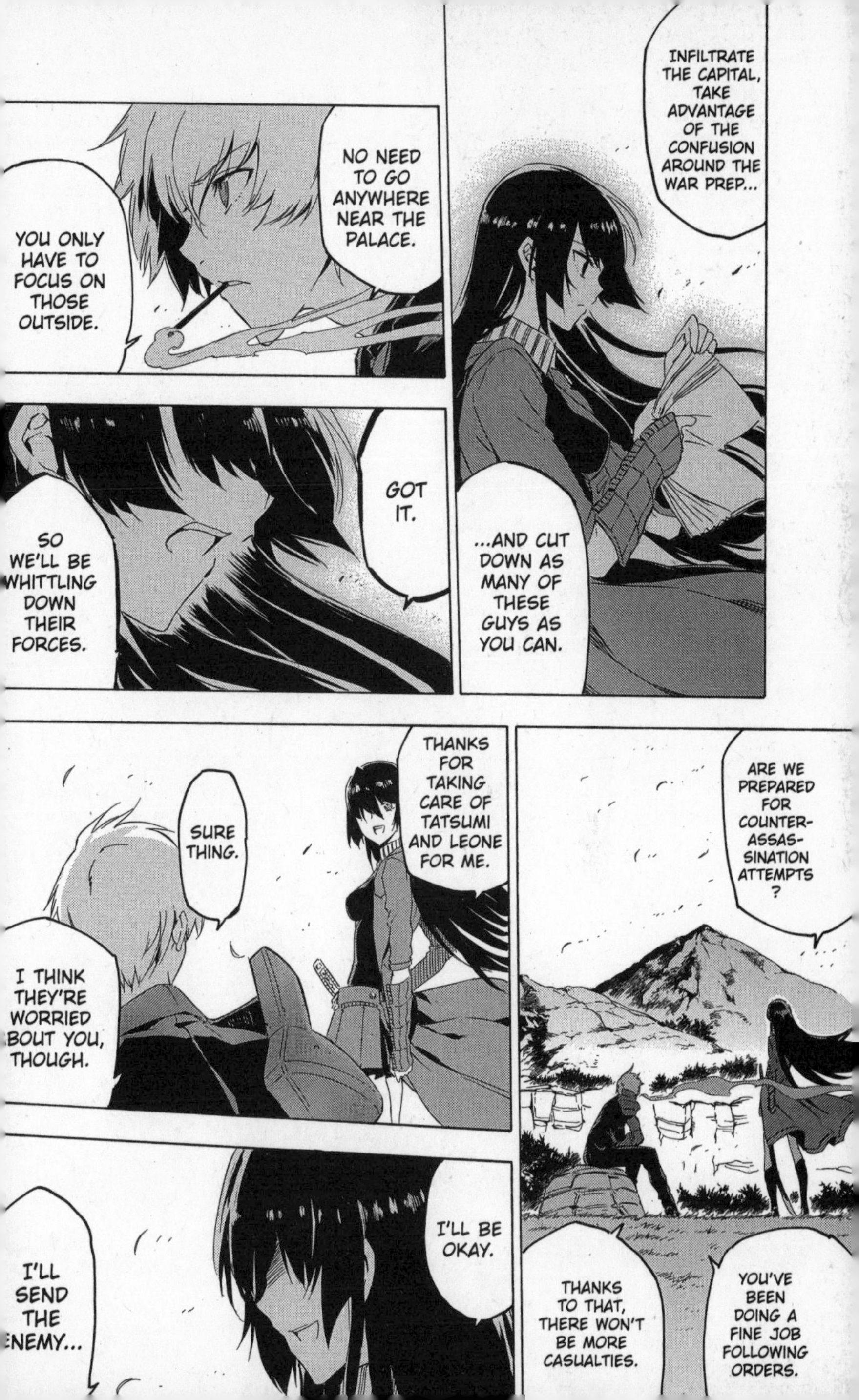
INFILTRATE THE CAPITAL, TAKE ADVANTAGE OF THE CONFUSION AROUND THE WAR PREP...
...AND CUT DOWN AS MANY OF THESE GUYS AS YOU CAN.
NO NEED TO GO ANYWHERE NEAR THE PALACE.
YOU ONLY HAVE TO FOCUS ON THOSE OUTSIDE.
GOT IT.
SO WE'LL BE WHITTLING DOWN THEIR FORCES.
ARE WE PREPARED FOR COUNTER-ASSAS-SINATION ATTEMPTS?
YOU'VE BEEN DOING A FINE JOB FOLLOWING ORDERS.
THANKS TO THAT, THERE WON'T BE MORE CASUALTIES.
THANKS FOR TAKING CARE OF TATSUMI AND LEONE FOR ME.
SURE THING.
I THINK THEY'RE WORRIED 'BOUT YOU, THOUGH.
I'LL BE OKAY.
I'LL SEND THE ENEMY...

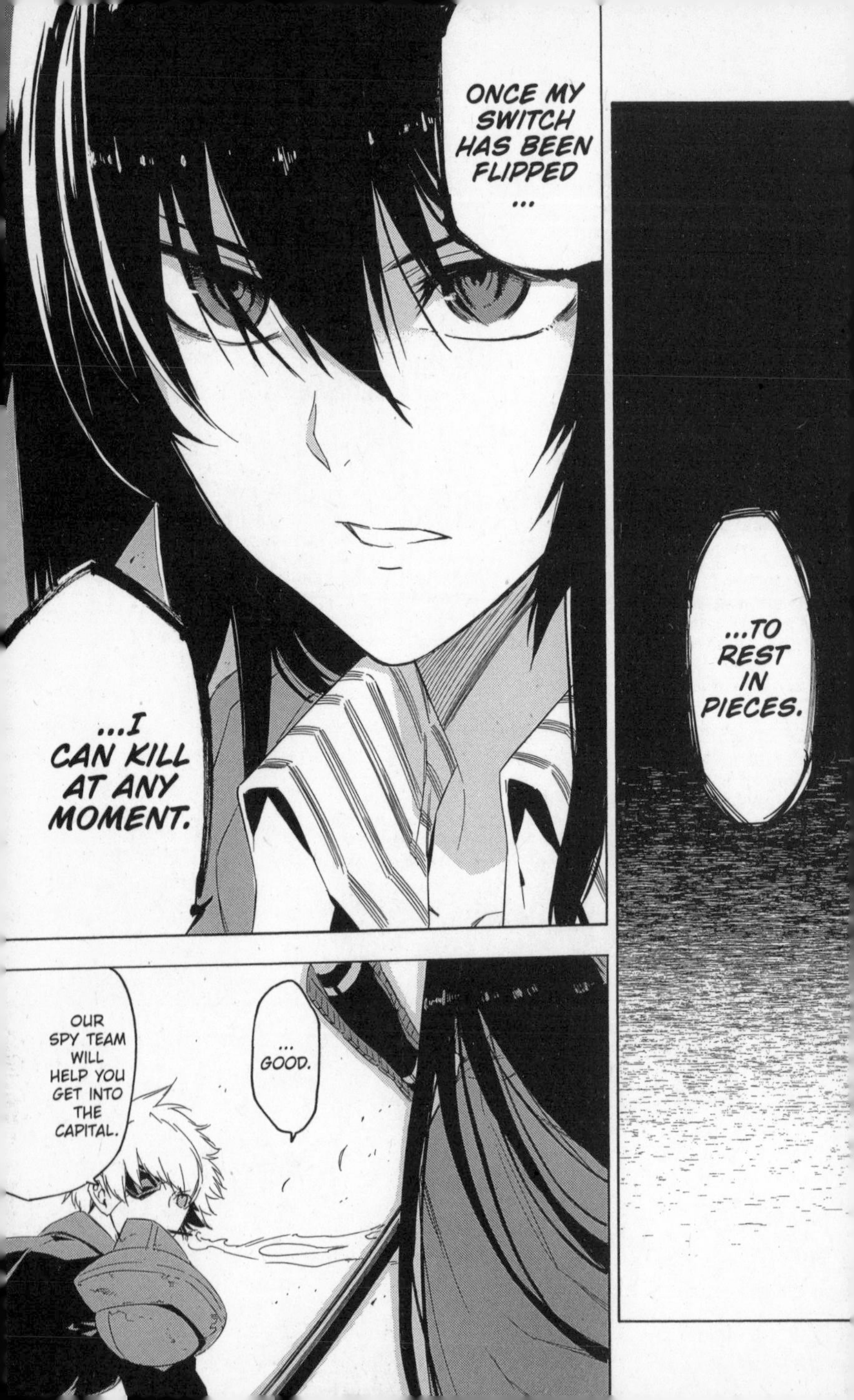
...TO REST IN PIECES.
ONCE MY SWITCH HAS BEEN FLIPPED...
...I CAN KILL AT ANY MOMENT.
...GOOD.
OUR SPY TEAM WILL HELP YOU GET INTO THE CAPITAL.

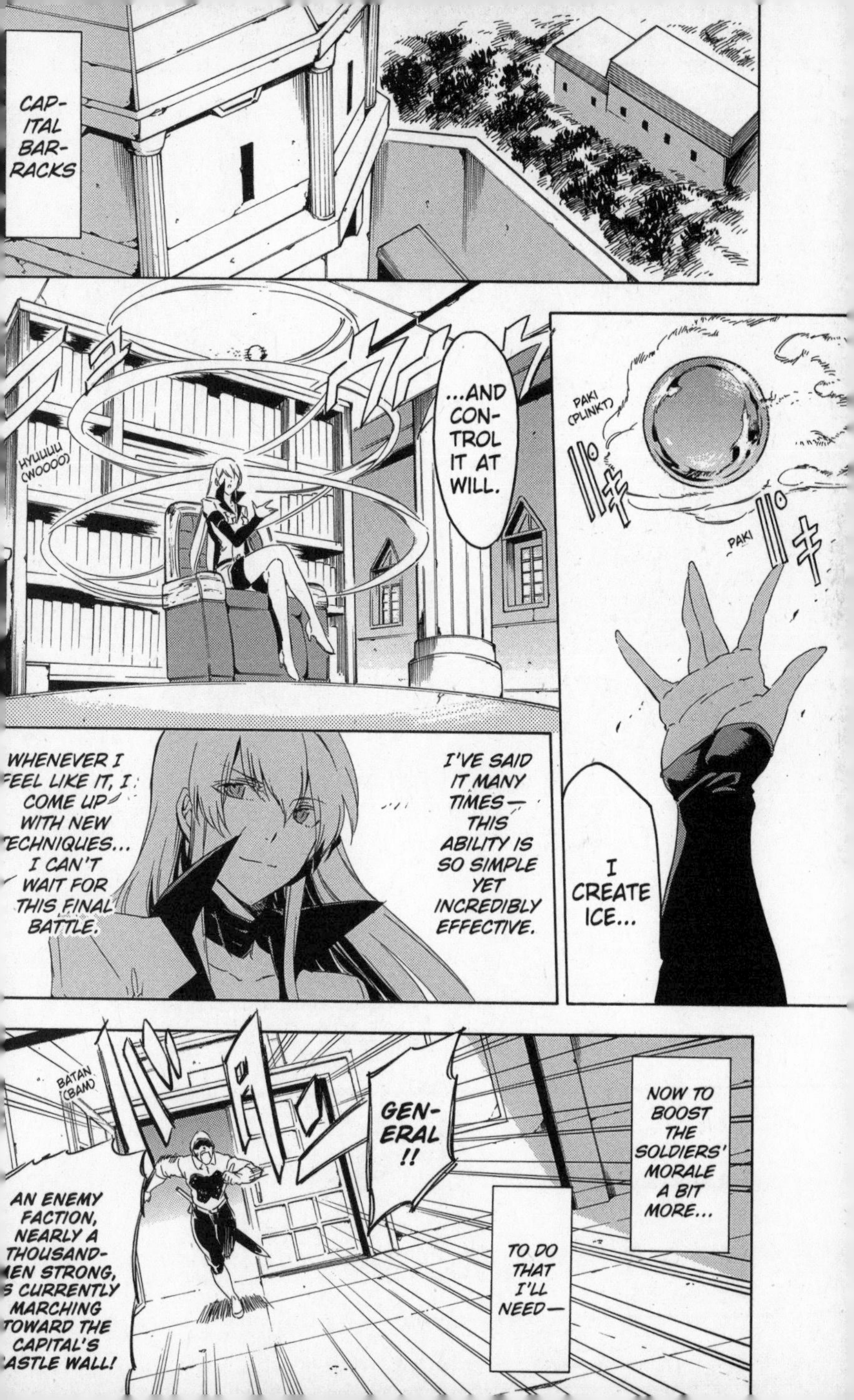
CAP-ITAL BAR-RACKS
PAKI (PLINKT)
PAKI
I CREATE ICE...
...AND CON-TROL IT AT WILL.
HYUUUU (WOOOO)
I'VE SAID IT MANY TIMES— THIS ABILITY IS SO SIMPLE YET INCREDIBLY EFFECTIVE.
WHENEVER I EEL LIKE IT, I COME UP WITH NEW ECHNIQUES... I CAN'T WAIT FOR THIS FINAL BATTLE.
NOW TO BOOST THE SOLDIERS' MORALE A BIT MORE...
TO DO THAT I'LL NEED—
GEN-ERAL !!
BATAN (BAM)
AN ENEMY FACTION, NEARLY A THOUSAND-EN STRONG, S CURRENTLY MARCHING TOWARD THE CAPITAL'S ASTLE WALL!

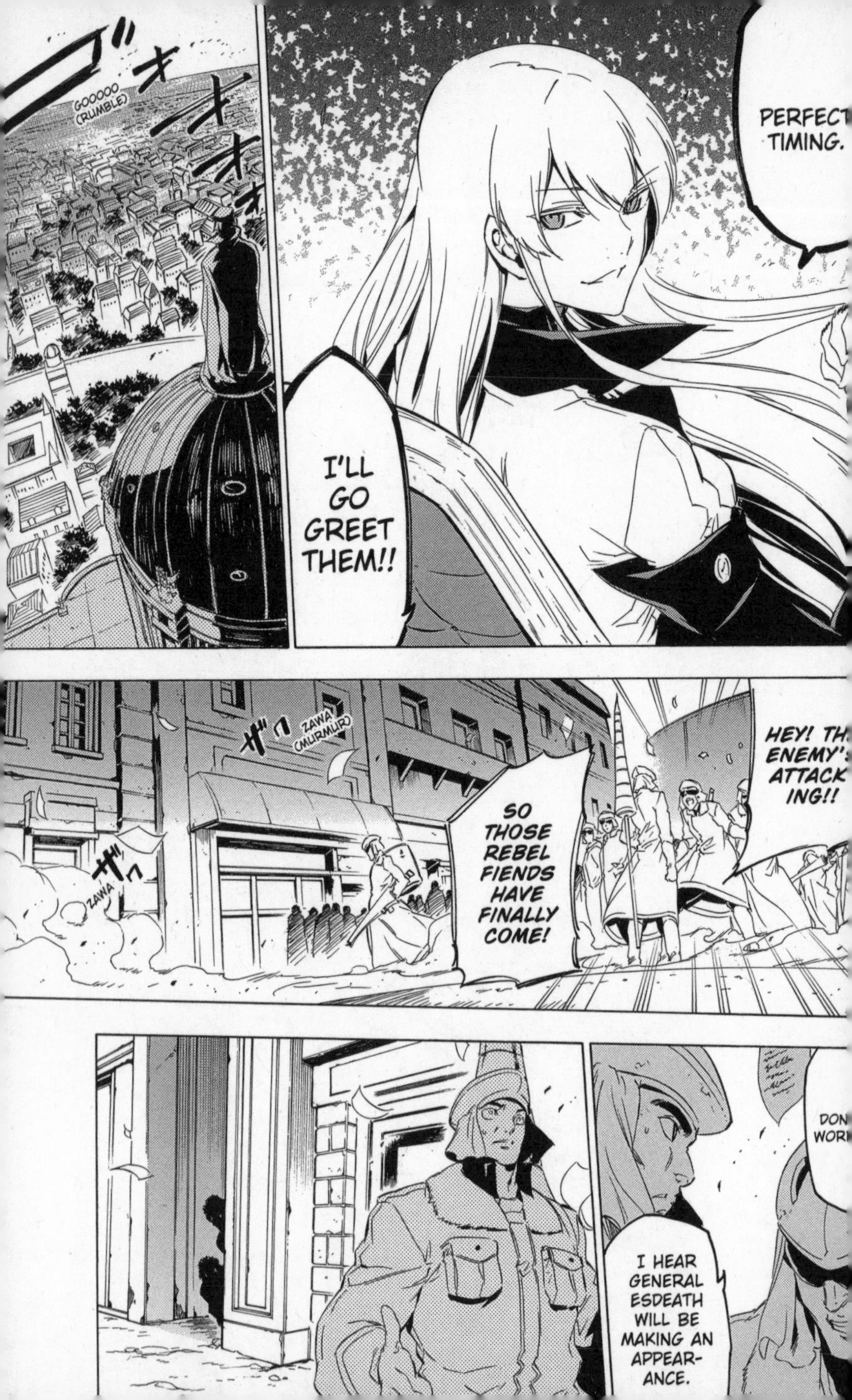
PERFECT TIMING.
I'LL GO GREET THEM!!
GOOOOO (RUMBLE)
HEY! TH ENEMY'S ATTACKING!!
SO THOSE REBEL FIENDS HAVE FINALLY COME!
ZAWA (MURMUR)
ZAWA
DON WORK
I HEAR GENERAL ESDEATH WILL BE MAKING AN APPEARANCE.

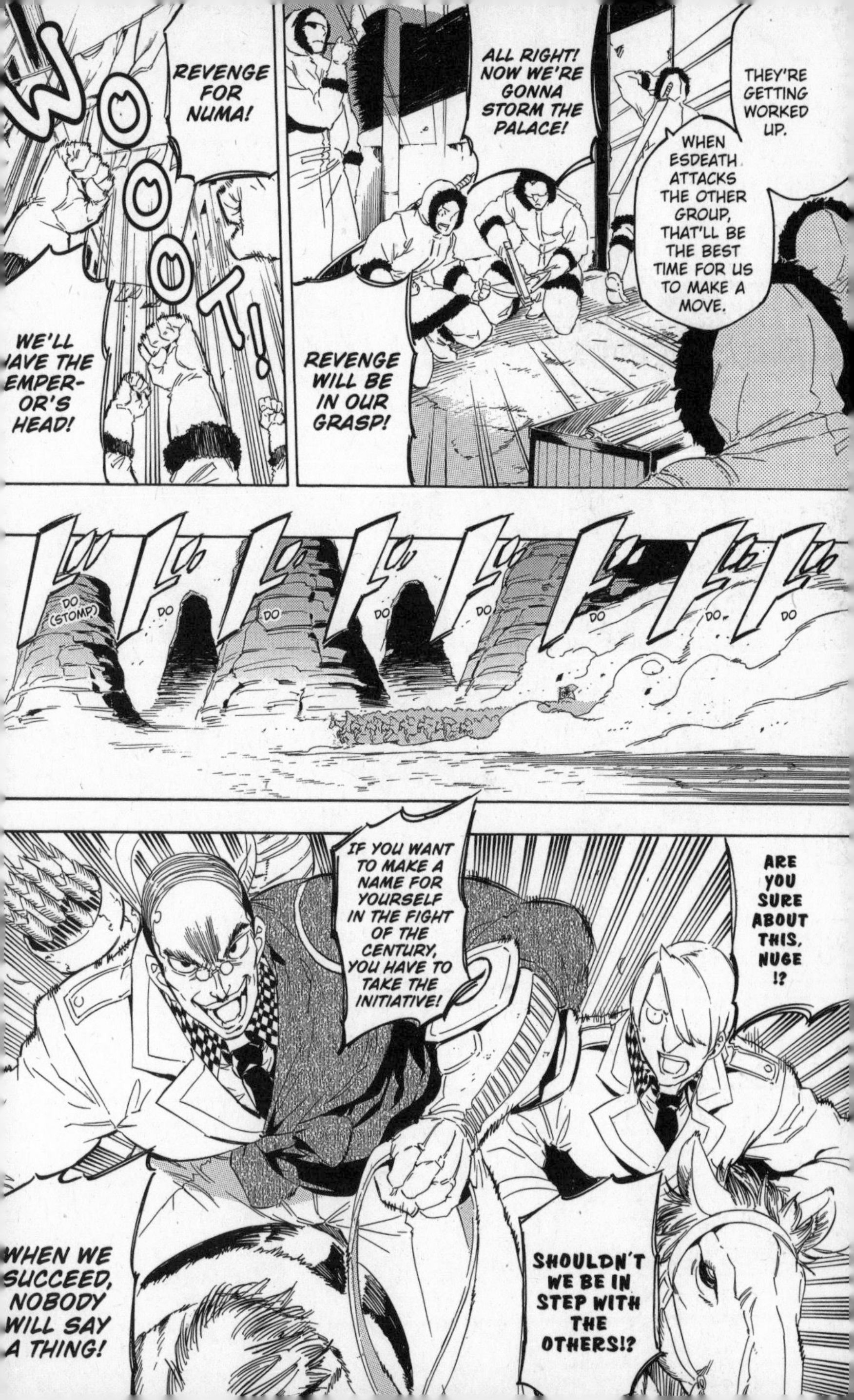
THEY'RE GETTING WORKED UP.
WHEN ESDEATH ATTACKS THE OTHER GROUP, THAT'LL BE THE BEST TIME FOR US TO MAKE A MOVE.
ALL RIGHT! NOW WE'RE GONNA STORM THE PALACE!
REVENGE WILL BE IN OUR GRASP!
REVENGE FOR NUMA!
WOOOT!!
WE'LL AVE THE EMPER-OR'S HEAD!
DO
DO
DO
DO
DO
DO
DO
DO (STOMP)
ARE YOU SURE ABOUT THIS, NUGE!?
SHOULDN'T WE BE IN STEP WITH THE OTHERS!?
IF YOU WANT TO MAKE A NAME FOR YOURSELF IN THE FIGHT OF THE CENTURY, YOU HAVE TO TAKE THE INITIATIVE!
WHEN WE SUCCEED, NOBODY WILL SAY A THING!

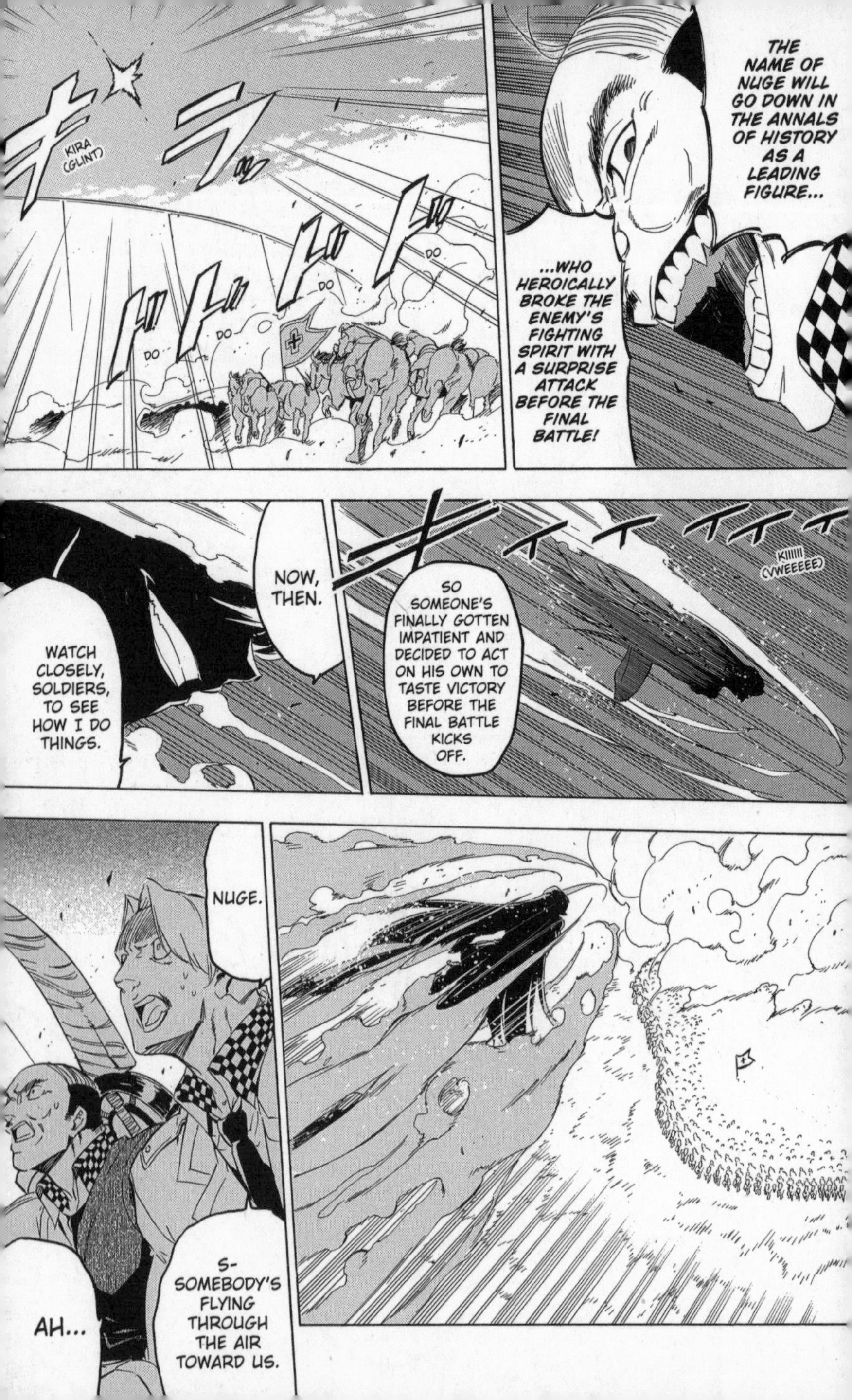
THE NAME OF NUGE WILL GO DOWN IN THE ANNALS OF HISTORY AS A LEADING FIGURE...
...WHO HEROICALLY BROKE THE ENEMY'S FIGHTING SPIRIT WITH A SURPRISE ATTACK BEFORE THE FINAL BATTLE!
KIRA (GLINT)
DO
DO
DO
DO
KIIIIII (VWEEEEE)
SO SOMEONE'S FINALLY GOTTEN IMPATIENT AND DECIDED TO ACT ON HIS OWN TO TASTE VICTORY BEFORE THE FINAL BATTLE KICKS OFF.
NOW, THEN.
WATCH CLOSELY, SOLDIERS, TO SEE HOW I DO THINGS.
NUGE.
S-SOMEBODY'S FLYING THROUGH THE AIR TOWARD US.
AH...

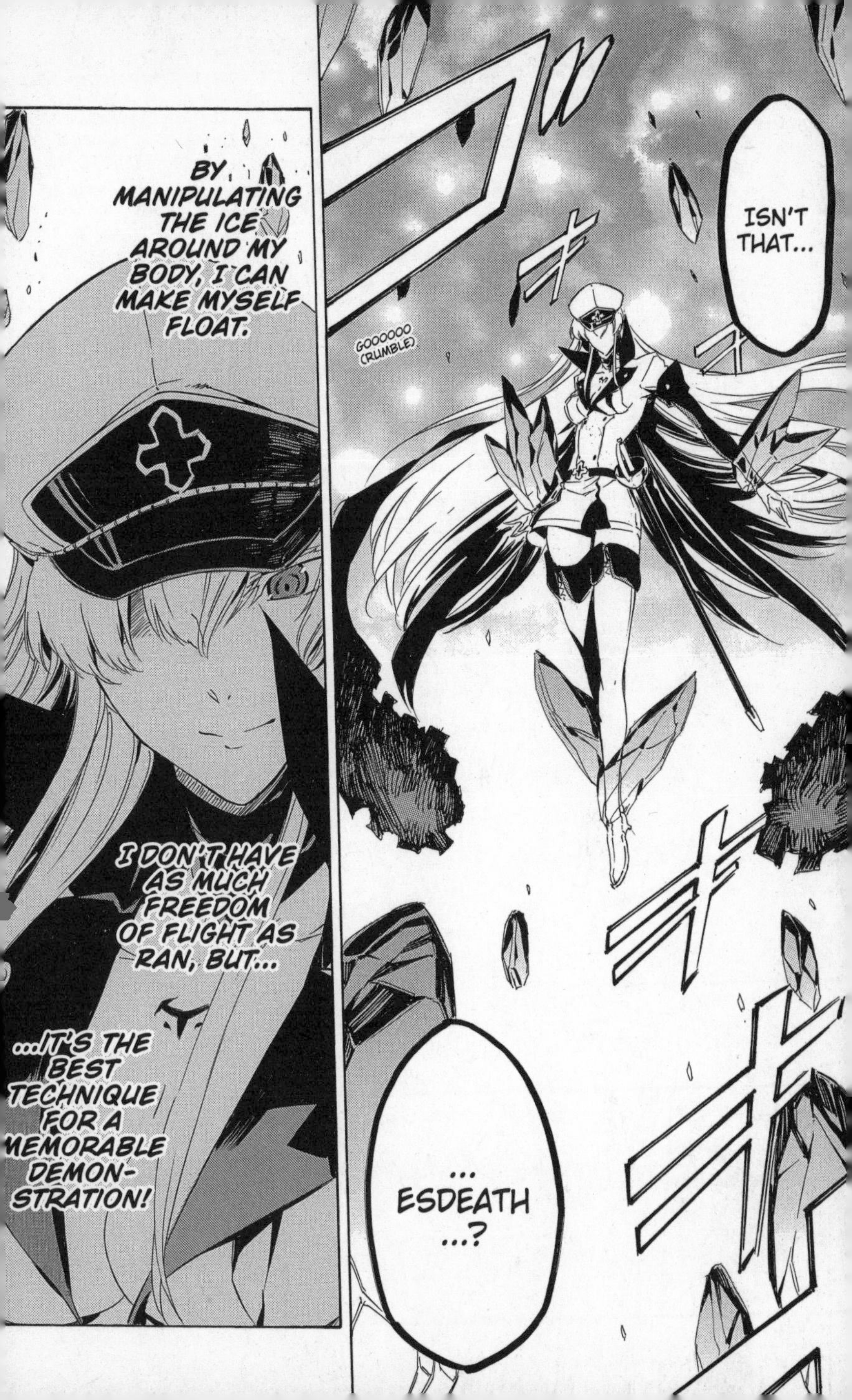
ISN'T THAT...
GOOOOOO (RUMBLE)
... ESDEATH ...?
BY MANIPULATING THE ICE AROUND MY BODY, I CAN MAKE MYSELF FLOAT.
I DON'T HAVE AS MUCH FREEDOM OF FLIGHT AS RAN, BUT...
...IT'S THE BEST TECHNIQUE FOR A MEMORABLE DEMON-STRATION!

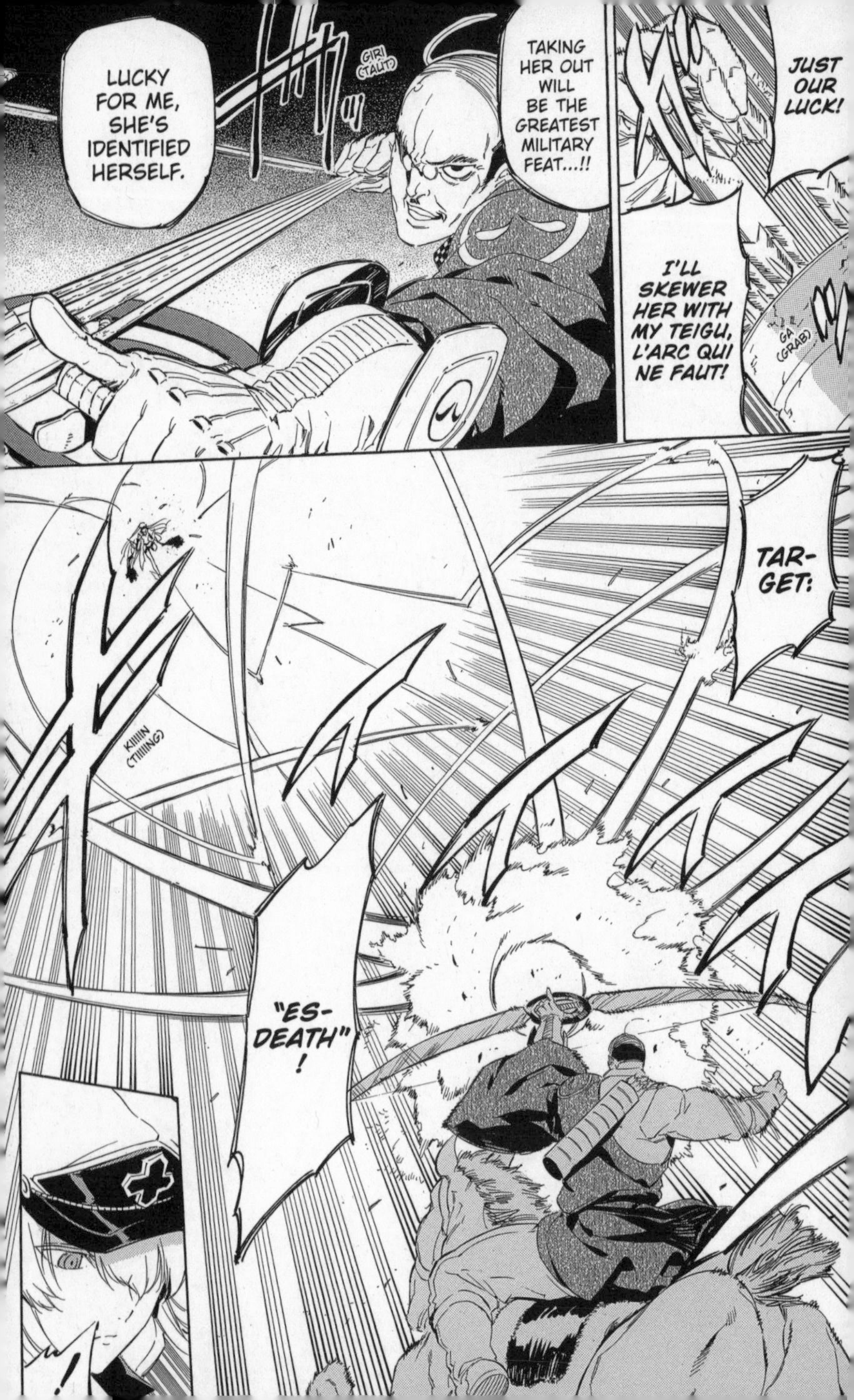
JUST OUR LUCK!
I'LL SKEWER HER WITH MY TEIGU, L'ARC QUI NE FAUT!
GA (GRAB)
TAKING HER OUT WILL BE THE GREATEST MILITARY FEAT...!!
GIRI (TAUT)
LUCKY FOR ME, SHE'S IDENTIFIED HERSELF.
TAR-GET:
KIIIIN (TIIIING)
"ES-DEATH"!
!

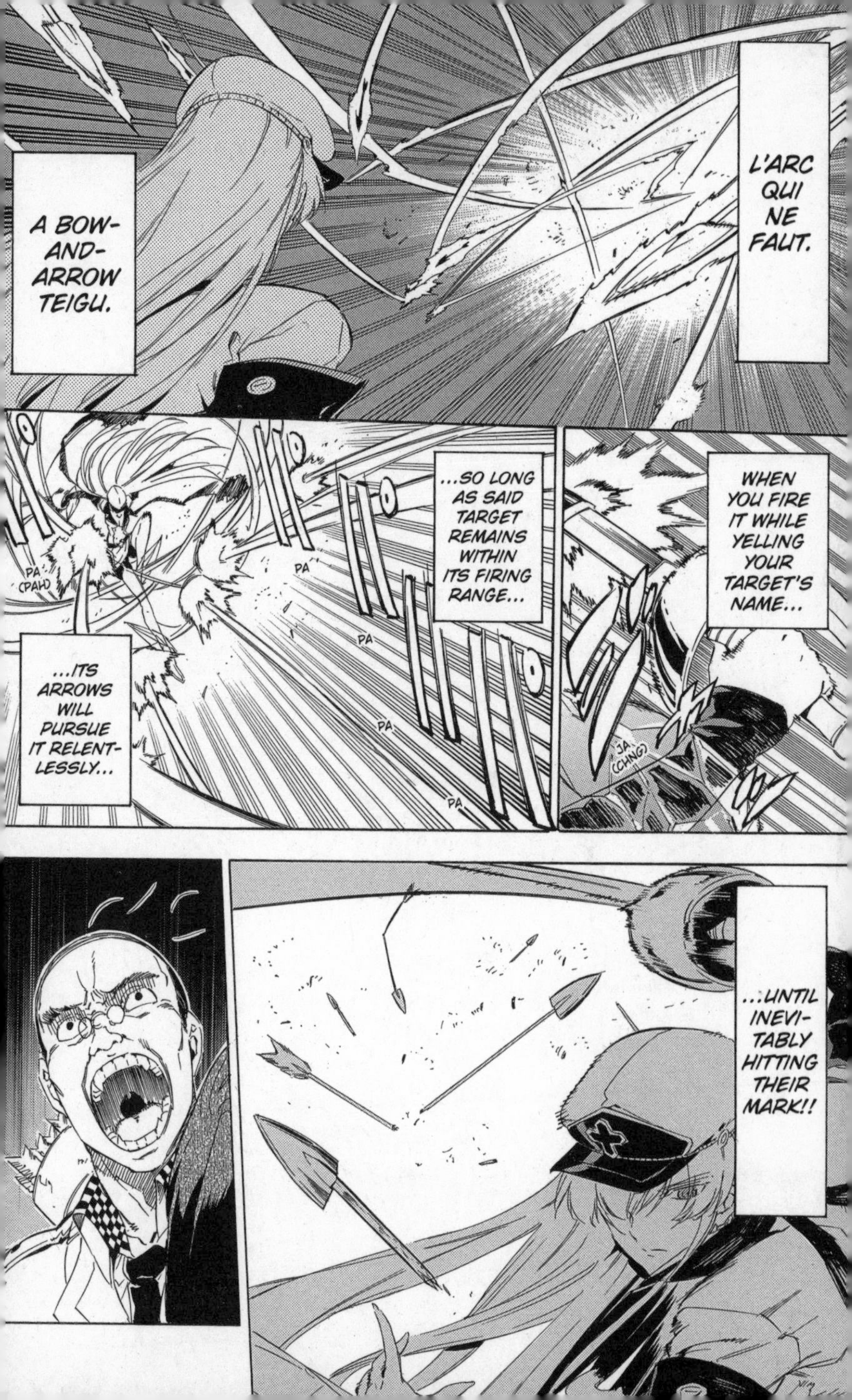
L'ARC QUI NE FAUT.
A BOW-AND-ARROW TEIGU.
WHEN YOU FIRE IT WHILE YELLING YOUR TARGET'S NAME...
JA (CHNG)
...SO LONG AS SAID TARGET REMAINS WITHIN ITS FIRING RANGE...
PA
PA (PAH)
PA
PA
PA
...ITS ARROWS WILL PURSUE IT RELENT-LESSLY...
...UNTIL INEVI-TABLY HITTING THEIR MARK!!

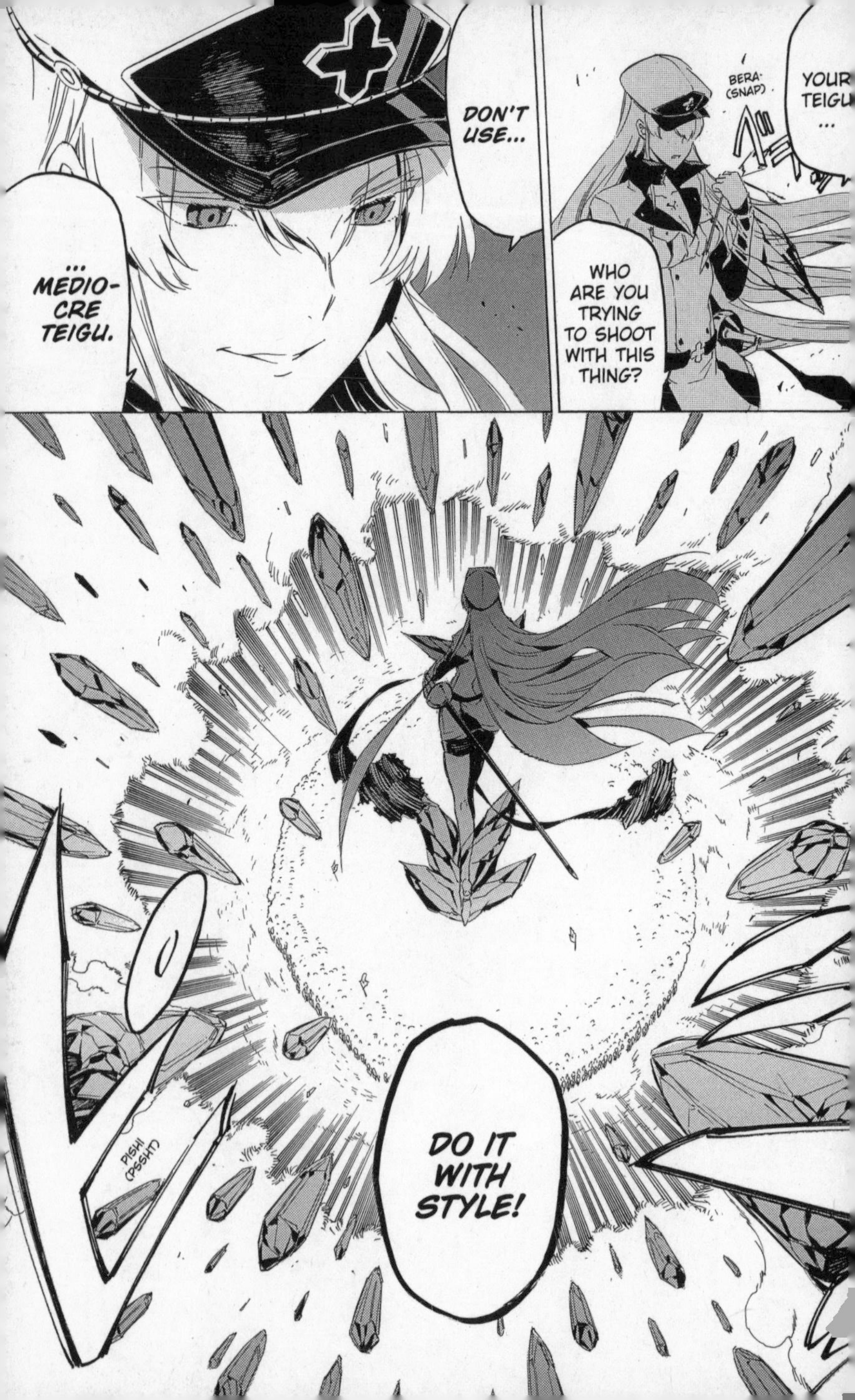
YOUR TEIGU ...
BERA (SNAP)
WHO ARE YOU TRYING TO SHOOT WITH THIS THING?
DON'T USE...
... MEDIOCRE TEIGU.
DO IT WITH STYLE!
PISHI (PSSHT)

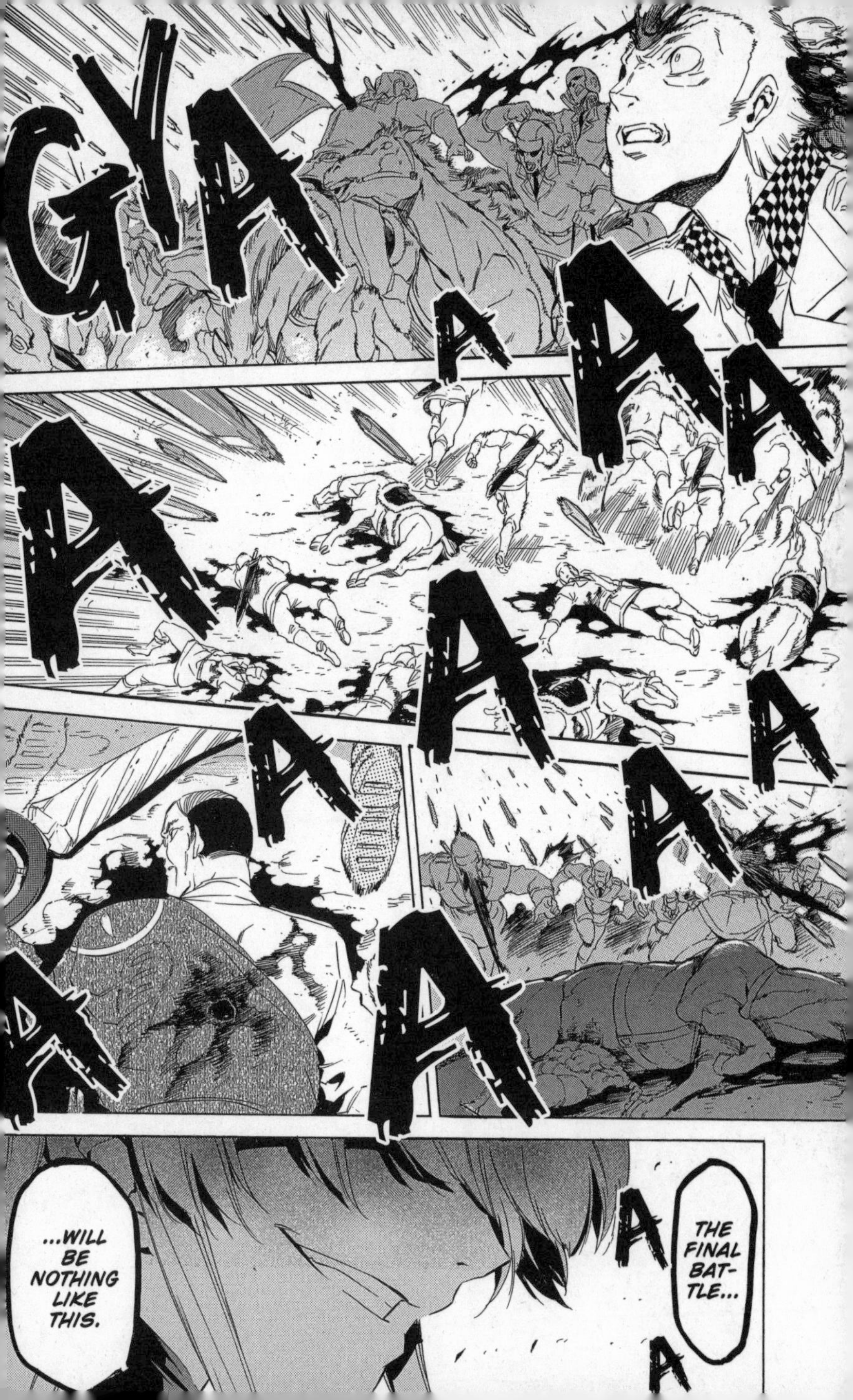
GYAAAAAAAAAAAAA
THE FINAL BATTLE...
...WILL BE NOTHING LIKE THIS.

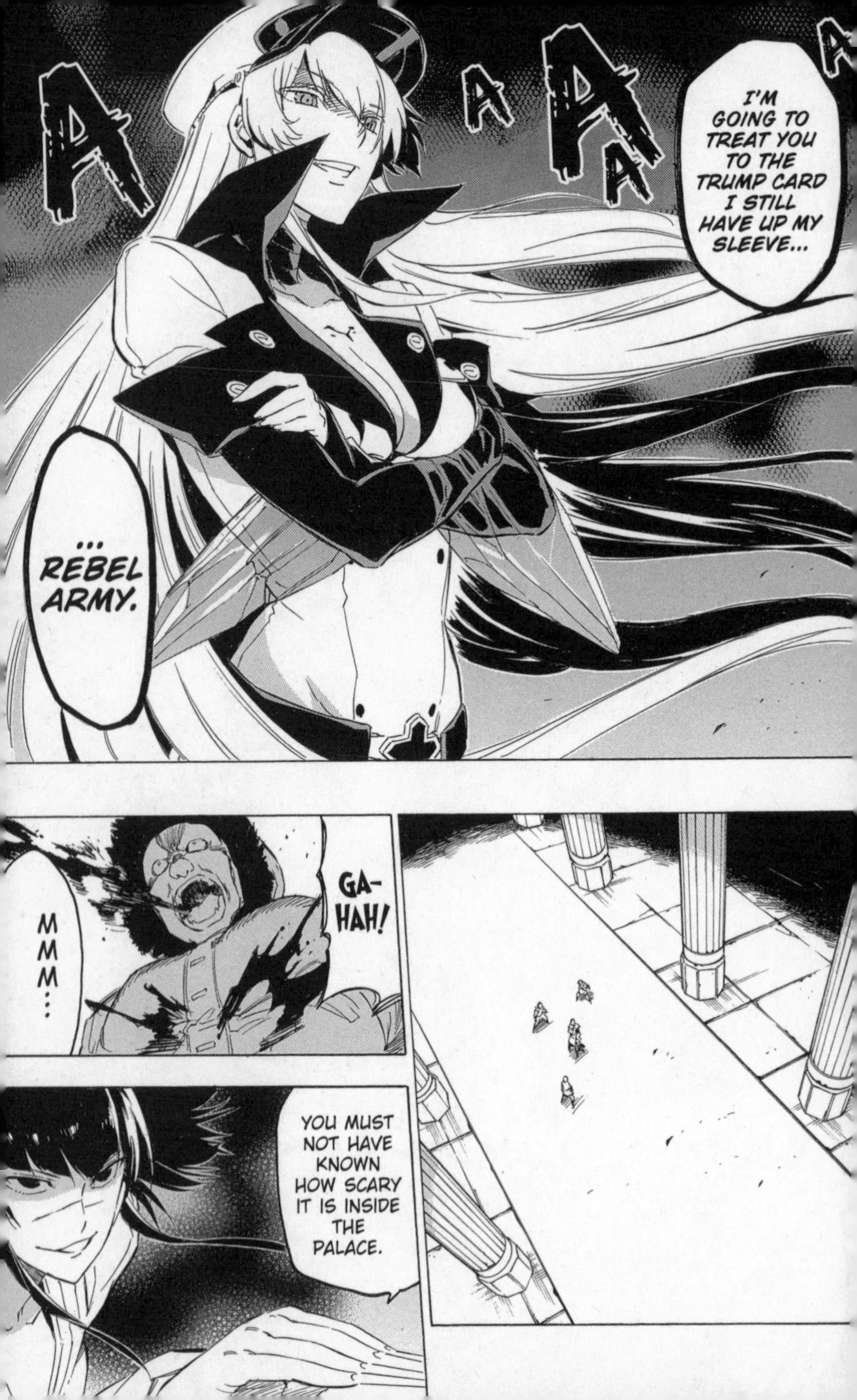
AAAAAA
I'M GOING TO TREAT YOU TO THE TRUMP CARD I STILL HAVE UP MY SLEEVE...
... REBEL ARMY.
GA-HAH!
MMM...
YOU MUST NOT HAVE KNOWN HOW SCARY IT IS INSIDE THE PALACE.

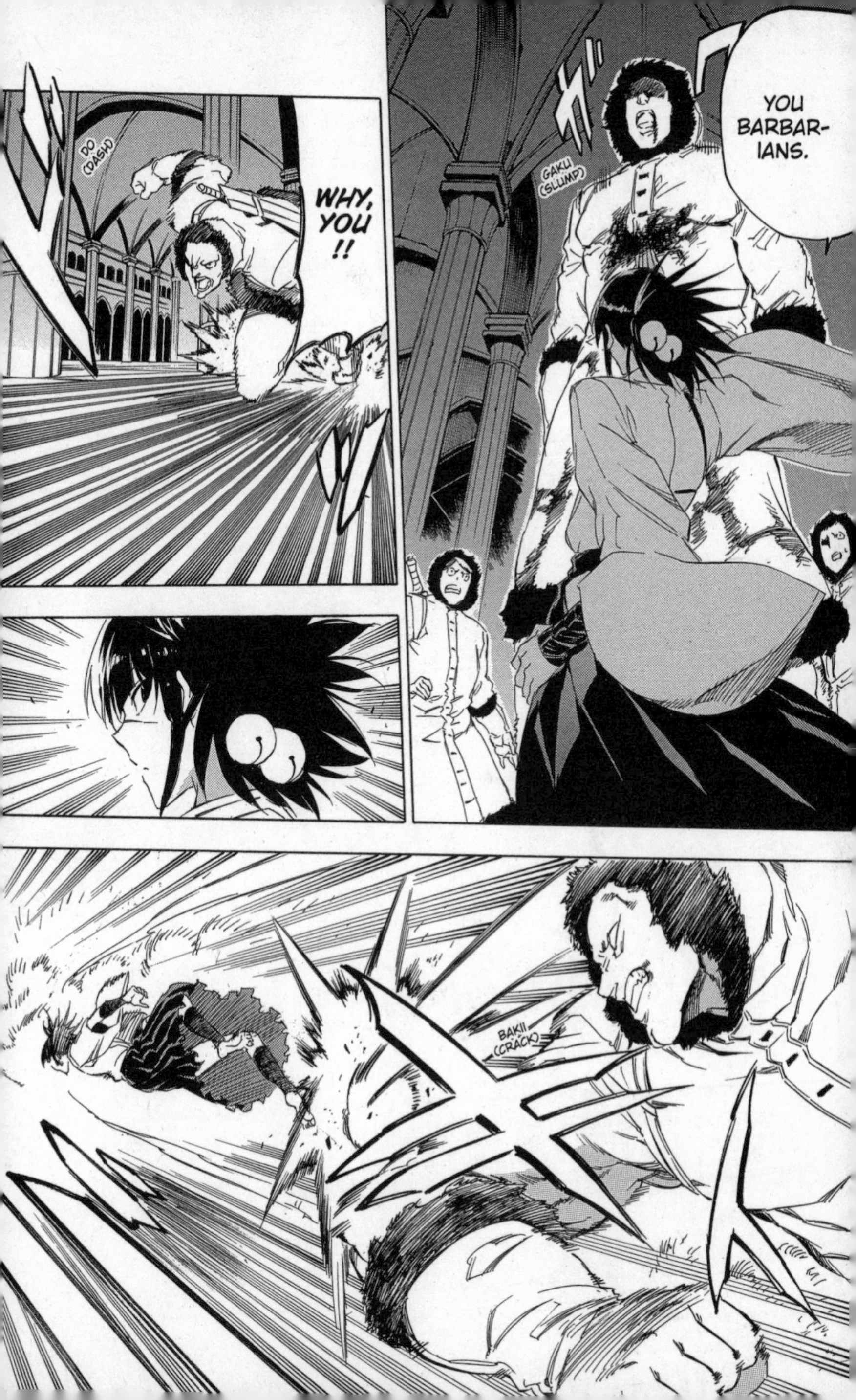
YOU BARBAR-IANS.
GAKU (SLUMP)
DO (DASH)
WHY, YOU !!
BAKII (CRACK)

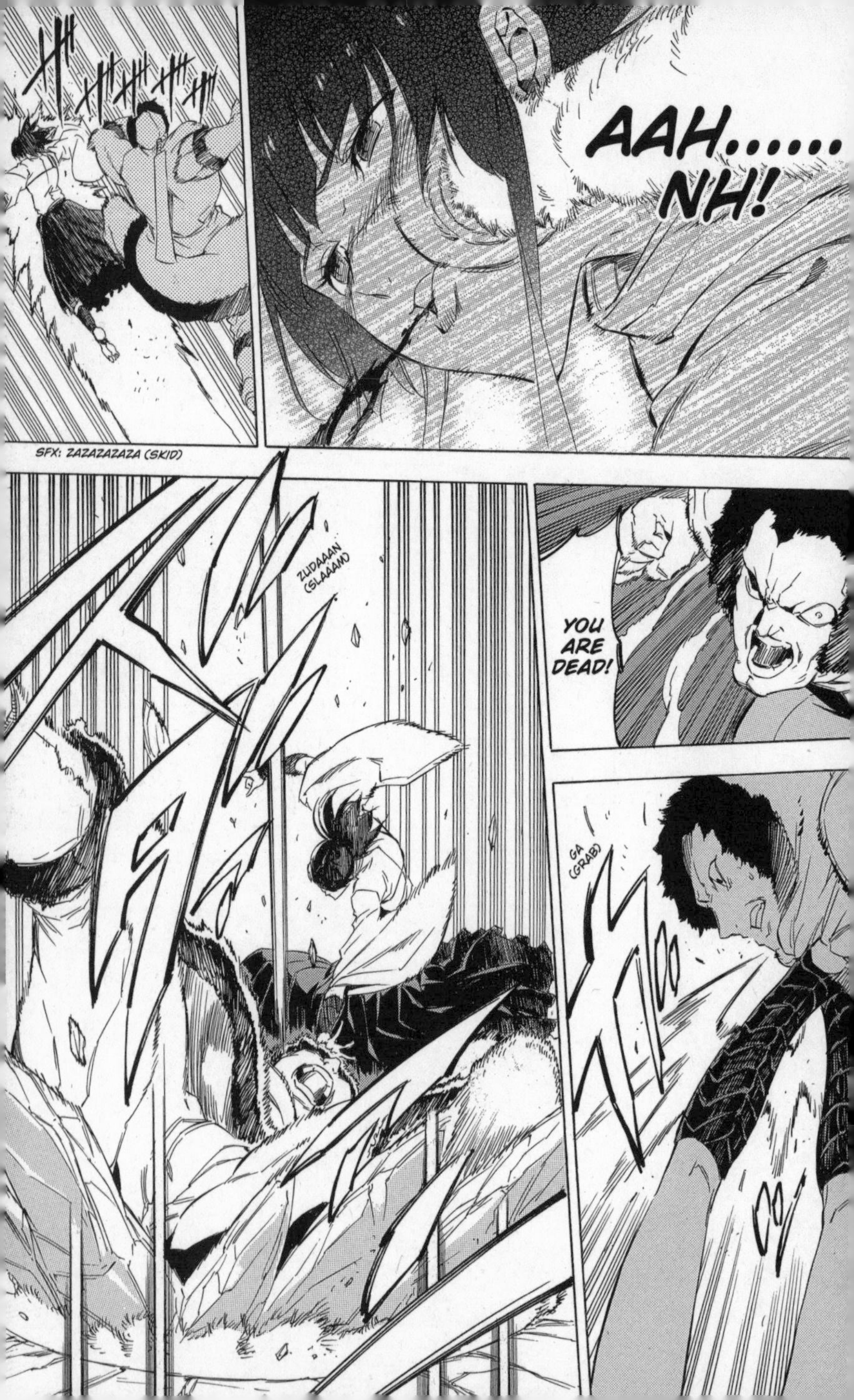
AAH......
NH!
SFX: ZAZAZAZAZA (SKID)
YOU ARE DEAD!
GA (GRAB)
ZUDAAAN (SLAAAM)

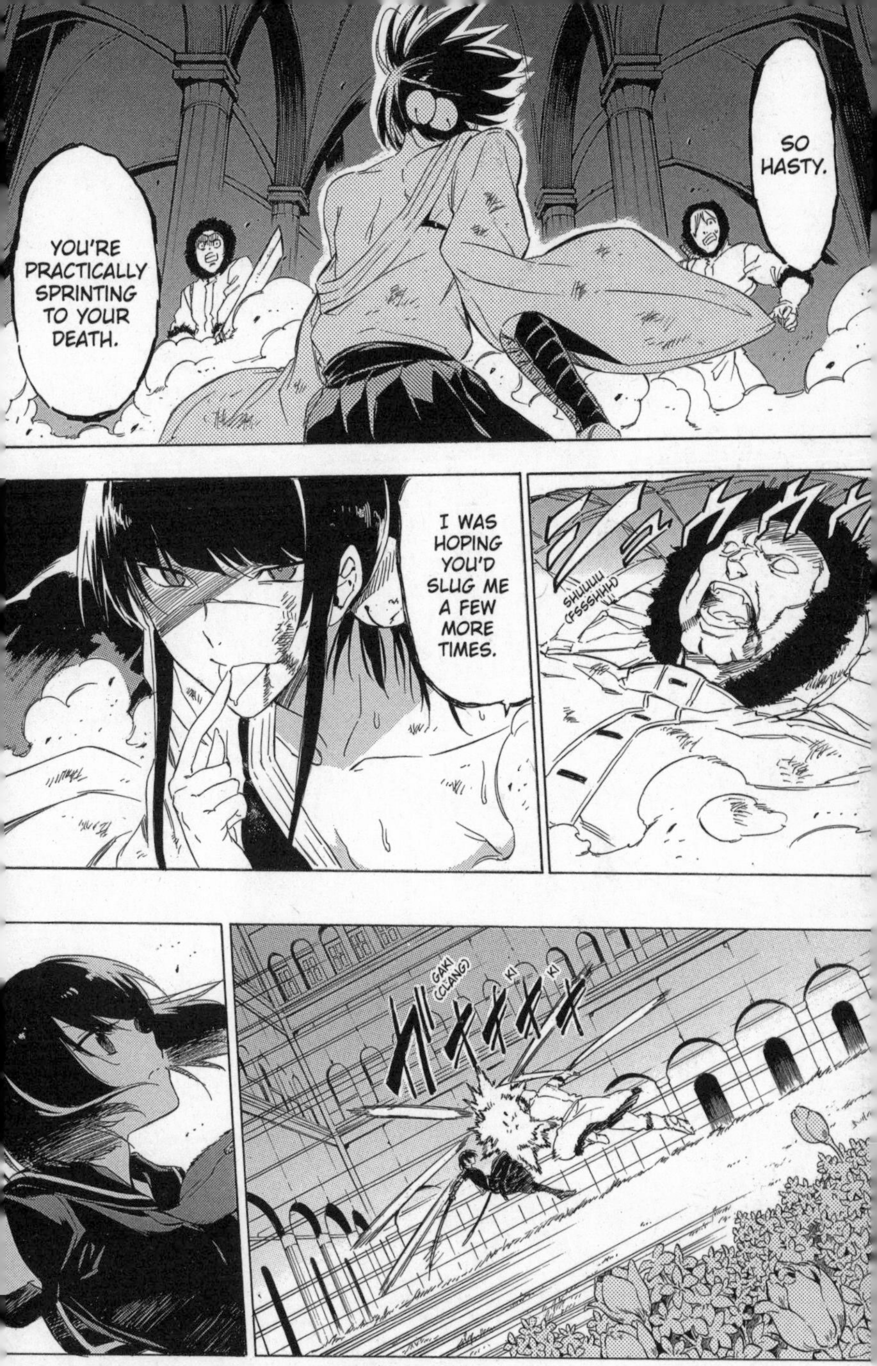
SO HASTY.
YOU'RE PRACTICALLY SPRINTING TO YOUR DEATH.
SHUUUU (FSSSHHH)
I WAS HOPING YOU'D SLUG ME A FEW MORE TIMES.
GAKI (CLANG)
KI
KI

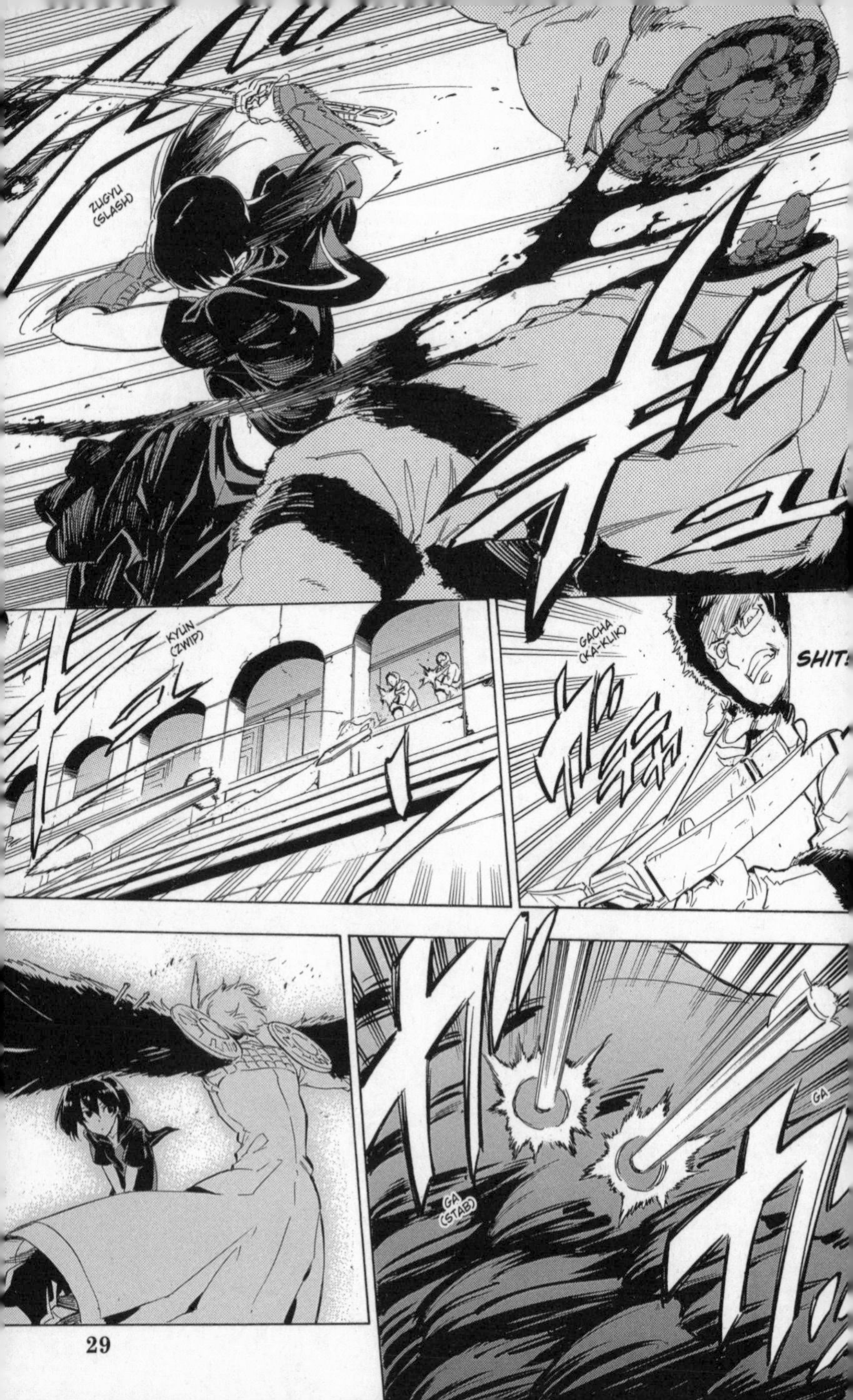
ZUGYU (SLASH)
GACHA (KA-KLIK)
SHIT!
KYUN (ZWIP)
GA
GA (STAB)

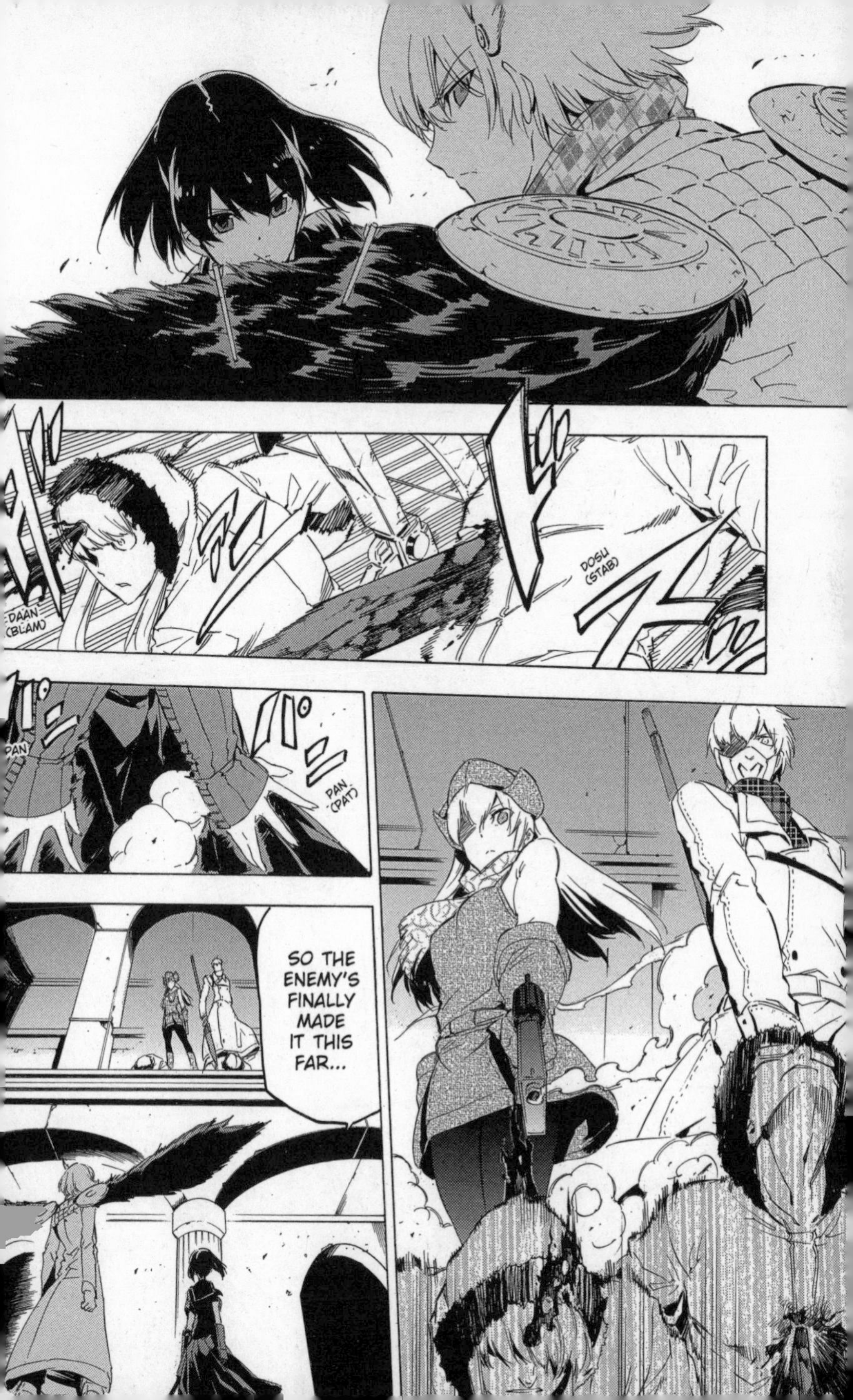
DOSU (STAB)
DAAN (BLAM)
PAN (PAT)
PAN
SO THE ENEMY'S FINALLY MADE IT THIS FAR...

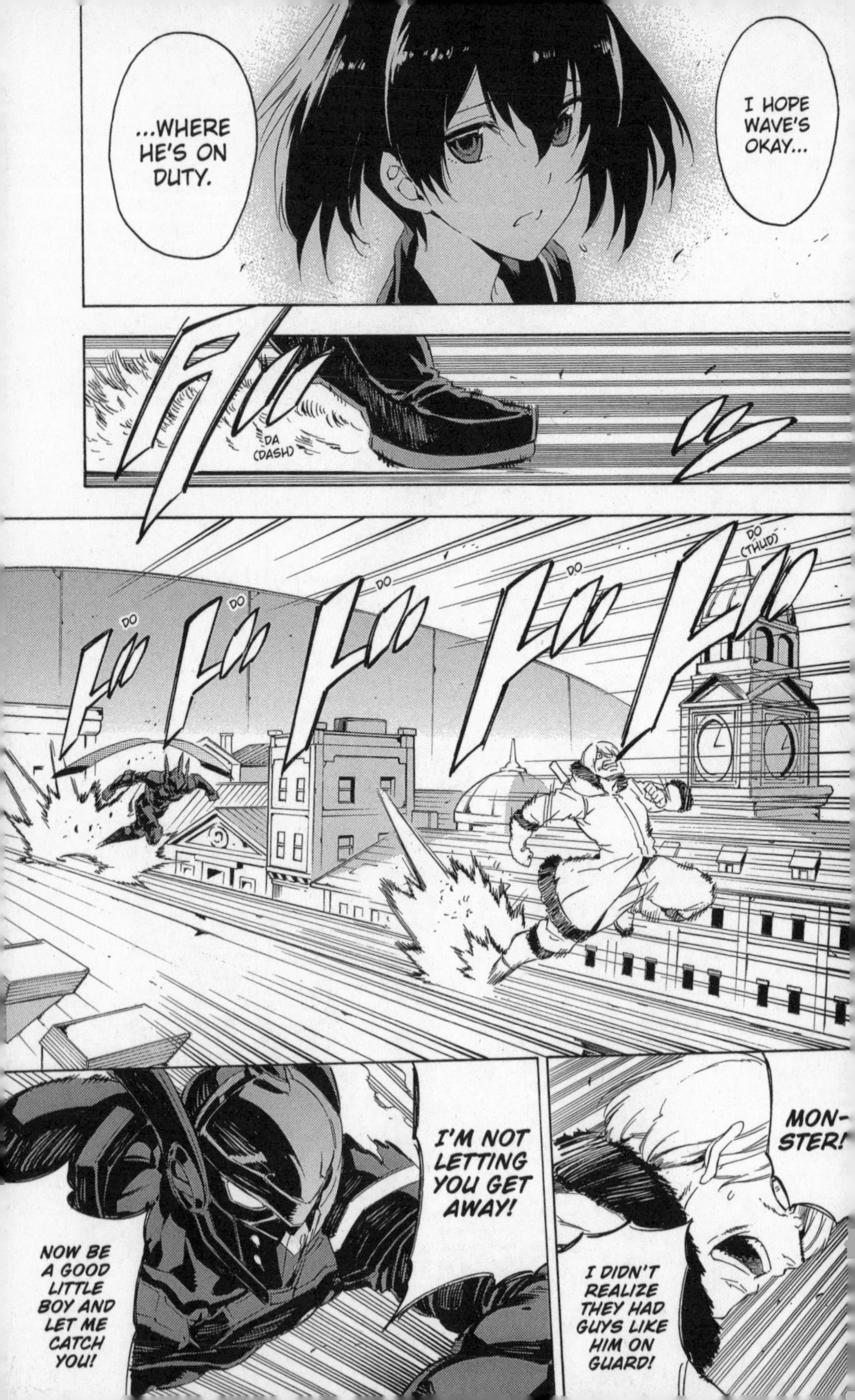
I HOPE WAVE'S OKAY...
...WHERE HE'S ON DUTY.
DA (DASH)
DO (THUD)
DO
DO
DO
DO
MON-STER!
I DIDN'T REALIZE THEY HAD GUYS LIKE HIM ON GUARD!
I'M NOT LETTING YOU GET AWAY!
NOW BE A GOOD LITTLE BOY AND LET ME CATCH YOU!

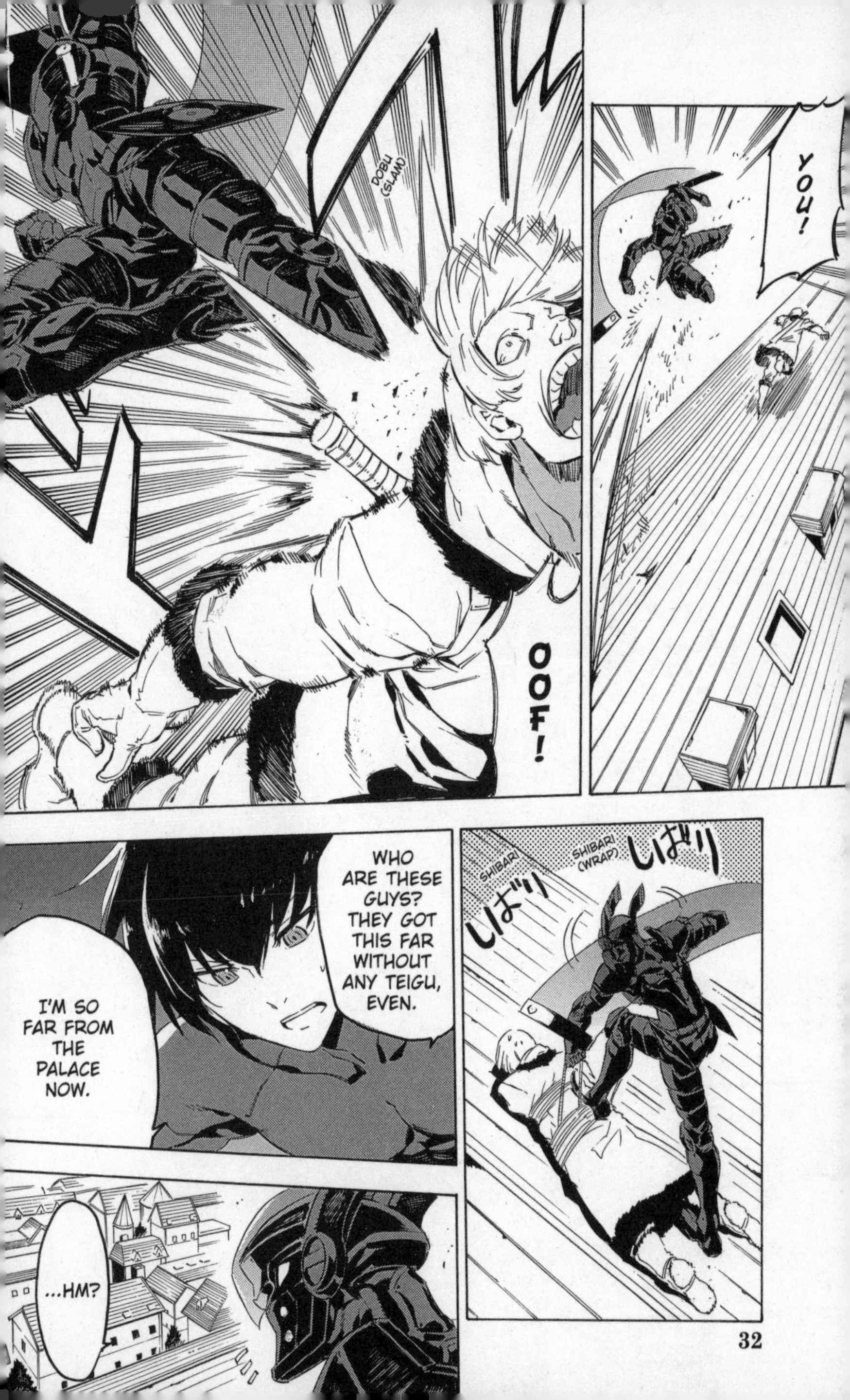
YOU!
DOBU (SLAM)
OOF!
SHIBARI (WRAP)
しばり
SHIBARI
しばり
WHO ARE THESE GUYS? THEY GOT THIS FAR WITHOUT ANY TEIGU, EVEN.
I'M SO FAR FROM THE PALACE NOW.
...HM?

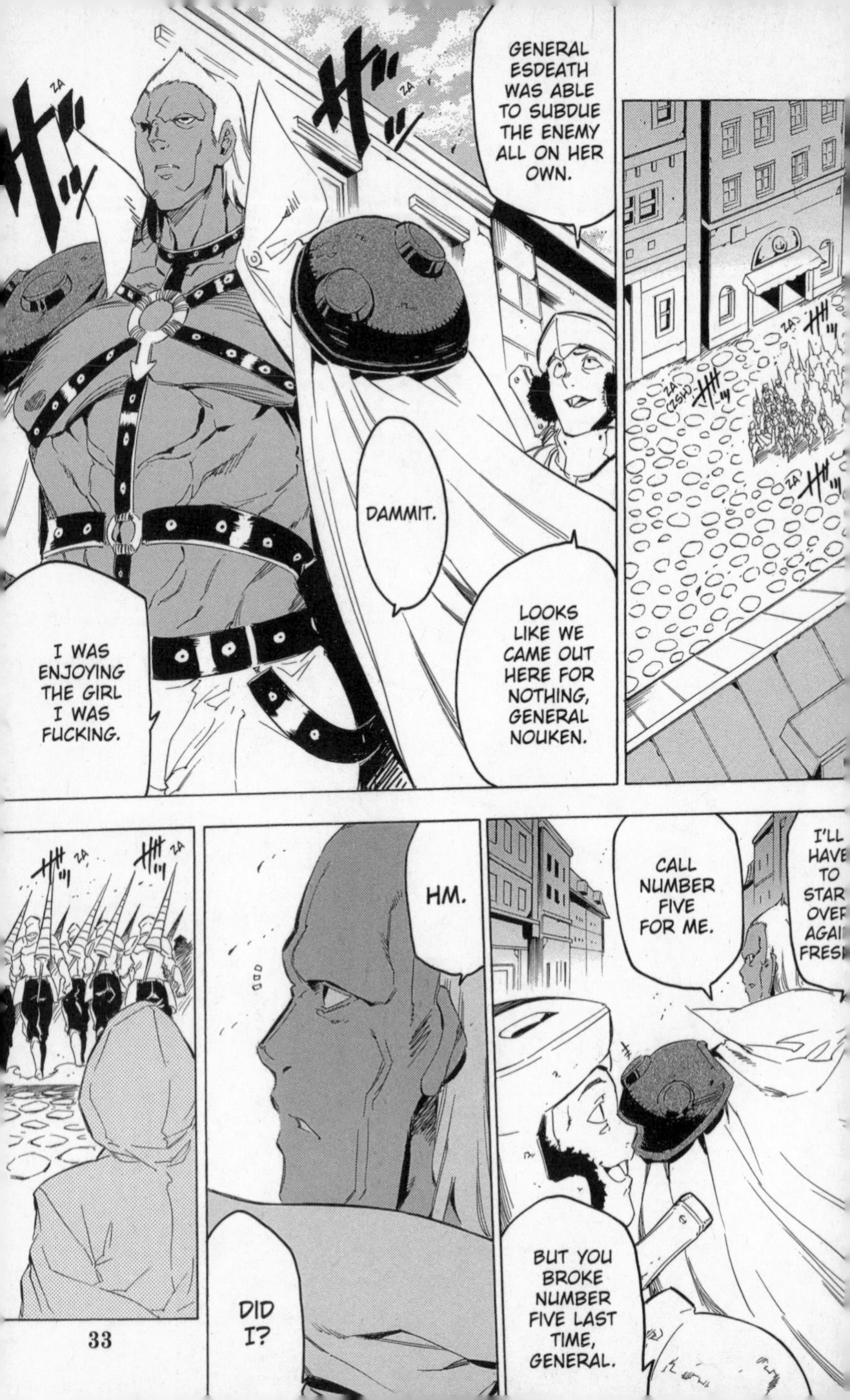
ZA
ZA (ZSH)
ZA
ZA
ZA
GENERAL ESDEATH WAS ABLE TO SUBDUE THE ENEMY ALL ON HER OWN.
DAMMIT.
LOOKS LIKE WE CAME OUT HERE FOR NOTHING, GENERAL NOUKEN.
I WAS ENJOYING THE GIRL I WAS FUCKING.
I'LL HAVE TO STAR OVER AGAI FRES
CALL NUMBER FIVE FOR ME.
BUT YOU BROKE NUMBER FIVE LAST TIME, GENERAL.
HM.
DID I?
ZA
ZA

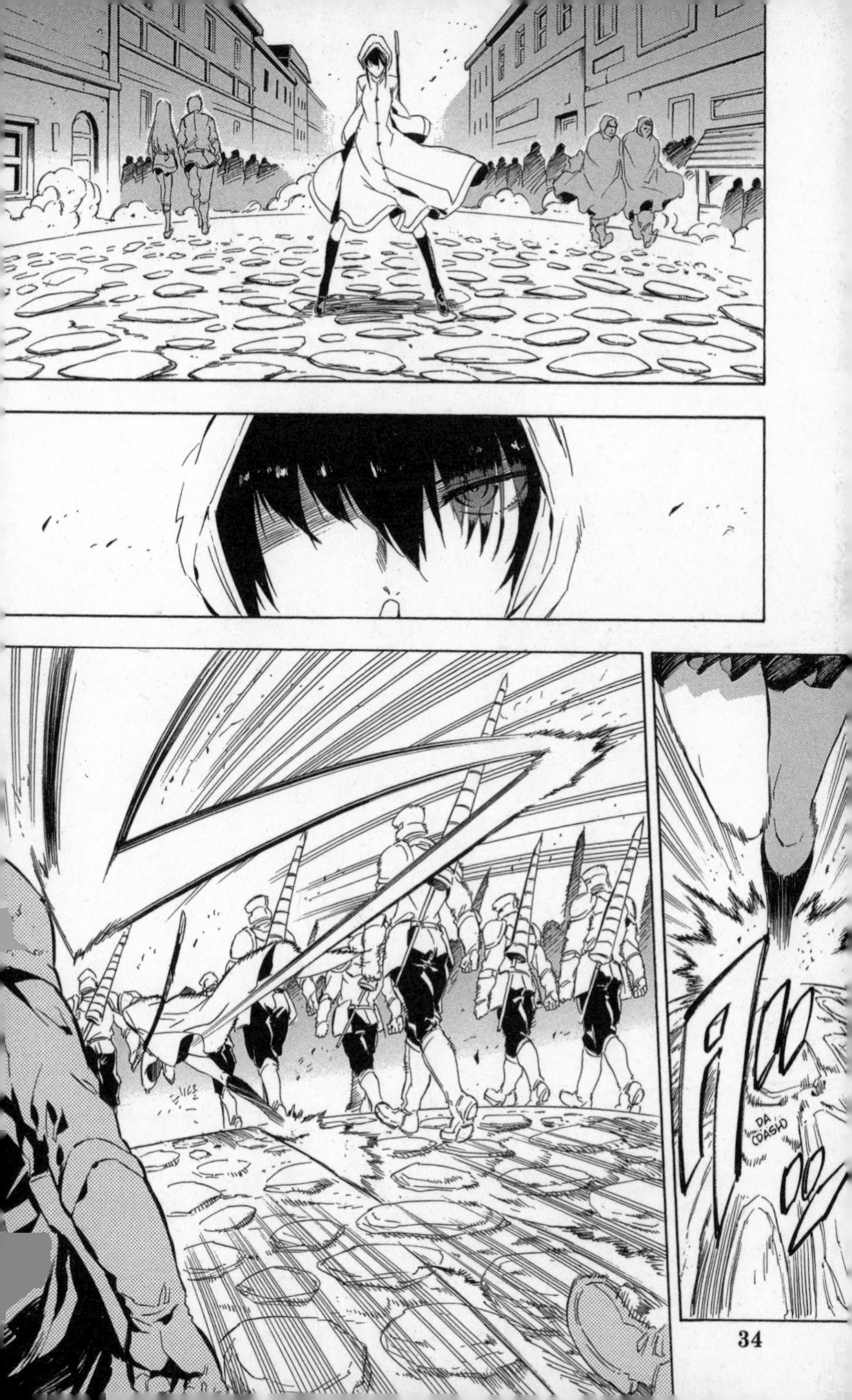
DA
DASH

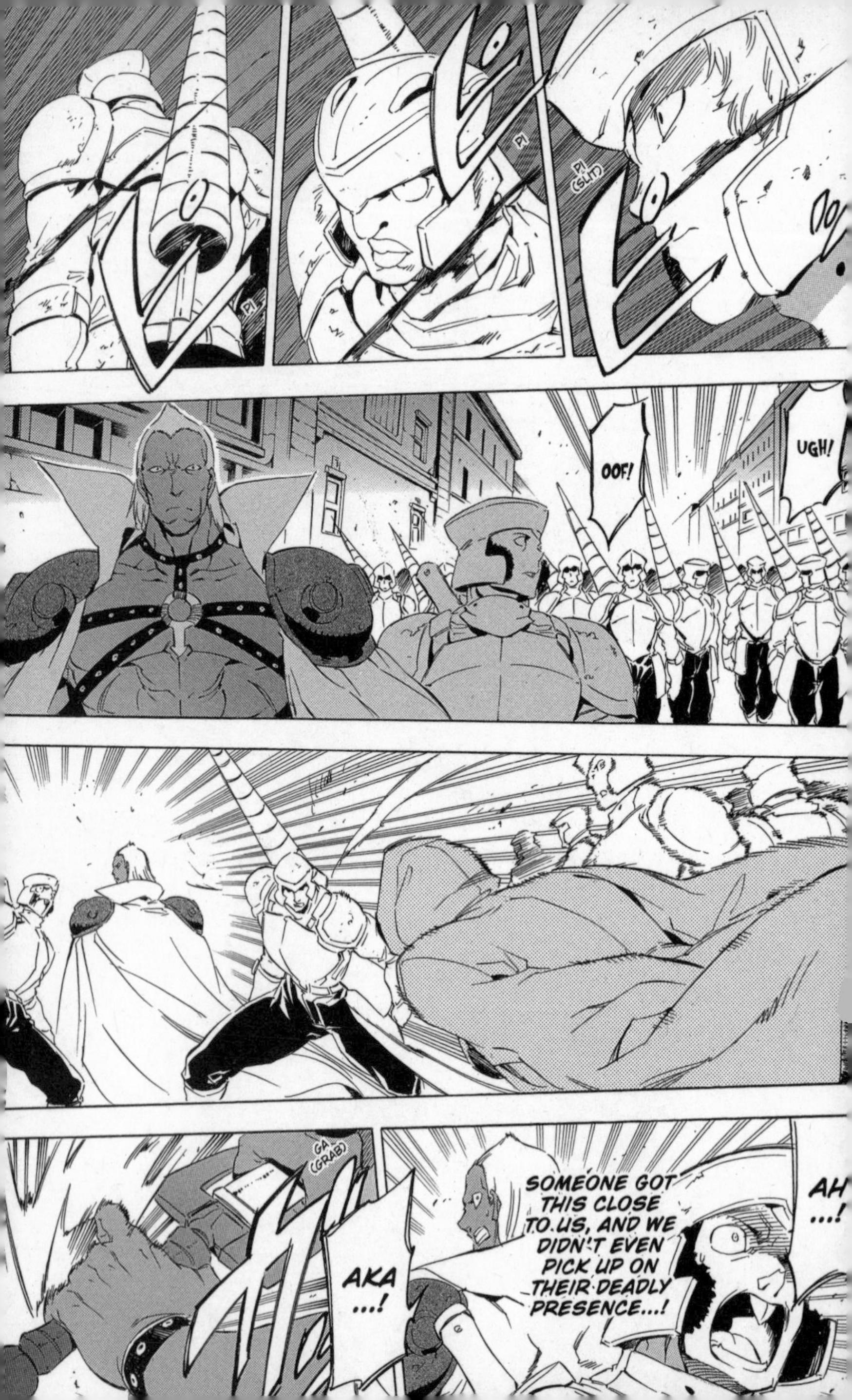
PI (SLIT)
PI
PI
UGH!
OOF!
AH ...!
SOMEONE GOT THIS CLOSE TO US, AND WE DIDN'T EVEN PICK UP ON THEIR DEADLY PRESENCE...!
GA (GRAB)
AKA ...!

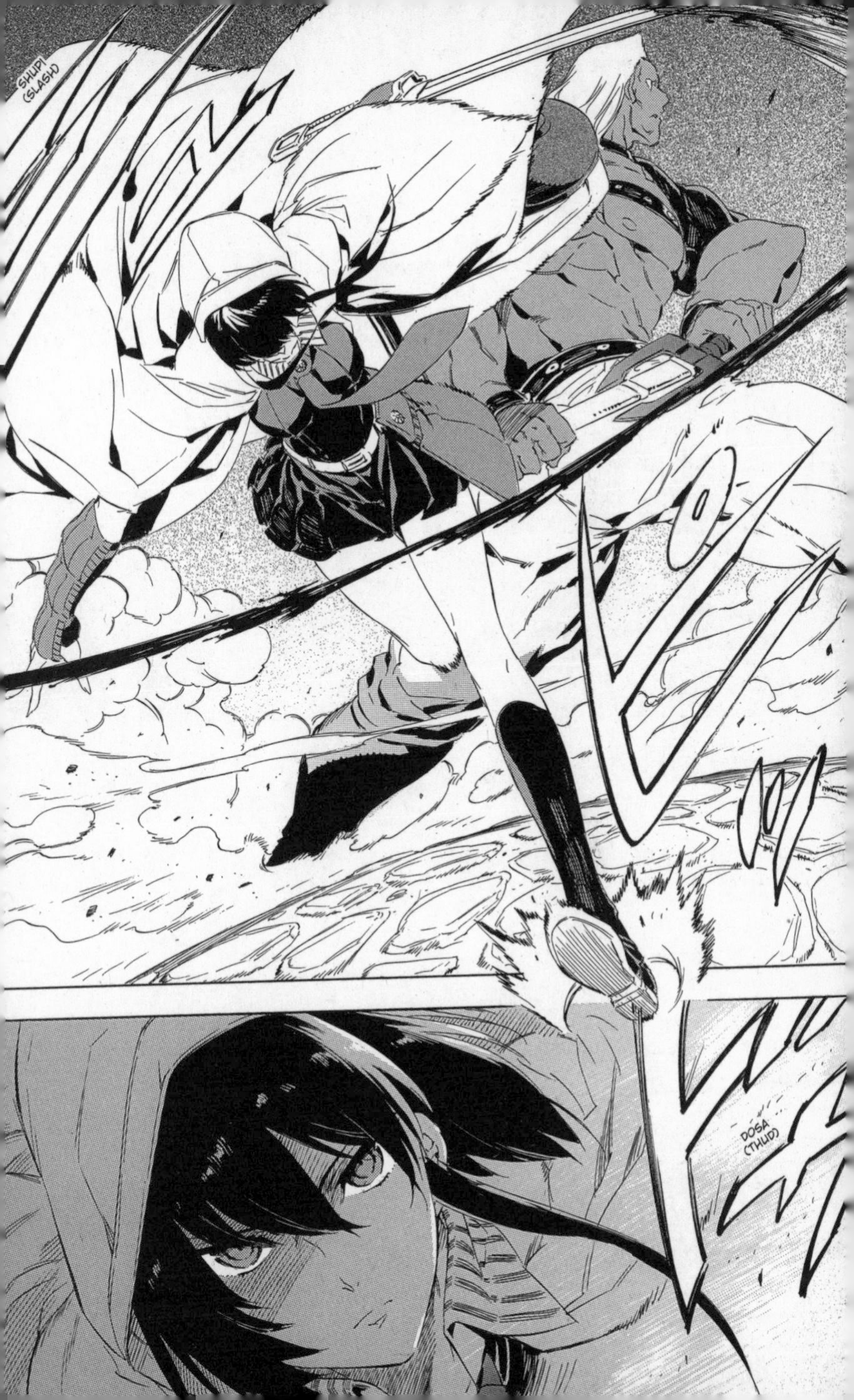
SHUP! (SLASH)
DOSA (THUD)

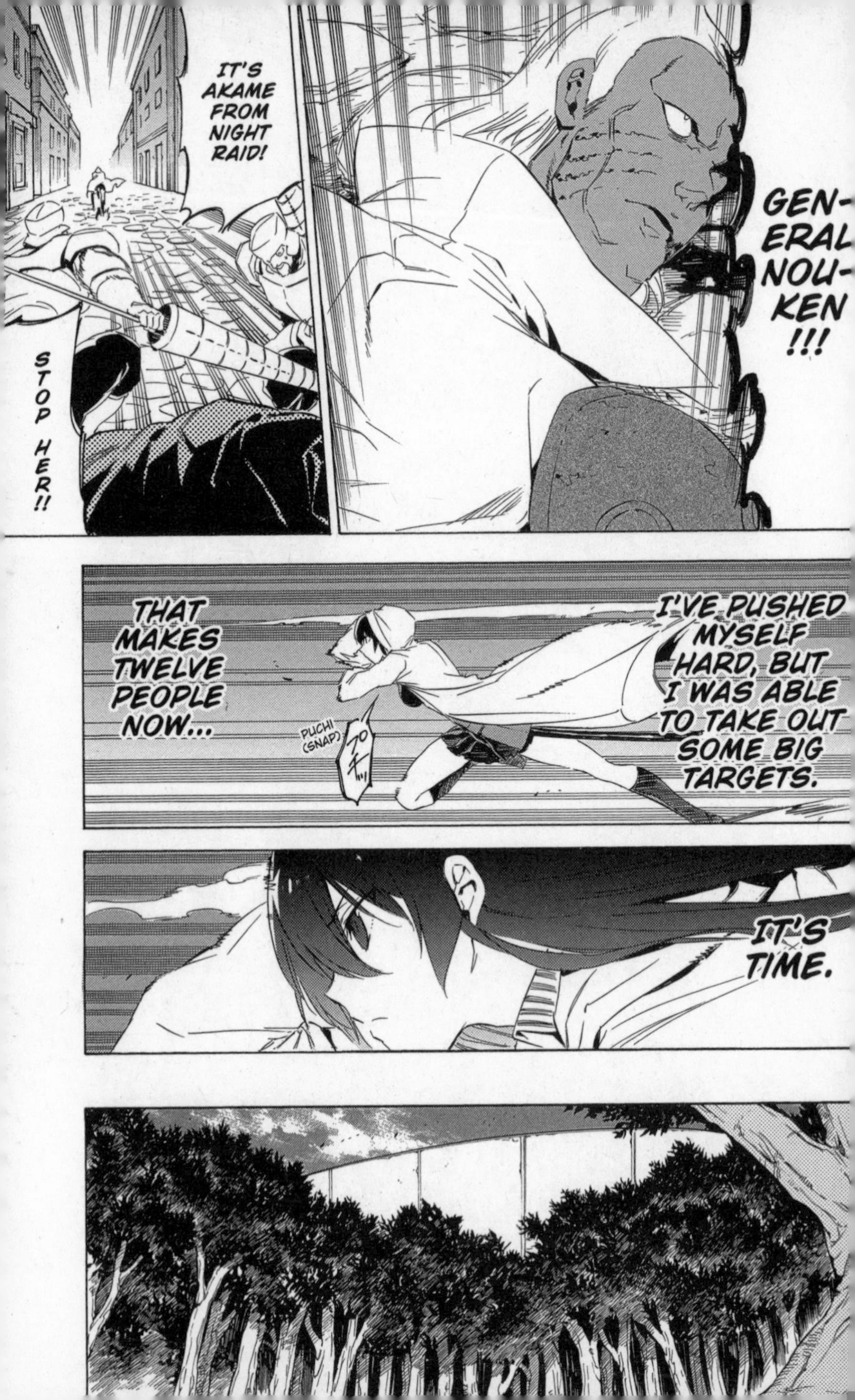
GENERAL NOUKEN!!!
IT'S AKAME FROM NIGHT RAID!
STOP HER!!
I'VE PUSHED MYSELF HARD, BUT I WAS ABLE TO TAKE OUT SOME BIG TARGETS.
THAT MAKES TWELVE PEOPLE NOW...
PUCHI (SNAP)
プチ
IT'S TIME.

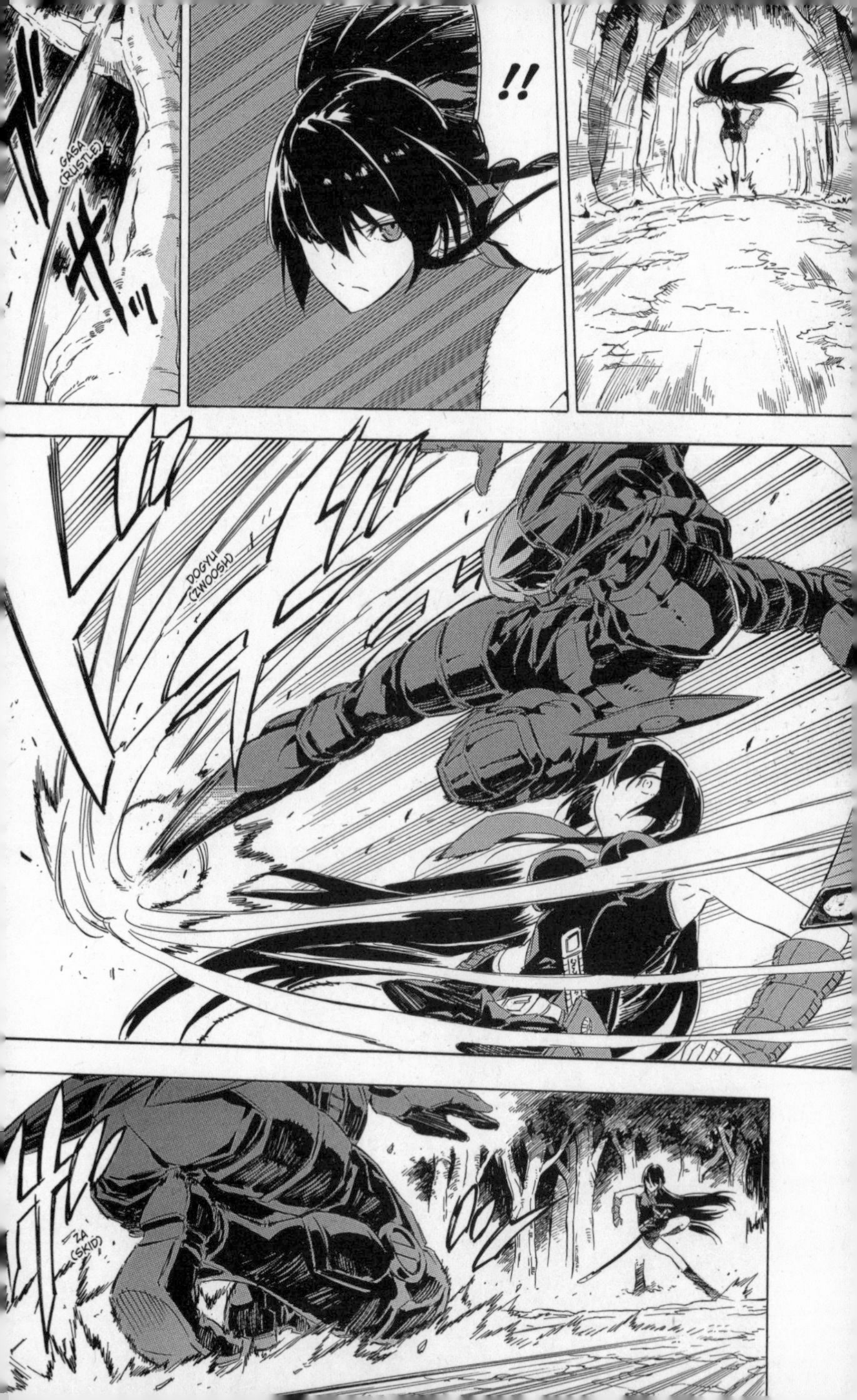
!!
GASA (RUSTLE)
DOGYU (ZWOOSH)
ZA (SKID)

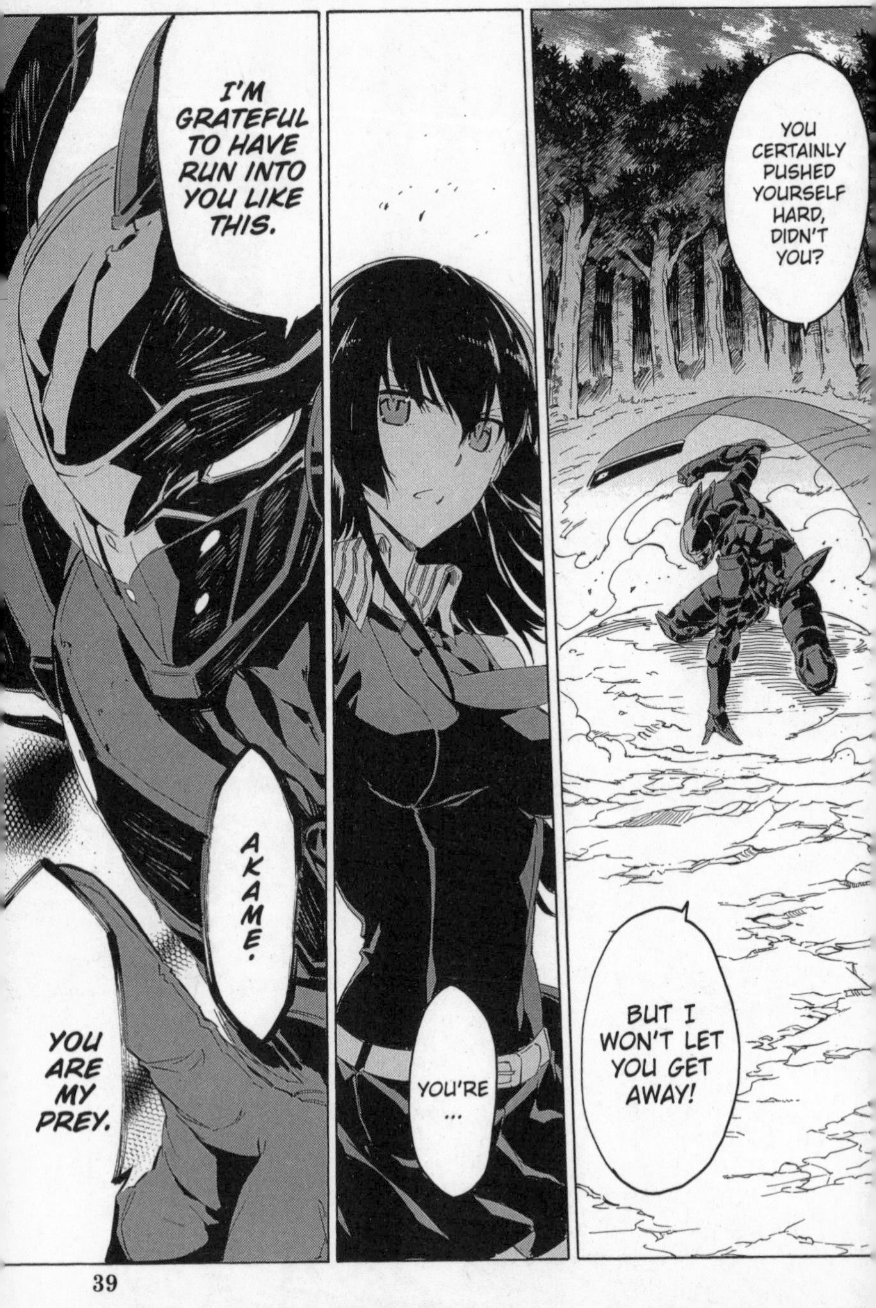
YOU CERTAINLY PUSHED YOURSELF HARD, DIDN'T YOU?
BUT I WON'T LET YOU GET AWAY!
YOU'RE ...
I'M GRATEFUL TO HAVE RUN INTO YOU LIKE THIS.
AKAME.
YOU ARE MY PREY.

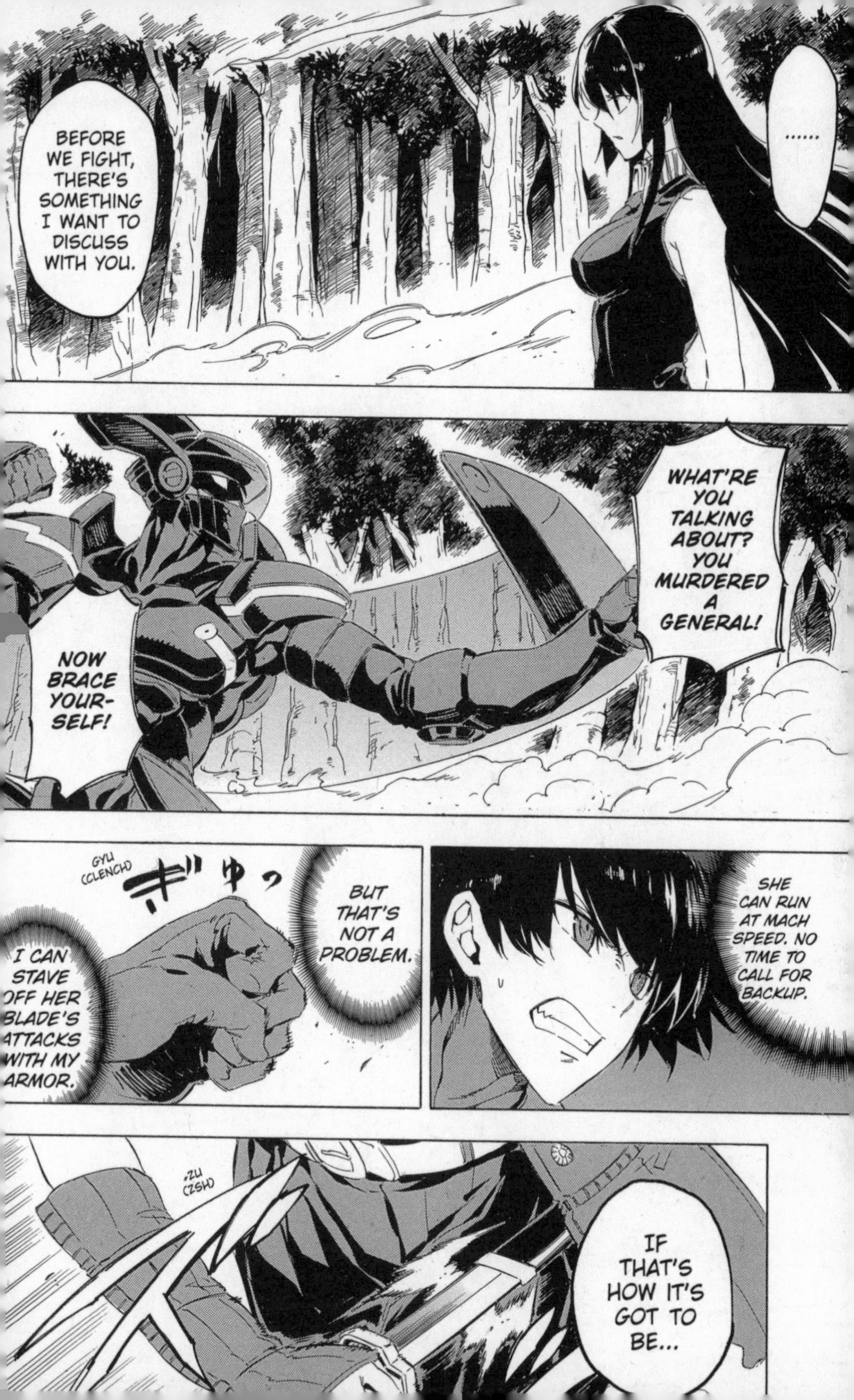
......
BEFORE WE FIGHT, THERE'S SOMETHING I WANT TO DISCUSS WITH YOU.
WHAT'RE YOU TALKING ABOUT? YOU MURDERED A GENERAL!
NOW BRACE YOURSELF!
SHE CAN RUN AT MACH SPEED. NO TIME TO CALL FOR BACKUP.
GYU (CLENCH)
BUT THAT'S NOT A PROBLEM.
I CAN STAVE OFF HER BLADE'S ATTACKS WITH MY ARMOR.
IF THAT'S HOW IT'S GOT TO BE...
ZU (ZSH)

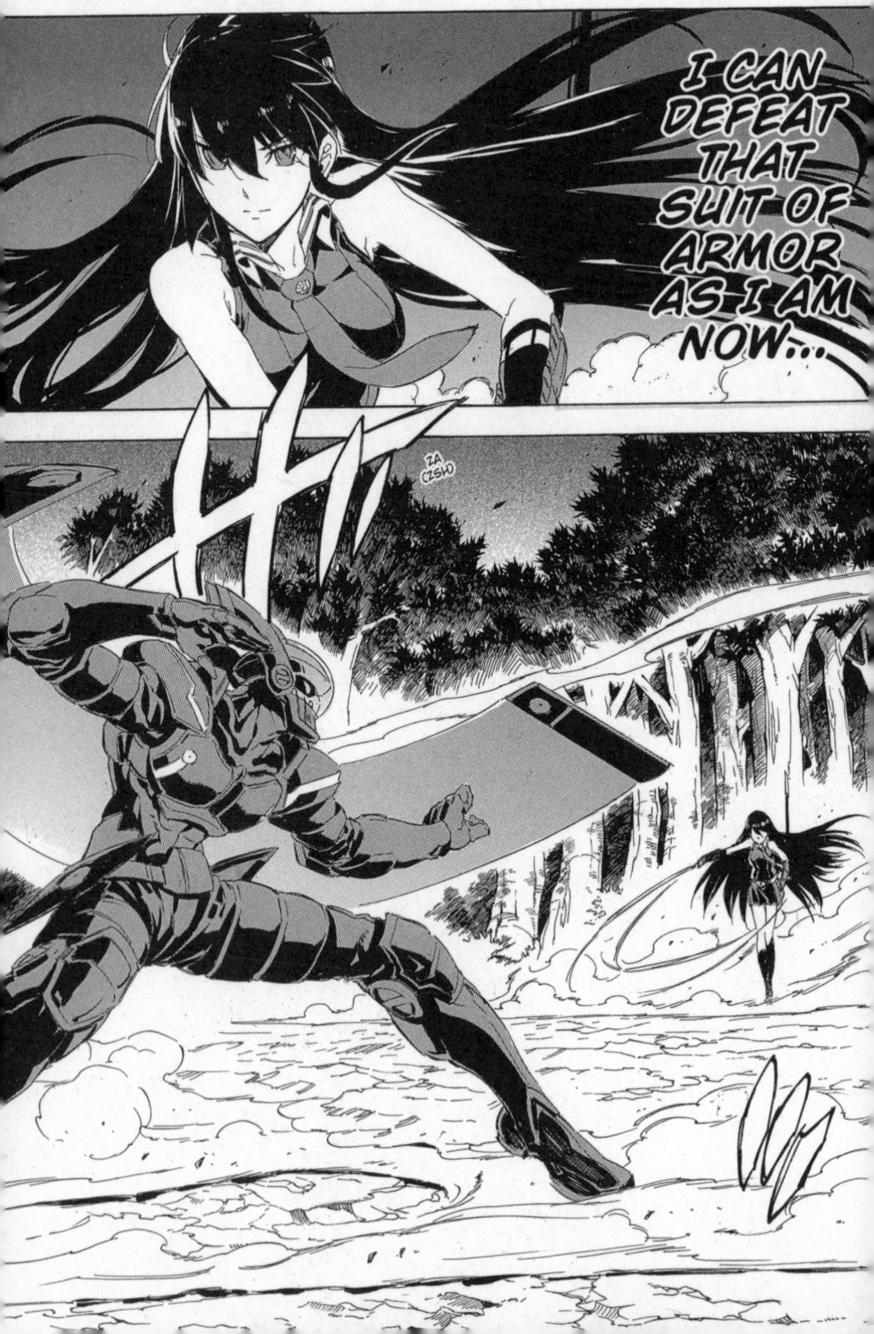
I CAN DEFEAT THAT SUIT OF ARMOR AS I AM NOW...
ZA (ZSH)

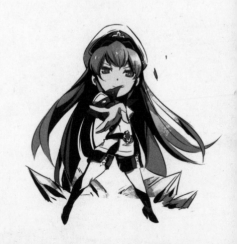

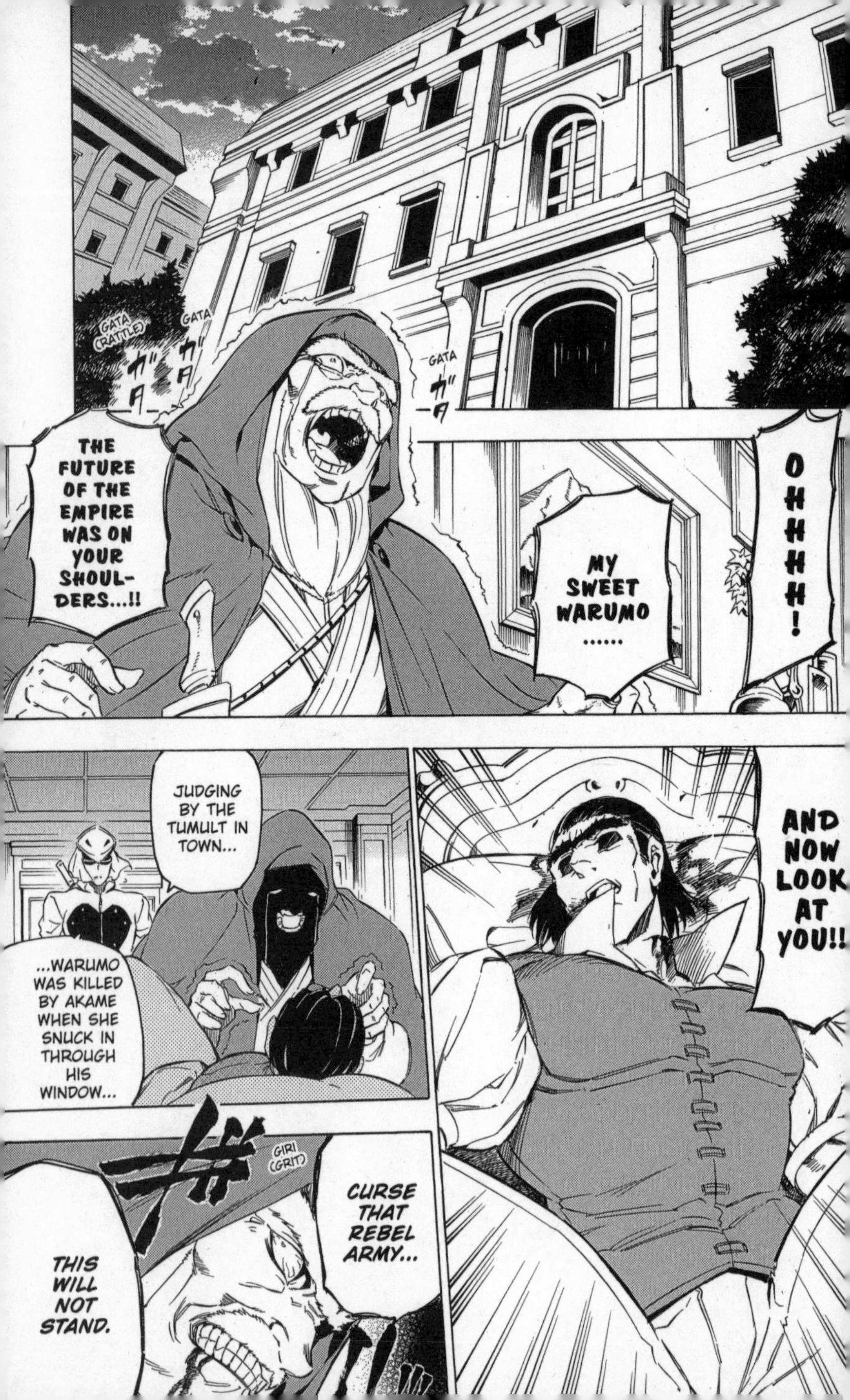
GATA
GATA
GATA (RATTLE)
OHHHHH!
MY SWEET WARUMO ......
THE FUTURE OF THE EMPIRE WAS ON YOUR SHOULDERS...!!
AND NOW LOOK AT YOU!!
JUDGING BY THE TUMULT IN TOWN...
...WARUMO WAS KILLED BY AKAME WHEN SHE SNUCK IN THROUGH HIS WINDOW...
CURSE THAT REBEL ARMY...
GIRI (GRIT)
THIS WILL NOT STAND.

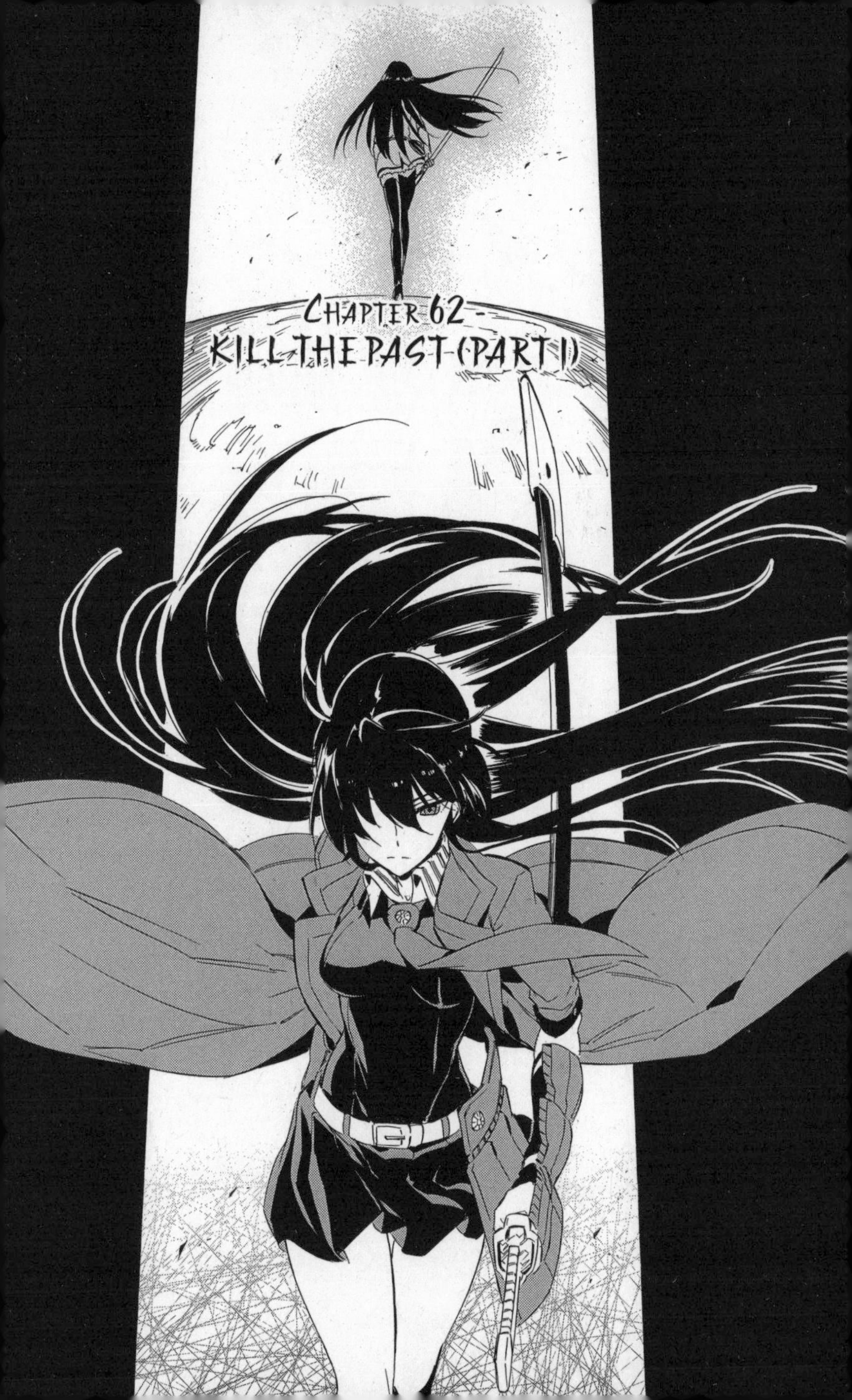
Chapter 62
Kill the Past (Part 1)

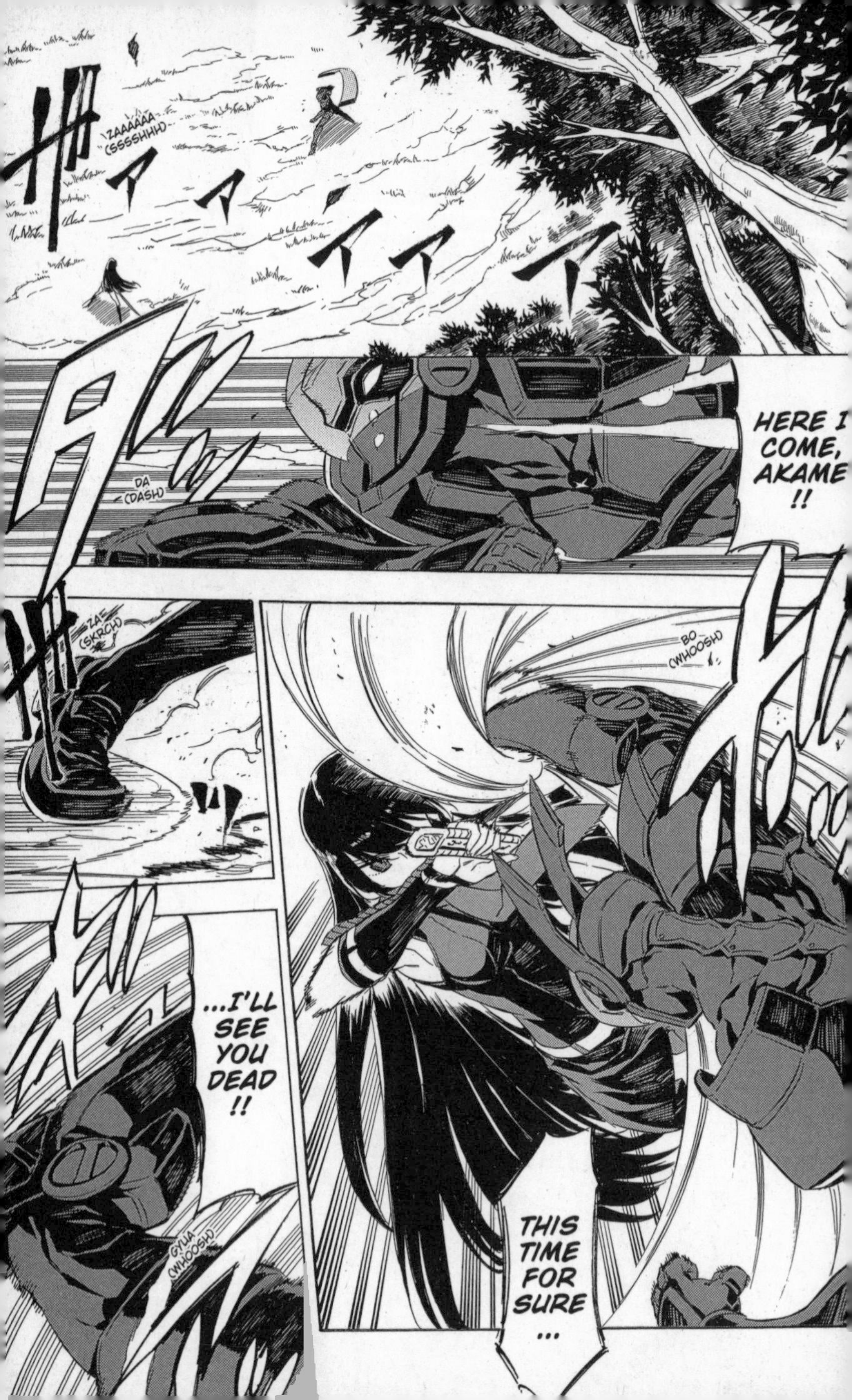
ZAAAAAA (SSSSHHH)
HERE I COME, AKAME!!
DA (DASH)
BO (WHOOSH)
THIS TIME FOR SURE...
ZA (SKRCH)
...I'LL SEE YOU DEAD!!
GYUA (WHOOSH)

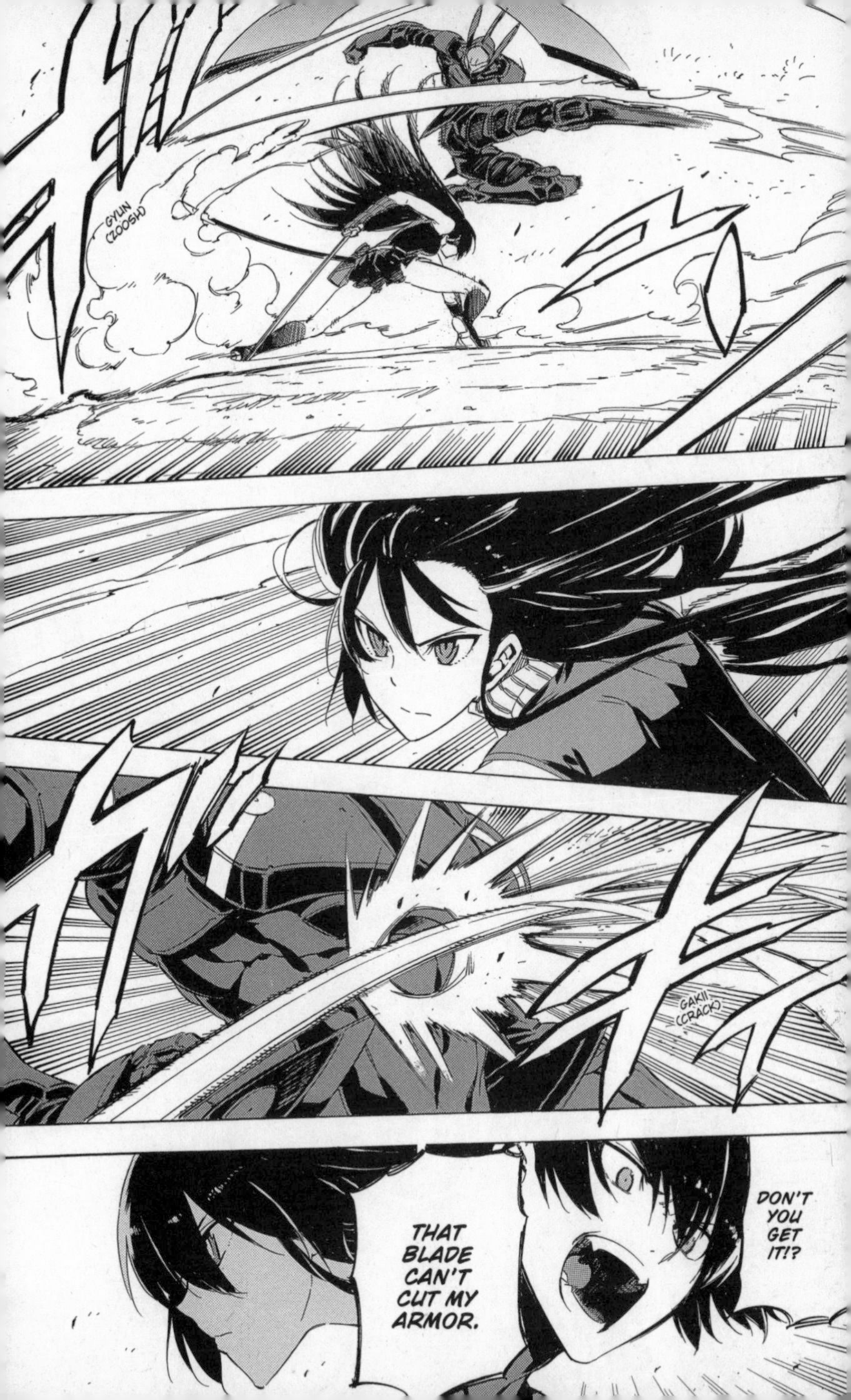
GYUN (ZOOSH)
GAKII (CRACK)
DON'T YOU GET IT!?
THAT BLADE CAN'T CUT MY ARMOR.

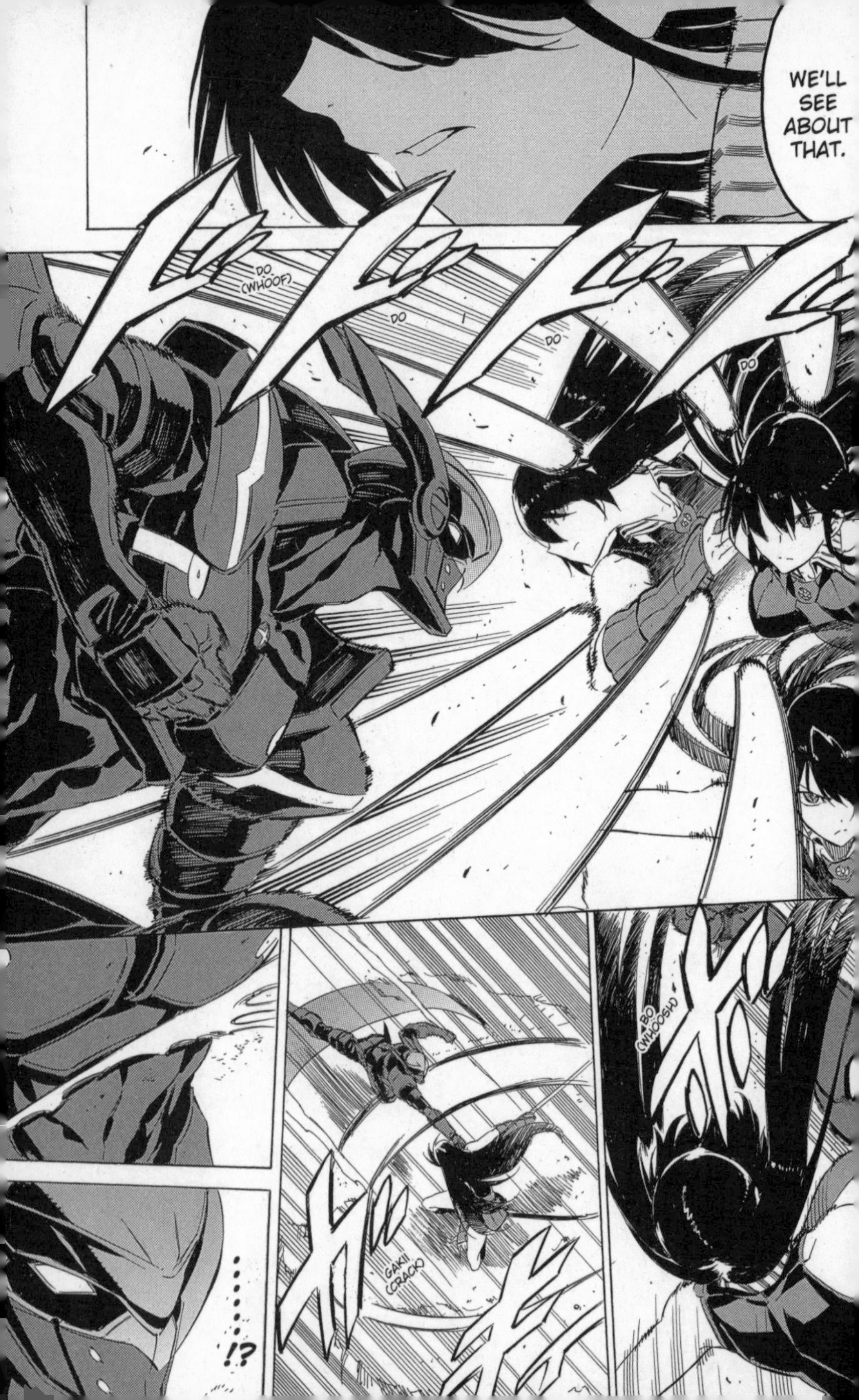
WE'LL SEE ABOUT THAT.
DO
DO
DO
DO (WHOOF)
BO (WHOOSH)
GAKII (CRACK)
......!?

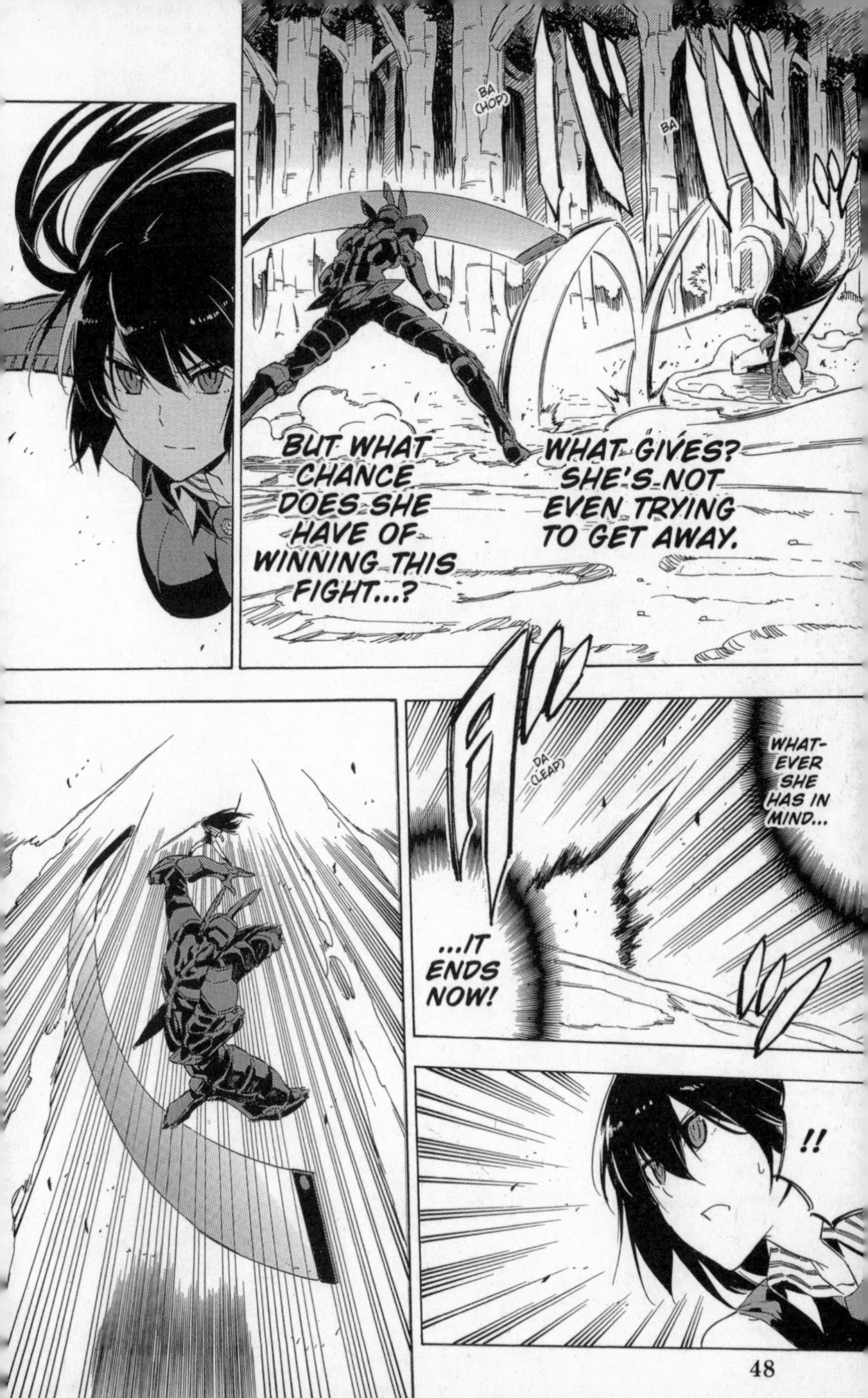
BA (HOP)
BA
WHAT GIVES? SHE'S NOT EVEN TRYING TO GET AWAY.
BUT WHAT CHANCE DOES SHE HAVE OF WINNING THIS FIGHT...?
DA (LEAP)
WHAT-EVER SHE HAS IN MIND...
...IT ENDS NOW!
!!
...

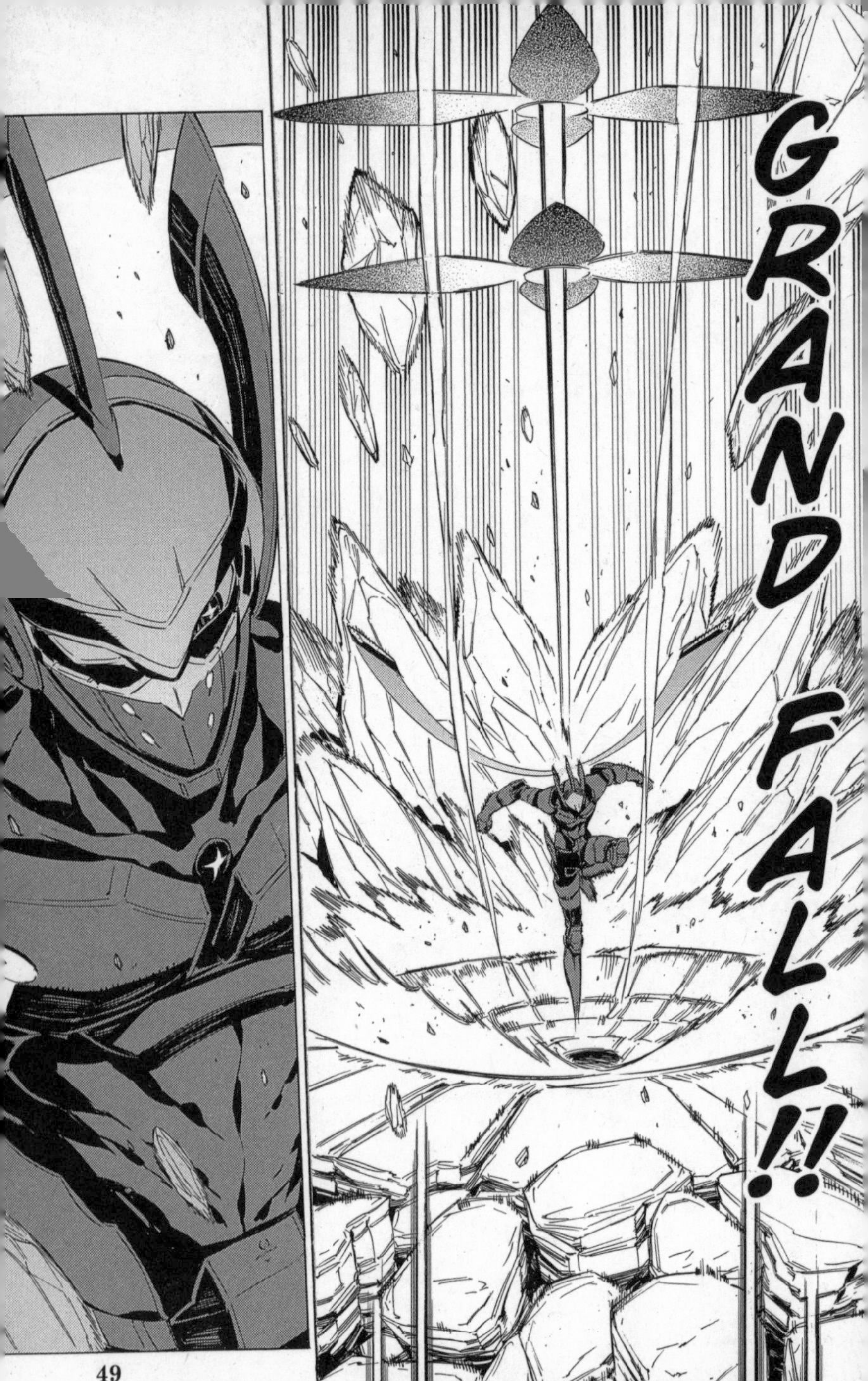
GRAND FALL!!

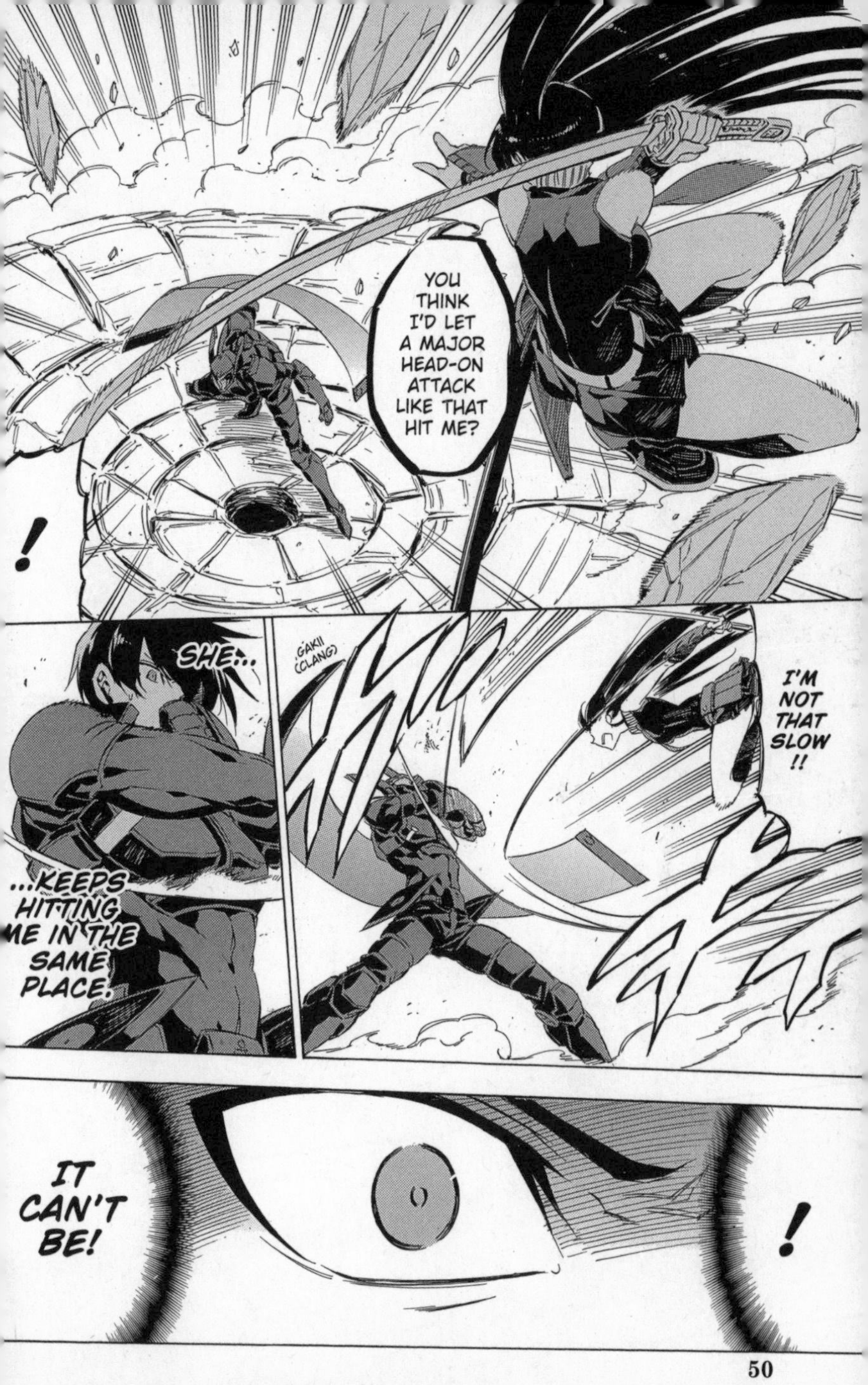
YOU THINK I'D LET A MAJOR HEAD-ON ATTACK LIKE THAT HIT ME?
!
I'M NOT THAT SLOW !!
GAKII (CLANG)
SHE...
...KEEPS HITTING ME IN THE SAME PLACE.
!
IT CAN'T BE!

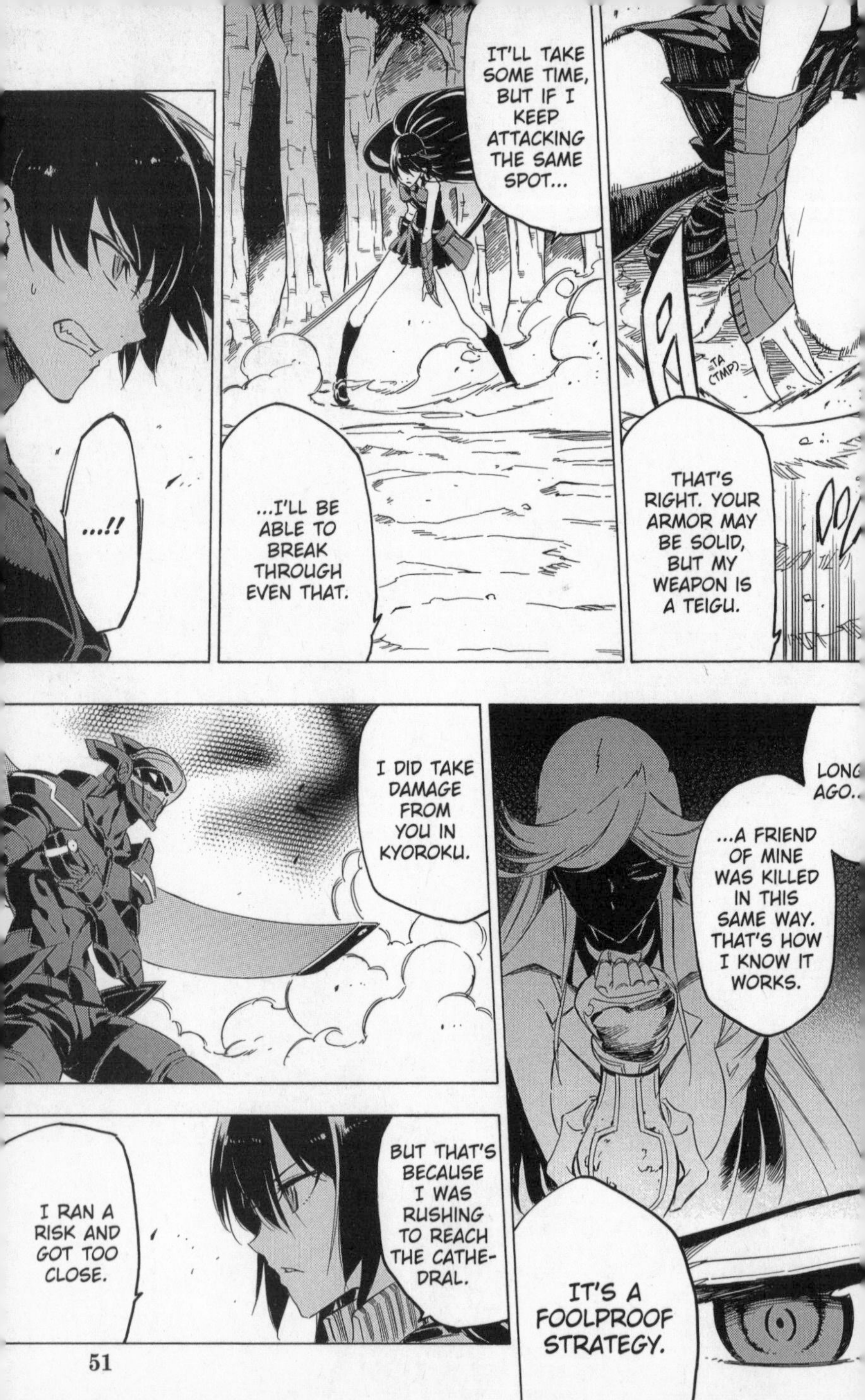
TA (TMP)
THAT'S RIGHT. YOUR ARMOR MAY BE SOLID, BUT MY WEAPON IS A TEIGU.
IT'LL TAKE SOME TIME, BUT IF I KEEP ATTACKING THE SAME SPOT...
...I'LL BE ABLE TO BREAK THROUGH EVEN THAT.
...!!
LONG AGO...
...A FRIEND OF MINE WAS KILLED IN THIS SAME WAY. THAT'S HOW I KNOW IT WORKS.
IT'S A FOOLPROOF STRATEGY.
I DID TAKE DAMAGE FROM YOU IN KYOROKU.
BUT THAT'S BECAUSE I WAS RUSHING TO REACH THE CATHE-DRAL.
I RAN A RISK AND GOT TOO CLOSE.

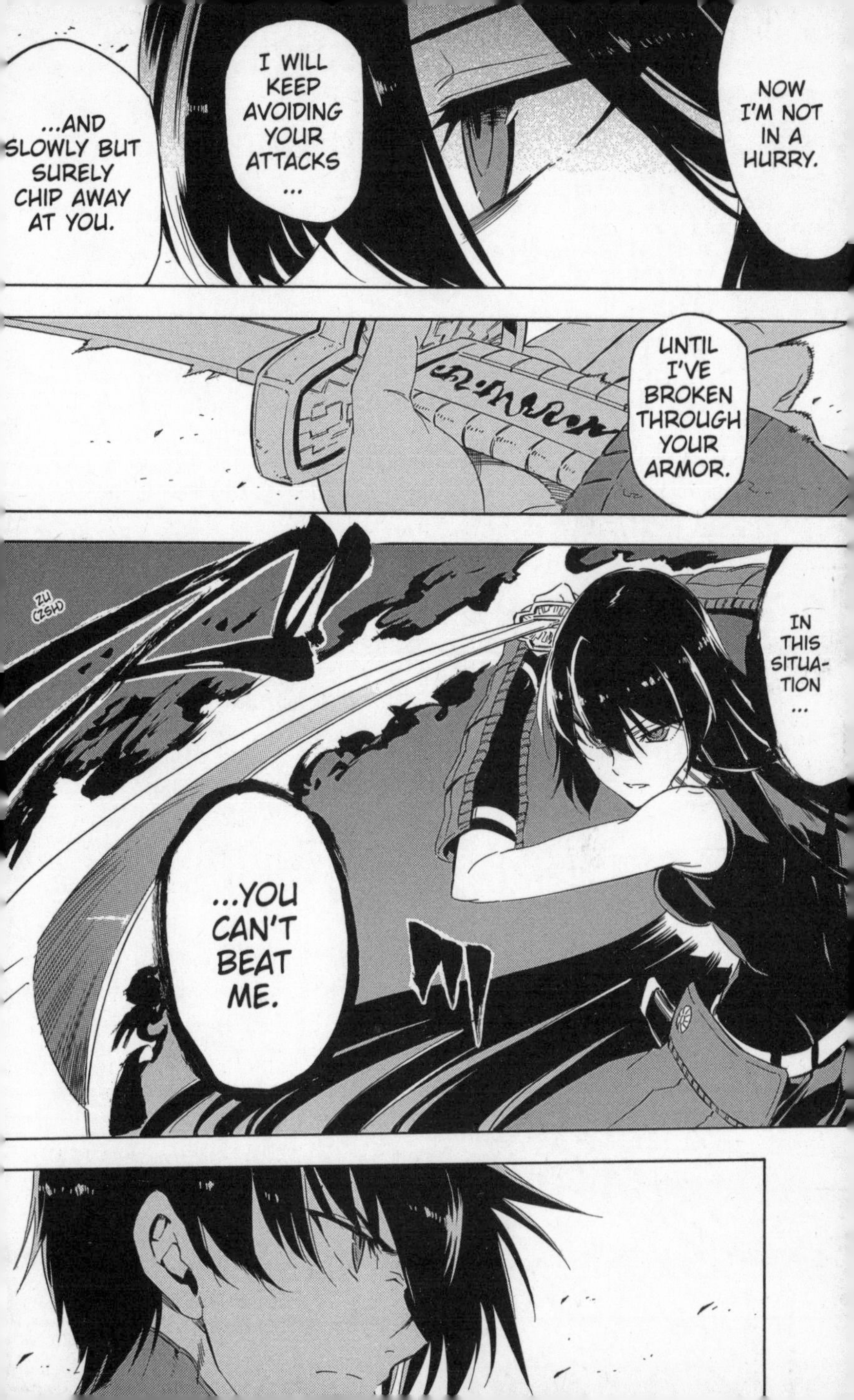
NOW I'M NOT IN A HURRY.
I WILL KEEP AVOIDING YOUR ATTACKS ...
...AND SLOWLY BUT SURELY CHIP AWAY AT YOU.
UNTIL I'VE BROKEN THROUGH YOUR ARMOR.
IN THIS SITUATION ...
ZU (ZSH)
...YOU CAN'T BEAT ME.

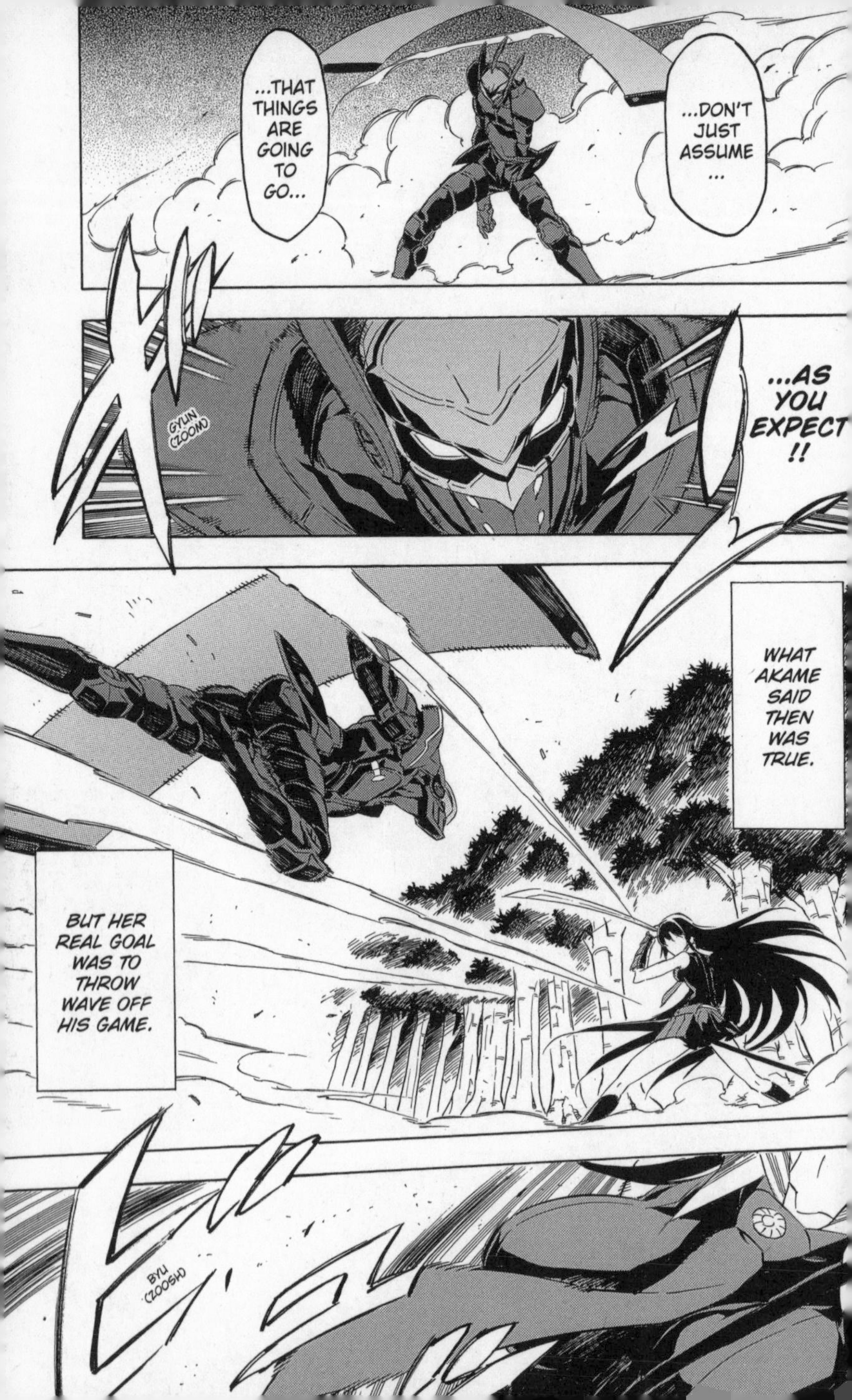
...DON'T JUST ASSUME ...
...THAT THINGS ARE GOING TO GO...
...AS YOU EXPECT !!
GYUN (ZOOM)
WHAT AKAME SAID THEN WAS TRUE.
BUT HER REAL GOAL WAS TO THROW WAVE OFF HIS GAME.
BYU (ZOOSH)

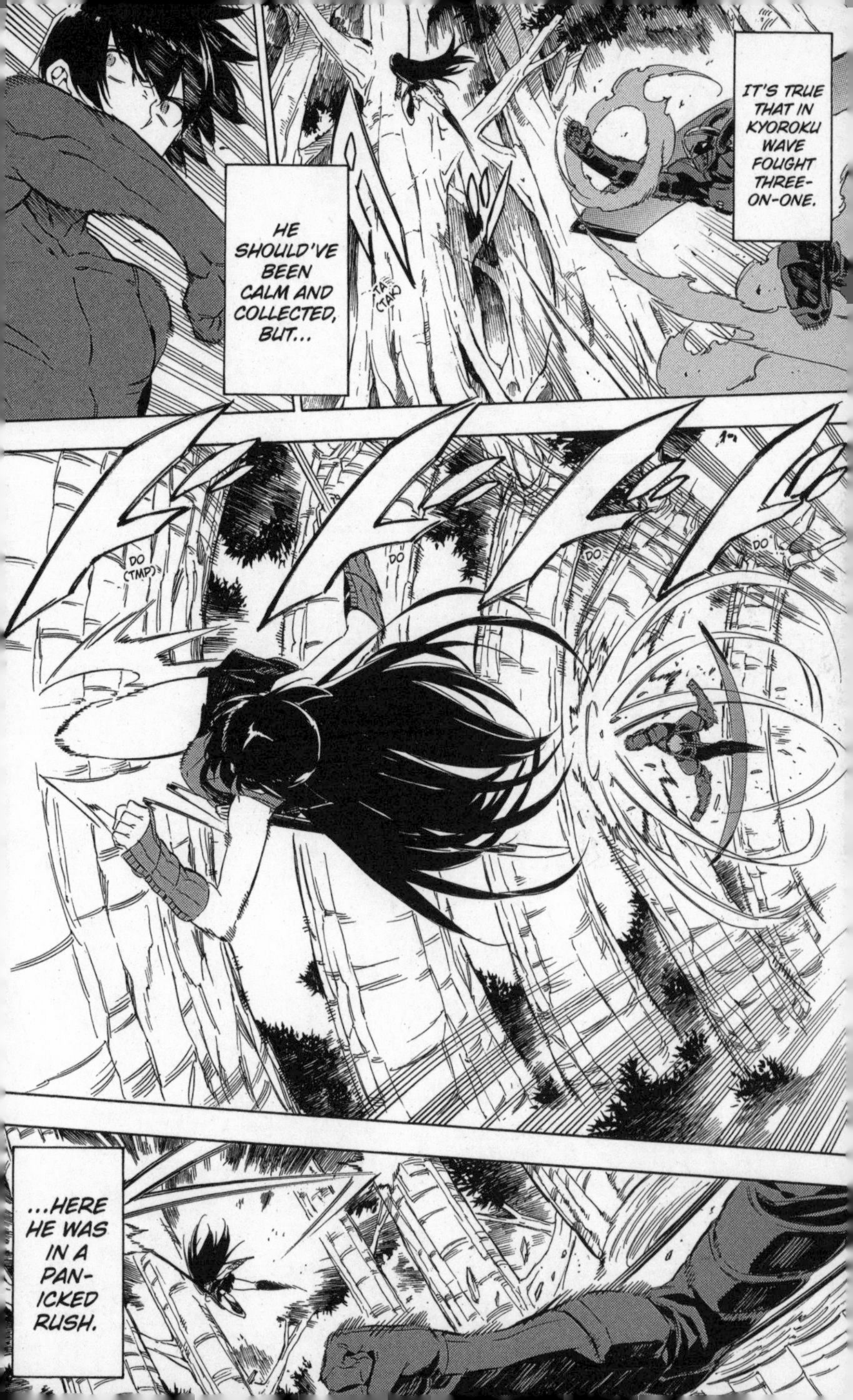
IT'S TRUE THAT IN KYOROKU WAVE FOUGHT THREE-ON-ONE.
HE SHOULD'VE BEEN CALM AND COLLECTED, BUT...
TA (TAK)
DO
DO
DO
DO (TMP)
...HERE HE WAS IN A PAN-ICKED RUSH.

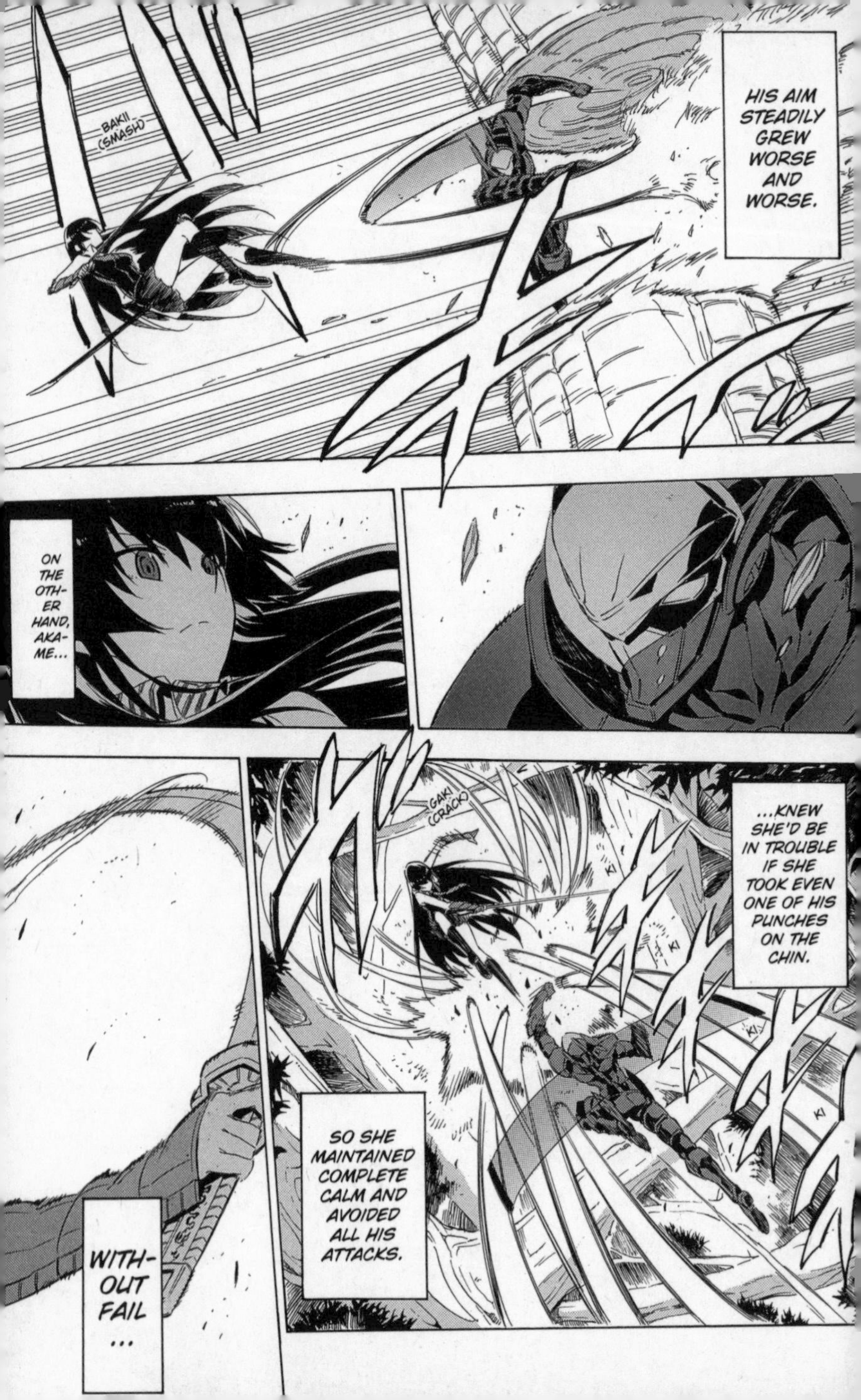
HIS AIM STEADILY GREW WORSE AND WORSE.
BAKII (SMASH)
ON THE OTH-ER HAND, AKA-ME...
...KNEW SHE'D BE IN TROUBLE IF SHE TOOK EVEN ONE OF HIS PUNCHES ON THE CHIN.
GAKI (CRACK)
KI
KI
KI
KI
SO SHE MAINTAINED COMPLETE CALM AND AVOIDED ALL HIS ATTACKS.
WITH-OUT FAIL ...

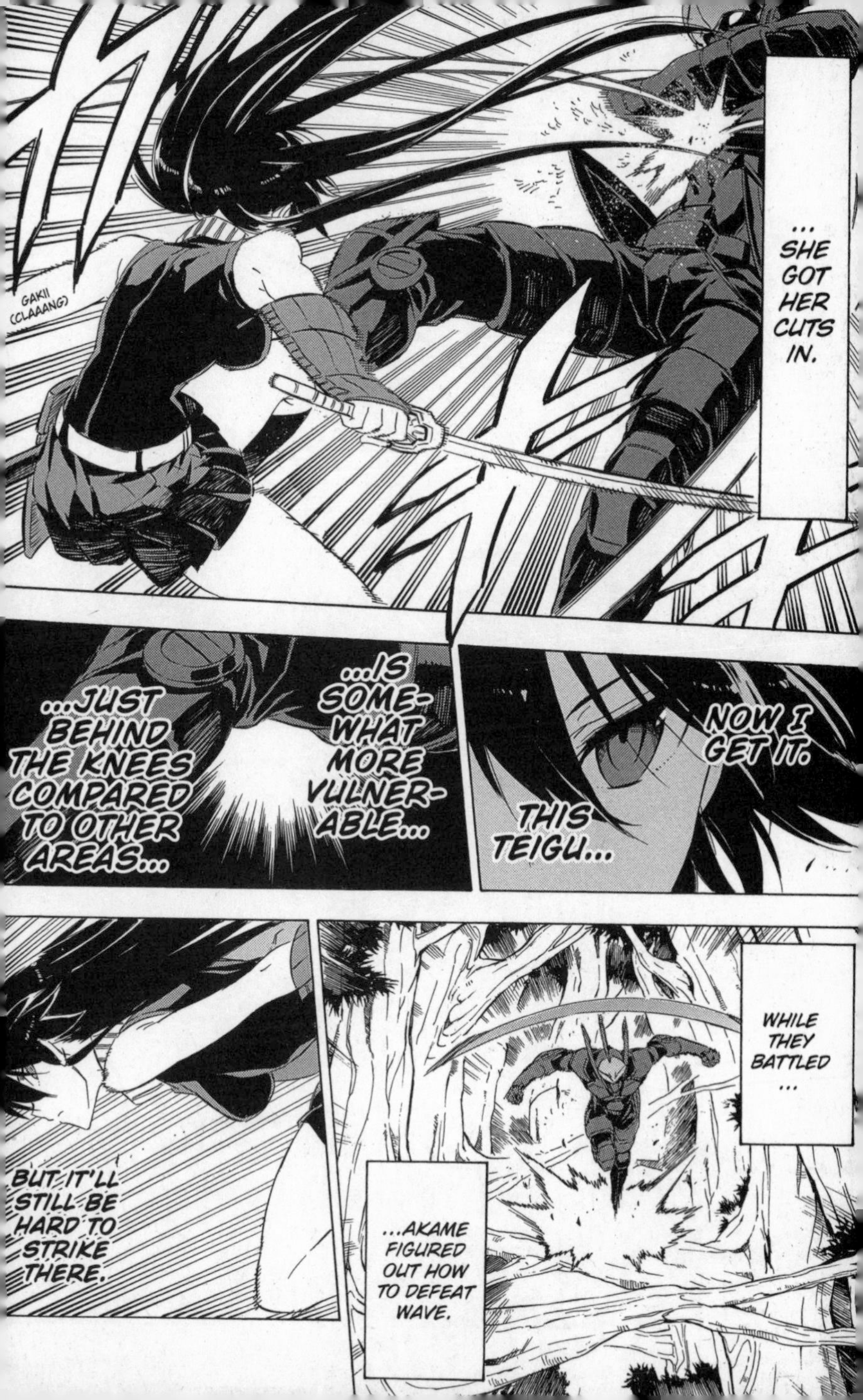
...SHE GOT HER CUTS IN.
GAKII (CLAAANG)
NOW I GET IT.
THIS TEIGU...
...IS SOMEWHAT MORE VULNERABLE...
...JUST BEHIND THE KNEES COMPARED TO OTHER AREAS...
WHILE THEY BATTLED...
...AKAME FIGURED OUT HOW TO DEFEAT WAVE.
BUT IT'LL STILL BE HARD TO STRIKE THERE.

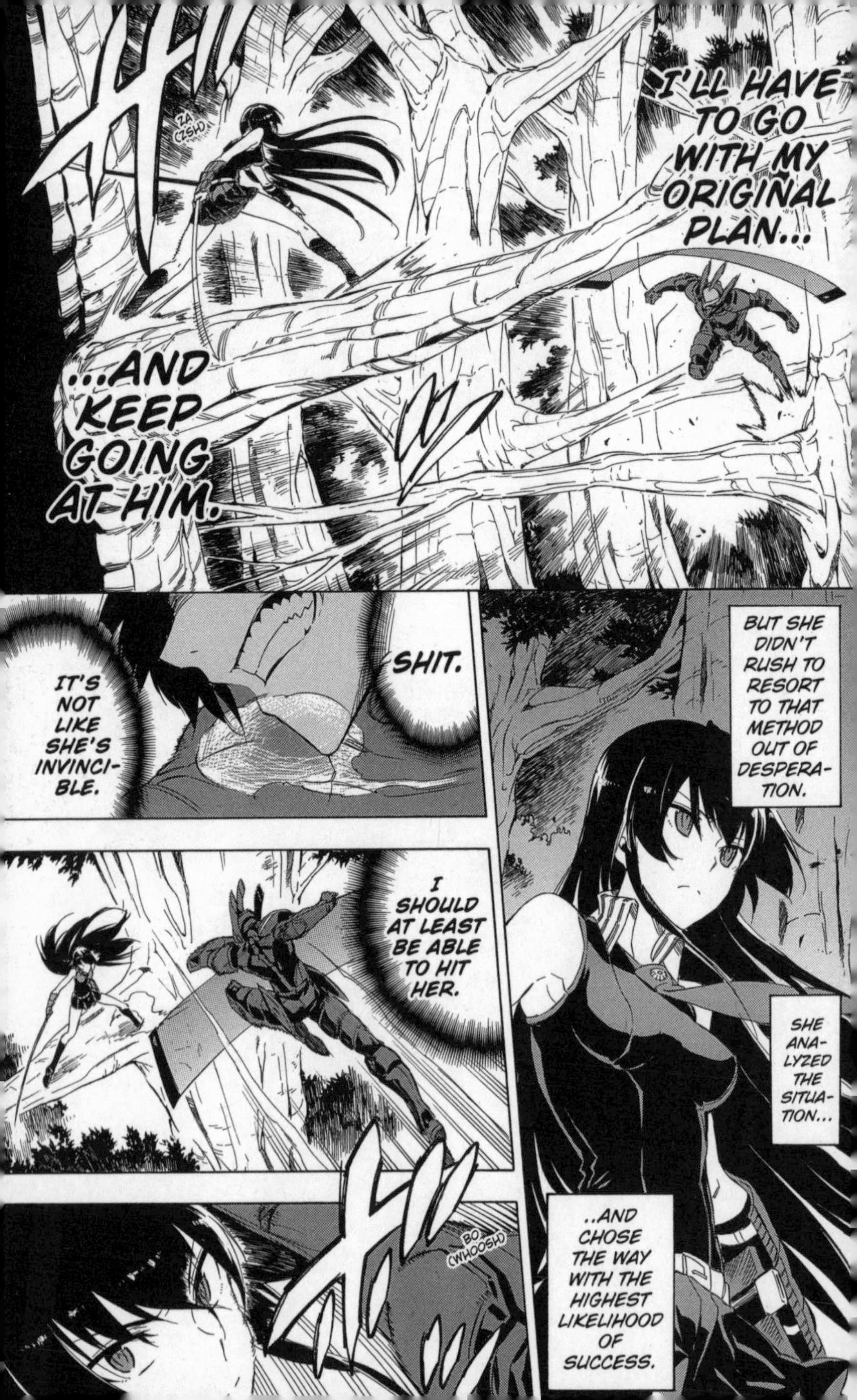
ZA (ZSHH)
I'LL HAVE TO GO WITH MY ORIGINAL PLAN...
...AND KEEP GOING AT HIM.
BUT SHE DIDN'T RUSH TO RESORT TO THAT METHOD OUT OF DESPERA-TION.
SHE ANA-LYZED THE SITUA-TION...
..AND CHOSE THE WAY WITH THE HIGHEST LIKELIHOOD OF SUCCESS.
SHIT.
IT'S NOT LIKE SHE'S INVINCI-BLE.
I SHOULD AT LEAST BE ABLE TO HIT HER.
BO (WHOOSH)

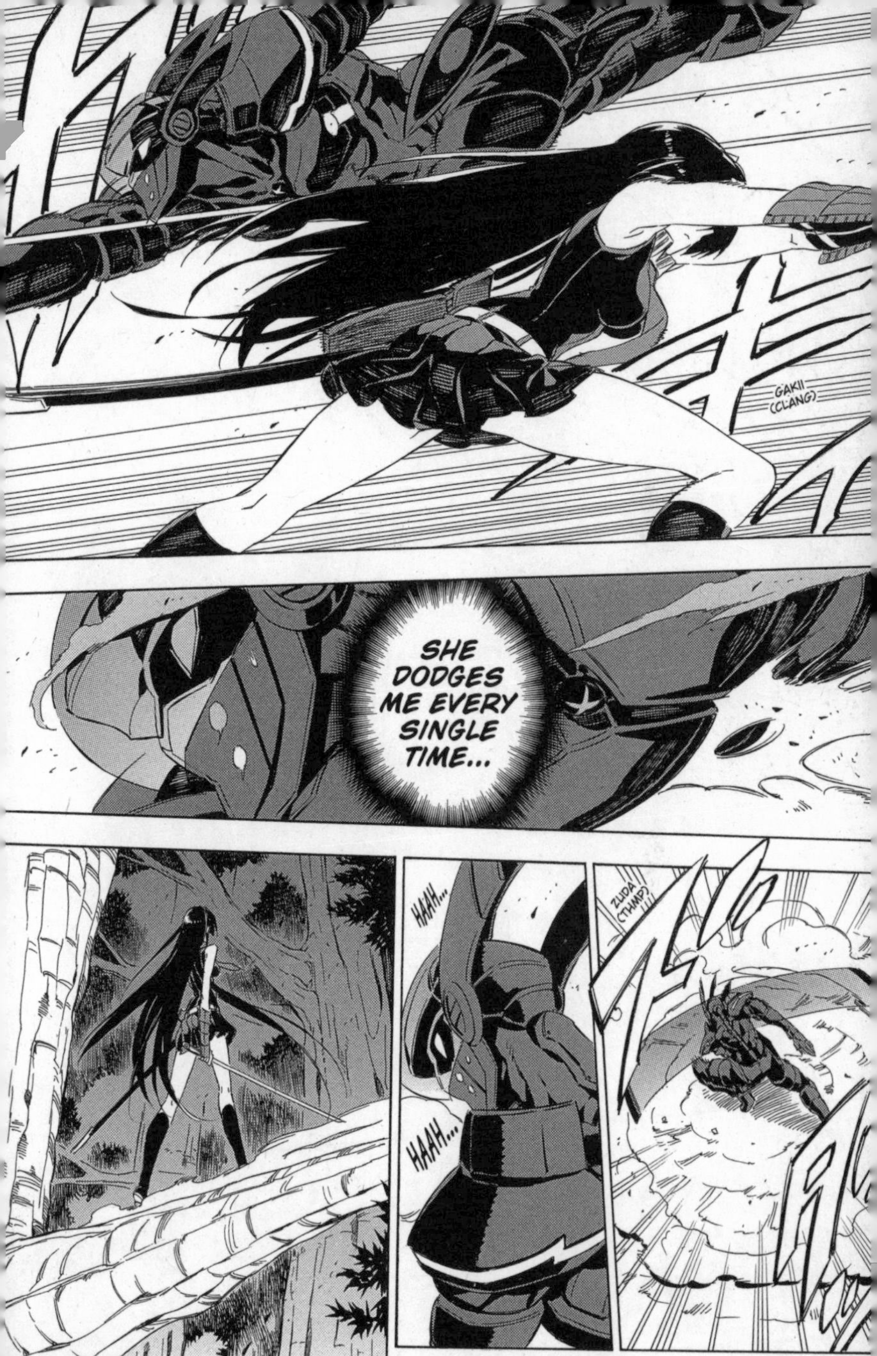
GAKII (CLANG)
SHE DODGES ME EVERY SINGLE TIME...
ZUDA (THUMP)
HAAH...
HAAH...

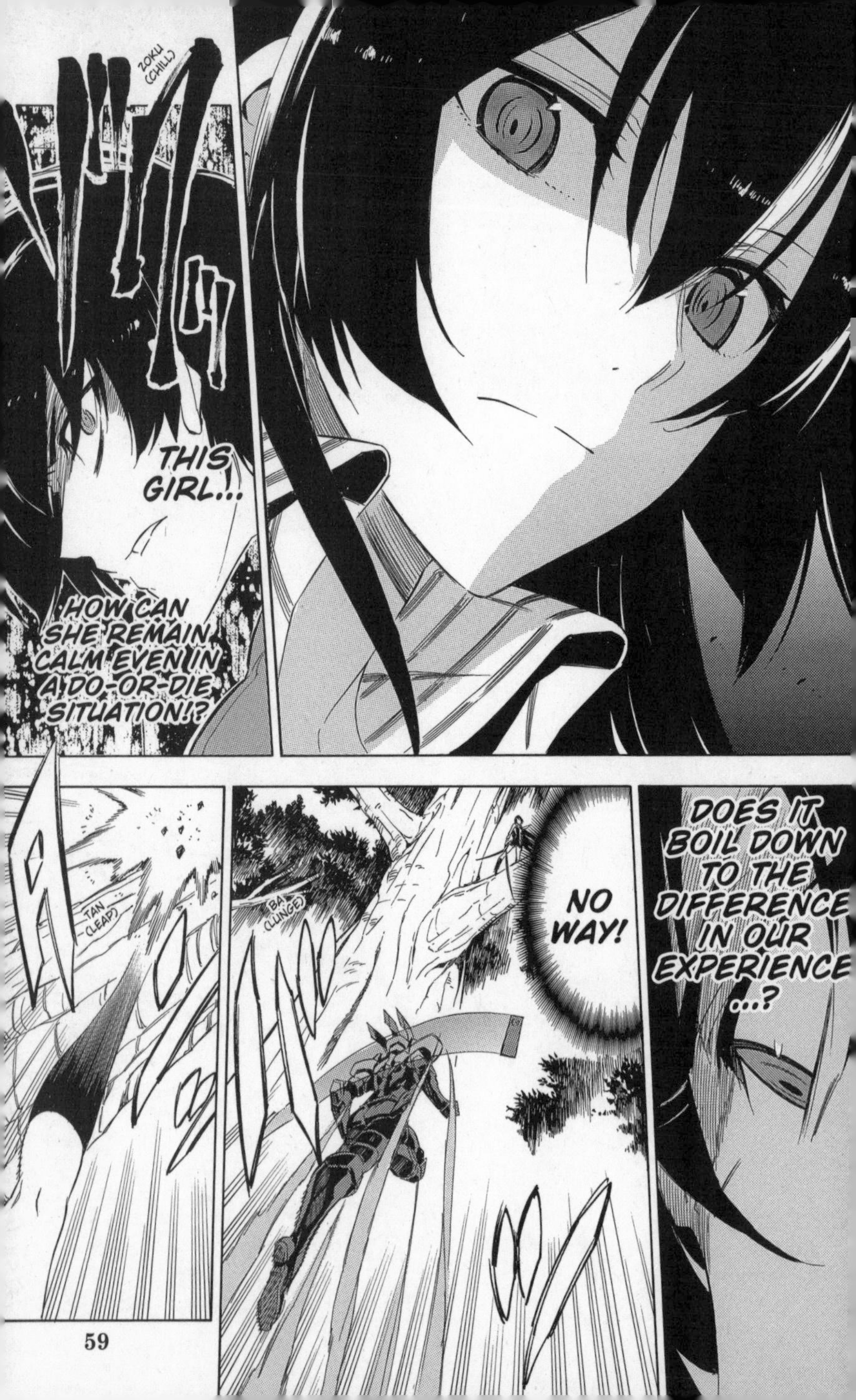
ZOKU (CHILL)
THIS GIRL...
HOW CAN SHE REMAIN CALM EVEN IN A DO-OR-DIE SITUATION!?
DOES IT BOIL DOWN TO THE DIFFERENCE IN OUR EXPERIENCE...?
NO WAY!
BA (LUNGE)
TAN (LEAP)

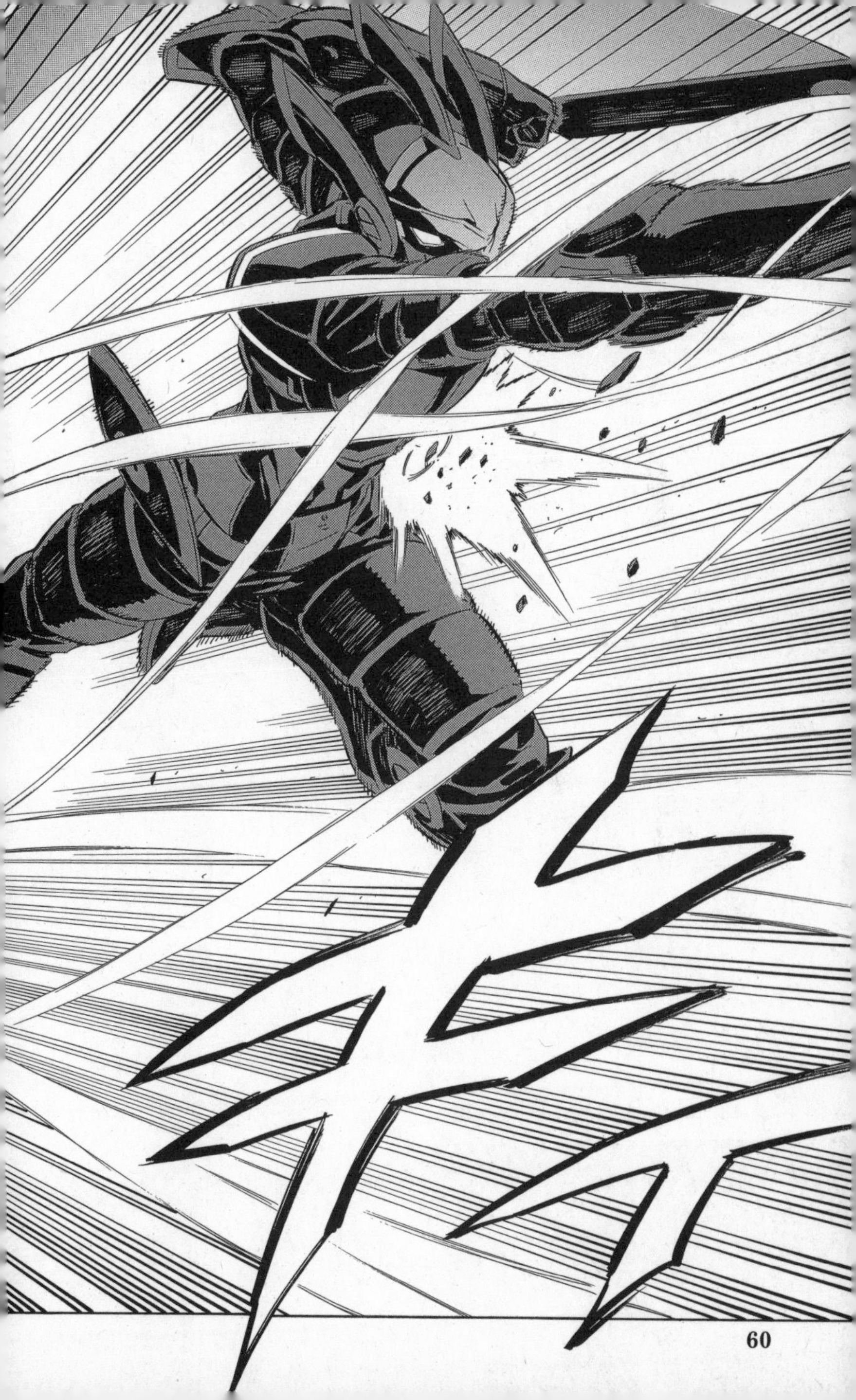

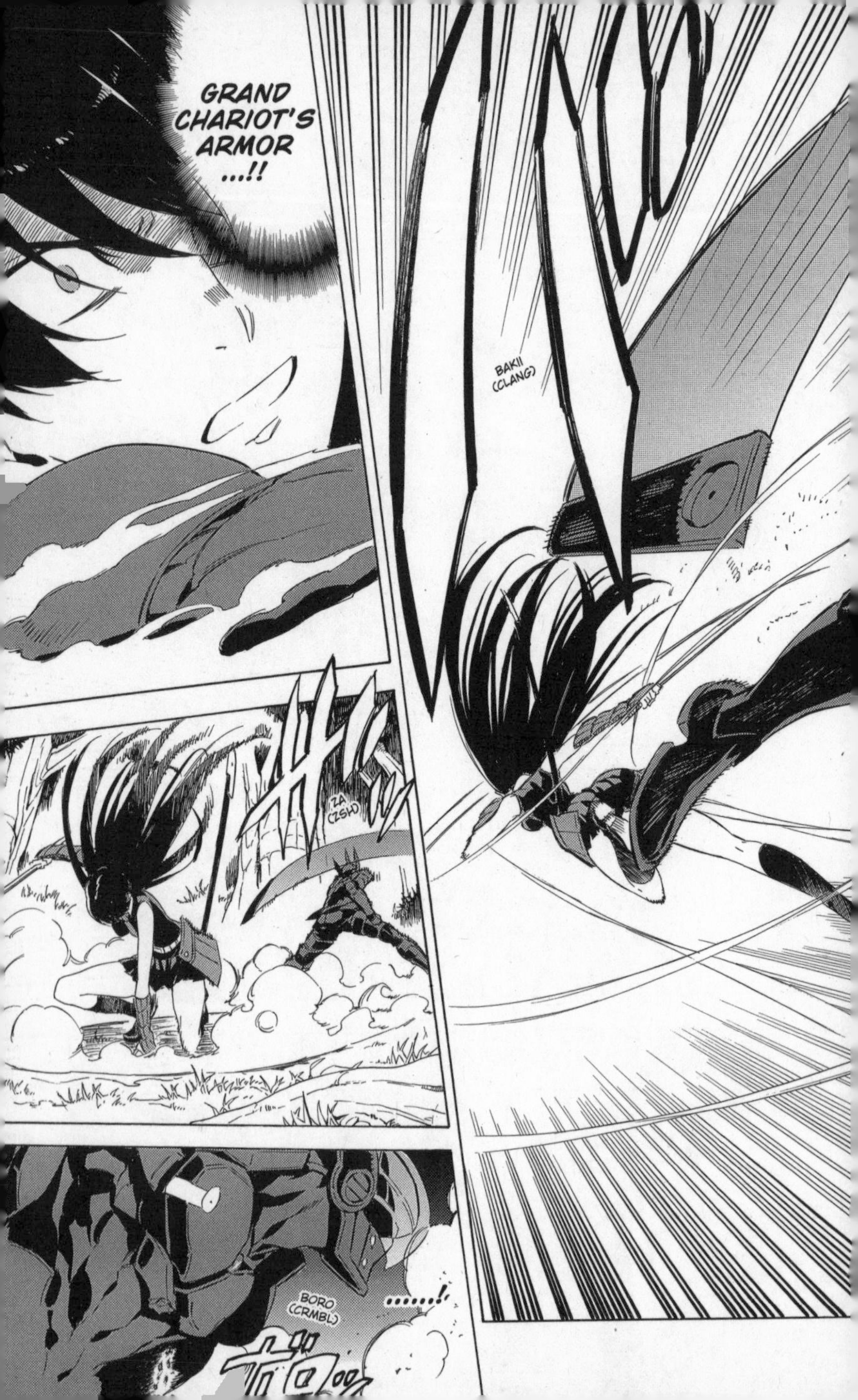
BAKII (CLANG)
GRAND CHARIOT'S ARMOR ...!!
ZA (ZSH)
......!
BORO (CRMBL)

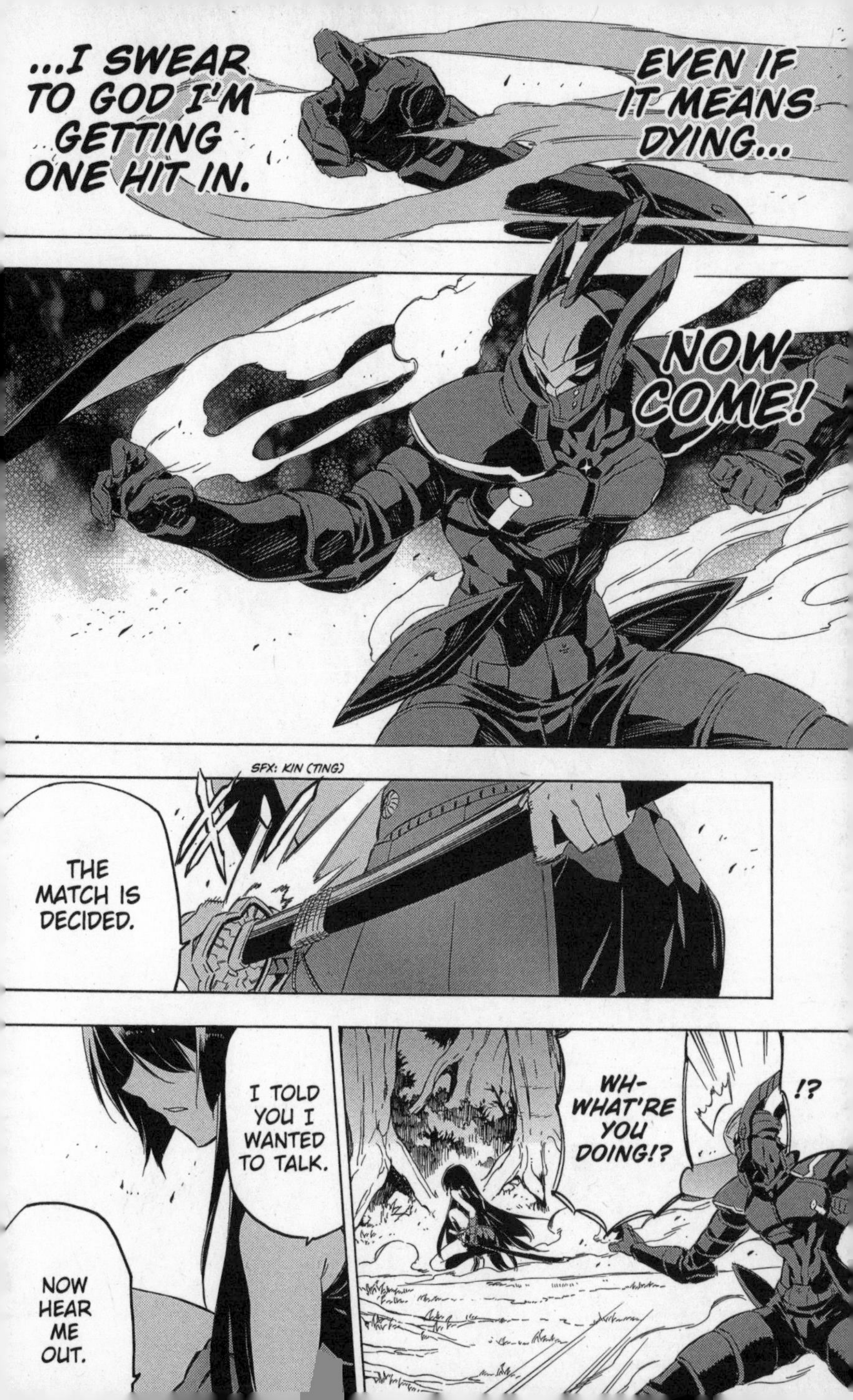
EVEN IF IT MEANS DYING...
...I SWEAR TO GOD I'M GETTING ONE HIT IN.
NOW COME!
SFX: KIN (TING)
THE MATCH IS DECIDED.
!?
WH- WHAT'RE YOU DOING!?
I TOLD YOU I WANTED TO TALK.
NOW HEAR ME OUT.

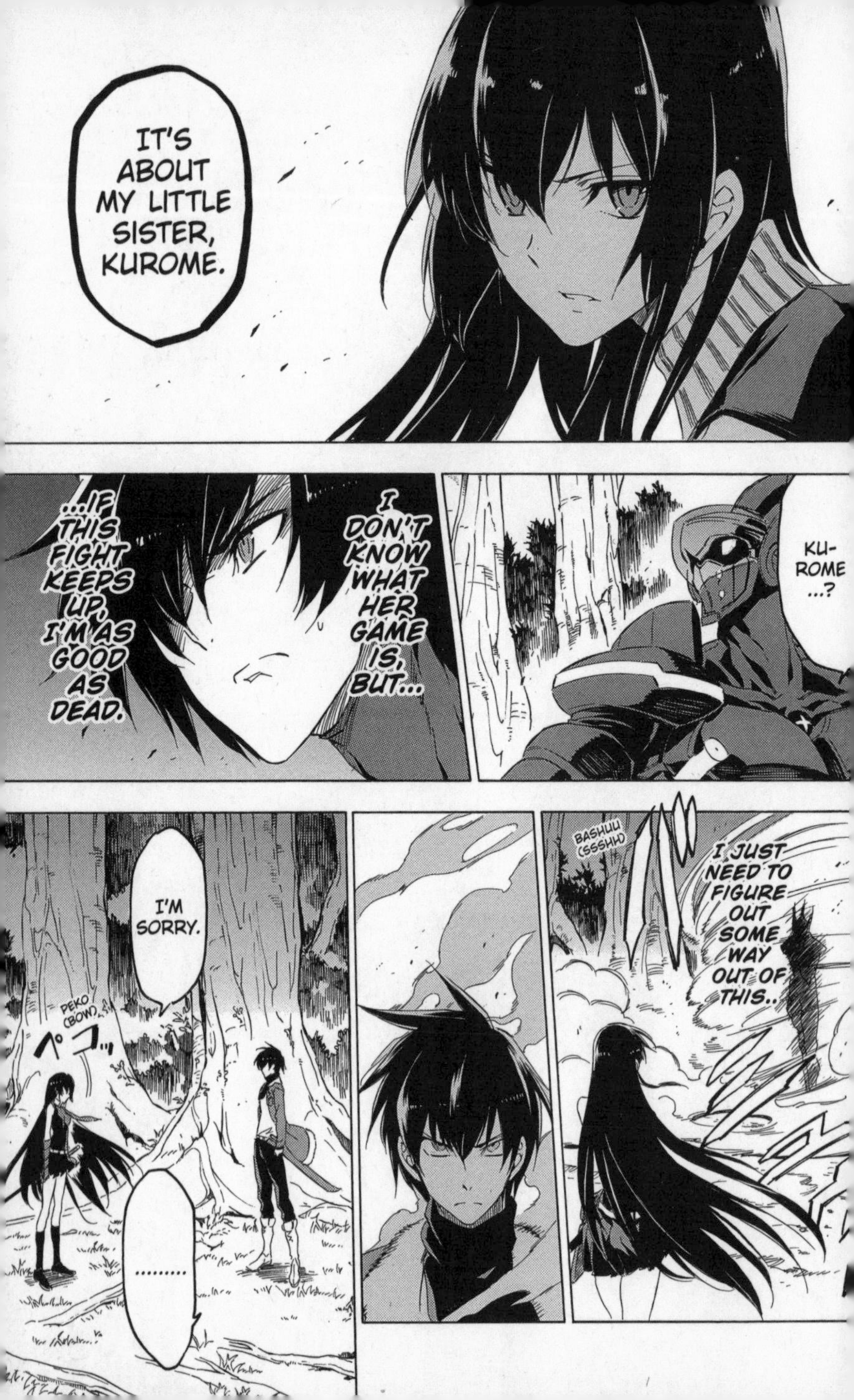
IT'S ABOUT MY LITTLE SISTER, KUROME.
KU-ROME ...?
I DON'T KNOW WHAT HER GAME IS, BUT...
...IF THIS FIGHT KEEPS UP, I'M AS GOOD AS DEAD.
BASHUU (SSSHH)
I JUST NEED TO FIGURE OUT SOME WAY OUT OF THIS..
I'M SORRY.
PEKO (BOW)
ペコッ
....

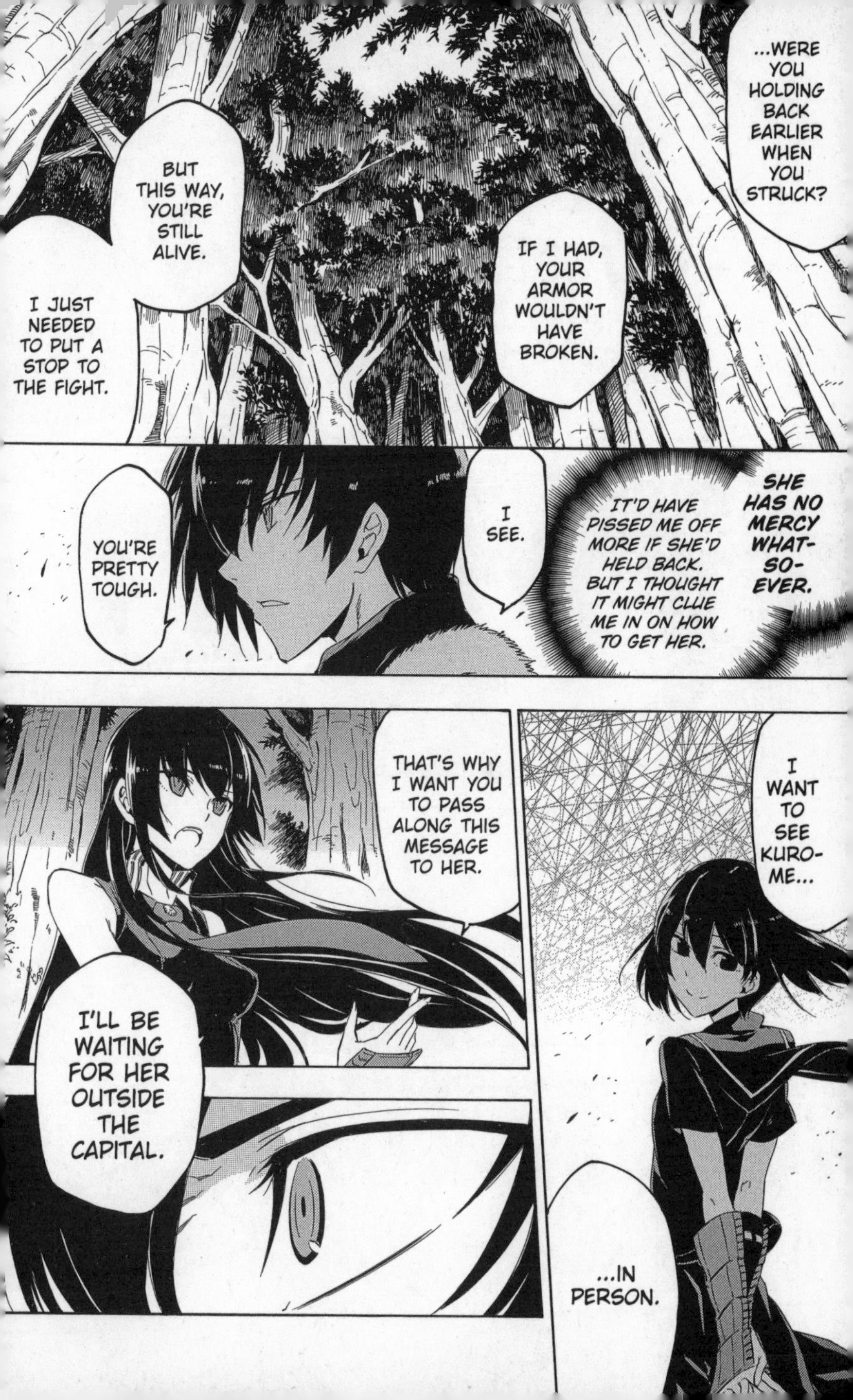
...WERE YOU HOLDING BACK EARLIER WHEN YOU STRUCK?
IF I HAD, YOUR ARMOR WOULDN'T HAVE BROKEN.
BUT THIS WAY, YOU'RE STILL ALIVE.
I JUST NEEDED TO PUT A STOP TO THE FIGHT.
SHE HAS NO MERCY WHAT-SO-EVER.
IT'D HAVE PISSED ME OFF MORE IF SHE'D HELD BACK. BUT I THOUGHT IT MIGHT CLUE ME IN ON HOW TO GET HER.
I SEE.
YOU'RE PRETTY TOUGH.
I WANT TO SEE KURO-ME...
...IN PERSON.
THAT'S WHY I WANT YOU TO PASS ALONG THIS MESSAGE TO HER.
I'LL BE WAITING FOR HER OUTSIDE THE CAPITAL.

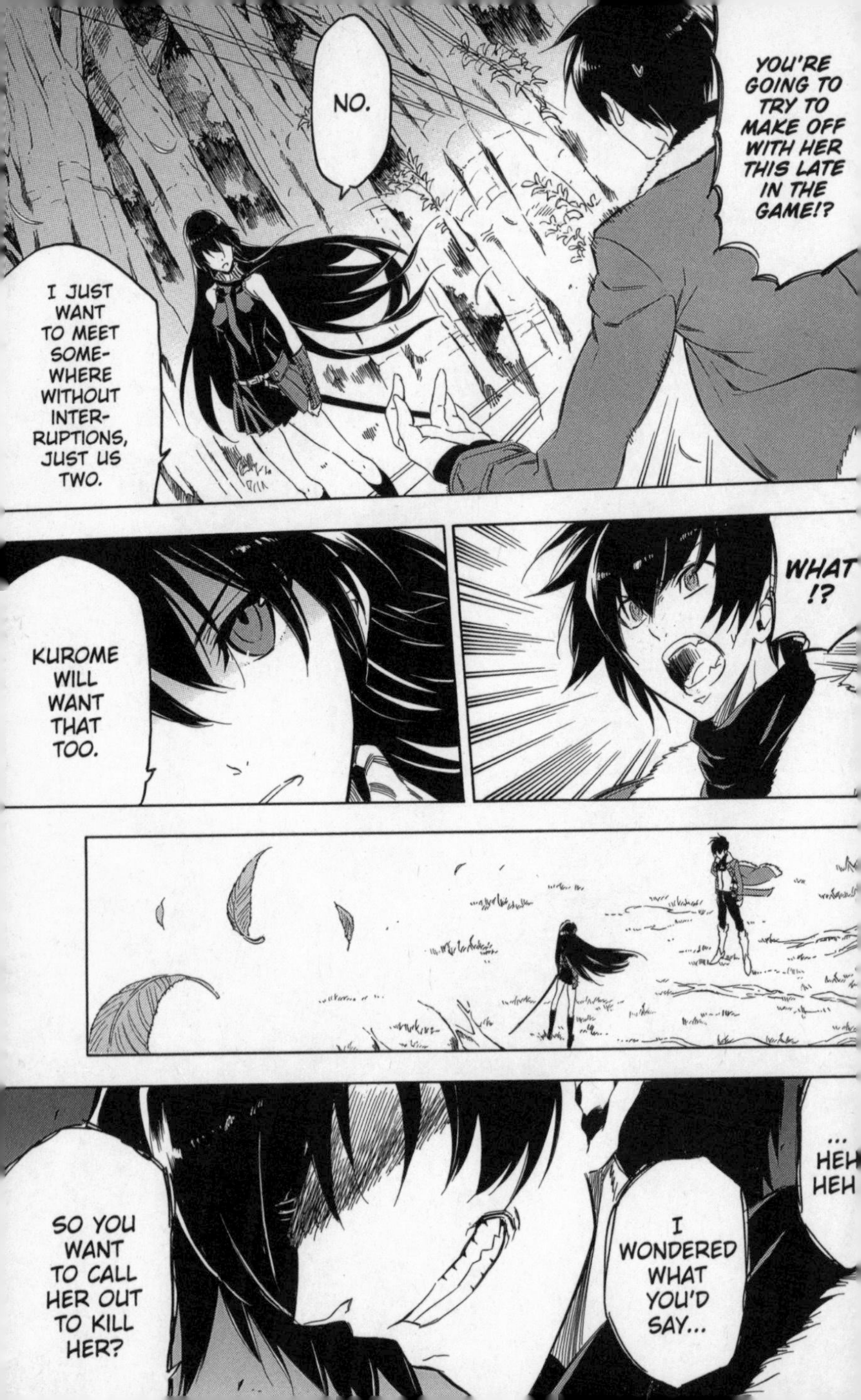
YOU'RE GOING TO TRY TO MAKE OFF WITH HER THIS LATE IN THE GAME!?
NO.
I JUST WANT TO MEET SOME-WHERE WITHOUT INTER-RUPTIONS, JUST US TWO.
WHAT!?
KUROME WILL WANT THAT TOO.
...HEH HEH
I WONDERED WHAT YOU'D SAY...
SO YOU WANT TO CALL HER OUT TO KILL HER?

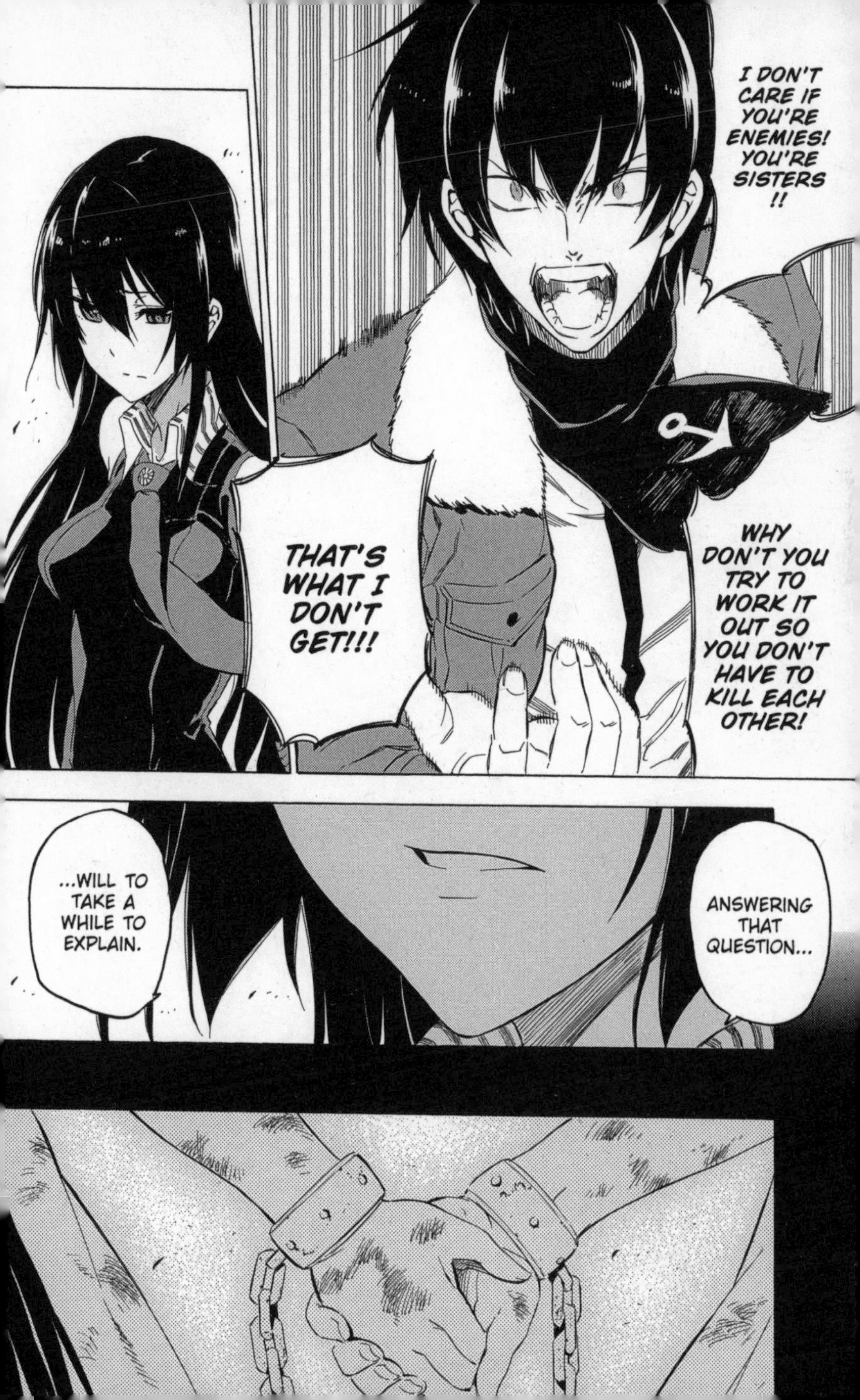
I DON'T CARE IF YOU'RE ENEMIES! YOU'RE SISTERS !!
WHY DON'T YOU TRY TO WORK IT OUT SO YOU DON'T HAVE TO KILL EACH OTHER!
THAT'S WHAT I DON'T GET!!!
ANSWERING THAT QUESTION...
...WILL TO TAKE A WHILE TO EXPLAIN.

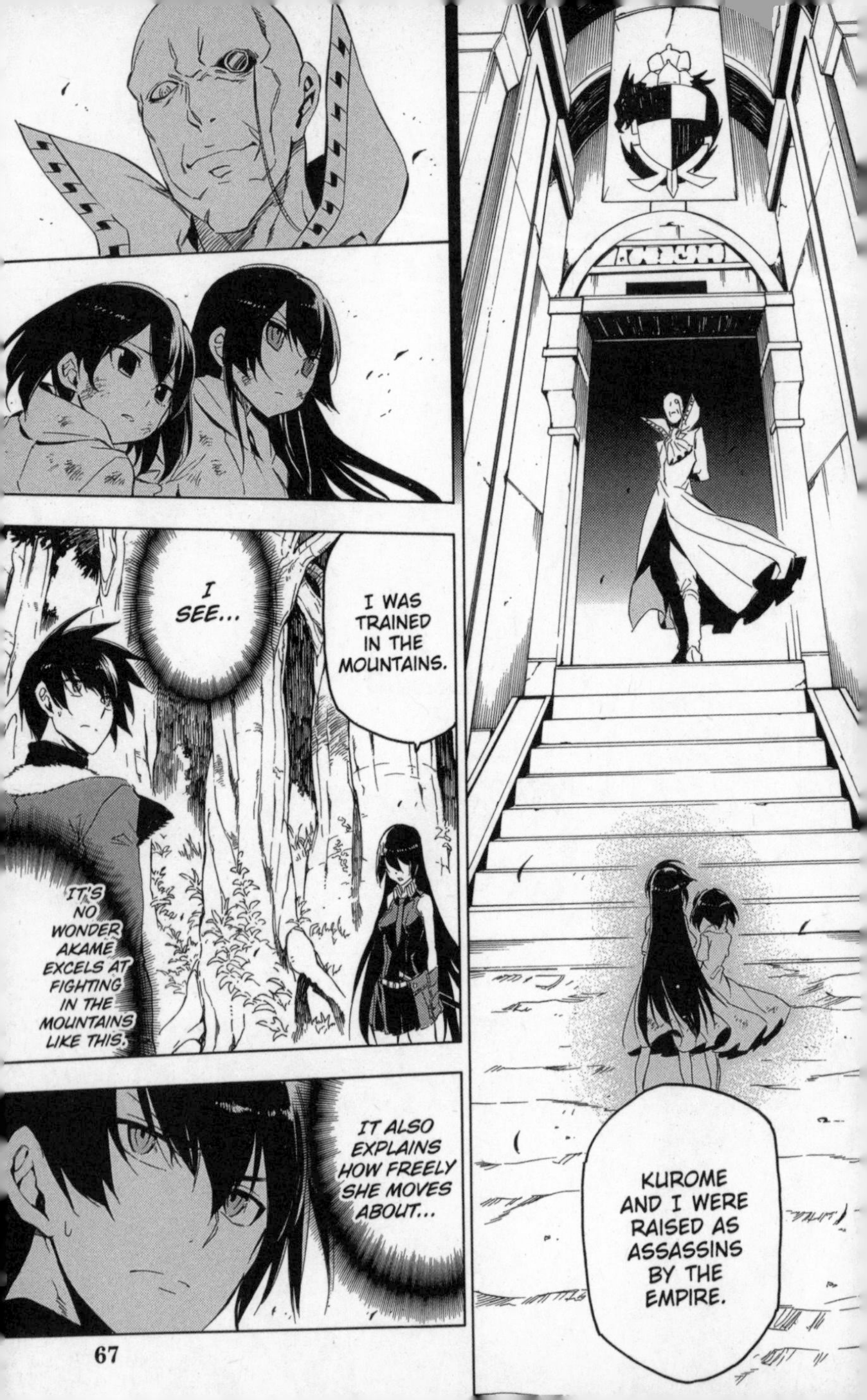
KUROME AND I WERE RAISED AS ASSASSINS BY THE EMPIRE.
I WAS TRAINED IN THE MOUNTAINS.
I SEE...
IT'S NO WONDER AKAME EXCELS AT FIGHTING IN THE MOUNTAINS LIKE THIS.
IT ALSO EXPLAINS HOW FREELY SHE MOVES ABOUT...

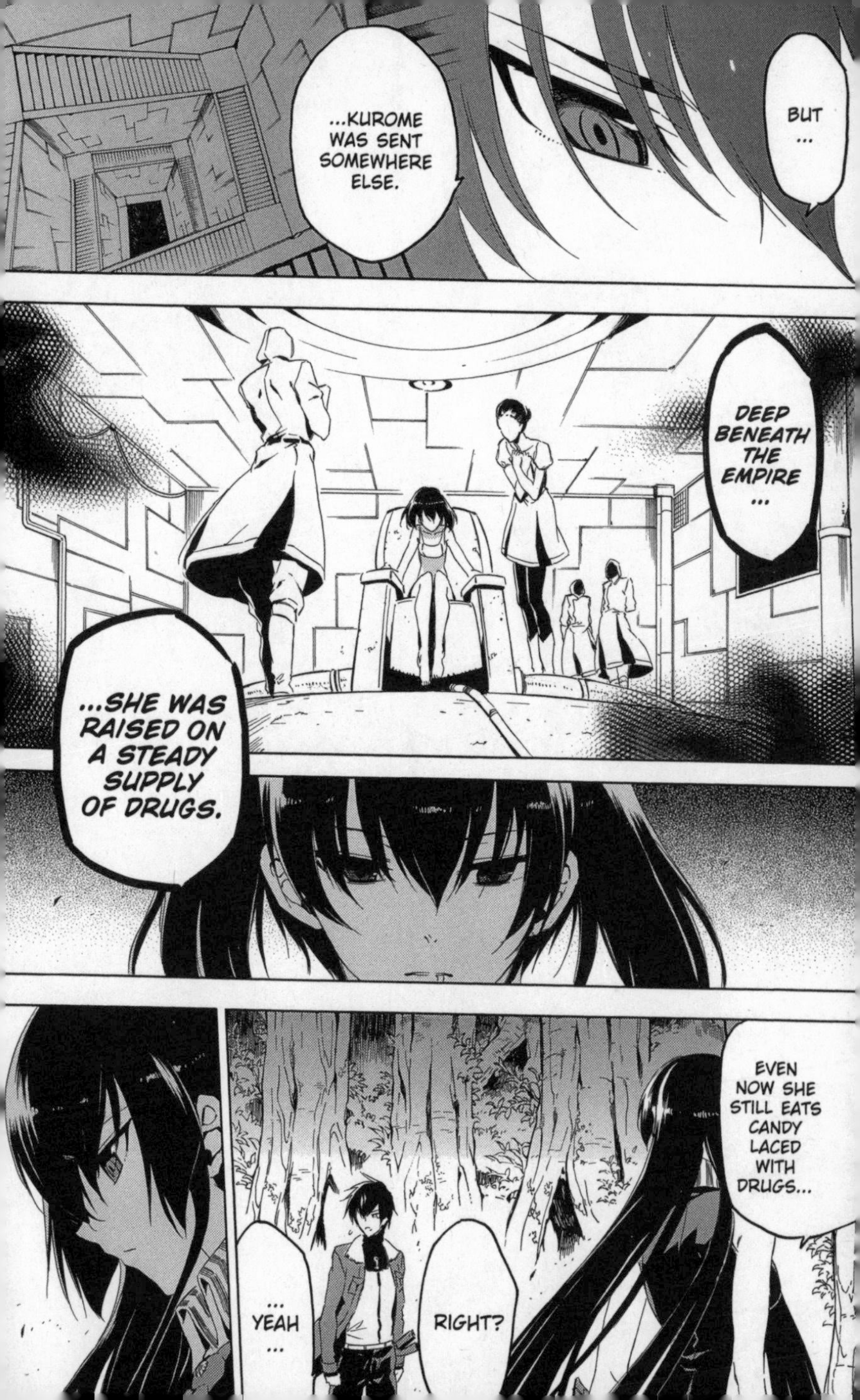
BUT ...
...KUROME WAS SENT SOMEWHERE ELSE.
DEEP BENEATH THE EMPIRE ...
...SHE WAS RAISED ON A STEADY SUPPLY OF DRUGS.
EVEN NOW SHE STILL EATS CANDY LACED WITH DRUGS...
RIGHT?
... YEAH ...

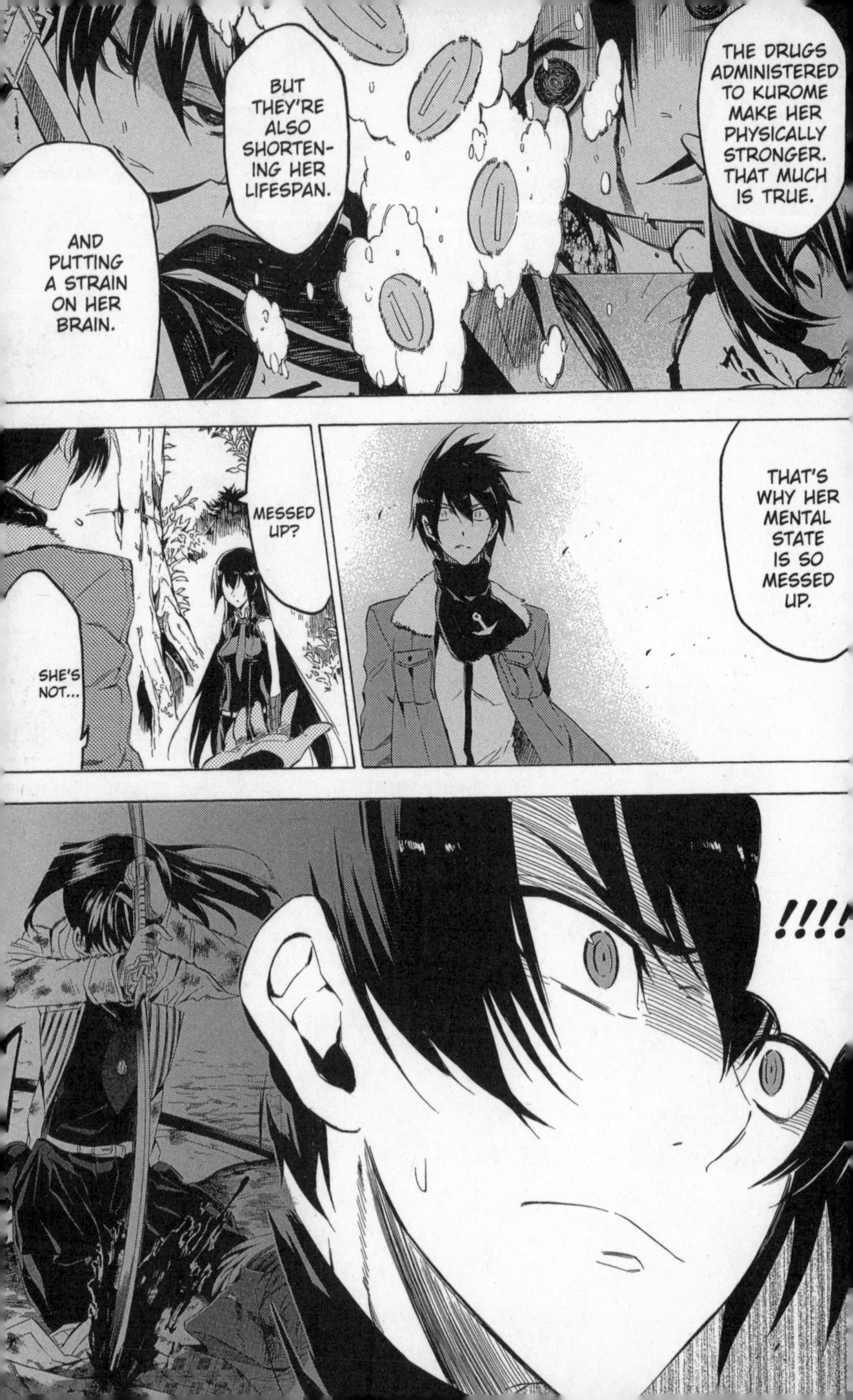
THE DRUGS ADMINISTERED TO KUROME MAKE HER PHYSICALLY STRONGER. THAT MUCH IS TRUE.
BUT THEY'RE ALSO SHORTENING HER LIFESPAN.
AND PUTTING A STRAIN ON HER BRAIN.
THAT'S WHY HER MENTAL STATE IS SO MESSED UP.
MESSED UP?
SHE'S NOT...
!!!!

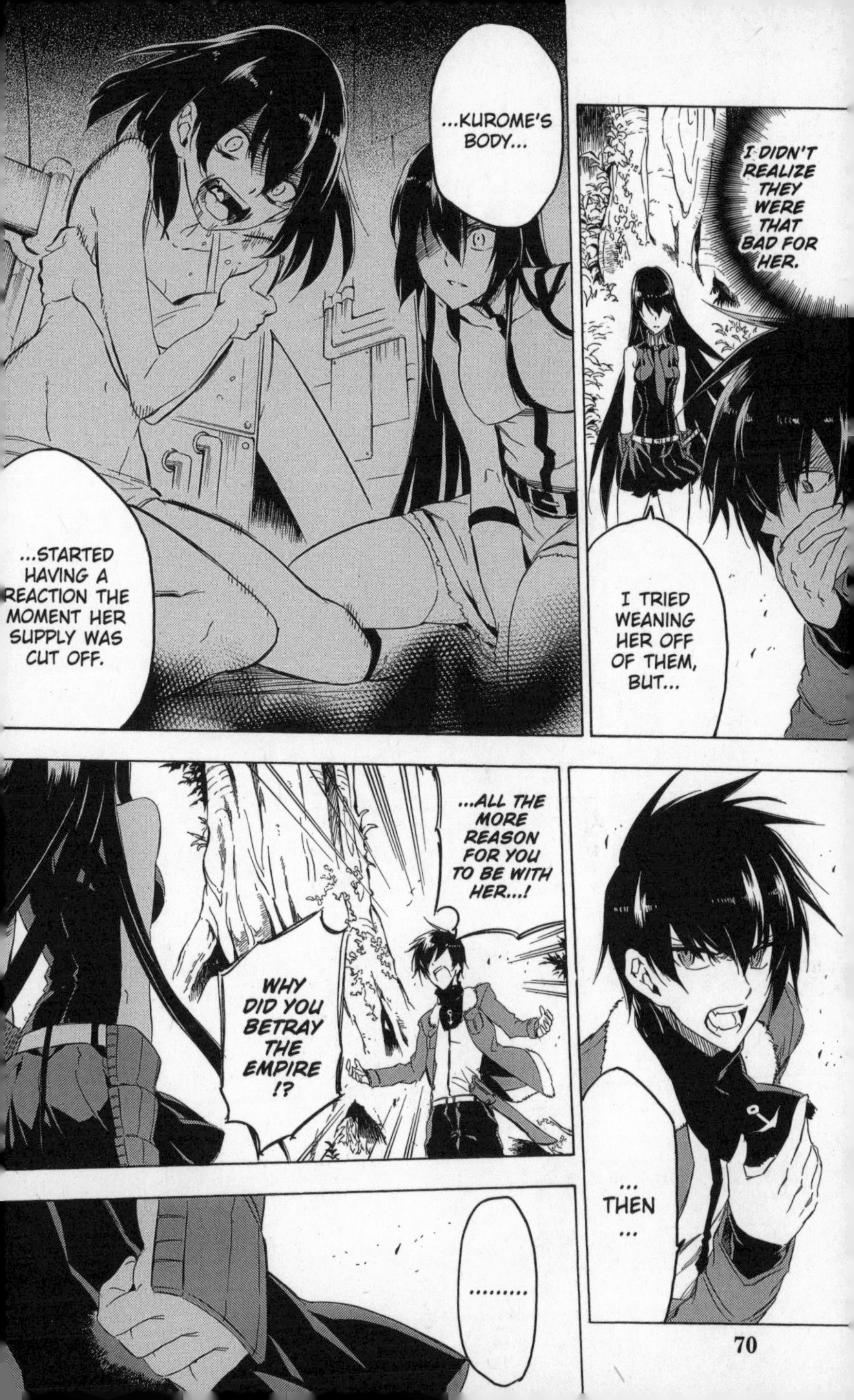
I DIDN'T REALIZE THEY WERE THAT BAD FOR HER.
I TRIED WEANING HER OFF OF THEM, BUT...
...KUROME'S BODY...
...STARTED HAVING A REACTION THE MOMENT HER SUPPLY WAS CUT OFF.
...THEN...
...ALL THE MORE REASON FOR YOU TO BE WITH HER...!
WHY DID YOU BETRAY THE EMPIRE!?
....

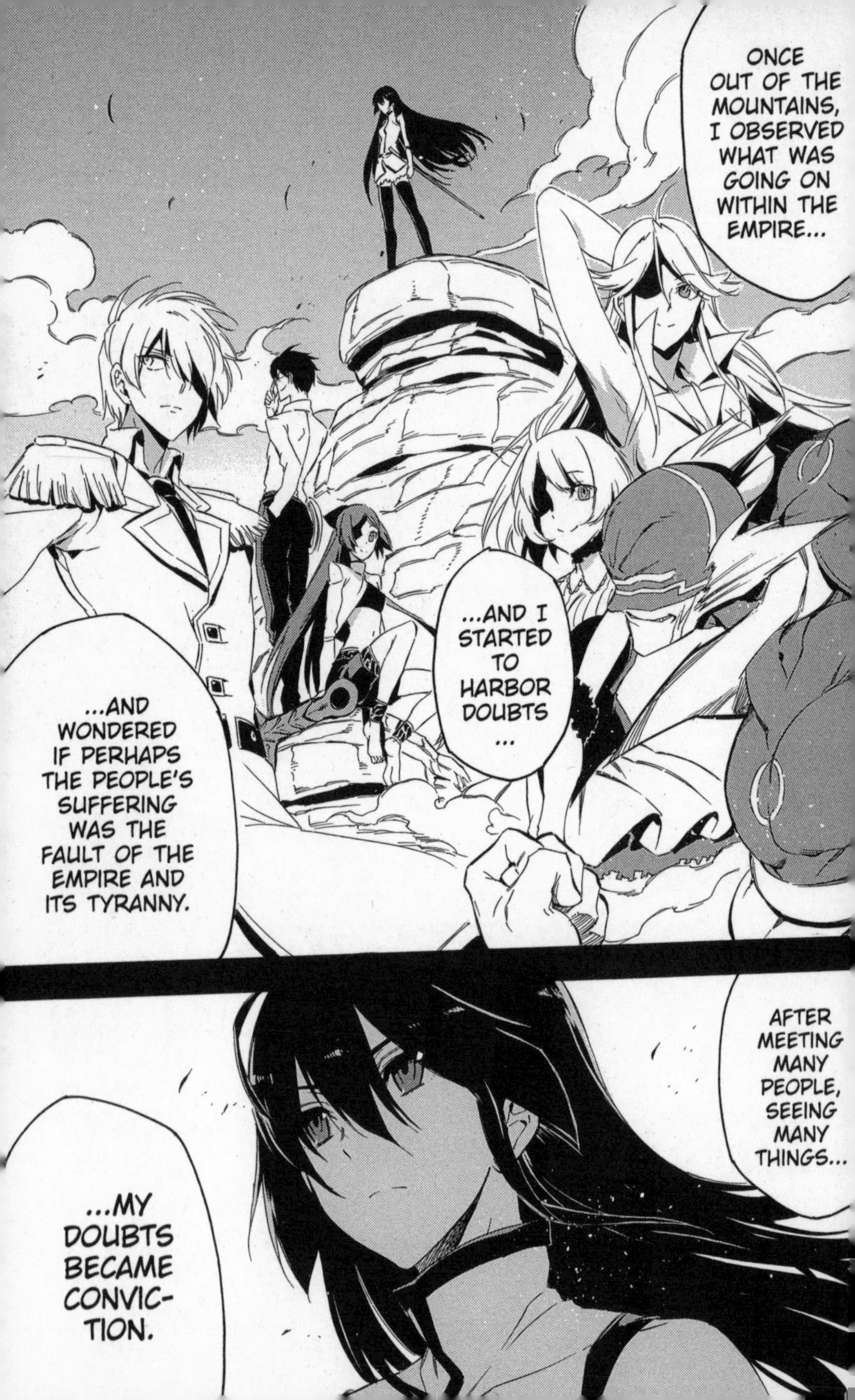
ONCE OUT OF THE MOUNTAINS, I OBSERVED WHAT WAS GOING ON WITHIN THE EMPIRE...
...AND I STARTED TO HARBOR DOUBTS...
...AND WONDERED IF PERHAPS THE PEOPLE'S SUFFERING WAS THE FAULT OF THE EMPIRE AND ITS TYRANNY.
AFTER MEETING MANY PEOPLE, SEEING MANY THINGS...
...MY DOUBTS BECAME CONVIC-TION.

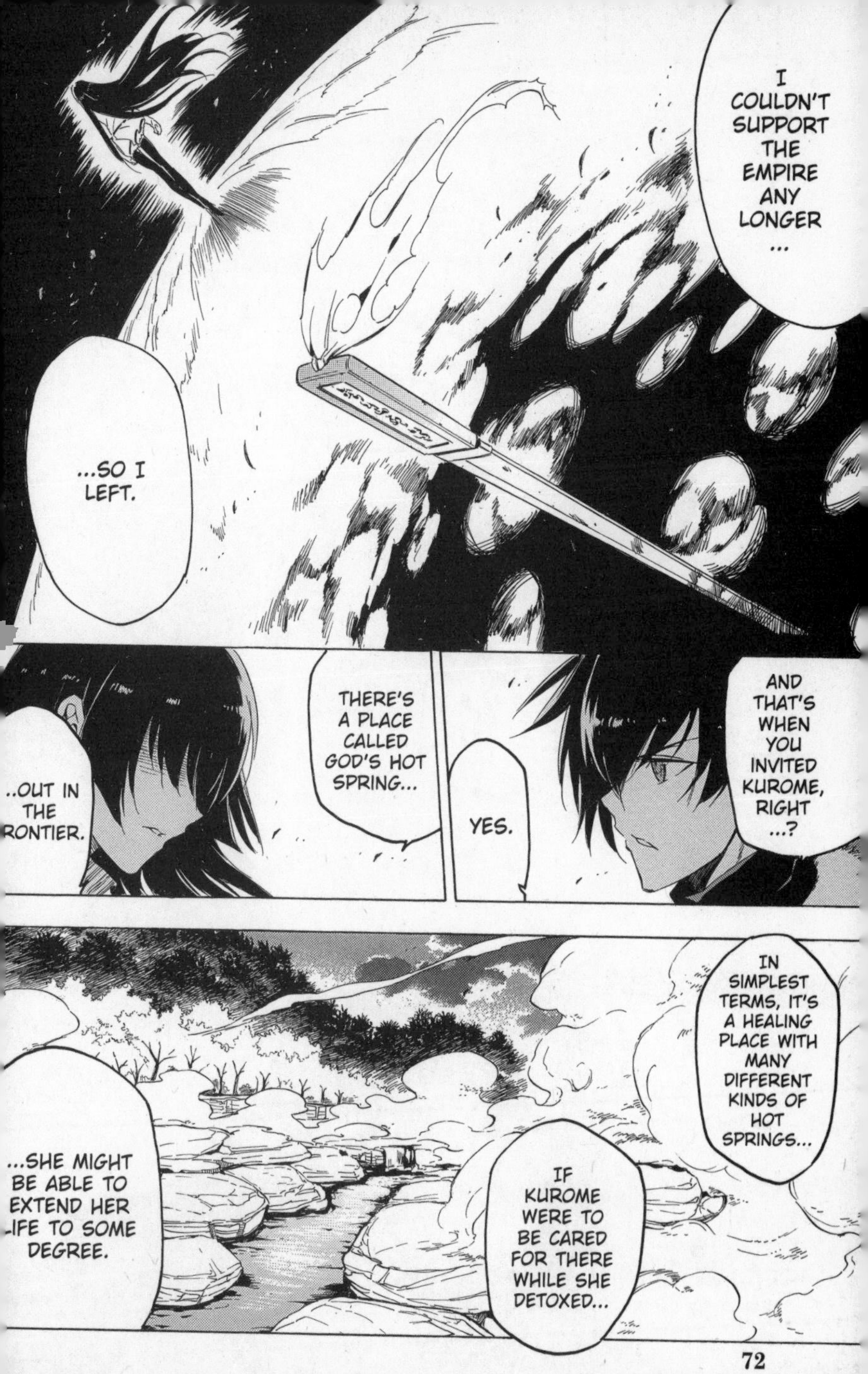
I COULDN'T SUPPORT THE EMPIRE ANY LONGER ...
...SO I LEFT.
AND THAT'S WHEN YOU INVITED KUROME, RIGHT ...?
YES.
THERE'S A PLACE CALLED GOD'S HOT SPRING...
..OUT IN THE RONTIER.
IN SIMPLEST TERMS, IT'S A HEALING PLACE WITH MANY DIFFERENT KINDS OF HOT SPRINGS...
IF KUROME WERE TO BE CARED FOR THERE WHILE SHE DETOXED...
...SHE MIGHT BE ABLE TO EXTEND HER IFE TO SOME DEGREE.

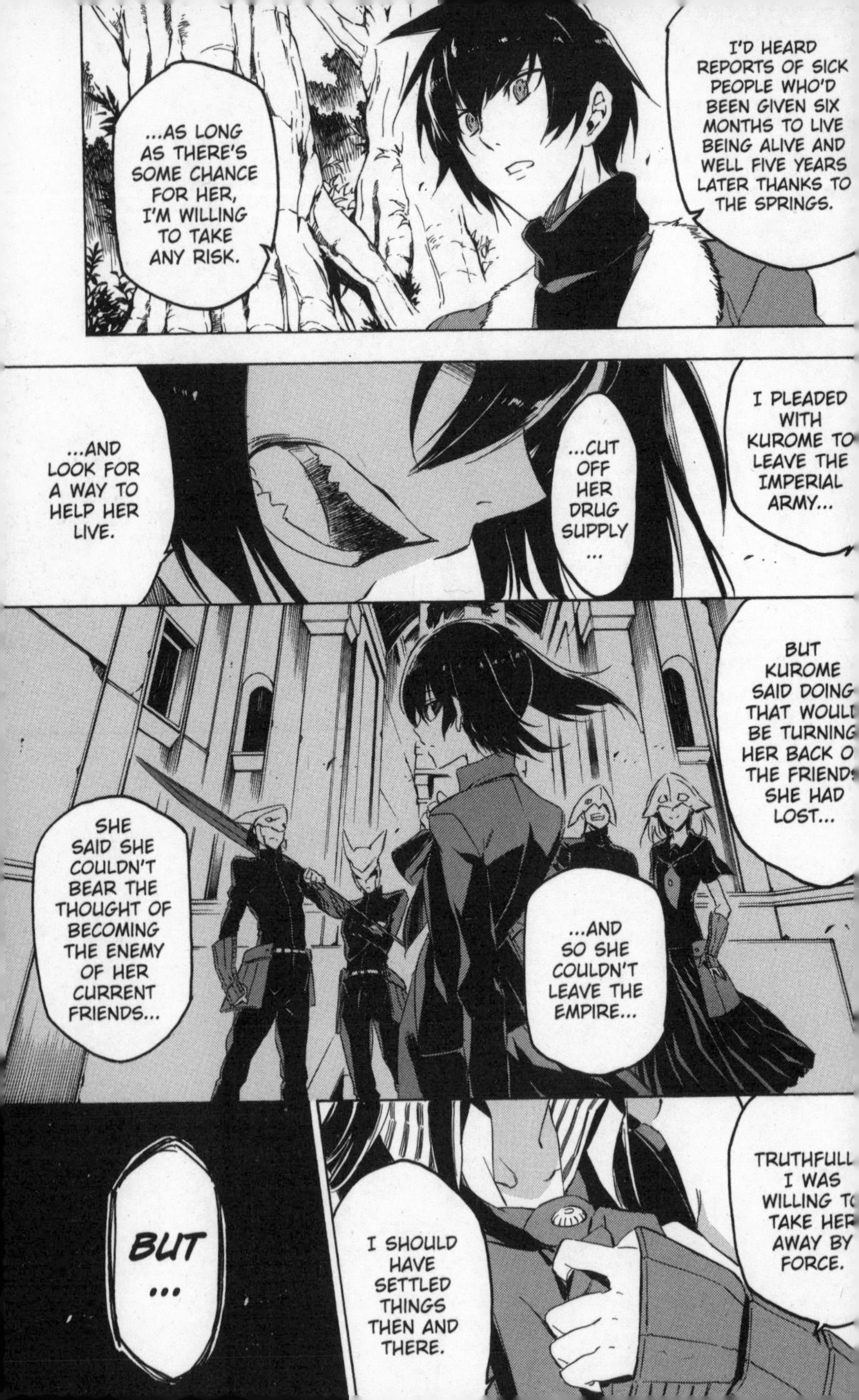
I'D HEARD REPORTS OF SICK PEOPLE WHO'D BEEN GIVEN SIX MONTHS TO LIVE BEING ALIVE AND WELL FIVE YEARS LATER THANKS TO THE SPRINGS.
...AS LONG AS THERE'S SOME CHANCE FOR HER, I'M WILLING TO TAKE ANY RISK.
I PLEADED WITH KUROME TO LEAVE THE IMPERIAL ARMY...
...CUT OFF HER DRUG SUPPLY ...
...AND LOOK FOR A WAY TO HELP HER LIVE.
BUT KUROME SAID DOING THAT WOULI BE TURNING HER BACK O THE FRIENDS SHE HAD LOST...
SHE SAID SHE COULDN'T BEAR THE THOUGHT OF BECOMING THE ENEMY OF HER CURRENT FRIENDS...
...AND SO SHE COULDN'T LEAVE THE EMPIRE...
TRUTHFULL I WAS WILLING T TAKE HER AWAY BY FORCE.
I SHOULD HAVE SETTLED THINGS THEN AND THERE.
BUT ...

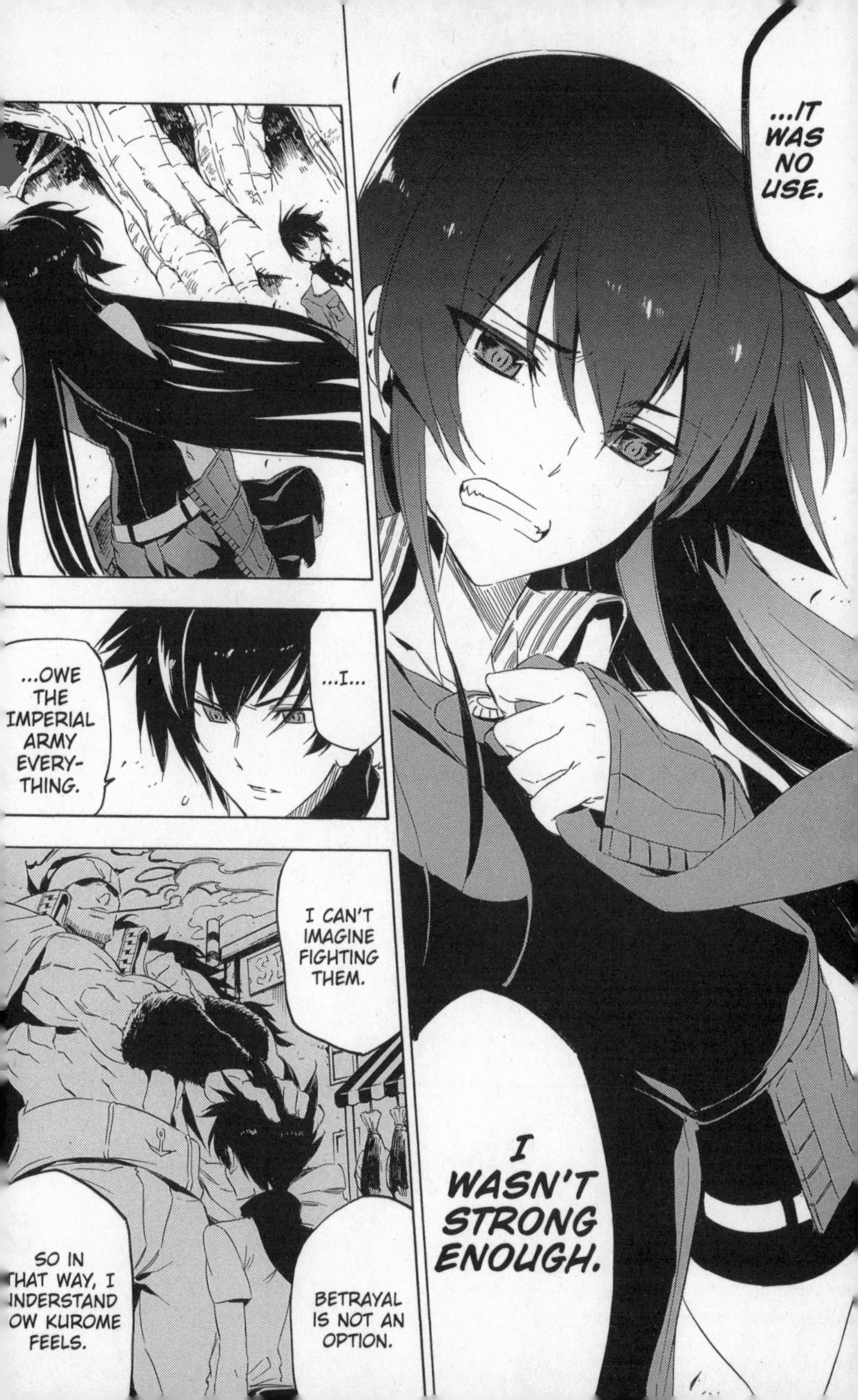
...IT WAS NO USE.
I WASN'T STRONG ENOUGH.
...I...
...OWE THE IMPERIAL ARMY EVERYTHING.
I CAN'T IMAGINE FIGHTING THEM.
BETRAYAL IS NOT AN OPTION.
SO IN THAT WAY, I INDERSTAND OW KUROME FEELS.

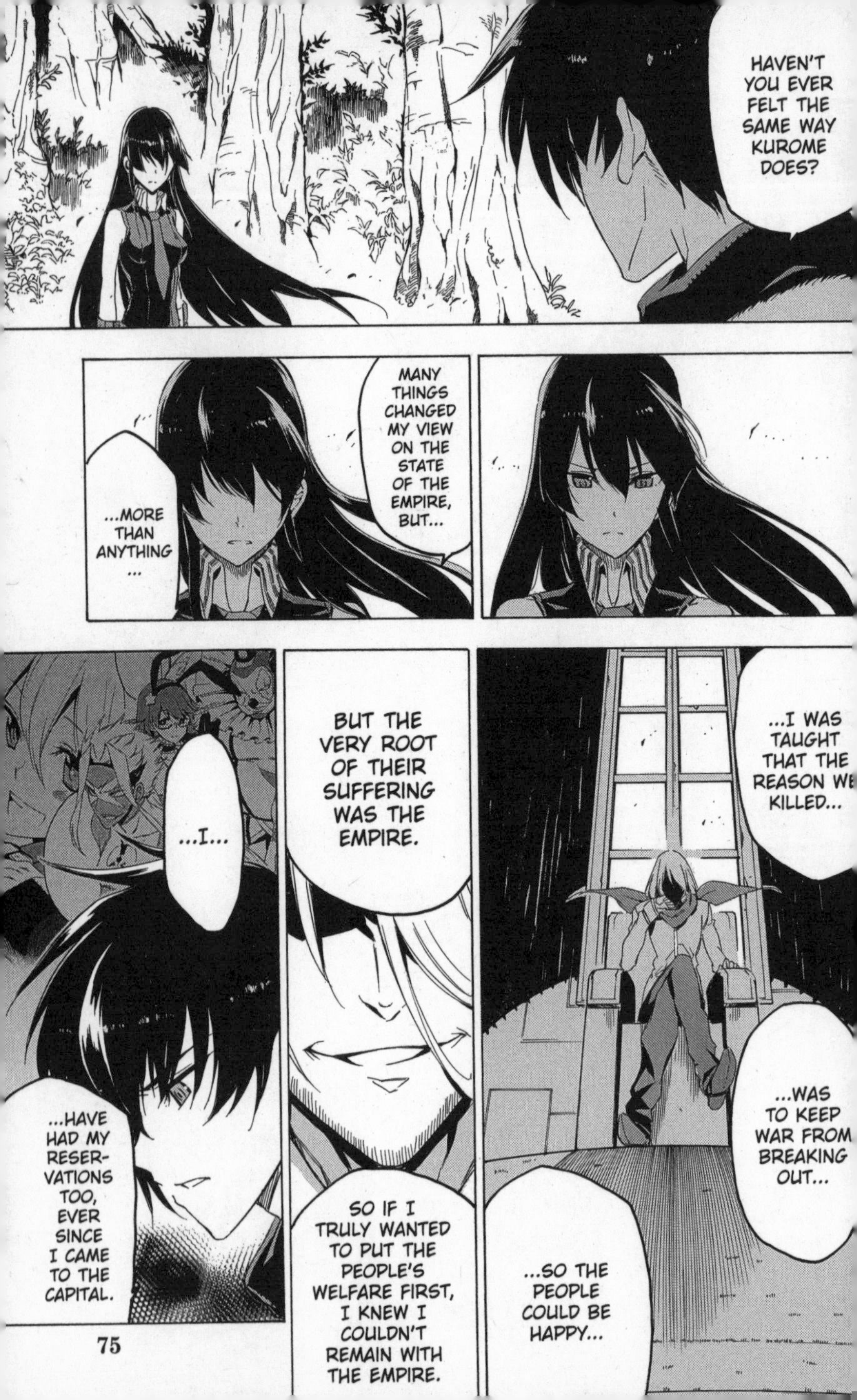
HAVEN'T YOU EVER FELT THE SAME WAY KUROME DOES?
MANY THINGS CHANGED MY VIEW ON THE STATE OF THE EMPIRE, BUT...
...MORE THAN ANYTHING...
...I WAS TAUGHT THAT THE REASON WE KILLED...
...WAS TO KEEP WAR FROM BREAKING OUT...
...SO THE PEOPLE COULD BE HAPPY...
BUT THE VERY ROOT OF THEIR SUFFERING WAS THE EMPIRE.
SO IF I TRULY WANTED TO PUT THE PEOPLE'S WELFARE FIRST, I KNEW I COULDN'T REMAIN WITH THE EMPIRE.
...I...
...HAVE HAD MY RESER-VATIONS TOO, EVER SINCE I CAME TO THE CAPITAL.

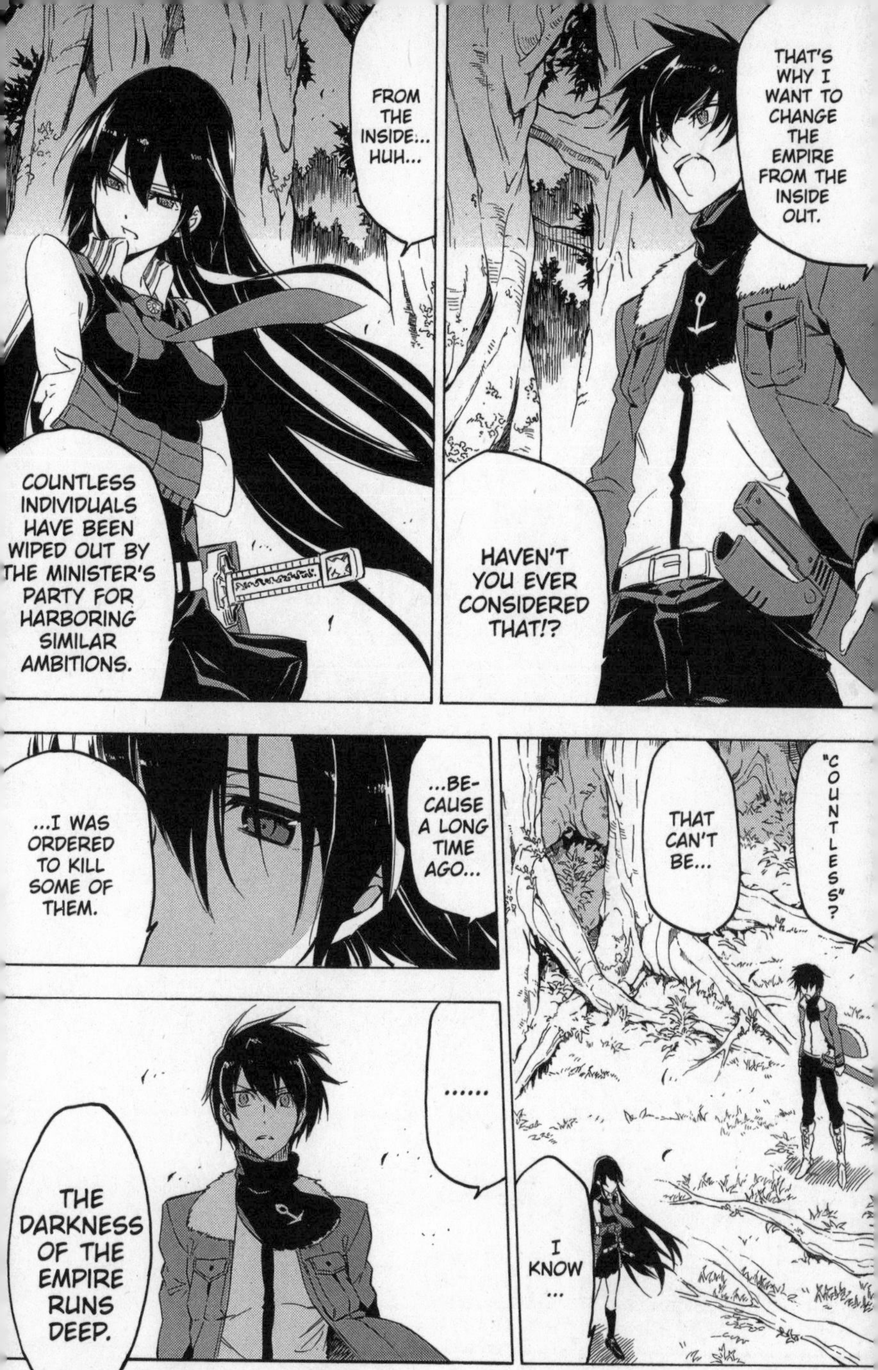
THAT'S WHY I WANT TO CHANGE THE EMPIRE FROM THE INSIDE OUT.
HAVEN'T YOU EVER CONSIDERED THAT!?
FROM THE INSIDE... HUH...
COUNTLESS INDIVIDUALS HAVE BEEN WIPED OUT BY THE MINISTER'S PARTY FOR HARBORING SIMILAR AMBITIONS.
"COUNTLESS"?
THAT CAN'T BE...
I KNOW...
...BE-CAUSE A LONG TIME AGO...
...I WAS ORDERED TO KILL SOME OF THEM.
......
THE DARKNESS OF THE EMPIRE RUNS DEEP.

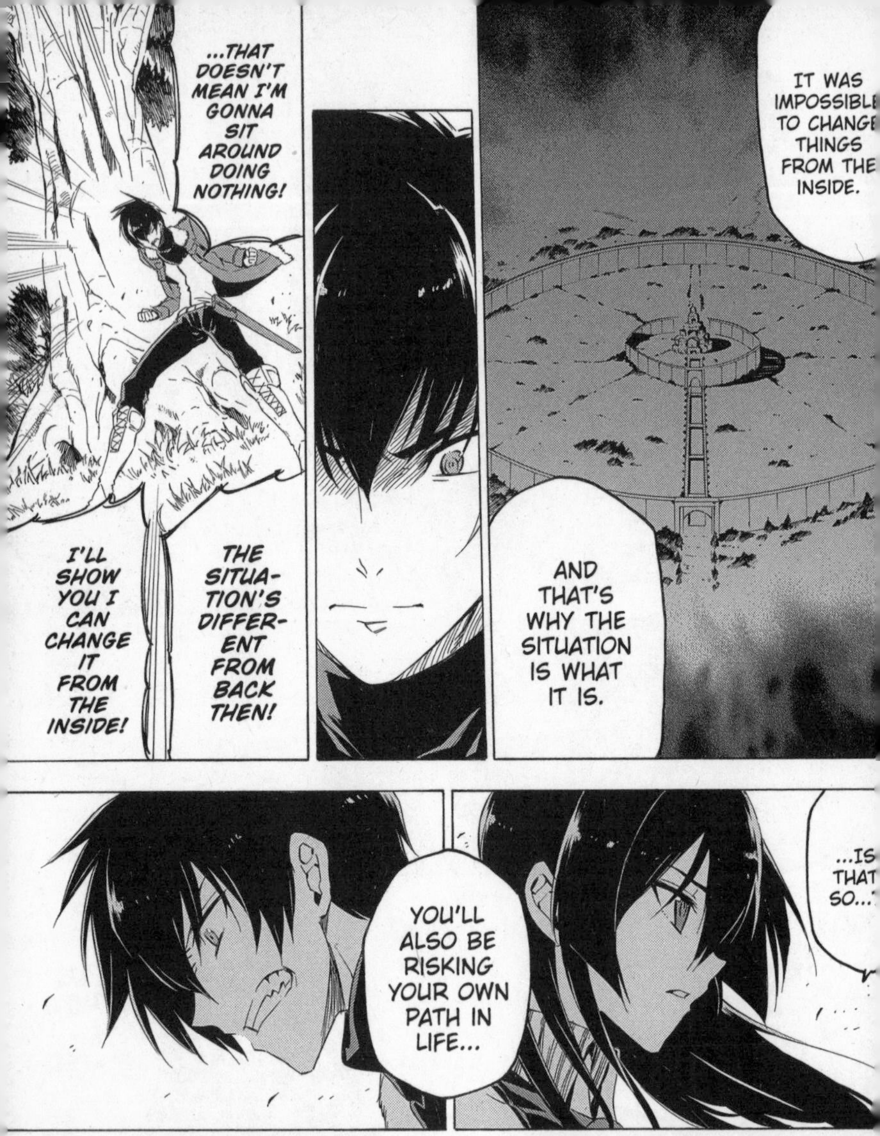
IT WAS IMPOSSIBLE TO CHANGE THINGS FROM THE INSIDE.
AND THAT'S WHY THE SITUATION IS WHAT IT IS.
...THAT DOESN'T MEAN I'M GONNA SIT AROUND DOING NOTHING!
THE SITUATION'S DIFFERENT FROM BACK THEN!
I'LL SHOW YOU I CAN CHANGE IT FROM THE INSIDE!
...IS THAT SO...
YOU'LL ALSO BE RISKING YOUR OWN PATH IN LIFE...

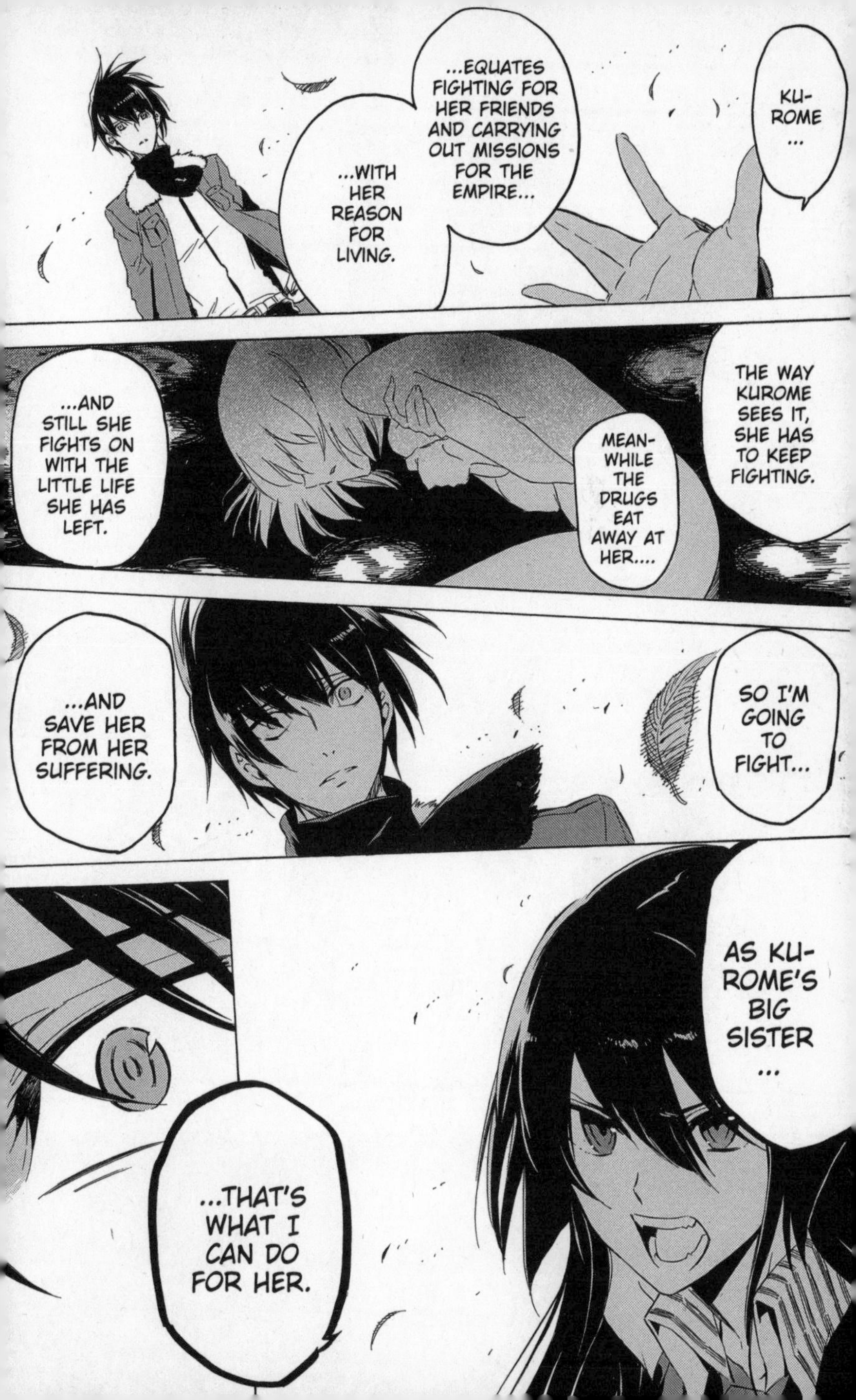

KUROME...
...EQUATES FIGHTING FOR HER FRIENDS AND CARRYING OUT MISSIONS FOR THE EMPIRE...
...WITH HER REASON FOR LIVING.
THE WAY KUROME SEES IT, SHE HAS TO KEEP FIGHTING.
MEANWHILE THE DRUGS EAT AWAY AT HER....
...AND STILL SHE FIGHTS ON WITH THE LITTLE LIFE SHE HAS LEFT.
SO I'M GOING TO FIGHT...
...AND SAVE HER FROM HER SUFFERING.
AS KUROME'S BIG SISTER...
...THAT'S WHAT I CAN DO FOR HER.

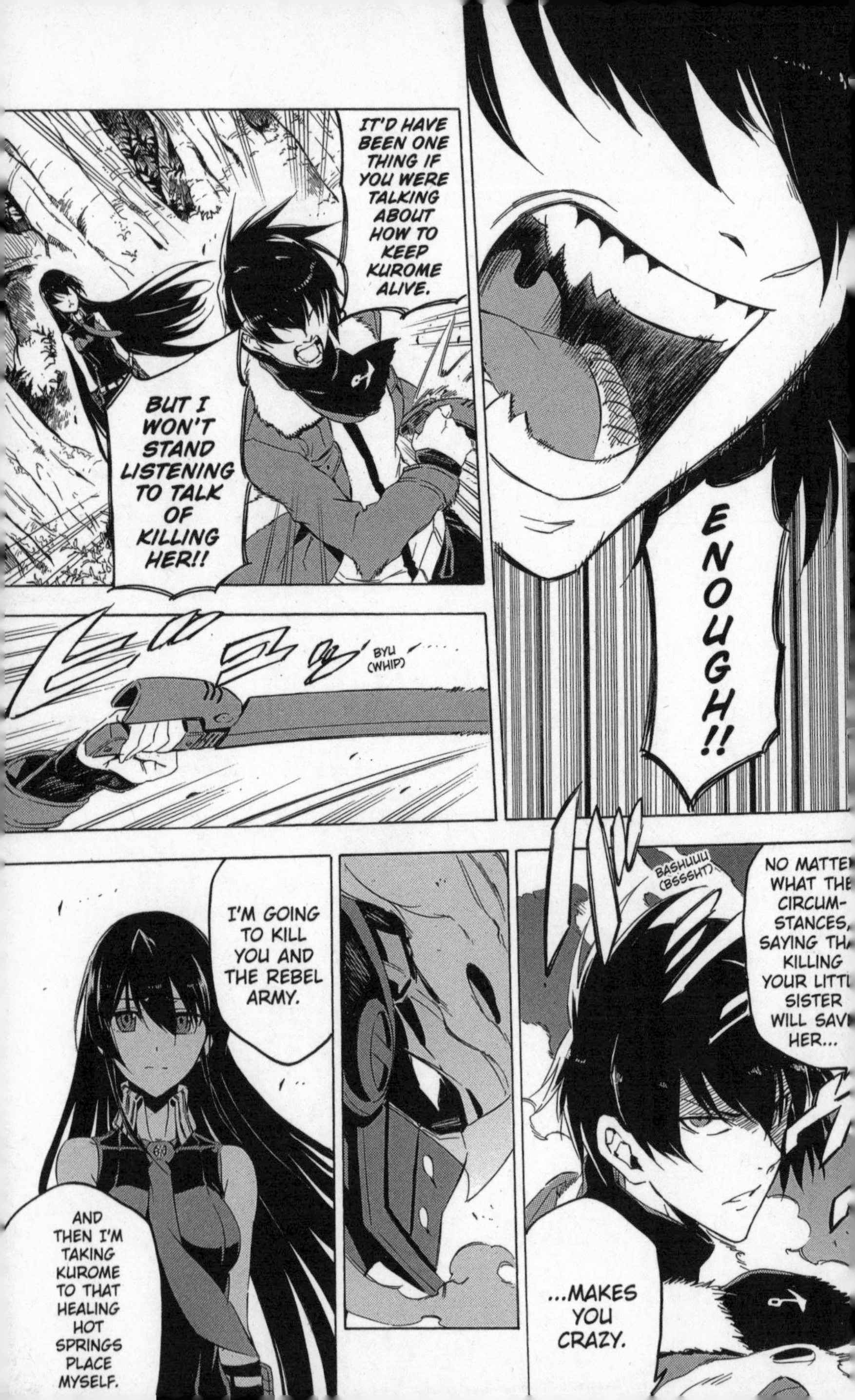
ENOUGH!!
IT'D HAVE BEEN ONE THING IF YOU WERE TALKING ABOUT HOW TO KEEP KUROME ALIVE.
BUT I WON'T STAND LISTENING TO TALK OF KILLING HER!!
BYU (WHIP)
BASHUUU (BSSSHT)
NO MATTE WHAT THE CIRCUM- STANCES, SAYING TH KILLING YOUR LITT SISTER WILL SAV HER...
...MAKES YOU CRAZY.
I'M GOING TO KILL YOU AND THE REBEL ARMY.
AND THEN I'M TAKING KUROME TO THAT HEALING HOT SPRINGS PLACE MYSELF.

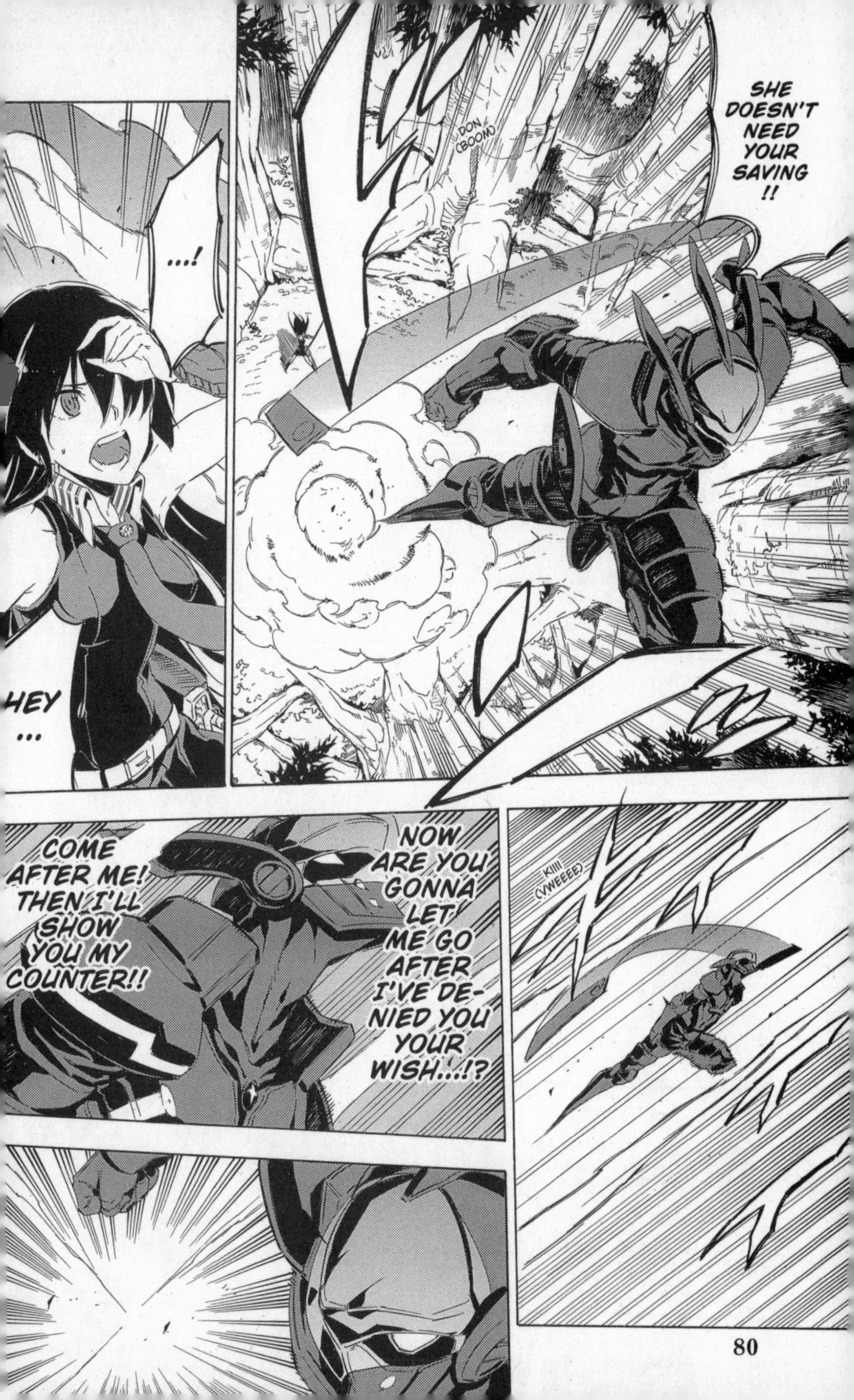
SHE DOESN'T NEED YOUR SAVING !!
DON (BOOM)
...!
HEY ...
KIIII (VWEEEE)
NOW ARE YOU GONNA LET ME GO AFTER I'VE DE-NIED YOU YOUR WISH...!?
COME AFTER ME! THEN I'LL SHOW YOU MY COUNTER!!
...

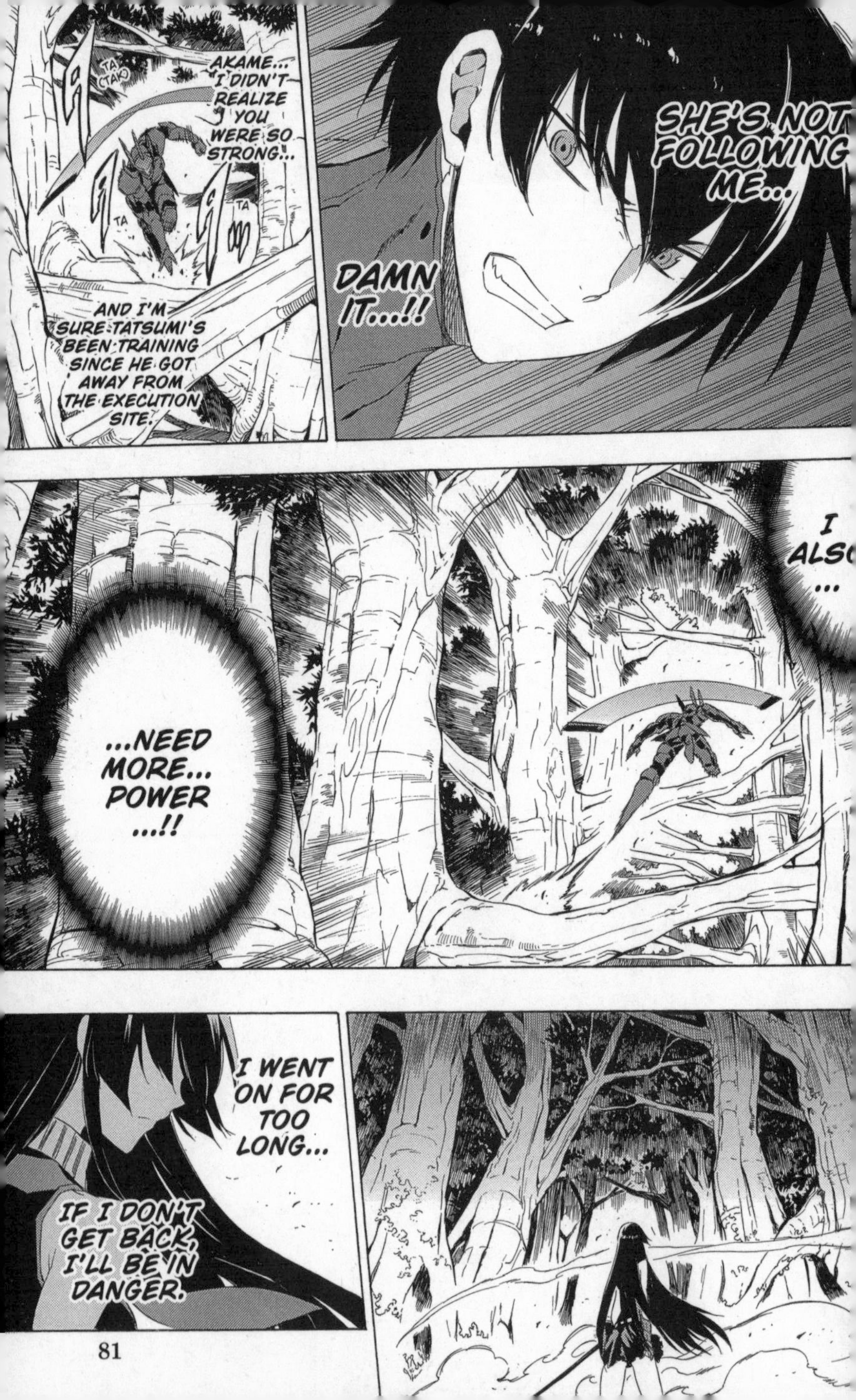
SHE'S NOT FOLLOWING ME...
DAMN IT...!!
AKAME... I DIDN'T REALIZE YOU WERE SO STRONG...
TA TAK
TA
TA
AND I'M SURE TATSUMI'S BEEN TRAINING SINCE HE GOT AWAY FROM THE EXECUTION SITE.
I ALSO ...
...NEED MORE... POWER ...!!
I WENT ON FOR TOO LONG...
IF I DON'T GET BACK, I'LL BE IN DANGER.

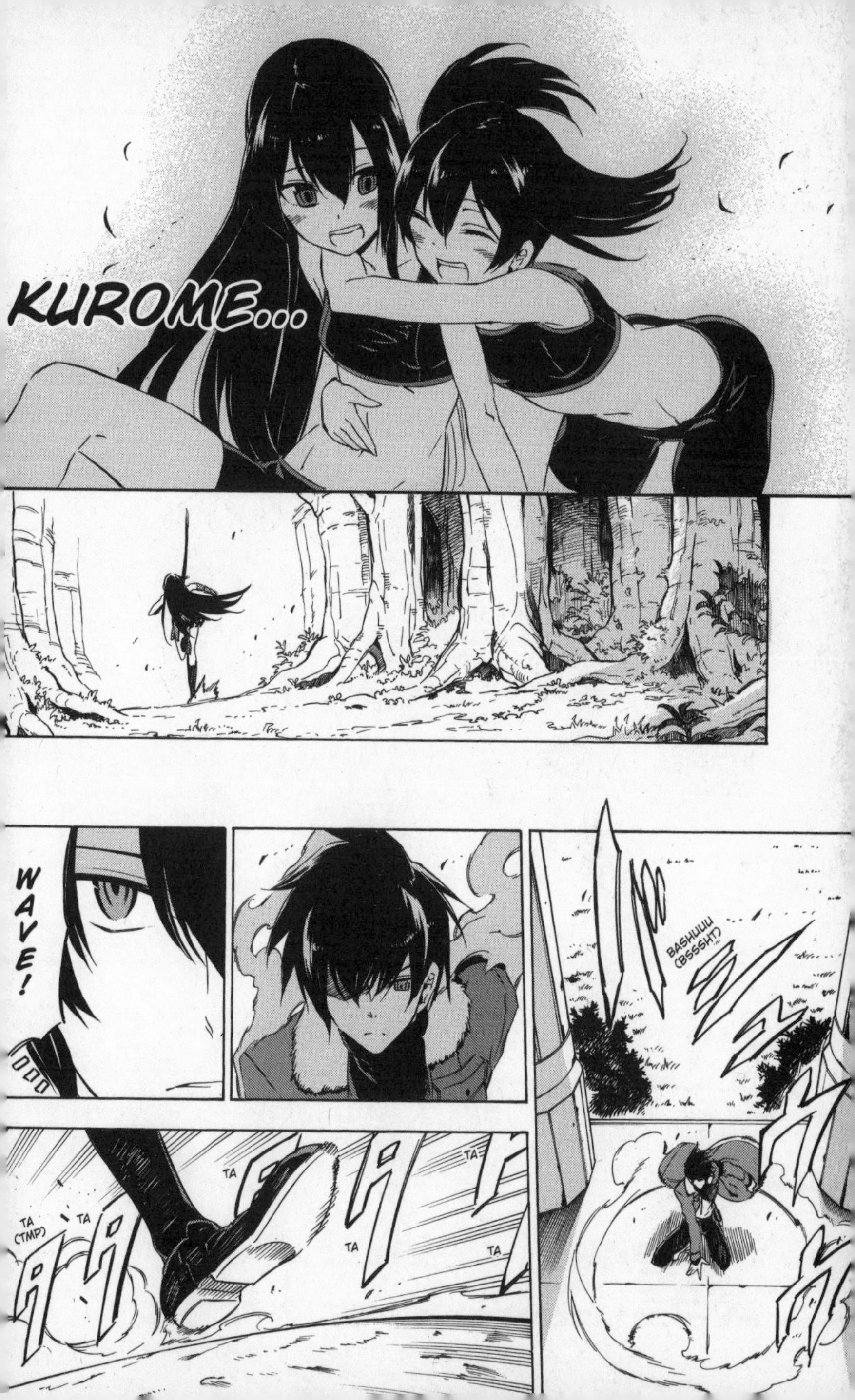
KUROME...
BASHUUU (BSSSHT)
WAVE!
TA
TA
TA
TA
TA
TA (TMP)

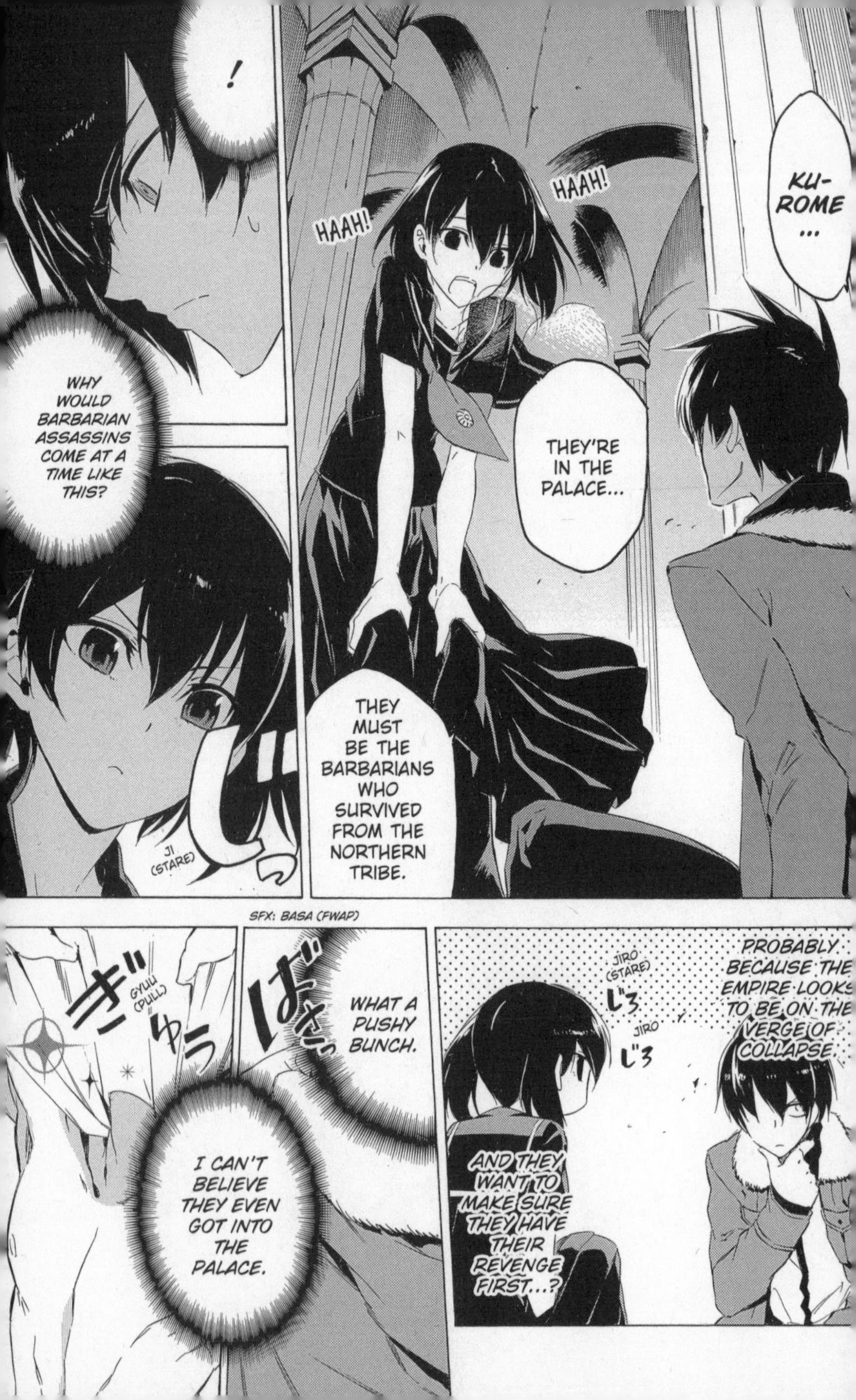
KU-ROME ...
HAAH!
HAAH!
THEY'RE IN THE PALACE...
THEY MUST BE THE BARBARIANS WHO SURVIVED FROM THE NORTHERN TRIBE.
!
WHY WOULD BARBARIAN ASSASSINS COME AT A TIME LIKE THIS?
JI (STARE)
SFX: BASA (FWAP)
PROBABLY BECAUSE THE EMPIRE LOOKS TO BE ON THE VERGE OF COLLAPSE.
JIRO (STARE)
JIRO
AND THEY WANT TO MAKE SURE THEY HAVE THEIR REVENGE FIRST...?
WHAT A PUSHY BUNCH.
I CAN'T BELIEVE THEY EVEN GOT INTO THE PALACE.
GYUU (PULL)

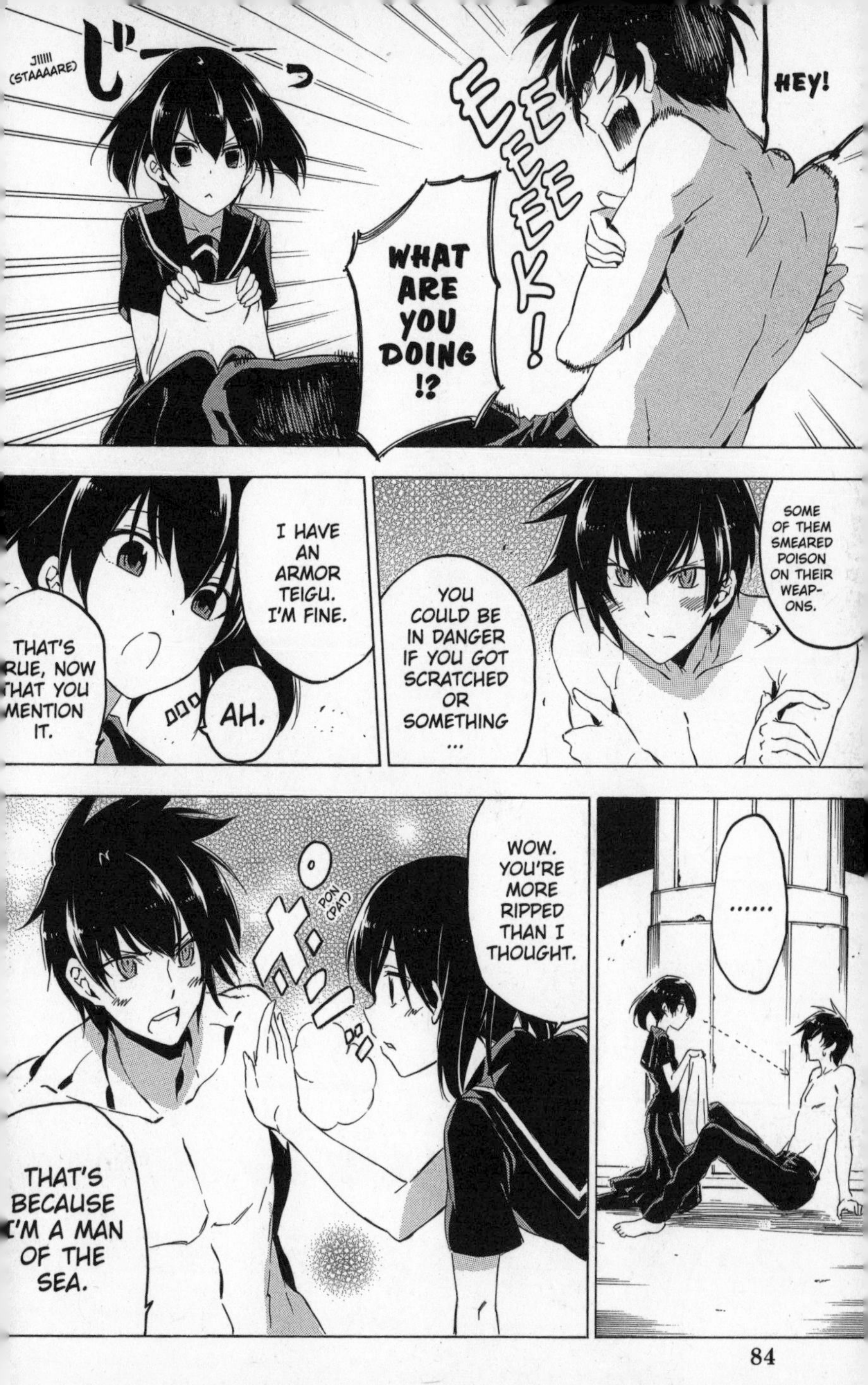
HEY!
EEEEEEK!
WHAT ARE YOU DOING!?
JIIIII (STAAAARE)
SOME OF THEM SMEARED POISON ON THEIR WEAP-ONS.
YOU COULD BE IN DANGER IF YOU GOT SCRATCHED OR SOMETHING...
I HAVE AN ARMOR TEIGU. I'M FINE.
AH.
THAT'S RUE, NOW HAT YOU MENTION IT.
......
WOW. YOU'RE MORE RIPPED THAN I THOUGHT.
PON (PAT)
THAT'S BECAUSE I'M A MAN OF THE SEA.

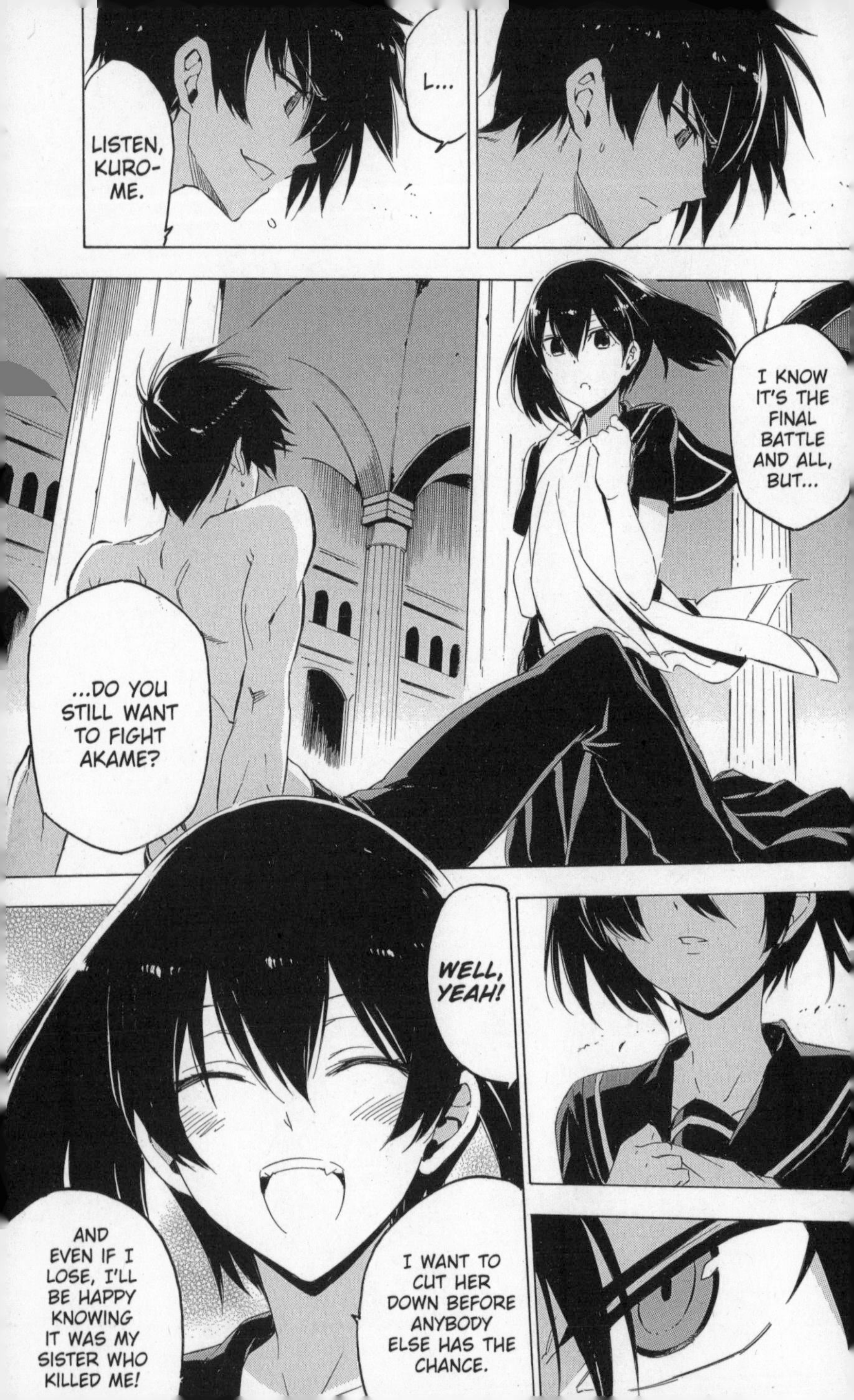
L...
LISTEN, KURO-ME.
I KNOW IT'S THE FINAL BATTLE AND ALL, BUT...
...DO YOU STILL WANT TO FIGHT AKAME?
WELL, YEAH!
I WANT TO CUT HER DOWN BEFORE ANYBODY ELSE HAS THE CHANCE.
AND EVEN IF I LOSE, I'LL BE HAPPY KNOWING IT WAS MY SISTER WHO KILLED ME!

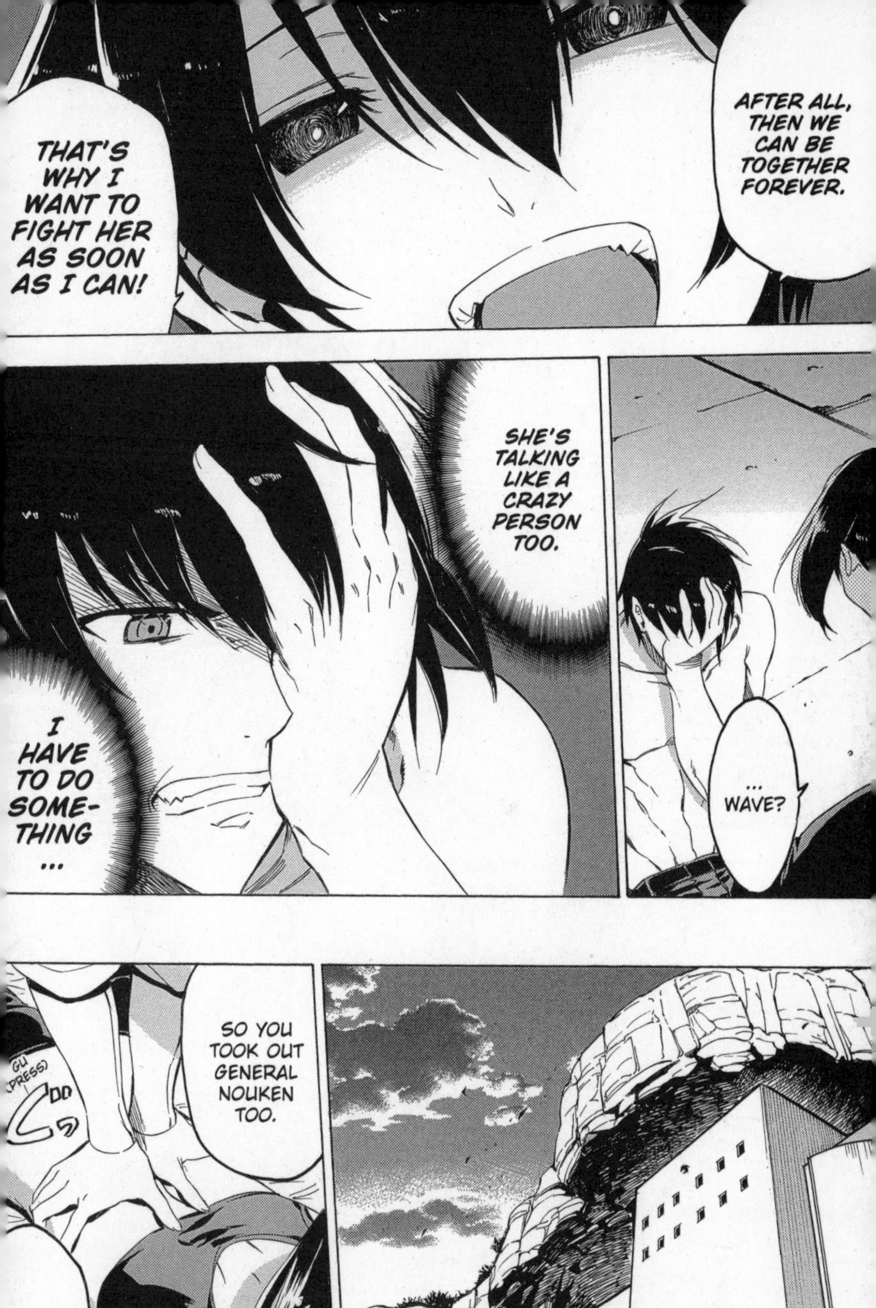
AFTER ALL, THEN WE CAN BE TOGETHER FOREVER.
THAT'S WHY I WANT TO FIGHT HER AS SOON AS I CAN!
... WAVE?
SHE'S TALKING LIKE A CRAZY PERSON TOO.
I HAVE TO DO SOME-THING ...
SO YOU TOOK OUT GENERAL NOUKEN TOO.
GU (PRESS)
THANKS.

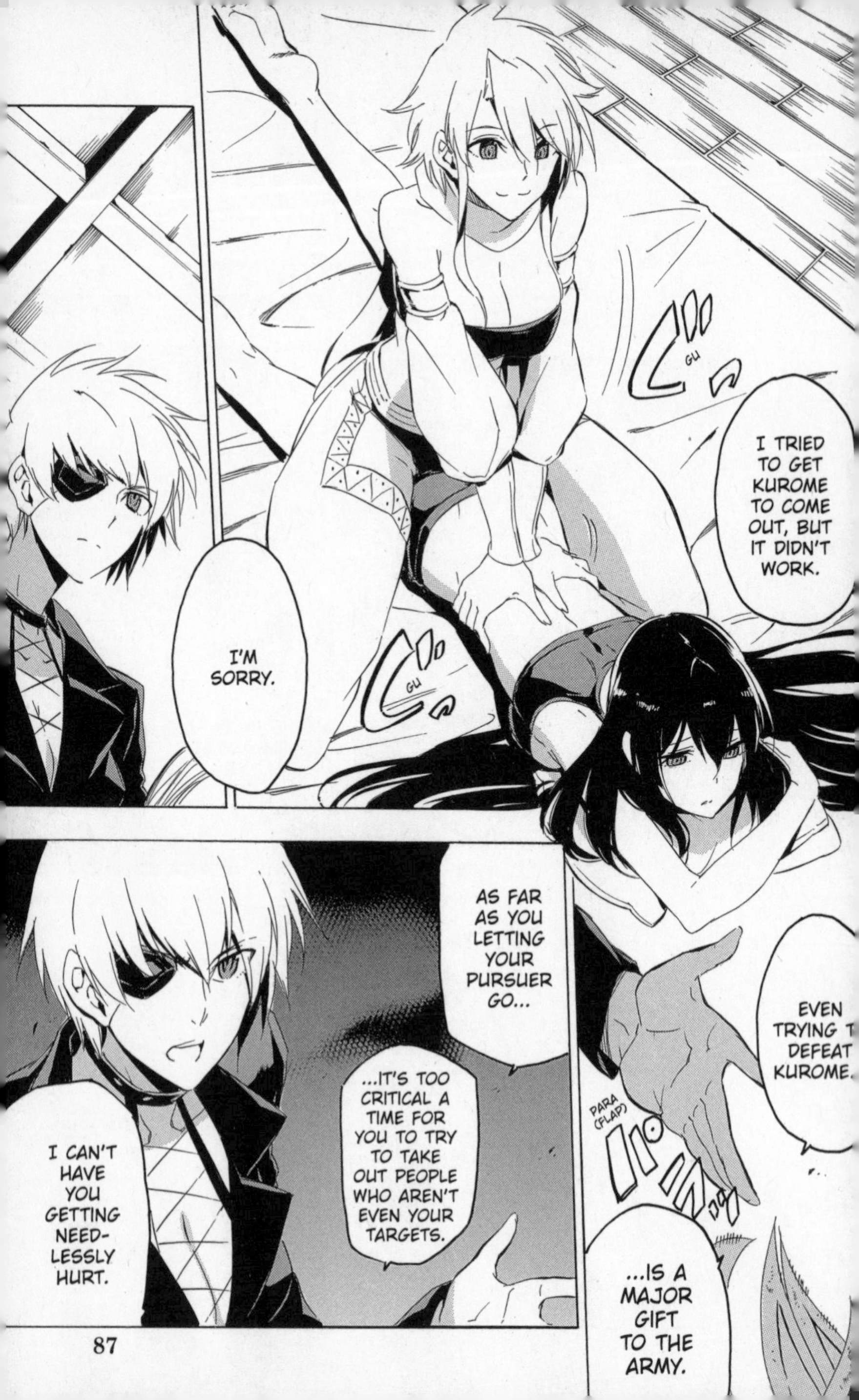
GU
I TRIED TO GET KUROME TO COME OUT, BUT IT DIDN'T WORK.
GU
I'M SORRY.
EVEN TRYING T DEFEAT KUROME.
PARA (FLAP)
...IS A MAJOR GIFT TO THE ARMY.
AS FAR AS YOU LETTING YOUR PURSUER GO...
...IT'S TOO CRITICAL A TIME FOR YOU TO TRY TO TAKE OUT PEOPLE WHO AREN'T EVEN YOUR TARGETS.
I CAN'T HAVE YOU GETTING NEED-LESSLY HURT.

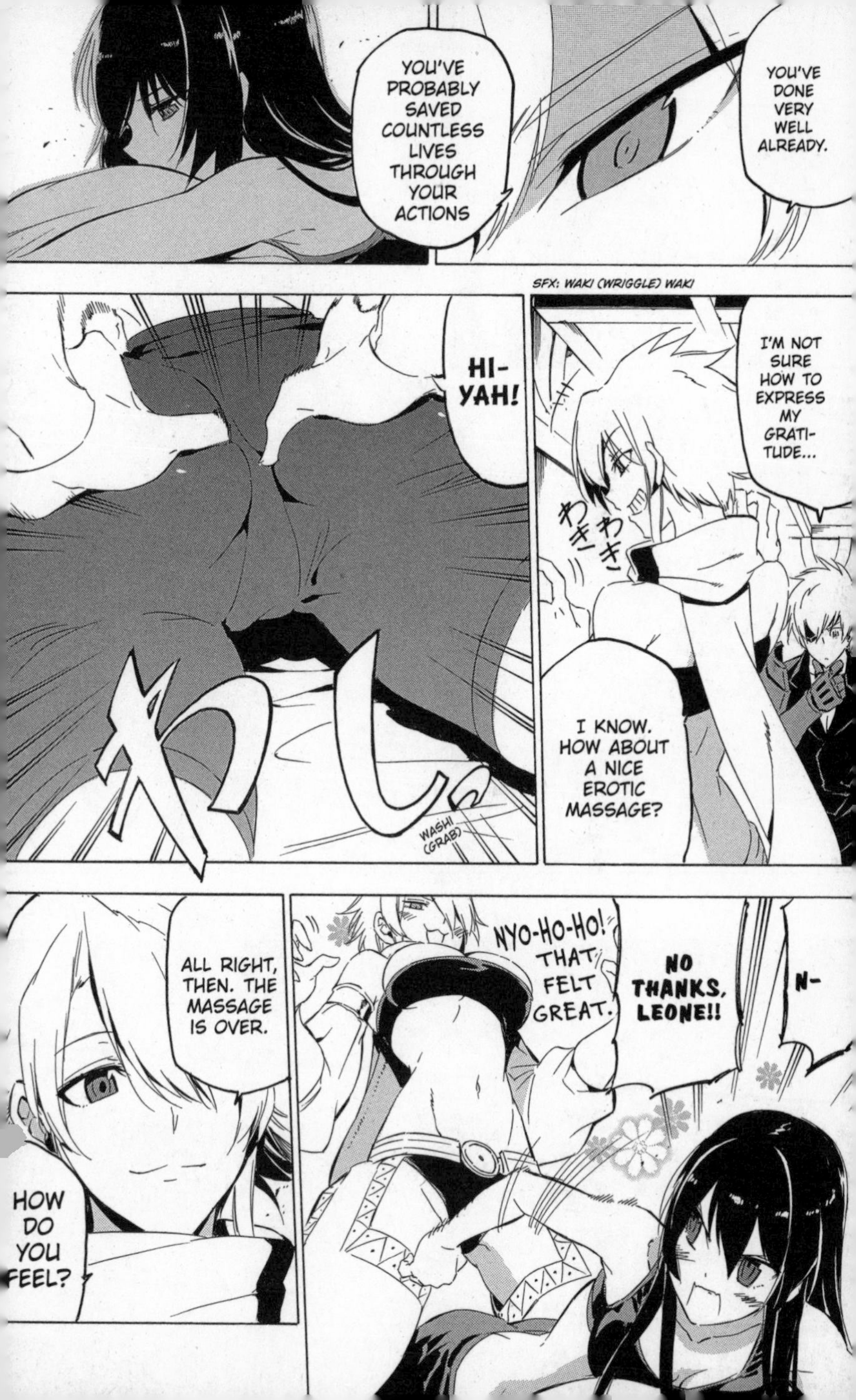
YOU'VE DONE VERY WELL ALREADY.
YOU'VE PROBABLY SAVED COUNTLESS LIVES THROUGH YOUR ACTIONS
SFX: WAKI (WRIGGLE) WAKI
I'M NOT SURE HOW TO EXPRESS MY GRATI-TUDE...
わきわき
I KNOW. HOW ABOUT A NICE EROTIC MASSAGE?
HI-YAH!
WASHI (GRAB)
N-
NO THANKS, LEONE!!
NYO-HO-HO! THAT FELT GREAT.
ALL RIGHT, THEN. THE MASSAGE IS OVER.
HOW DO YOU FEEL?

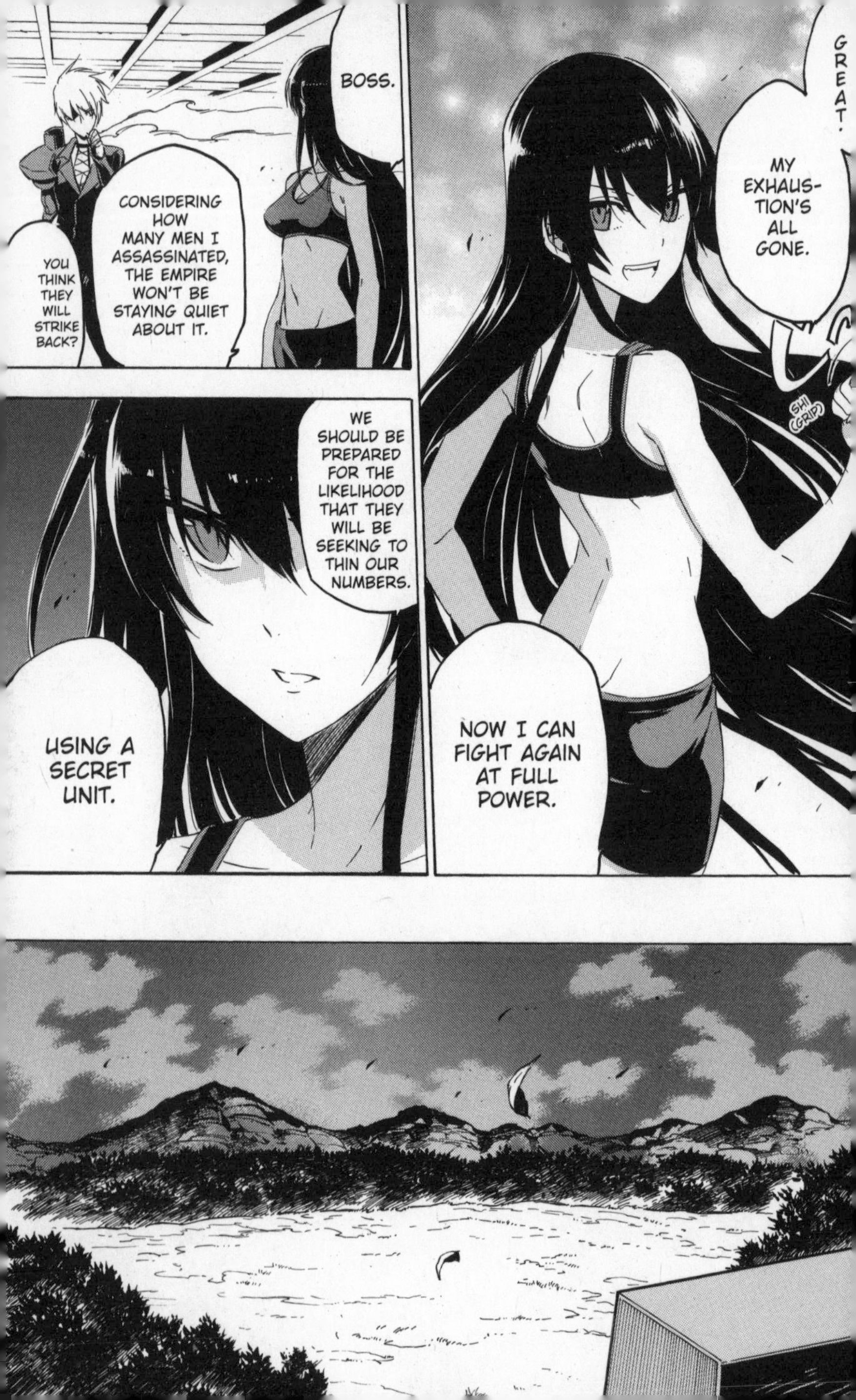
GREAT.
MY EXHAUSTION'S ALL GONE.
SHI (GRIP)
NOW I CAN FIGHT AGAIN AT FULL POWER.
BOSS.
CONSIDERING HOW MANY MEN I ASSASSINATED, THE EMPIRE WON'T BE STAYING QUIET ABOUT IT.
YOU THINK THEY WILL STRIKE BACK?
WE SHOULD BE PREPARED FOR THE LIKELIHOOD THAT THEY WILL BE SEEKING TO THIN OUR NUMBERS.
USING A SECRET UNIT.

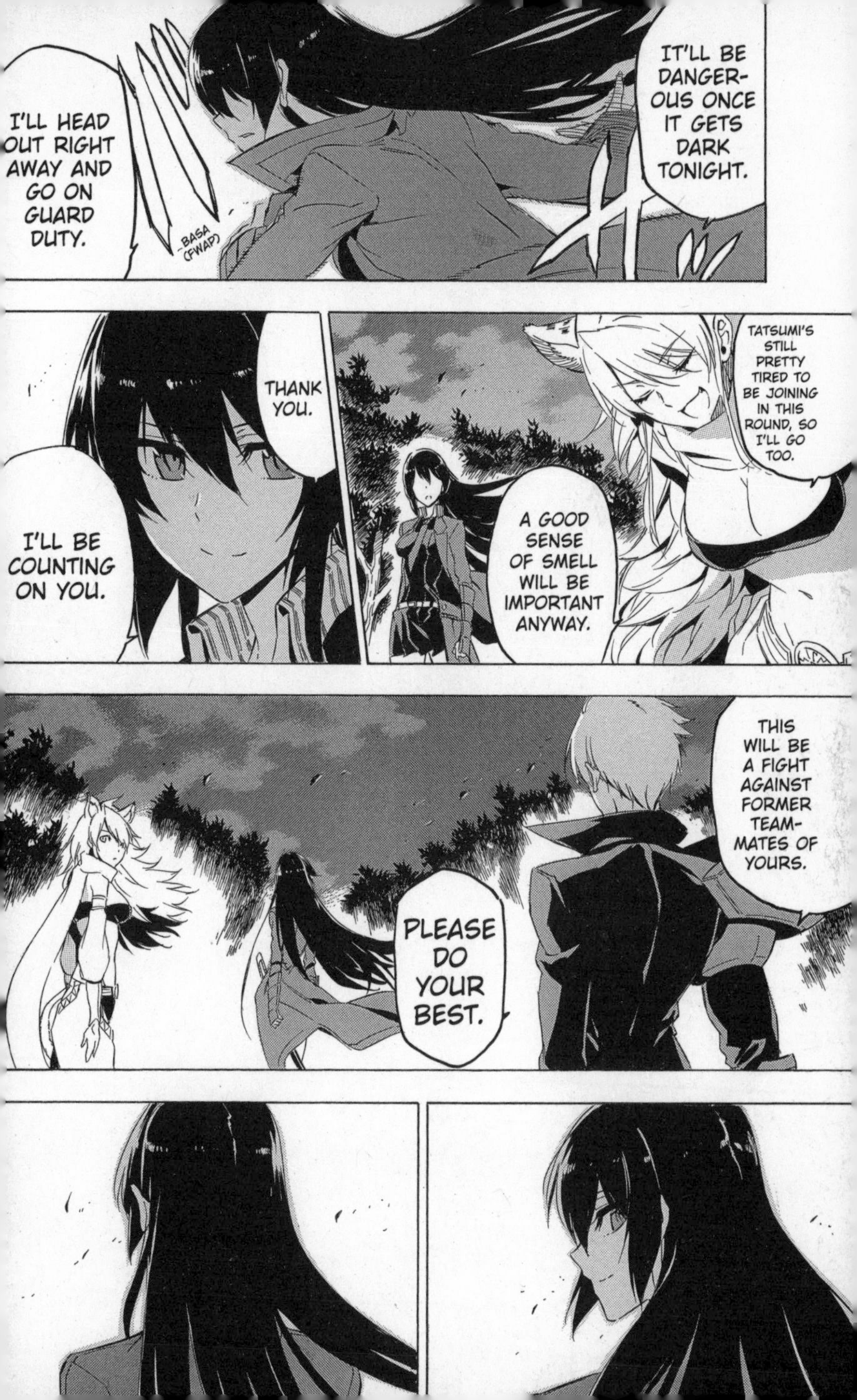
IT'LL BE DANGER-OUS ONCE IT GETS DARK TONIGHT.
I'LL HEAD OUT RIGHT AWAY AND GO ON GUARD DUTY.
BASA (FWAP)
TATSUMI'S STILL PRETTY TIRED TO BE JOINING IN THIS ROUND, SO I'LL GO TOO.
A GOOD SENSE OF SMELL WILL BE IMPORTANT ANYWAY.
THANK YOU.
I'LL BE COUNTING ON YOU.
THIS WILL BE A FIGHT AGAINST FORMER TEAM-MATES OF YOURS.
PLEASE DO YOUR BEST.

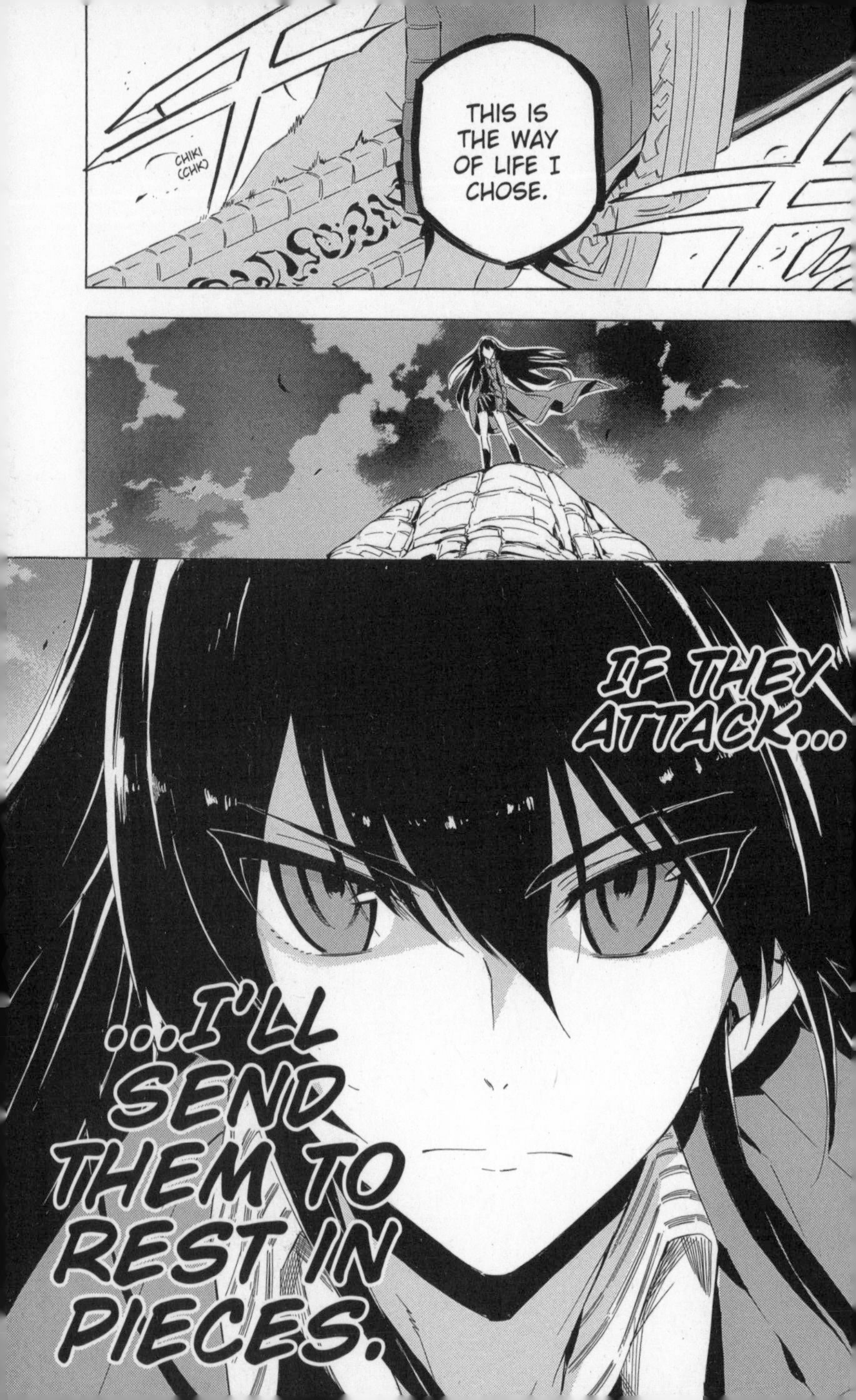
THIS IS THE WAY OF LIFE I CHOSE.
CHIKI (CHK)
IF THEY ATTACK...
...I'LL SEND THEM TO REST IN PIECES.

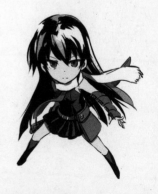

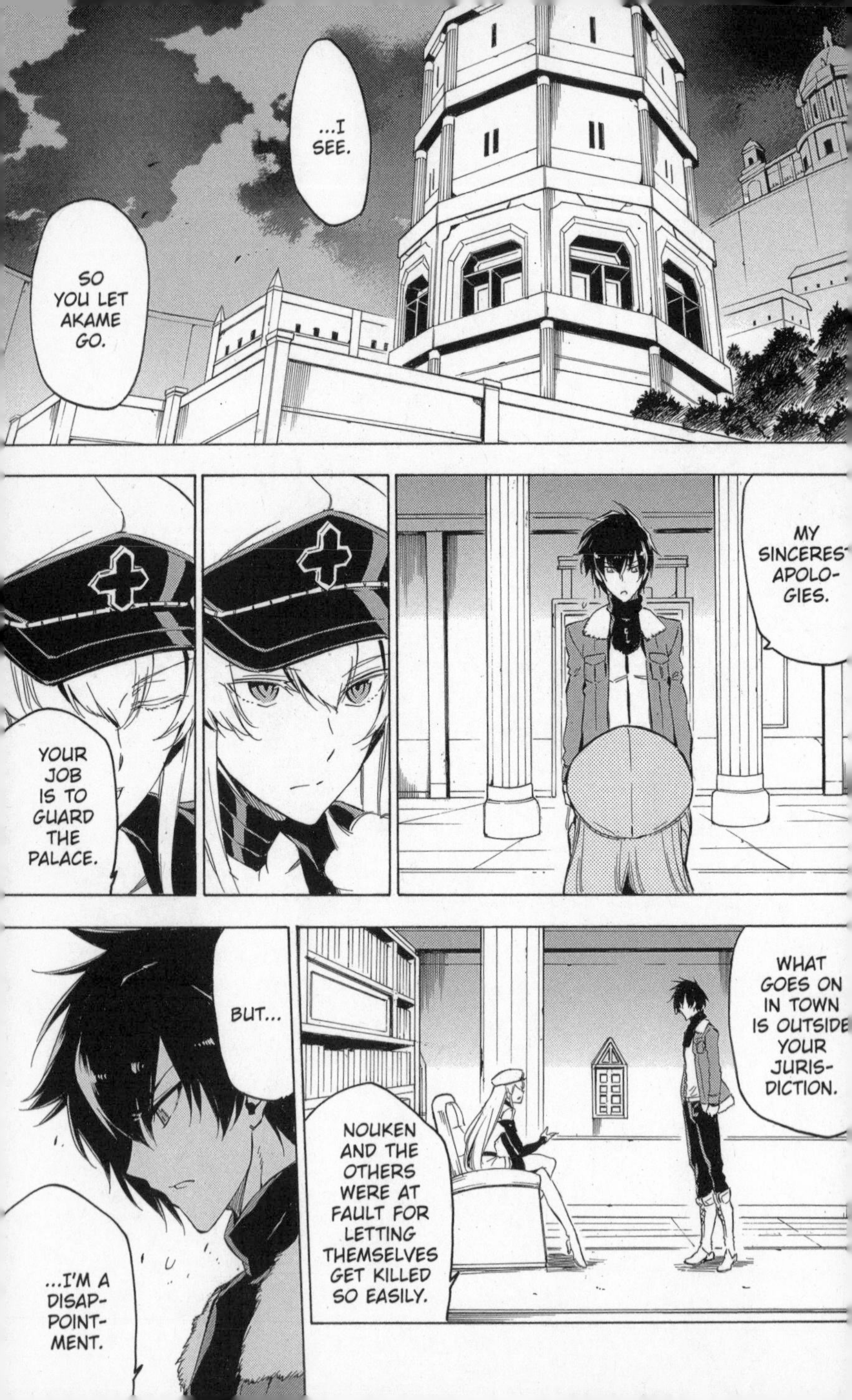
...I SEE.
SO YOU LET AKAME GO.
MY SINCEREST APOLOGIES.
YOUR JOB IS TO GUARD THE PALACE.
WHAT GOES ON IN TOWN IS OUTSIDE YOUR JURISDICTION.
NOUKEN AND THE OTHERS WERE AT FAULT FOR LETTING THEMSELVES GET KILLED SO EASILY.
BUT...
...I'M A DISAPPOINTMENT.

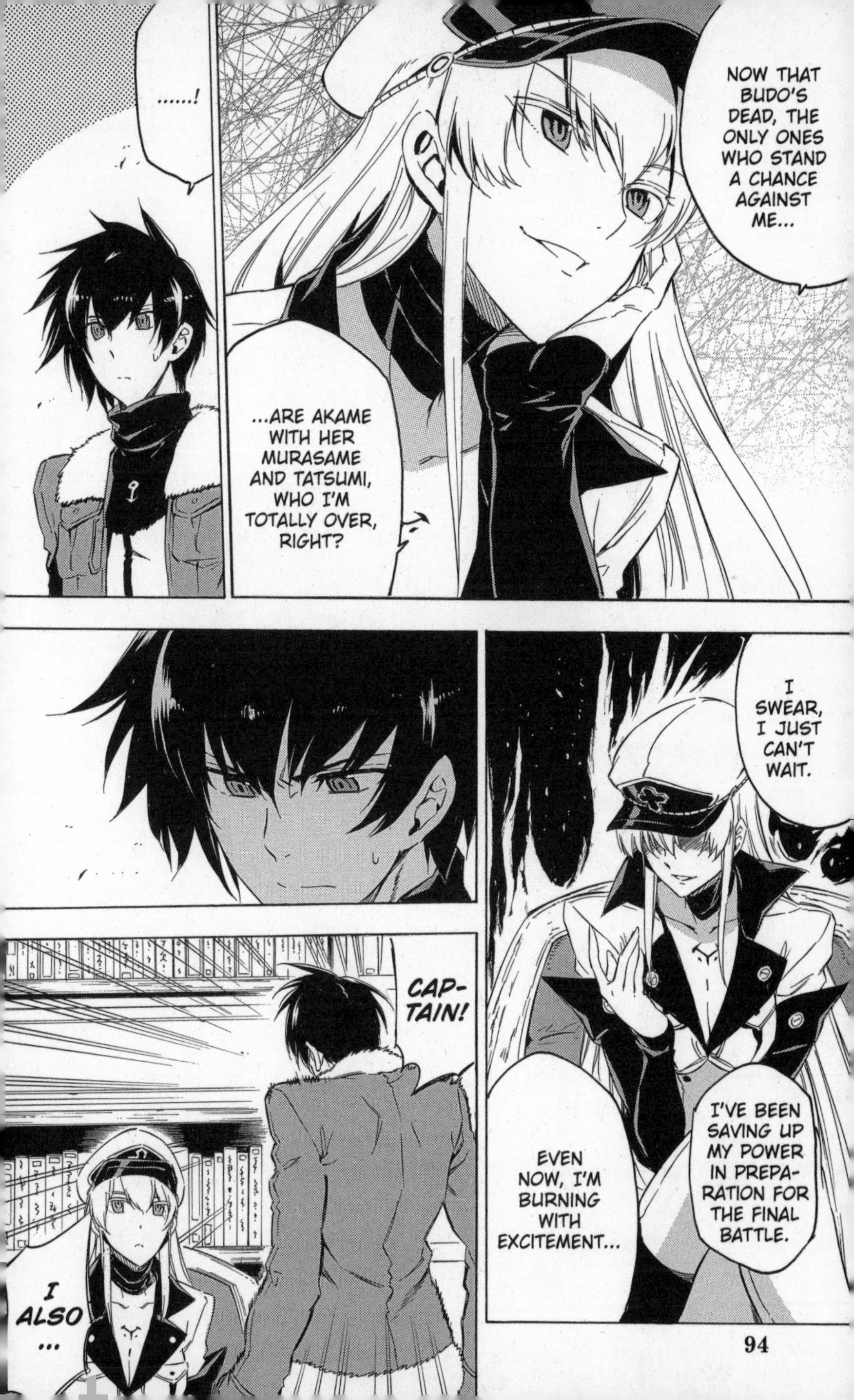
NOW THAT BUDO'S DEAD, THE ONLY ONES WHO STAND A CHANCE AGAINST ME...
...ARE AKAME WITH HER MURASAME AND TATSUMI, WHO I'M TOTALLY OVER, RIGHT?
......!
I SWEAR, I JUST CAN'T WAIT.
I'VE BEEN SAVING UP MY POWER IN PREPARATION FOR THE FINAL BATTLE.
EVEN NOW, I'M BURNING WITH EXCITEMENT...
CAP-TAIN!
I ALSO ...

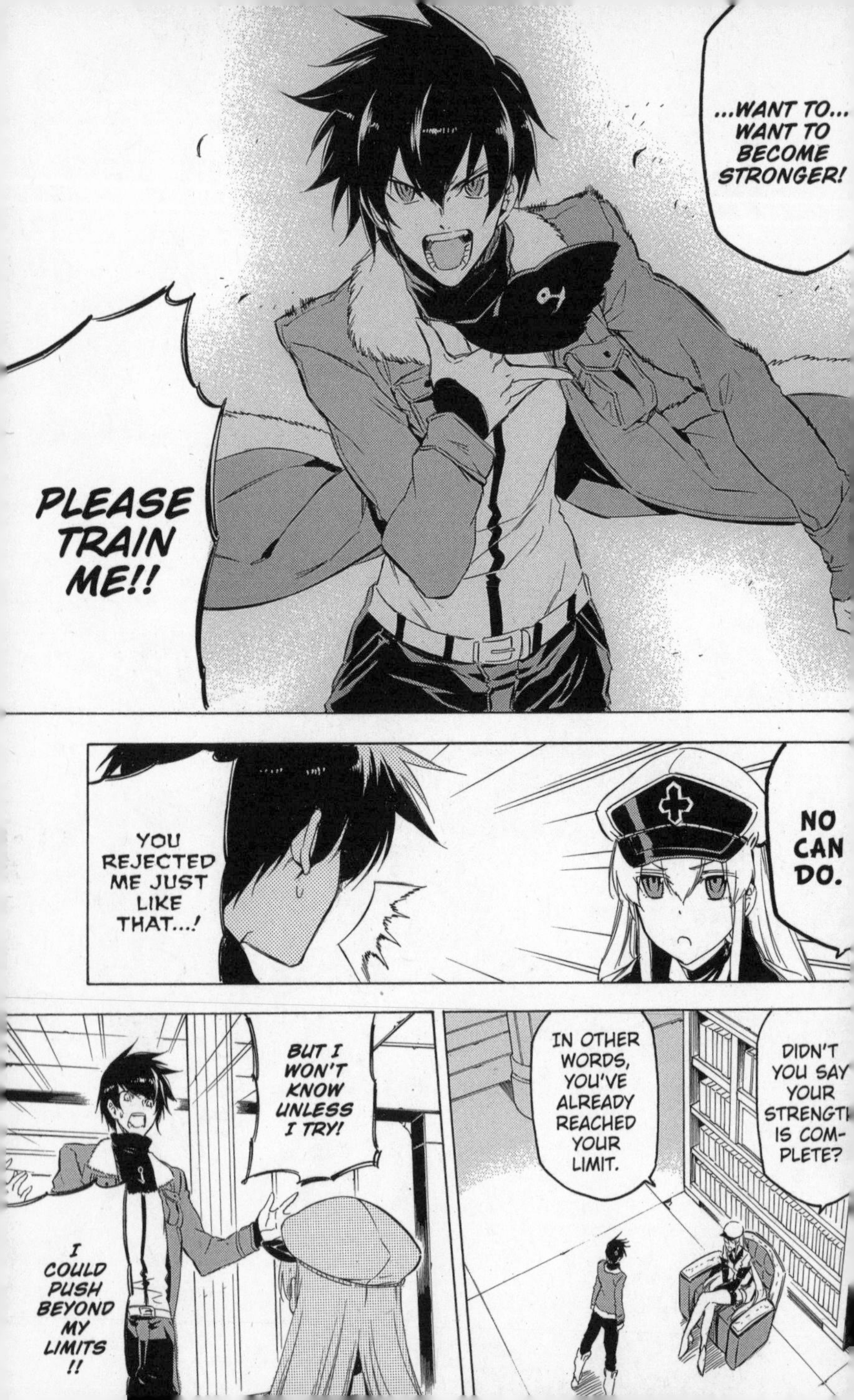
...WANT TO... WANT TO BECOME STRONGER!
PLEASE TRAIN ME!!
NO CAN DO.
YOU REJECTED ME JUST LIKE THAT...!
DIDN'T YOU SAY YOUR STRENGT IS COM-PLETE?
IN OTHER WORDS, YOU'VE ALREADY REACHED YOUR LIMIT.
BUT I WON'T KNOW UNLESS I TRY!
I COULD PUSH BEYOND MY LIMITS!!

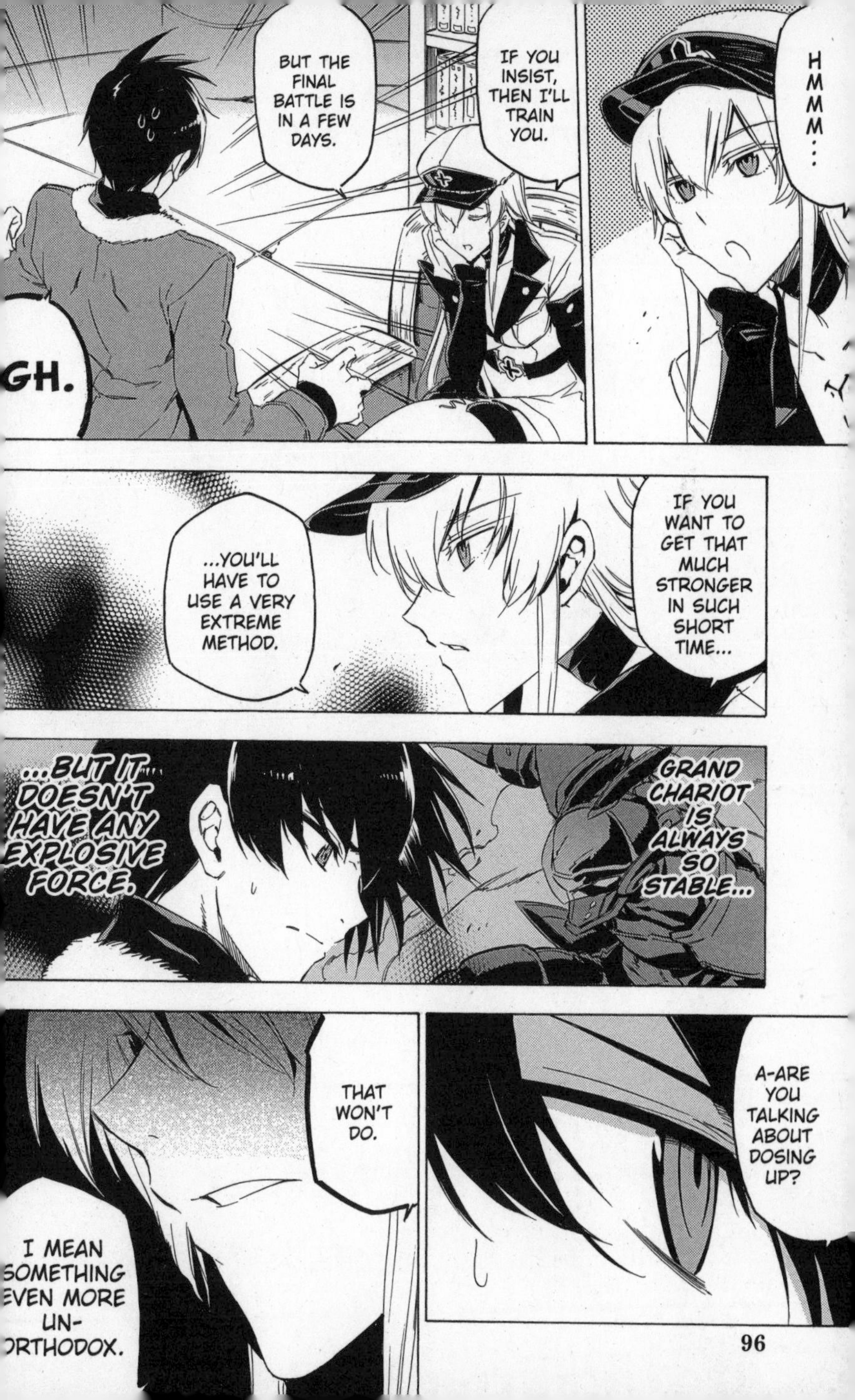

HMMM...
IF YOU INSIST, THEN I'LL TRAIN YOU.
BUT THE FINAL BATTLE IS IN A FEW DAYS.
GH.
IF YOU WANT TO GET THAT MUCH STRONGER IN SUCH SHORT TIME...
...YOU'LL HAVE TO USE A VERY EXTREME METHOD.
GRAND CHARIOT IS ALWAYS SO STABLE...
...BUT IT DOESN'T HAVE ANY EXPLOSIVE FORCE.
A-ARE YOU TALKING ABOUT DOSING UP?
THAT WON'T DO.
I MEAN SOMETHING EVEN MORE UN-ORTHODOX.

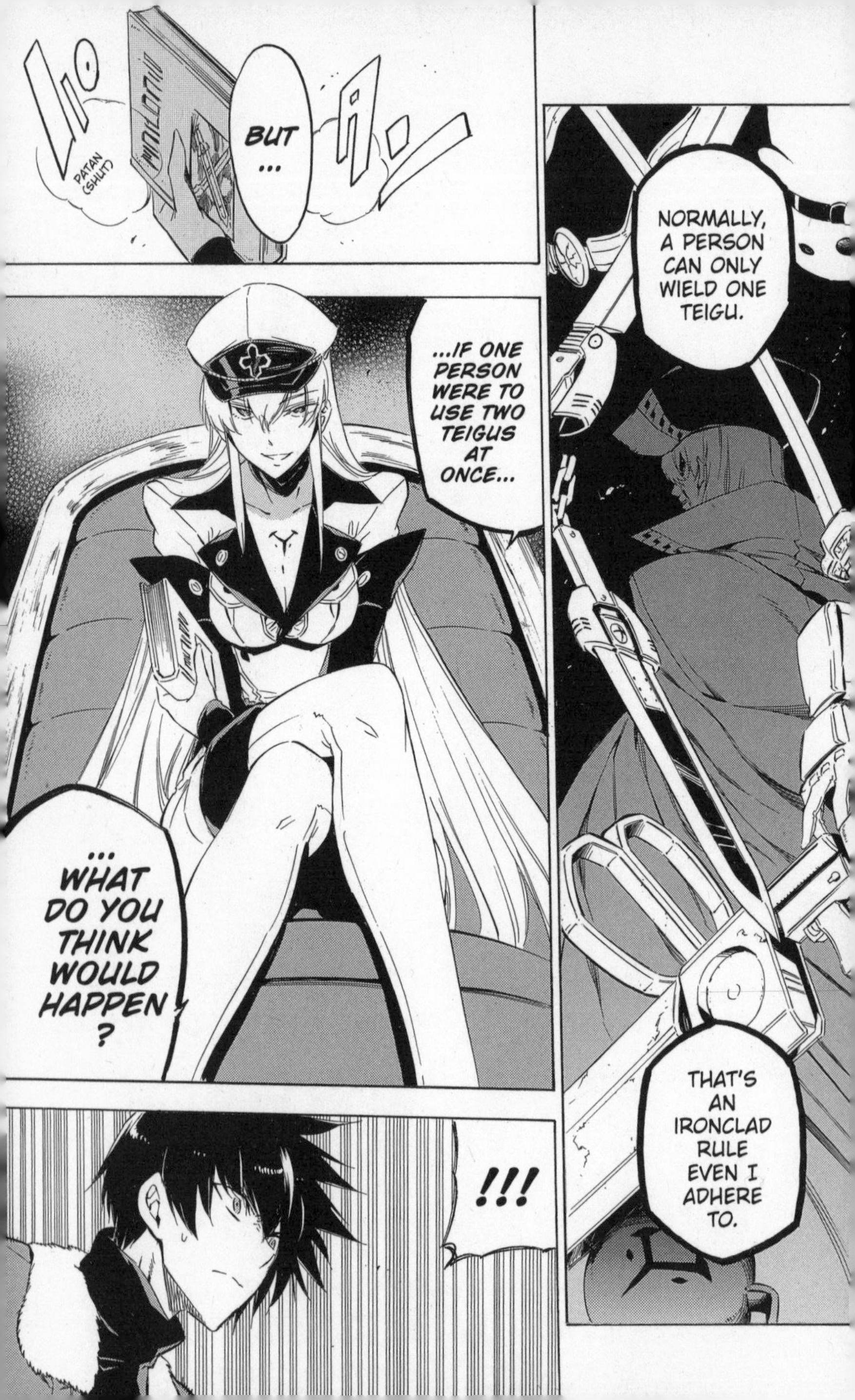

NORMALLY, A PERSON CAN ONLY WIELD ONE TEIGU.
THAT'S AN IRONCLAD RULE EVEN I ADHERE TO.
BUT ...
PATAN (SHUT)
...IF ONE PERSON WERE TO USE TWO TEIGUS AT ONCE...
... WHAT DO YOU THINK WOULD HAPPEN ?
!!!

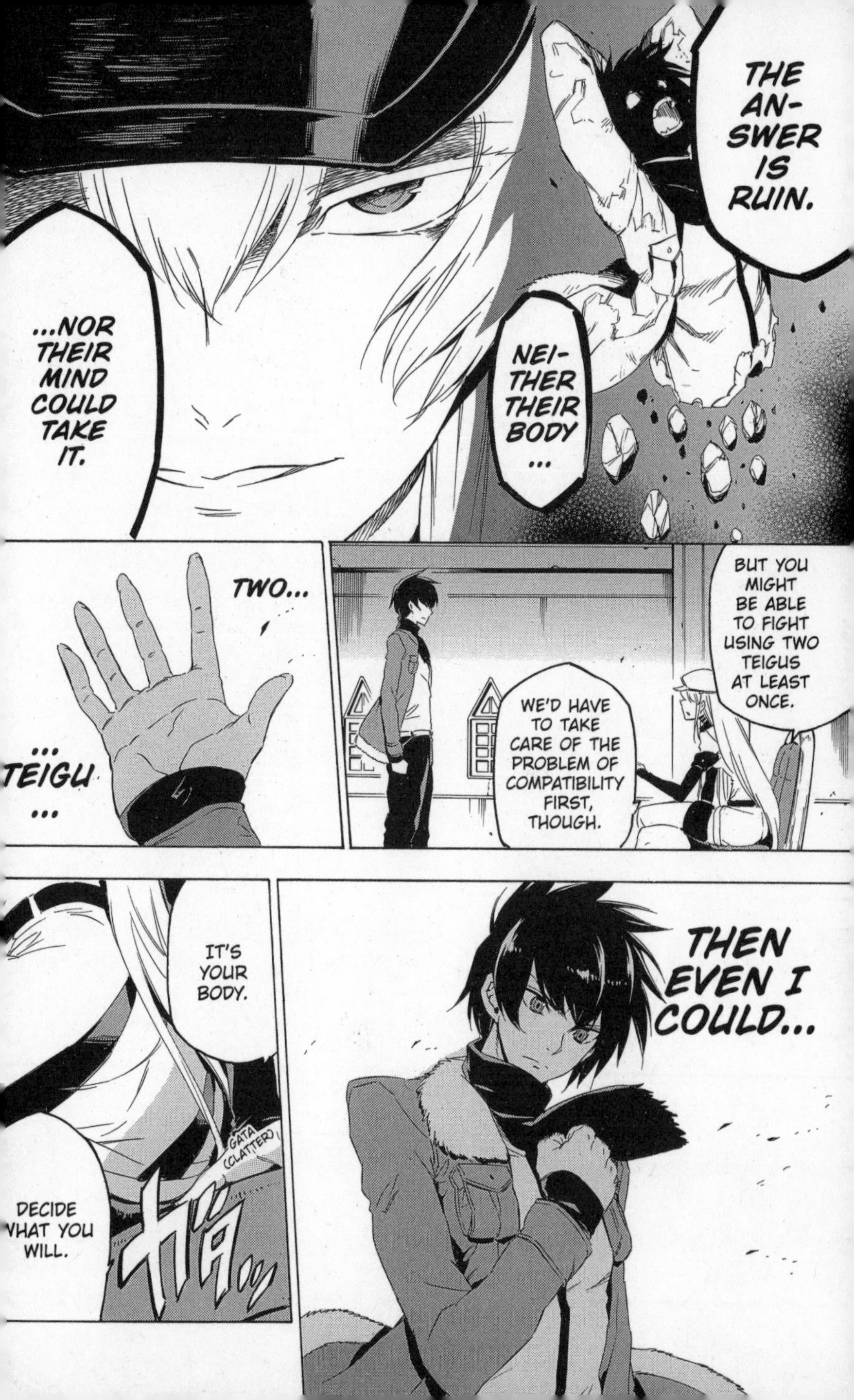
THE ANSWER IS RUIN.
NEITHER THEIR BODY...
...NOR THEIR MIND COULD TAKE IT.
BUT YOU MIGHT BE ABLE TO FIGHT USING TWO TEIGUS AT LEAST ONCE.
WE'D HAVE TO TAKE CARE OF THE PROBLEM OF COMPATIBILITY FIRST, THOUGH.
TWO...
...TEIGU...
THEN EVEN I COULD...
IT'S YOUR BODY.
GATA (CLATTER)
DECIDE WHAT YOU WILL.

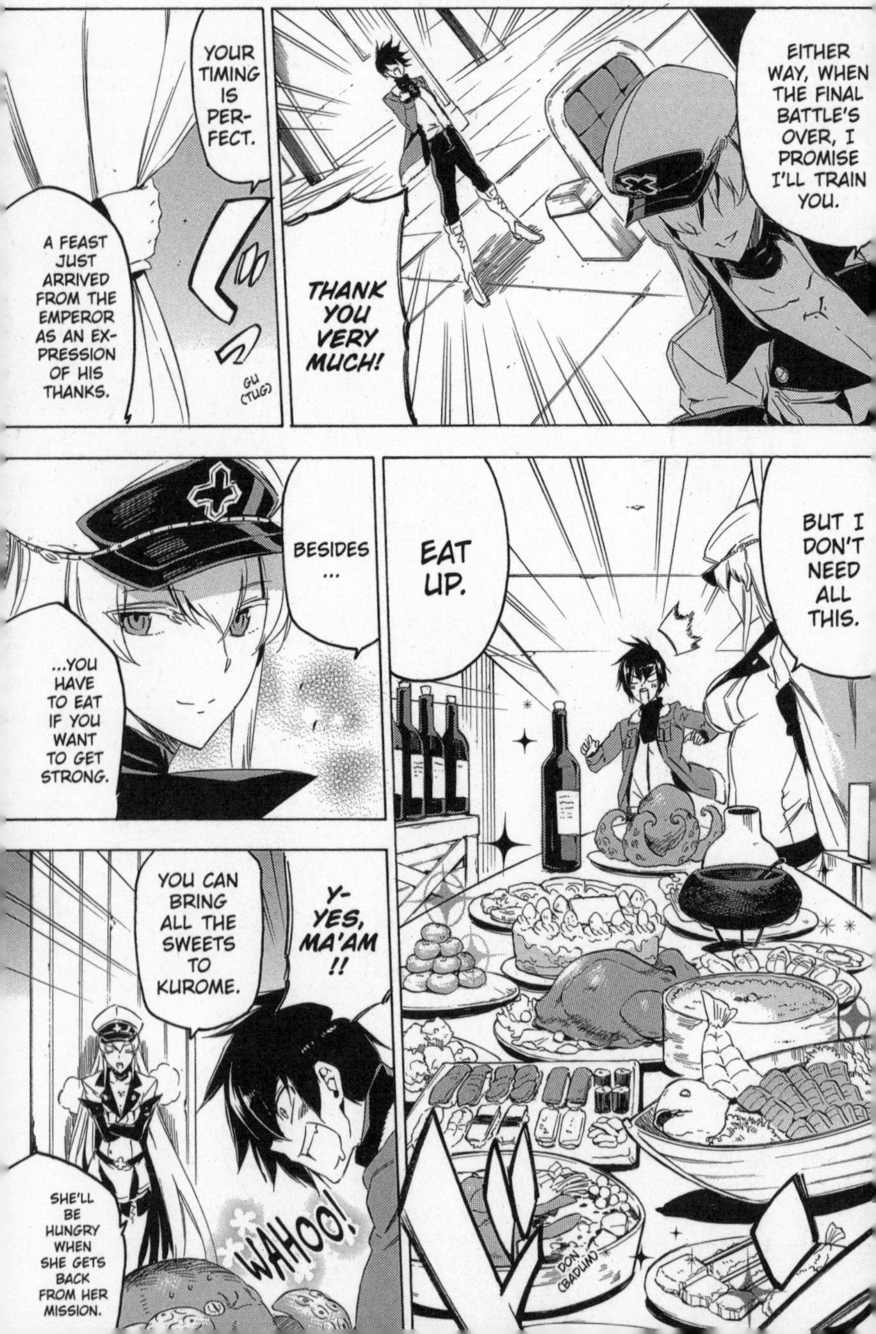
EITHER WAY, WHEN THE FINAL BATTLE'S OVER, I PROMISE I'LL TRAIN YOU.
THANK YOU VERY MUCH!
YOUR TIMING IS PER-FECT.
A FEAST JUST ARRIVED FROM THE EMPEROR AS AN EX-PRESSION OF HIS THANKS.
GU (TUG)
BUT I DON'T NEED ALL THIS.
EAT UP.
DON (BADUMP)
BESIDES...
...YOU HAVE TO EAT IF YOU WANT TO GET STRONG.
Y-YES, MA'AM!!
YOU CAN BRING ALL THE SWEETS TO KUROME.
SHE'LL BE HUNGRY WHEN SHE GETS BACK FROM HER MISSION.
WAHOO!

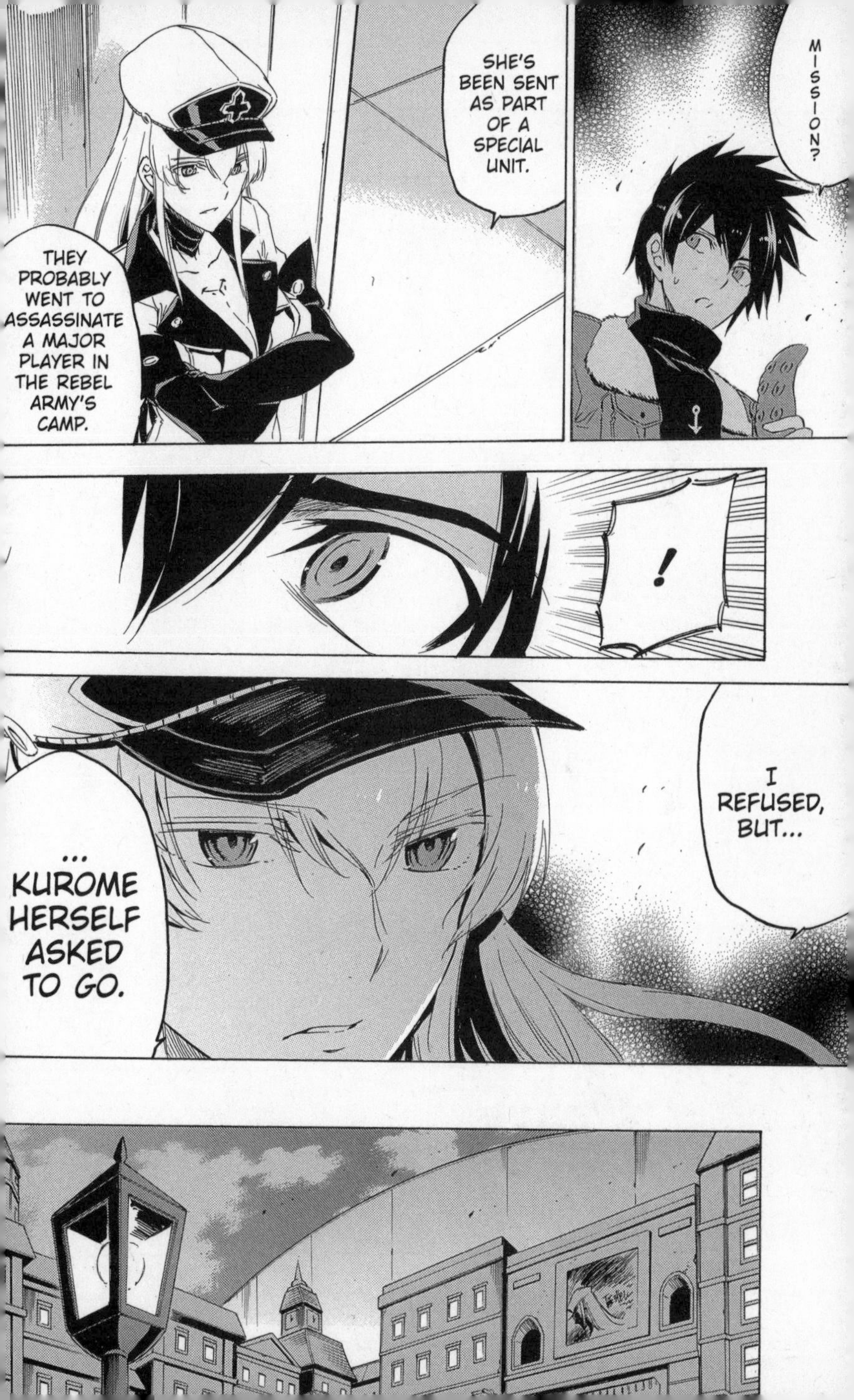
MISSION?
SHE'S BEEN SENT AS PART OF A SPECIAL UNIT.
THEY PROBABLY WENT TO ASSASSINATE A MAJOR PLAYER IN THE REBEL ARMY'S CAMP.
!
I REFUSED, BUT...
...KUROME HERSELF ASKED TO GO.

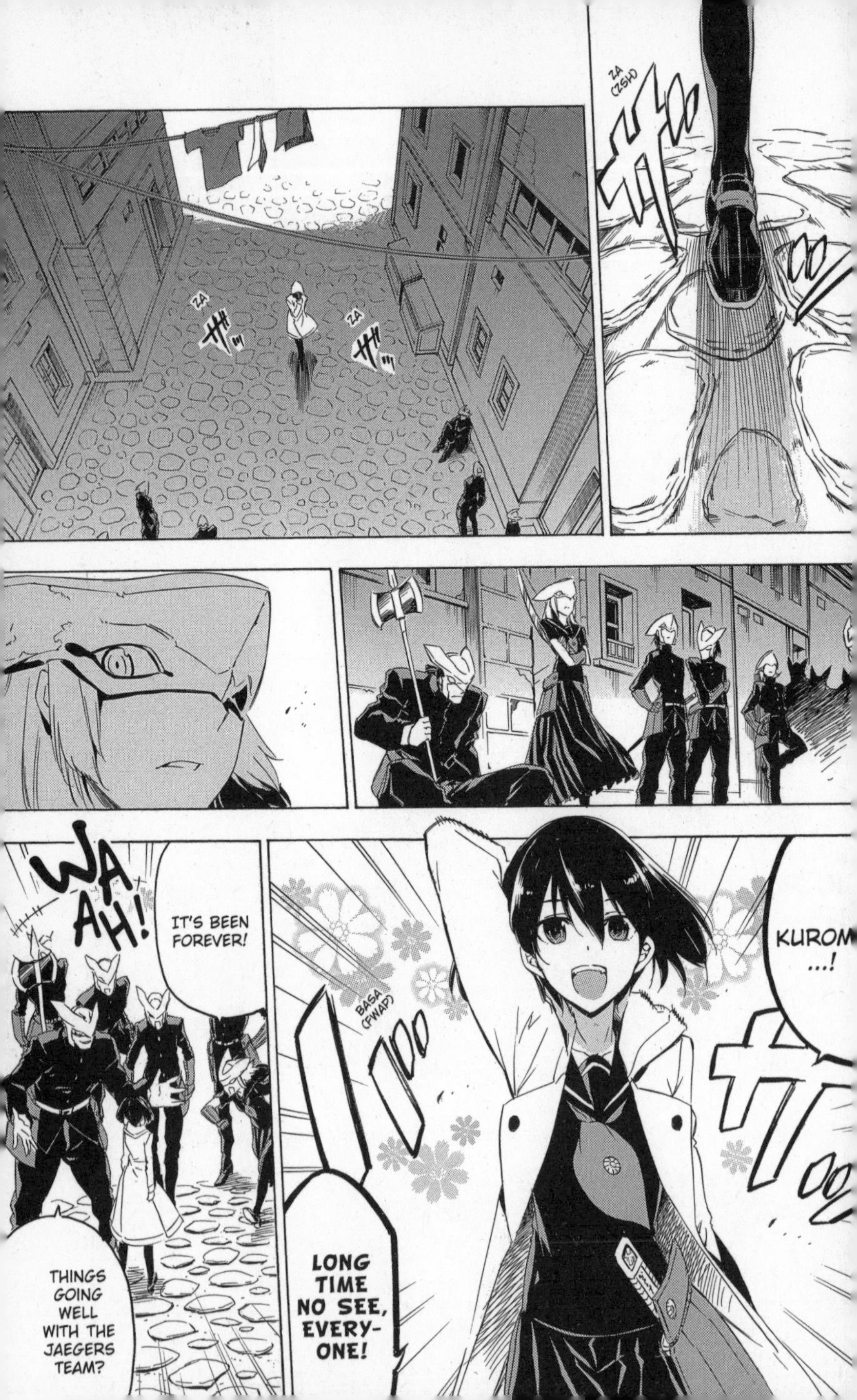
ZA (ZSH)
ZA
ZA
KUROM ...!
BASA (FWAP)
LONG TIME NO SEE, EVERY-ONE!
WAAH!
IT'S BEEN FOREVER!
THINGS GOING WELL WITH THE JAEGERS TEAM?

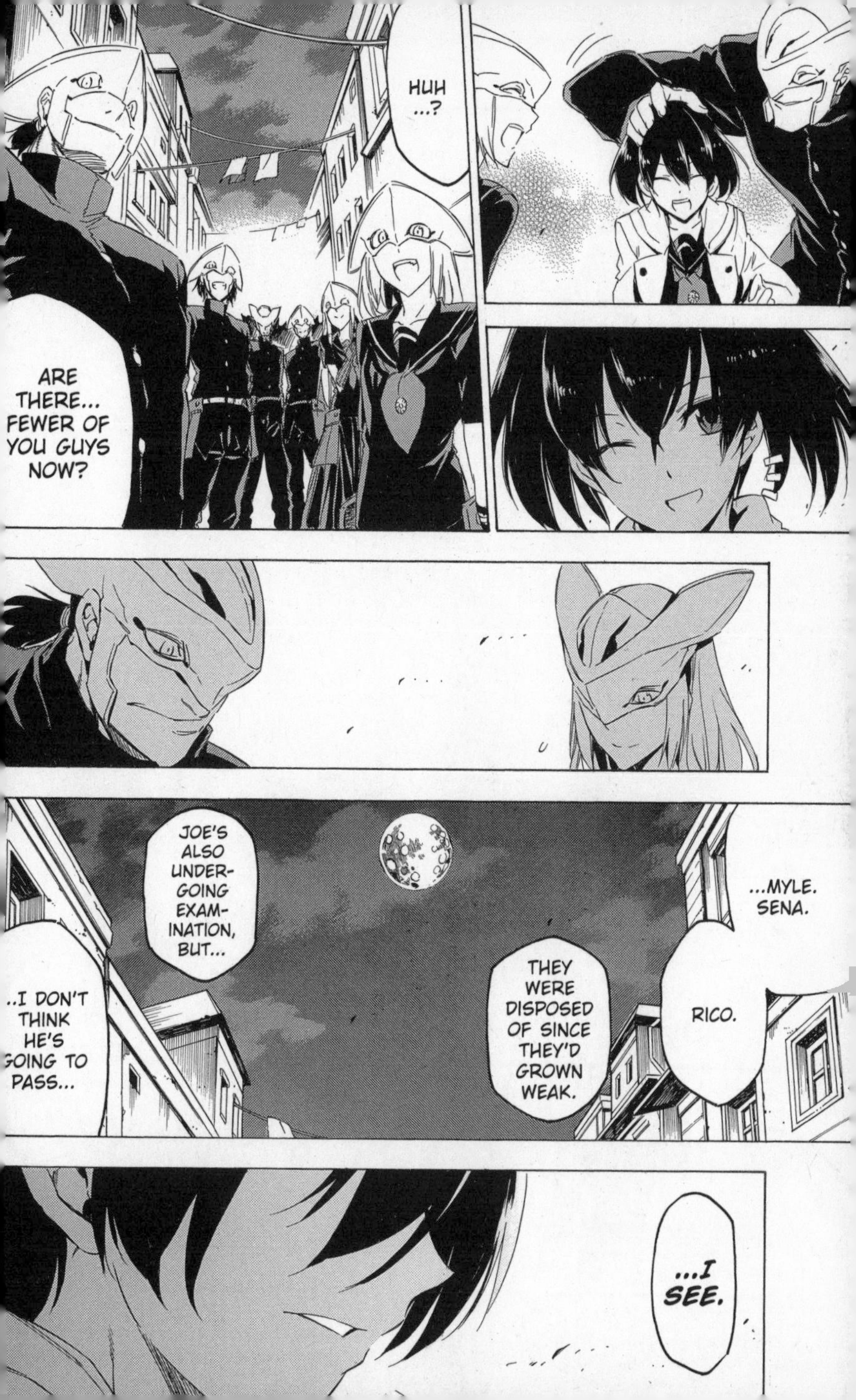
HUH ...?
ARE THERE... FEWER OF YOU GUYS NOW?
...MYLE. SENA.
RICO.
THEY WERE DISPOSED OF SINCE THEY'D GROWN WEAK.
JOE'S ALSO UNDER-GOING EXAM-INATION, BUT...
..I DON'T THINK HE'S GOING TO PASS...
...I SEE.

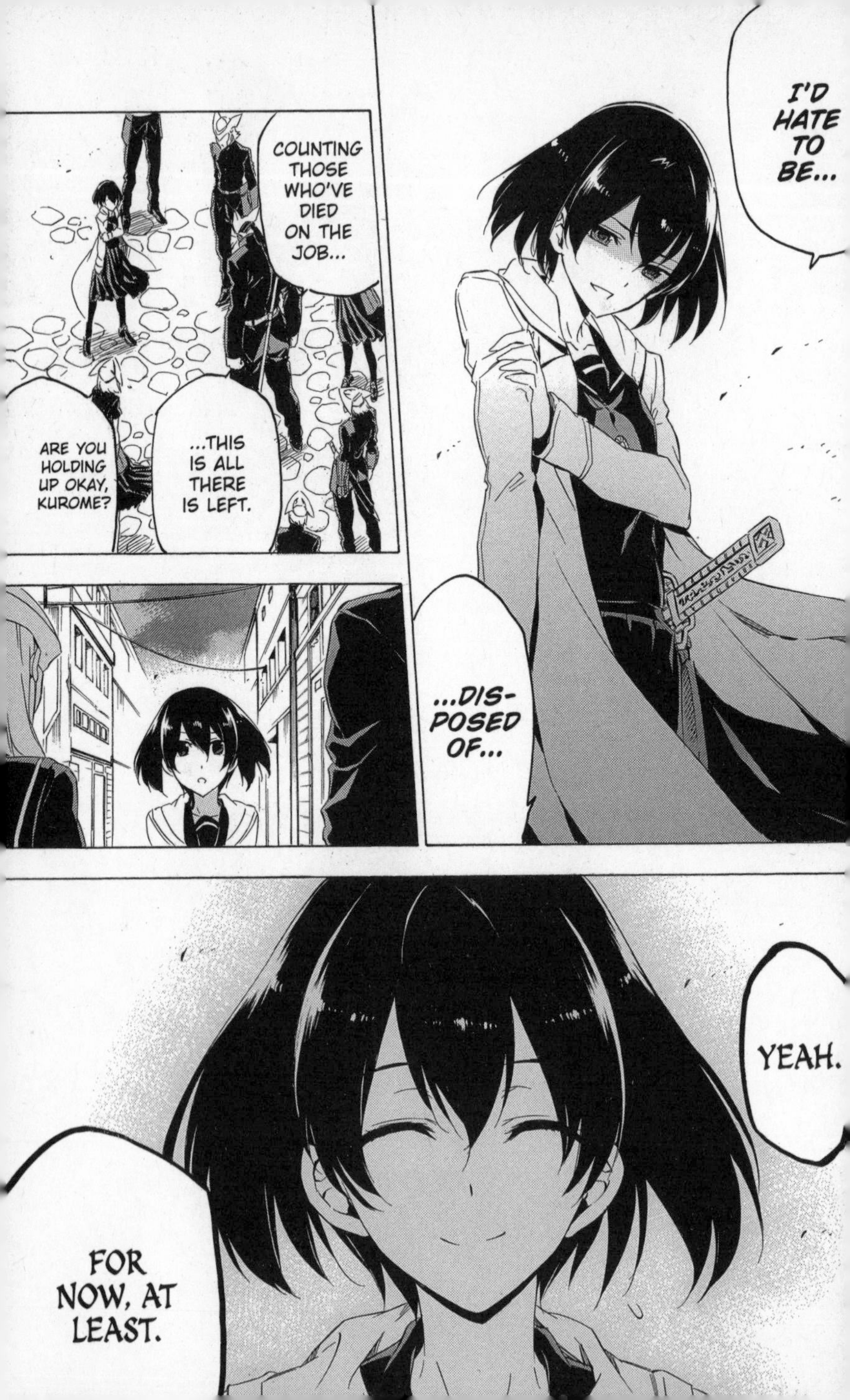
I'D HATE TO BE...
...DIS-POSED OF...
COUNTING THOSE WHO'VE DIED ON THE JOB...
...THIS IS ALL THERE IS LEFT.
ARE YOU HOLDING UP OKAY, KUROME?
YEAH.
FOR NOW, AT LEAST.

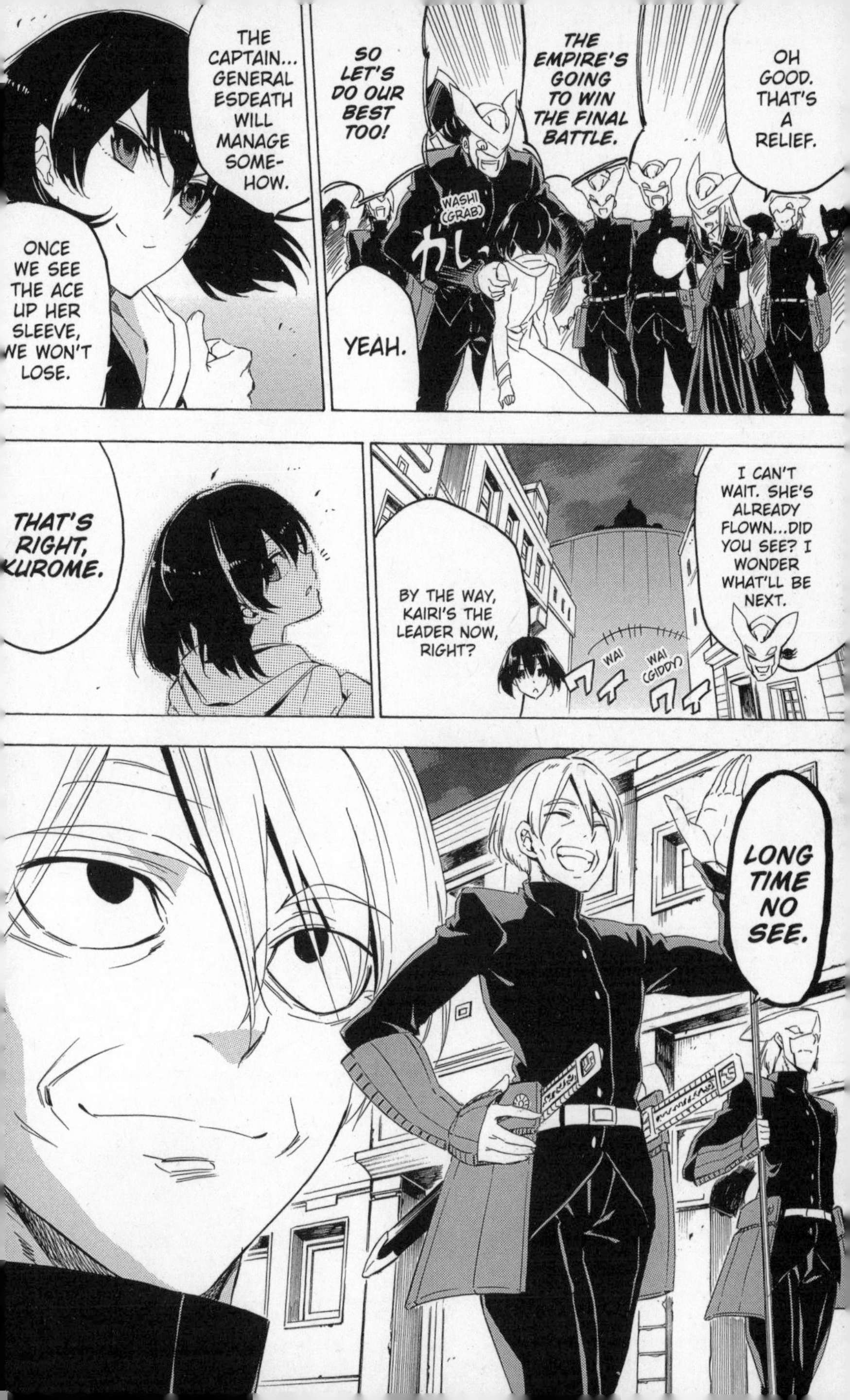
OH GOOD. THAT'S A RELIEF.
THE EMPIRE'S GOING TO WIN THE FINAL BATTLE.
SO LET'S DO OUR BEST TOO!
WASHI (GRAB)
YEAH.
THE CAPTAIN... GENERAL ESDEATH WILL MANAGE SOME-HOW.
ONCE WE SEE THE ACE UP HER SLEEVE, WE WON'T LOSE.
I CAN'T WAIT. SHE'S ALREADY FLOWN...DID YOU SEE? I WONDER WHAT'LL BE NEXT.
WAI WAI (GIDDY)
BY THE WAY, KAIRI'S THE LEADER NOW, RIGHT?
THAT'S RIGHT, KUROME.
LONG TIME NO SEE.

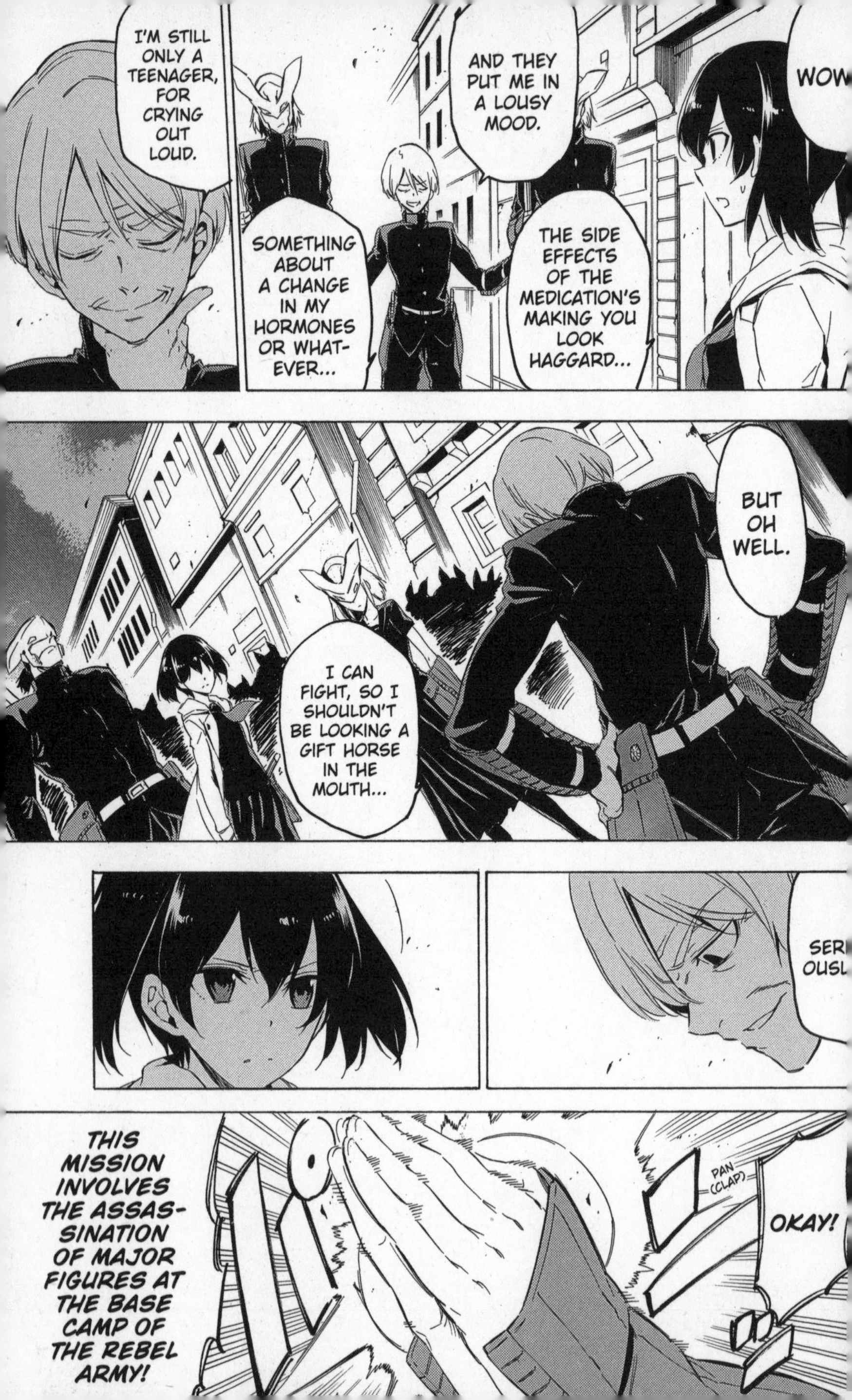
WOW
THE SIDE EFFECTS OF THE MEDICATION'S MAKING YOU LOOK HAGGARD...
SOMETHING ABOUT A CHANGE IN MY HORMONES OR WHAT-EVER...
AND THEY PUT ME IN A LOUSY MOOD.
I'M STILL ONLY A TEENAGER, FOR CRYING OUT LOUD.
BUT OH WELL.
I CAN FIGHT, SO I SHOULDN'T BE LOOKING A GIFT HORSE IN THE MOUTH...
SER OUSL
OKAY!
PAN (CLAP)
THIS MISSION INVOLVES THE ASSAS-SINATION OF MAJOR FIGURES AT THE BASE CAMP OF THE REBEL ARMY!

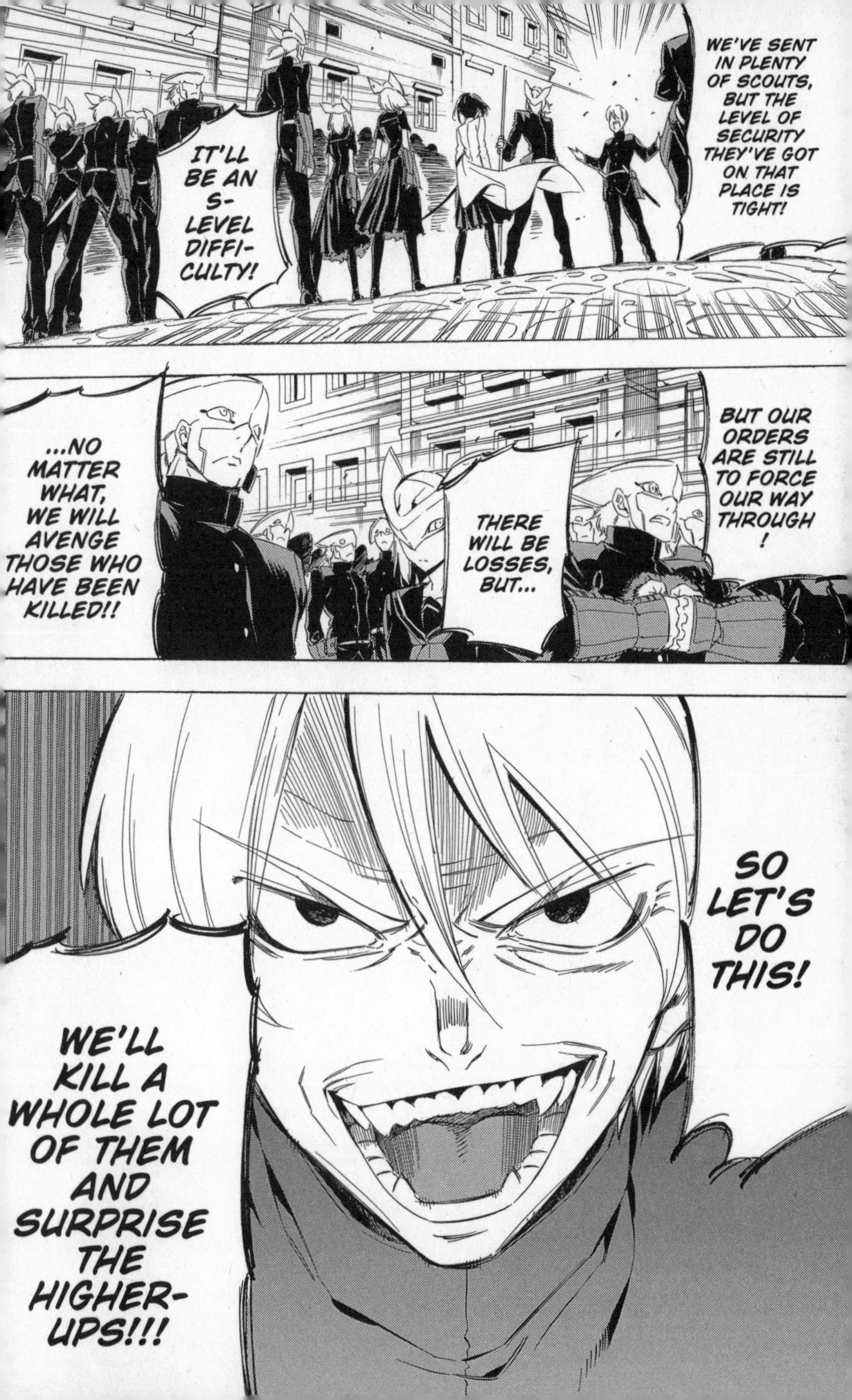
WE'VE SENT IN PLENTY OF SCOUTS, BUT THE LEVEL OF SECURITY THEY'VE GOT ON THAT PLACE IS TIGHT!
IT'LL BE AN S-LEVEL DIFFICULTY!
BUT OUR ORDERS ARE STILL TO FORCE OUR WAY THROUGH!
THERE WILL BE LOSSES, BUT...
...NO MATTER WHAT, WE WILL AVENGE THOSE WHO HAVE BEEN KILLED!!
SO LET'S DO THIS!
WE'LL KILL A WHOLE LOT OF THEM AND SURPRISE THE HIGHER-UPS!!!

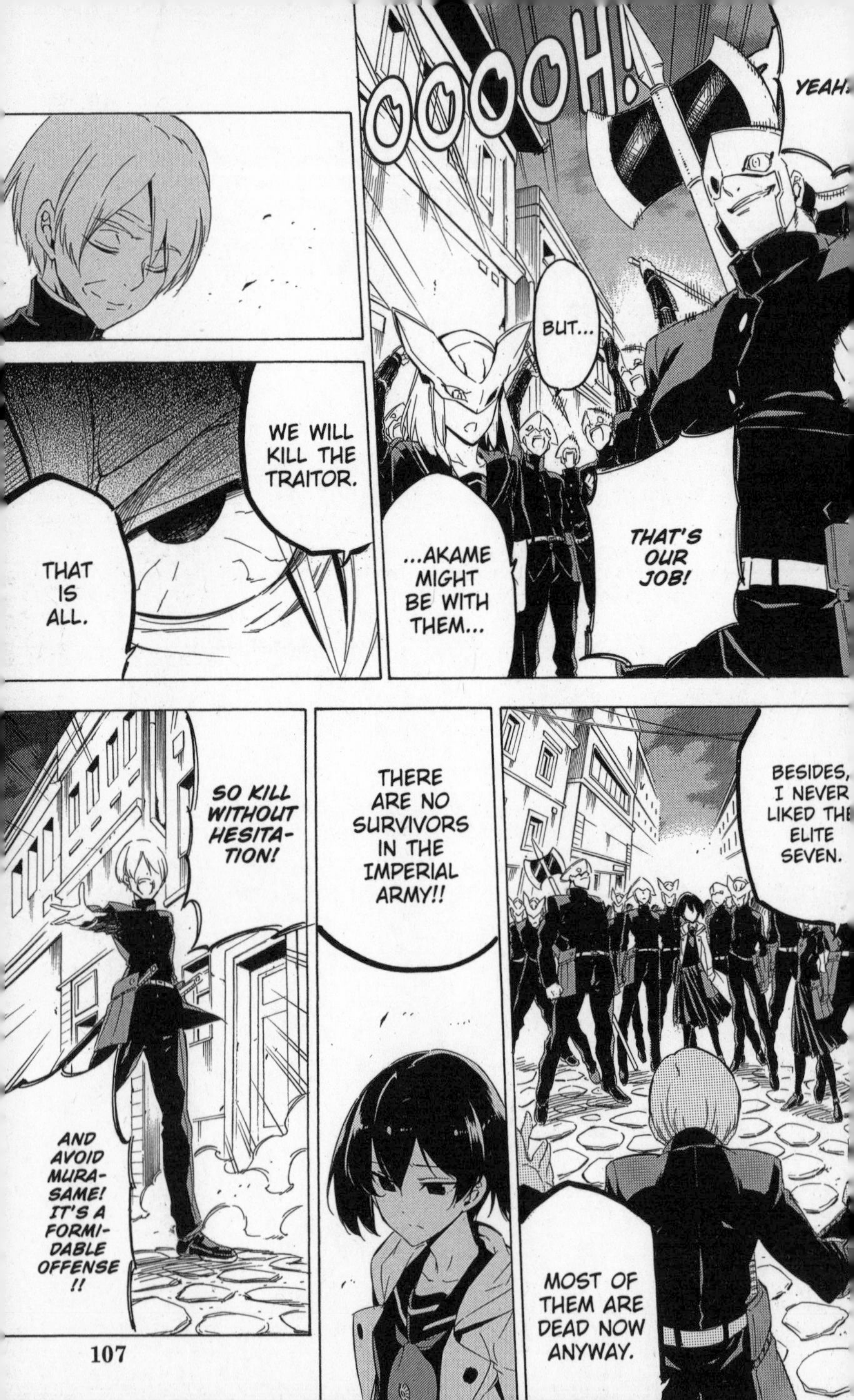
YEAH!
OOOOH!
BUT...
THAT'S OUR JOB!
...AKAME MIGHT BE WITH THEM...
WE WILL KILL THE TRAITOR.
THAT IS ALL.
BESIDES, I NEVER LIKED THE ELITE SEVEN.
MOST OF THEM ARE DEAD NOW ANYWAY.
THERE ARE NO SURVIVORS IN THE IMPERIAL ARMY!!
SO KILL WITHOUT HESITATION!
AND AVOID MURASAME! IT'S A FORMIDABLE OFFENSE!!

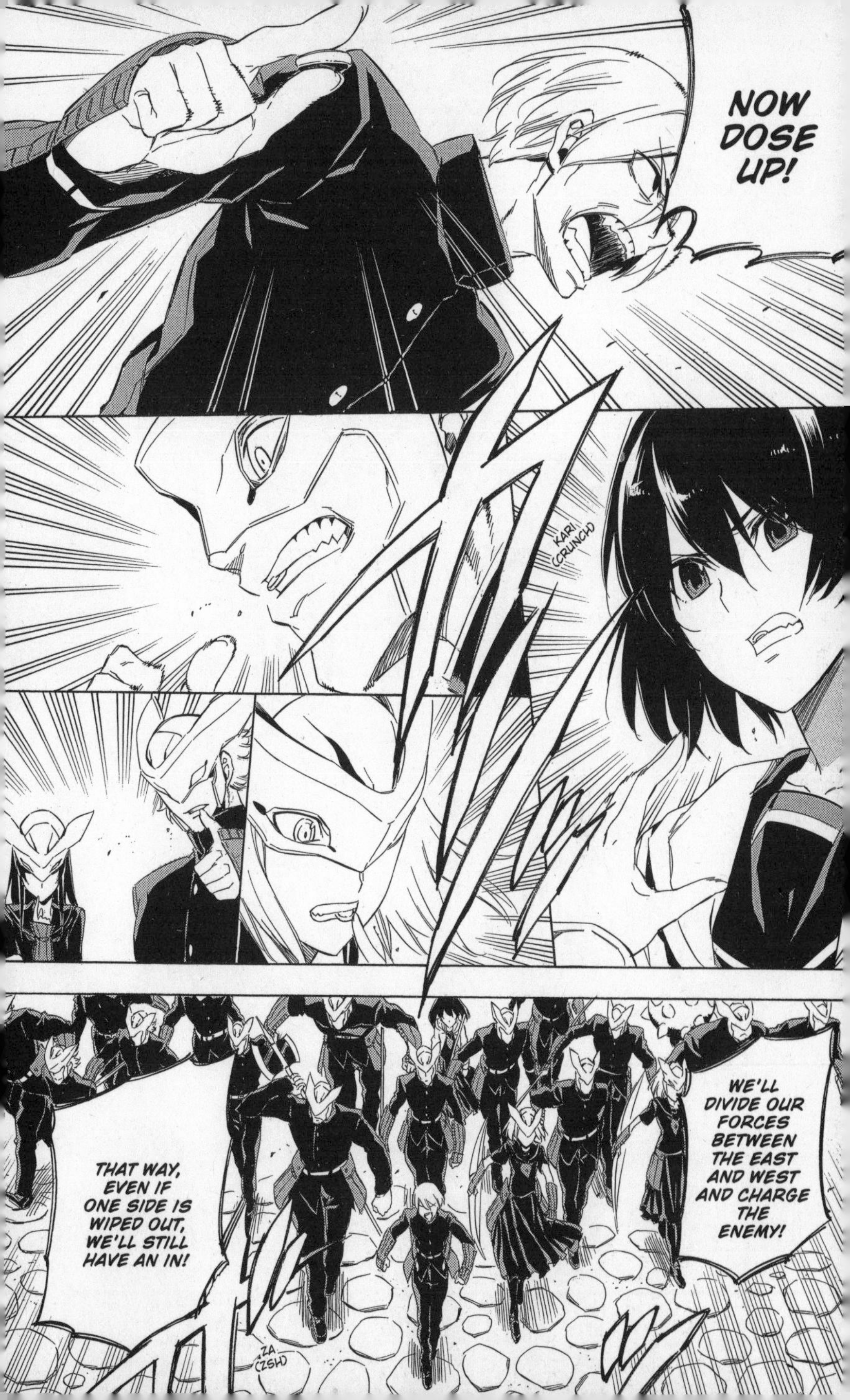
NOW DOSE UP!
KARI (CRUNCH)
WE'LL DIVIDE OUR FORCES BETWEEN THE EAST AND WEST AND CHARGE THE ENEMY!
THAT WAY, EVEN IF ONE SIDE IS WIPED OUT, WE'LL STILL HAVE AN IN!
ZA (ZSH)

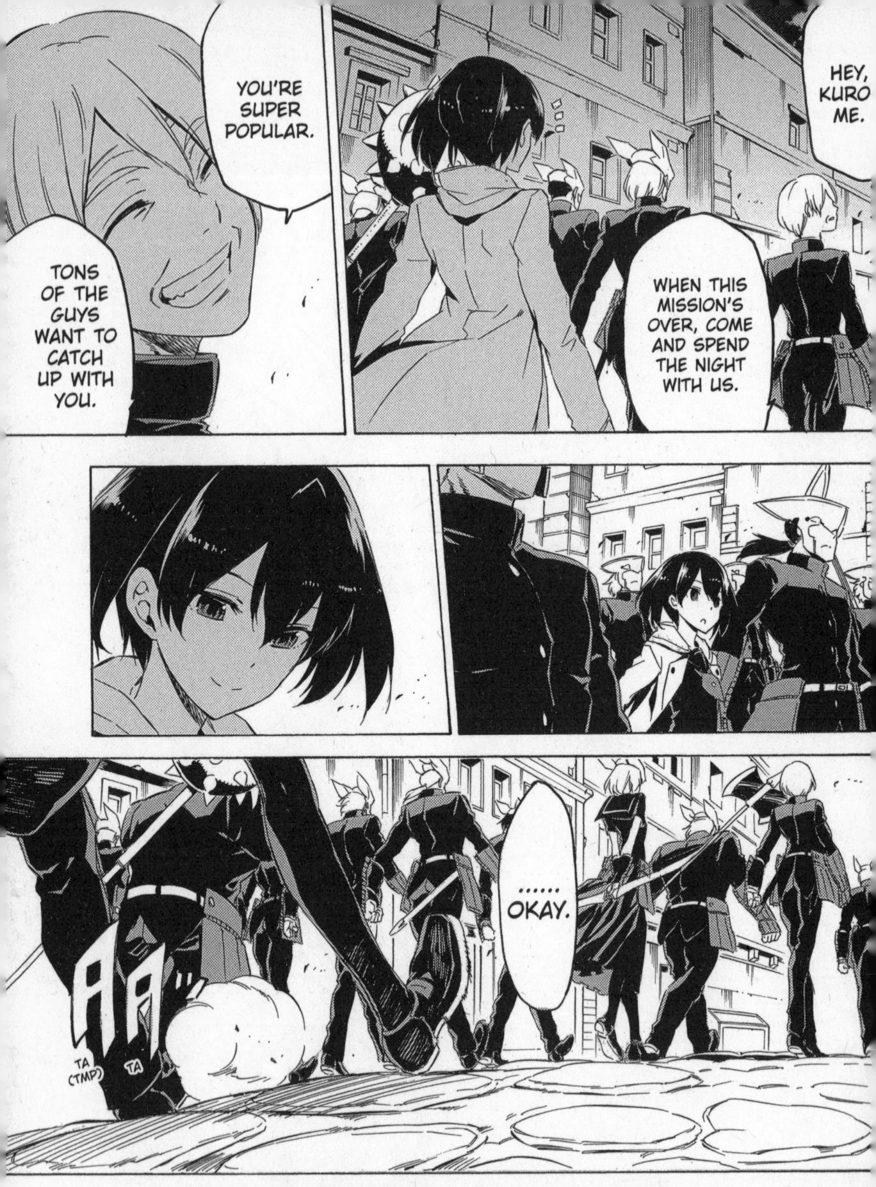
HEY, KURO ME.
WHEN THIS MISSION'S OVER, COME AND SPEND THE NIGHT WITH US.
YOU'RE SUPER POPULAR.
TONS OF THE GUYS WANT TO CATCH UP WITH YOU.
...... OKAY.
TA (TMP) TA

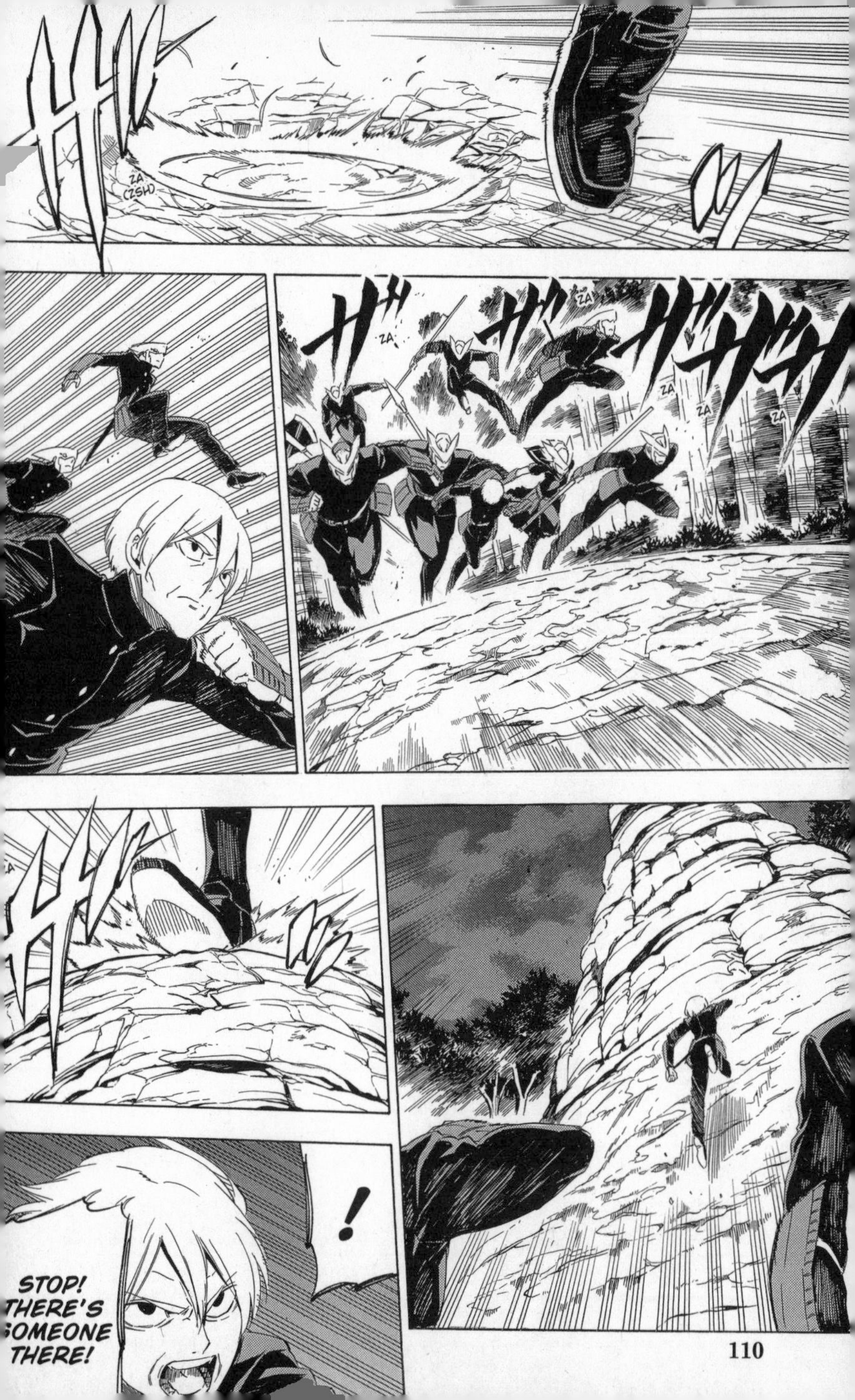
ZA
(ZSH)
ZA
ZA
ZA
ZA
ZA
!
STOP! THERE'S SOMEONE THERE!

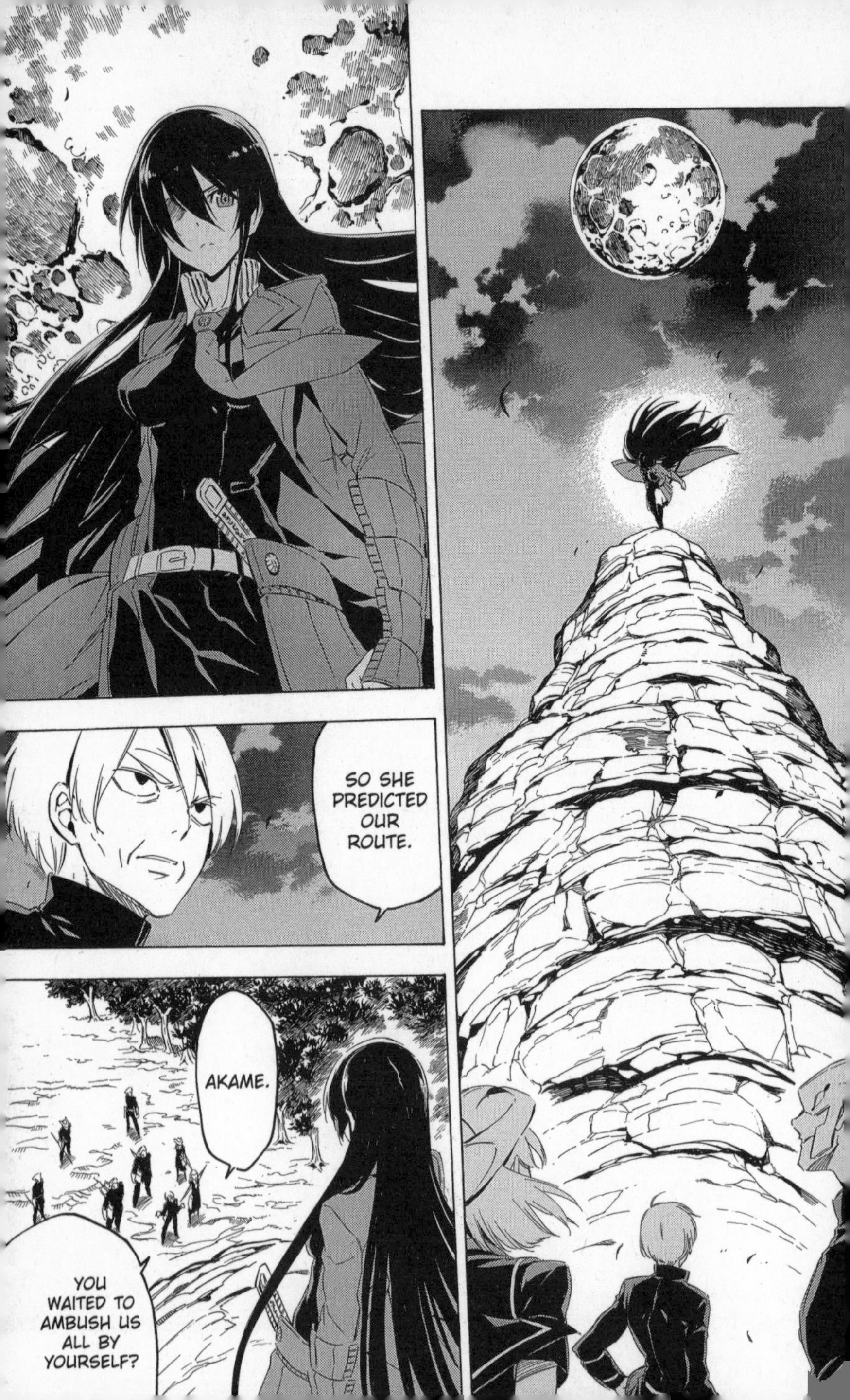
SO SHE PREDICTED OUR ROUTE.
AKAME.
YOU WAITED TO AMBUSH US ALL BY YOURSELF?

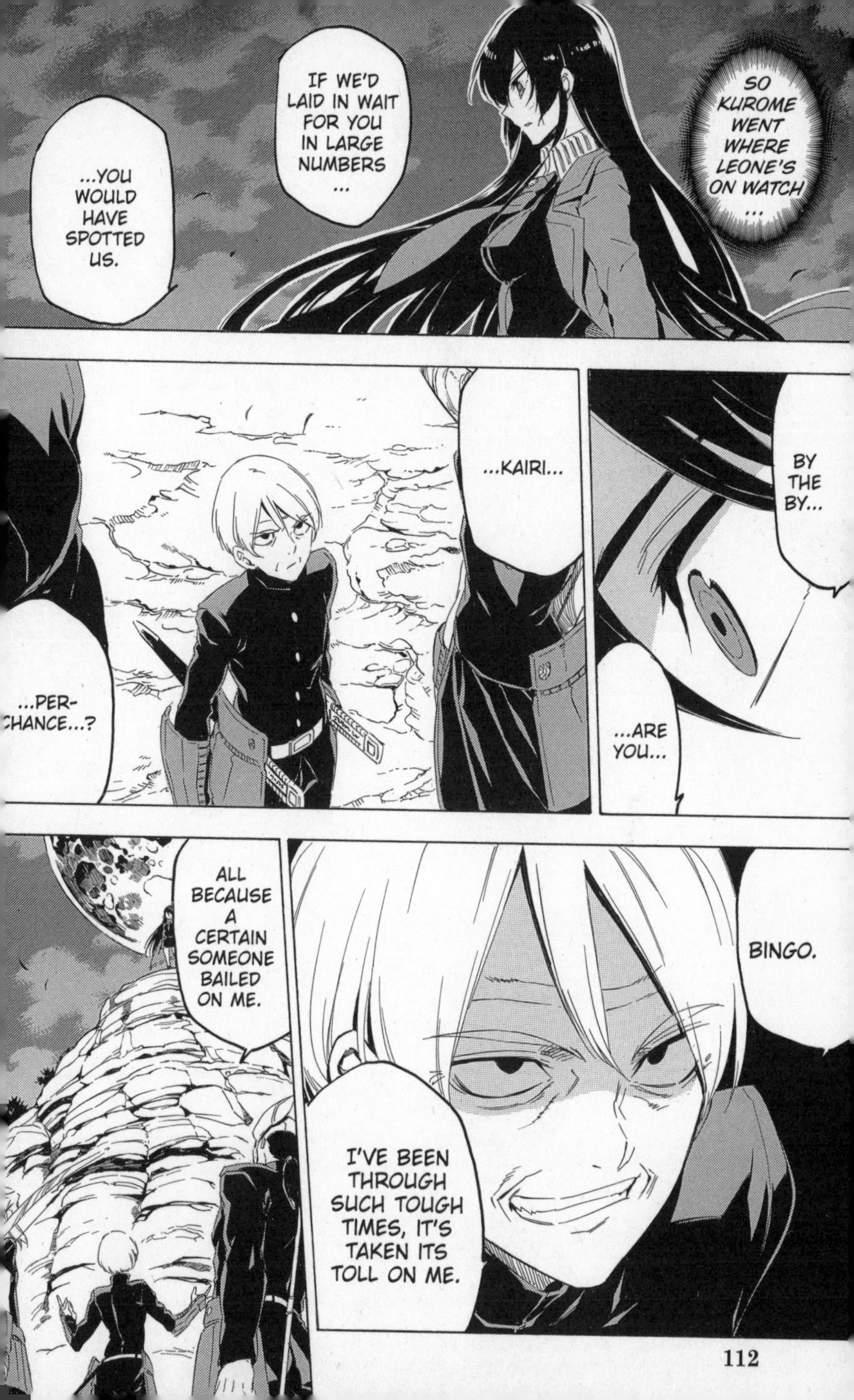
SO KUROME WENT WHERE LEONE'S ON WATCH ...
IF WE'D LAID IN WAIT FOR YOU IN LARGE NUMBERS ...
...YOU WOULD HAVE SPOTTED US.
BY THE BY...
...ARE YOU...
...KAIRI...
...PER-CHANCE...?
BINGO.
I'VE BEEN THROUGH SUCH TOUGH TIMES, IT'S TAKEN ITS TOLL ON ME.
ALL BECAUSE A CERTAIN SOMEONE BAILED ON ME.

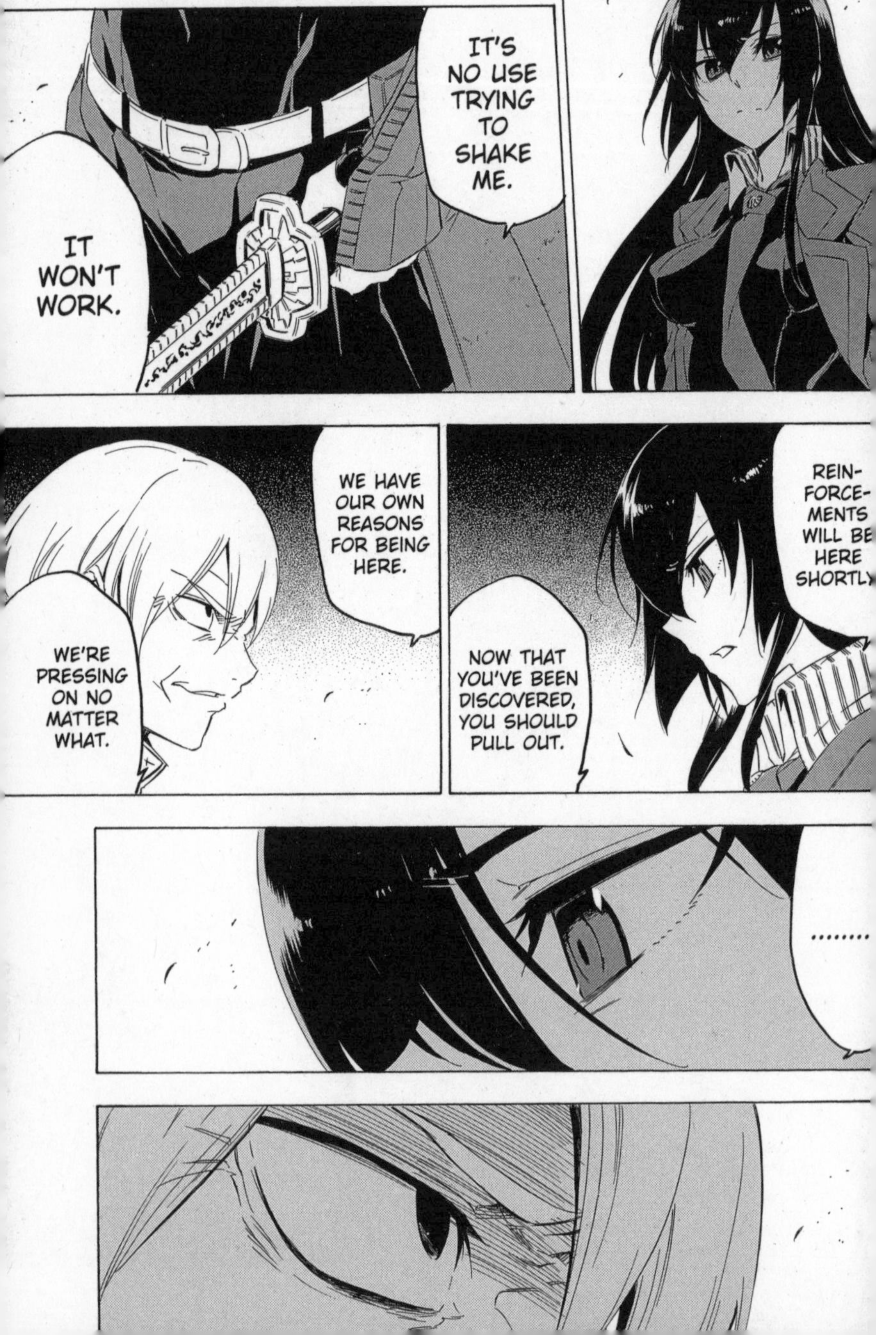
IT'S NO USE TRYING TO SHAKE ME.
IT WON'T WORK.
REIN-FORCE-MENTS WILL BE HERE SHORTLY.
NOW THAT YOU'VE BEEN DISCOVERED, YOU SHOULD PULL OUT.
WE HAVE OUR OWN REASONS FOR BEING HERE.
WE'RE PRESSING ON NO MATTER WHAT.
....

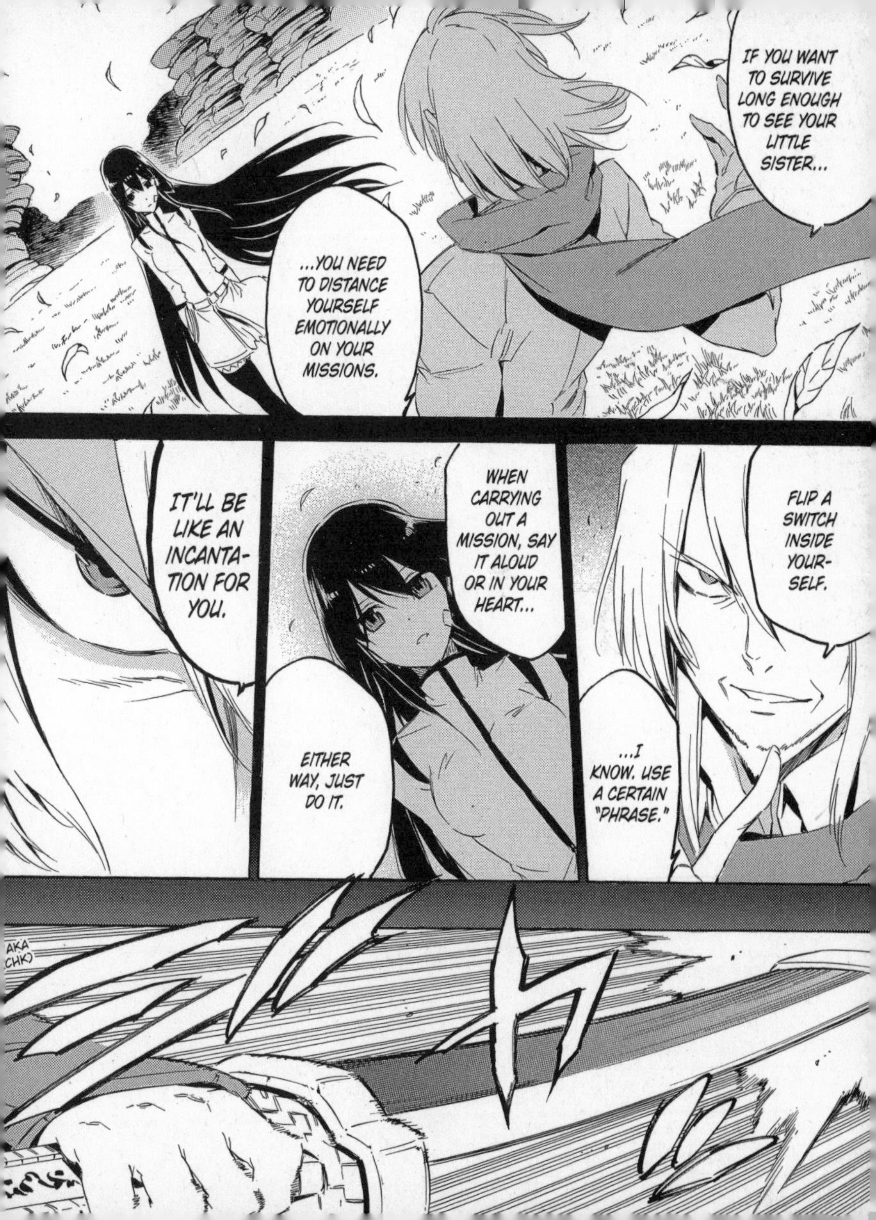
IF YOU WANT TO SURVIVE LONG ENOUGH TO SEE YOUR LITTLE SISTER...
...YOU NEED TO DISTANCE YOURSELF EMOTIONALLY ON YOUR MISSIONS.
FLIP A SWITCH INSIDE YOURSELF.
...I KNOW. USE A CERTAIN "PHRASE."
WHEN CARRYING OUT A MISSION, SAY IT ALOUD OR IN YOUR HEART...
EITHER WAY, JUST DO IT.
IT'LL BE LIKE AN INCANTATION FOR YOU.

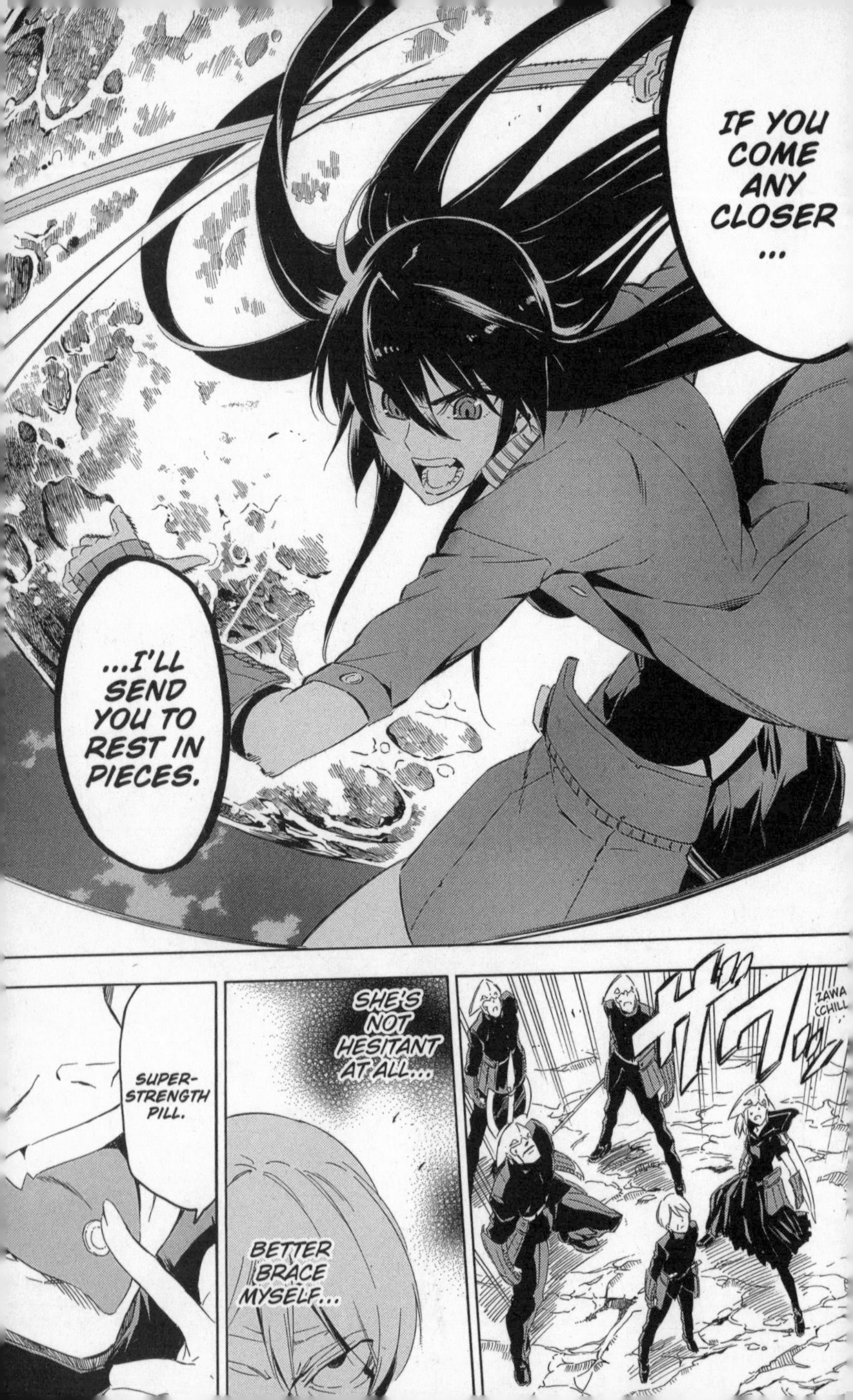
IF YOU COME ANY CLOSER...
...I'LL SEND YOU TO REST IN PIECES.
ZAWA
(CHILL
SHE'S NOT HESITANT AT ALL...
BETTER BRACE MYSELF...
SUPER-STRENGTH PILL.

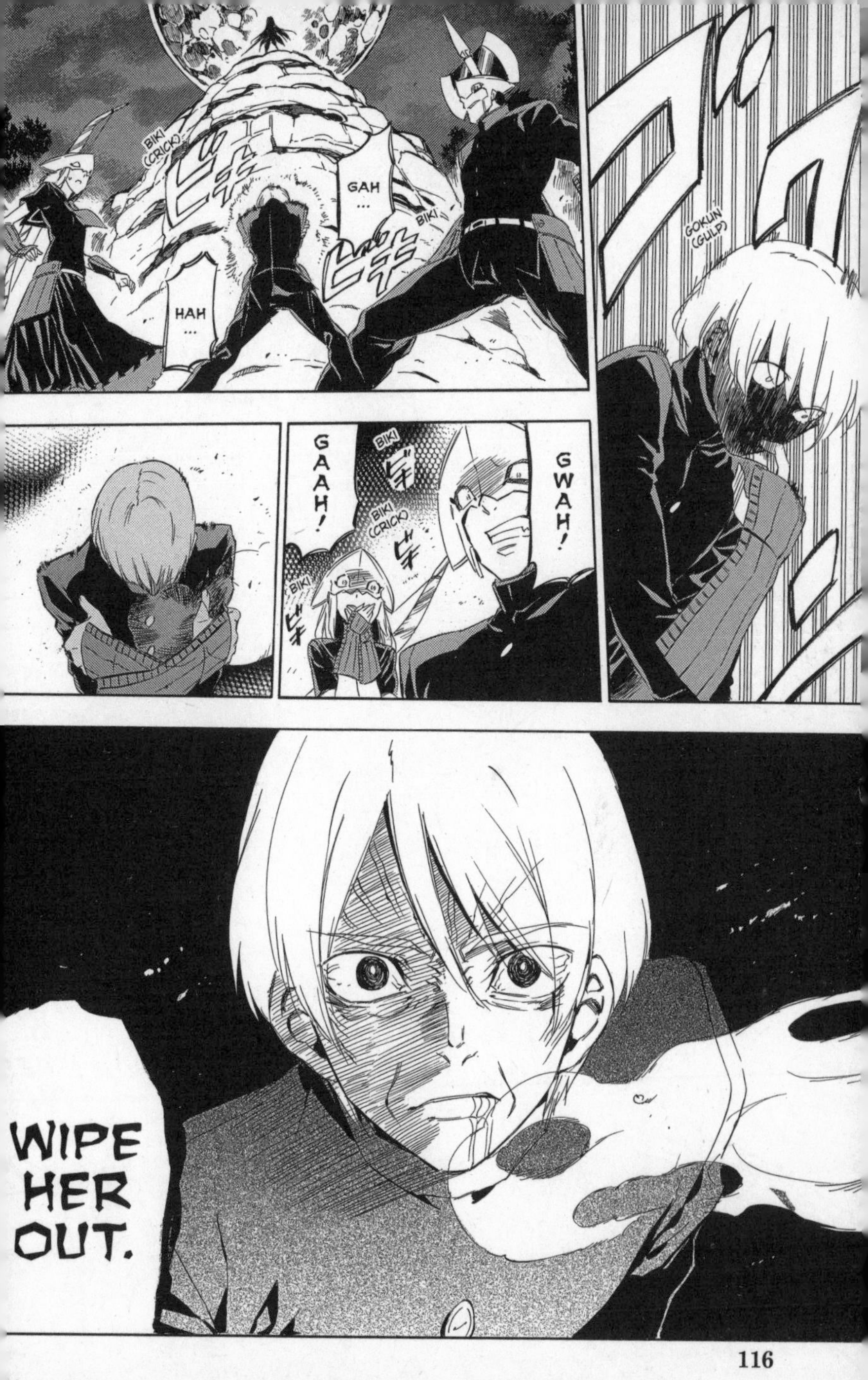
GOKUN (GULP)
BIKI (CRICK)
GAH ...
BIKI
HAH ...
GWAH!
BIKI
GAAH!
BIKI (CRICK)
BIKI
WIPE HER OUT.

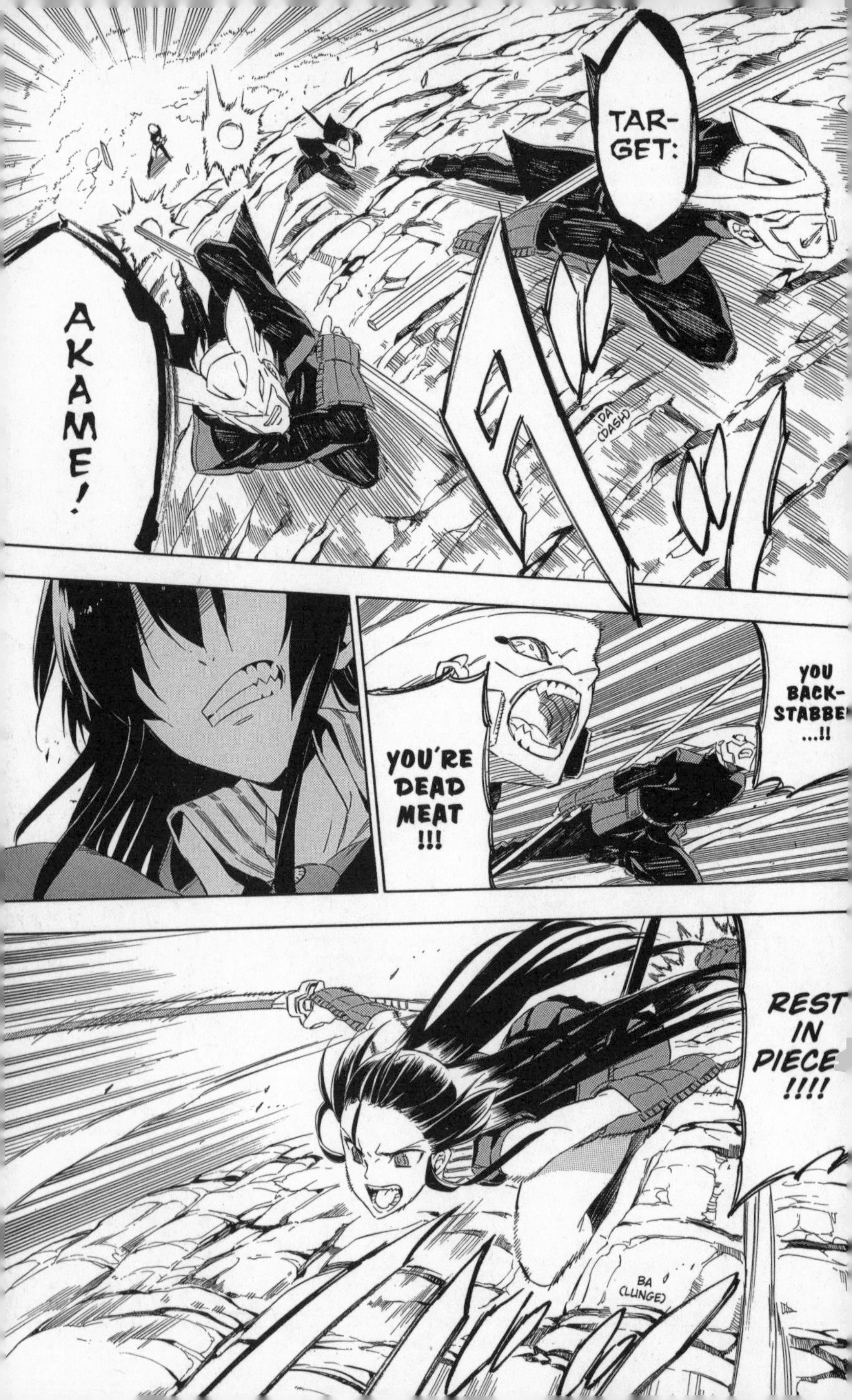
TAR-GET:
DA (DASH)
AKAME!
YOU BACK-STABBE ...!!
YOU'RE DEAD MEAT !!!
REST IN PIECE !!!!
BA (LUNGE)

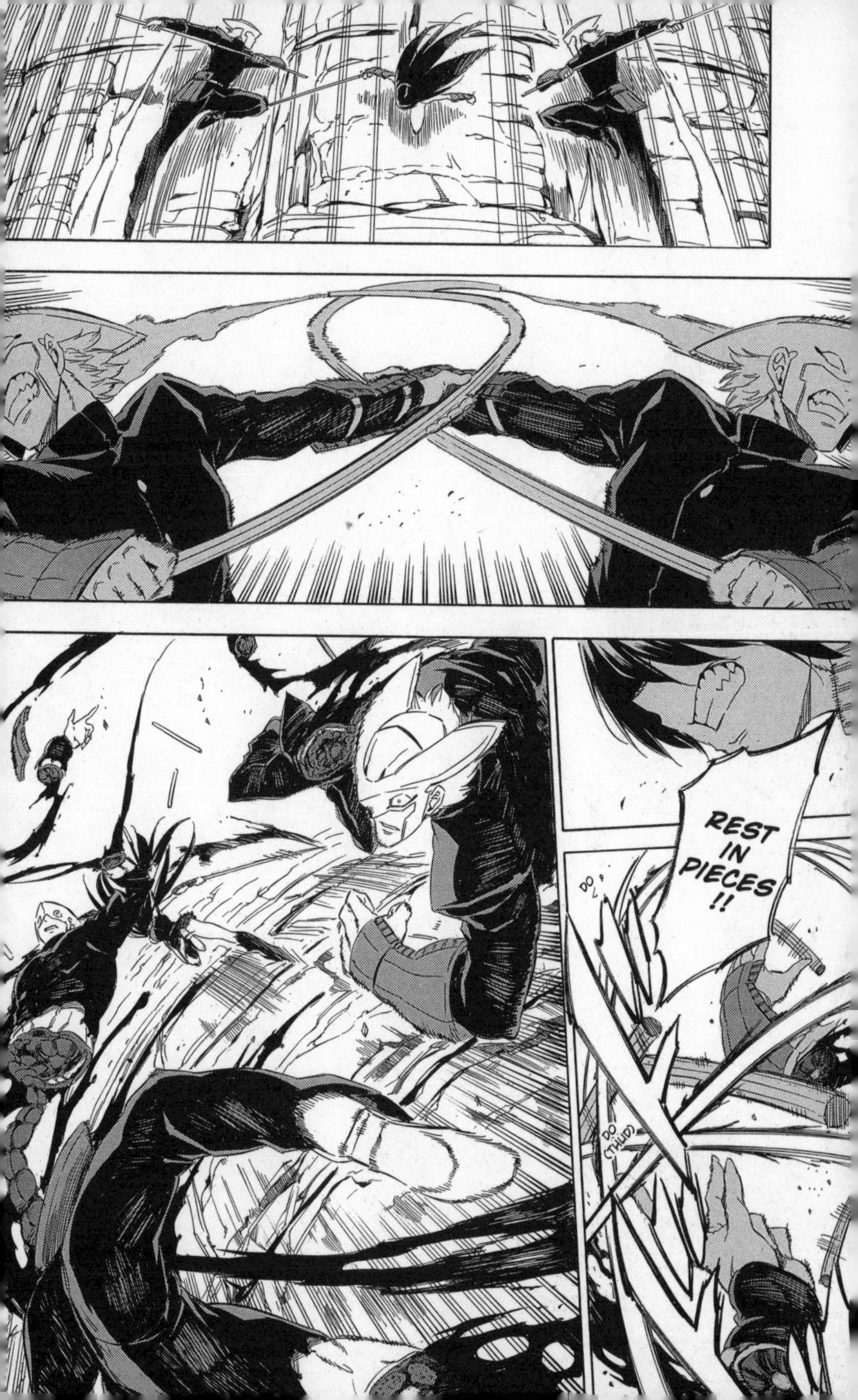
REST IN PIECES!!
DO
DO (THUD)

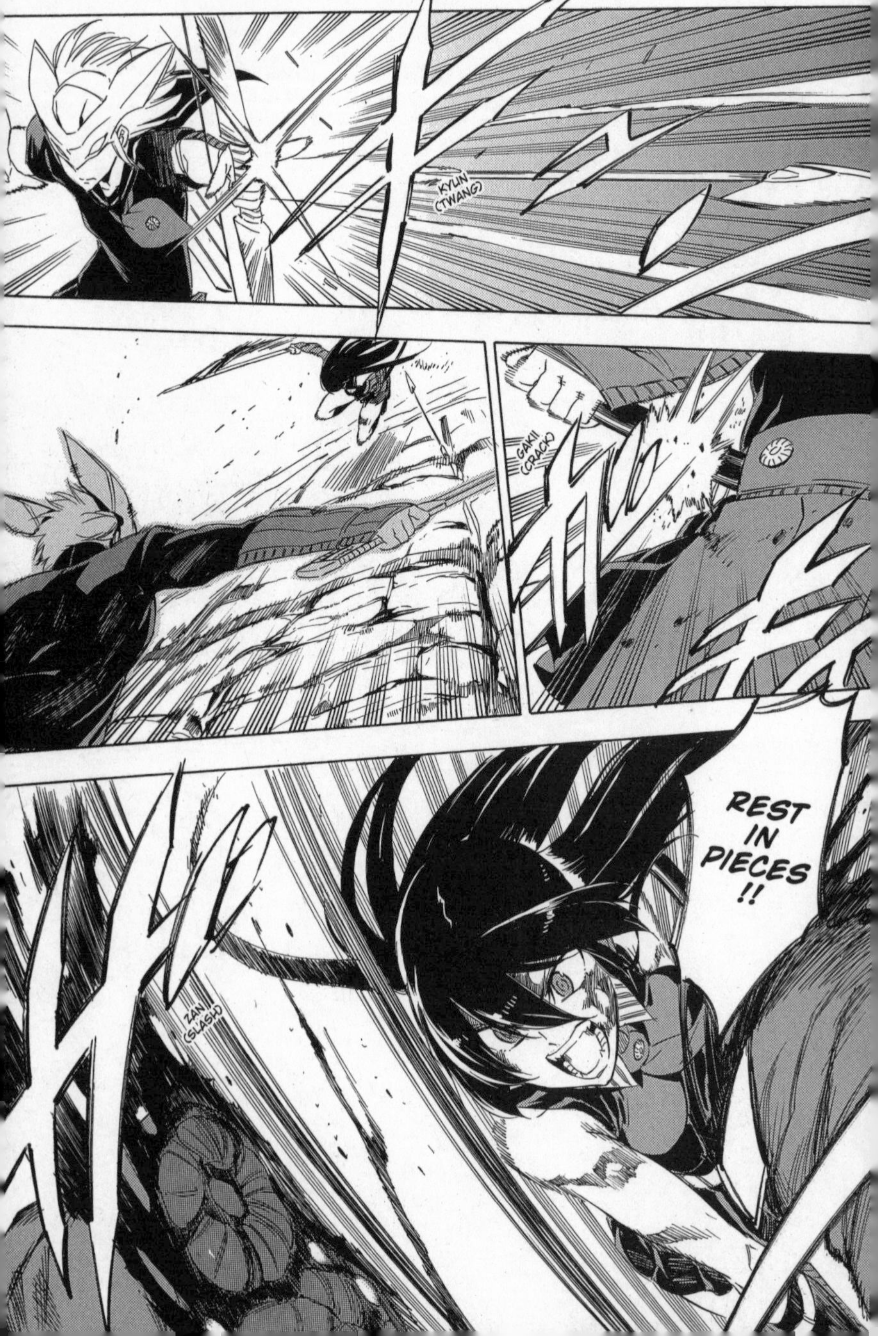
KYUN
(TWANG)
GAKI!
(CRACK)
REST IN PIECES !!
ZAN
(SLASH)

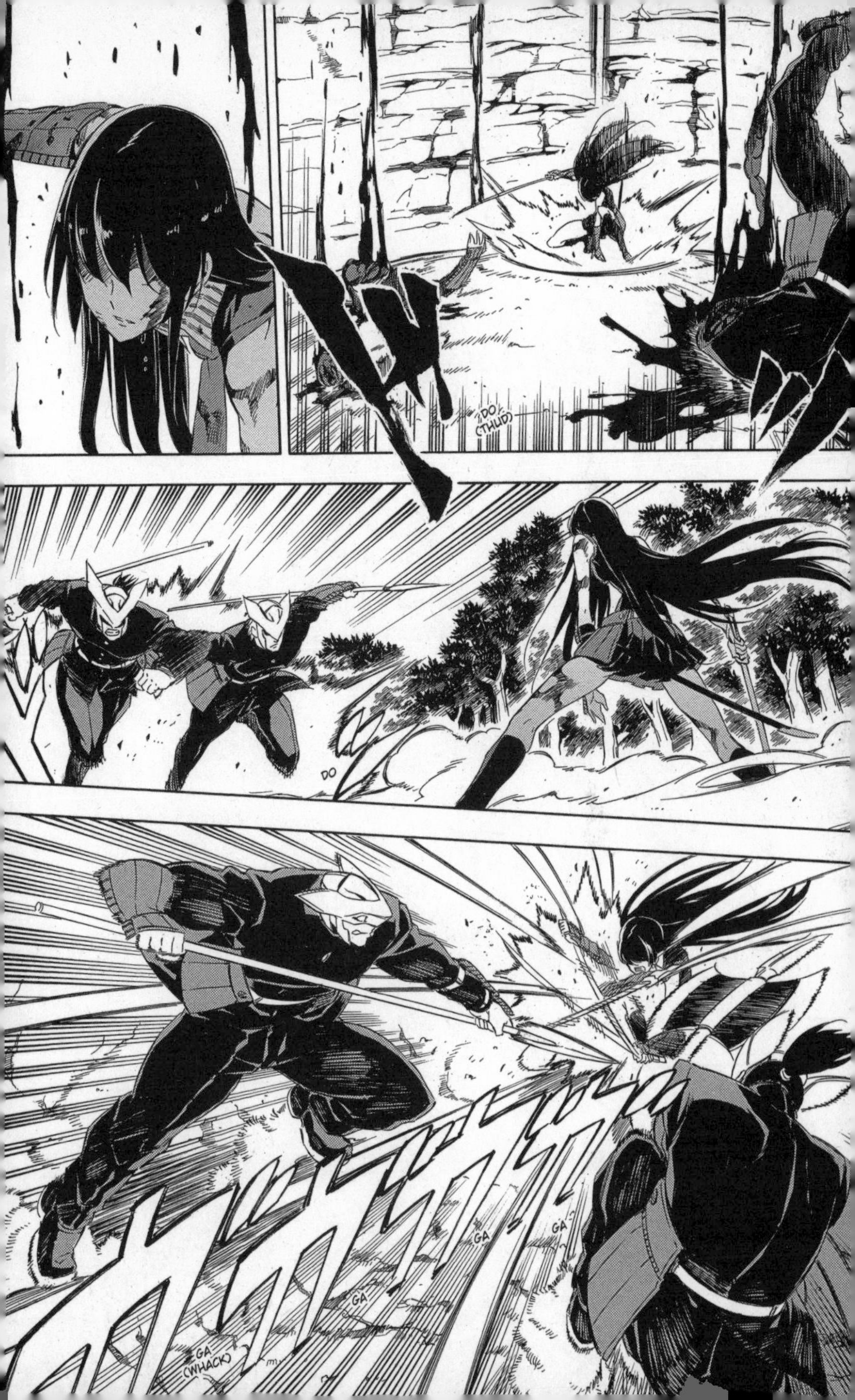
DO
(THUD)
DO
GA
GA
GA
GA
(WHACK)

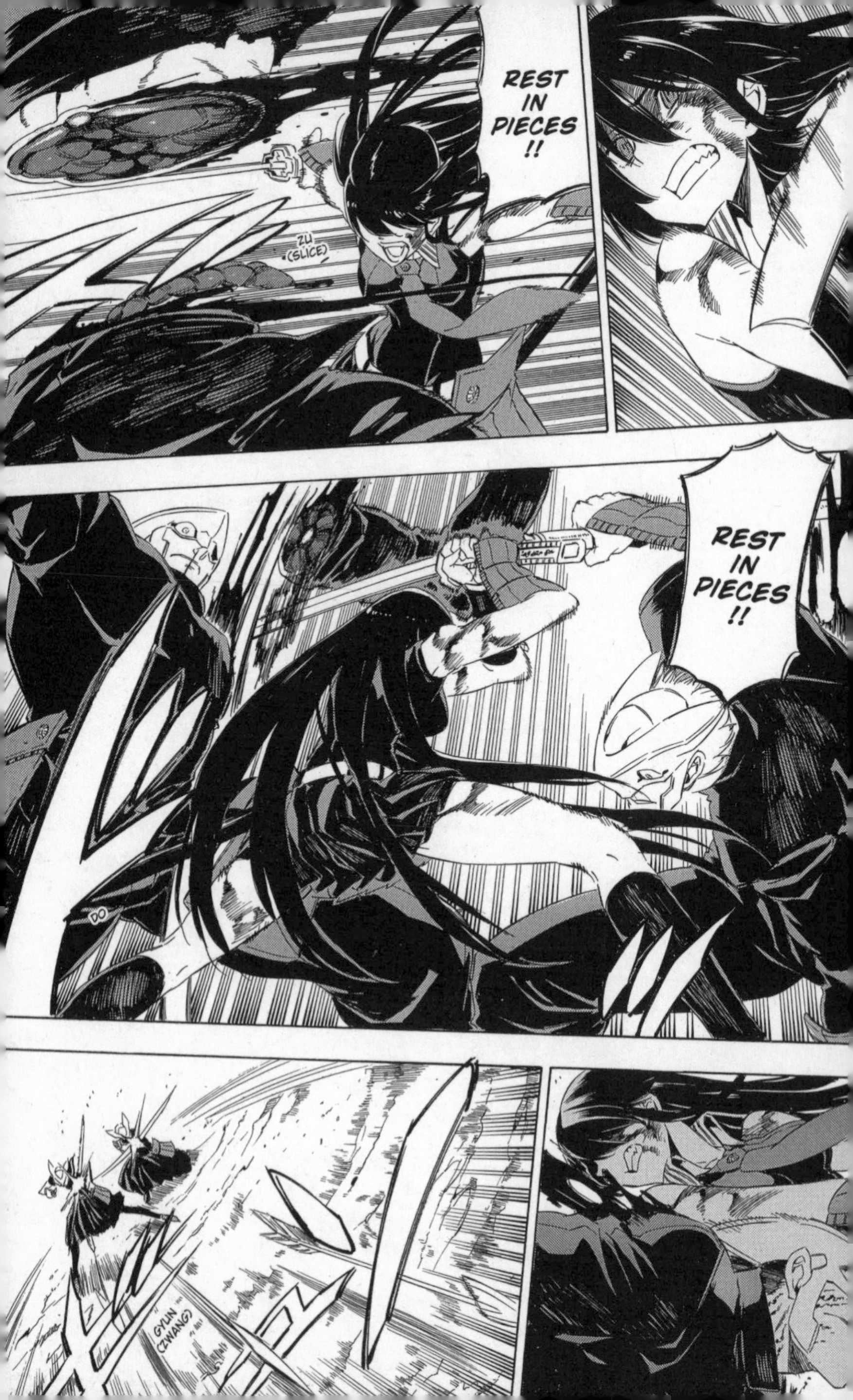
REST IN PIECES!!
ZU (SLICE)
REST IN PIECES!!
DO
GYUN (ZWANG)

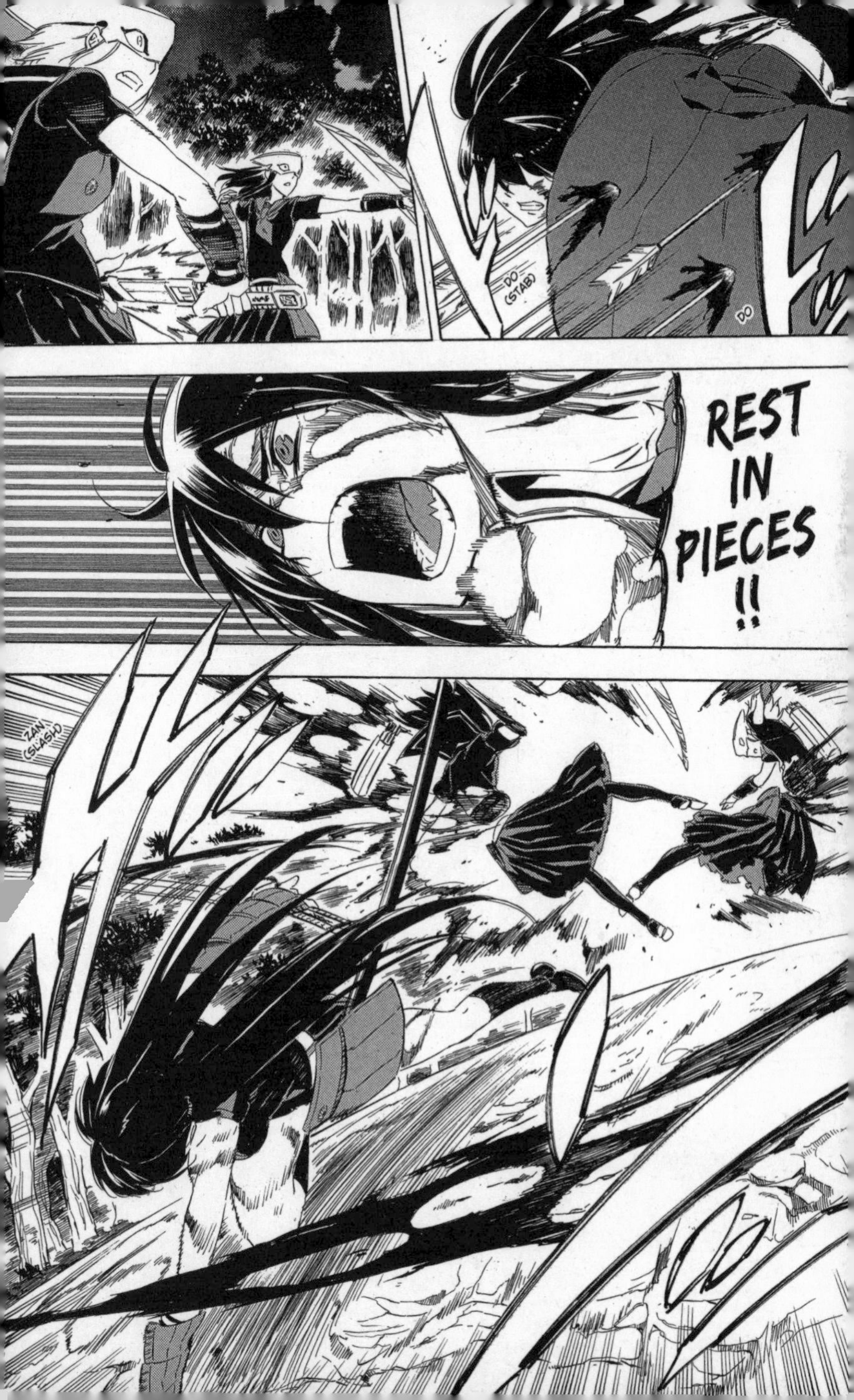
DO
DO (STAB)
REST IN PIECES!!
ZAN (SLASH)

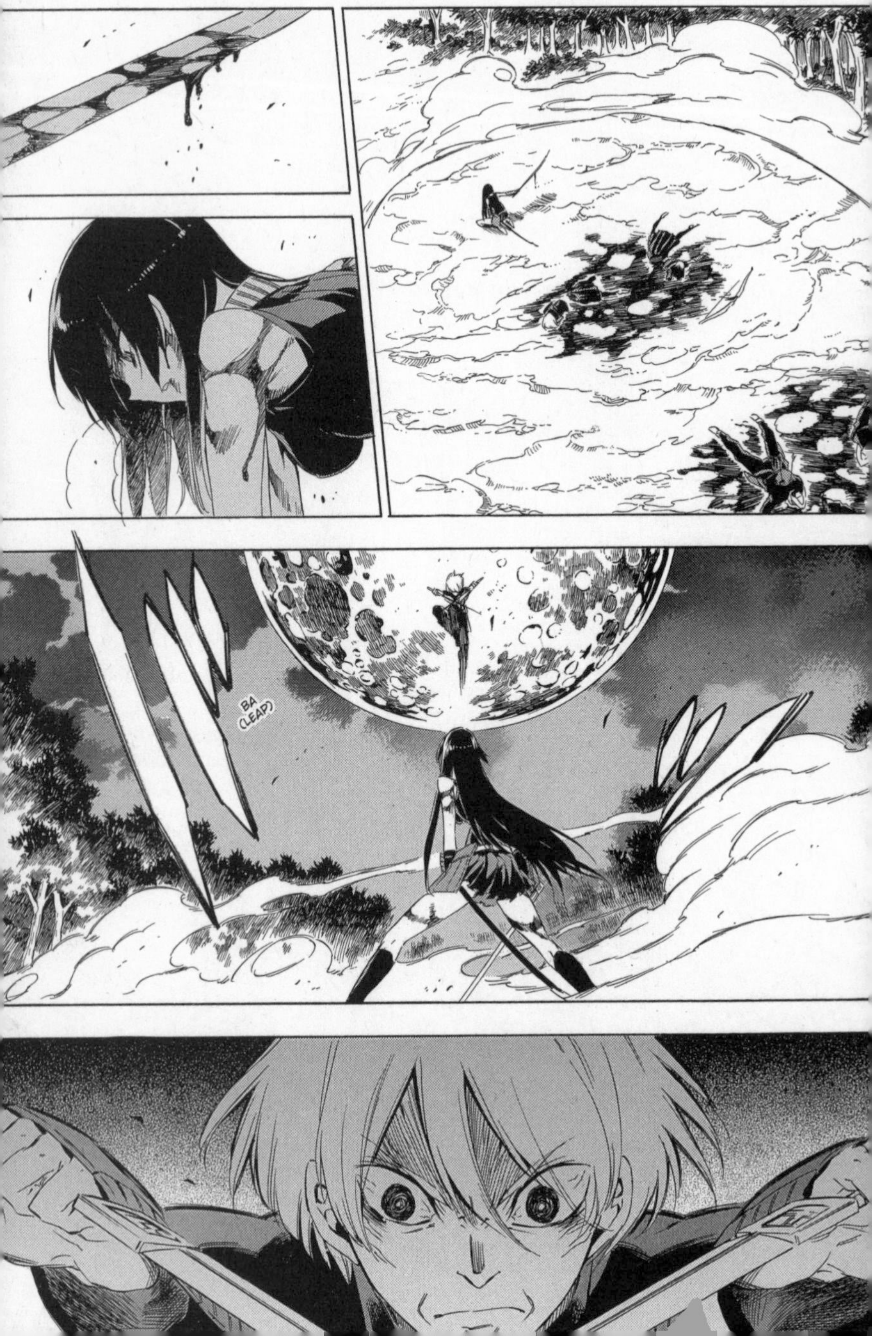
BA
(LEAP)

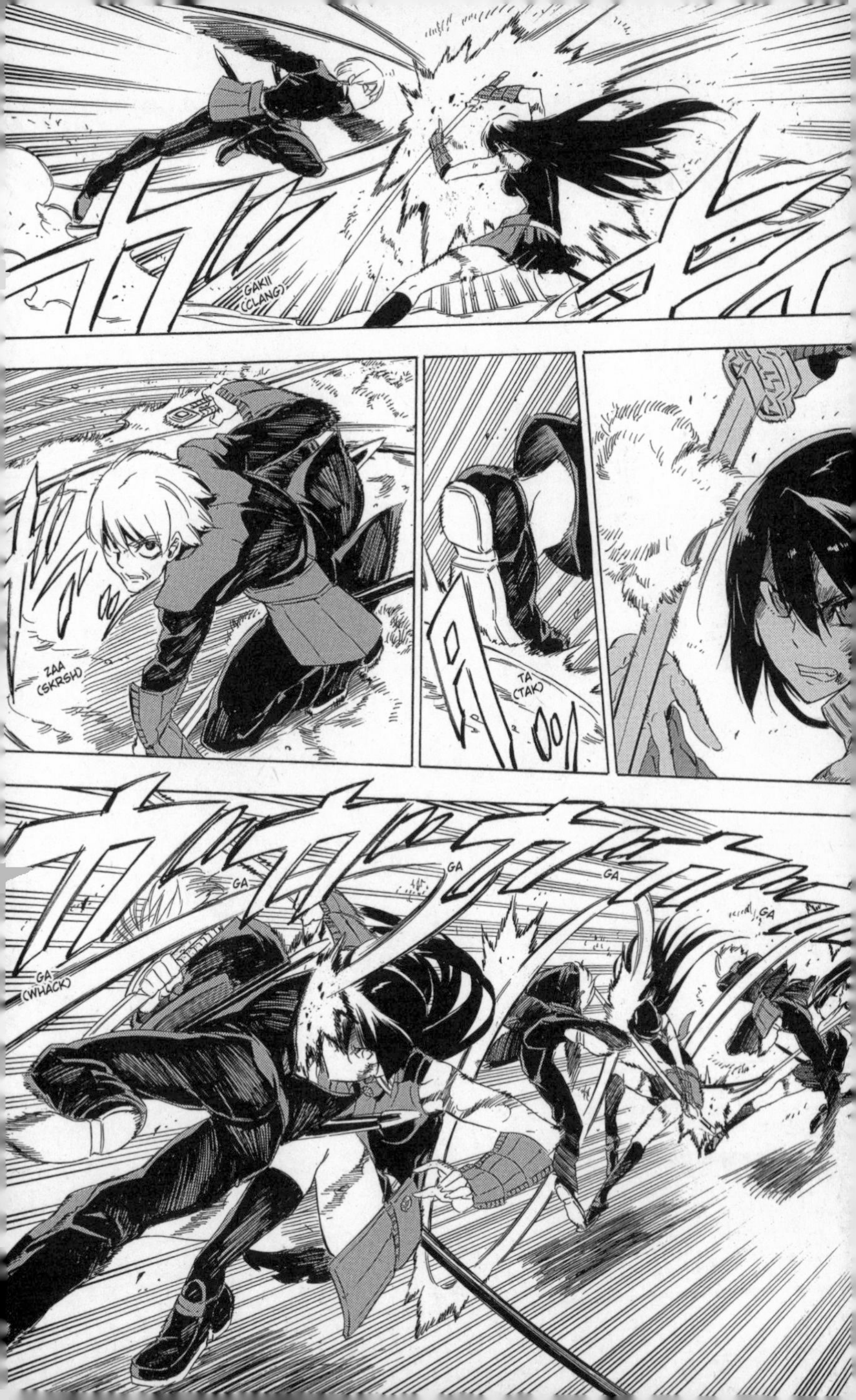
GAKII (CLANG)
TA (TAK)
ZAA (SKRSH)
GA
GA
GA
GA
GA (WHACK)

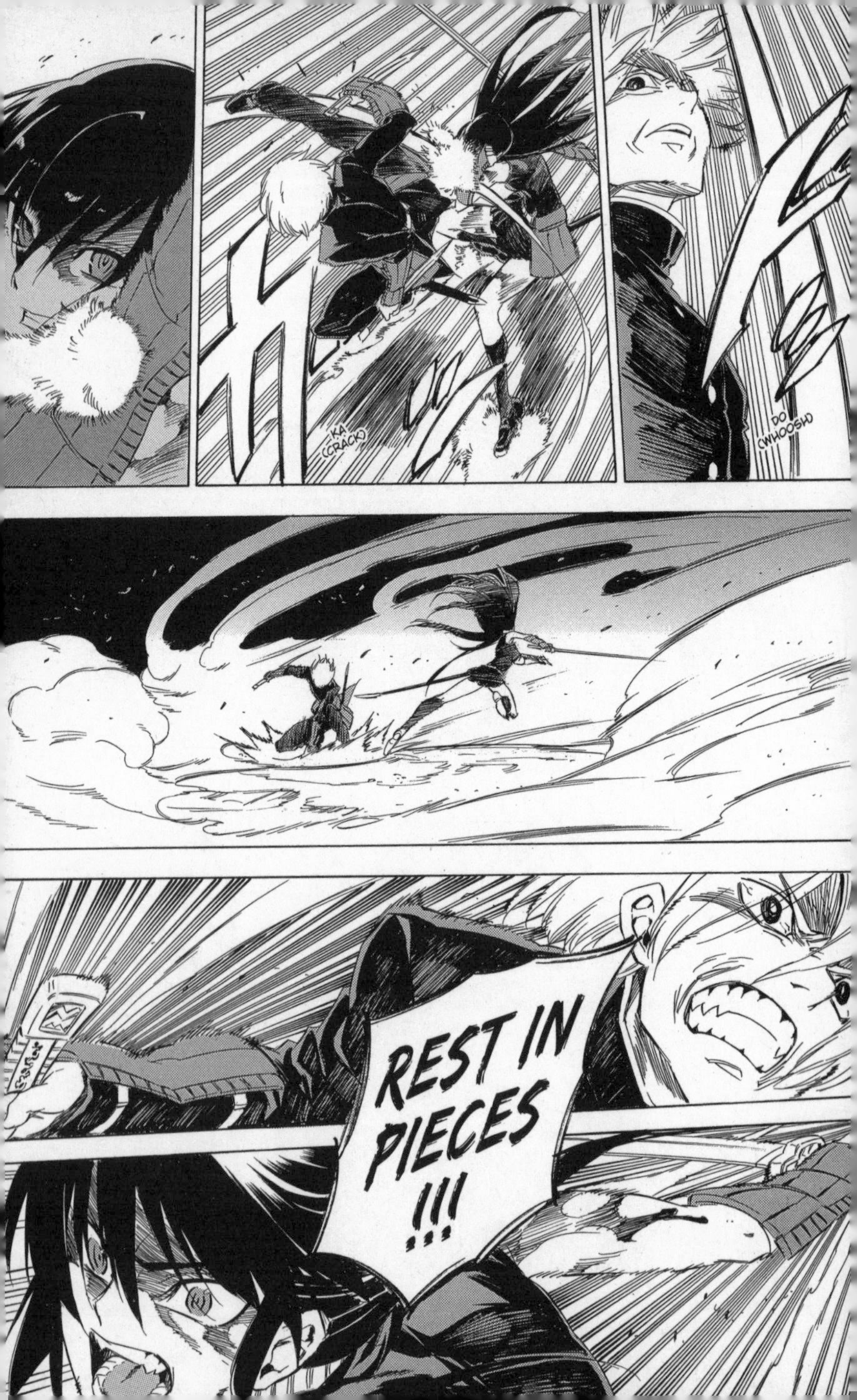
DO (WHOOSH)
KA (CRACK)
REST IN PIECES !!!

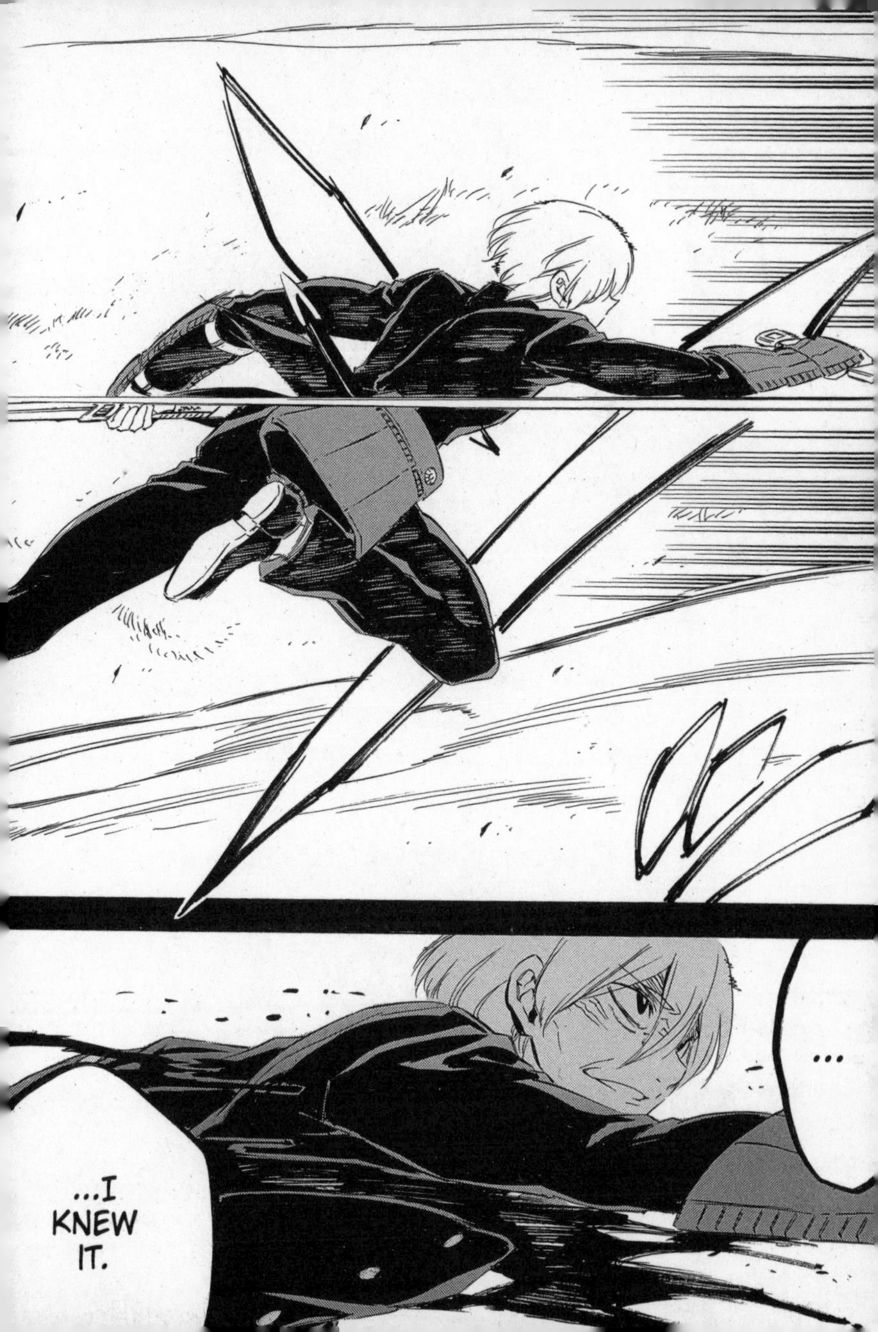
...
...I KNEW IT.

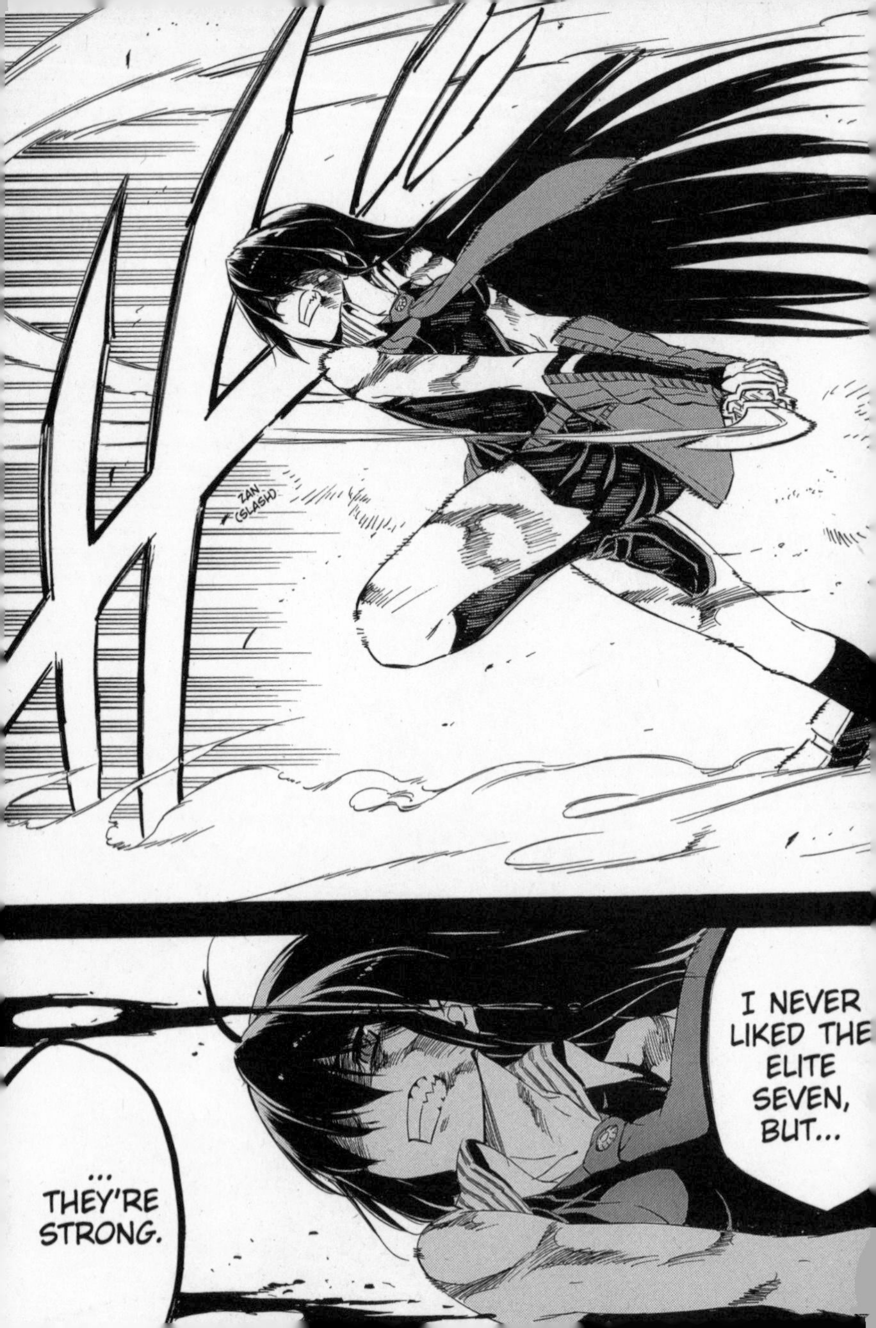
ZAN (SLASH)
I NEVER LIKED THE ELITE SEVEN, BUT...
... THEY'RE STRONG.

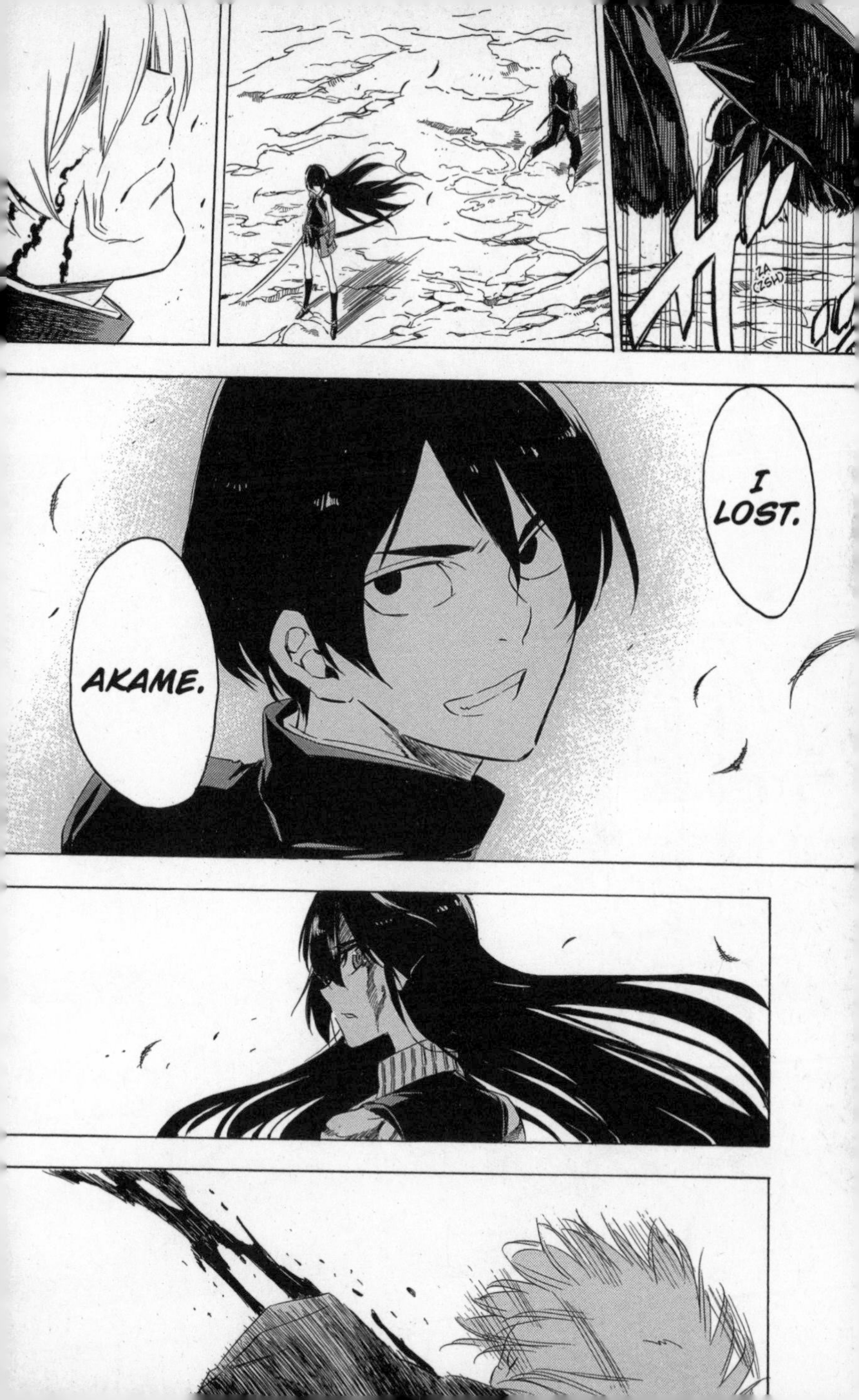
ZA (ZSH)
I LOST.
AKAME.

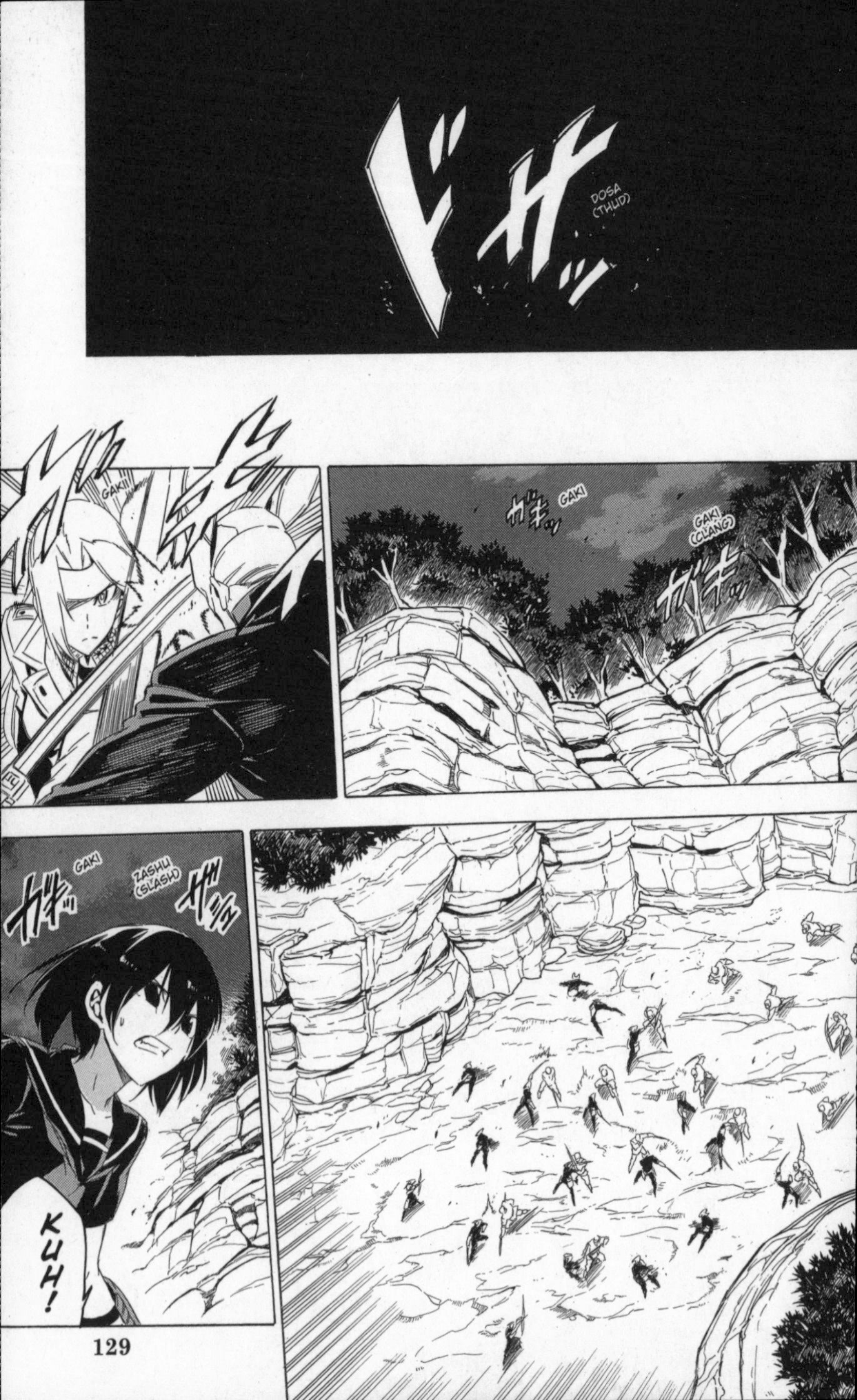
DOSA (THUD)
GAKI
GAKI (CLANG)
GAKI
GAKI
ZASHU (SLASH)
KUH!

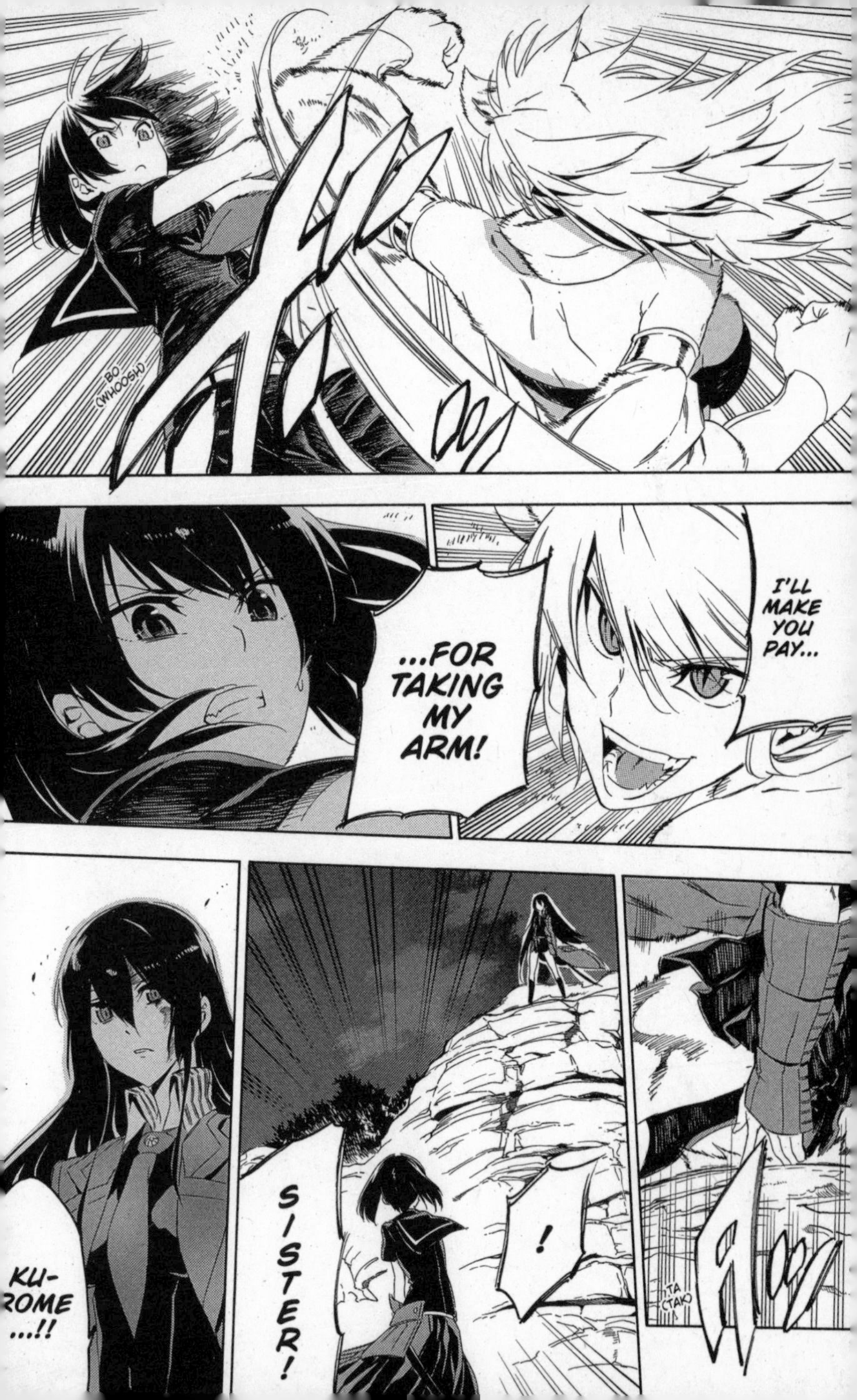
BO (WHOOSH)
I'LL MAKE YOU PAY...
...FOR TAKING MY ARM!
TA TAK
!
SISTER!
KU-ROME ...!!

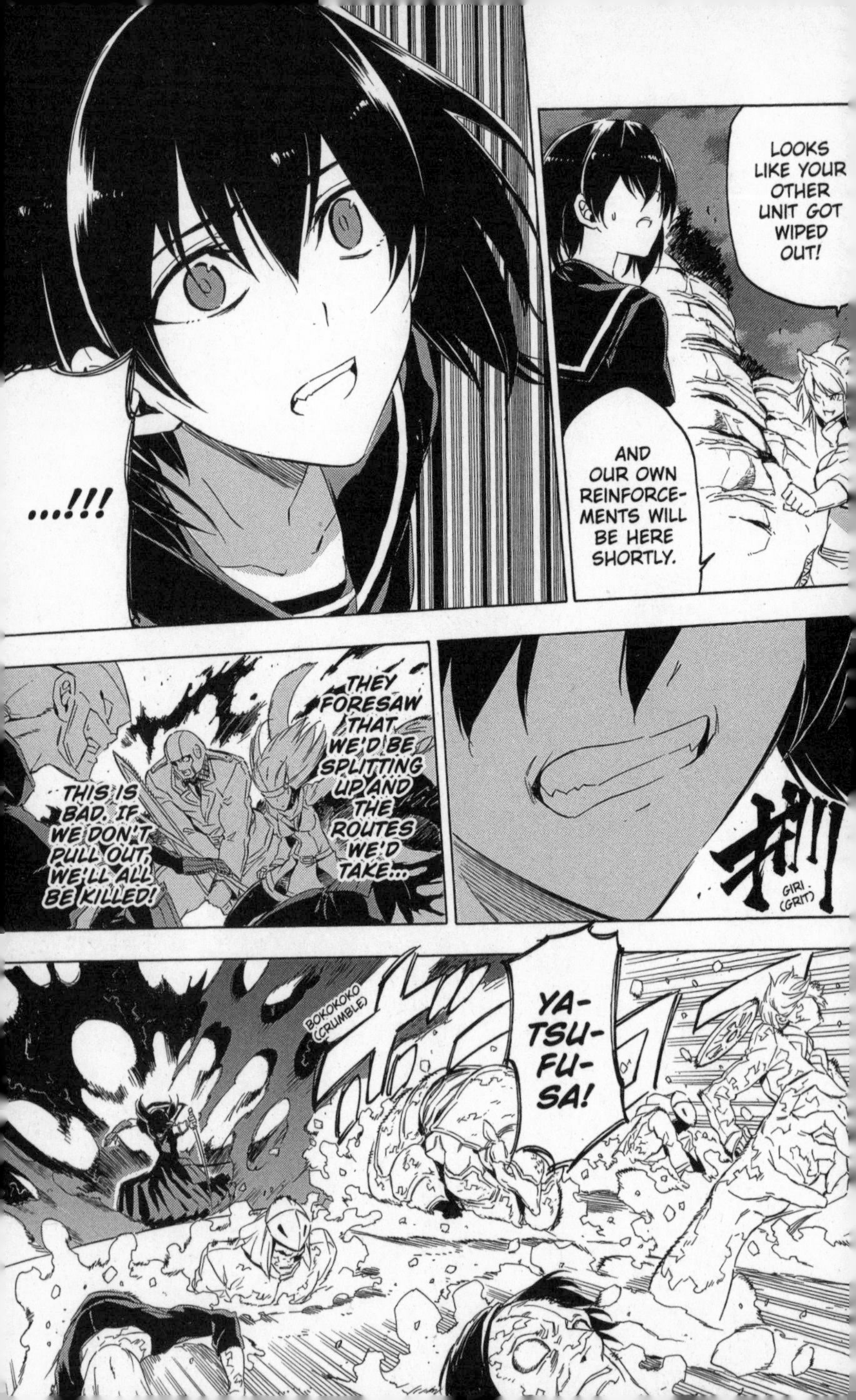
LOOKS LIKE YOUR OTHER UNIT GOT WIPED OUT!
AND OUR OWN REINFORCEMENTS WILL BE HERE SHORTLY.
...!!!
GIRI (GRIT)
THEY FORESAW THAT WE'D BE SPLITTING UP AND THE ROUTES WE'D TAKE...
THIS IS BAD. IF WE DON'T PULL OUT, WE'LL ALL BE KILLED!
YA-TSU-FU-SA!
BOKOKOKO (CRUMBLE)

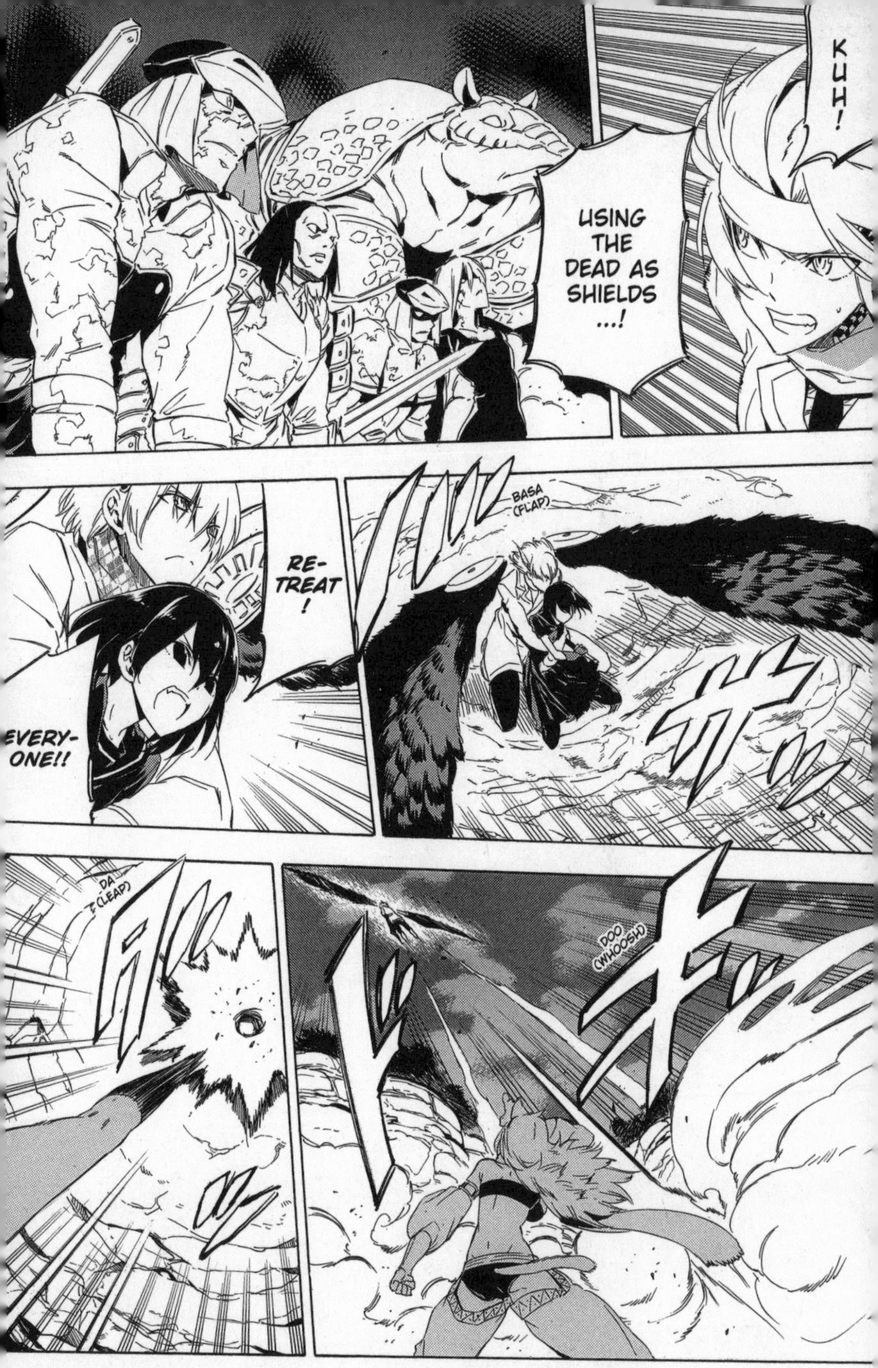
KUH!
USING THE DEAD AS SHIELDS ...!
BASA (FLAP)
RE-TREAT!
EVERYONE!!
DOO (WHOOSH)
DA (LEAP)

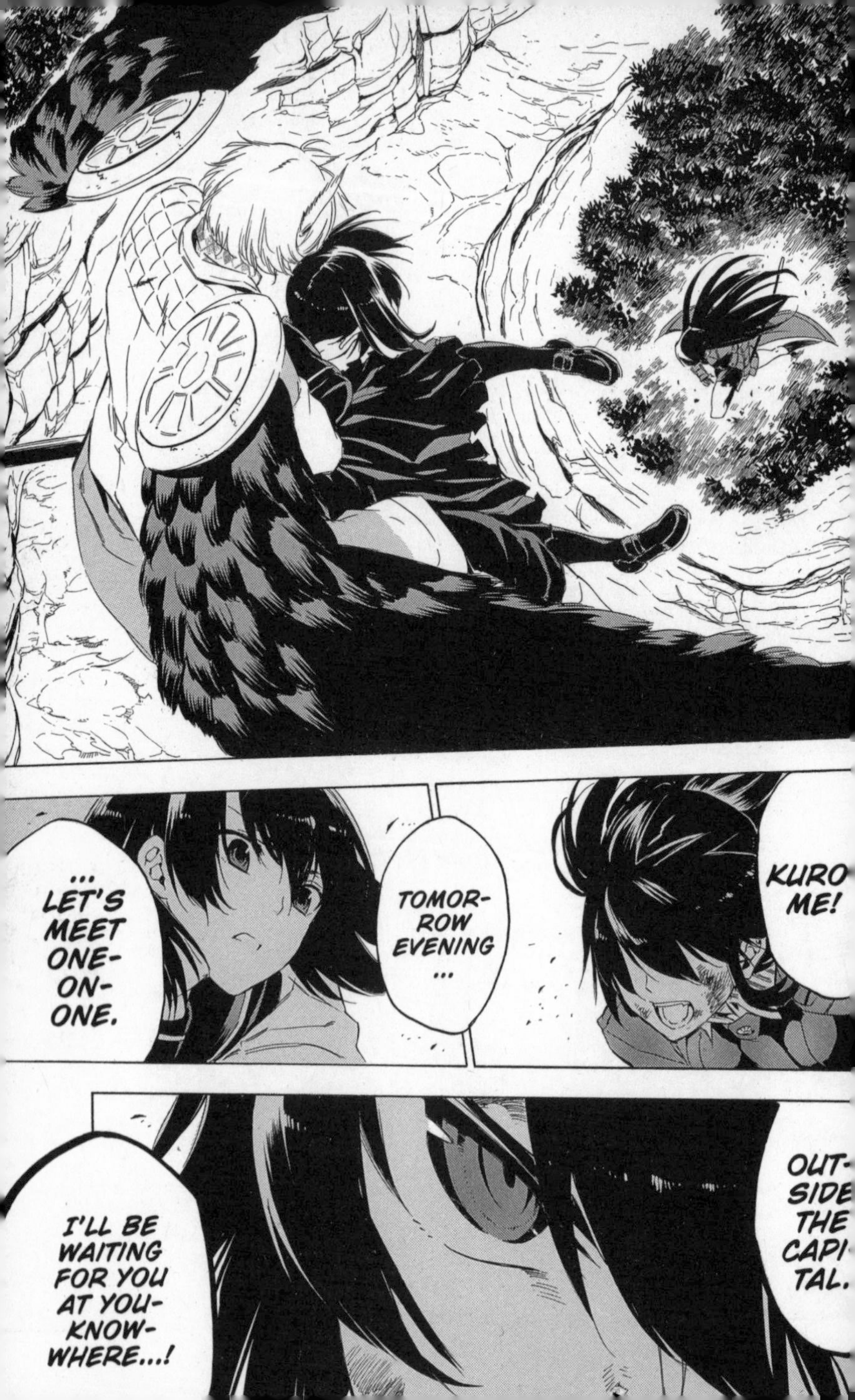
KURO ME!
TOMOR- ROW EVENING ...
... LET'S MEET ONE- ON- ONE.
OUT- SIDE THE CAPI- TAL.
I'LL BE WAITING FOR YOU AT YOU- KNOW- WHERE...!

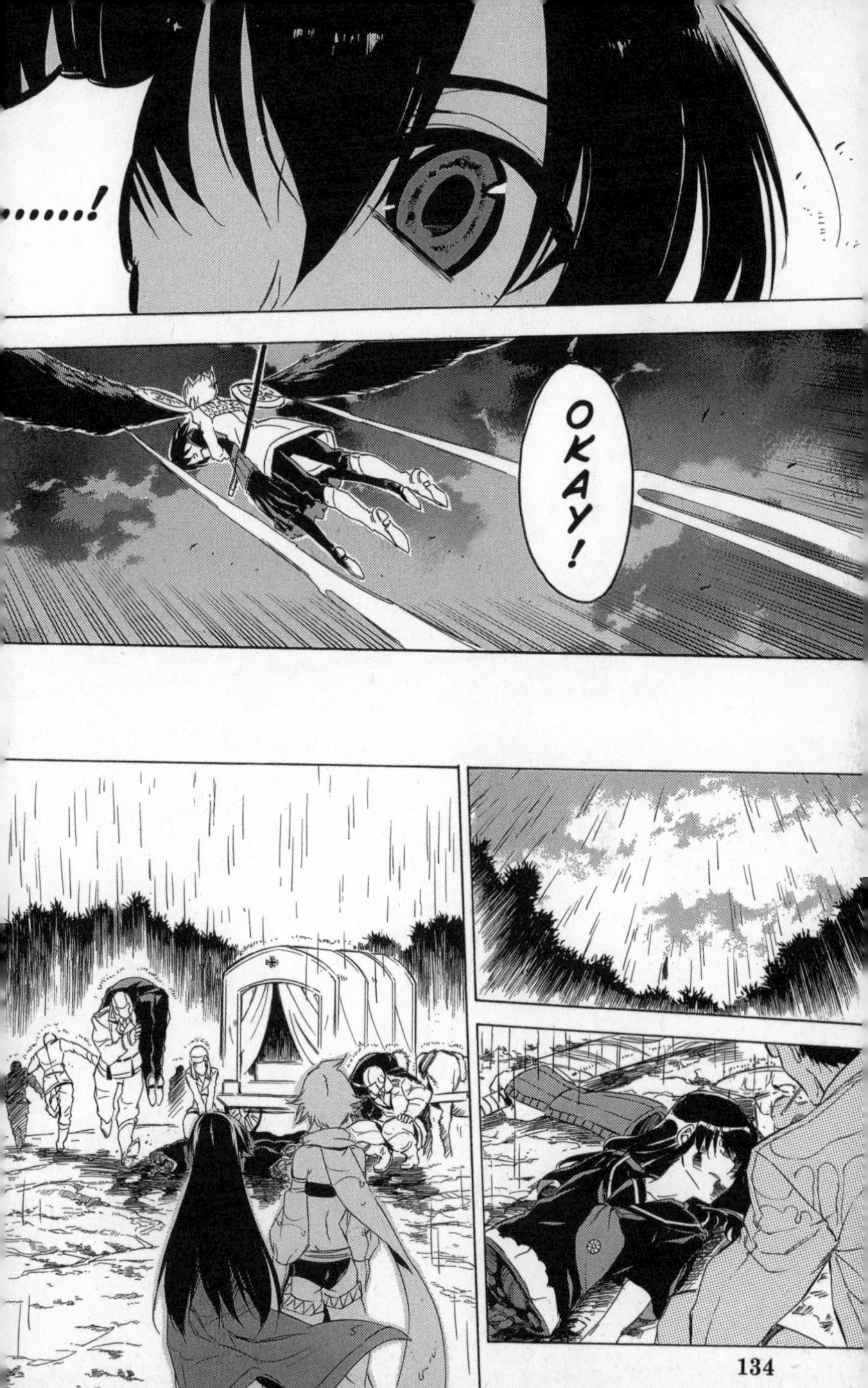
......!
OKAY!

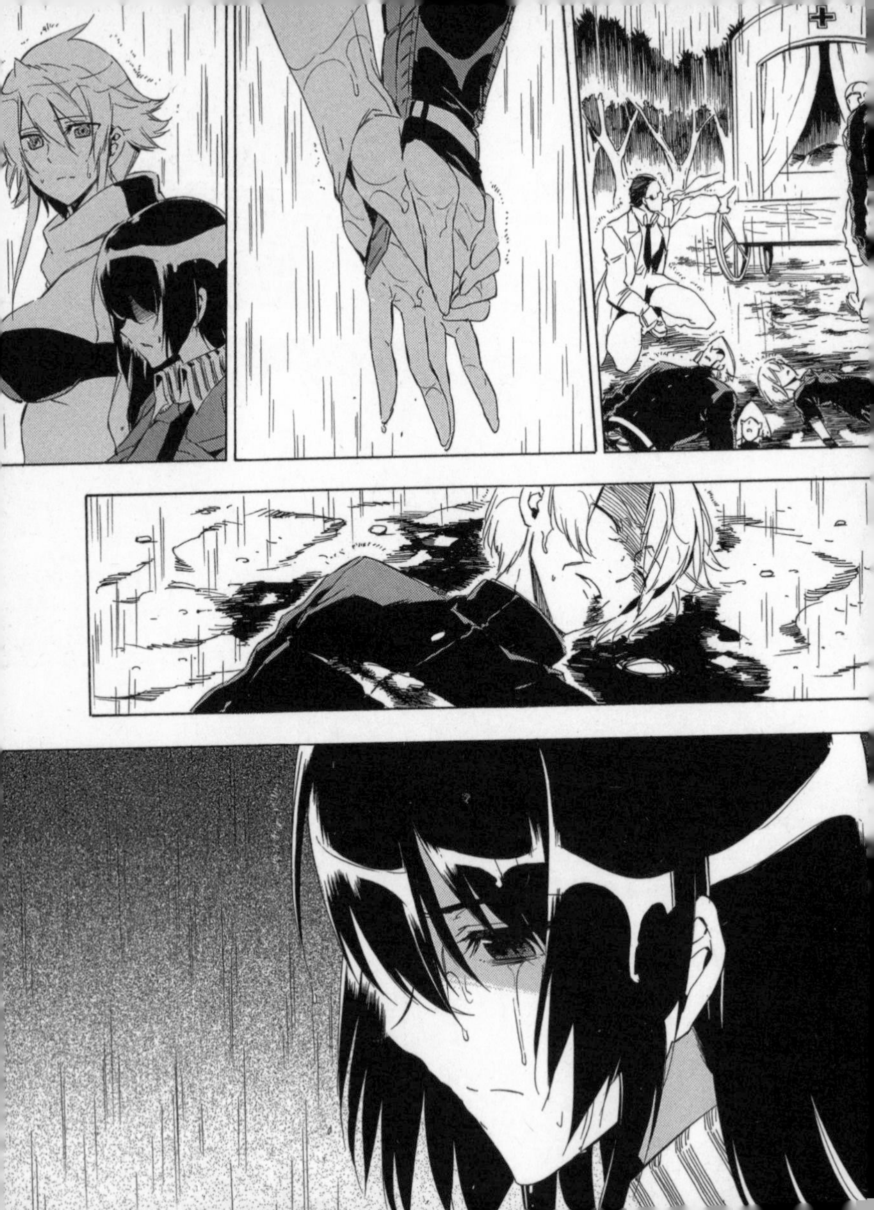

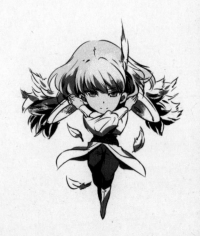

Chapter 64 - Kill the Little Sister (Part 1)

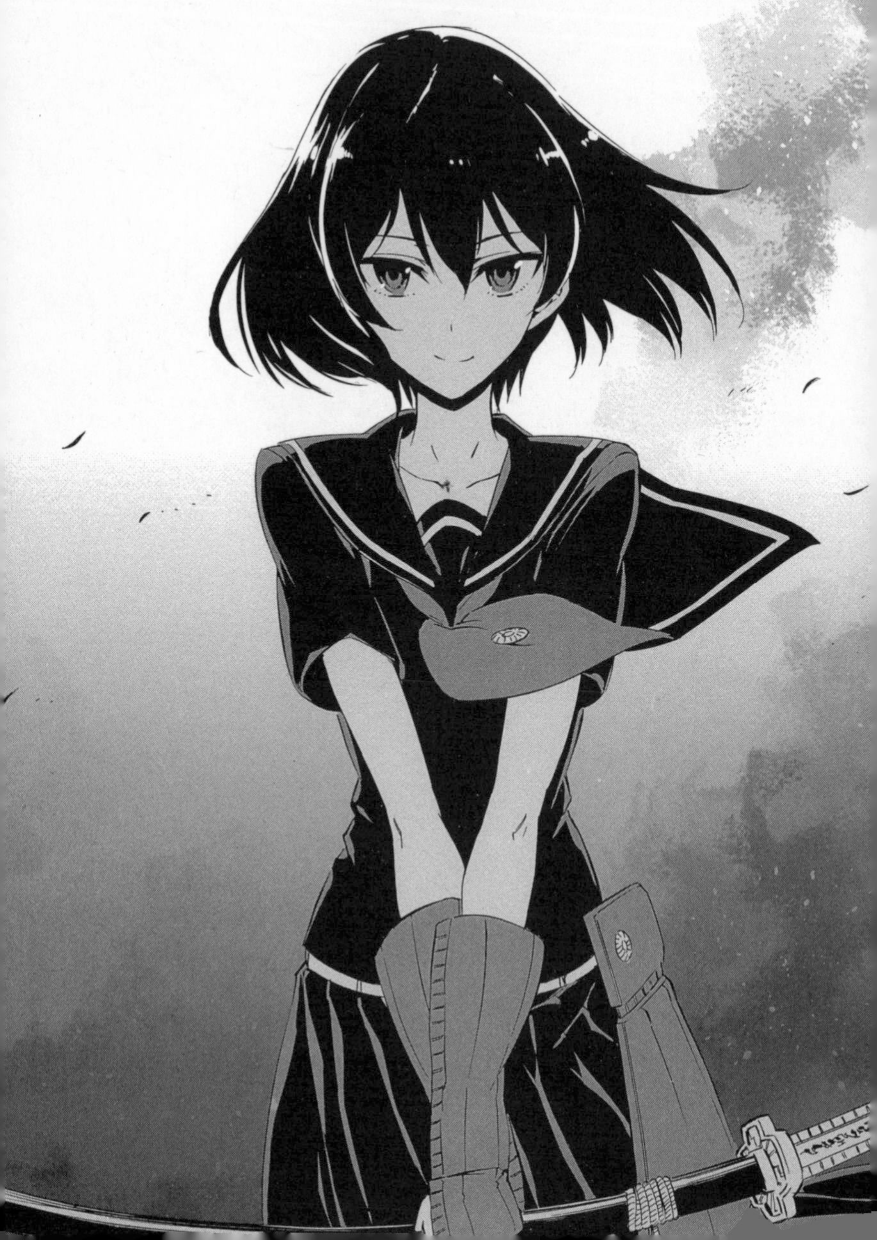

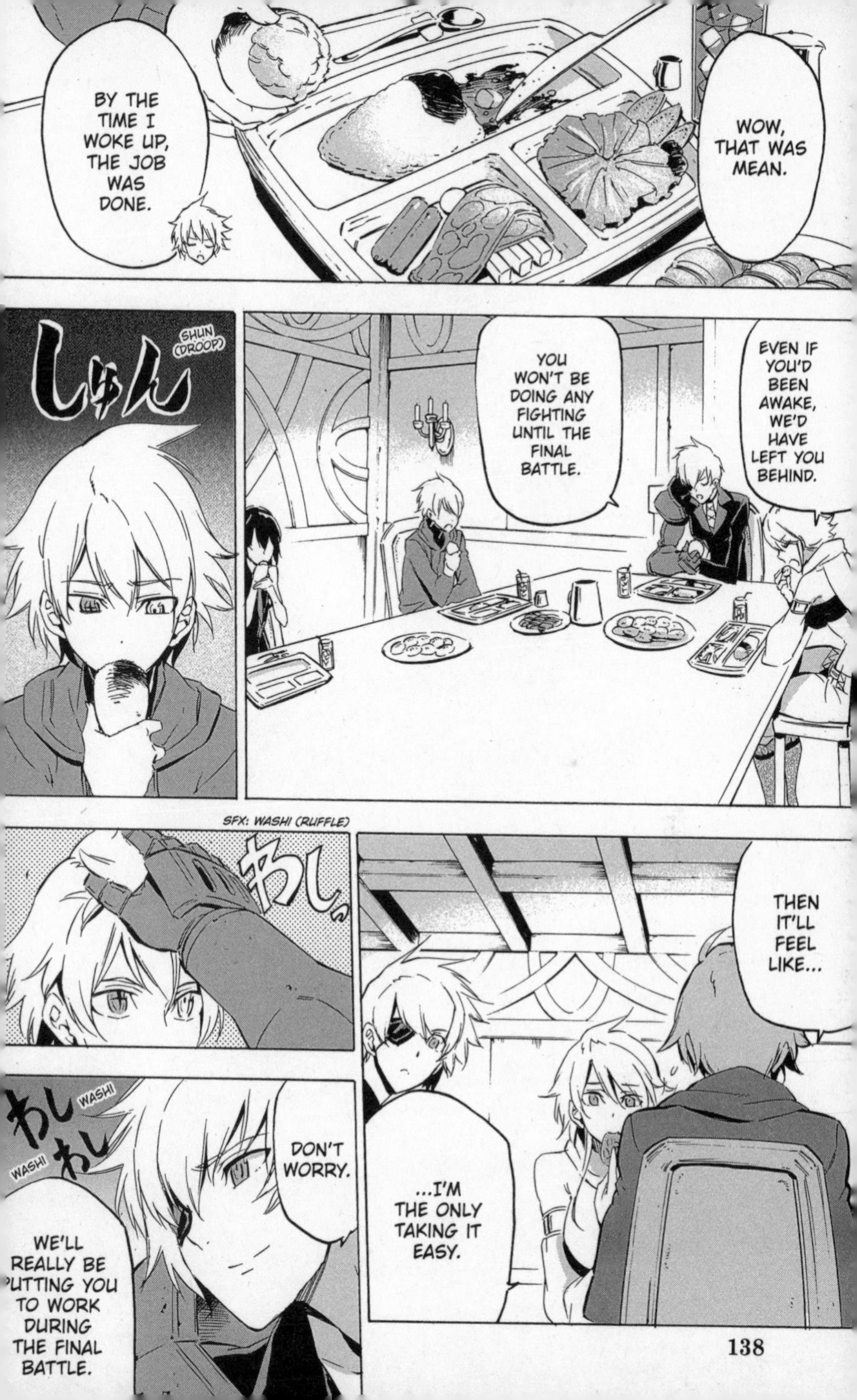
WOW, THAT WAS MEAN.
BY THE TIME I WOKE UP, THE JOB WAS DONE.
EVEN IF YOU'D BEEN AWAKE, WE'D HAVE LEFT YOU BEHIND.
YOU WON'T BE DOING ANY FIGHTING UNTIL THE FINAL BATTLE.
しゅん
SHUN (DROOP)
THEN IT'LL FEEL LIKE...
...I'M THE ONLY TAKING IT EASY.
SFX: WASHI (RUFFLE)
わしっ
わしわし
WASHI
WASHI
DON'T WORRY.
WE'LL REALLY BE PUTTING YOU TO WORK DURING THE FINAL BATTLE.

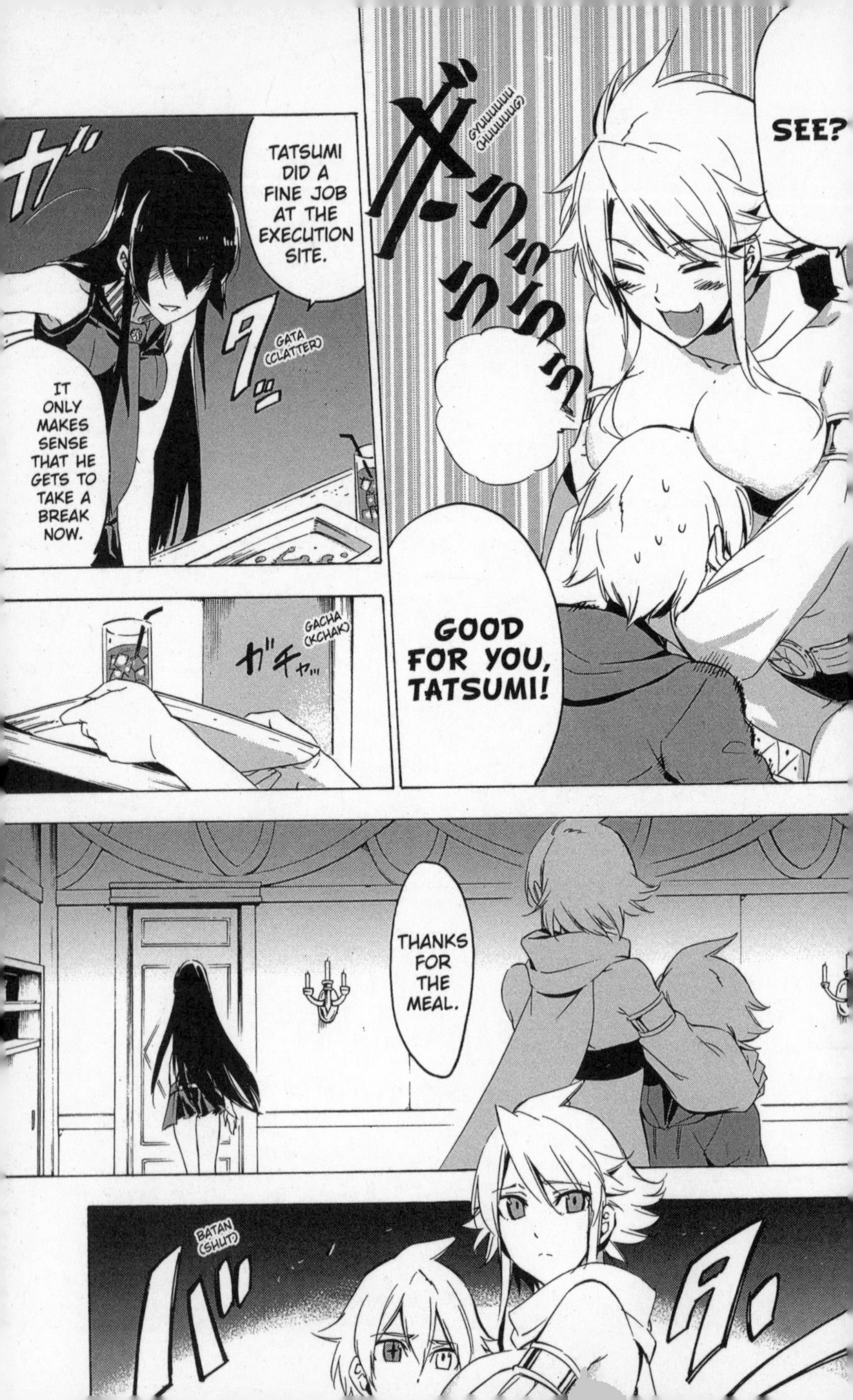
SEE?
GYUUUUUN (GYUUUUNG)
GOOD FOR YOU, TATSUMI!
TATSUMI DID A FINE JOB AT THE EXECUTION SITE.
GATA (CLATTER)
IT ONLY MAKES SENSE THAT HE GETS TO TAKE A BREAK NOW.
GACHA (KCHAK)
THANKS FOR THE MEAL.
BATAN (SHUT)

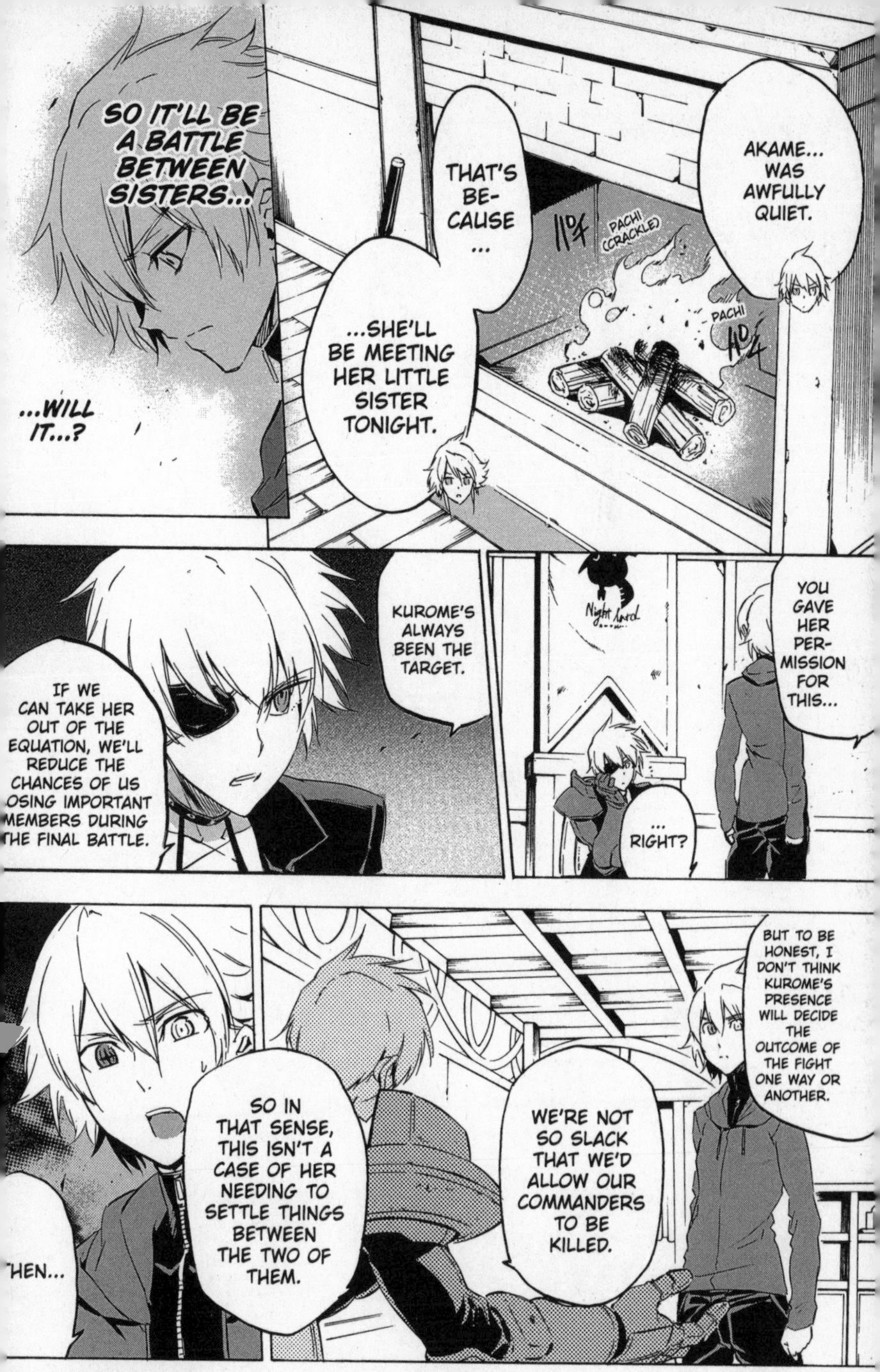
AKAME... WAS AWFULLY QUIET.
PACHI (CRACKLE)
PACHI
THAT'S BE-CAUSE ...
...SHE'LL BE MEETING HER LITTLE SISTER TONIGHT.
SO IT'LL BE A BATTLE BETWEEN SISTERS...
...WILL IT...?
YOU GAVE HER PER-MISSION FOR THIS...
Night Raid
...RIGHT?
KUROME'S ALWAYS BEEN THE TARGET.
IF WE CAN TAKE HER OUT OF THE EQUATION, WE'LL REDUCE THE CHANCES OF US OSING IMPORTANT MEMBERS DURING THE FINAL BATTLE.
BUT TO BE HONEST, I DON'T THINK KUROME'S PRESENCE WILL DECIDE THE OUTCOME OF THE FIGHT ONE WAY OR ANOTHER.
WE'RE NOT SO SLACK THAT WE'D ALLOW OUR COMMANDERS TO BE KILLED.
SO IN THAT SENSE, THIS ISN'T A CASE OF HER NEEDING TO SETTLE THINGS BETWEEN THE TWO OF THEM.
HEN...

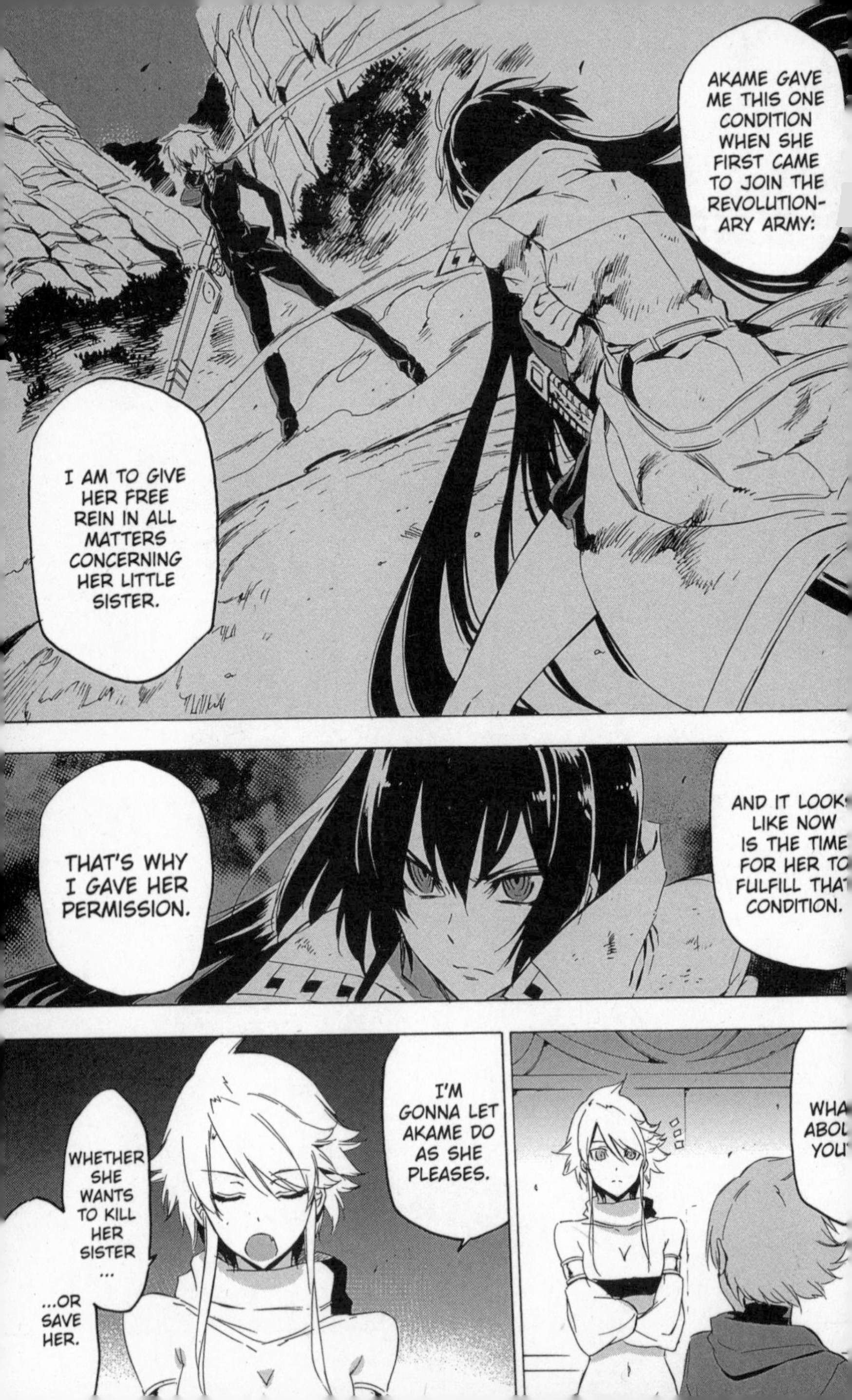
AKAME GAVE ME THIS ONE CONDITION WHEN SHE FIRST CAME TO JOIN THE REVOLUTION-ARY ARMY:
I AM TO GIVE HER FREE REIN IN ALL MATTERS CONCERNING HER LITTLE SISTER.
AND IT LOOK LIKE NOW IS THE TIME FOR HER TO FULFILL THA CONDITION.
THAT'S WHY I GAVE HER PERMISSION.
WHA ABOU YOU
I'M GONNA LET AKAME DO AS SHE PLEASES.
WHETHER SHE WANTS TO KILL HER SISTER ...
...OR SAVE HER.

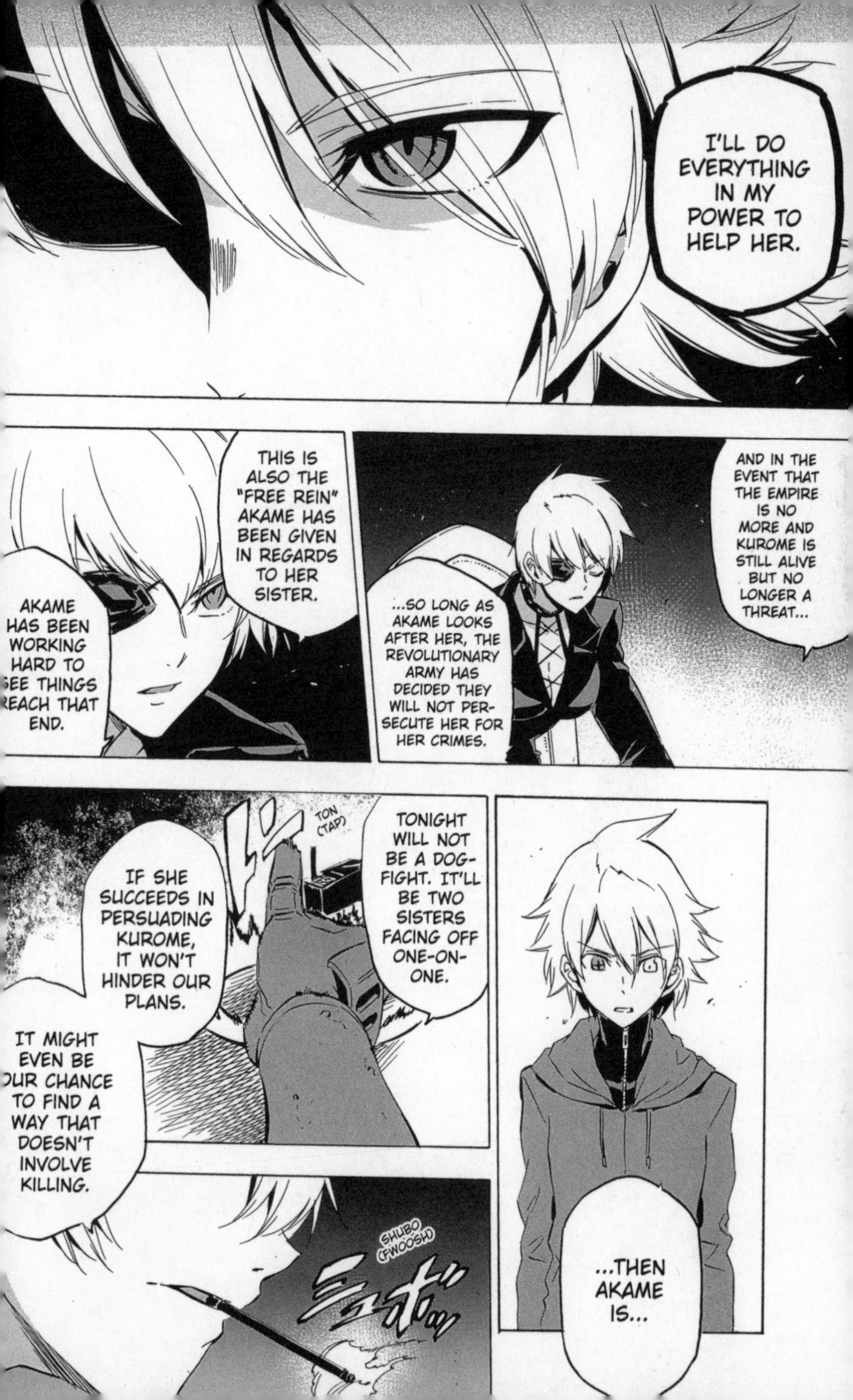
I'LL DO EVERYTHING IN MY POWER TO HELP HER.
AND IN THE EVENT THAT THE EMPIRE IS NO MORE AND KUROME IS STILL ALIVE BUT NO LONGER A THREAT...
...SO LONG AS AKAME LOOKS AFTER HER, THE REVOLUTIONARY ARMY HAS DECIDED THEY WILL NOT PER-SECUTE HER FOR HER CRIMES.
THIS IS ALSO THE "FREE REIN" AKAME HAS BEEN GIVEN IN REGARDS TO HER SISTER.
AKAME HAS BEEN WORKING HARD TO SEE THINGS REACH THAT END.
...THEN AKAME IS...
TON (TAP)
TONIGHT WILL NOT BE A DOG-FIGHT. IT'LL BE TWO SISTERS FACING OFF ONE-ON-ONE.
IF SHE SUCCEEDS IN PERSUADING KUROME, IT WON'T HINDER OUR PLANS.
IT MIGHT EVEN BE OUR CHANCE TO FIND A WAY THAT DOESN'T INVOLVE KILLING.
SHUBO (FWOOSH)

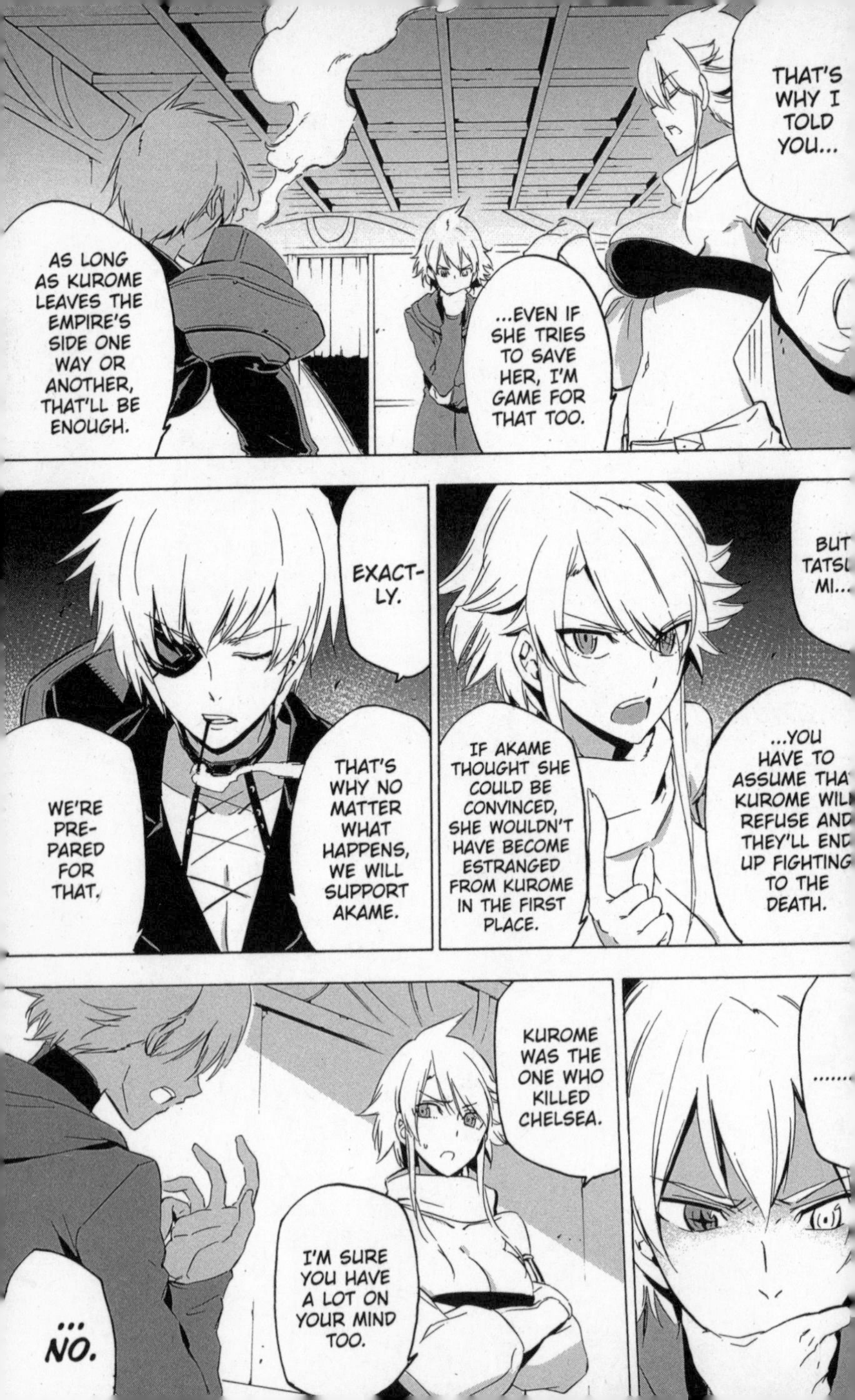
THAT'S WHY I TOLD YOU...
AS LONG AS KUROME LEAVES THE EMPIRE'S SIDE ONE WAY OR ANOTHER, THAT'LL BE ENOUGH.
...EVEN IF SHE TRIES TO SAVE HER, I'M GAME FOR THAT TOO.
BUT TATSU-MI...
...YOU HAVE TO ASSUME THA KUROME WIL REFUSE AND THEY'LL END UP FIGHTING TO THE DEATH.
IF AKAME THOUGHT SHE COULD BE CONVINCED, SHE WOULDN'T HAVE BECOME ESTRANGED FROM KUROME IN THE FIRST PLACE.
EXACT-LY.
THAT'S WHY NO MATTER WHAT HAPPENS, WE WILL SUPPORT AKAME.
WE'RE PRE-PARED FOR THAT.
......
KUROME WAS THE ONE WHO KILLED CHELSEA.
I'M SURE YOU HAVE A LOT ON YOUR MIND TOO.
...NO.

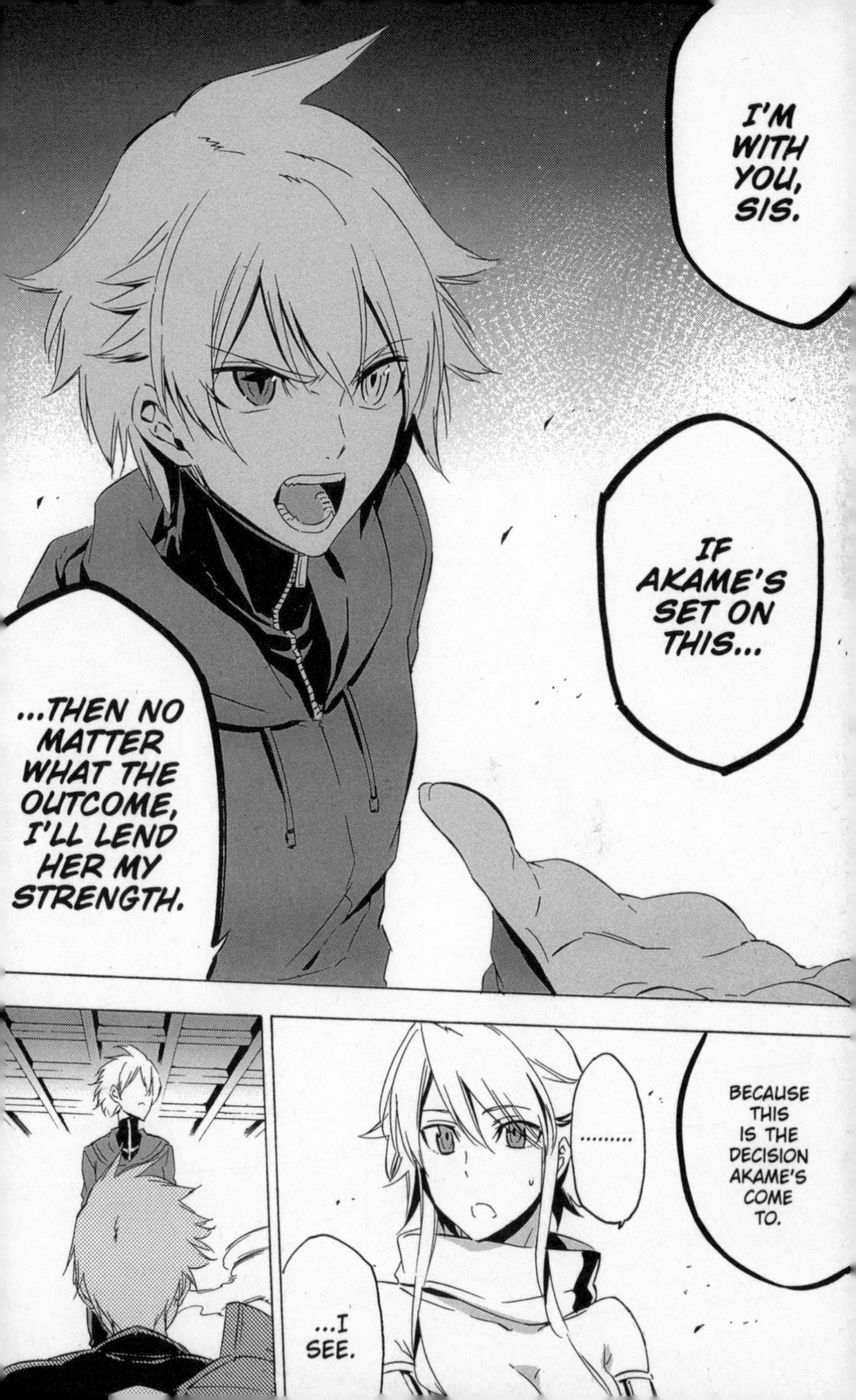
I'M WITH YOU, SIS.
IF AKAME'S SET ON THIS...
...THEN NO MATTER WHAT THE OUTCOME, I'LL LEND HER MY STRENGTH.
BECAUSE THIS IS THE DECISION AKAME'S COME TO.
....
...I SEE.

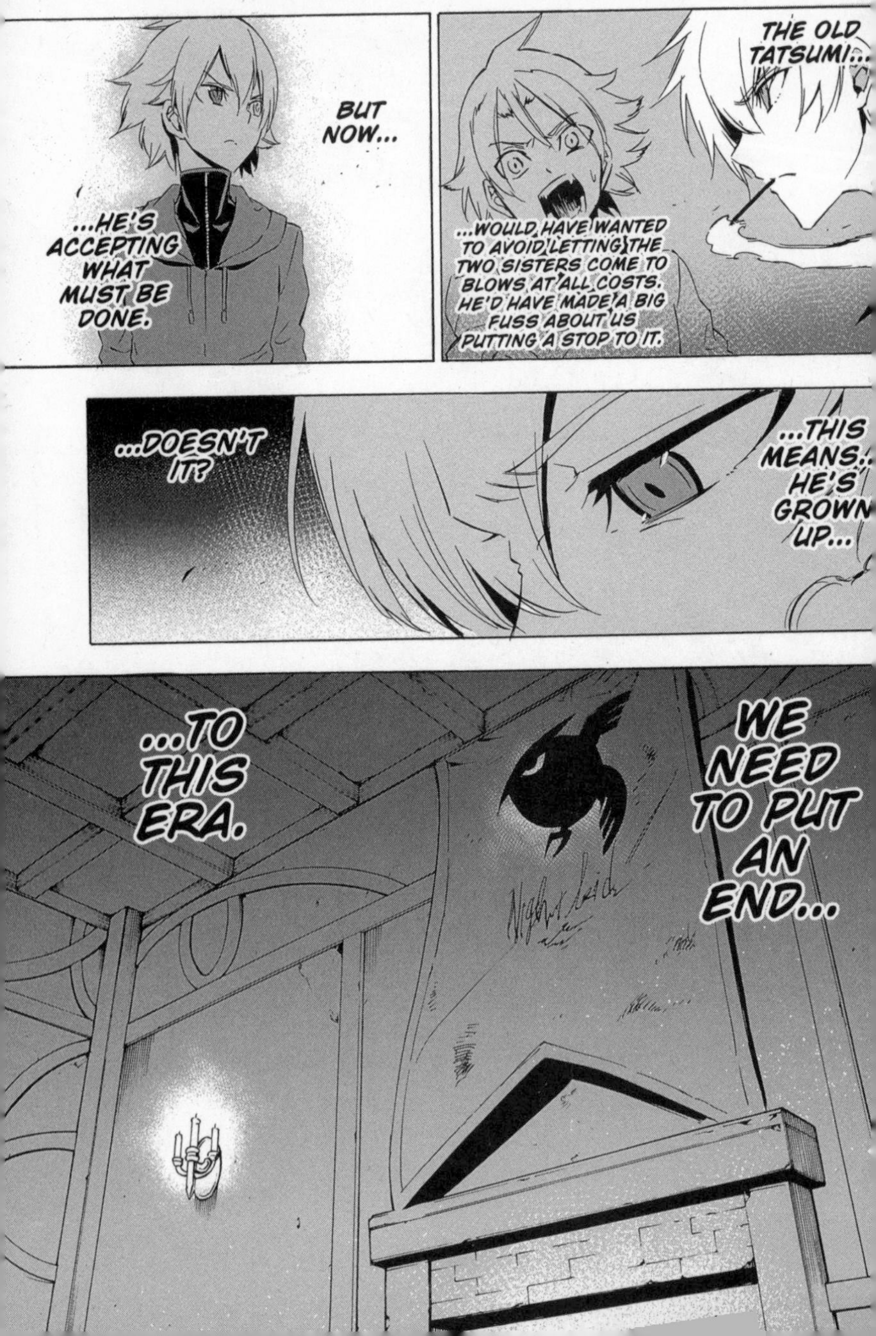
THE OLD TATSUMI...
...WOULD HAVE WANTED TO AVOID LETTING THE TWO SISTERS COME TO BLOWS AT ALL COSTS. HE'D HAVE MADE A BIG FUSS ABOUT US PUTTING A STOP TO IT.
BUT NOW...
...HE'S ACCEPTING WHAT MUST BE DONE.
...THIS MEANS... HE'S GROWN UP...
...DOESN'T IT?
WE NEED TO PUT AN END...
...TO THIS ERA.

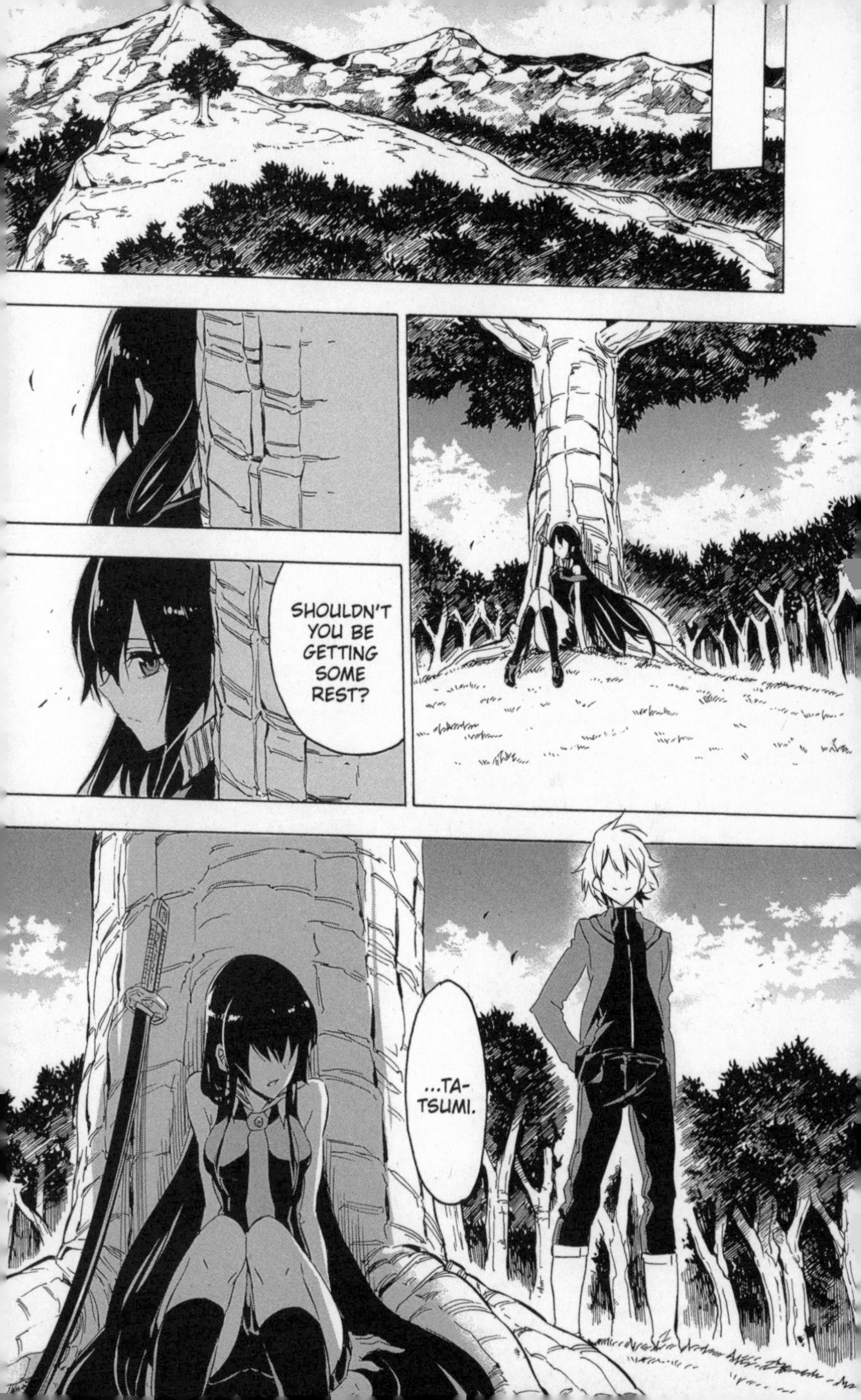
SHOULDN'T YOU BE GETTING SOME REST?
...TA-TSUMI.

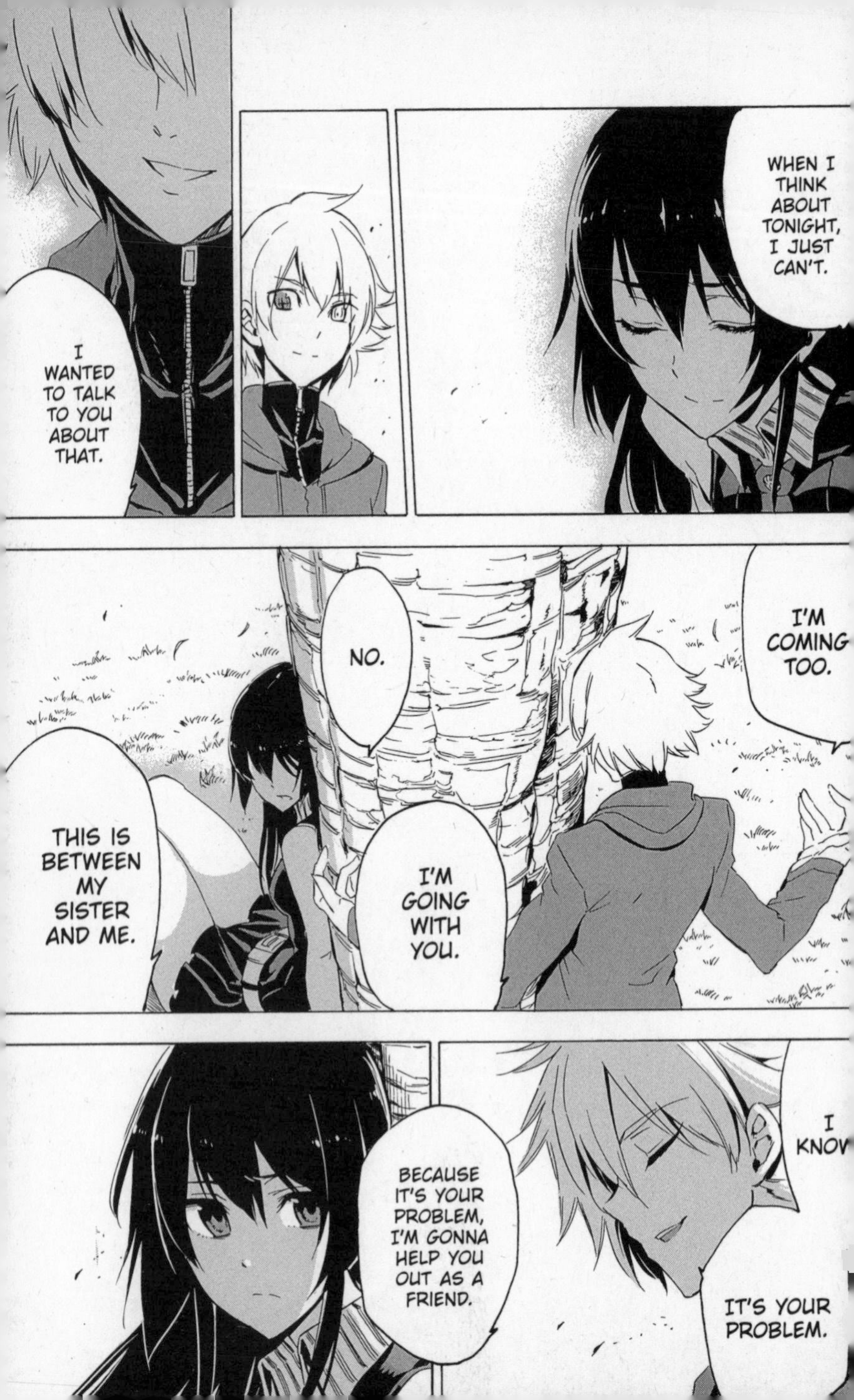
WHEN I THINK ABOUT TONIGHT, I JUST CAN'T.
I WANTED TO TALK TO YOU ABOUT THAT.
I'M COMING TOO.
NO.
I'M GOING WITH YOU.
THIS IS BETWEEN MY SISTER AND ME.
I KNOW
IT'S YOUR PROBLEM.
BECAUSE IT'S YOUR PROBLEM, I'M GONNA HELP YOU OUT AS A FRIEND.

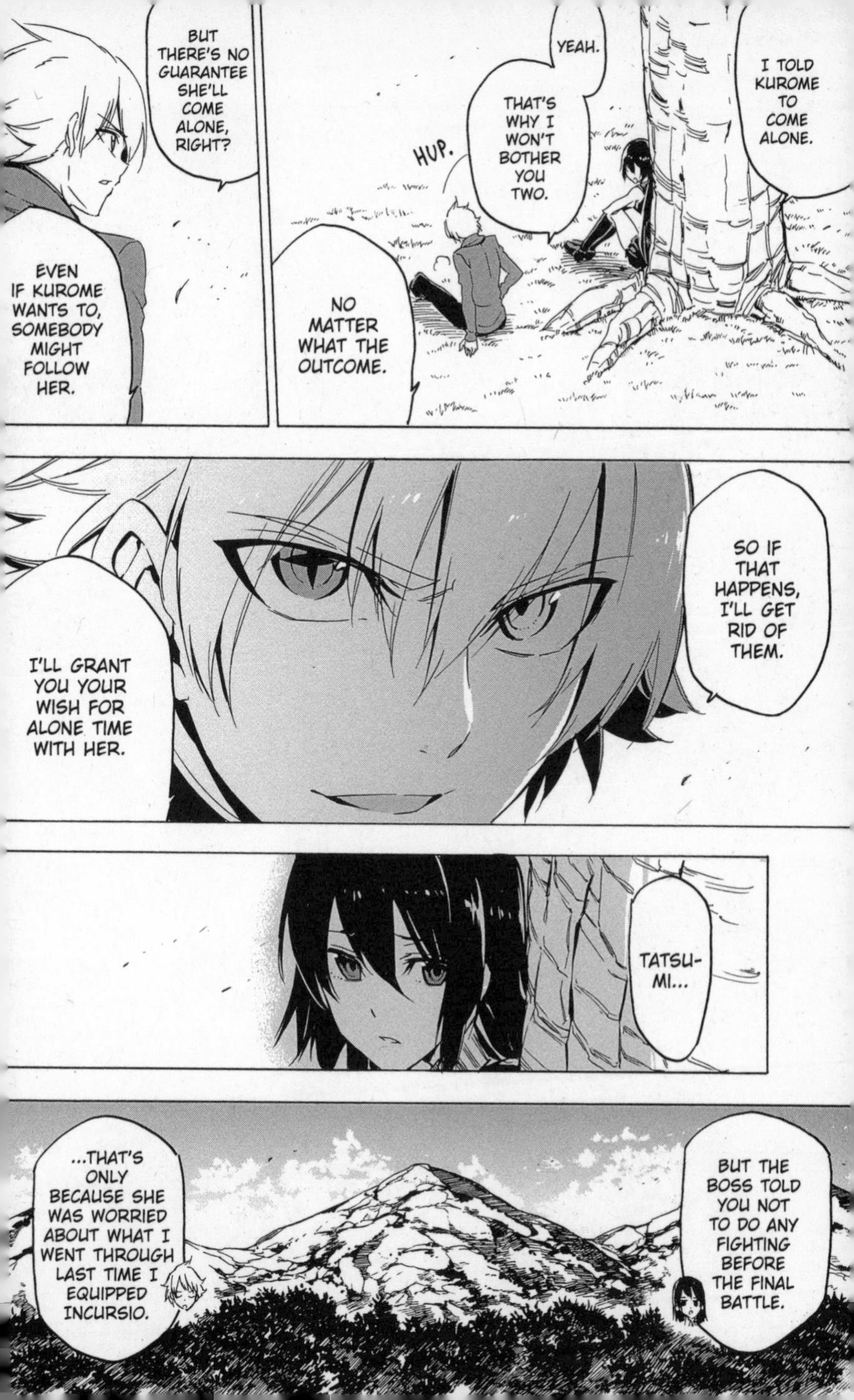
I TOLD KUROME TO COME ALONE.
YEAH.
THAT'S WHY I WON'T BOTHER YOU TWO.
HUP.
NO MATTER WHAT THE OUTCOME.
BUT THERE'S NO GUARANTEE SHE'LL COME ALONE, RIGHT?
EVEN IF KUROME WANTS TO, SOMEBODY MIGHT FOLLOW HER.
SO IF THAT HAPPENS, I'LL GET RID OF THEM.
I'LL GRANT YOU YOUR WISH FOR ALONE TIME WITH HER.
TATSU-MI...
BUT THE BOSS TOLD YOU NOT TO DO ANY FIGHTING BEFORE THE FINAL BATTLE.
...THAT'S ONLY BECAUSE SHE WAS WORRIED ABOUT WHAT I WENT THROUGH LAST TIME I EQUIPPED INCURSIO.

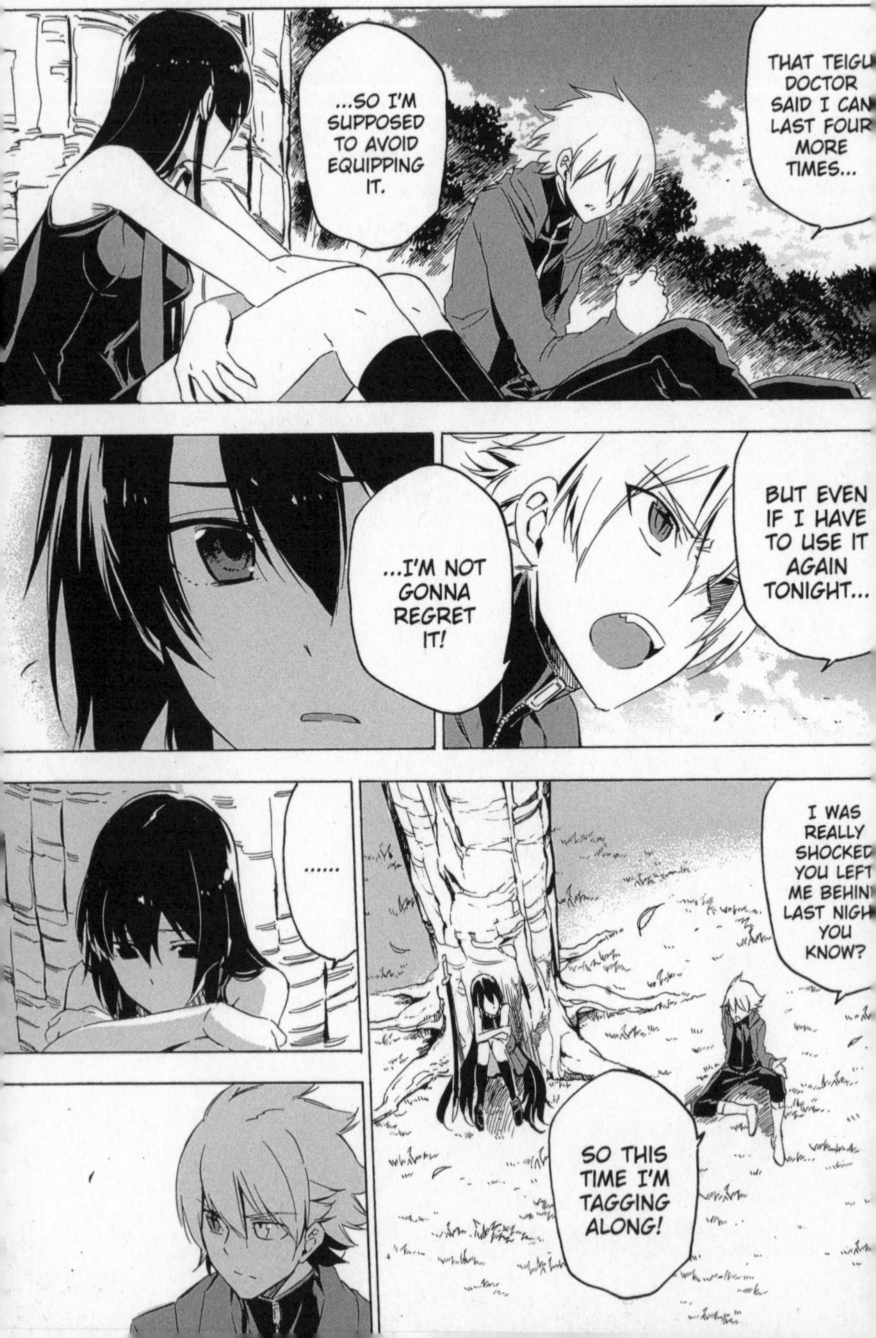
THAT TEIGU DOCTOR SAID I CAN LAST FOUR MORE TIMES...
...SO I'M SUPPOSED TO AVOID EQUIPPING IT.
BUT EVEN IF I HAVE TO USE IT AGAIN TONIGHT...
...I'M NOT GONNA REGRET IT!
I WAS REALLY SHOCKED YOU LEFT ME BEHIN LAST NIGH YOU KNOW?
SO THIS TIME I'M TAGGING ALONG!
......

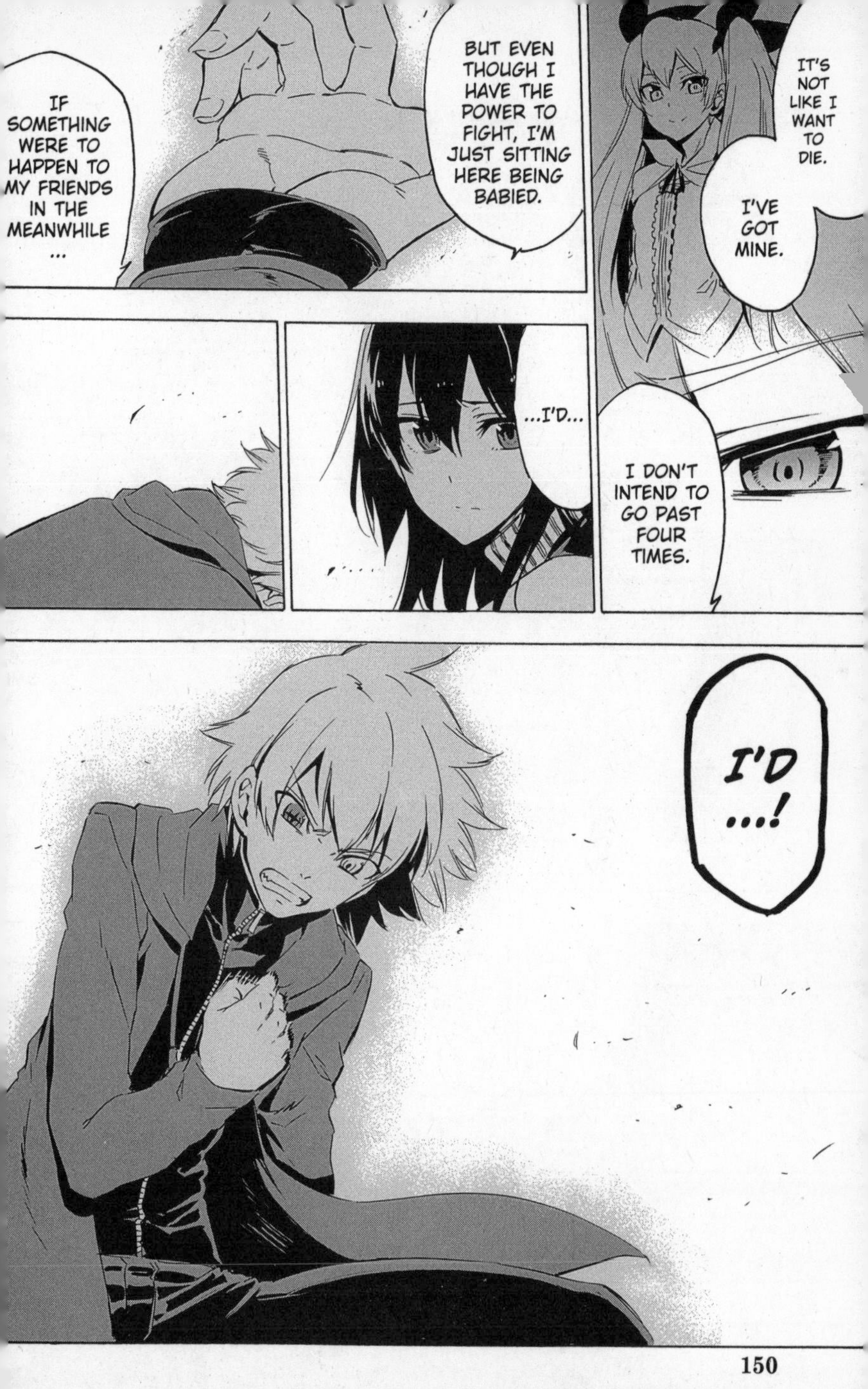
IT'S NOT LIKE I WANT TO DIE.
I'VE GOT MINE.
BUT EVEN THOUGH I HAVE THE POWER TO FIGHT, I'M JUST SITTING HERE BEING BABIED.
IF SOMETHING WERE TO HAPPEN TO MY FRIENDS IN THE MEANWHILE ...
I DON'T INTEND TO GO PAST FOUR TIMES.
...I'D...
I'D ...!

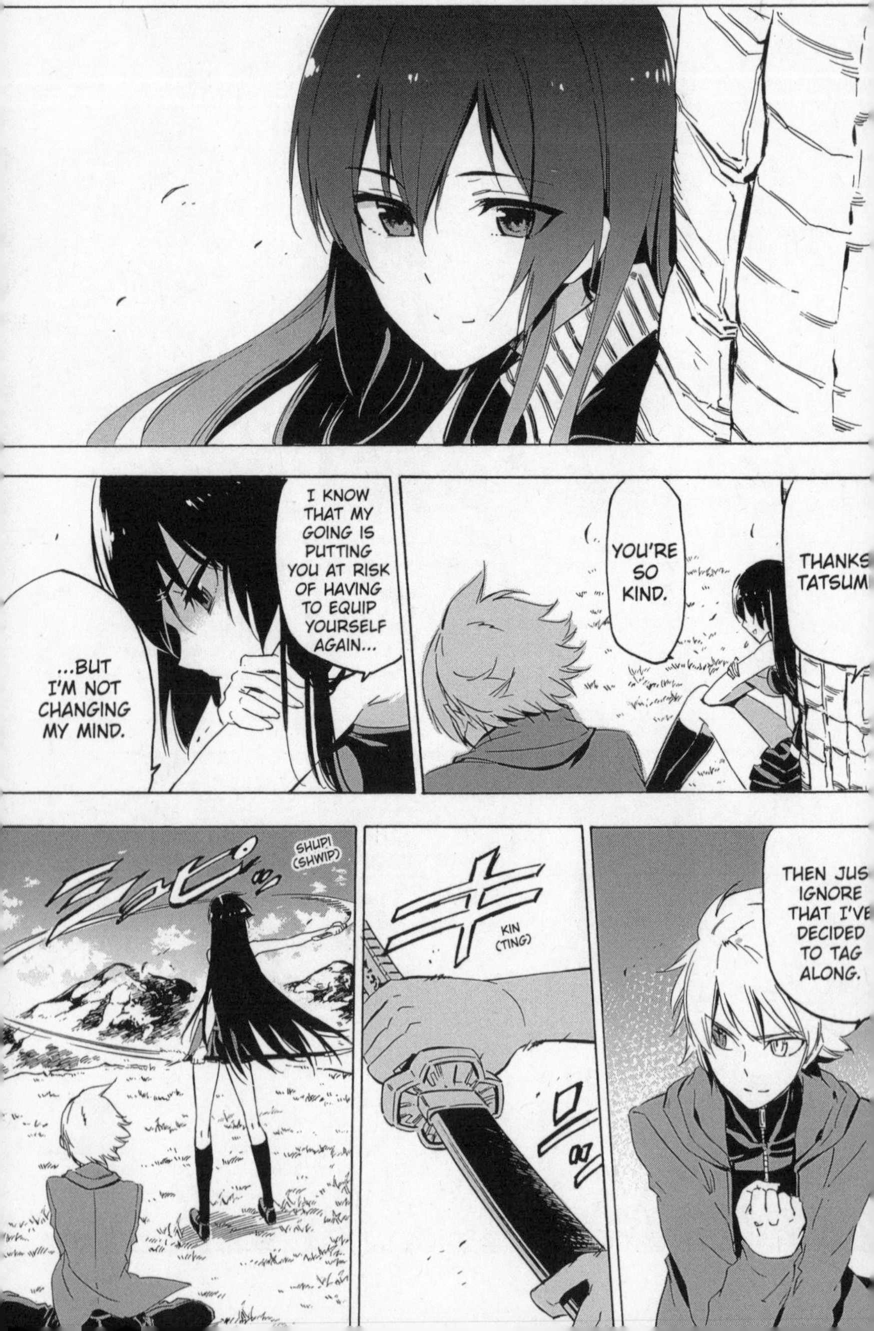
THANKS TATSUM
YOU'RE SO KIND.
I KNOW THAT MY GOING IS PUTTING YOU AT RISK OF HAVING TO EQUIP YOURSELF AGAIN...
...BUT I'M NOT CHANGING MY MIND.
THEN JUS IGNORE THAT I'VE DECIDED TO TAG ALONG.
KIN (TING)
SHUP! (SHWIP)

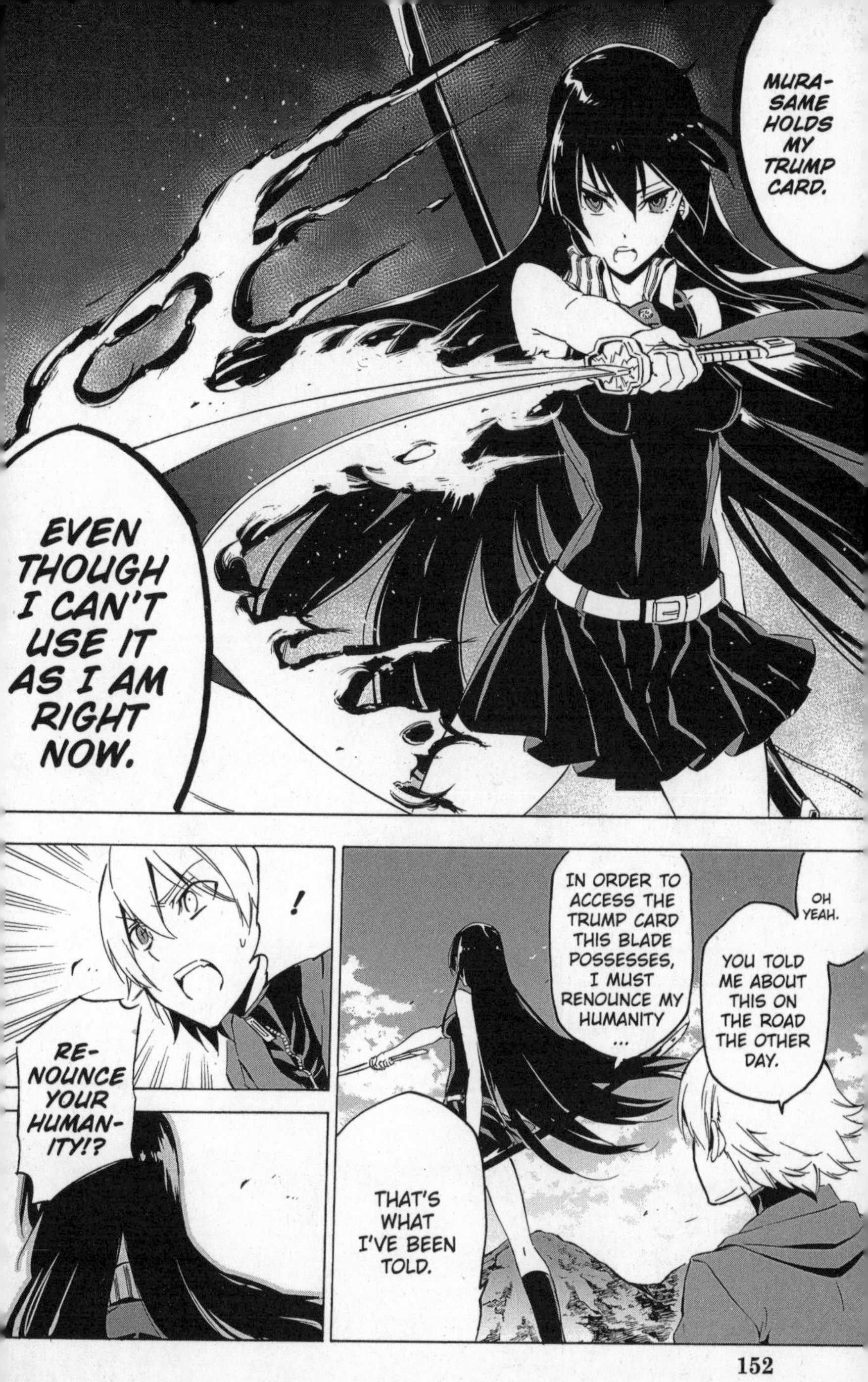
MURA-SAME HOLDS MY TRUMP CARD.
EVEN THOUGH I CAN'T USE IT AS I AM RIGHT NOW.
OH YEAH.
YOU TOLD ME ABOUT THIS ON THE ROAD THE OTHER DAY.
IN ORDER TO ACCESS THE TRUMP CARD THIS BLADE POSSESSES, I MUST RENOUNCE MY HUMANITY ...
THAT'S WHAT I'VE BEEN TOLD.
!
RE-NOUNCE YOUR HUMAN-ITY!?
...

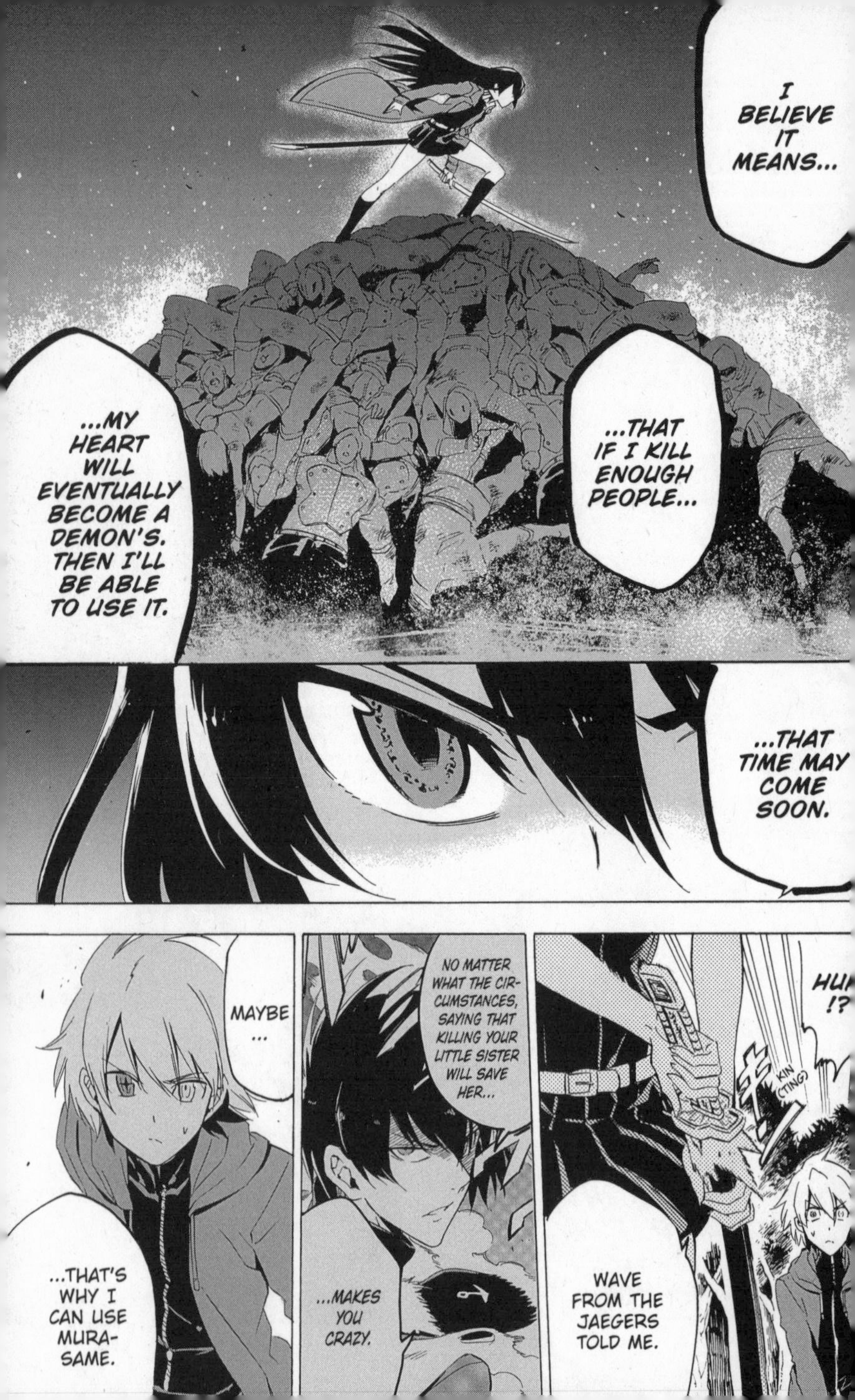
I BELIEVE IT MEANS...
...THAT IF I KILL ENOUGH PEOPLE...
...MY HEART WILL EVENTUALLY BECOME A DEMON'S. THEN I'LL BE ABLE TO USE IT.
...THAT TIME MAY COME SOON.
HU!?
KIN (TING)
WAVE FROM THE JAEGERS TOLD ME.
NO MATTER WHAT THE CIR-CUMSTANCES, SAYING THAT KILLING YOUR LITTLE SISTER WILL SAVE HER...
...MAKES YOU CRAZY.
MAYBE...
...THAT'S WHY I CAN USE MURA-SAME.

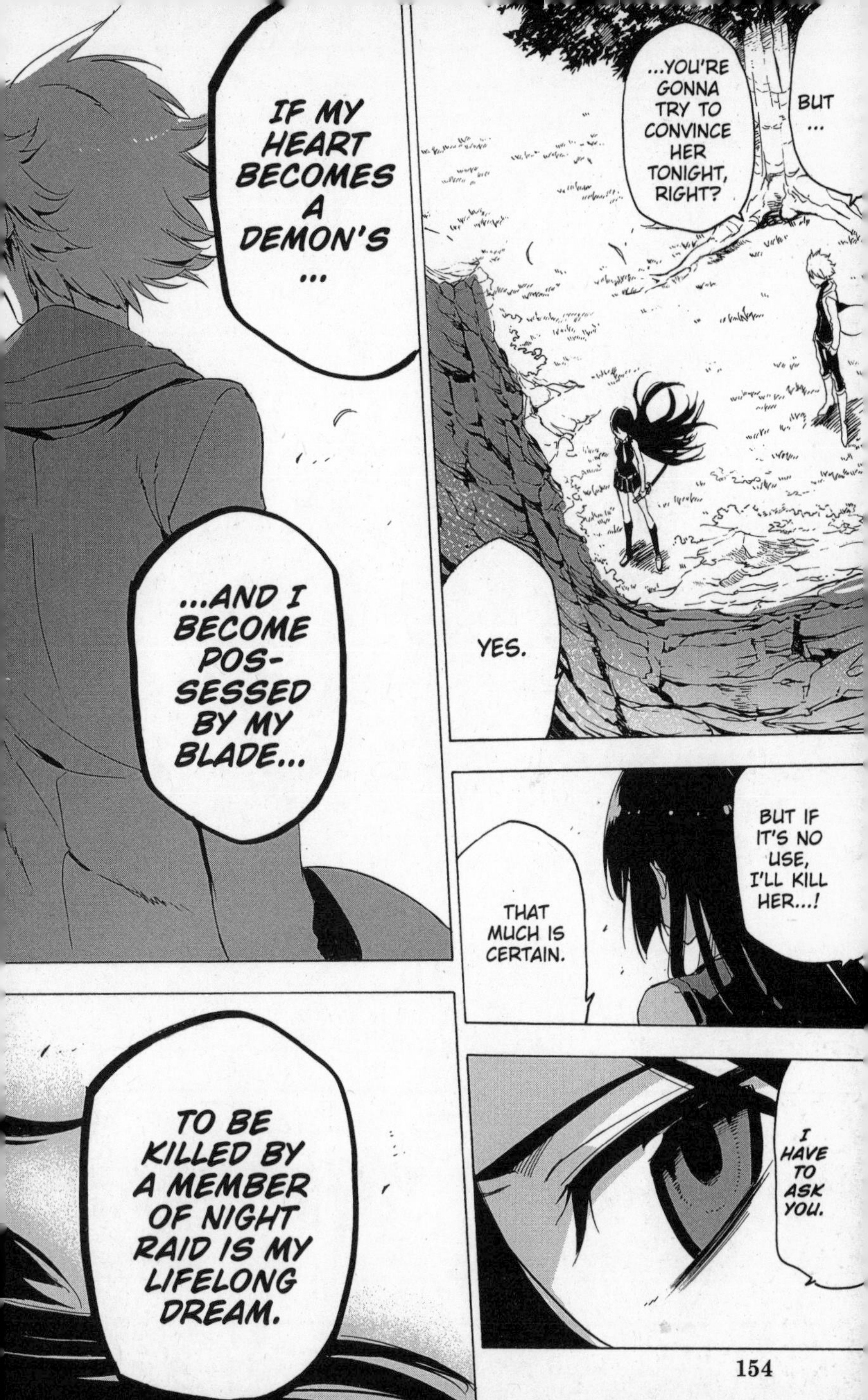
BUT ...
...YOU'RE GONNA TRY TO CONVINCE HER TONIGHT, RIGHT?
YES.
BUT IF IT'S NO USE, I'LL KILL HER...!
THAT MUCH IS CERTAIN.
IF MY HEART BECOMES A DEMON'S ...
...AND I BECOME POS-SESSED BY MY BLADE...
I HAVE TO ASK YOU.
TO BE KILLED BY A MEMBER OF NIGHT RAID IS MY LIFELONG DREAM.

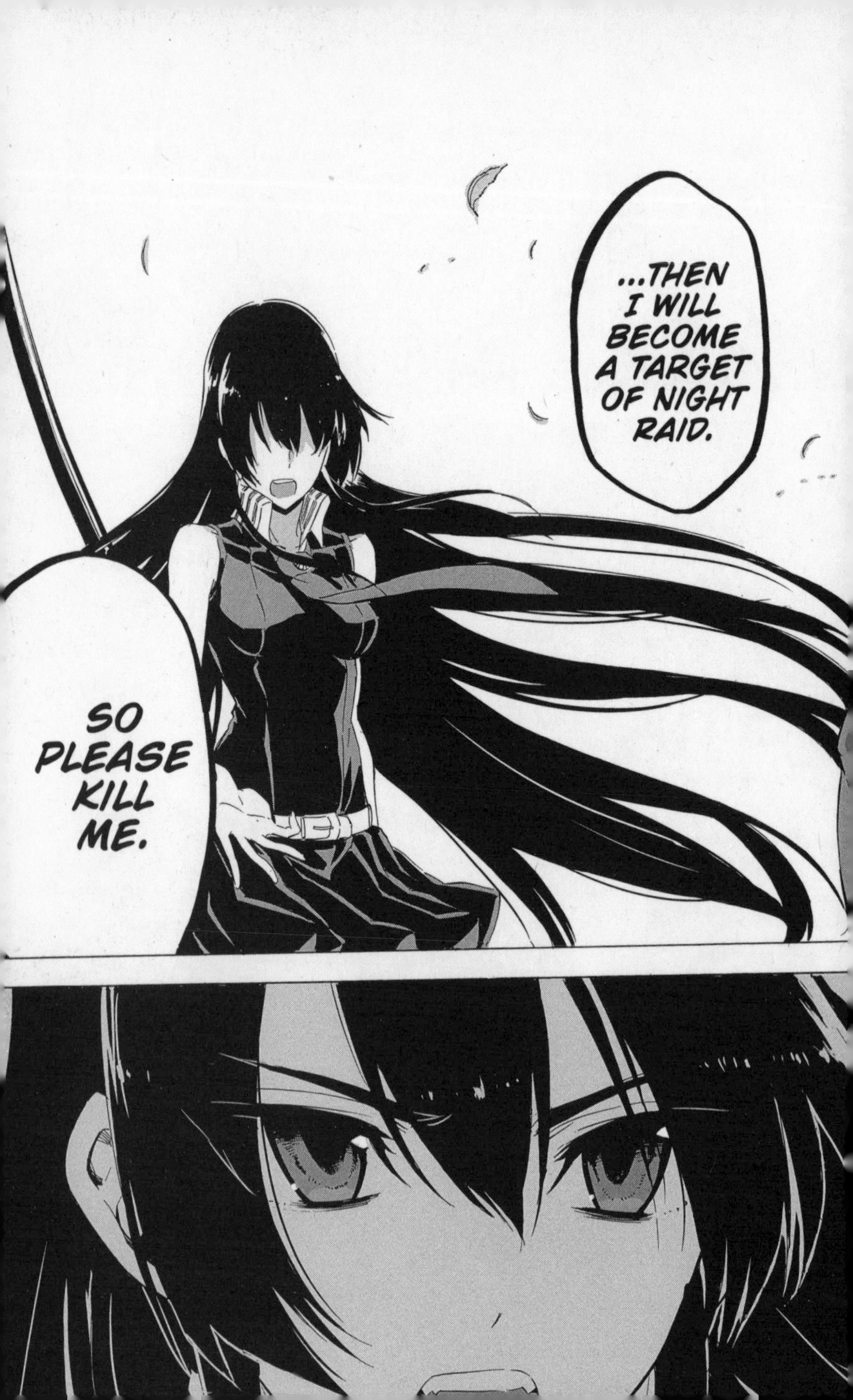
...THEN I WILL BECOME A TARGET OF NIGHT RAID.
SO PLEASE KILL ME.

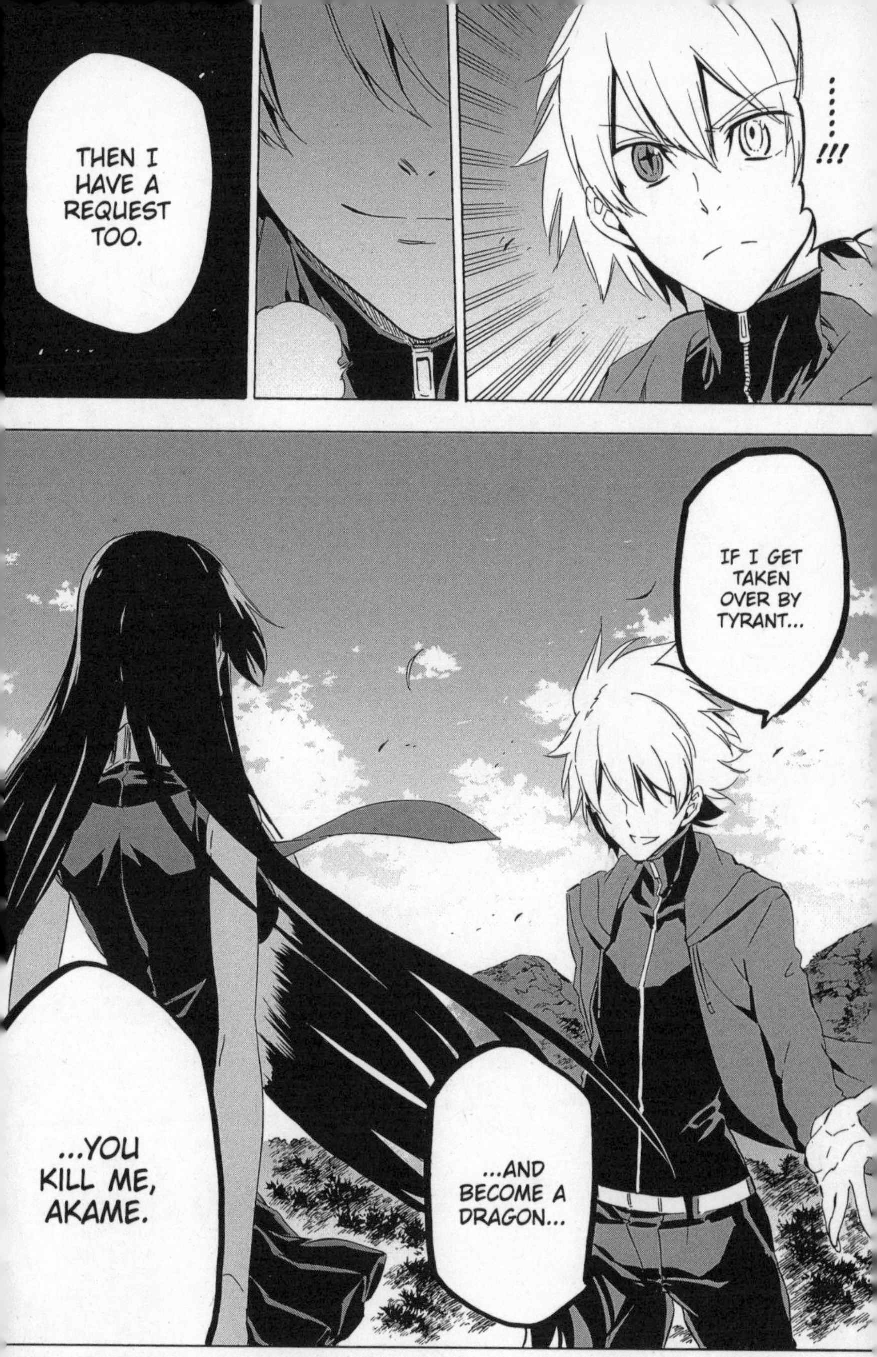
......!!!
THEN I HAVE A REQUEST TOO.
IF I GET TAKEN OVER BY TYRANT...
...AND BECOME A DRAGON...
...YOU KILL ME, AKAME.

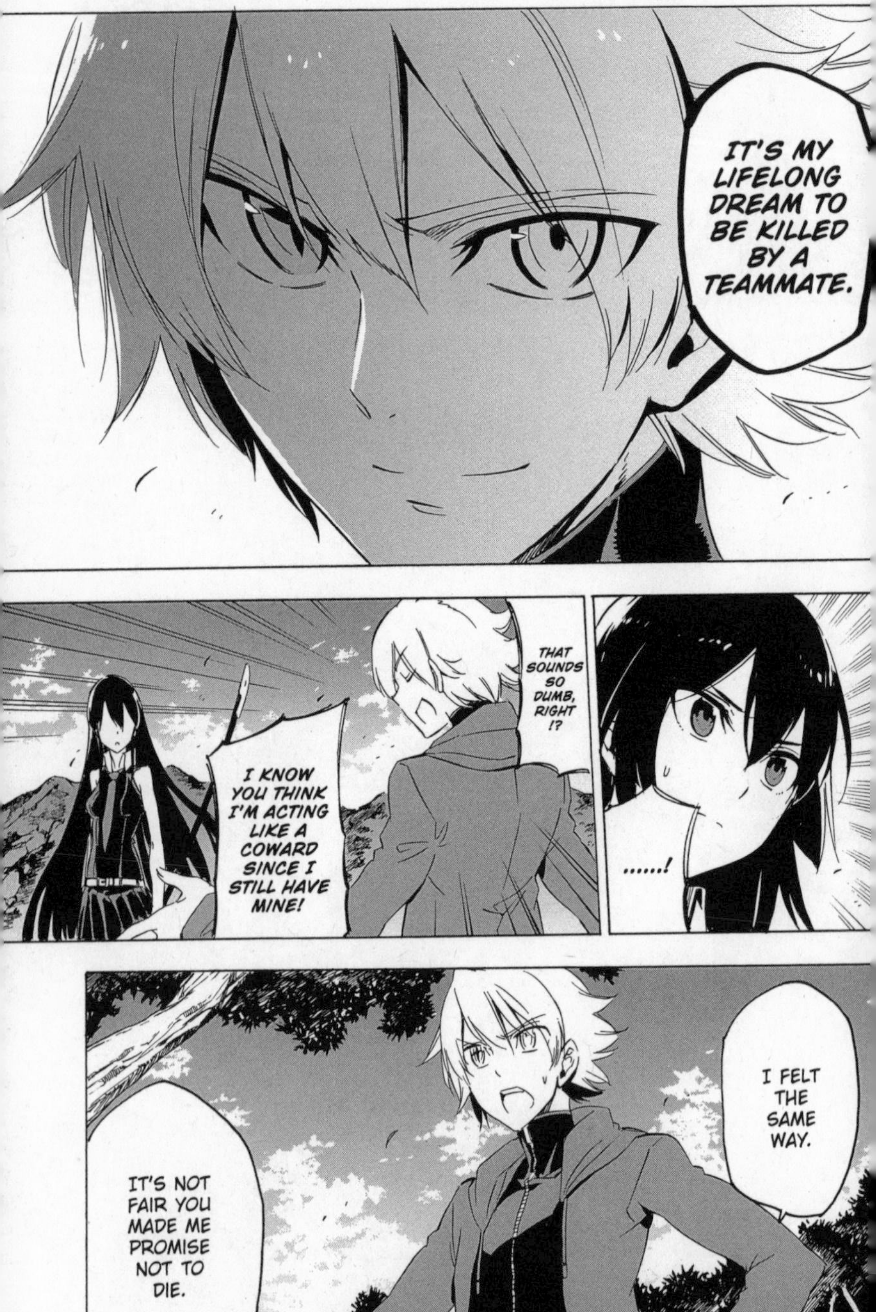
IT'S MY LIFELONG DREAM TO BE KILLED BY A TEAMMATE.
......!
THAT SOUNDS SO DUMB, RIGHT!?
I KNOW YOU THINK I'M ACTING LIKE A COWARD SINCE I STILL HAVE MINE!
I FELT THE SAME WAY.
IT'S NOT FAIR YOU MADE ME PROMISE NOT TO DIE.

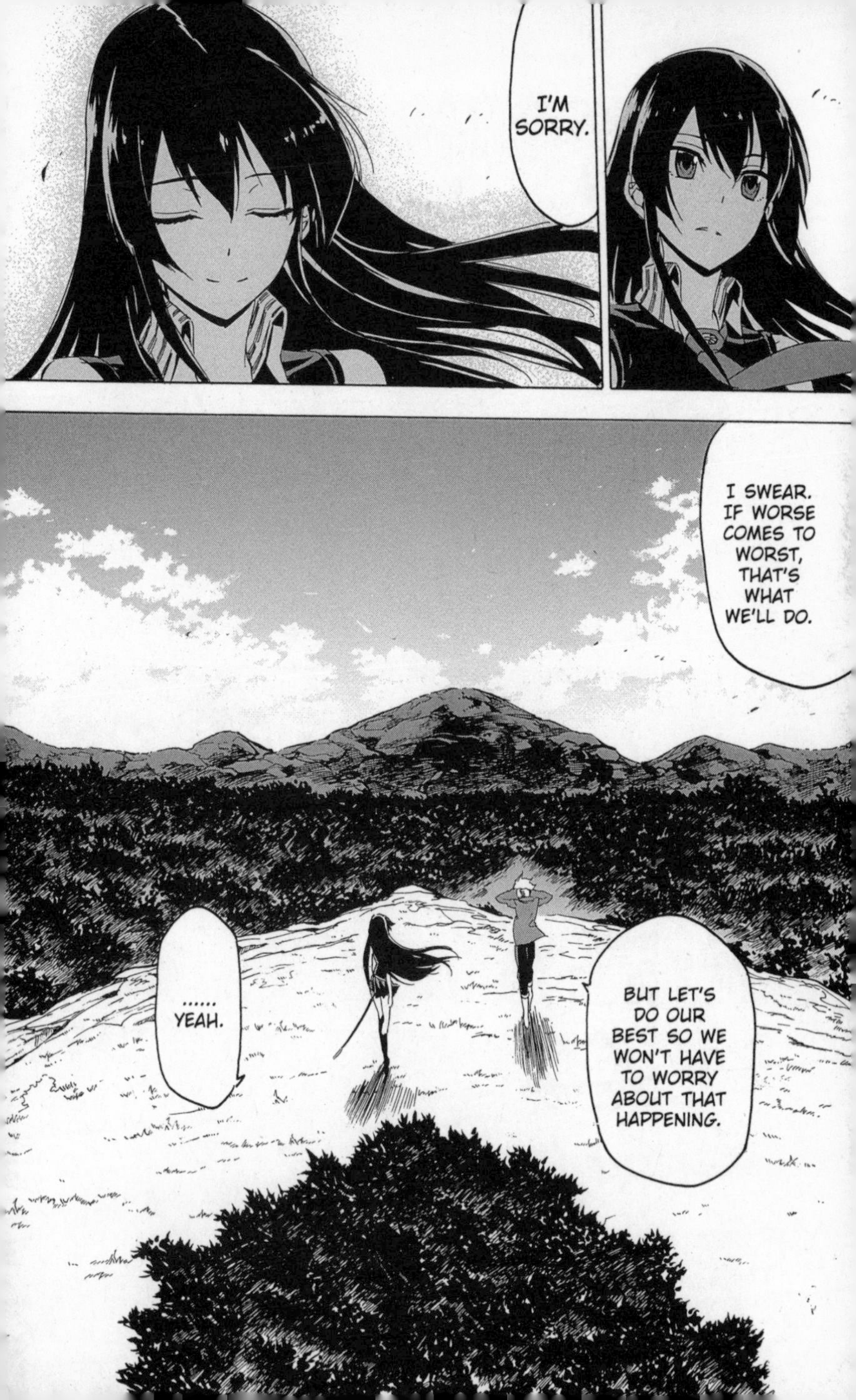
I'M SORRY.
I SWEAR. IF WORSE COMES TO WORST, THAT'S WHAT WE'LL DO.
BUT LET'S DO OUR BEST SO WE WON'T HAVE TO WORRY ABOUT THAT HAPPENING.
...... YEAH.

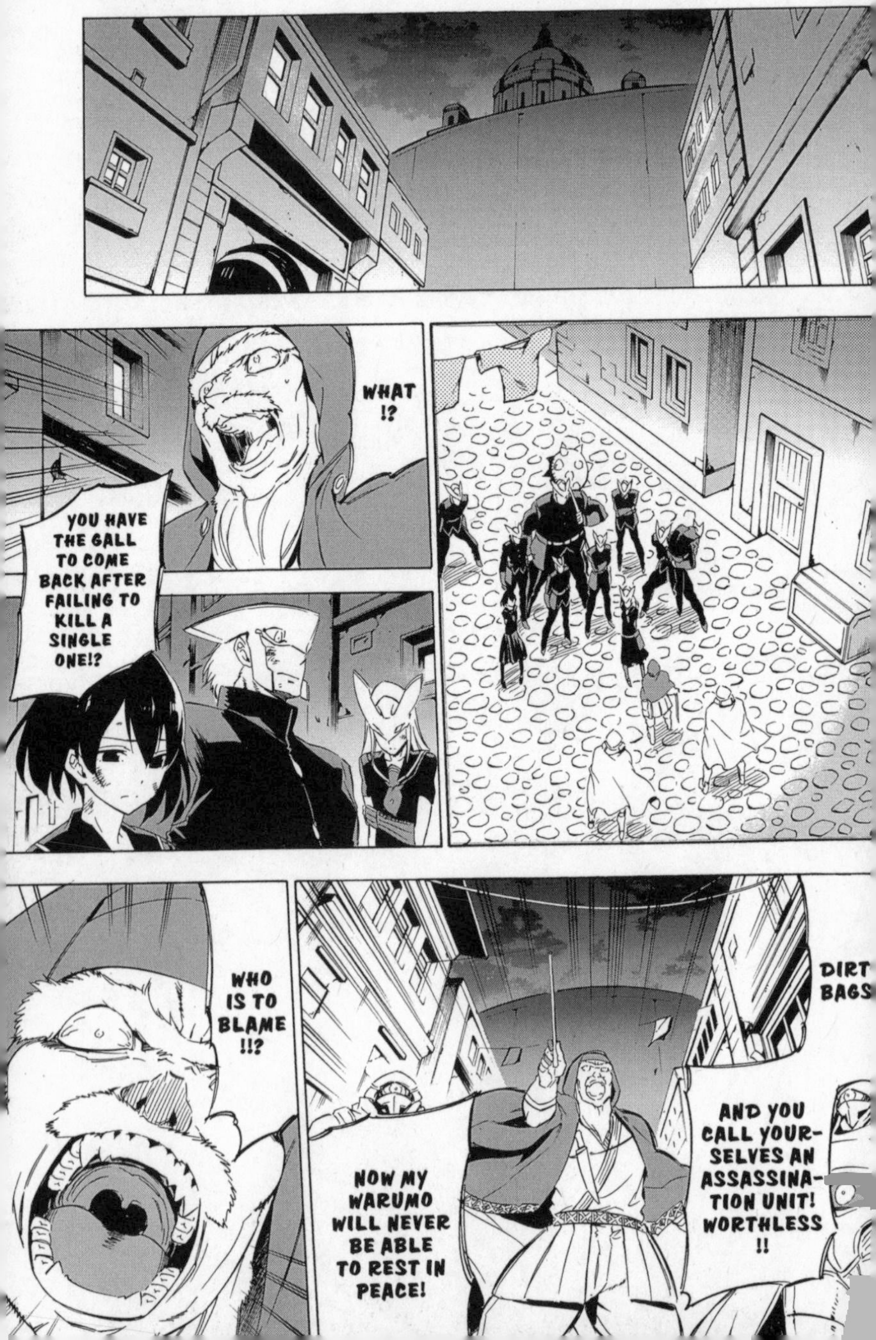
WHAT!?
YOU HAVE THE GALL TO COME BACK AFTER FAILING TO KILL A SINGLE ONE!?
DIRT BAGS
AND YOU CALL YOURSELVES AN ASSASSINATION UNIT! WORTHLESS!!
NOW MY WARUMO WILL NEVER BE ABLE TO REST IN PEACE!
WHO IS TO BLAME!!?

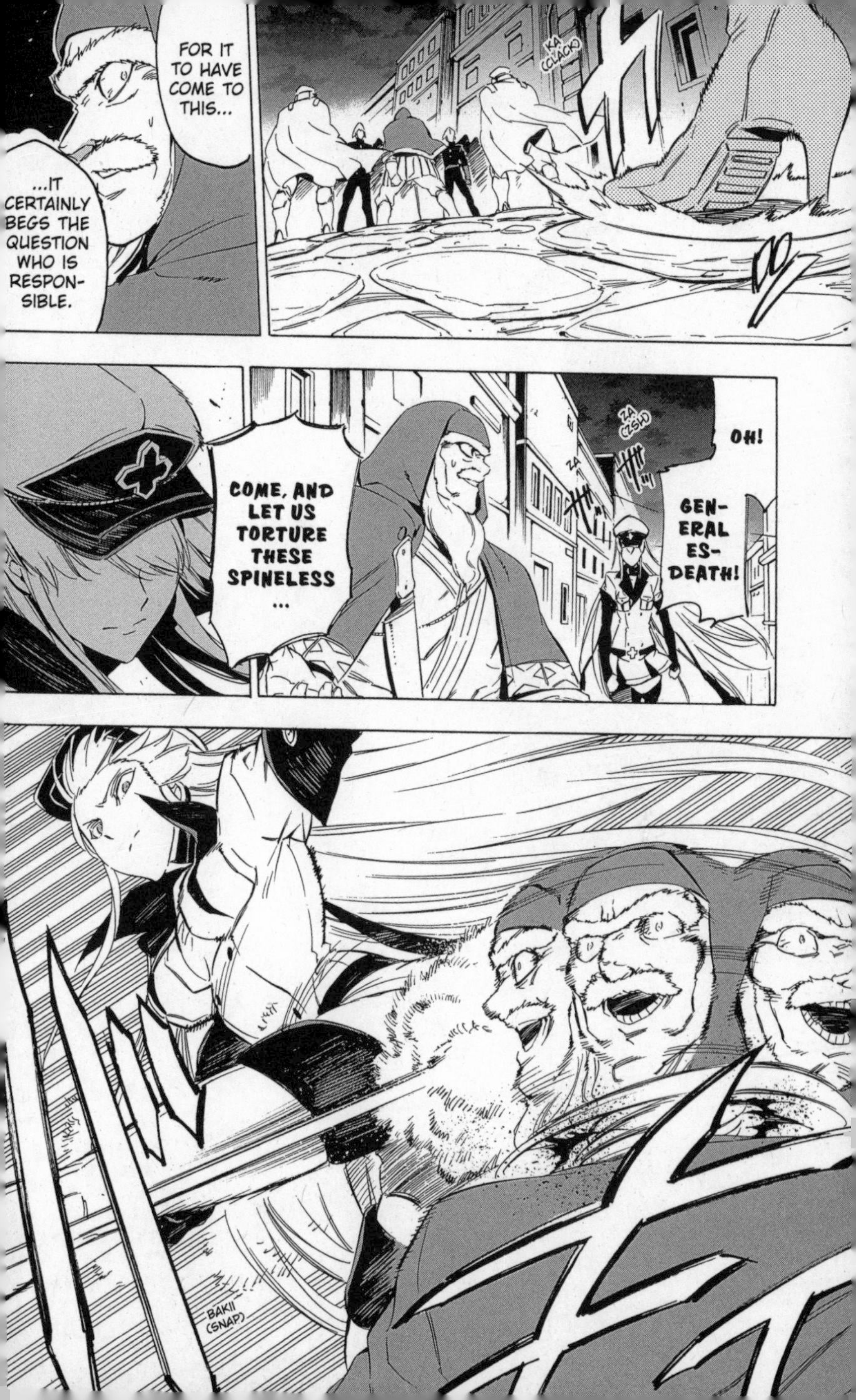
KA (CLACK)
FOR IT TO HAVE COME TO THIS...
...IT CERTAINLY BEGS THE QUESTION WHO IS RESPONSIBLE.
ZA (ZSH)
ZA
OH!
GENERAL ESDEATH!
COME, AND LET US TORTURE THESE SPINELESS ...
BAKII (SNAP)

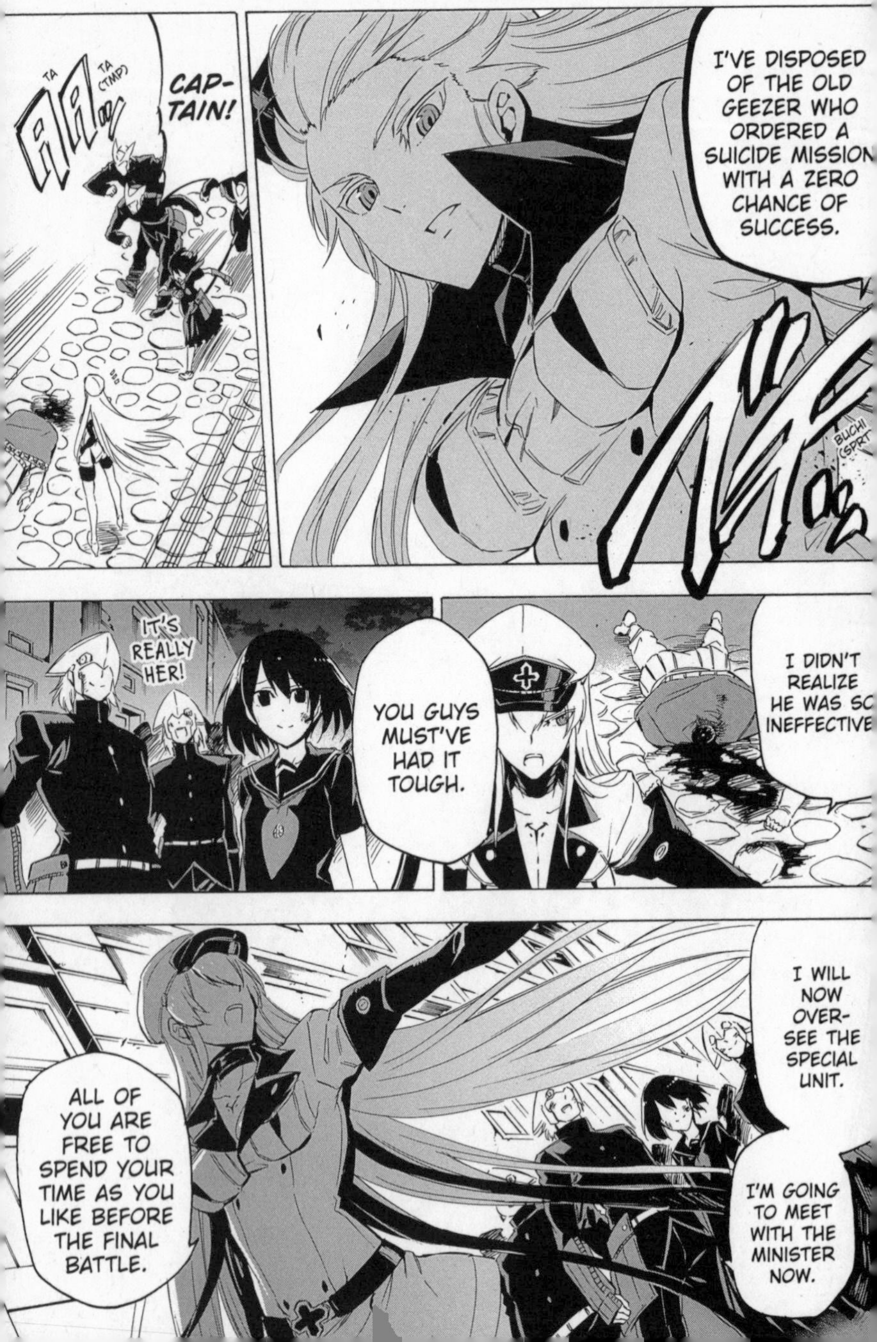
I'VE DISPOSED OF THE OLD GEEZER WHO ORDERED A SUICIDE MISSION WITH A ZERO CHANCE OF SUCCESS.
BUCHI (SPRT)
TA TA (TMP)
CAP-TAIN!
I DIDN'T REALIZE HE WAS SC INEFFECTIVE
YOU GUYS MUST'VE HAD IT TOUGH.
IT'S REALLY HER!
I WILL NOW OVER-SEE THE SPECIAL UNIT.
I'M GOING TO MEET WITH THE MINISTER NOW.
ALL OF YOU ARE FREE TO SPEND YOUR TIME AS YOU LIKE BEFORE THE FINAL BATTLE.

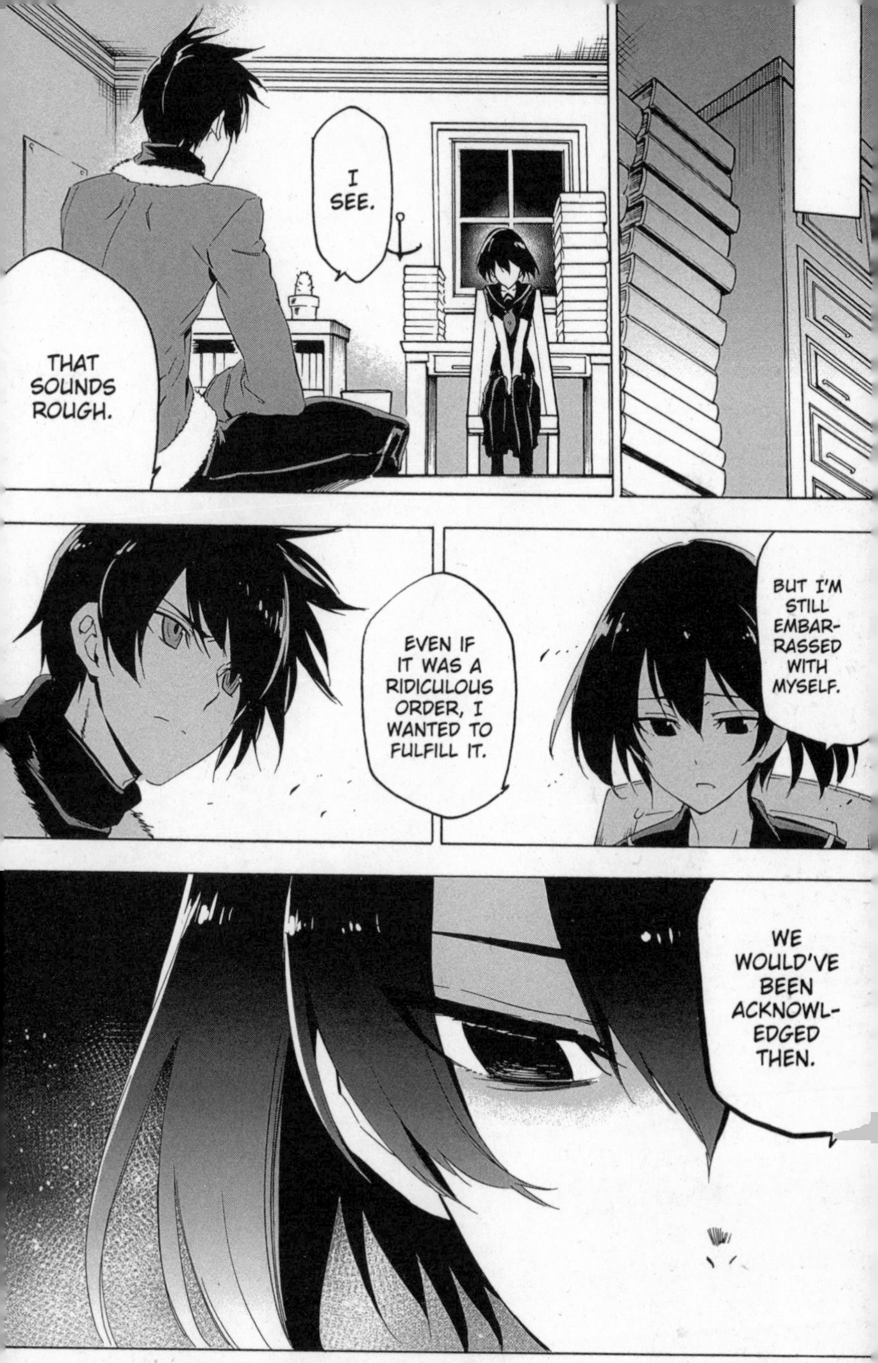
I SEE.
THAT SOUNDS ROUGH.
BUT I'M STILL EMBARRASSED WITH MYSELF.
EVEN IF IT WAS A RIDICULOUS ORDER, I WANTED TO FULFILL IT.
WE WOULD'VE BEEN ACKNOWLEDGED THEN.

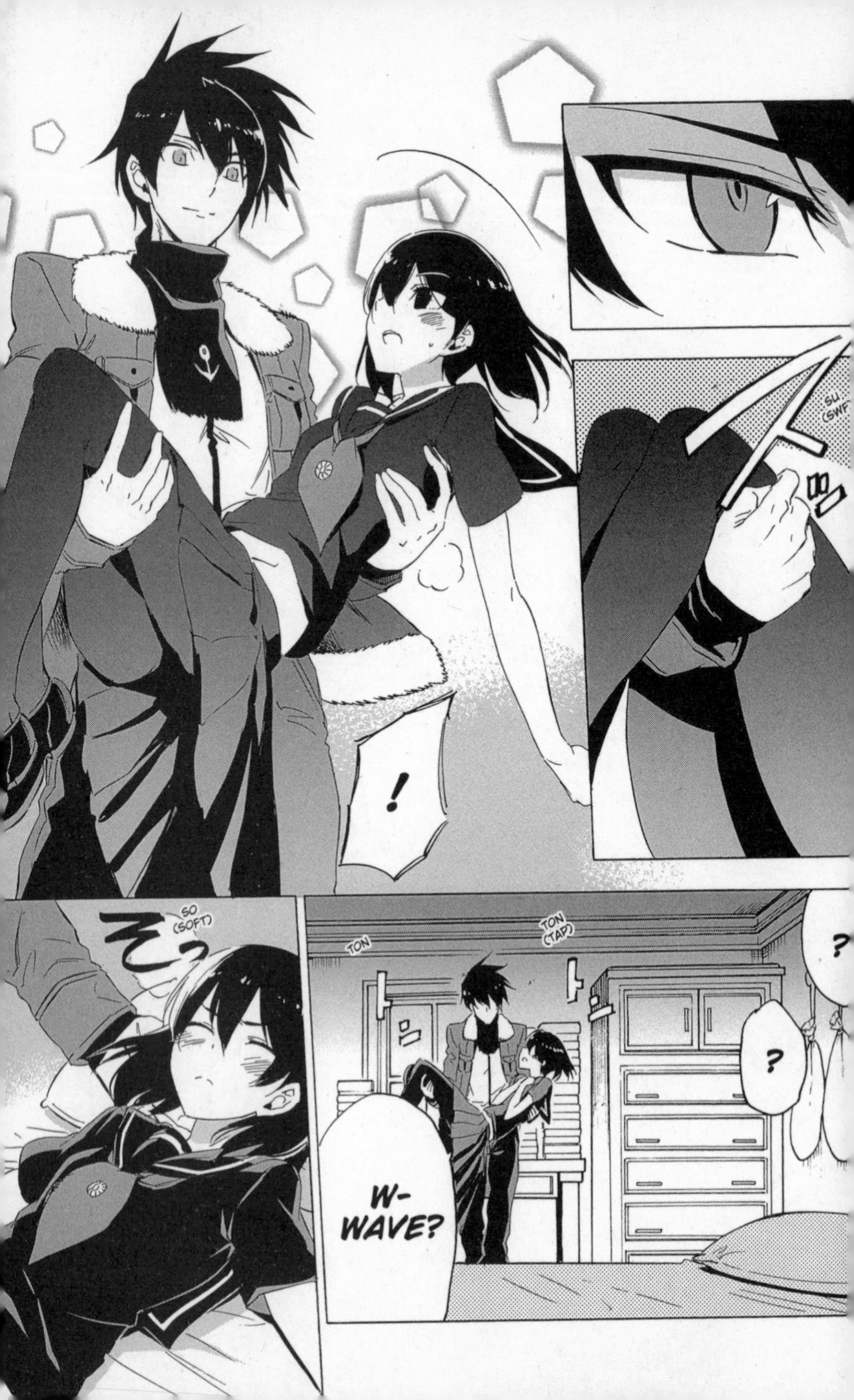
SU
(SWF
!
?
TON
(TAP)
?
TON
W-
WAVE?
SO
(SOFT)

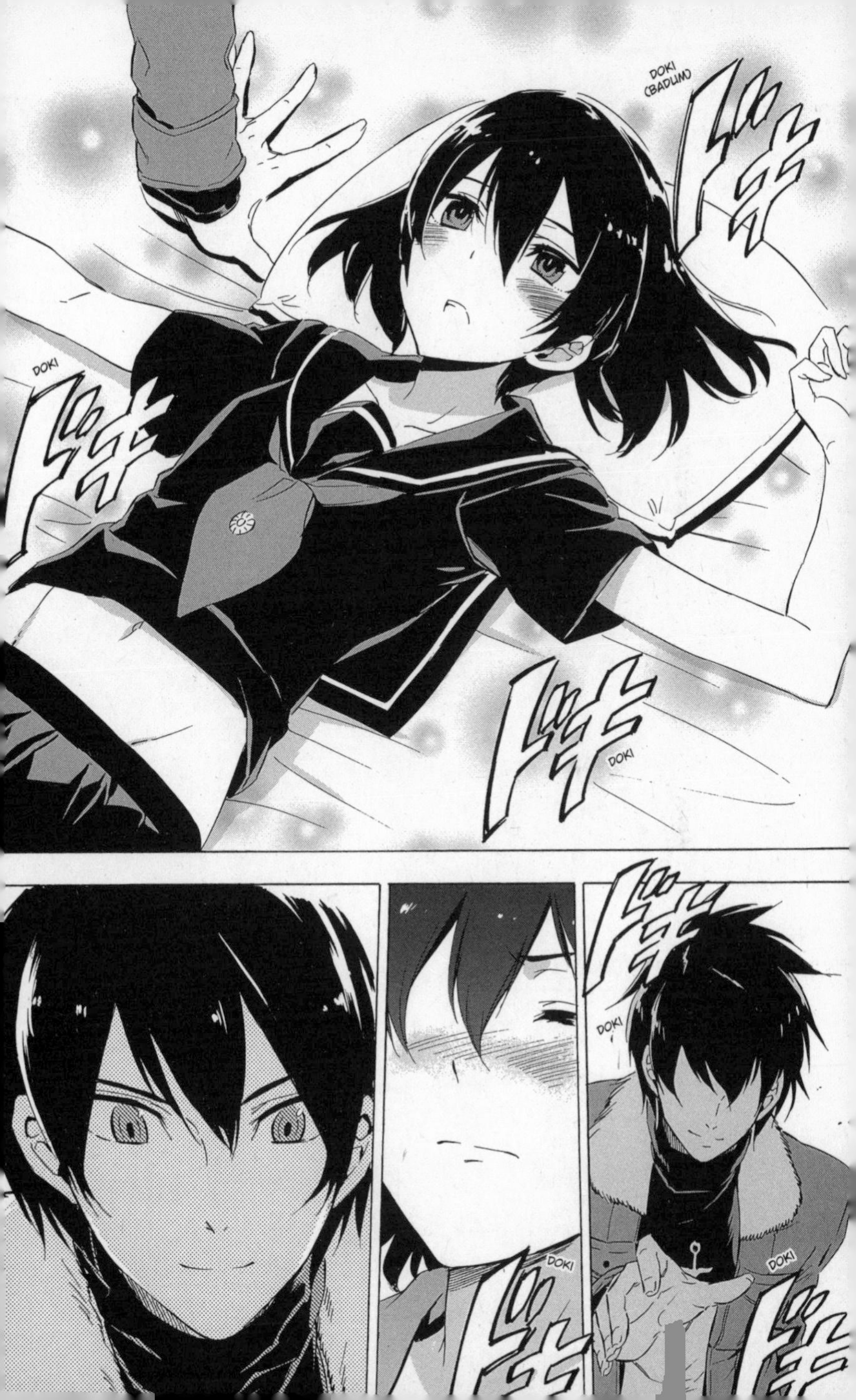
DOKI (BADUM)
DOKI
DOKI
DOKI
DOKI
DOKI

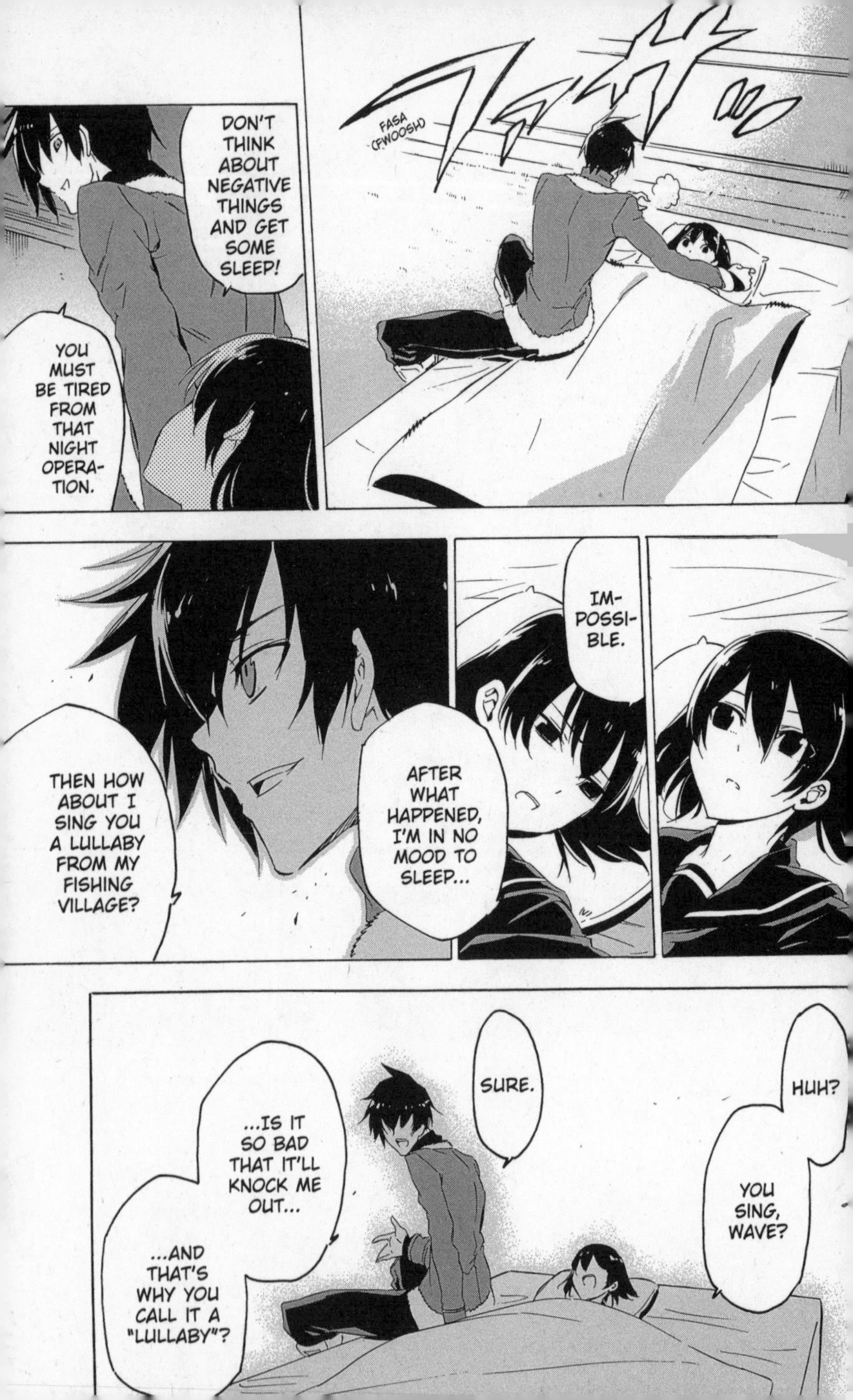
FASA (FWOOSH)
DON'T THINK ABOUT NEGATIVE THINGS AND GET SOME SLEEP!
YOU MUST BE TIRED FROM THAT NIGHT OPERATION.
IM-POSSI-BLE.
AFTER WHAT HAPPENED, I'M IN NO MOOD TO SLEEP...
THEN HOW ABOUT I SING YOU A LULLABY FROM MY FISHING VILLAGE?
HUH?
YOU SING, WAVE?
SURE.
...IS IT SO BAD THAT IT'LL KNOCK ME OUT...
...AND THAT'S WHY YOU CALL IT A "LULLABY"?

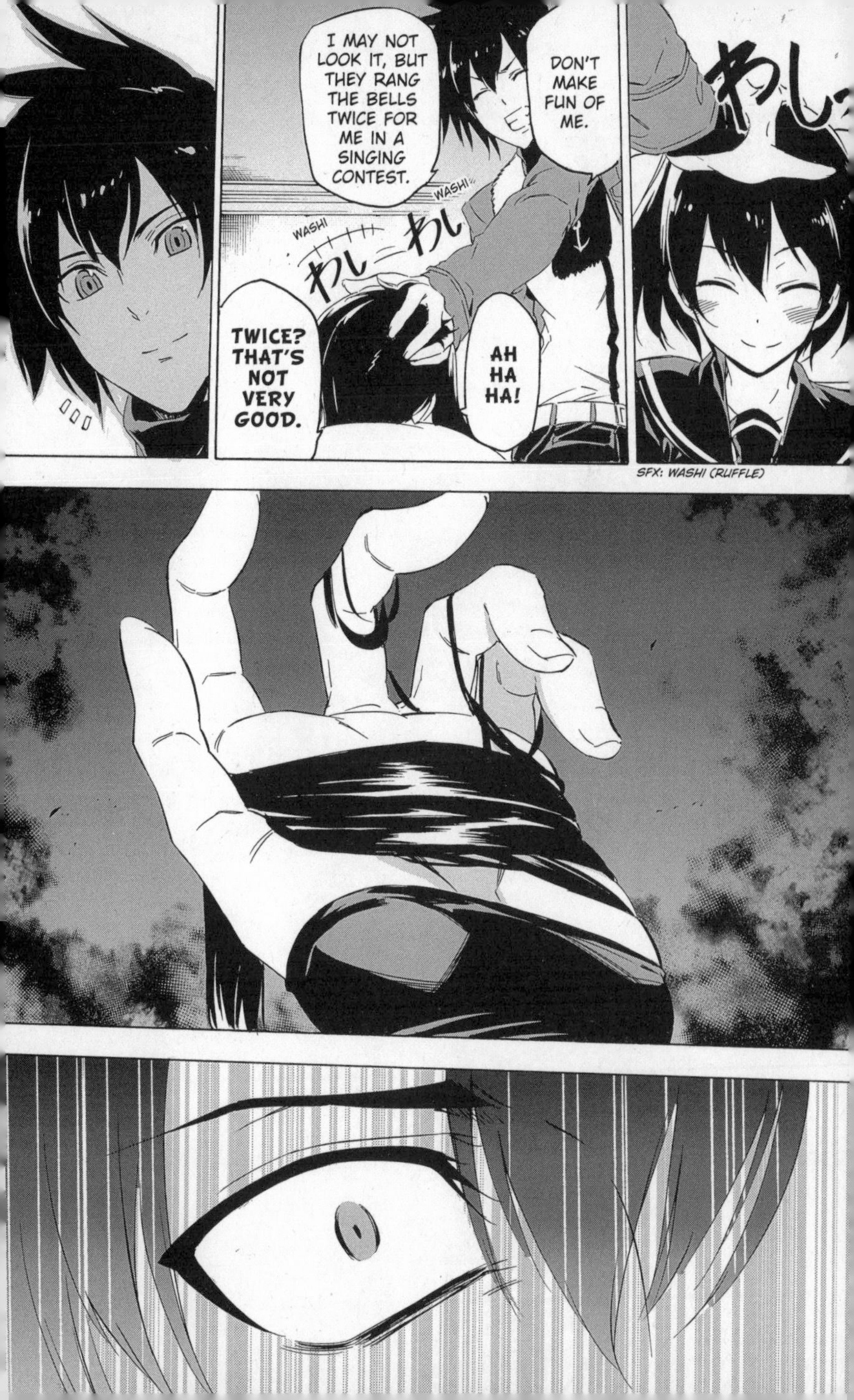
わし
I MAY NOT LOOK IT, BUT THEY RANG THE BELLS TWICE FOR ME IN A SINGING CONTEST.
TWICE? THAT'S NOT VERY GOOD.
DON'T MAKE FUN OF ME.
WASHI
わし
WASHI
わし
AH HA HA!
...
SFX: WASHI (RUFFLE)

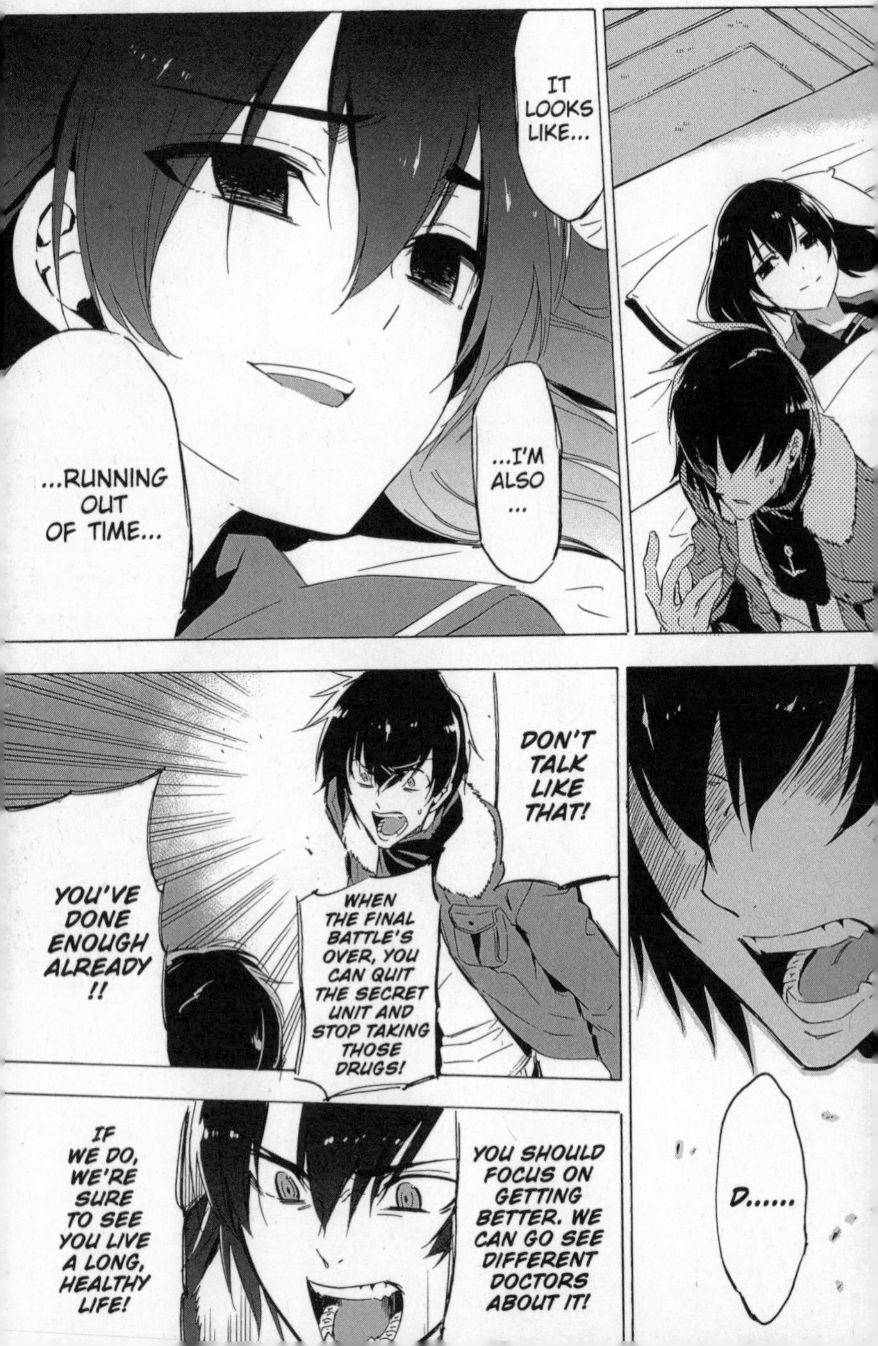
IT LOOKS LIKE...
...I'M ALSO ...
...RUNNING OUT OF TIME...
D......
DON'T TALK LIKE THAT!
WHEN THE FINAL BATTLE'S OVER, YOU CAN QUIT THE SECRET UNIT AND STOP TAKING THOSE DRUGS!
YOU'VE DONE ENOUGH ALREADY !!
YOU SHOULD FOCUS ON GETTING BETTER. WE CAN GO SEE DIFFERENT DOCTORS ABOUT IT!
IF WE DO, WE'RE SURE TO SEE YOU LIVE A LONG, HEALTHY LIFE!

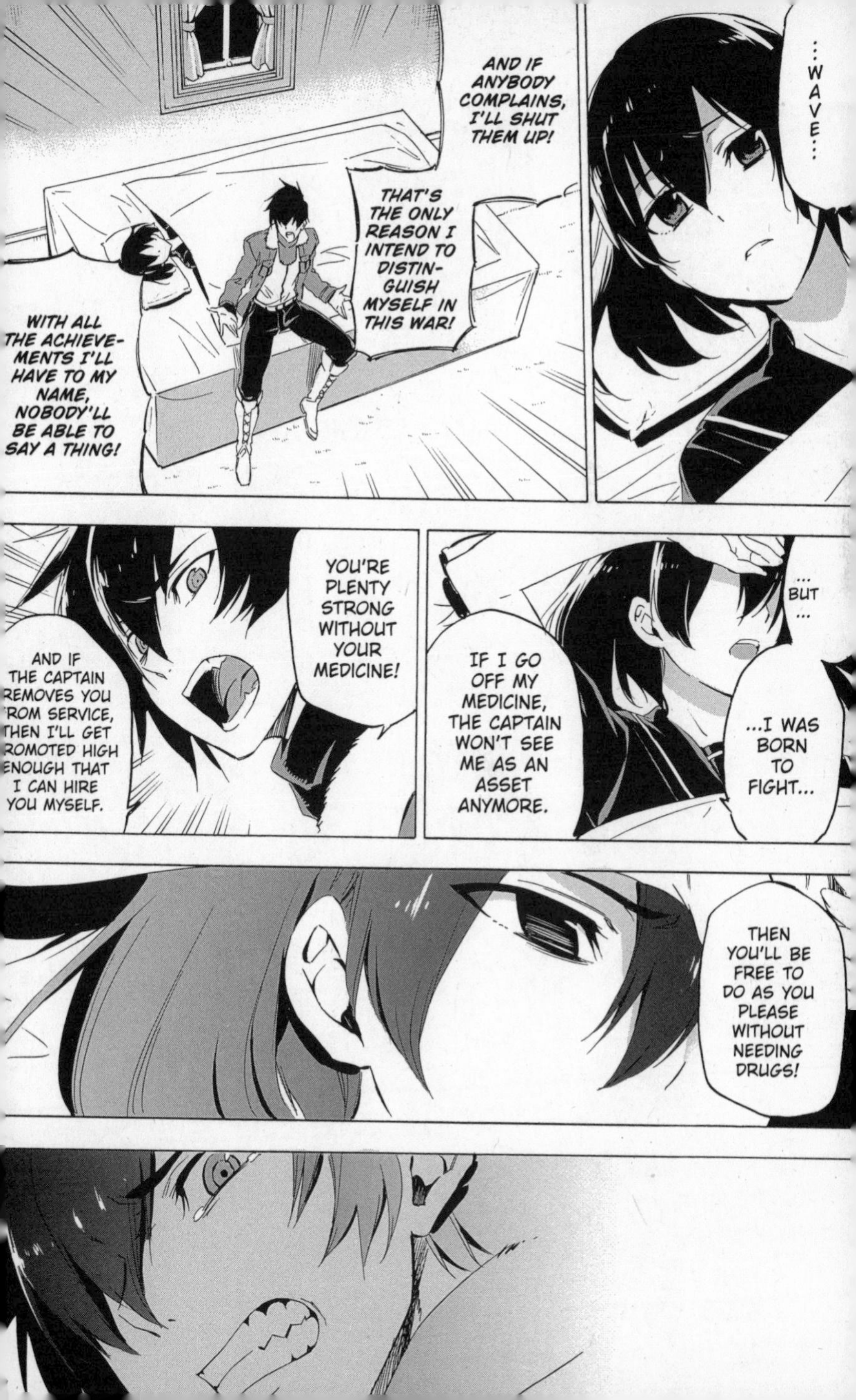
...WAVE...
AND IF ANYBODY COMPLAINS, I'LL SHUT THEM UP!
THAT'S THE ONLY REASON I INTEND TO DISTIN-GUISH MYSELF IN THIS WAR!
WITH ALL THE ACHIEVE-MENTS I'LL HAVE TO MY NAME, NOBODY'LL BE ABLE TO SAY A THING!
...BUT...
IF I GO OFF MY MEDICINE, THE CAPTAIN WON'T SEE ME AS AN ASSET ANYMORE.
...I WAS BORN TO FIGHT...
YOU'RE PLENTY STRONG WITHOUT YOUR MEDICINE!
AND IF THE CAPTAIN REMOVES YOU FROM SERVICE, THEN I'LL GET ROMOTED HIGH ENOUGH THAT I CAN HIRE YOU MYSELF.
THEN YOU'LL BE FREE TO DO AS YOU PLEASE WITHOUT NEEDING DRUGS!

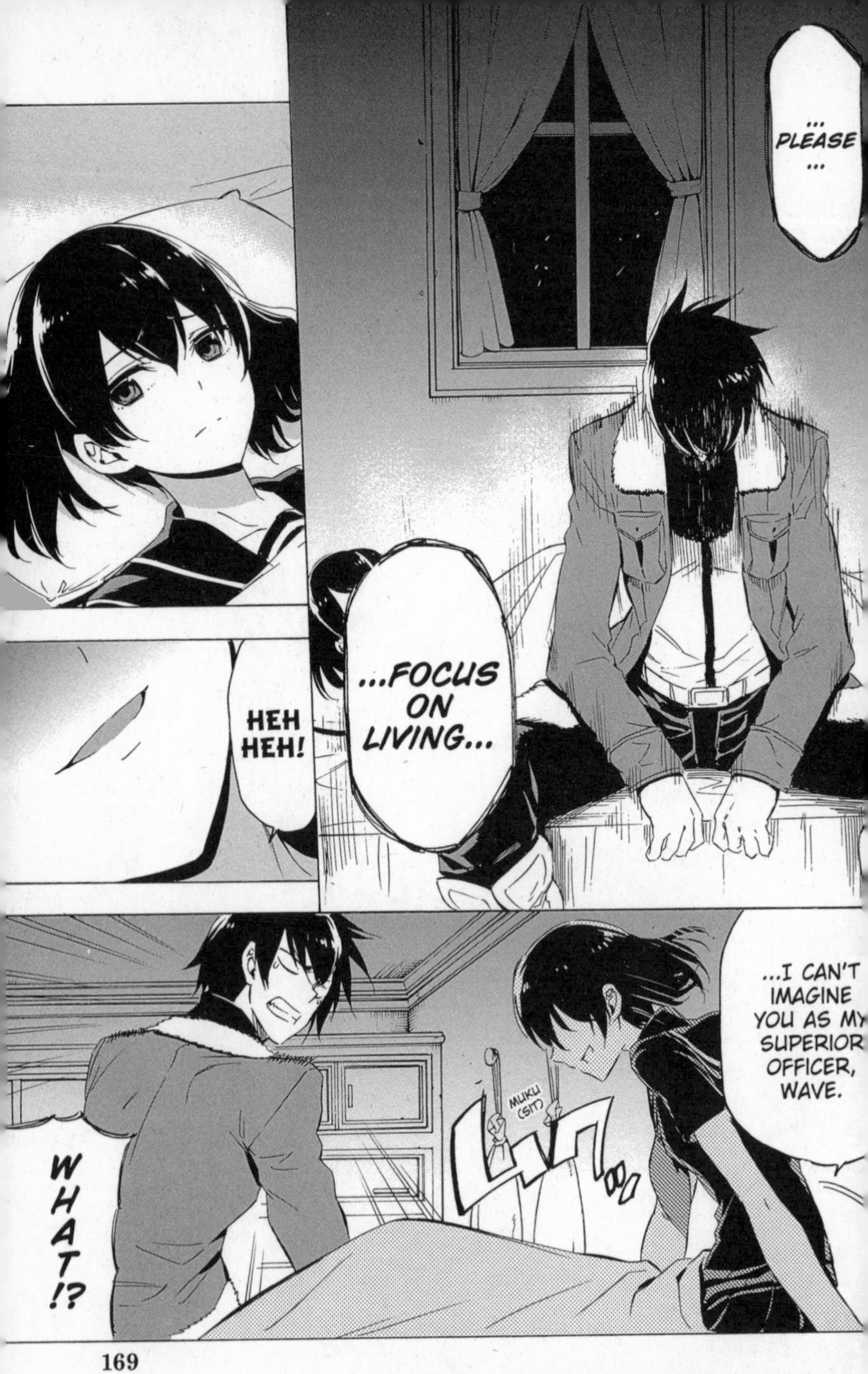
...PLEASE...
...FOCUS ON LIVING...
HEH HEH!
...I CAN'T IMAGINE YOU AS MY SUPERIOR OFFICER, WAVE.
MUKU (SIT)
WHAT!?

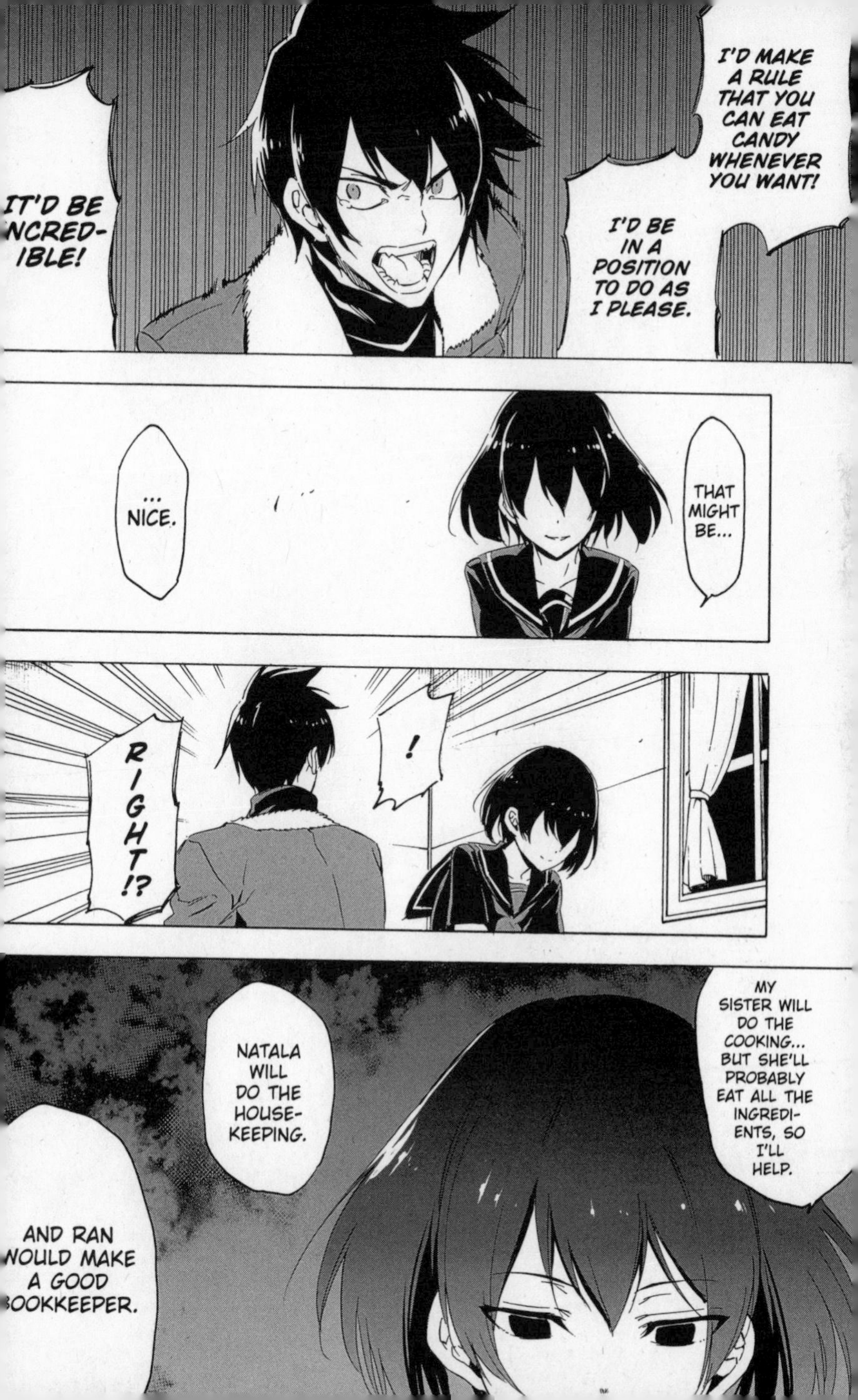
I'D MAKE A RULE THAT YOU CAN EAT CANDY WHENEVER YOU WANT!
I'D BE IN A POSITION TO DO AS I PLEASE.
IT'D BE NCRED-IBLE!
THAT MIGHT BE...
... NICE.
!
RIGHT!?
MY SISTER WILL DO THE COOKING... BUT SHE'LL PROBABLY EAT ALL THE INGREDI-ENTS, SO I'LL HELP.
NATALA WILL DO THE HOUSE-KEEPING.
AND RAN NOULD MAKE A GOOD OOKKEEPER.

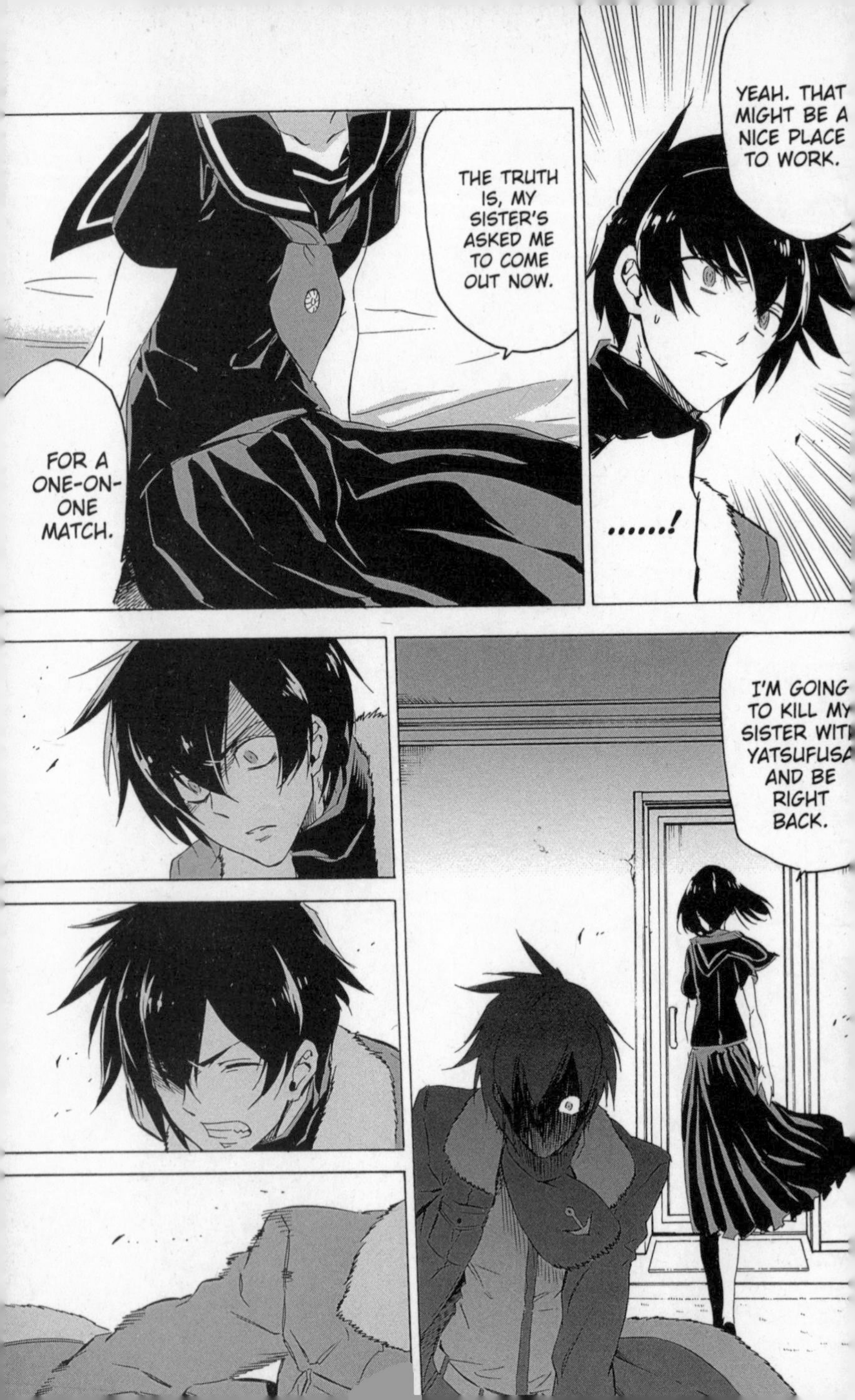
YEAH. THAT MIGHT BE A NICE PLACE TO WORK.
......!
THE TRUTH IS, MY SISTER'S ASKED ME TO COME OUT NOW.
FOR A ONE-ON-ONE MATCH.
I'M GOING TO KILL MY SISTER WITH YATSUFUSA AND BE RIGHT BACK.

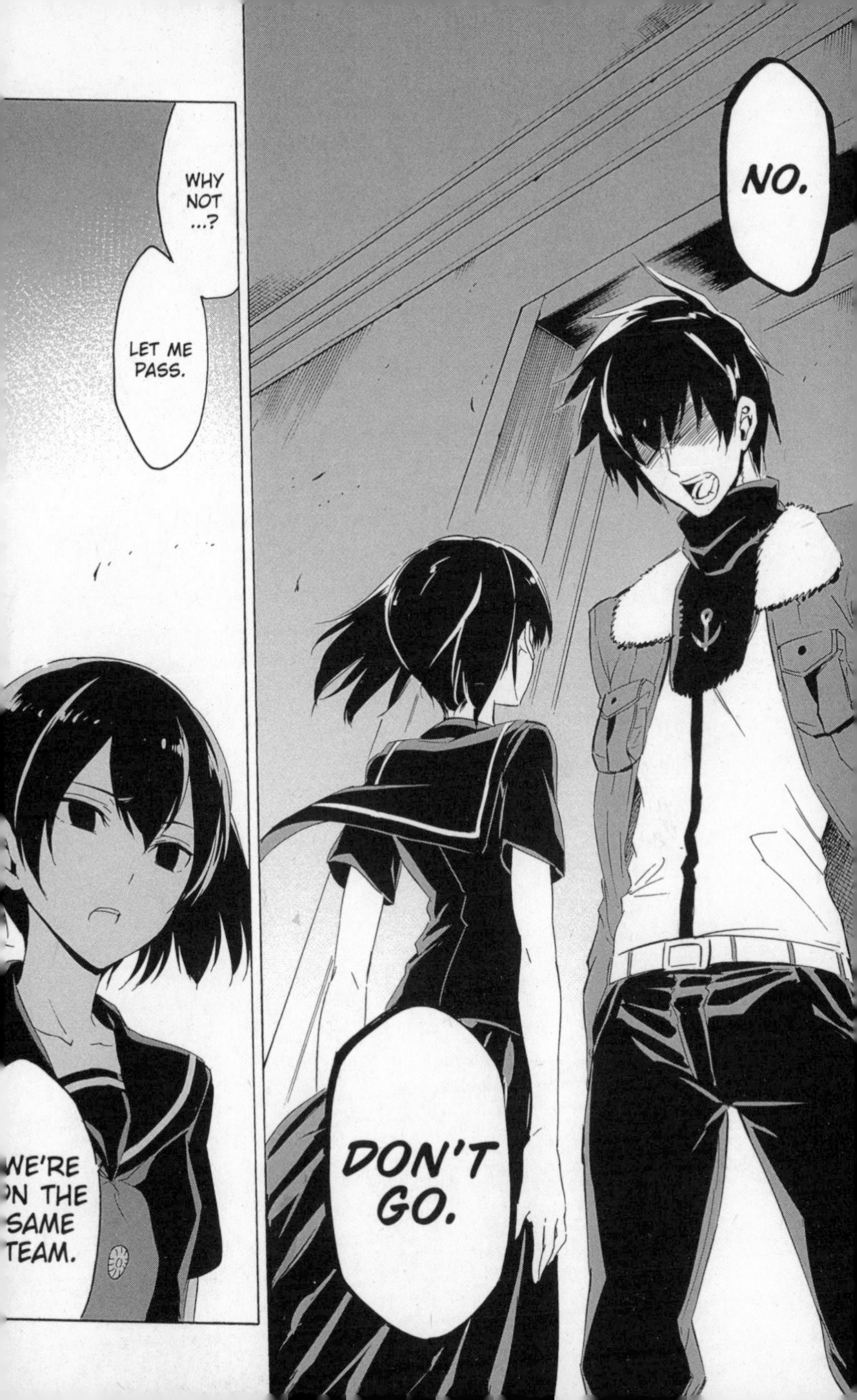
NO.
DON'T GO.
WHY NOT ...?
LET ME PASS.
WE'RE ON THE SAME TEAM.

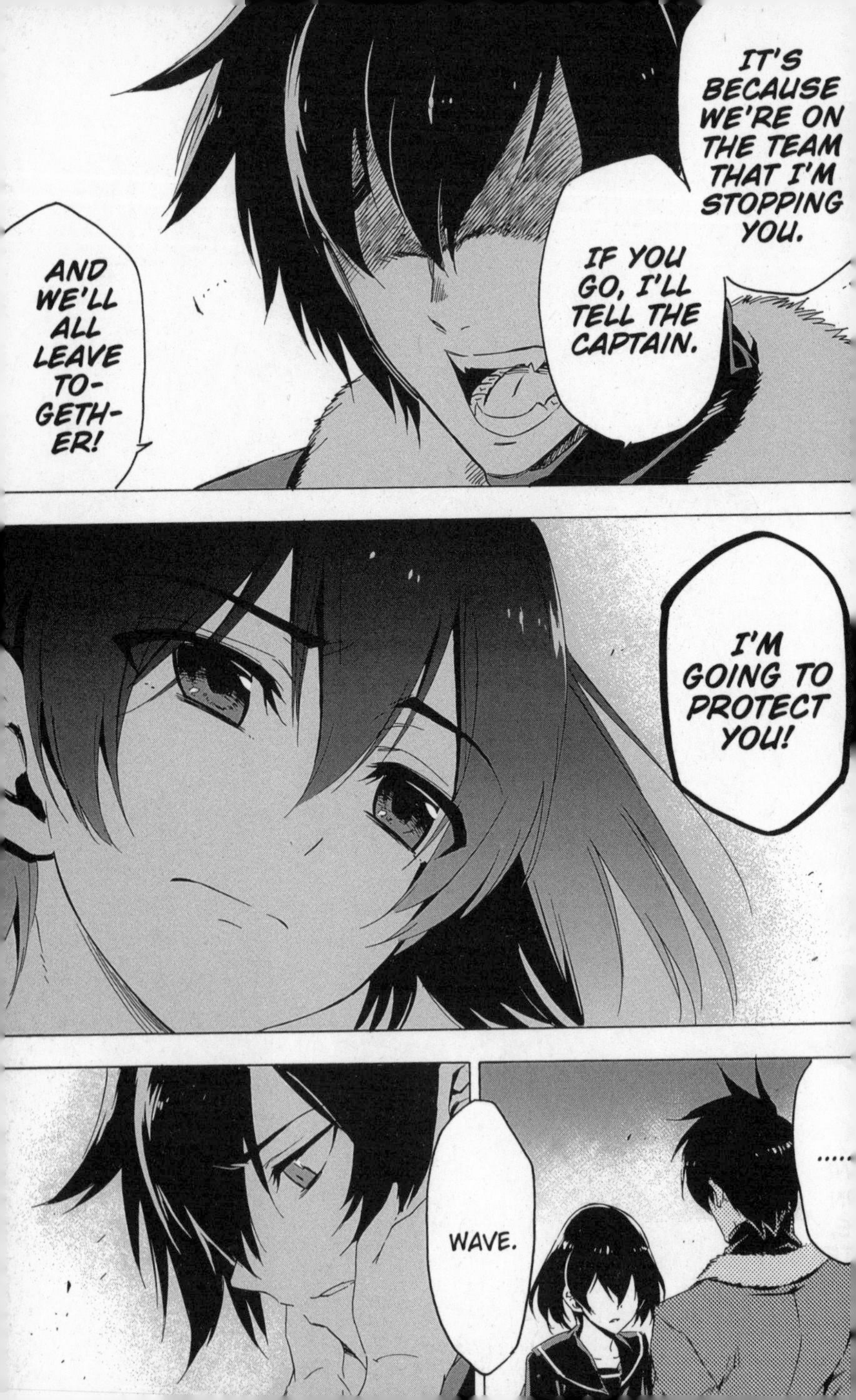
IT'S BECAUSE WE'RE ON THE TEAM THAT I'M STOPPING YOU.
IF YOU GO, I'LL TELL THE CAPTAIN.
AND WE'LL ALL LEAVE TO-GETH-ER!
I'M GOING TO PROTECT YOU!
.....
WAVE.

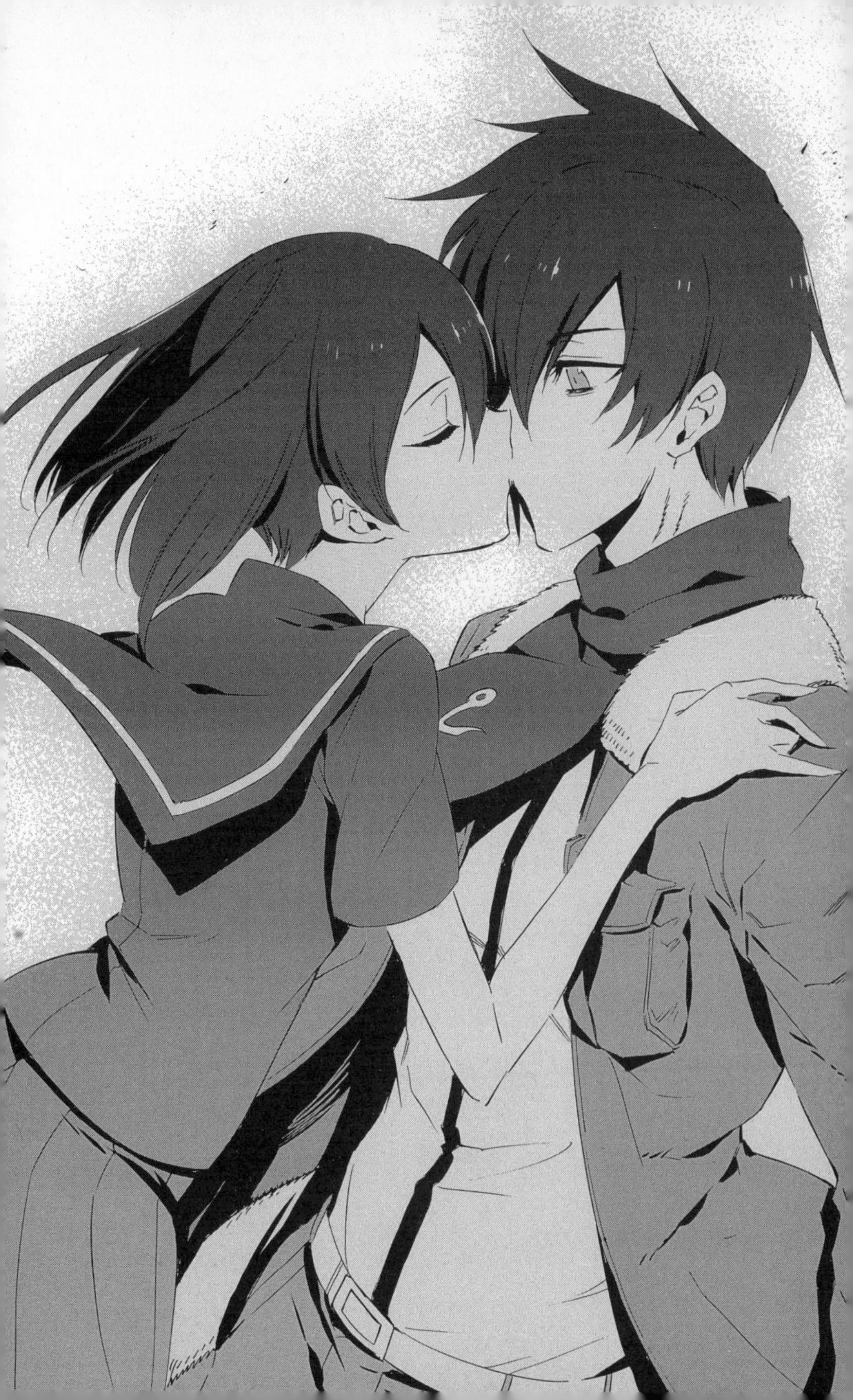

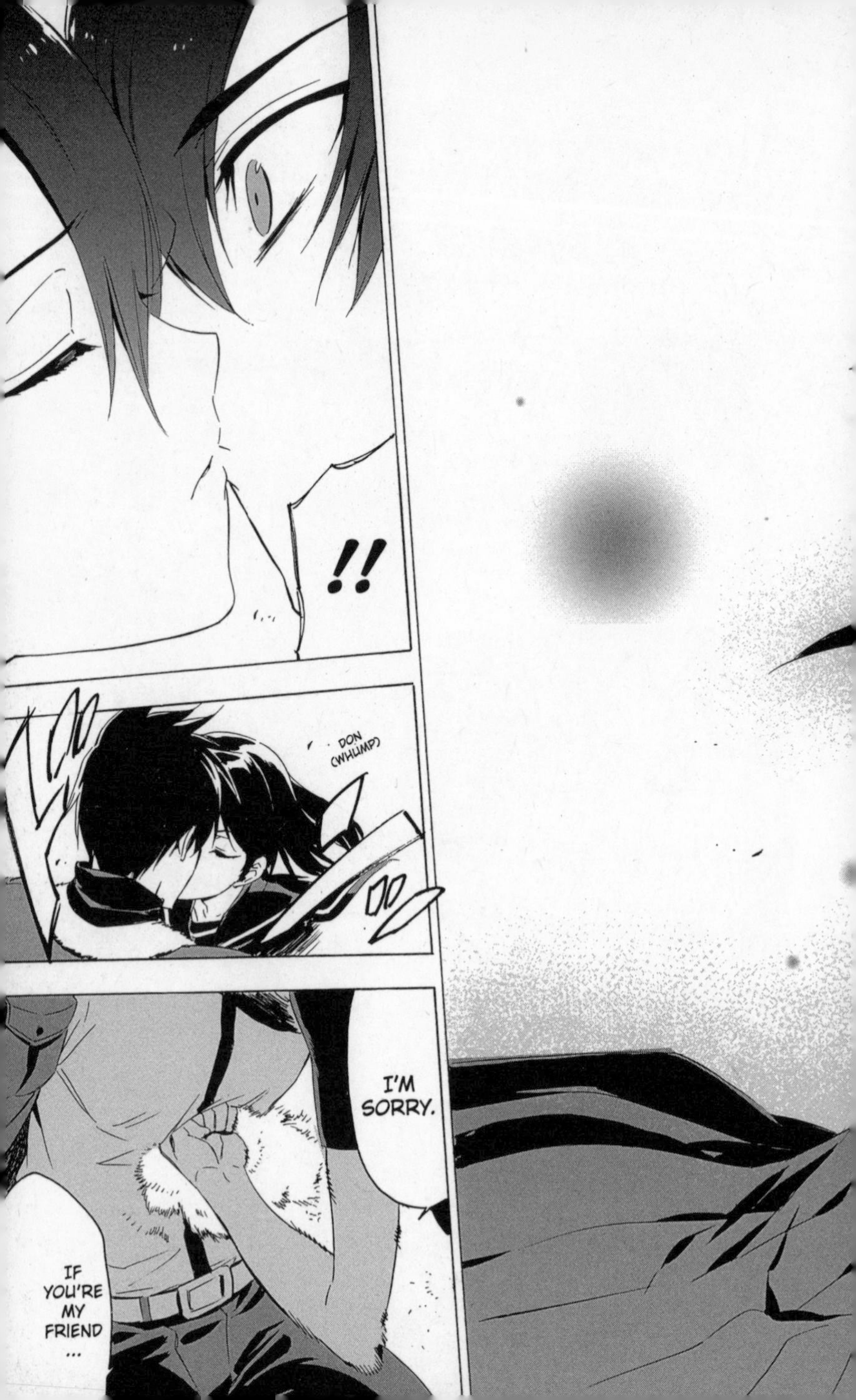
!!
DON (WHUMP)
I'M SORRY.
IF YOU'RE MY FRIEND ...

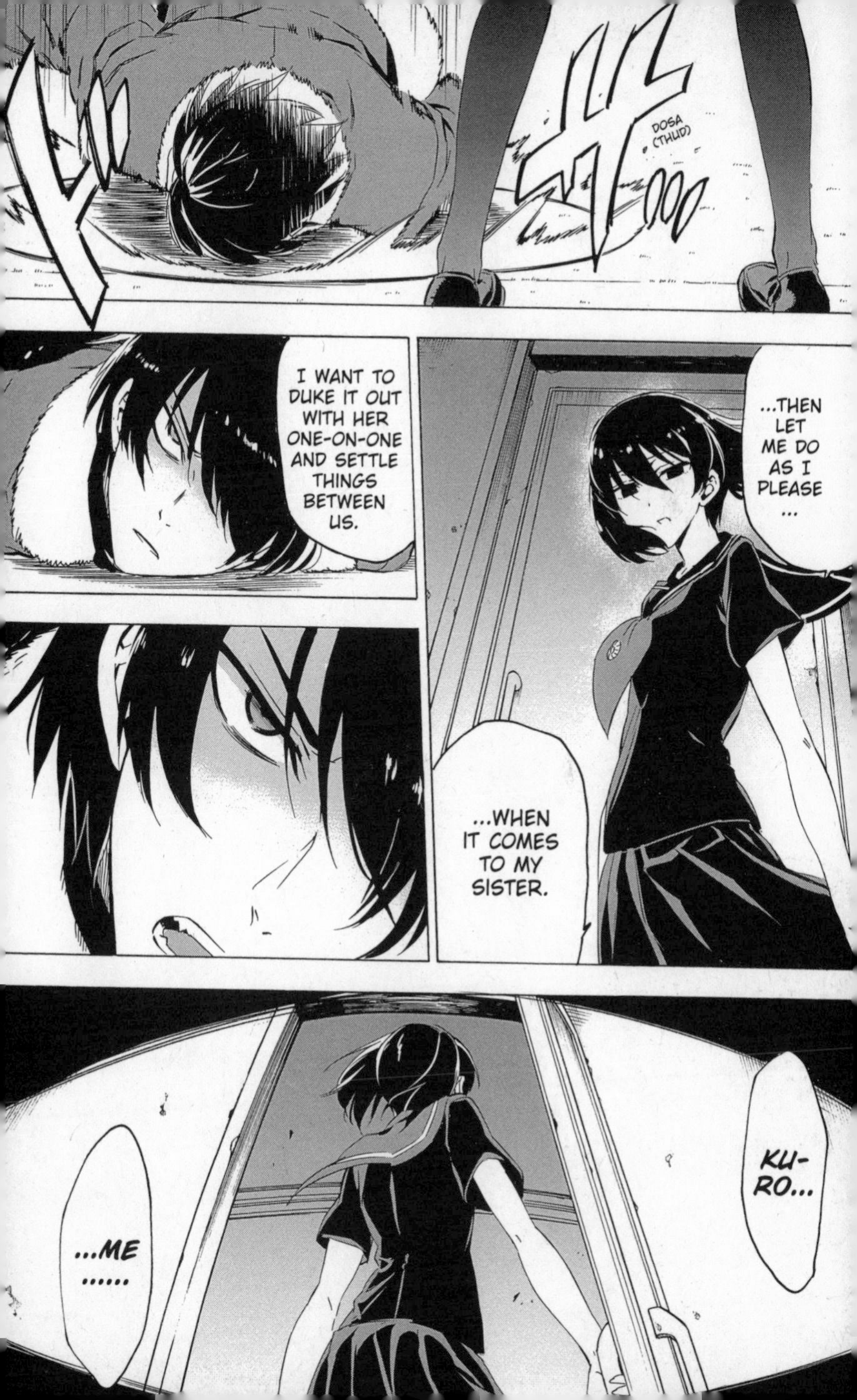
DOSA (THUD)
...THEN LET ME DO AS I PLEASE ...
I WANT TO DUKE IT OUT WITH HER ONE-ON-ONE AND SETTLE THINGS BETWEEN US.
...WHEN IT COMES TO MY SISTER.
KU-RO...
...ME ......

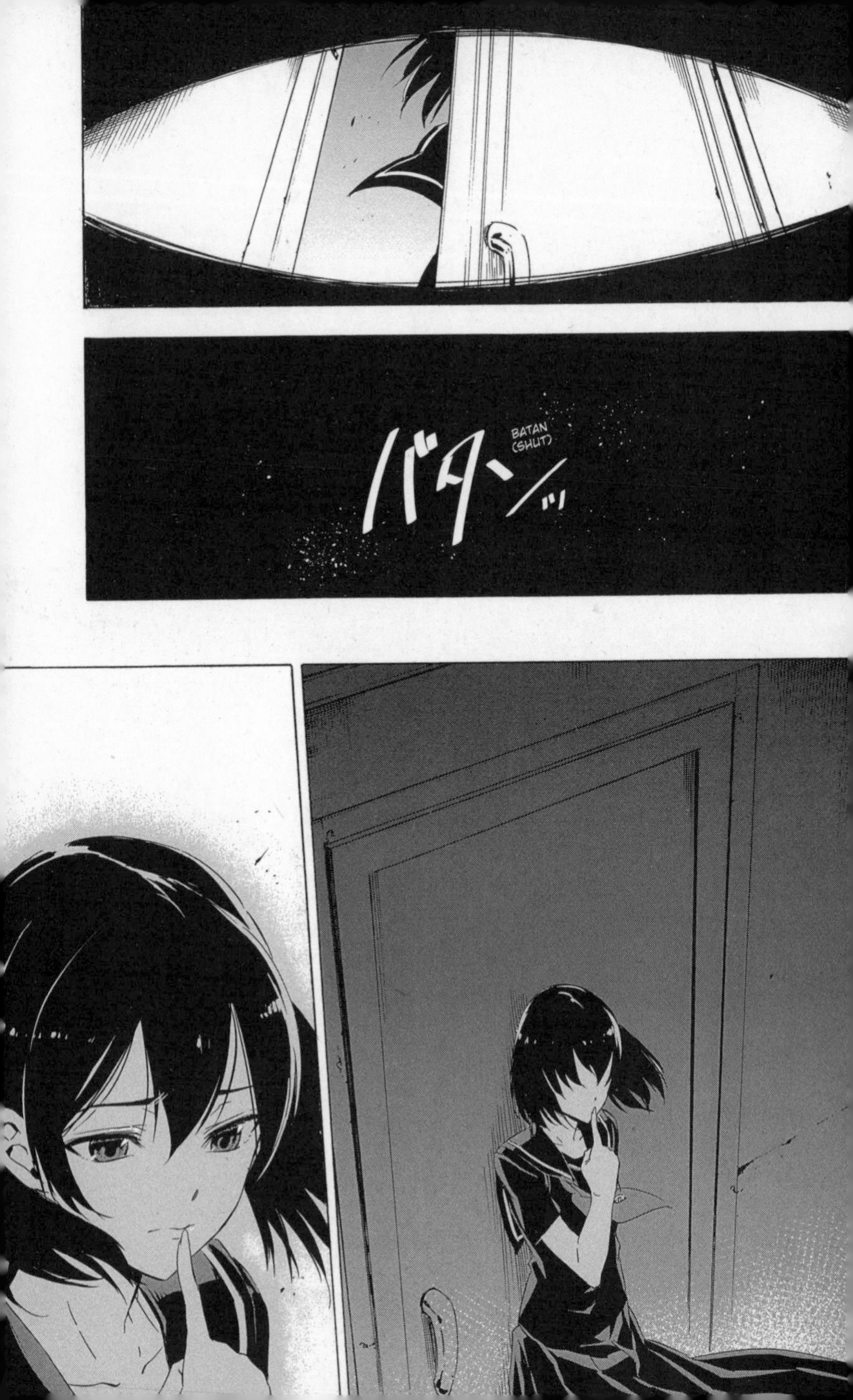
バタンッ
BATAN (SHUT)

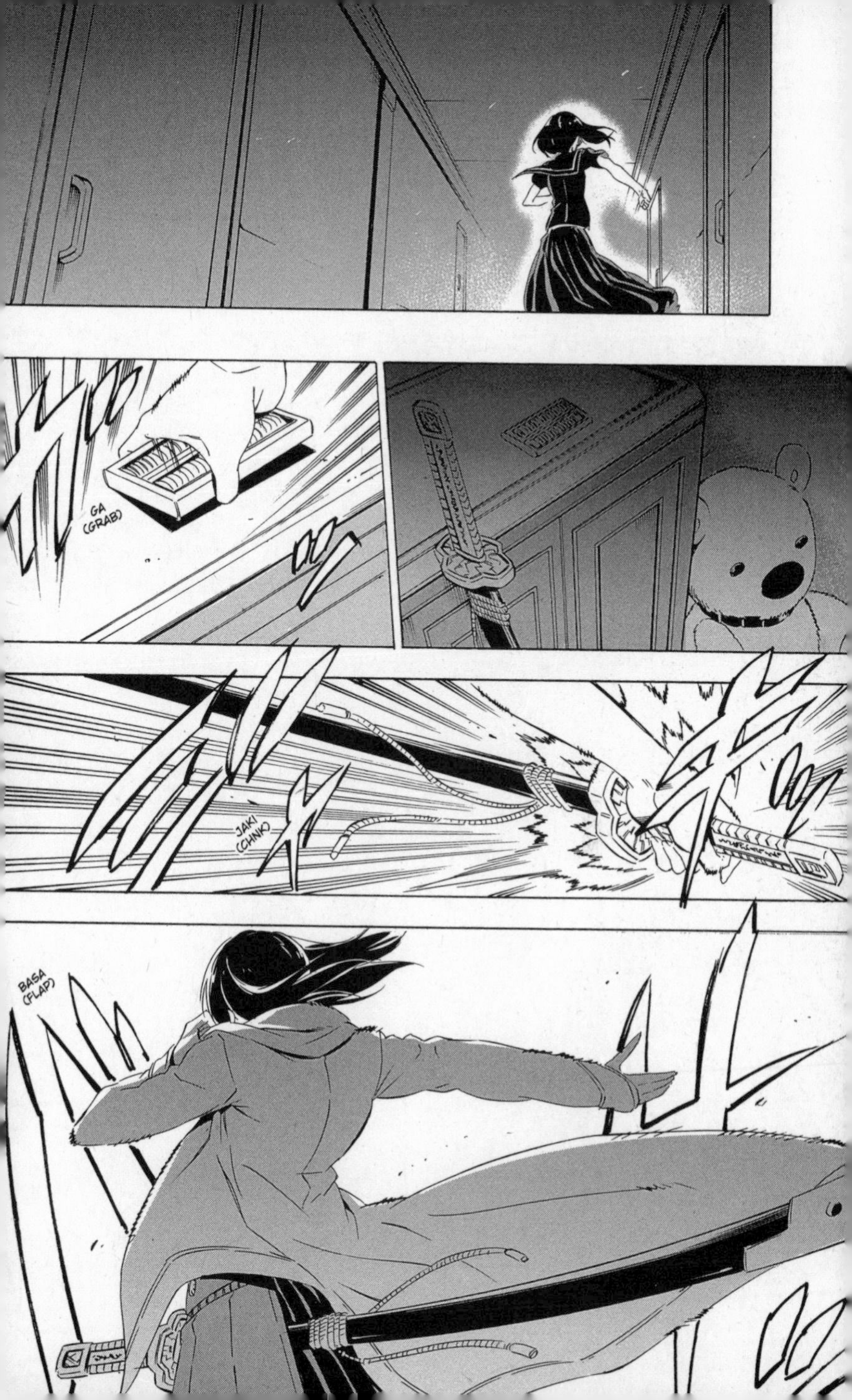
GA
(GRAB)
JAKI
(CHINK)
BASA
(FLAP)

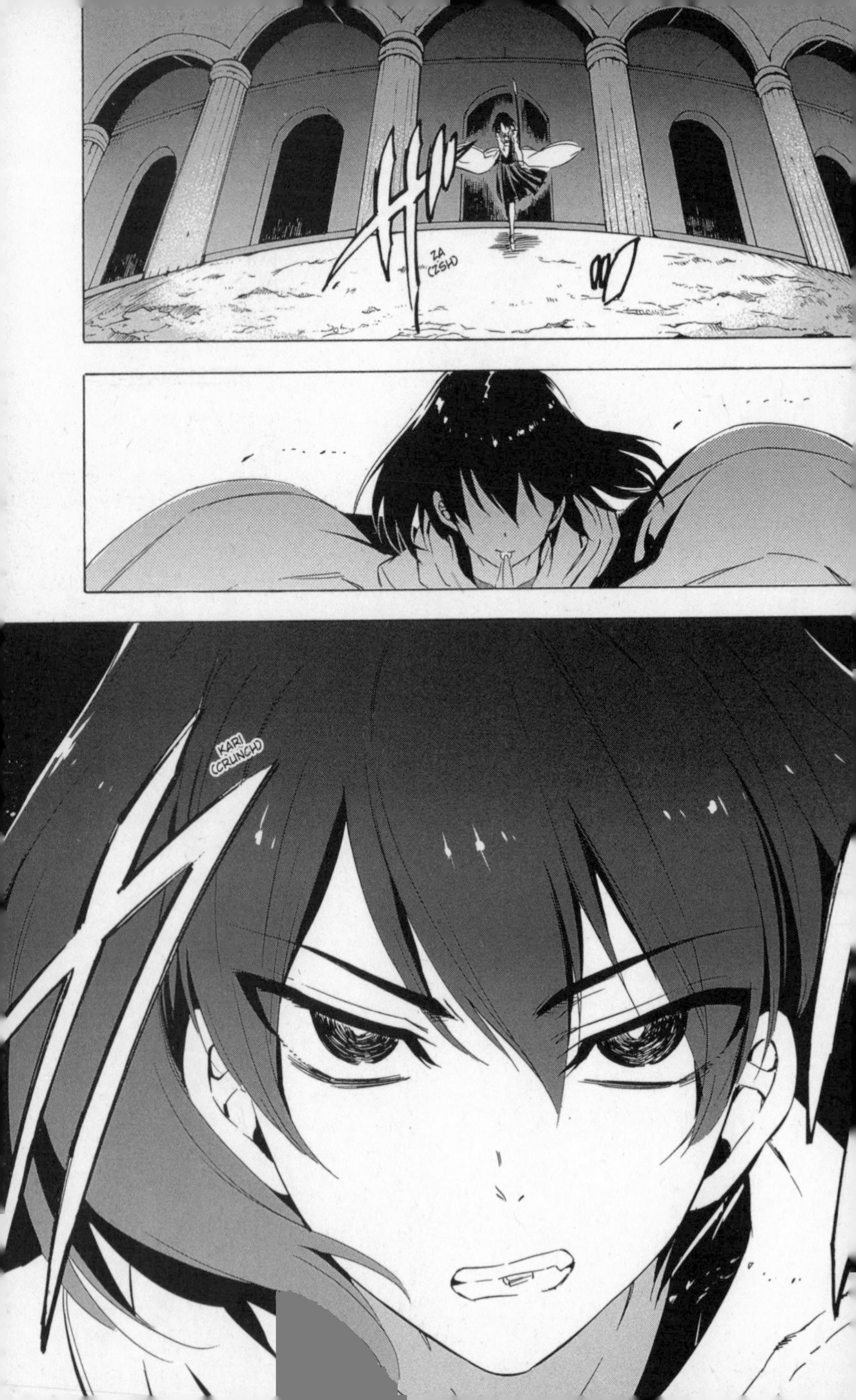
ZA (ZSH)
KARI (CRUNCH)

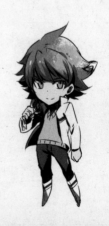

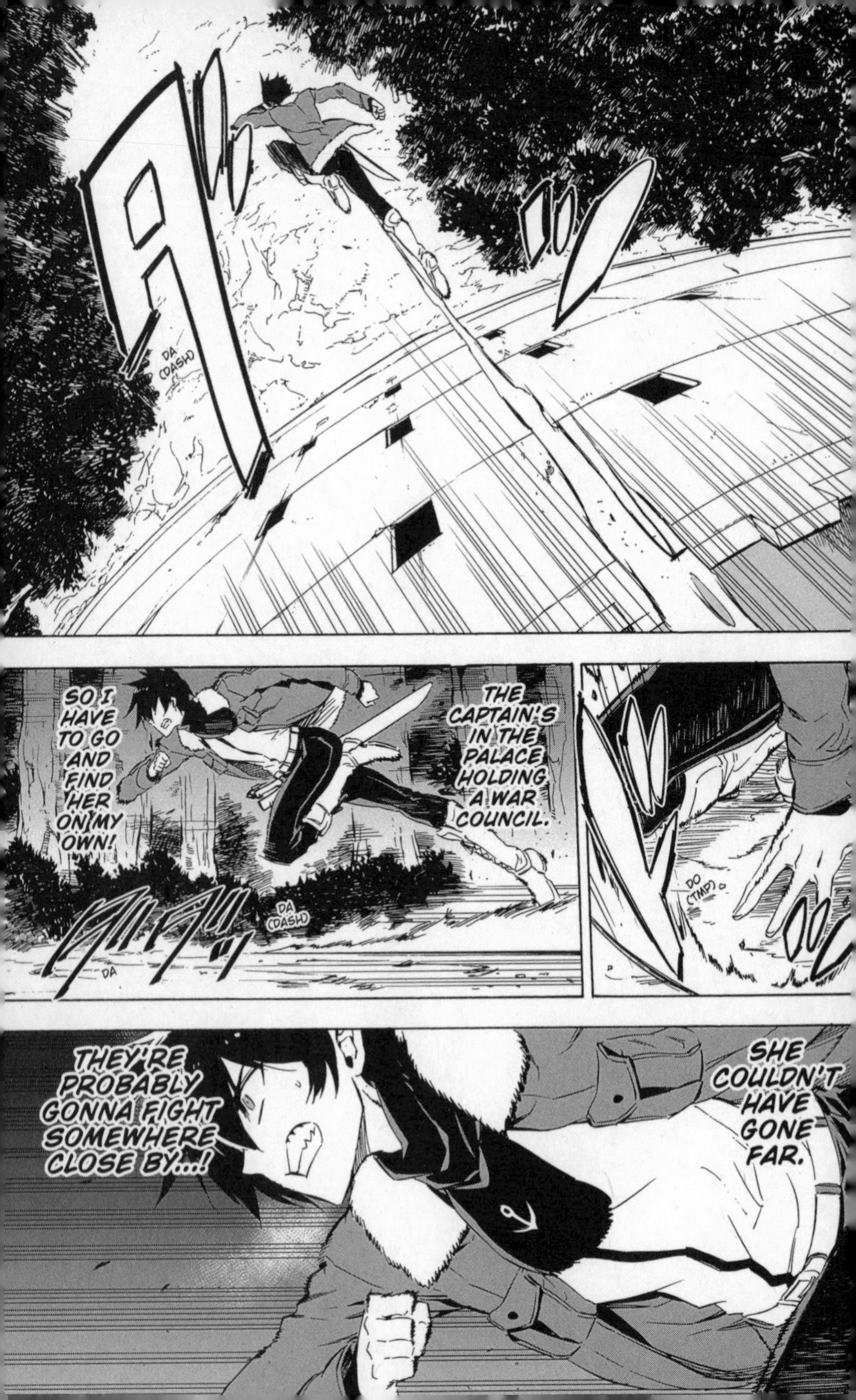
DA (DASH)
DO (TMP)
THE CAPTAIN'S IN THE PALACE HOLDING A WAR COUNCIL.
SO I HAVE TO GO AND FIND HER ON MY OWN!
DA (DASH)
DA
SHE COULDN'T HAVE GONE FAR.
THEY'RE PROBABLY GONNA FIGHT SOMEWHERE CLOSE BY...!

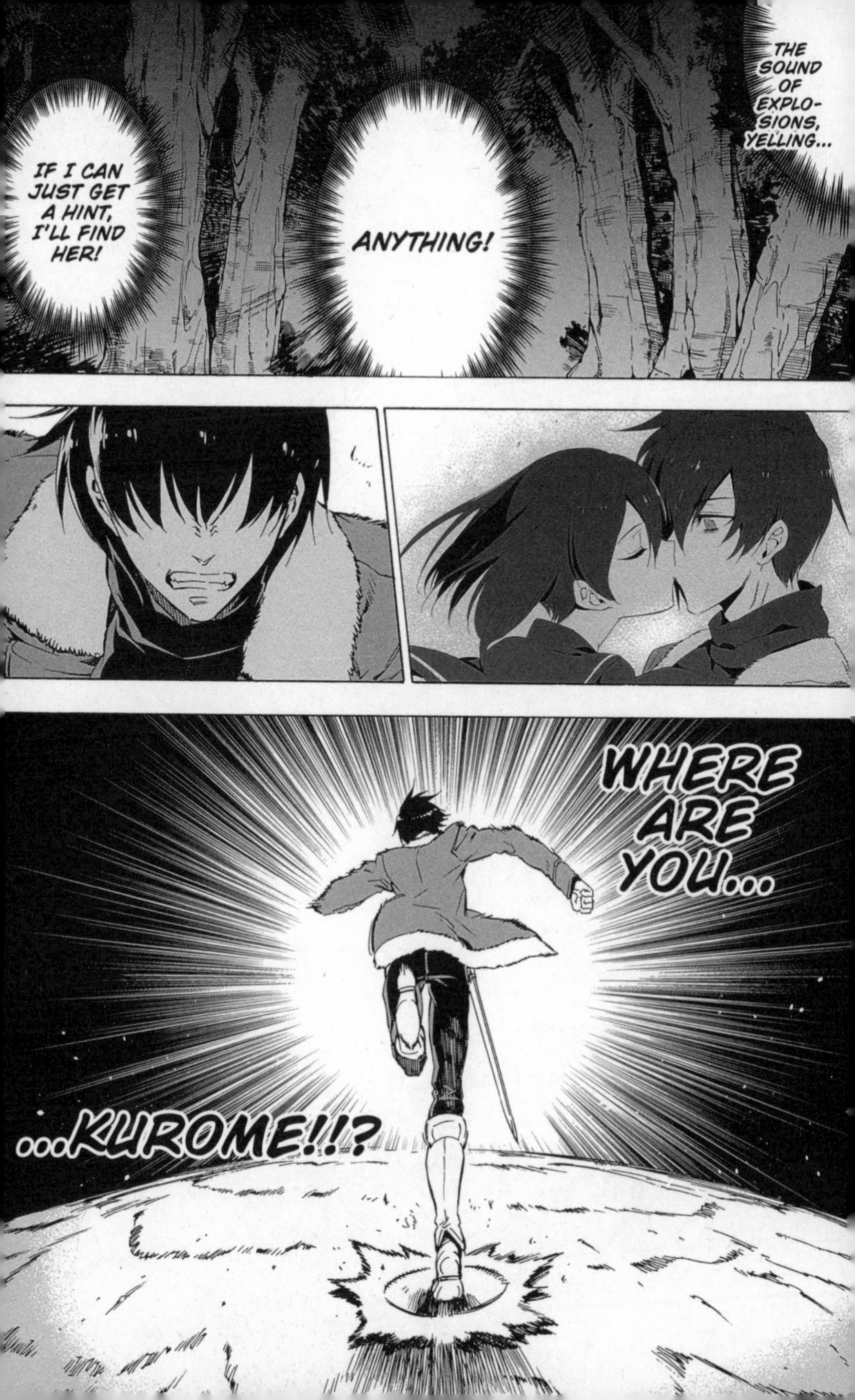
THE SOUND OF EXPLOSIONS, YELLING...
ANYTHING!
IF I CAN JUST GET A HINT, I'LL FIND HER!
WHERE ARE YOU...
...KUROME!!?

Chapter 65 - Kill the Little Sister (Part II)

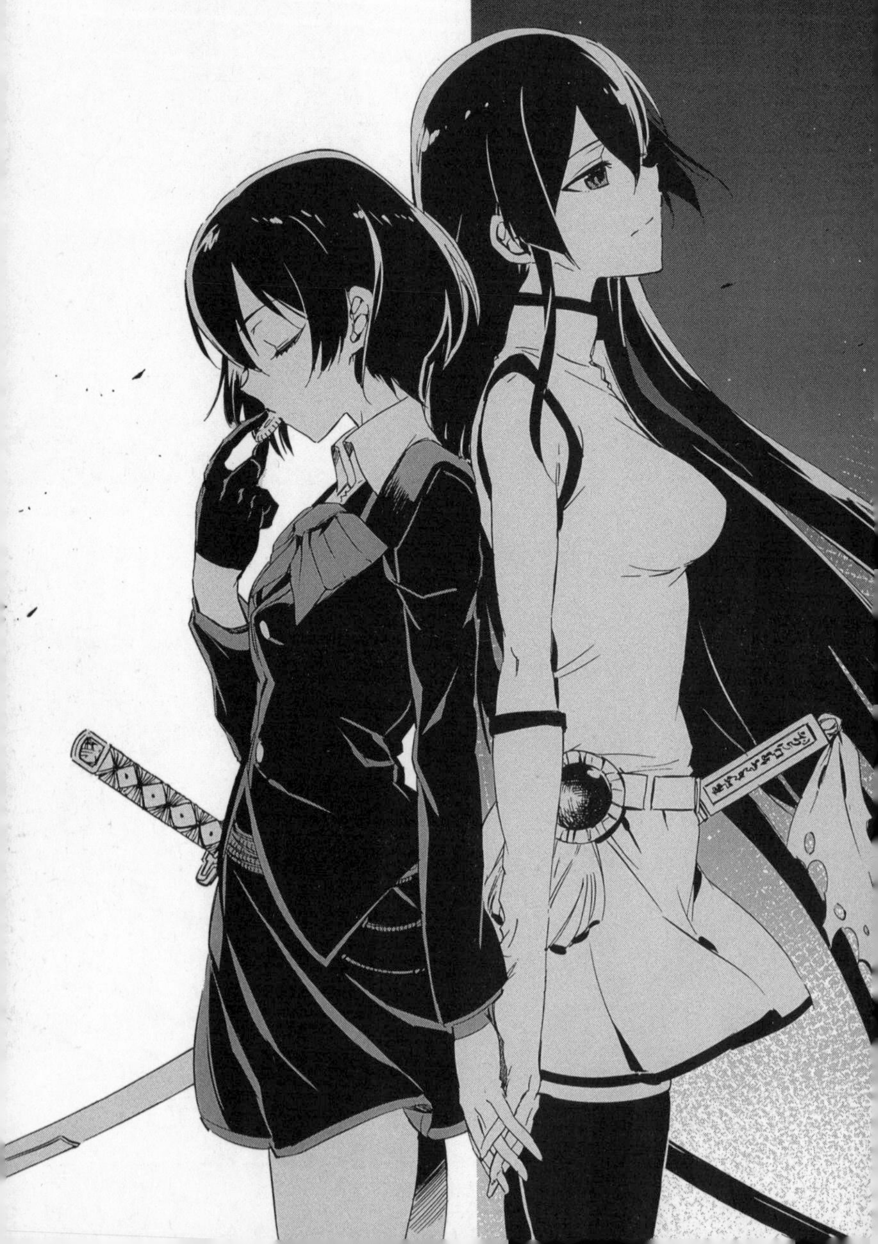

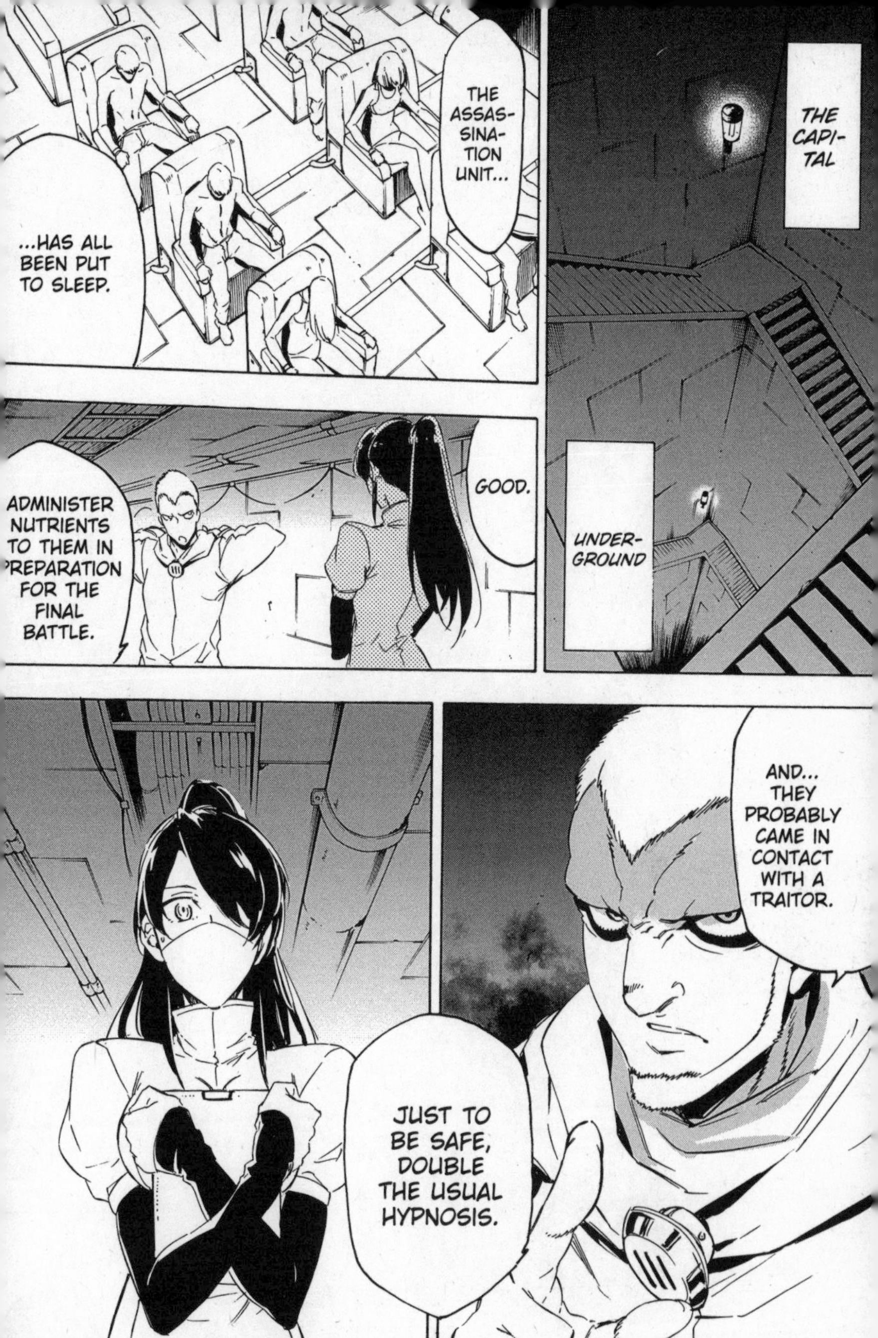
THE CAPI-TAL
UNDER-GROUND
THE ASSAS-SINA-TION UNIT...
...HAS ALL BEEN PUT TO SLEEP.
GOOD.
ADMINISTER NUTRIENTS TO THEM IN PREPARATION FOR THE FINAL BATTLE.
AND... THEY PROBABLY CAME IN CONTACT WITH A TRAITOR.
JUST TO BE SAFE, DOUBLE THE USUAL HYPNOSIS.

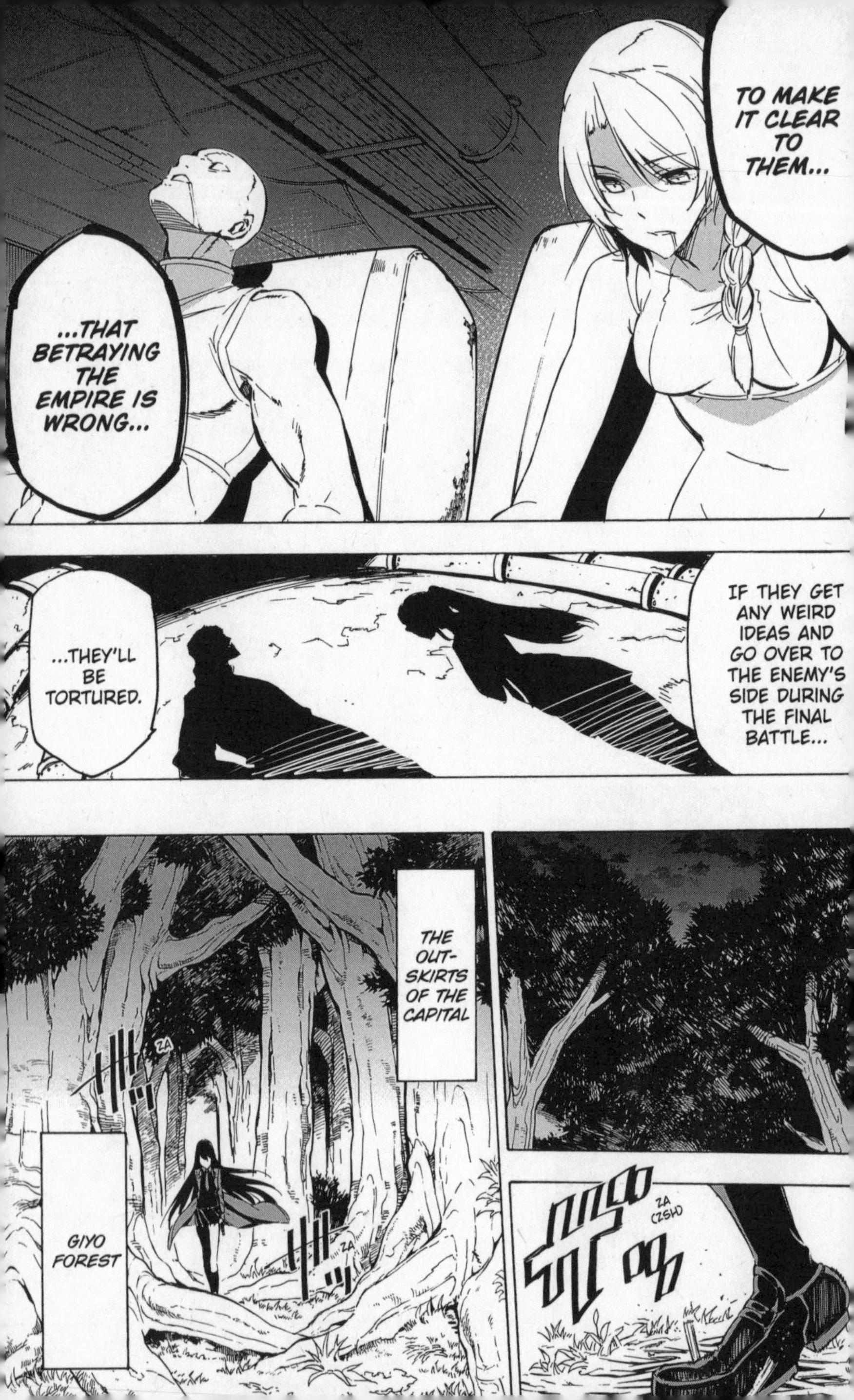
TO MAKE IT CLEAR TO THEM...
...THAT BETRAYING THE EMPIRE IS WRONG...
IF THEY GET ANY WEIRD IDEAS AND GO OVER TO THE ENEMY'S SIDE DURING THE FINAL BATTLE...
...THEY'LL BE TORTURED.
THE OUT-SKIRTS OF THE CAPITAL
ZA
GIYO FOREST
ZA
ZA (ZSH)

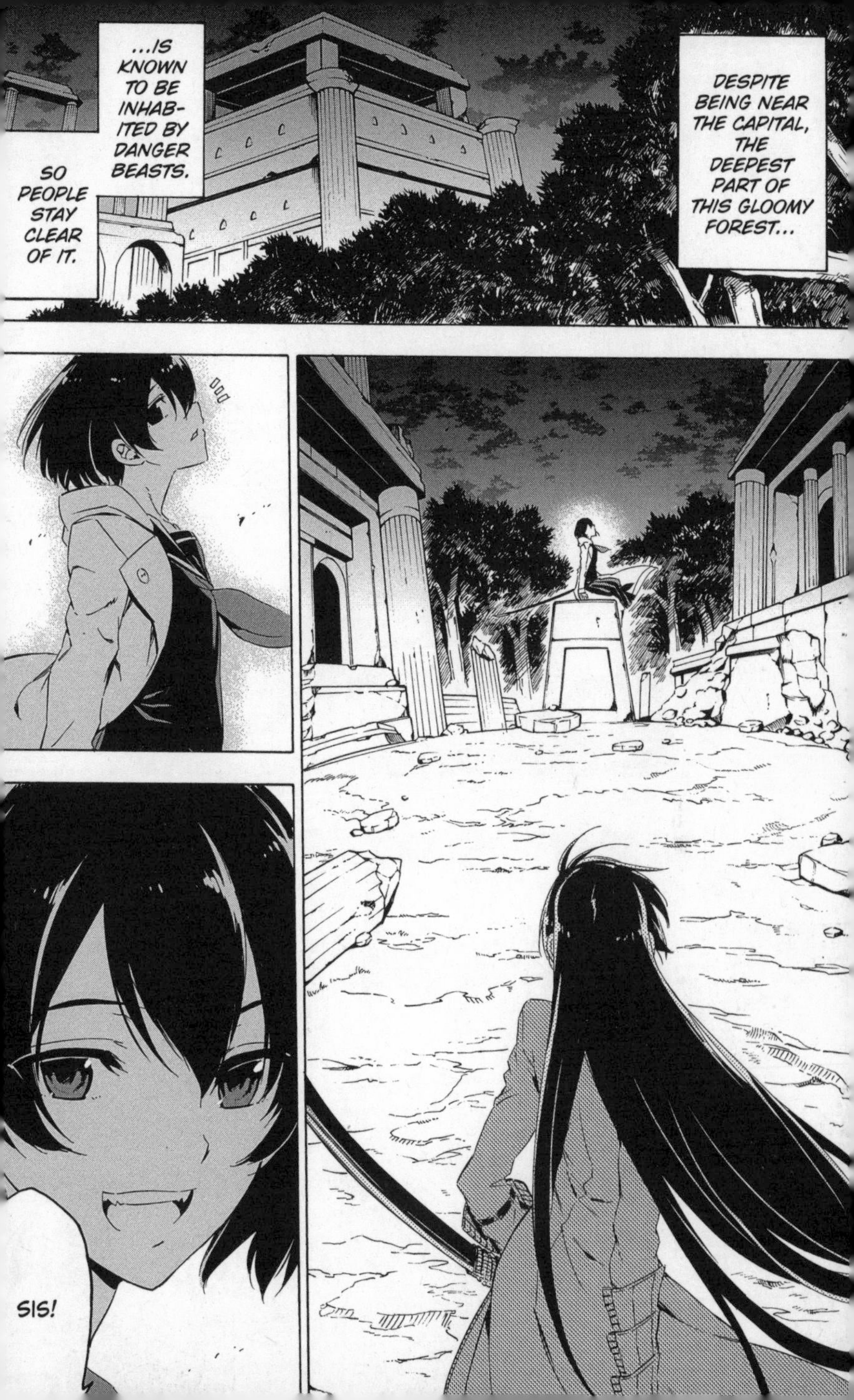
DESPITE BEING NEAR THE CAPITAL, THE DEEPEST PART OF THIS GLOOMY FOREST...
...IS KNOWN TO BE INHAB-ITED BY DANGER BEASTS.
SO PEOPLE STAY CLEAR OF IT.
SIS!

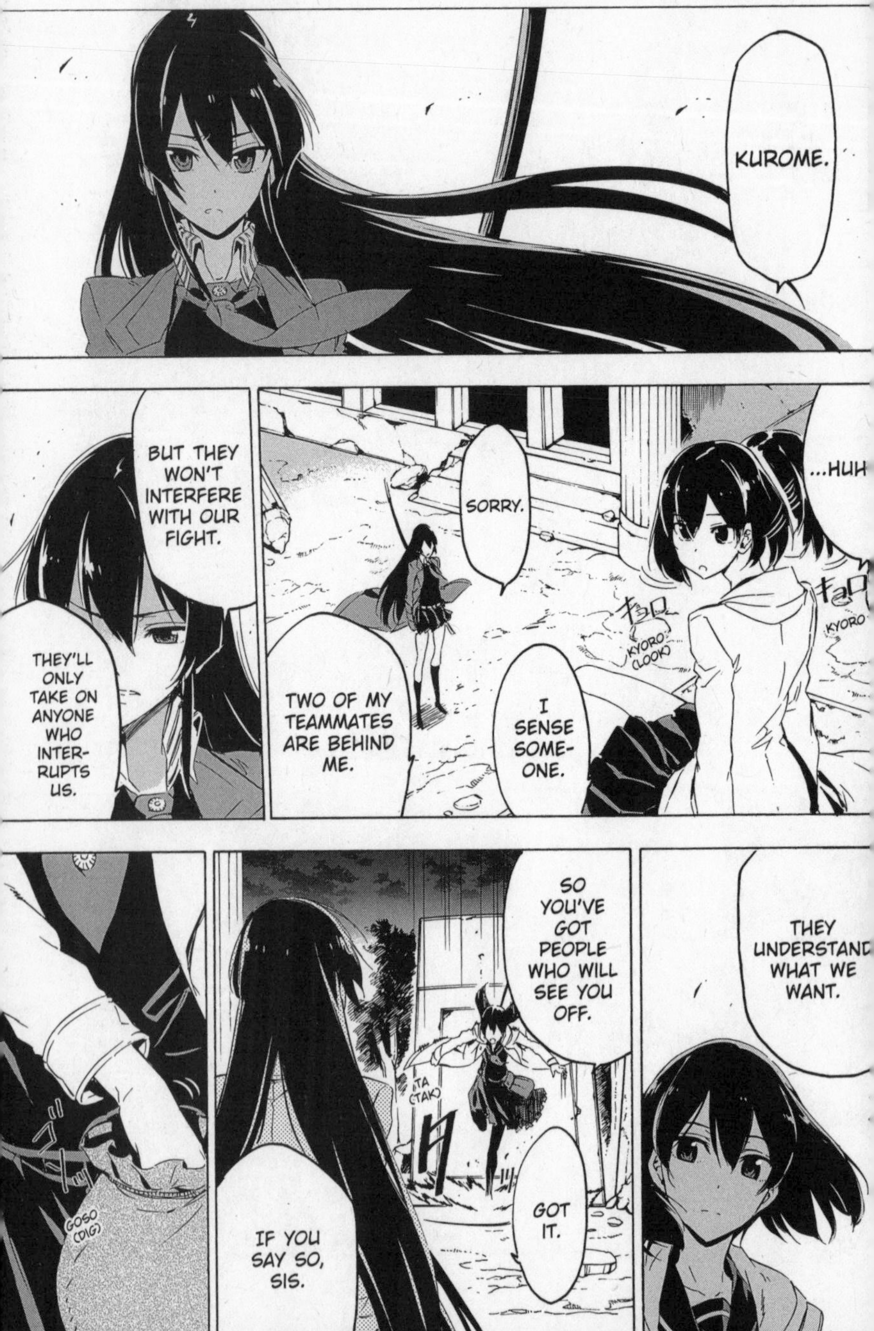
KUROME.
...HUH
KYORO
KYORO (LOOK)
I SENSE SOME-ONE.
SORRY.
TWO OF MY TEAMMATES ARE BEHIND ME.
BUT THEY WON'T INTERFERE WITH OUR FIGHT.
THEY'LL ONLY TAKE ON ANYONE WHO INTER-RUPTS US.
THEY UNDERSTAND WHAT WE WANT.
SO YOU'VE GOT PEOPLE WHO WILL SEE YOU OFF.
TA (TAK)
GOT IT.
IF YOU SAY SO, SIS.
GOSO (DIG)

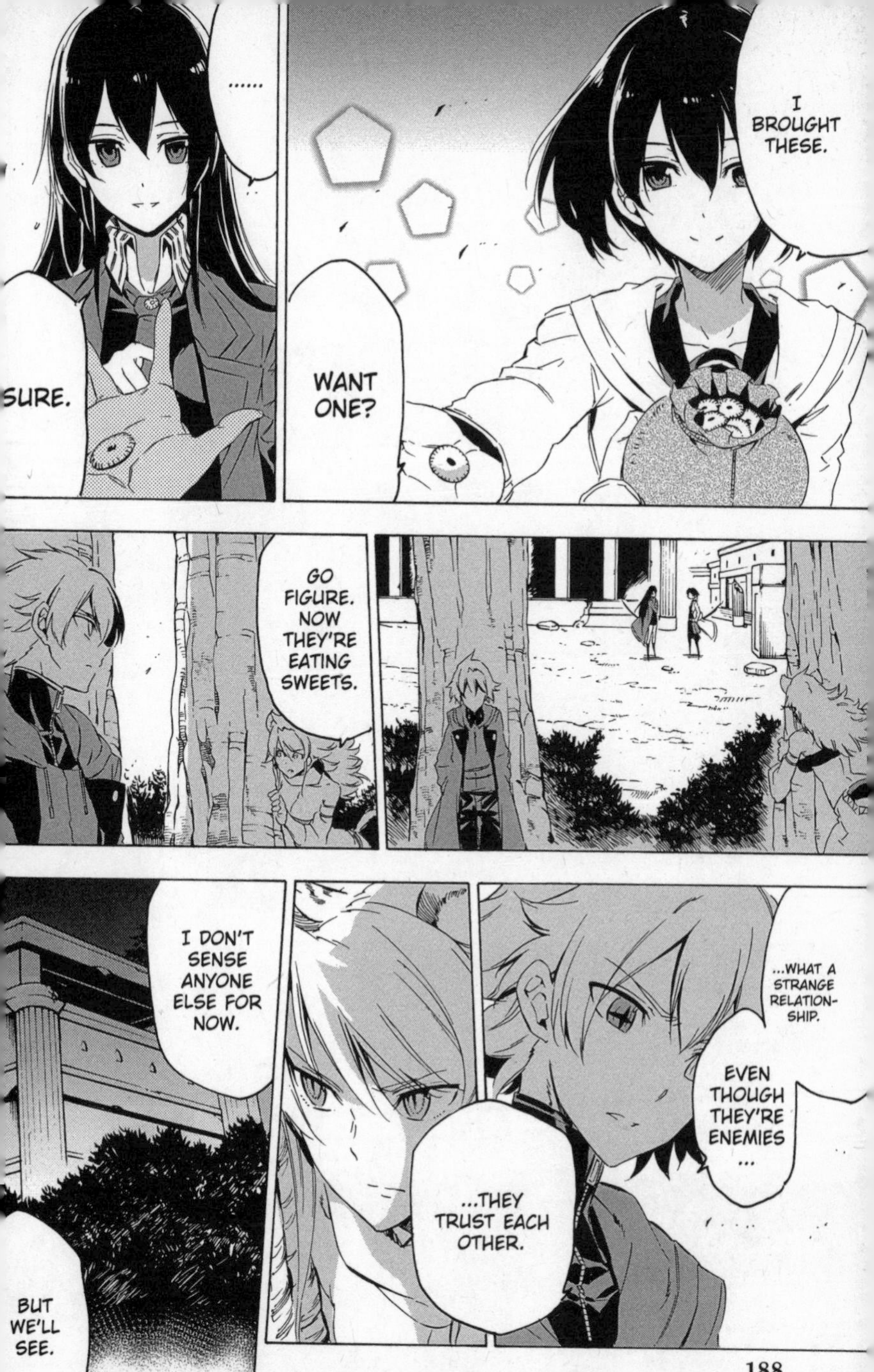
I BROUGHT THESE.
WANT ONE?
......
SURE.
GO FIGURE. NOW THEY'RE EATING SWEETS.
...WHAT A STRANGE RELATIONSHIP.
EVEN THOUGH THEY'RE ENEMIES...
...THEY TRUST EACH OTHER.
I DON'T SENSE ANYONE ELSE FOR NOW.
BUT WE'LL SEE.

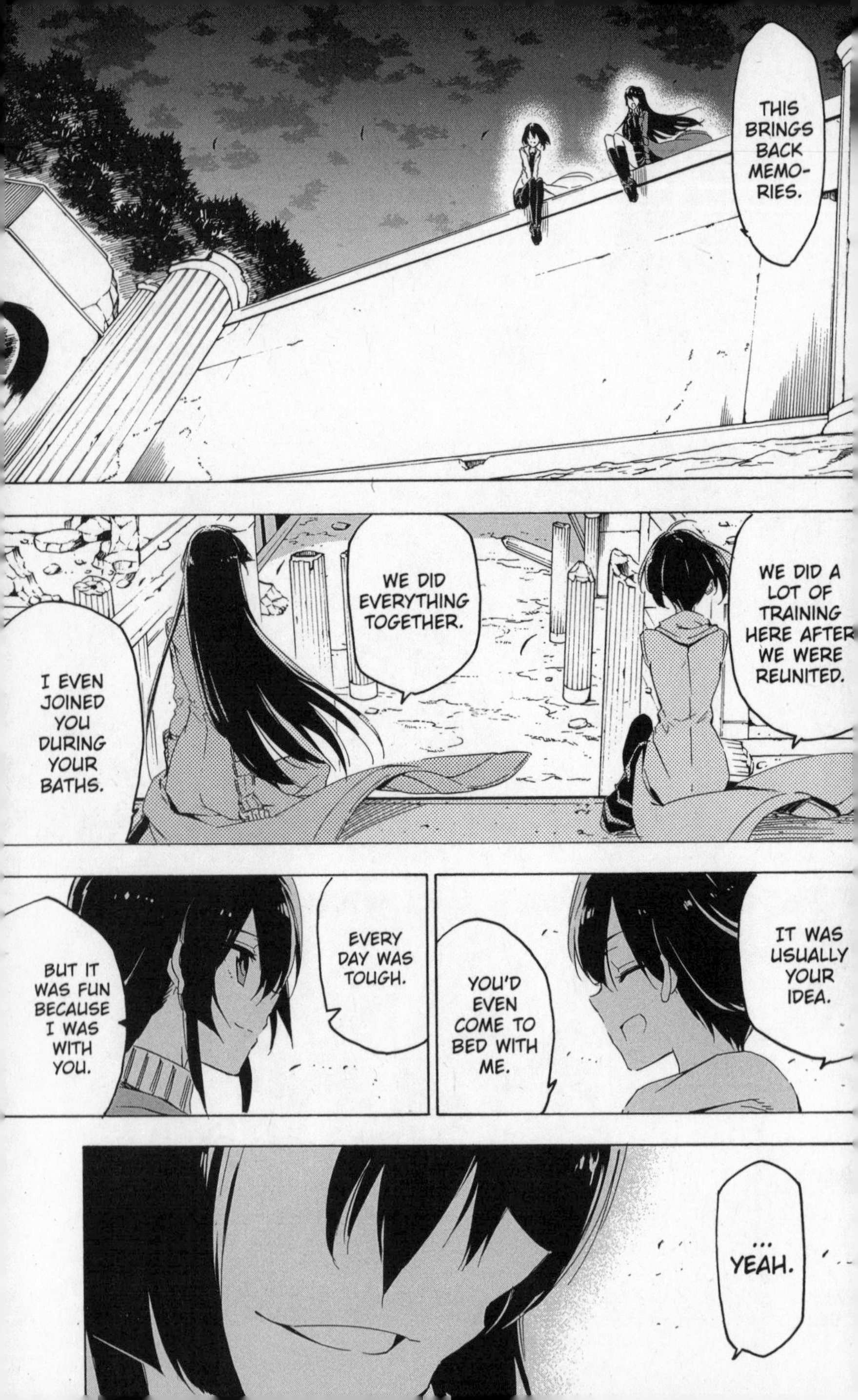
THIS BRINGS BACK MEMORIES.
WE DID A LOT OF TRAINING HERE AFTER WE WERE REUNITED.
WE DID EVERYTHING TOGETHER.
I EVEN JOINED YOU DURING YOUR BATHS.
IT WAS USUALLY YOUR IDEA.
YOU'D EVEN COME TO BED WITH ME.
EVERY DAY WAS TOUGH.
BUT IT WAS FUN BECAUSE I WAS WITH YOU.
... YEAH.

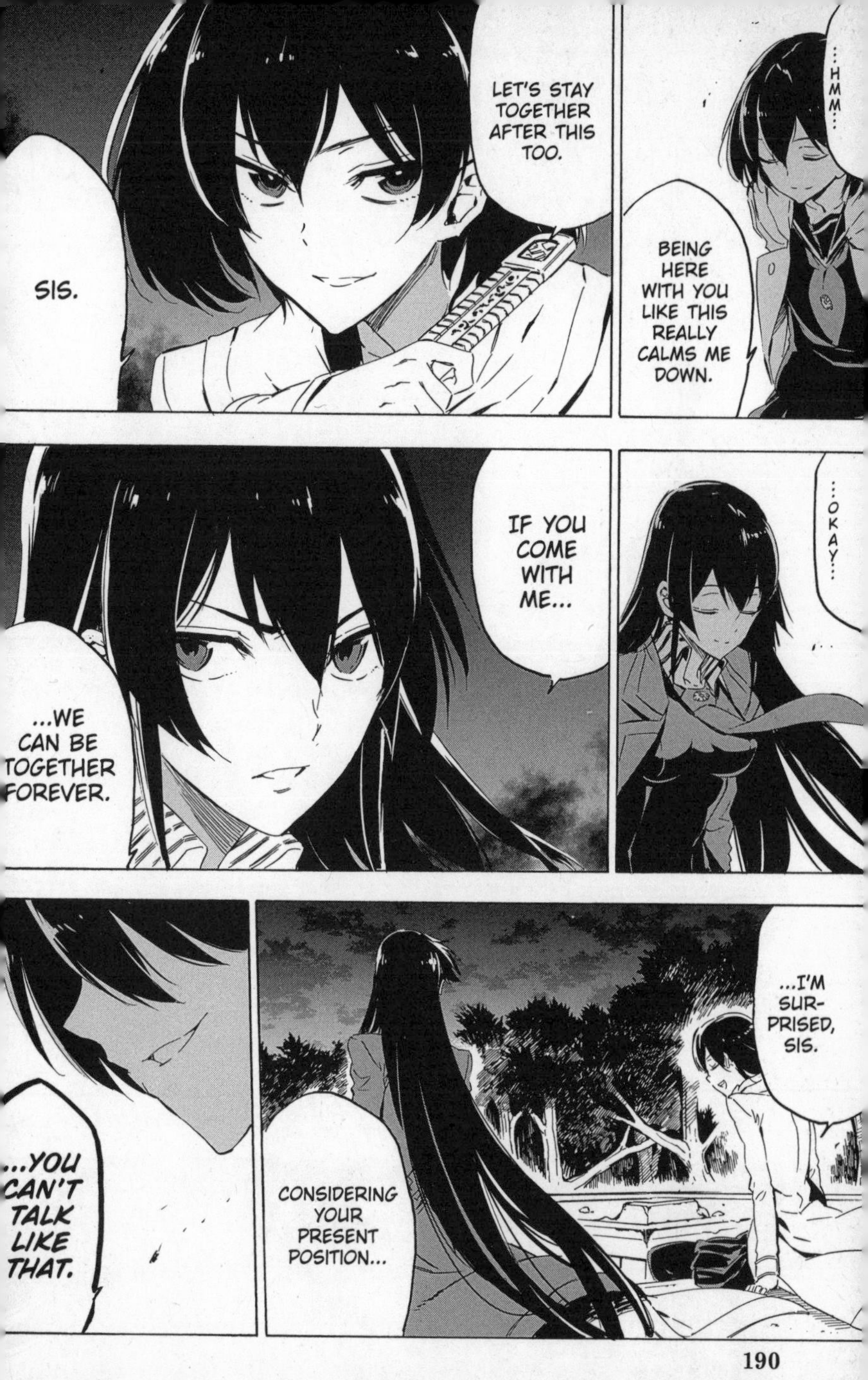
...HMM...
BEING HERE WITH YOU LIKE THIS REALLY CALMS ME DOWN.
LET'S STAY TOGETHER AFTER THIS TOO.
SIS.
...OKAY...
IF YOU COME WITH ME...
...WE CAN BE TOGETHER FOREVER.
...I'M SUR-PRISED, SIS.
CONSIDERING YOUR PRESENT POSITION...
...YOU CAN'T TALK LIKE THAT.

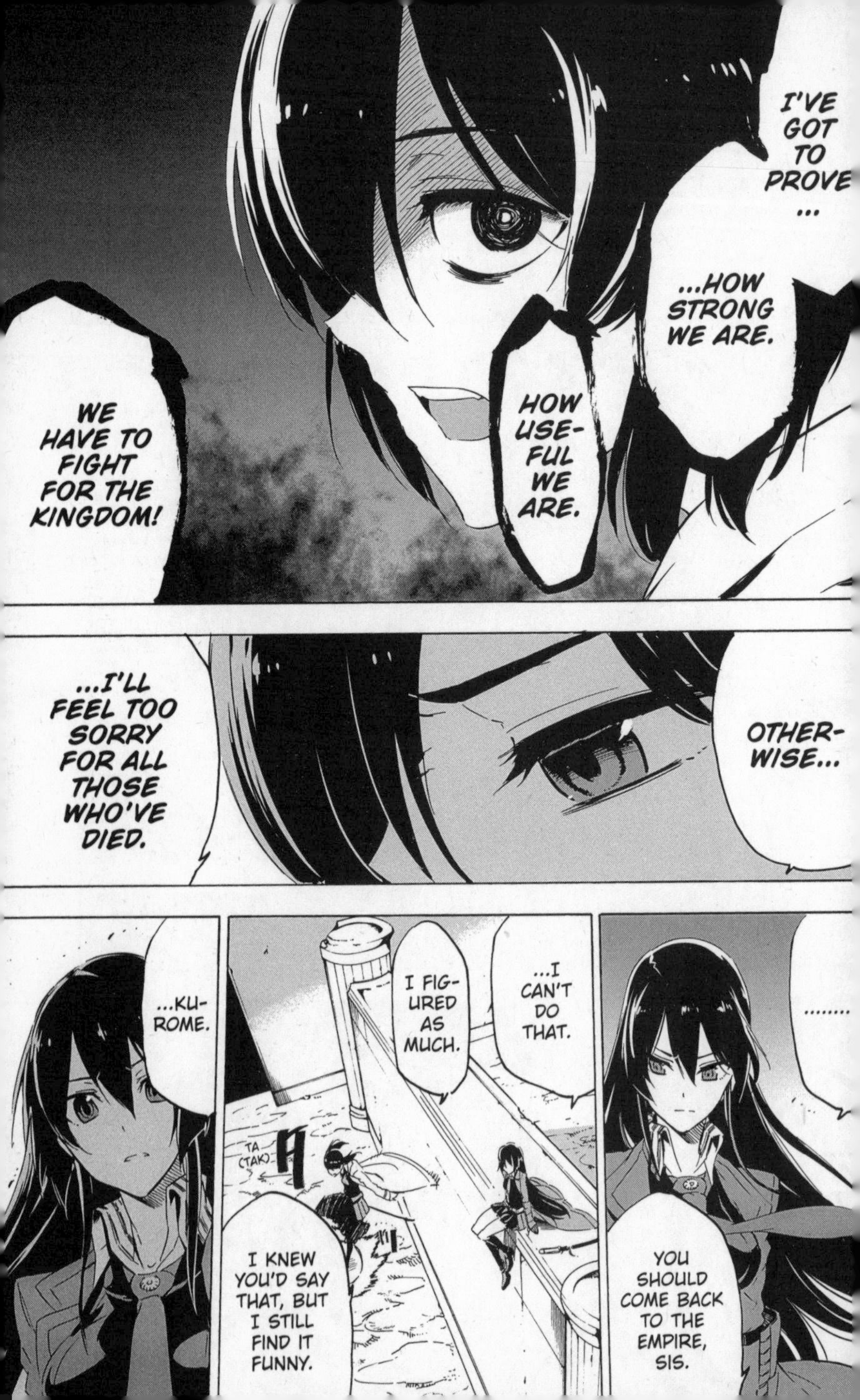

I'VE GOT TO PROVE ...
...HOW STRONG WE ARE.
HOW USE-FUL WE ARE.
WE HAVE TO FIGHT FOR THE KINGDOM!
OTHER-WISE...
...I'LL FEEL TOO SORRY FOR ALL THOSE WHO'VE DIED.
....
YOU SHOULD COME BACK TO THE EMPIRE, SIS.
...I CAN'T DO THAT.
I FIG-URED AS MUCH.
TA (TAK)
I KNEW YOU'D SAY THAT, BUT I STILL FIND IT FUNNY.
...KU-ROME.

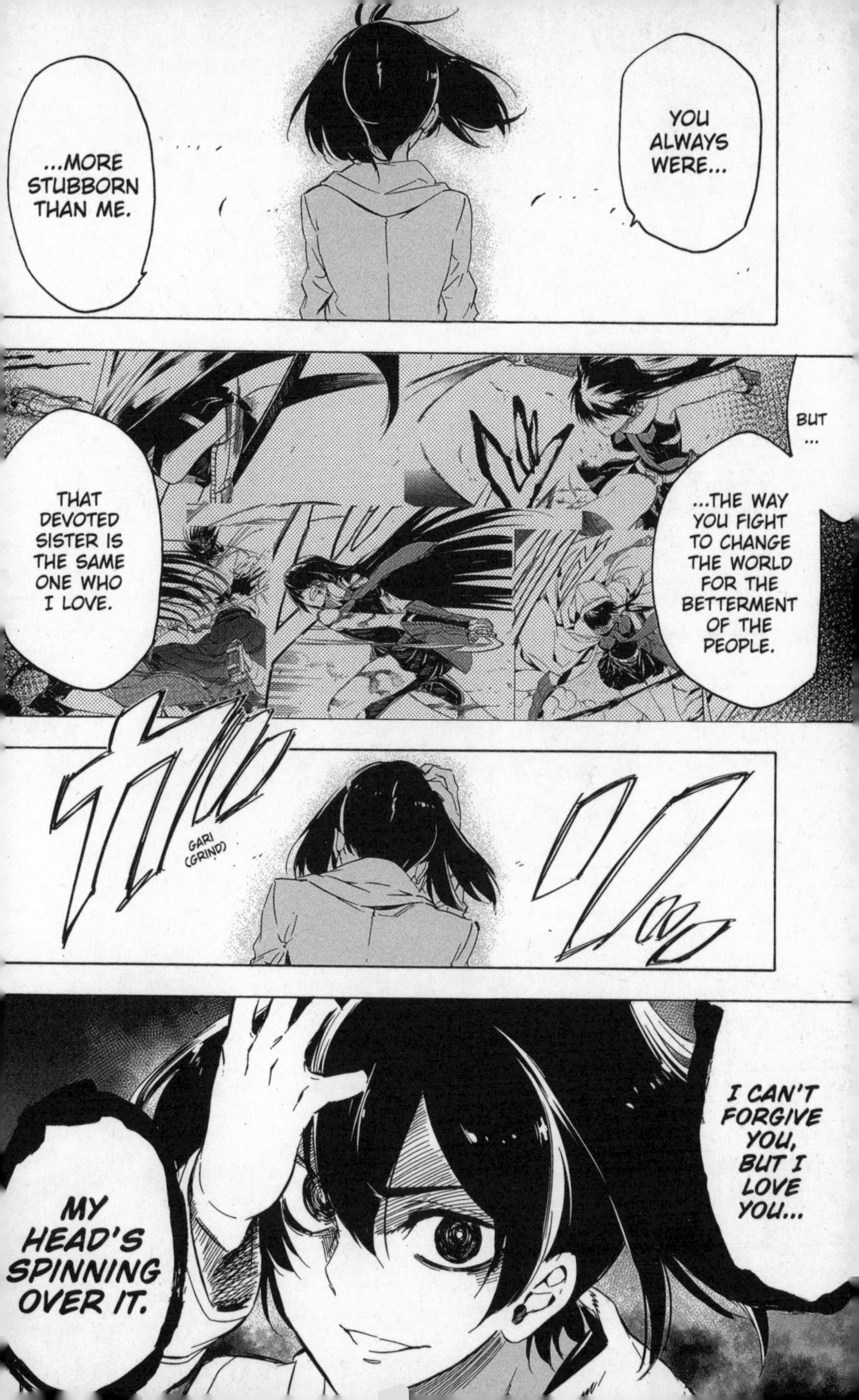
YOU ALWAYS WERE...
...MORE STUBBORN THAN ME.
BUT ...
...THE WAY YOU FIGHT TO CHANGE THE WORLD FOR THE BETTERMENT OF THE PEOPLE.
THAT DEVOTED SISTER IS THE SAME ONE WHO I LOVE.
GARI (GRIND)
I CAN'T FORGIVE YOU, BUT I LOVE YOU...
MY HEAD'S SPINNING OVER IT.

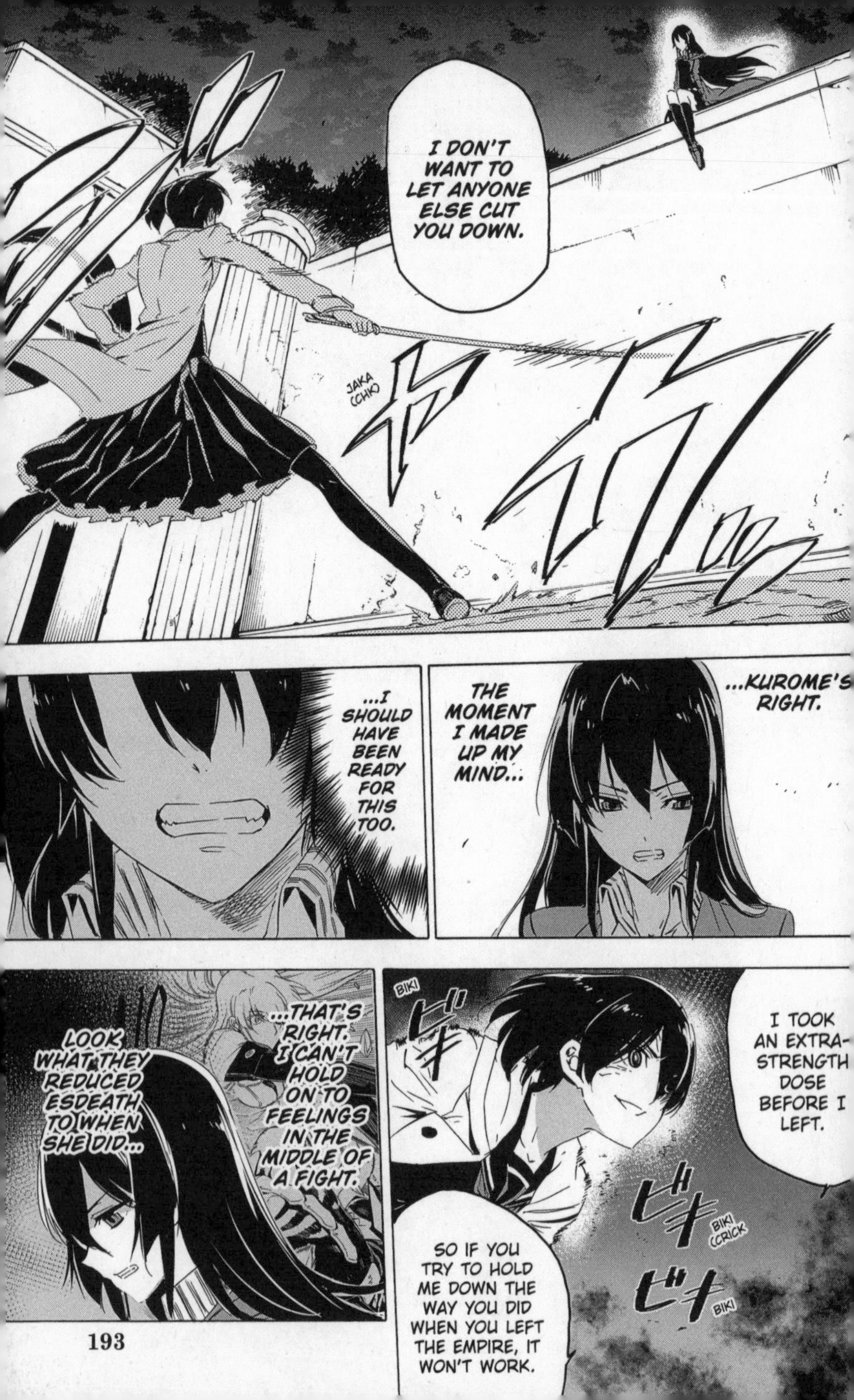
I DON'T WANT TO LET ANYONE ELSE CUT YOU DOWN.
JAKA (CHK)
...KUROME'S RIGHT.
THE MOMENT I MADE UP MY MIND...
...I SHOULD HAVE BEEN READY FOR THIS TOO.
BIKI
I TOOK AN EXTRA-STRENGTH DOSE BEFORE I LEFT.
BIKI (CRICK)
BIKI
SO IF YOU TRY TO HOLD ME DOWN THE WAY YOU DID WHEN YOU LEFT THE EMPIRE, IT WON'T WORK.
...THAT'S RIGHT. I CAN'T HOLD ON TO FEELINGS IN THE MIDDLE OF A FIGHT.
LOOK WHAT THEY REDUCED ESDEATH TO WHEN SHE DID...

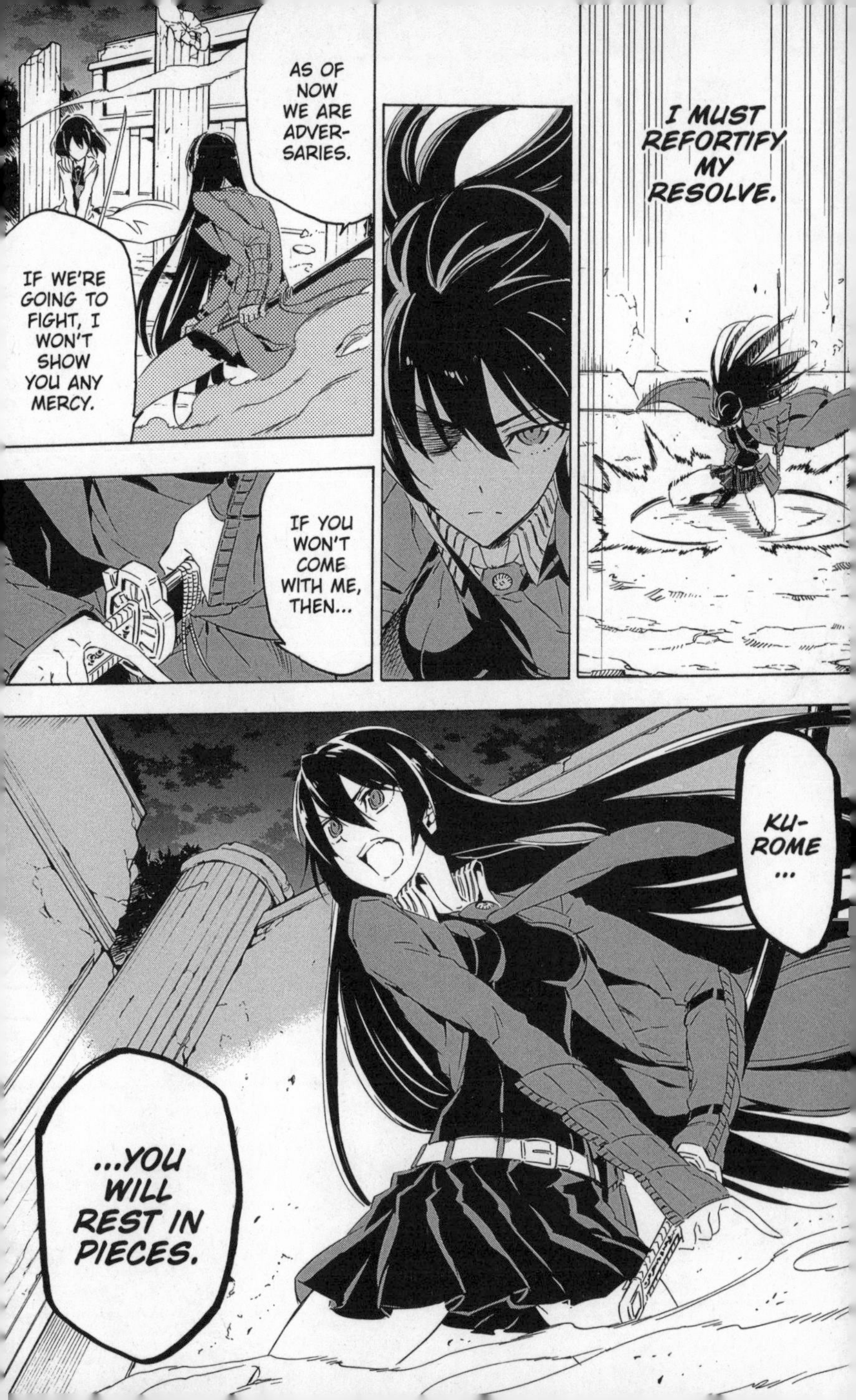
I MUST REFORTIFY MY RESOLVE.
AS OF NOW WE ARE ADVER-SARIES.
IF WE'RE GOING TO FIGHT, I WON'T SHOW YOU ANY MERCY.
IF YOU WON'T COME WITH ME, THEN...
KU-ROME...
...YOU WILL REST IN PIECES.

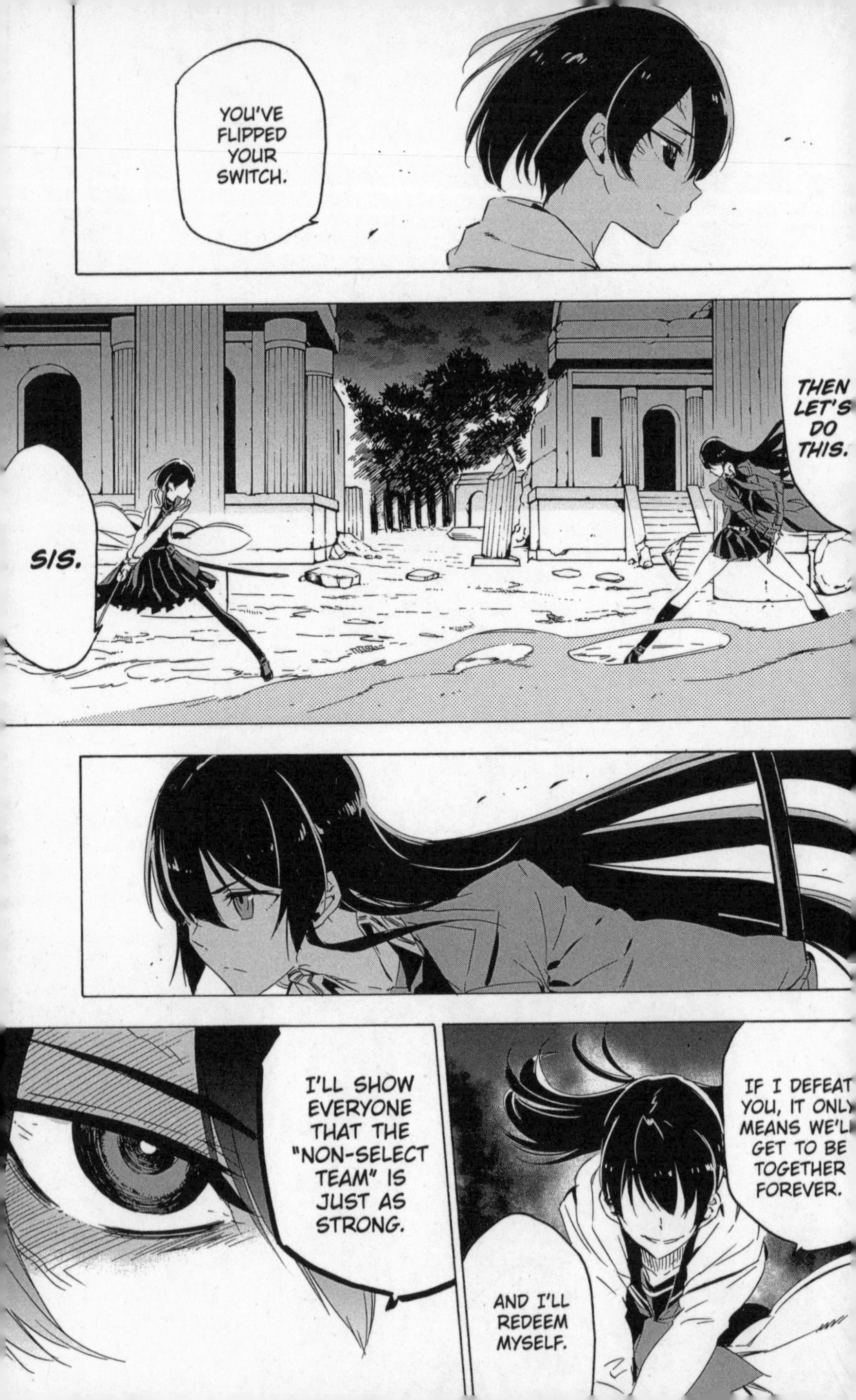
YOU'VE FLIPPED YOUR SWITCH.
THEN LET'S DO THIS.
SIS.
IF I DEFEAT YOU, IT ONLY MEANS WE'LL GET TO BE TOGETHER FOREVER.
AND I'LL REDEEM MYSELF.
I'LL SHOW EVERYONE THAT THE "NON-SELECT TEAM" IS JUST AS STRONG.

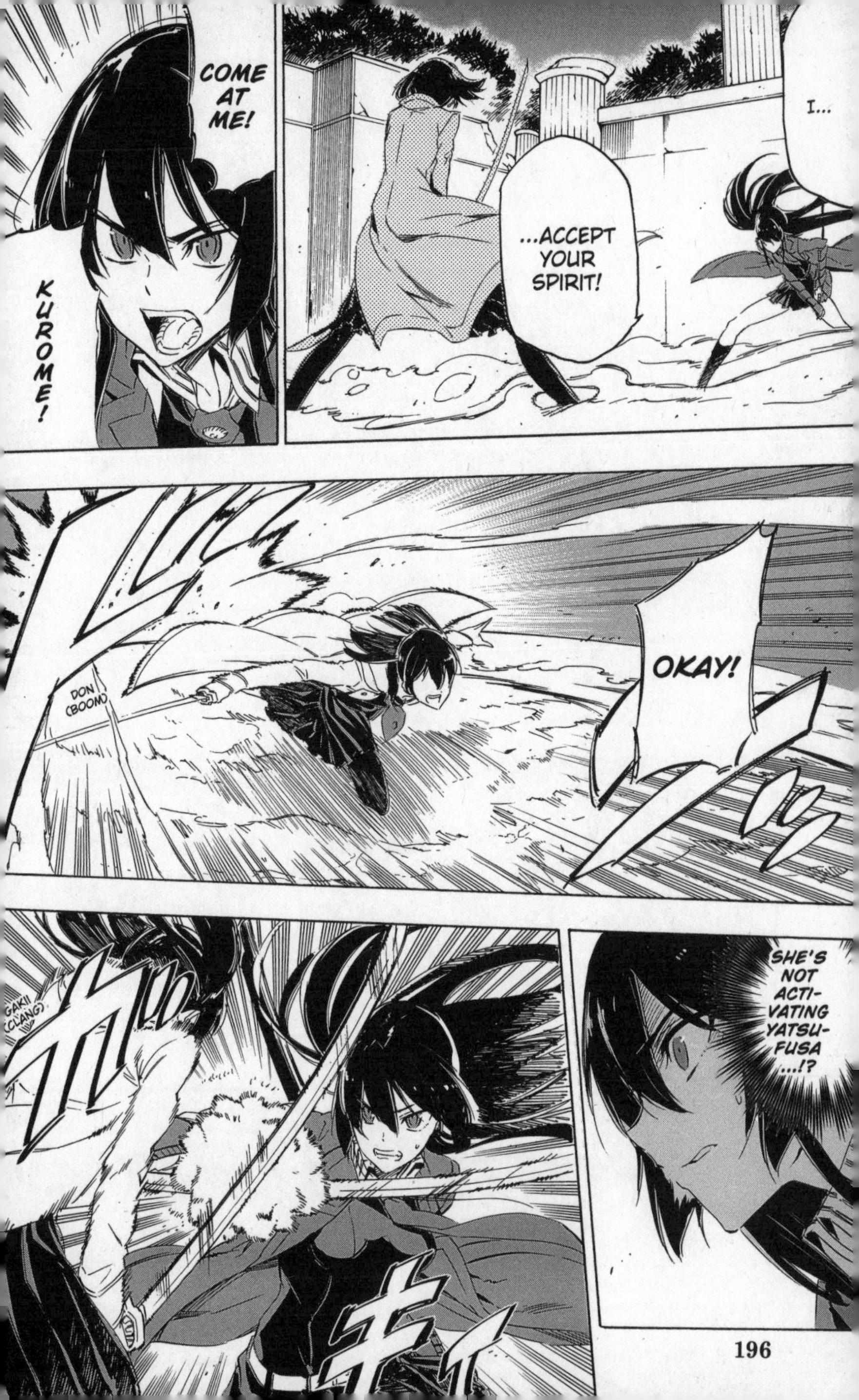
I...
...ACCEPT YOUR SPIRIT!
COME AT ME!
KUROME!
OKAY!
DON (BOOM)
SHE'S NOT ACTI-VATING YATSU-FUSA ...!?
GAKII (CLANG)

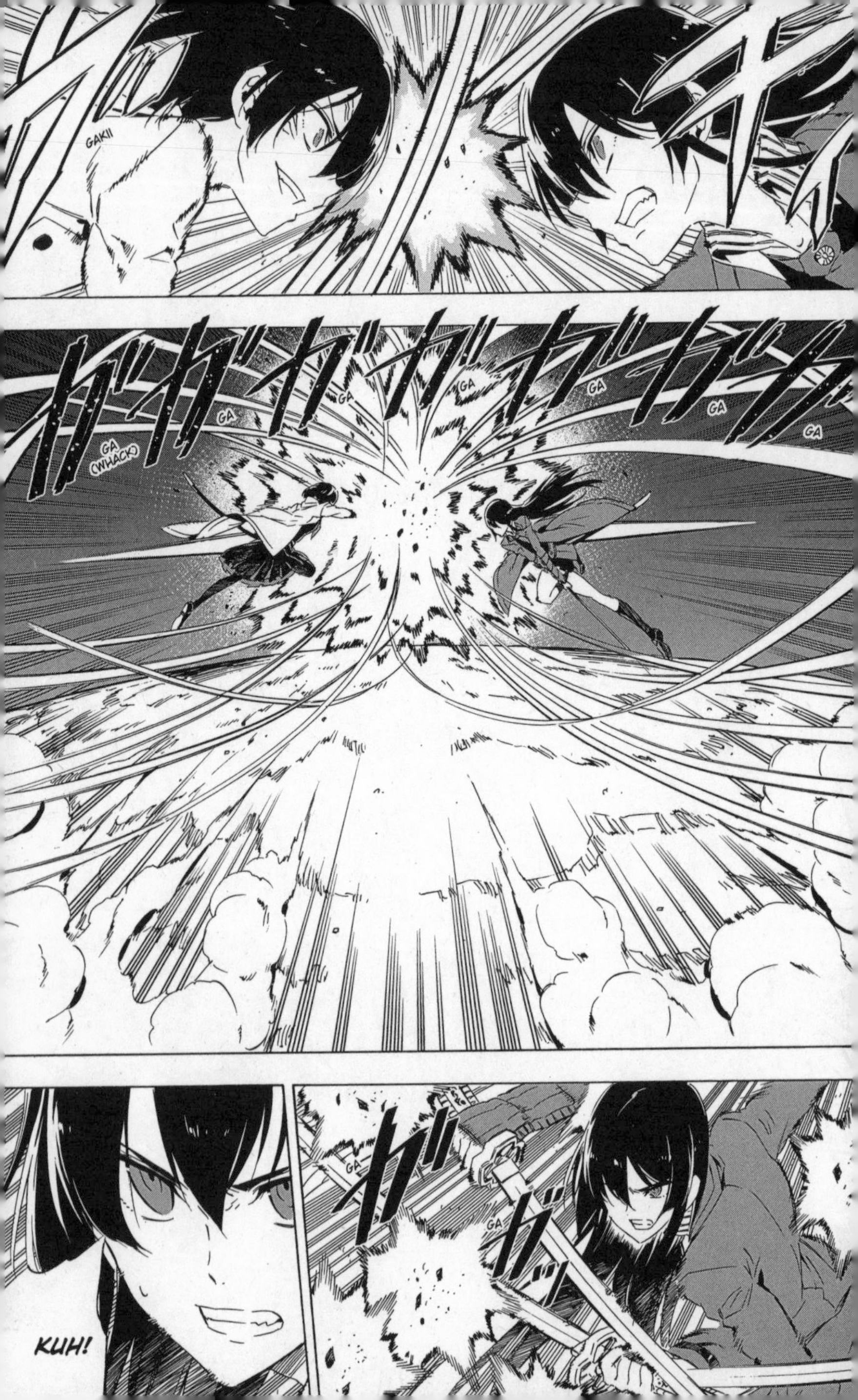
GAKII
GA
GA
GA
GA
GA
GA
GA (WHACK)
GA
GA
KUH!

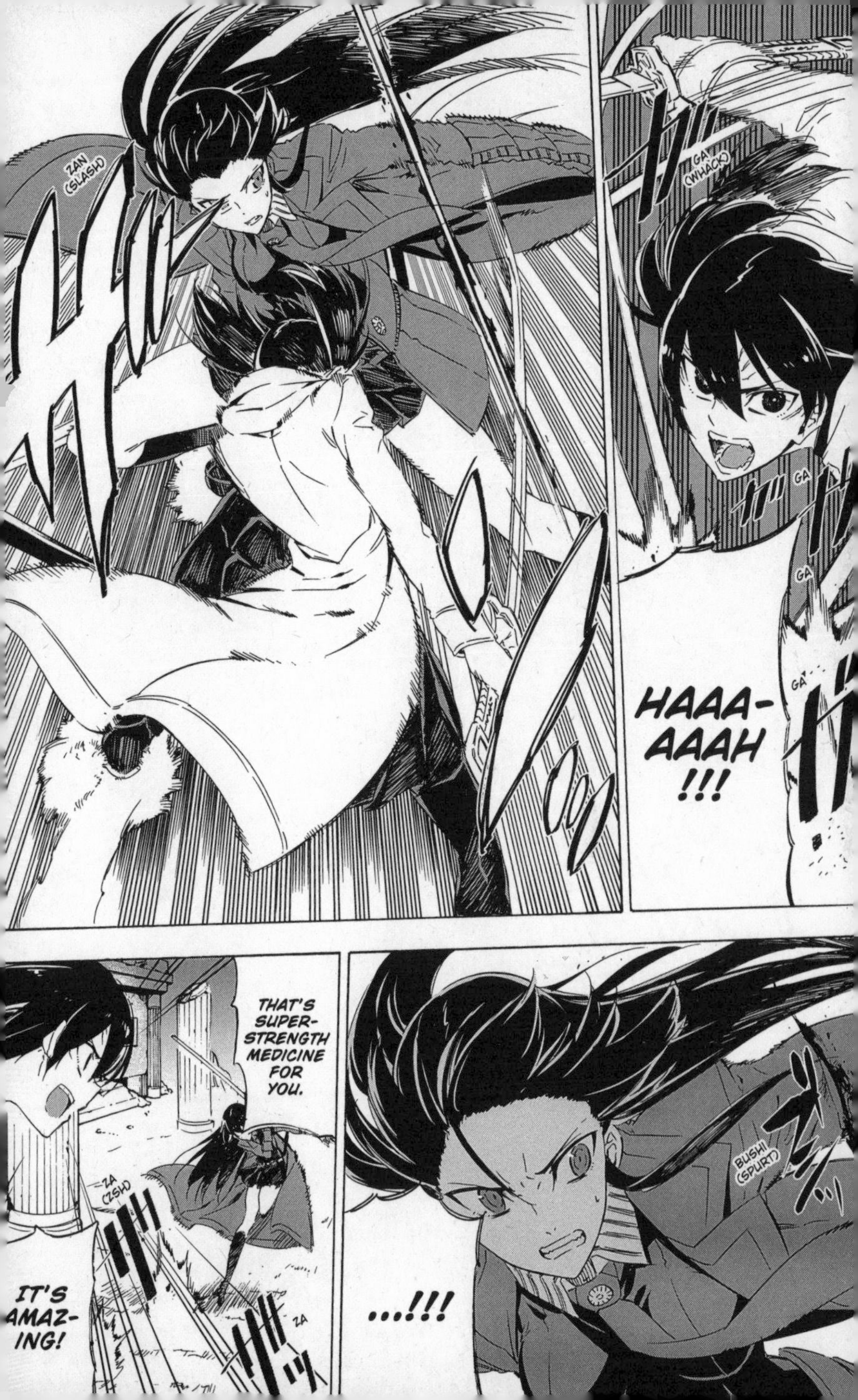
GA (WHACK)
GA
GA
GA
HAAAA-AAAH!!!
ZAN (SLASH)
BUSHI (SPURT)
...!!!
THAT'S SUPER-STRENGTH MEDICINE FOR YOU.
ZA (ZSH)
ZA
IT'S AMAZ-ING!

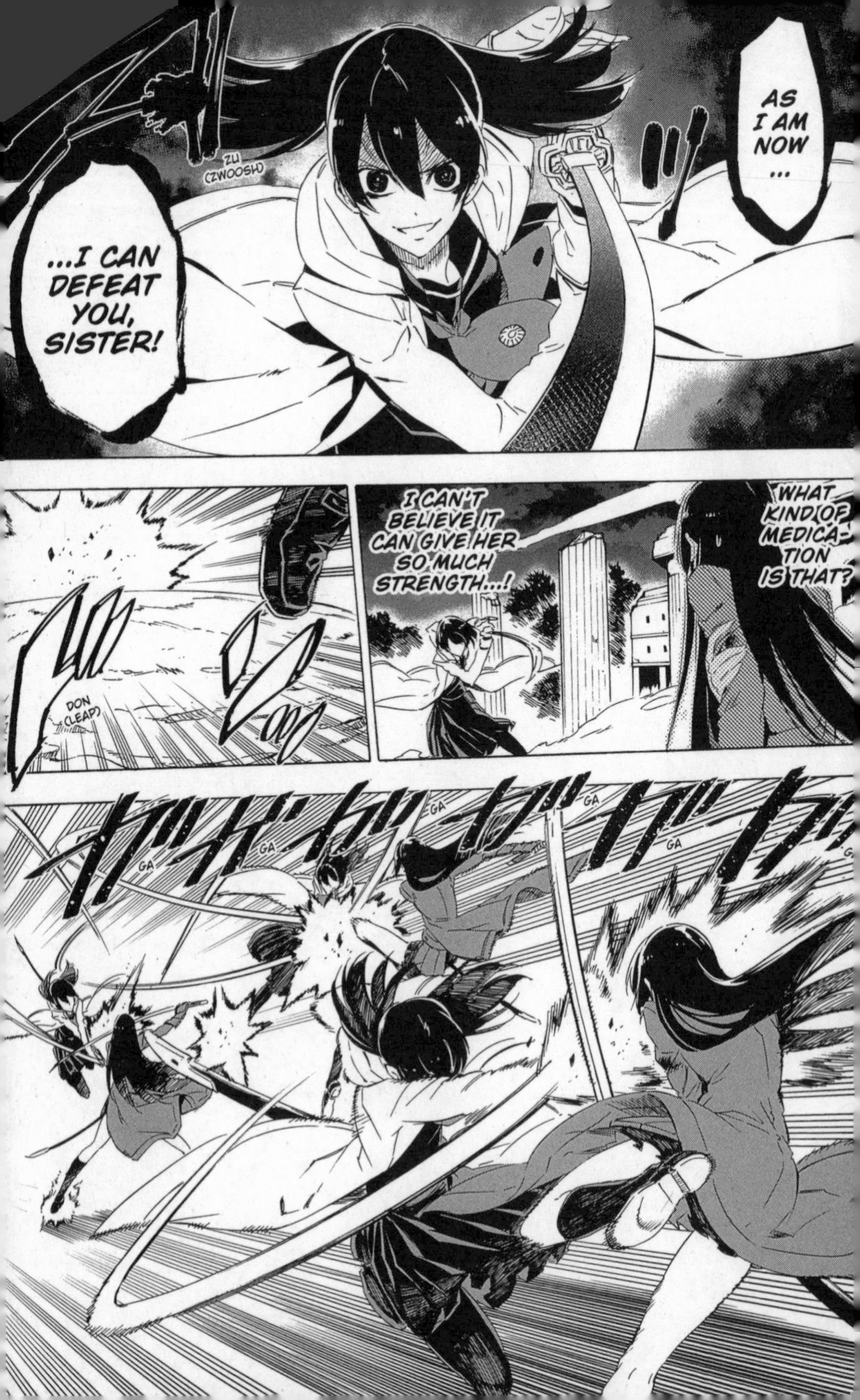
AS I AM NOW ...
ZU (ZWOOSH)
...I CAN DEFEAT YOU, SISTER!
WHAT KIND OF MEDICA-TION IS THAT?
I CAN'T BELIEVE IT CAN GIVE HER SO MUCH STRENGTH...!
DON (LEAP)
GA
GA
GA
GA
GA

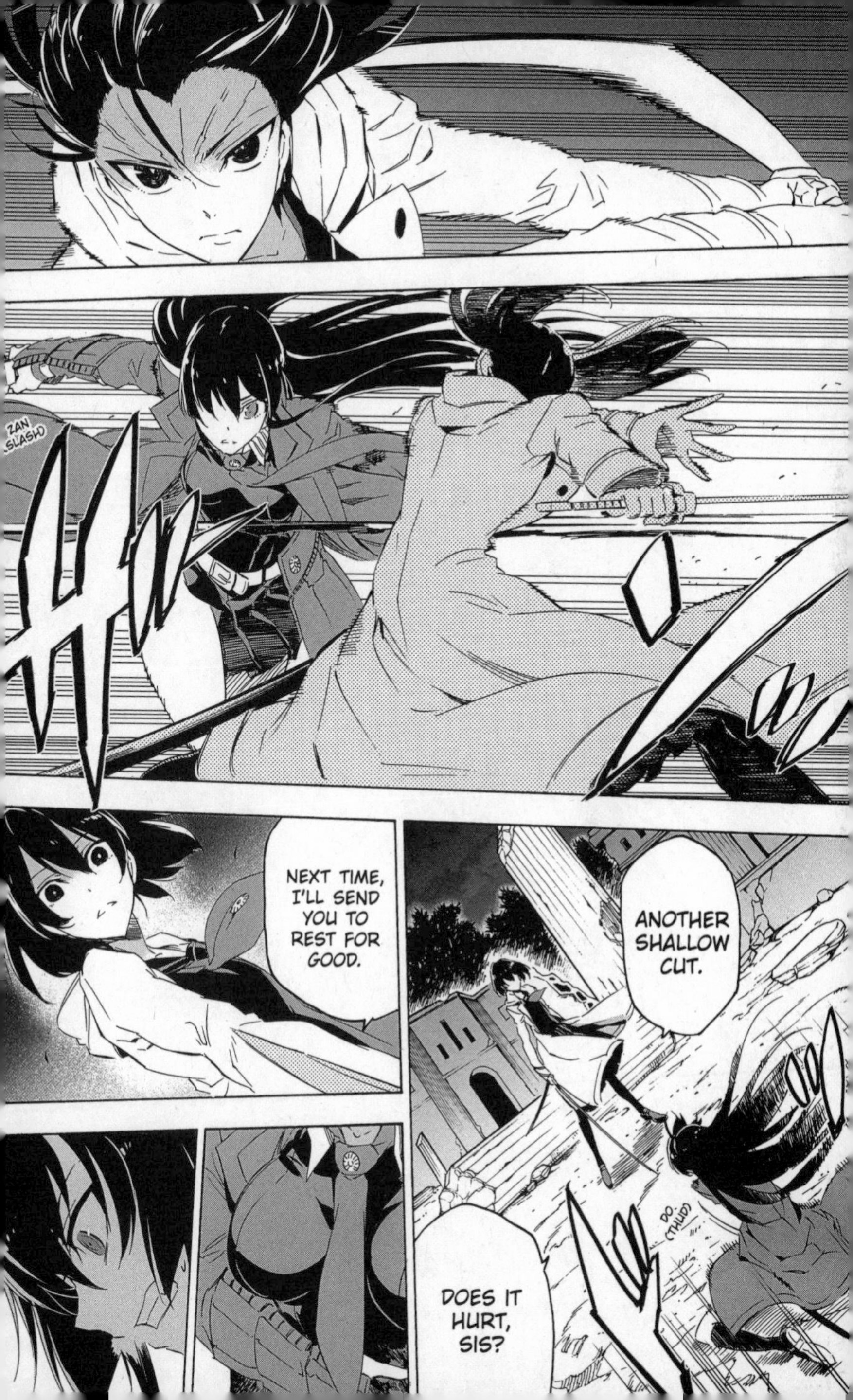
ZAN
SLASH
ANOTHER SHALLOW CUT.
DO-
(THUD)
DOES IT HURT, SIS?
NEXT TIME, I'LL SEND YOU TO REST FOR GOOD.

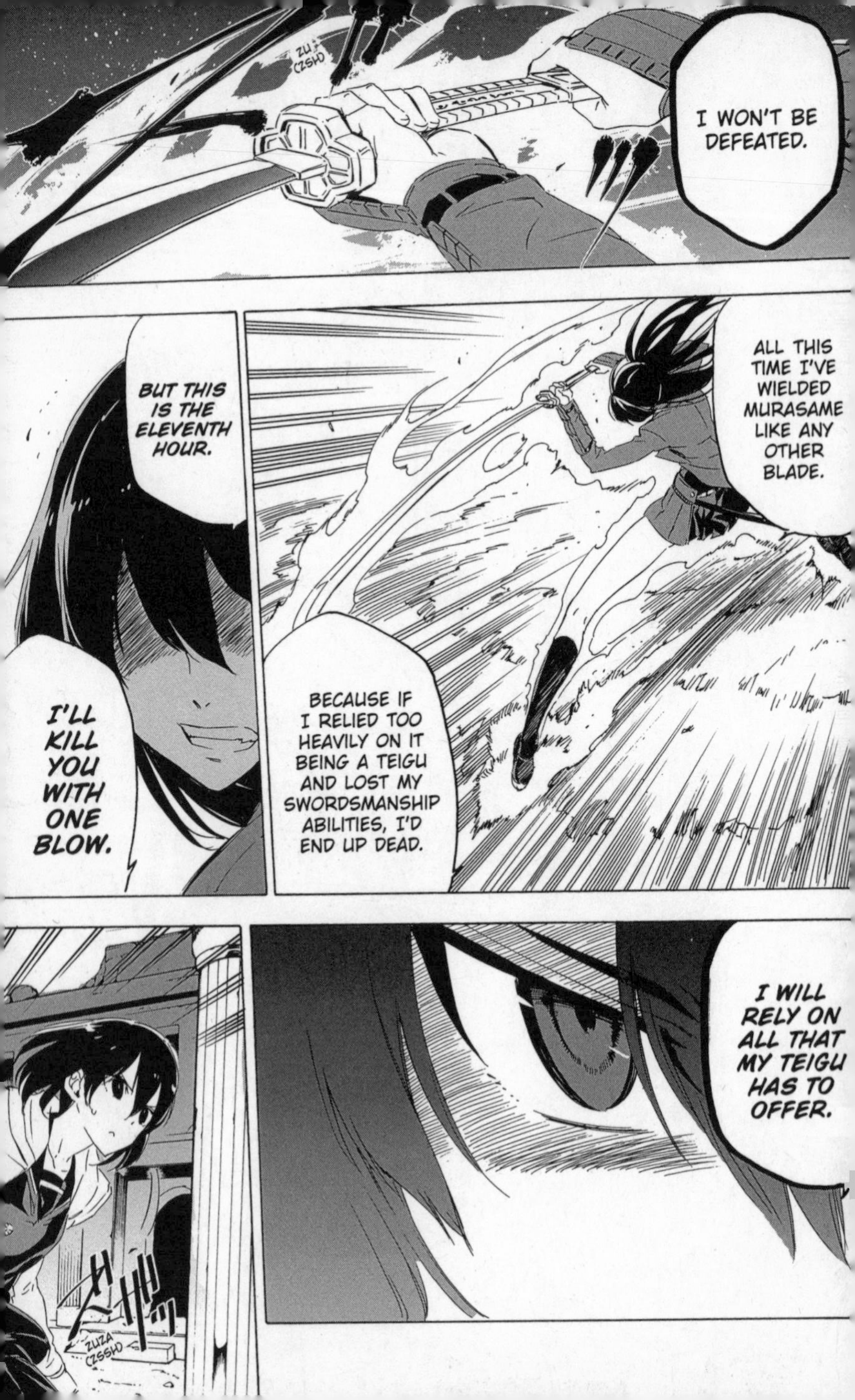
I WON'T BE DEFEATED.
ZU (ZSH)
ALL THIS TIME I'VE WIELDED MURASAME LIKE ANY OTHER BLADE.
BECAUSE IF I RELIED TOO HEAVILY ON IT BEING A TEIGU AND LOST MY SWORDSMANSHIP ABILITIES, I'D END UP DEAD.
BUT THIS IS THE ELEVENTH HOUR.
I'LL KILL YOU WITH ONE BLOW.
I WILL RELY ON ALL THAT MY TEIGU HAS TO OFFER.
ZUZA (ZSSH)

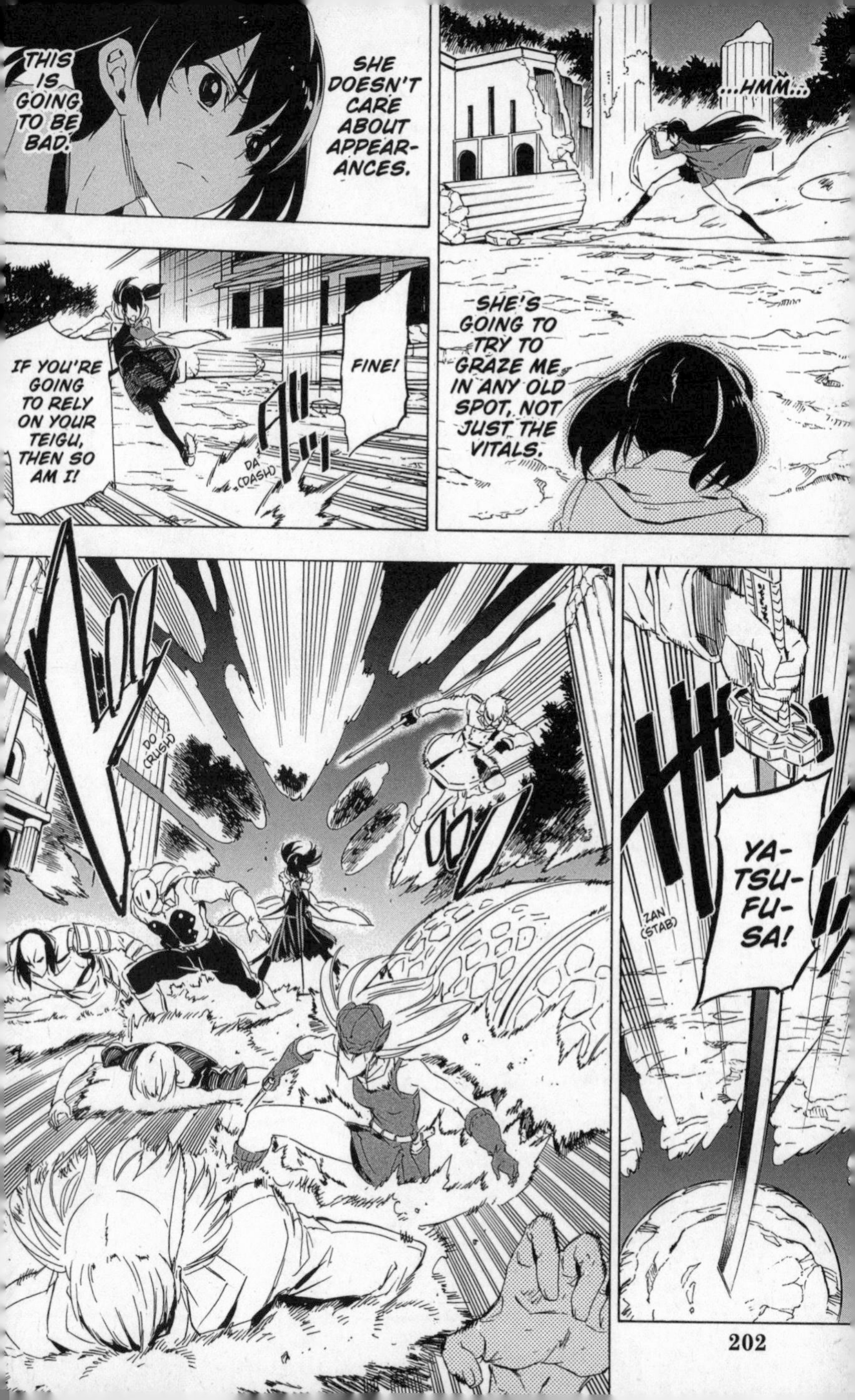
...HMM...
SHE DOESN'T CARE ABOUT APPEARANCES.
THIS IS GOING TO BE BAD.
SHE'S GOING TO TRY TO GRAZE ME IN ANY OLD SPOT, NOT JUST THE VITALS.
FINE!
IF YOU'RE GOING TO RELY ON YOUR TEIGU, THEN SO AM I!
DA (DASH)
ZAN (STAB)
YA-TSU-FU-SA!
DO (CRUSH)

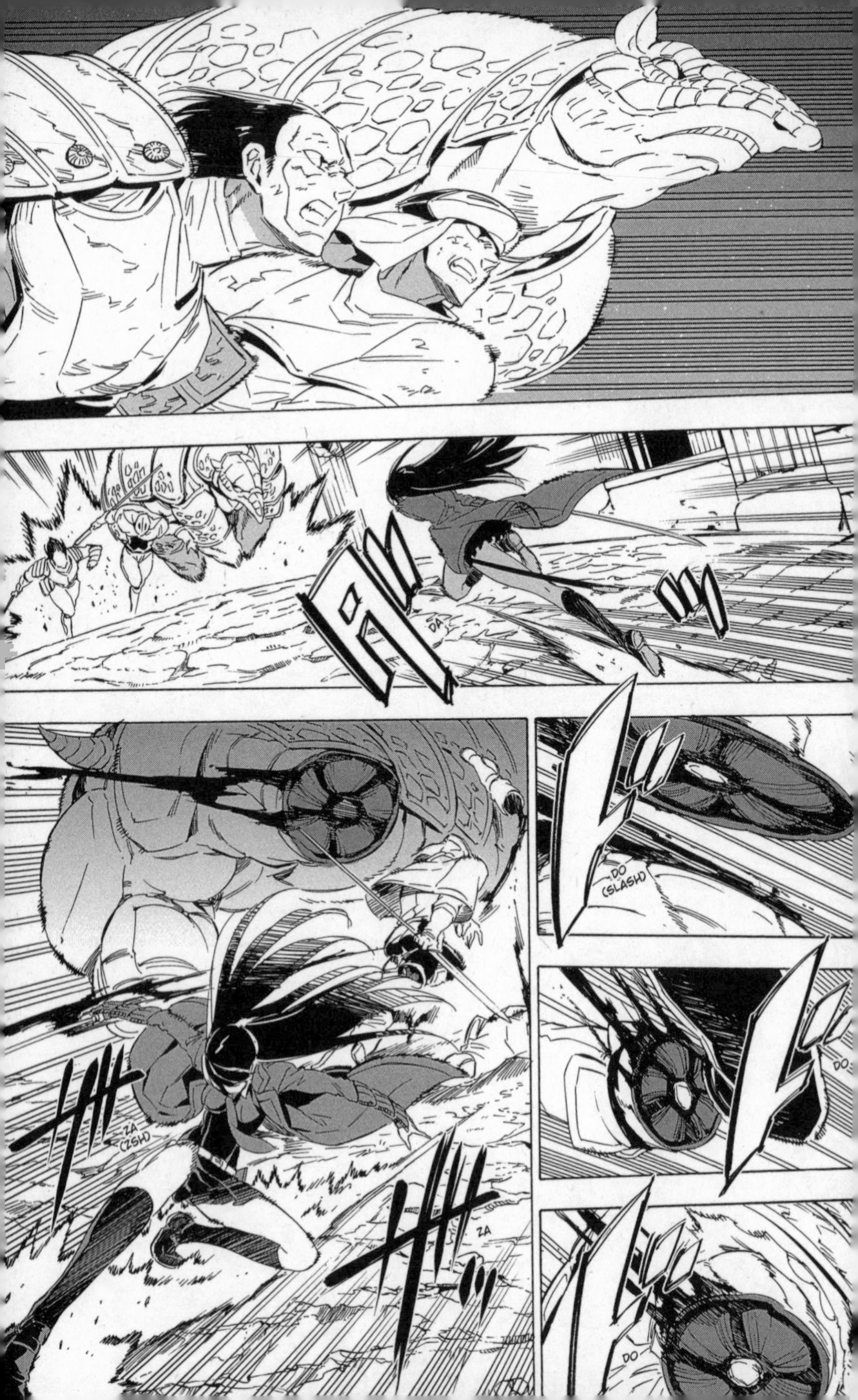
DA
DO (SLASH)
DO
DO
ZA (ZSH)
ZA

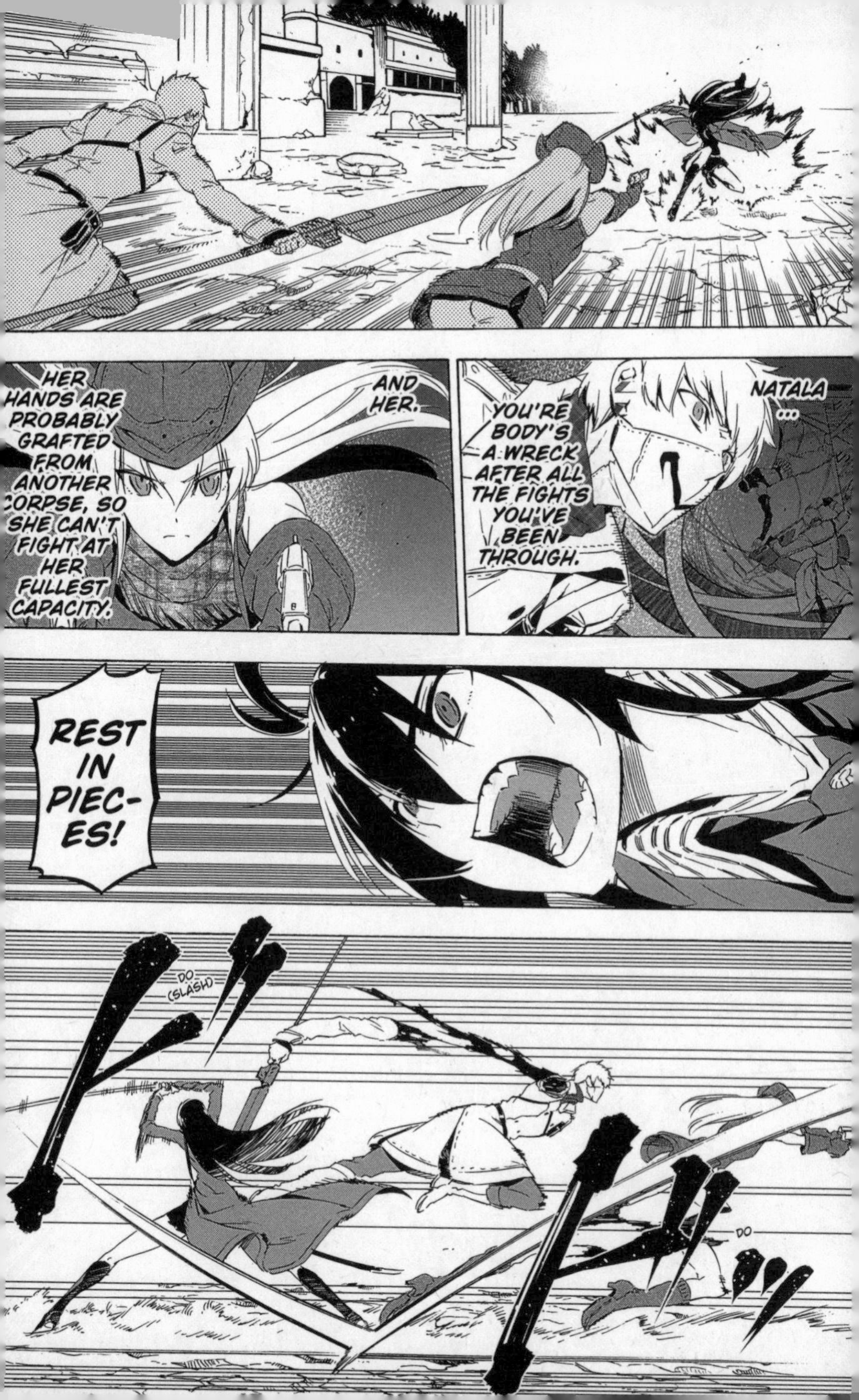
NATALA...
YOU'RE BODY'S A WRECK AFTER ALL THE FIGHTS YOU'VE BEEN THROUGH.
AND HER.
HER HANDS ARE PROBABLY GRAFTED FROM ANOTHER CORPSE, SO SHE CAN'T FIGHT AT HER FULLEST CAPACITY.
REST IN PIEC-ES!
DO (SLASH)
DO

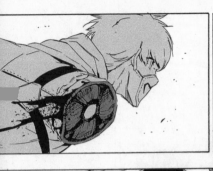
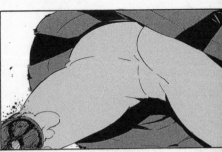

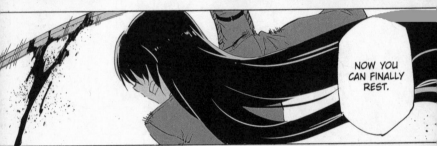

NOW YOU CAN FINALLY REST.

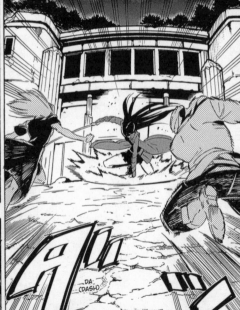

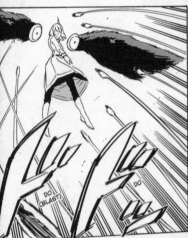

DO (BLAST)

DA (DASH)

I'VE EXPERIENCED THE STRENGTH AND SPEED OF THIS GUY'S WINGS BEFORE.

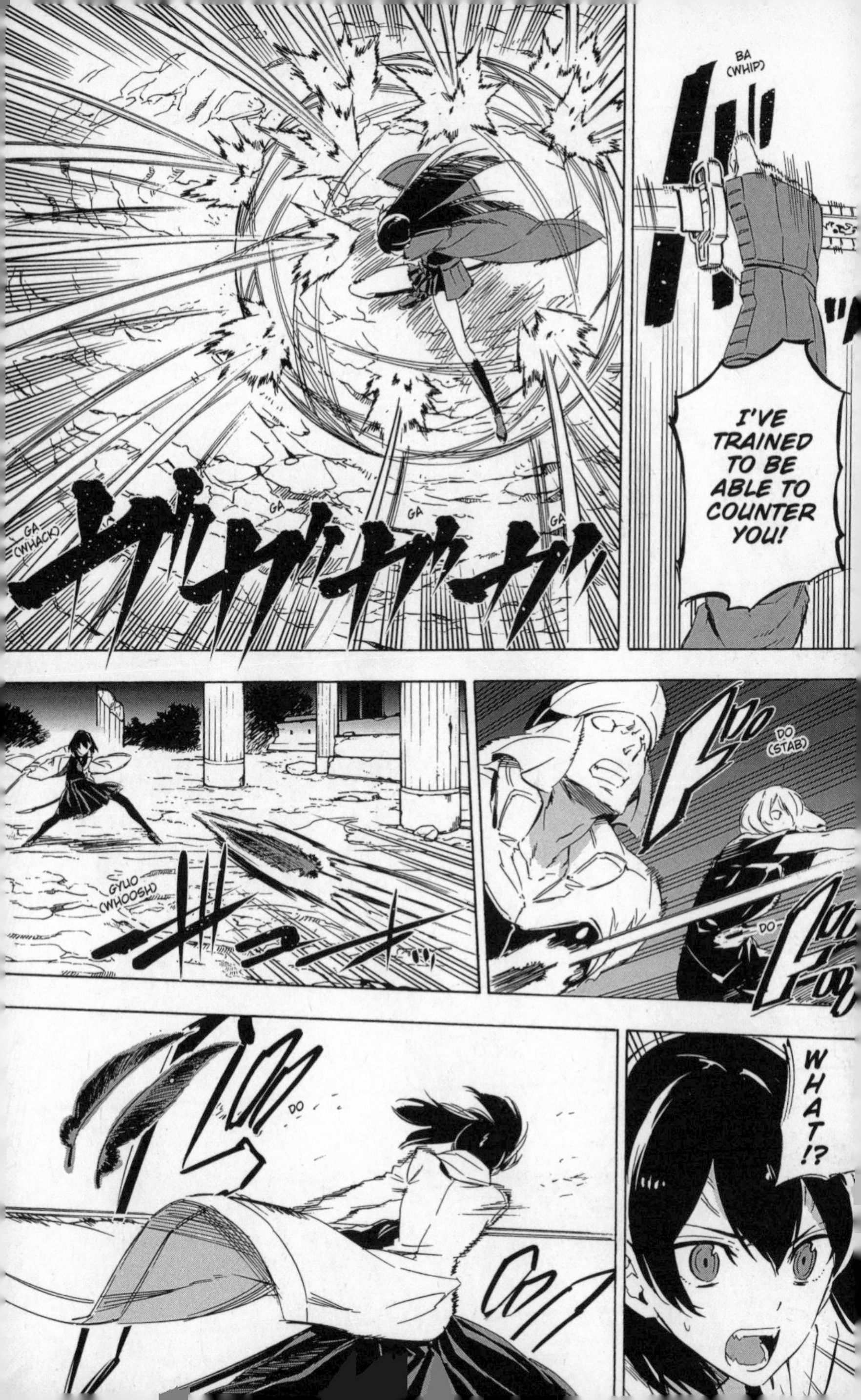
BA (WHIP)
I'VE TRAINED TO BE ABLE TO COUNTER YOU!
GA
GA
GA
GA (WHACK)
DO (STAB)
DO
GYUO (WHOOSH)
WHAT!?
DO

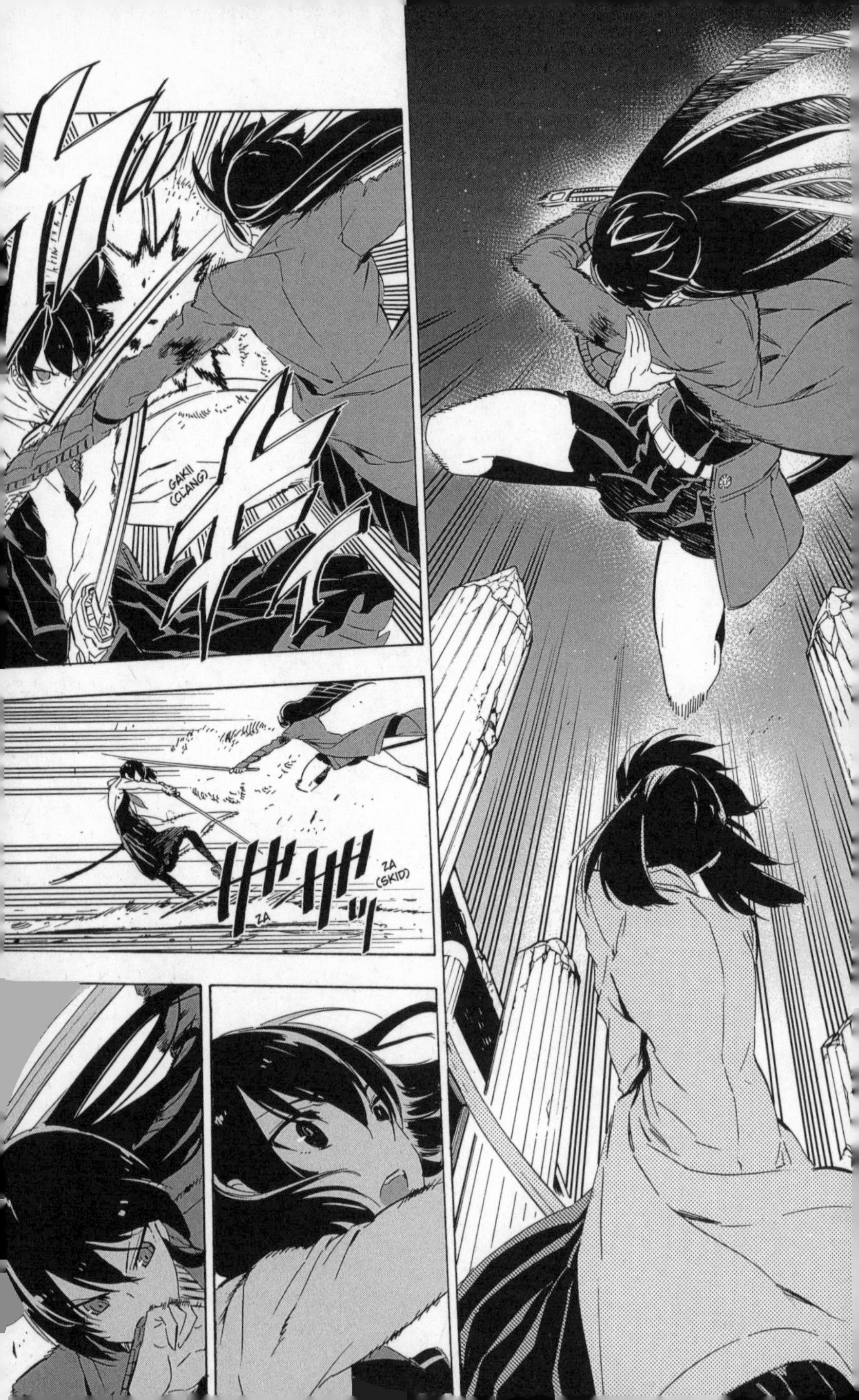
GAKII (CLANG)
ZA (SKID)
ZA

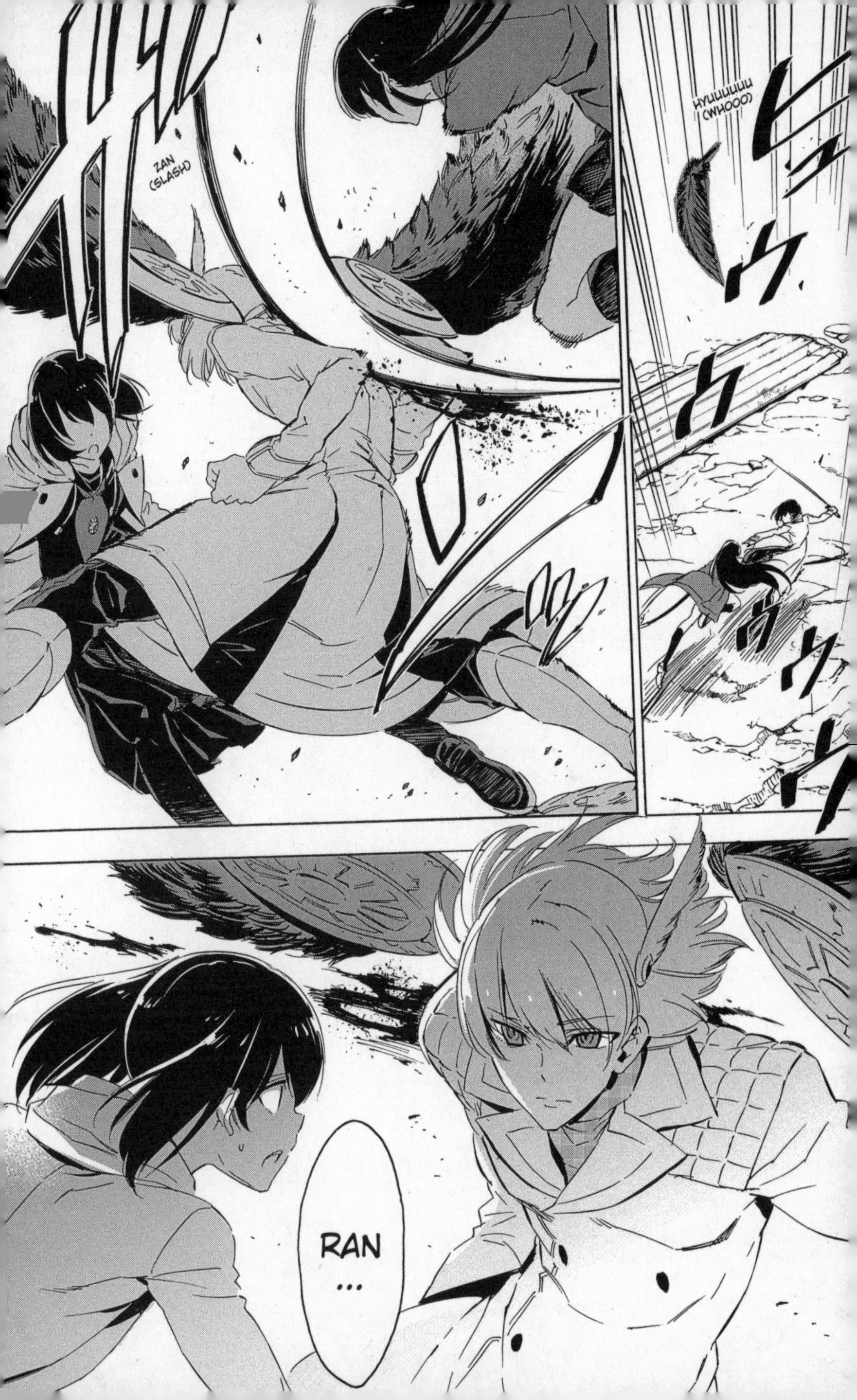
HYUUUUUUN (WHOOO)
ZAN (SLASH)
RAN ...

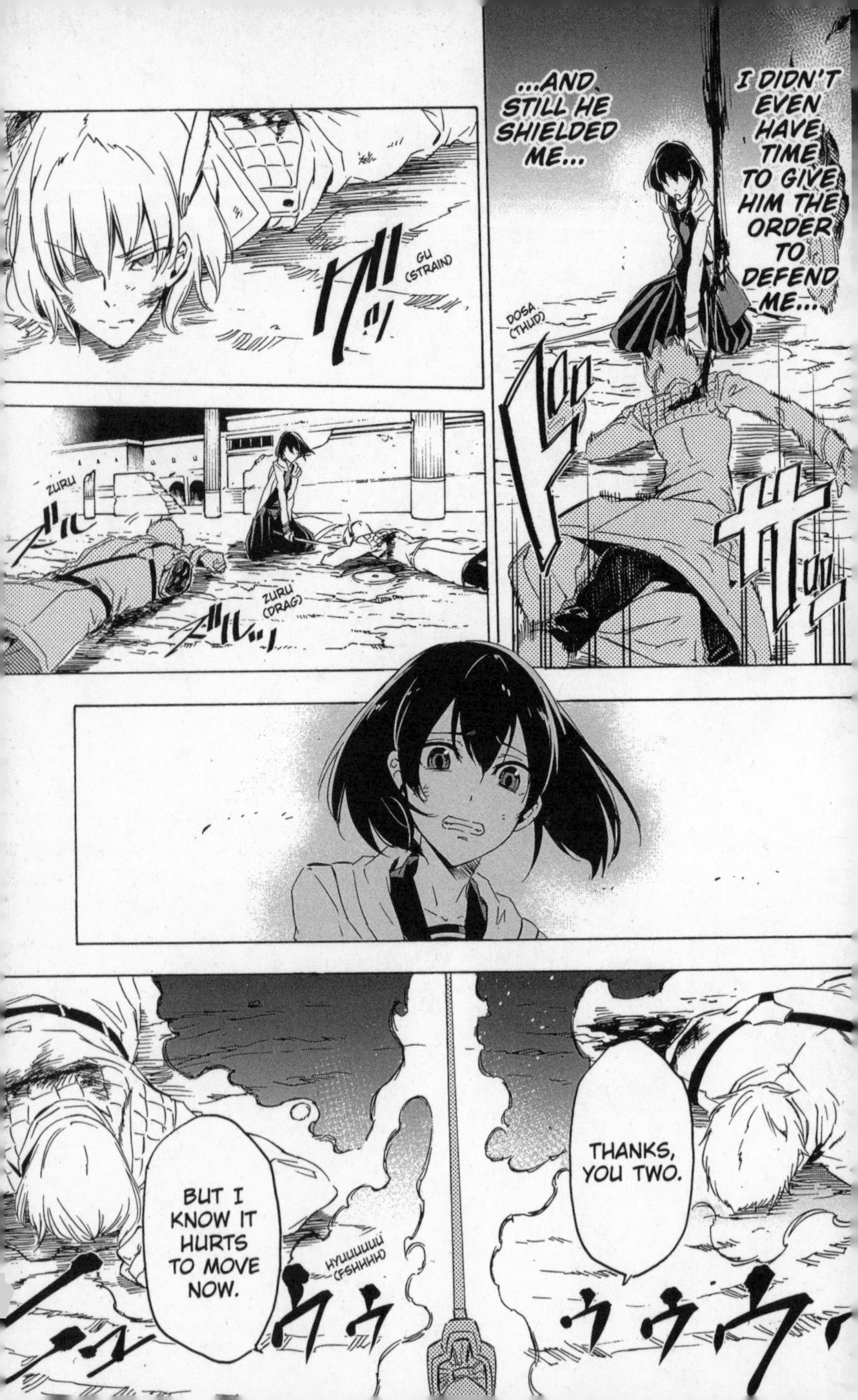
I DIDN'T EVEN HAVE TIME TO GIVE HIM THE ORDER TO DEFEND ME...
...AND STILL HE SHIELDED ME...
DOSA (THUD)
GU (STRAIN)
ZURU
ZURU (DRAG)
THANKS, YOU TWO.
HYUUUUUUU (FSHHHH)
BUT I KNOW IT HURTS TO MOVE NOW.

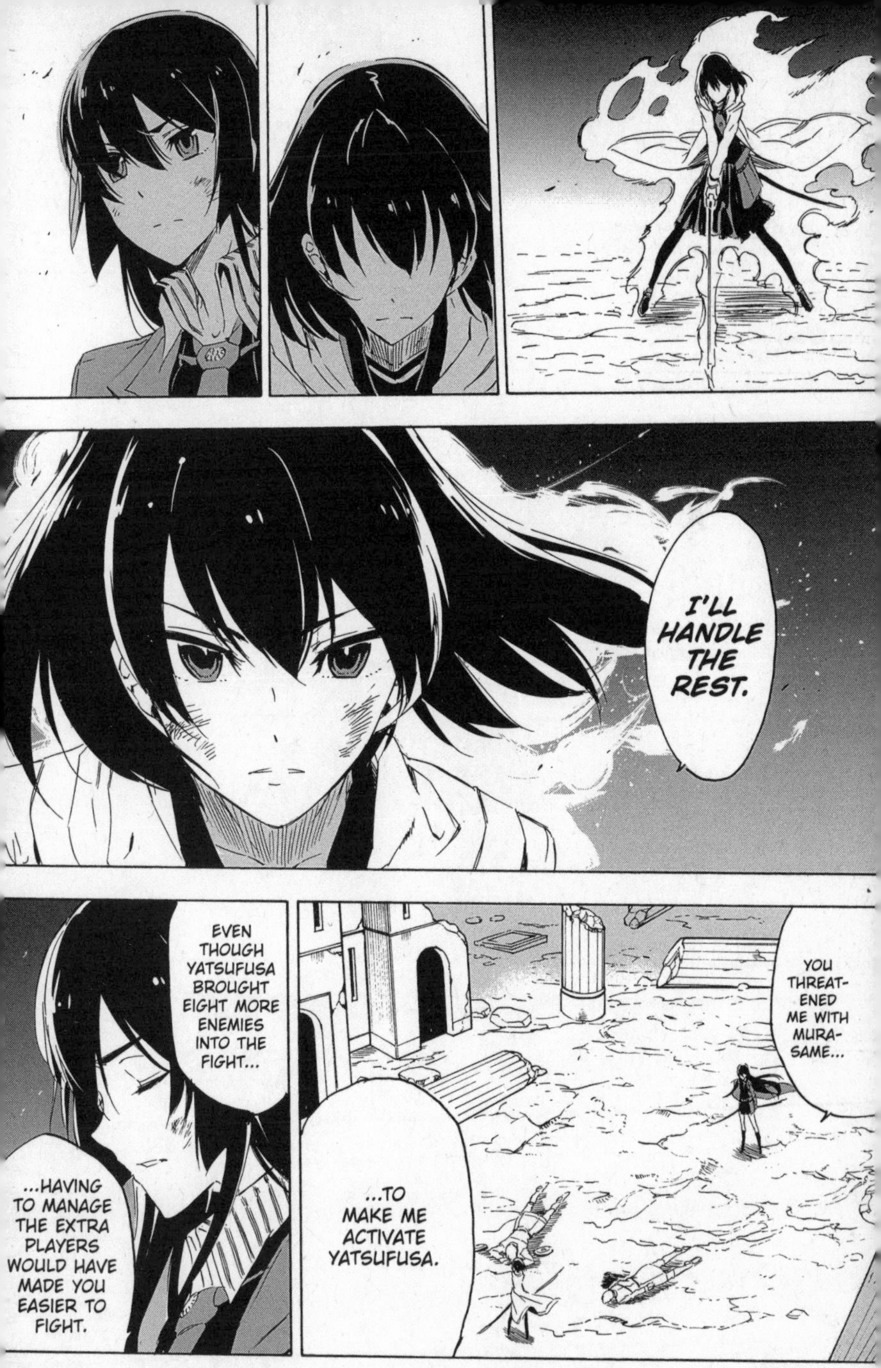
I'LL HANDLE THE REST.
YOU THREATENED ME WITH MURASAME...
...TO MAKE ME ACTIVATE YATSUFUSA.
EVEN THOUGH YATSUFUSA BROUGHT EIGHT MORE ENEMIES INTO THE FIGHT...
...HAVING TO MANAGE THE EXTRA PLAYERS WOULD HAVE MADE YOU EASIER TO FIGHT.

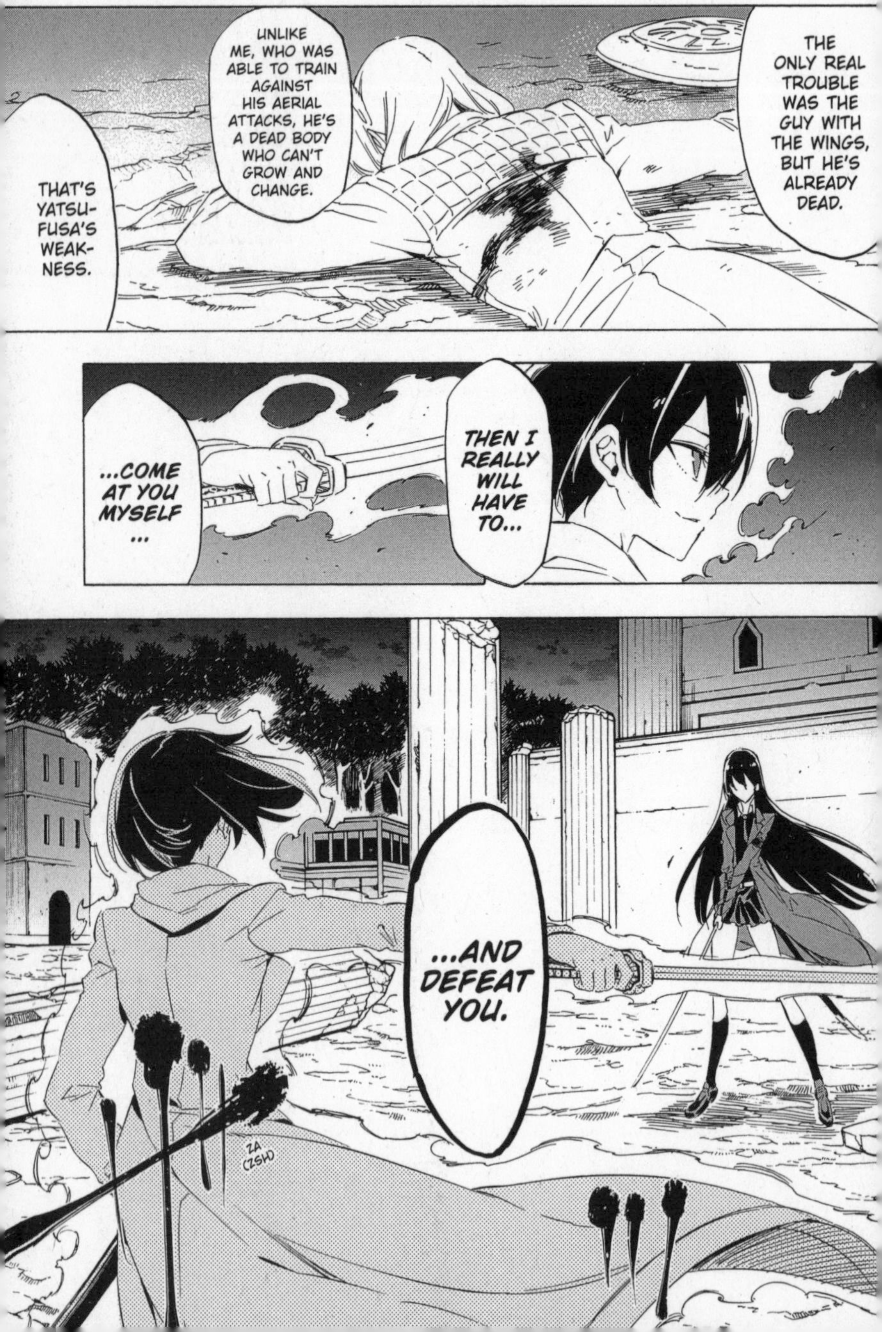
THE ONLY REAL TROUBLE WAS THE GUY WITH THE WINGS, BUT HE'S ALREADY DEAD.
UNLIKE ME, WHO WAS ABLE TO TRAIN AGAINST HIS AERIAL ATTACKS, HE'S A DEAD BODY WHO CAN'T GROW AND CHANGE.
THAT'S YATSU-FUSA'S WEAK-NESS.
THEN I REALLY WILL HAVE TO...
...COME AT YOU MYSELF...
...AND DEFEAT YOU.
ZA (ZSH)

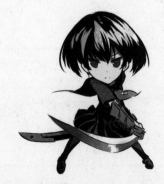

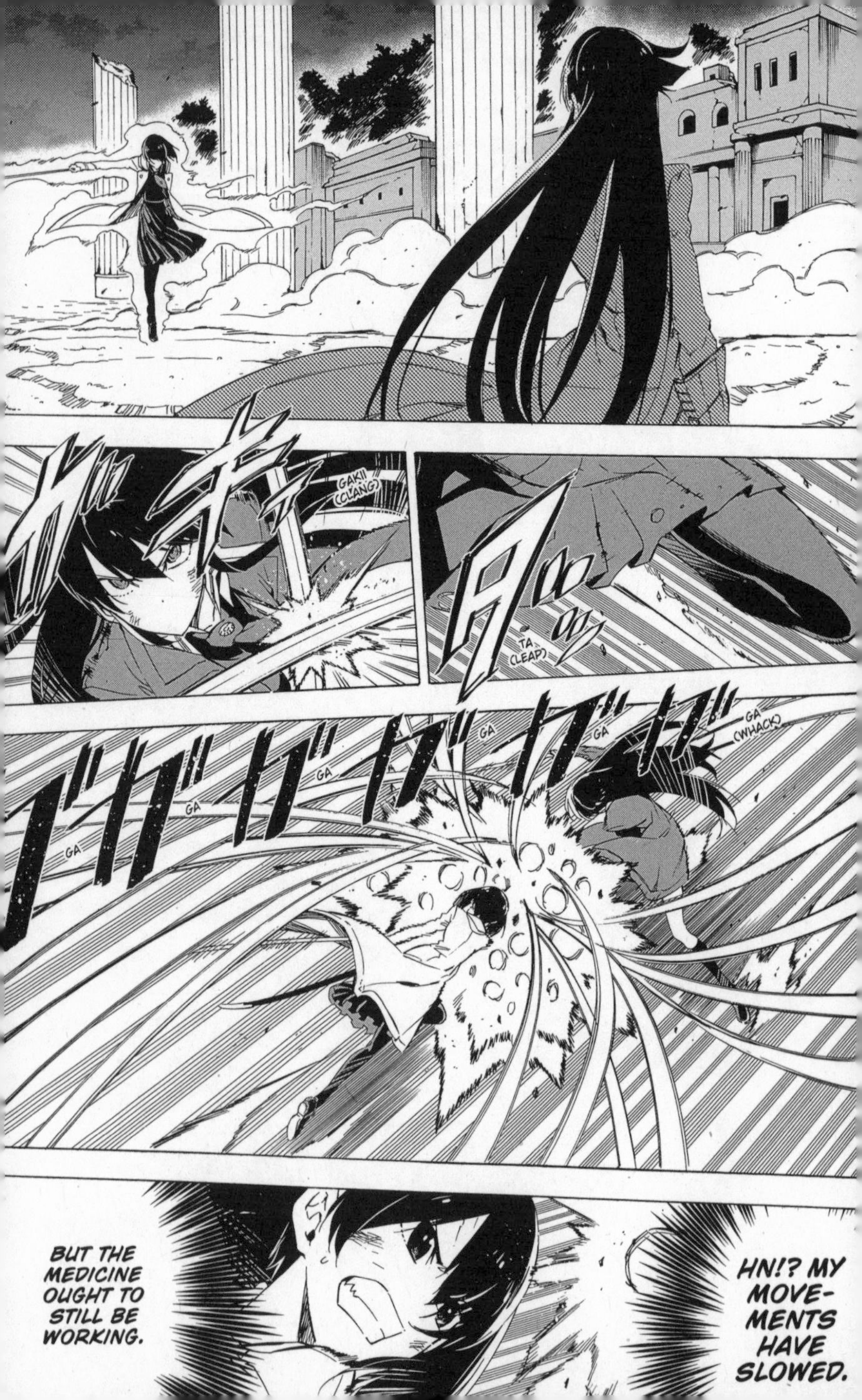
TA (LEAP)
GAKII (CLANG)
GA (WHACK)
GA
GA
GA
GA
GA
HN!? MY MOVE-MENTS HAVE SLOWED.
BUT THE MEDICINE OUGHT TO STILL BE WORKING.

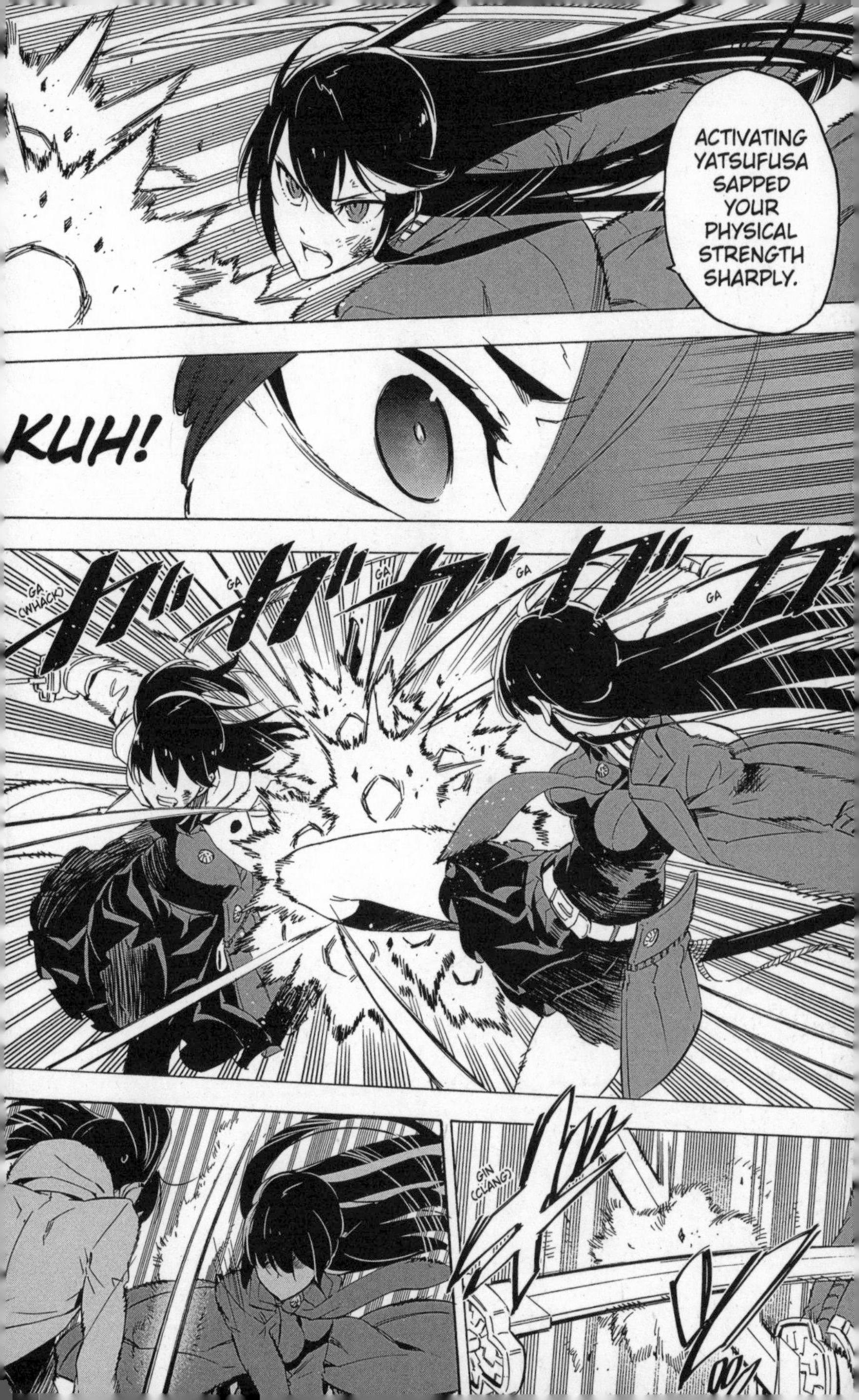
ACTIVATING YATSUFUSA SAPPED YOUR PHYSICAL STRENGTH SHARPLY.
KUH!
GA GA GA GA GA (WHACK)
GIN (CLANG)

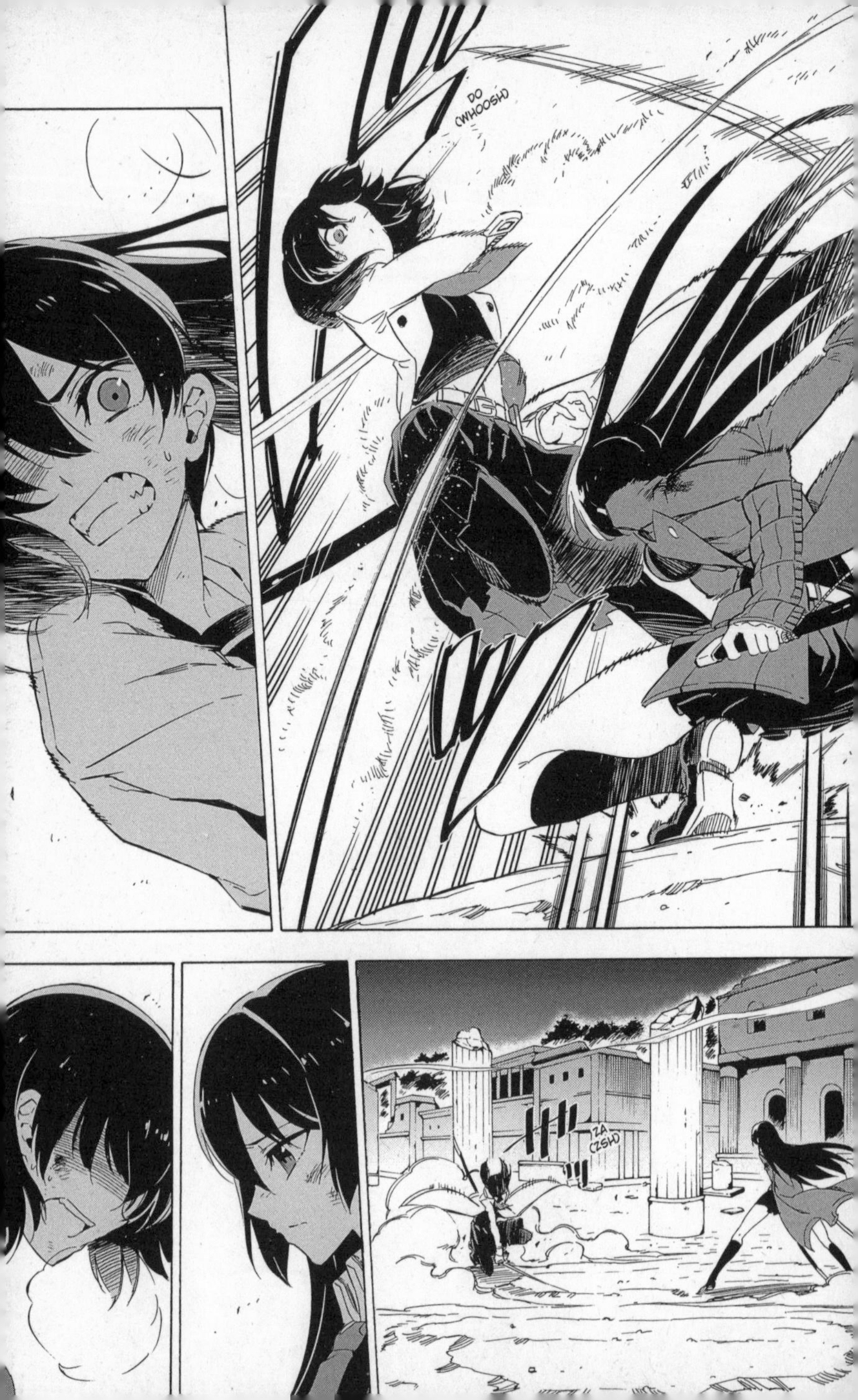
DO (WHOOSH)
ZA (ZSH)

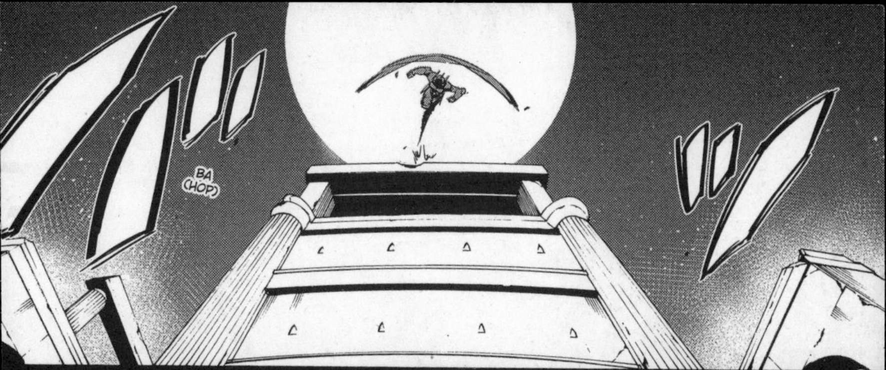
BA
(HOP)

Chapter 66

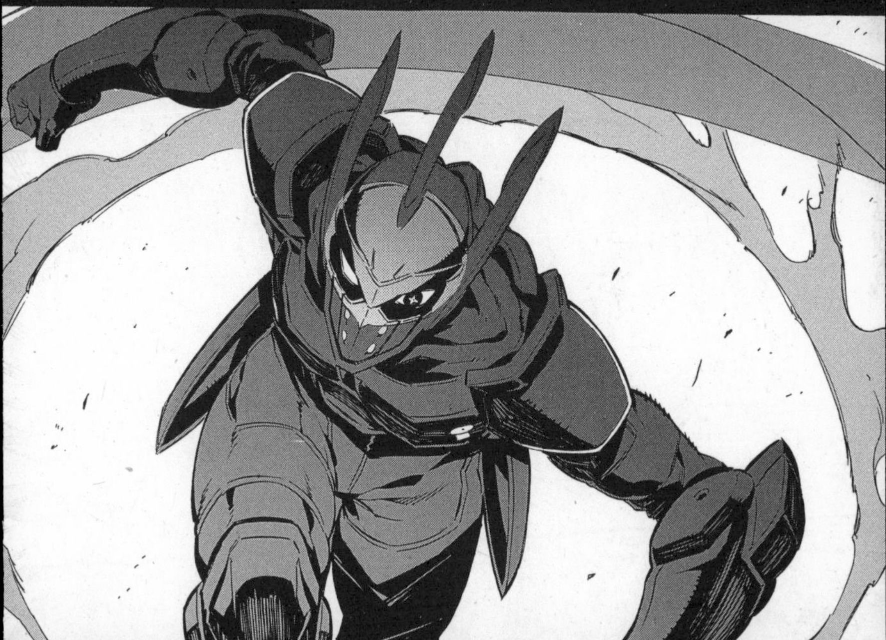

KILL THE FATE

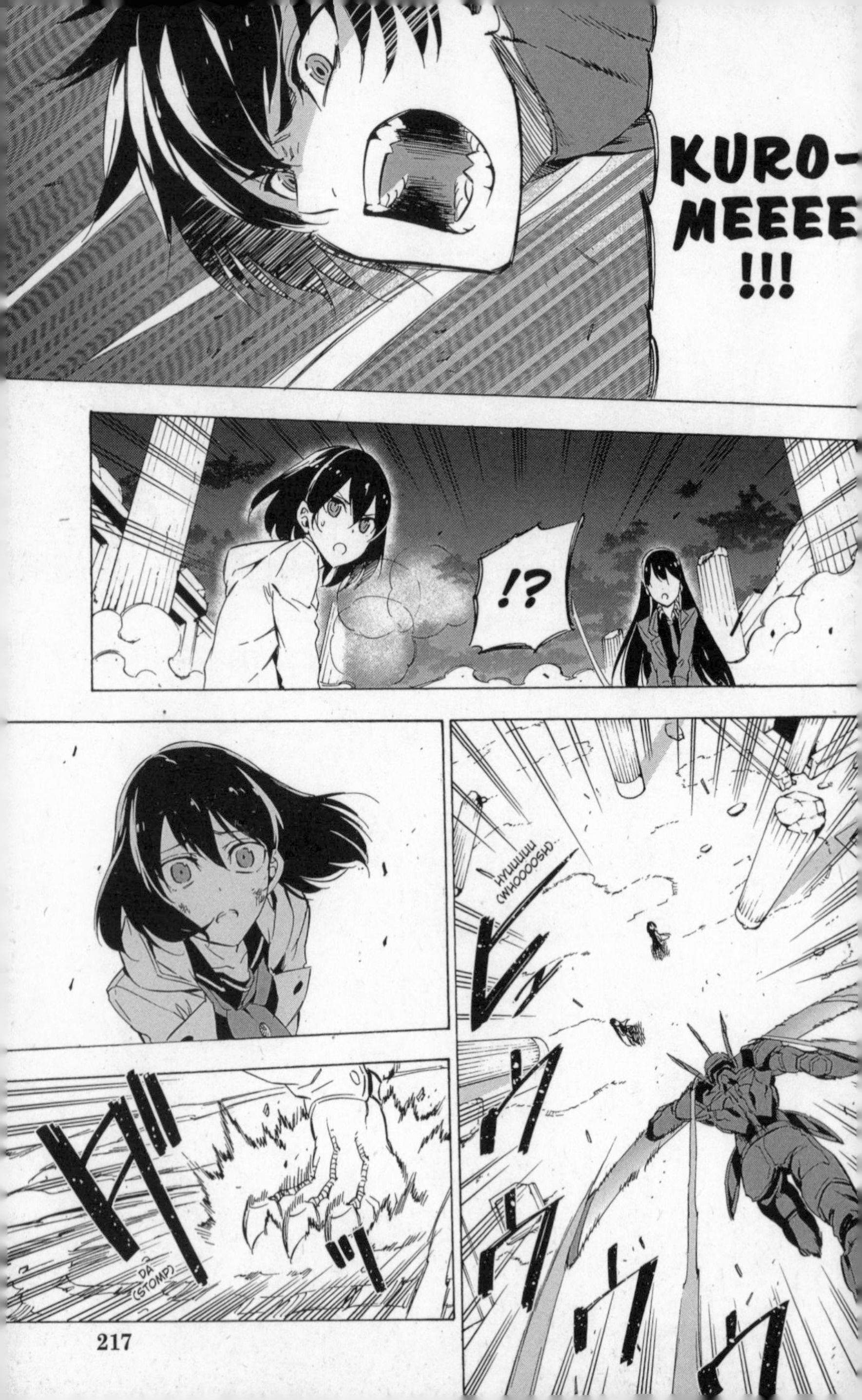
KURO-MEEEE!!!
!?
HYUUUUN (WHOOOOSH)
DA (STOMP)

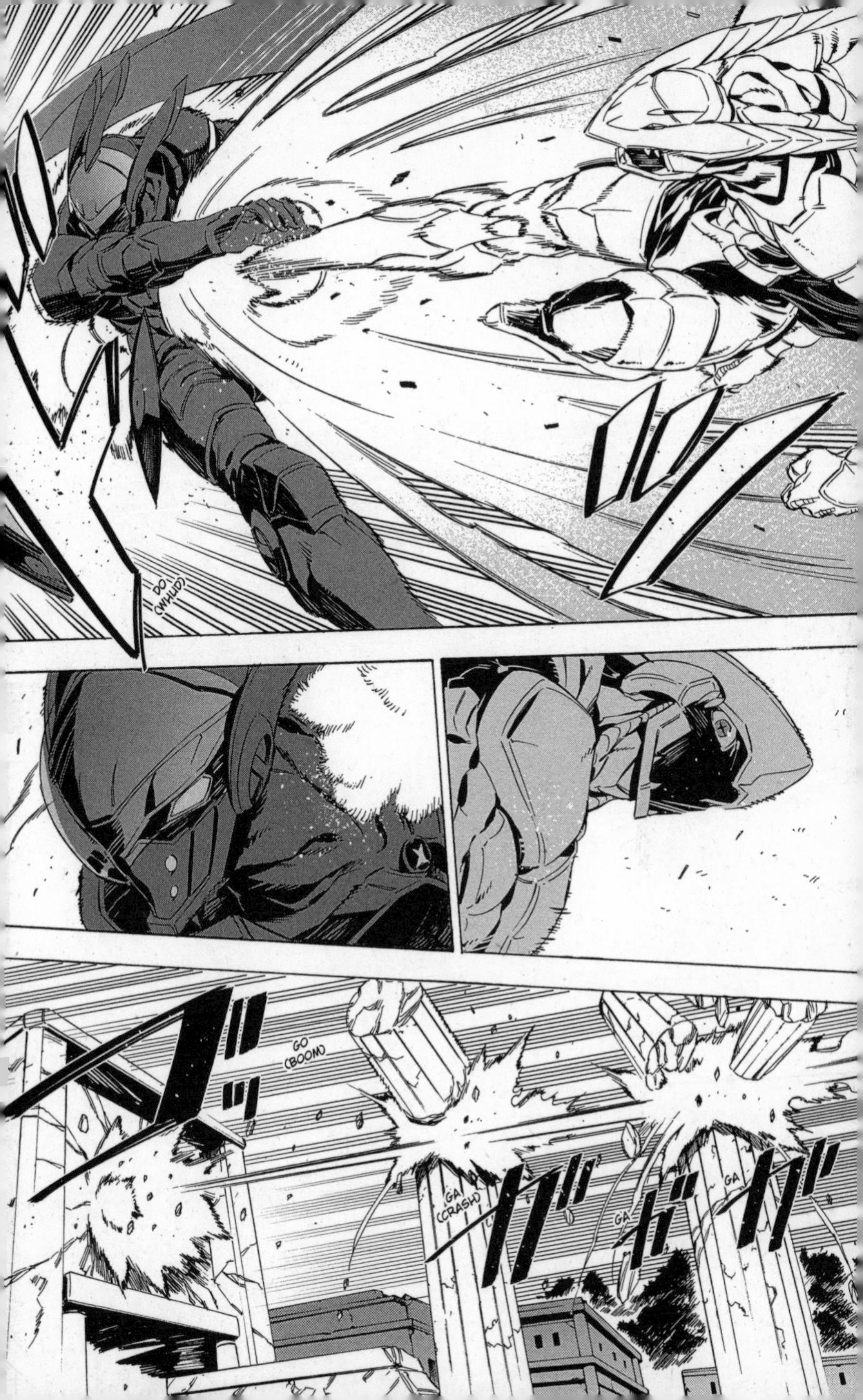
DO
(WHUD)
GO
(BOOM)
GA
GA
GA
(CRASH)

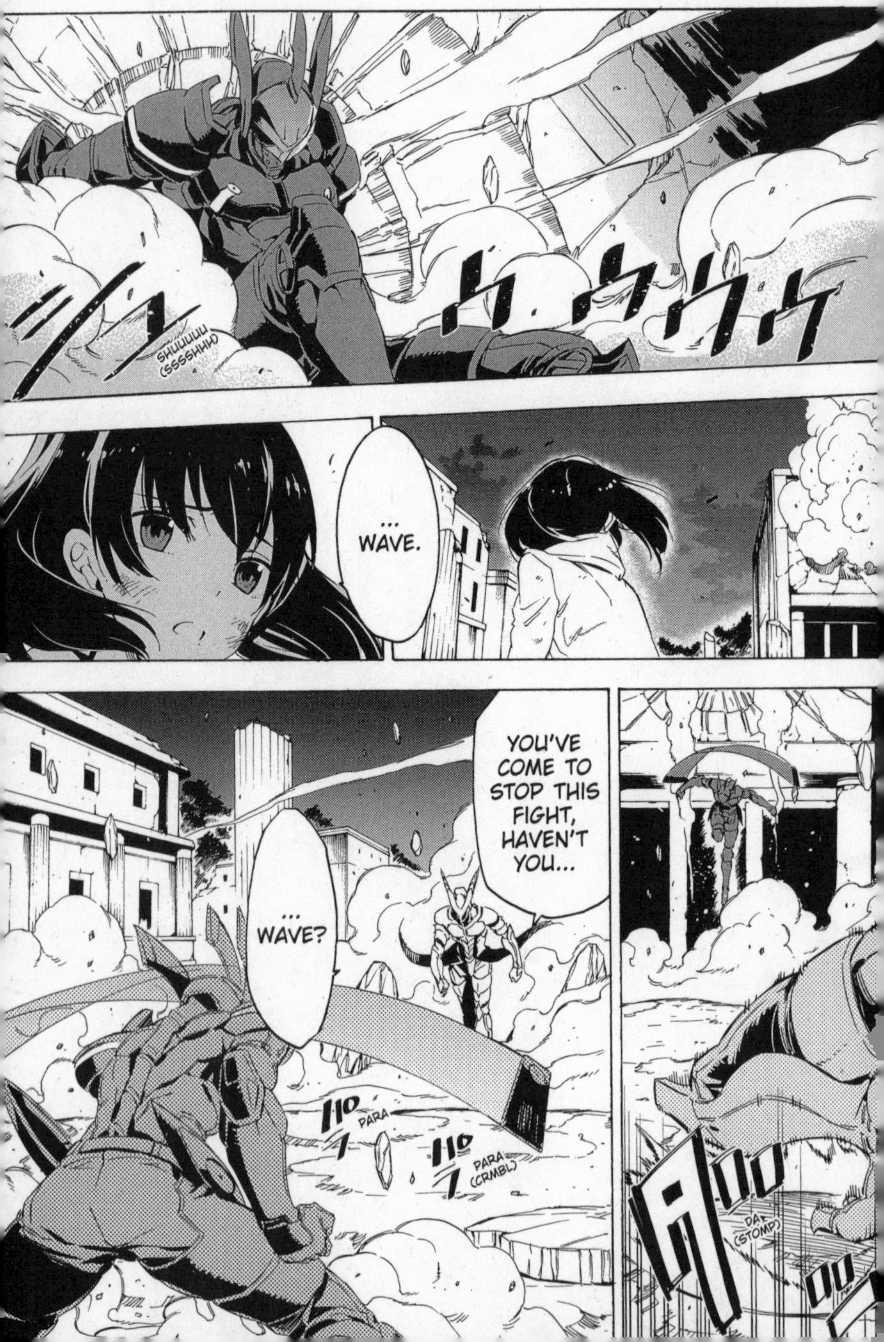
SHUUUUN (SSSSSHH)
... WAVE.
DA (STOMP)
YOU'VE COME TO STOP THIS FIGHT, HAVEN'T YOU...
... WAVE?
PARA
PARA (CRMBL)

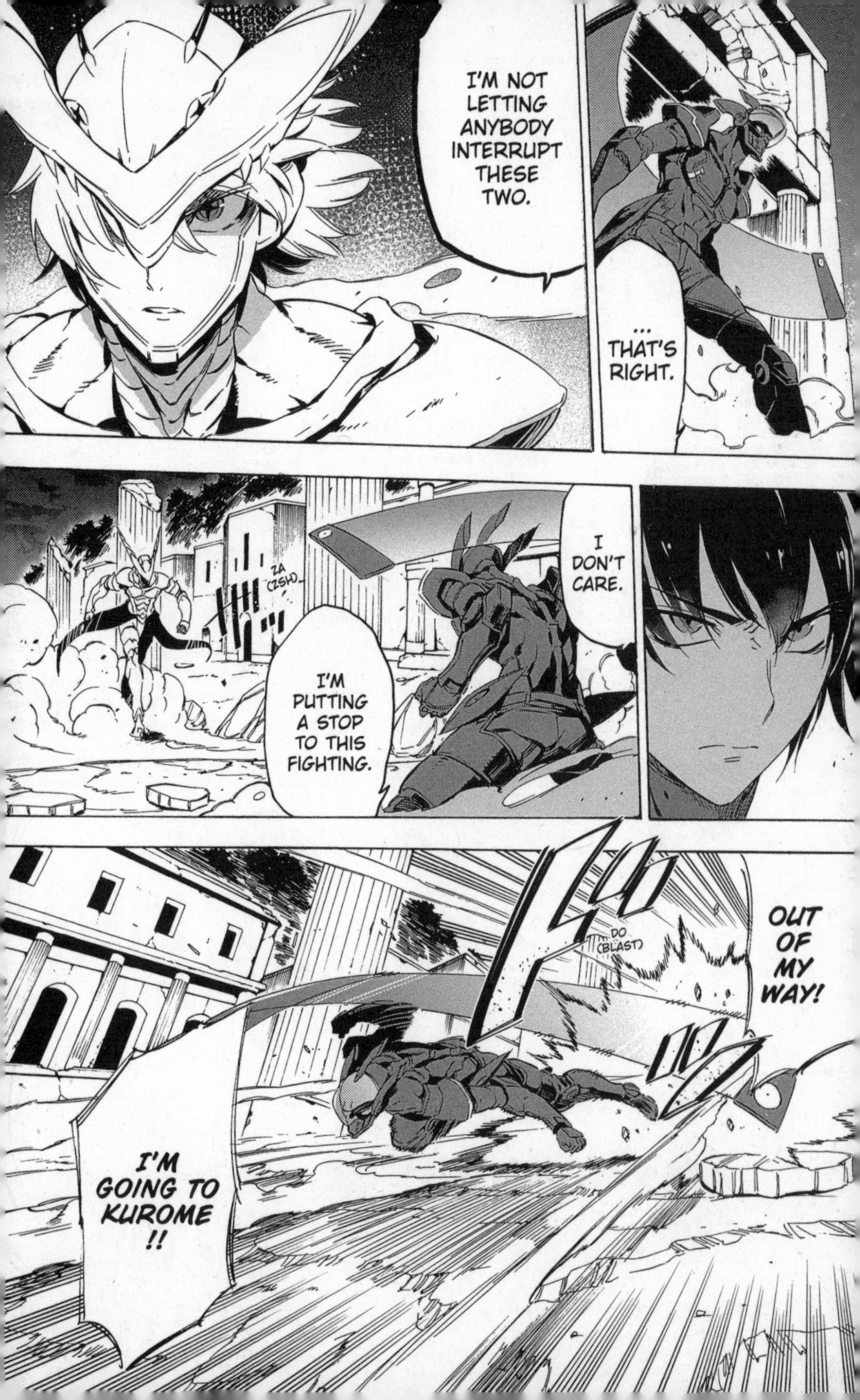
... THAT'S RIGHT.
I'M NOT LETTING ANYBODY INTERRUPT THESE TWO.
I DON'T CARE.
ZA (ZSH)
I'M PUTTING A STOP TO THIS FIGHTING.
OUT OF MY WAY!
DO (BLAST)
I'M GOING TO KUROME !!

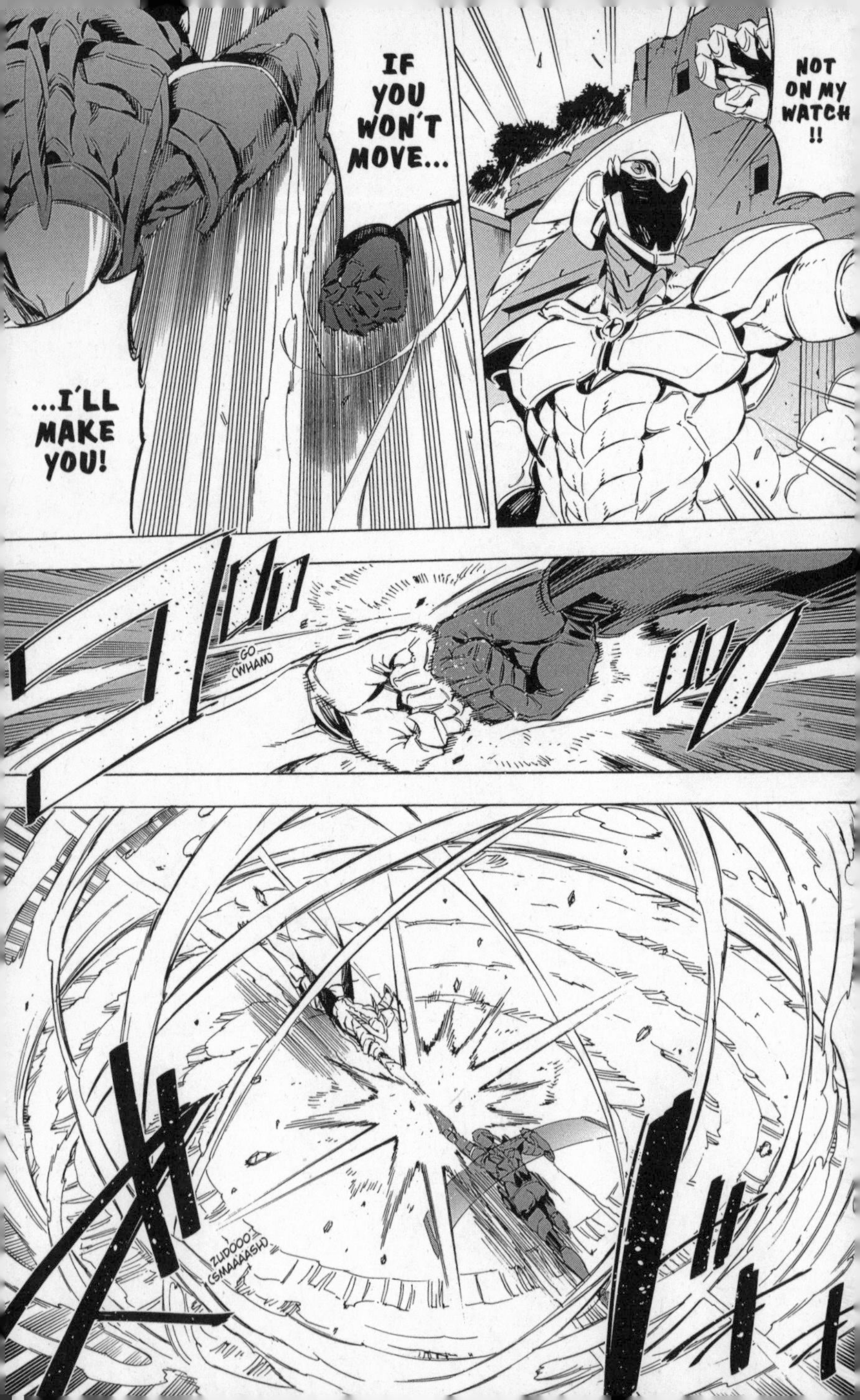
NOT ON MY WATCH!!
IF YOU WON'T MOVE...
...I'LL MAKE YOU!
GO (WHAM)
ZUDOOO (SMAAAASH)

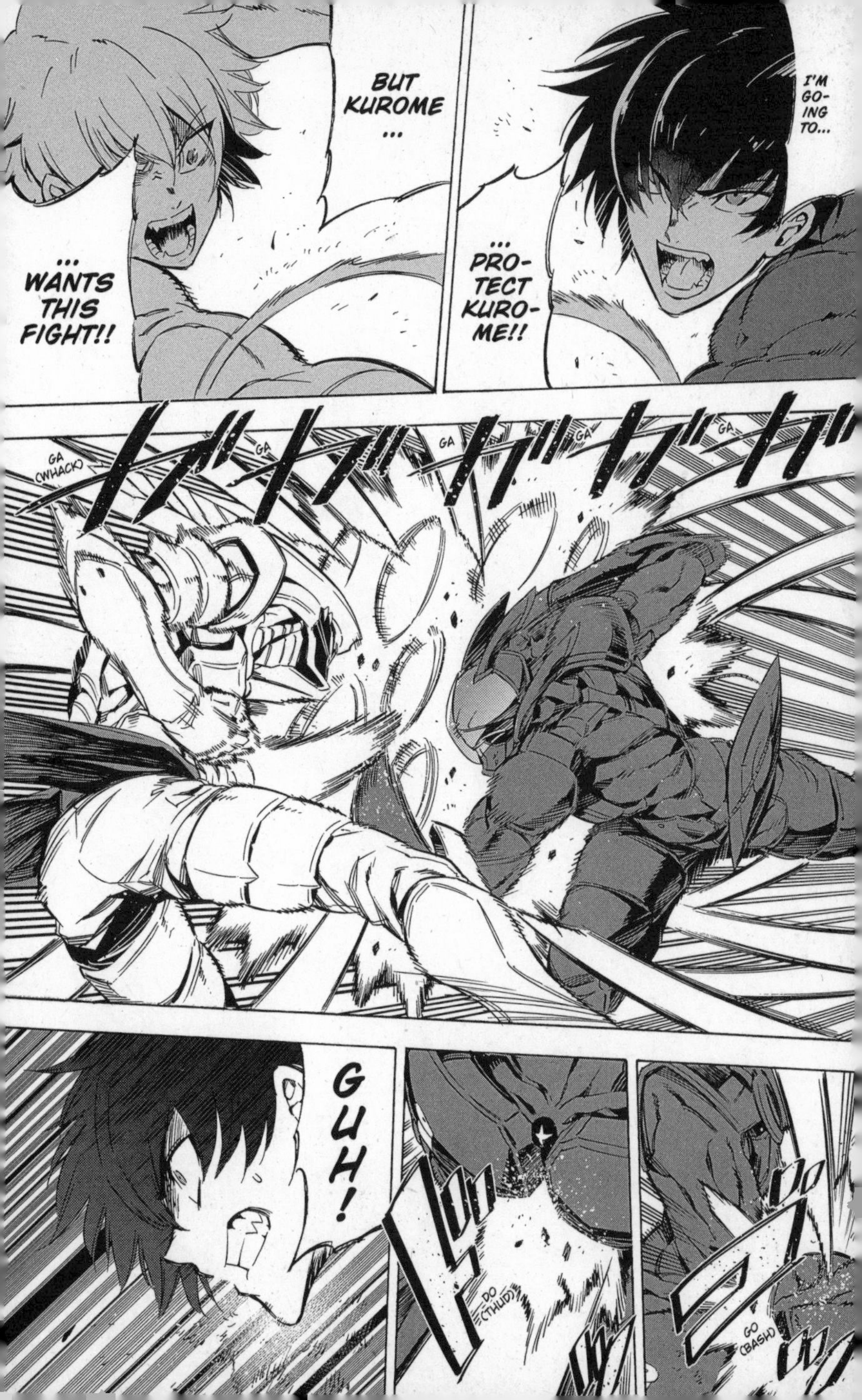
I'M GOING TO...
...PROTECT KUROME!!
BUT KUROME...
...WANTS THIS FIGHT!!
GA
GA
GA
GA
GA (WHACK)
GO (BASH)
DO (THUD)
GUH!

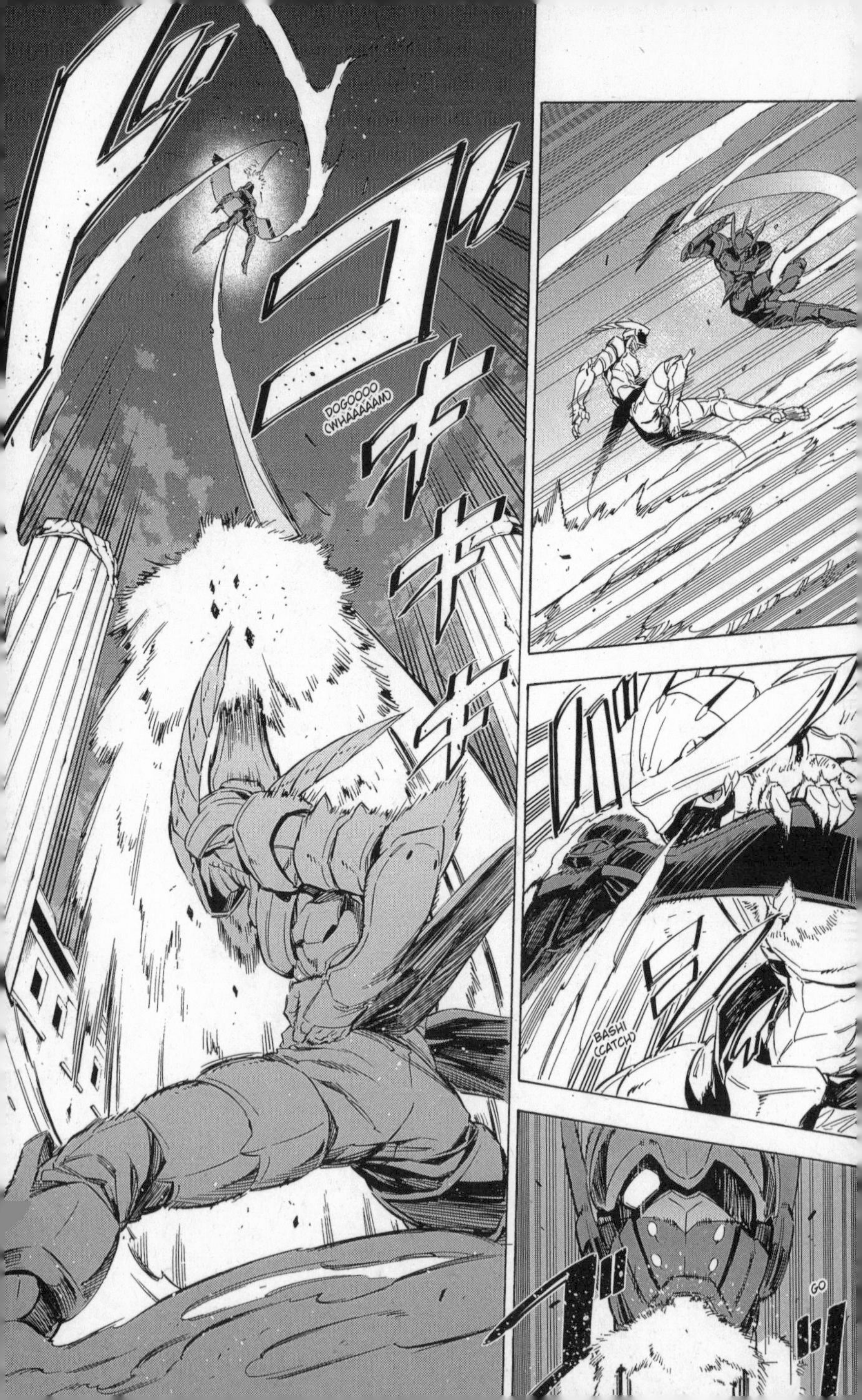
BASHI
(CATCH)
GO
DOGOOOO
(WHAAAAAM)

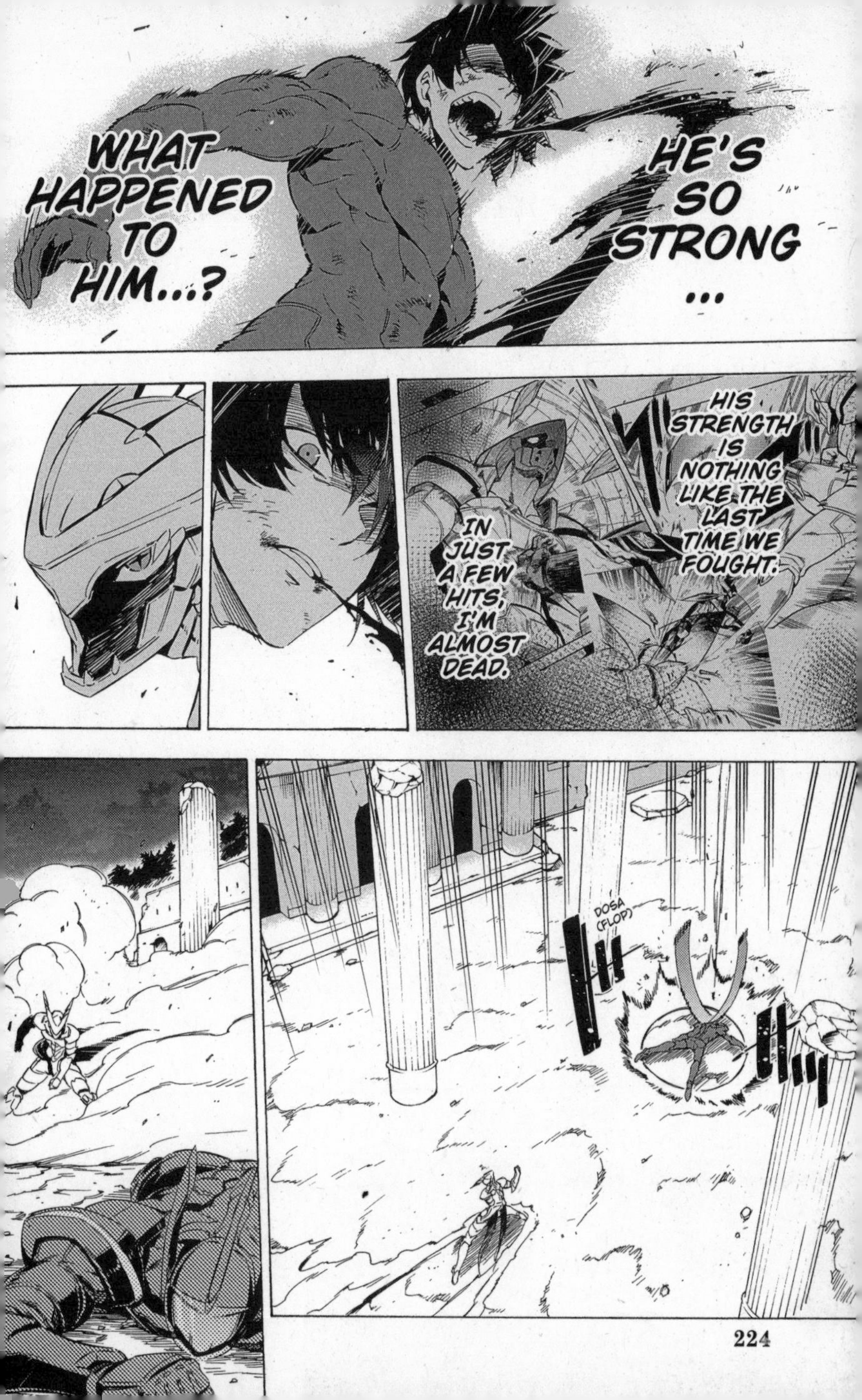
HE'S SO STRONG...
WHAT HAPPENED TO HIM...?
HIS STRENGTH IS NOTHING LIKE THE LAST TIME WE FOUGHT.
IN JUST A FEW HITS, I'M ALMOST DEAD.
DOSA (FLOP)

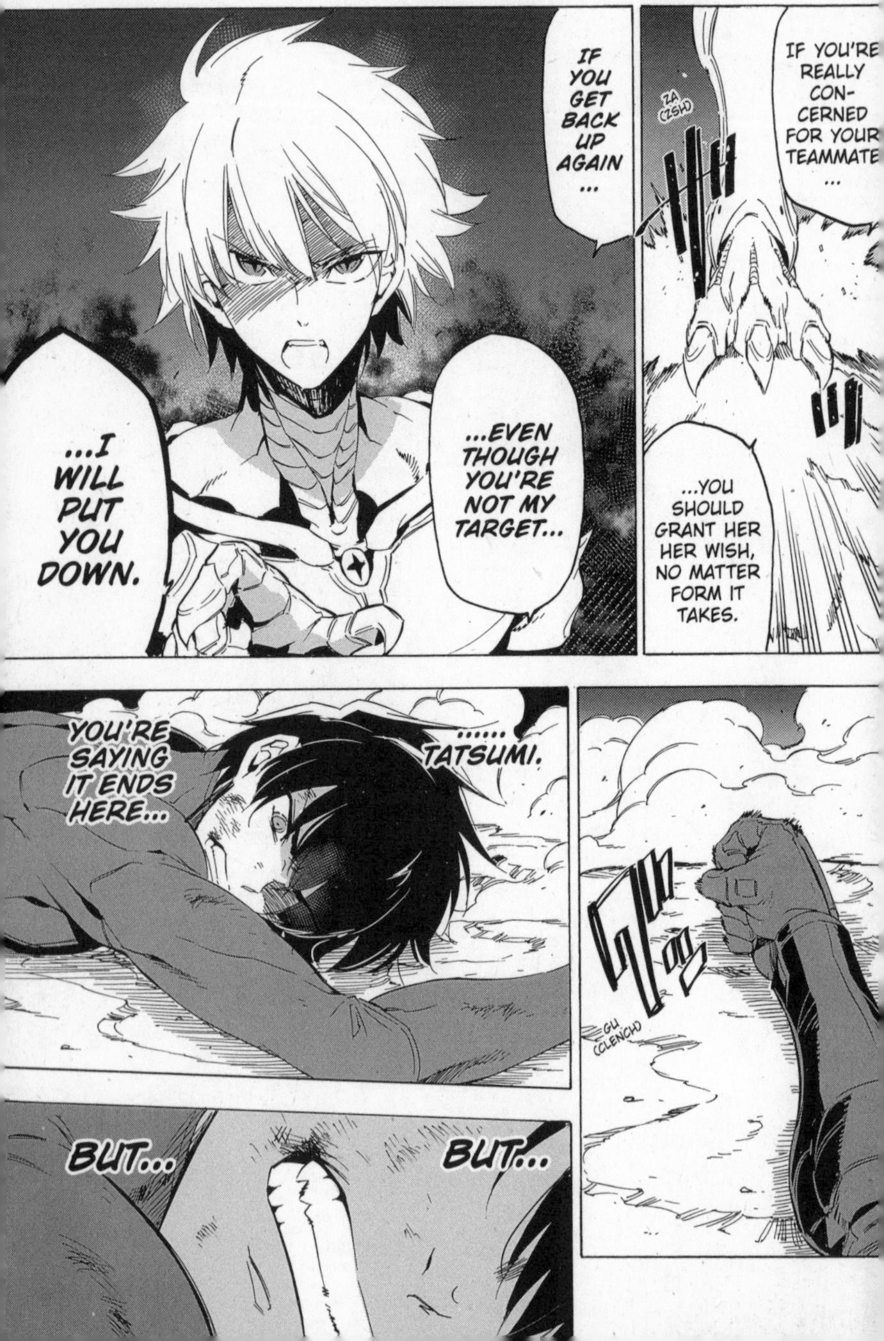
IF YOU'RE REALLY CON-CERNED FOR YOUR TEAMMATE...
ZA (ZSH)
...YOU SHOULD GRANT HER HER WISH, NO MATTER FORM IT TAKES.
IF YOU GET BACK UP AGAIN...
...EVEN THOUGH YOU'RE NOT MY TARGET...
...I WILL PUT YOU DOWN.
GU (CLENCH)
......TATSUMI.
YOU'RE SAYING IT ENDS HERE...
BUT...
BUT...

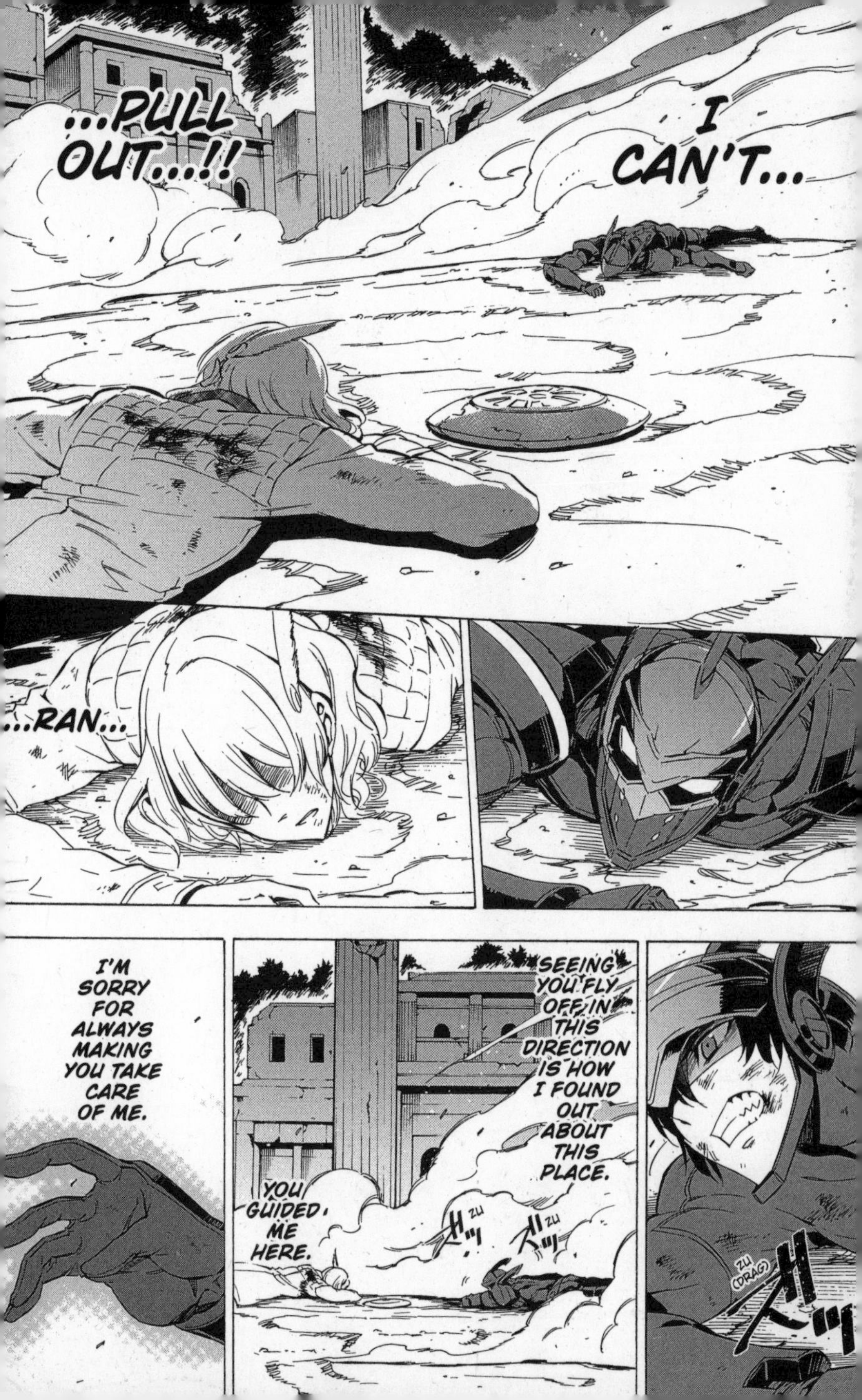
I CAN'T...
...PULL OUT...!!
...RAN...
ZU (DRAG)
SEEING YOU FLY OFF IN THIS DIRECTION IS HOW I FOUND OUT ABOUT THIS PLACE.
ZU
ZU
YOU GUIDED ME HERE.
I'M SORRY FOR ALWAYS MAKING YOU TAKE CARE OF ME.

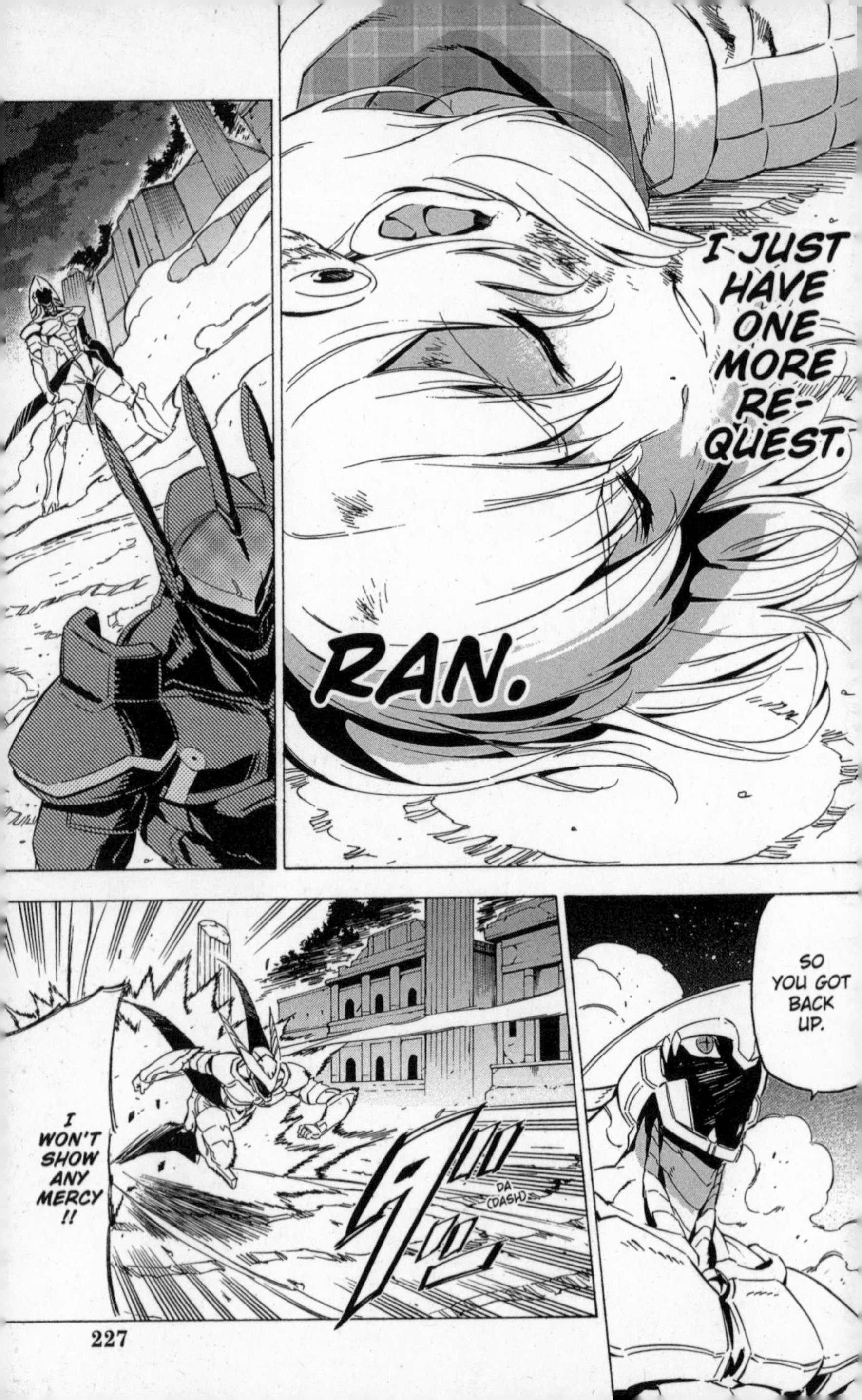
I JUST HAVE ONE MORE RE-QUEST.
RAN.
SO YOU GOT BACK UP.
I WON'T SHOW ANY MERCY!!
DA (DASH)

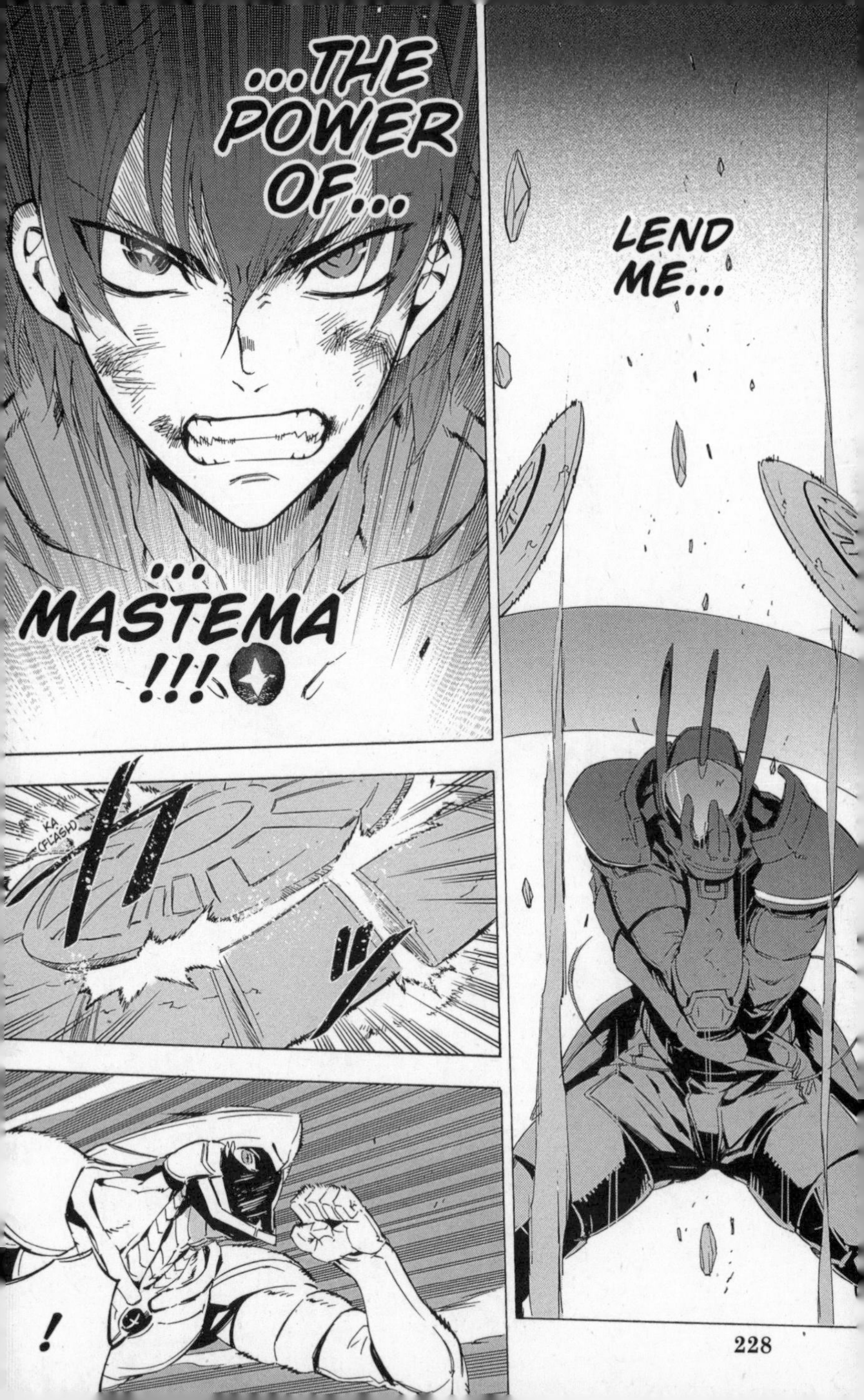
LEND ME...
...THE POWER OF...
...MASTEMA!!!
KA (FLASH)
!

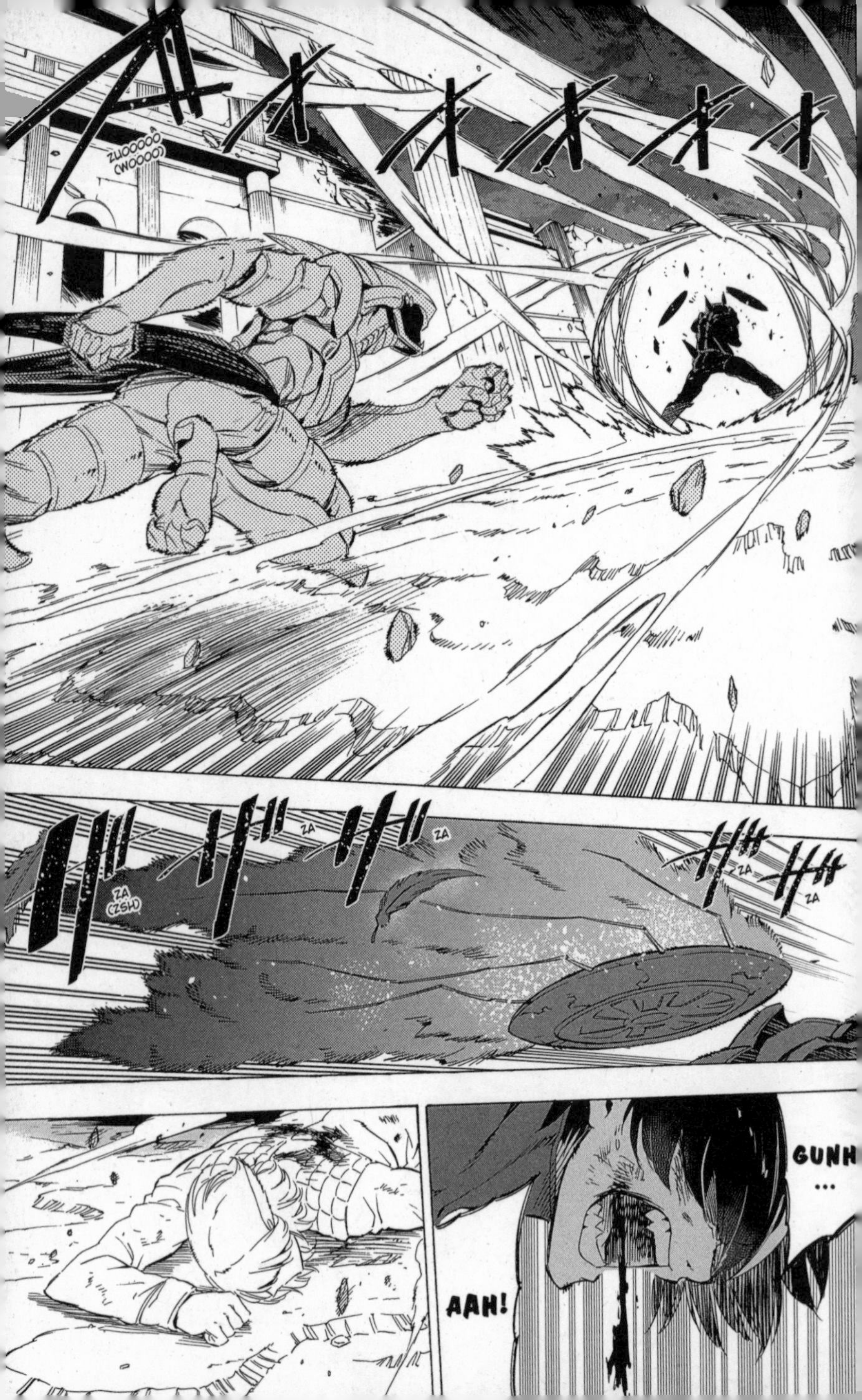
ZUOOOOO (WOOOOO)
ZA
ZA
ZA
ZA
ZA (ZSH)
GUNH...
AAH!

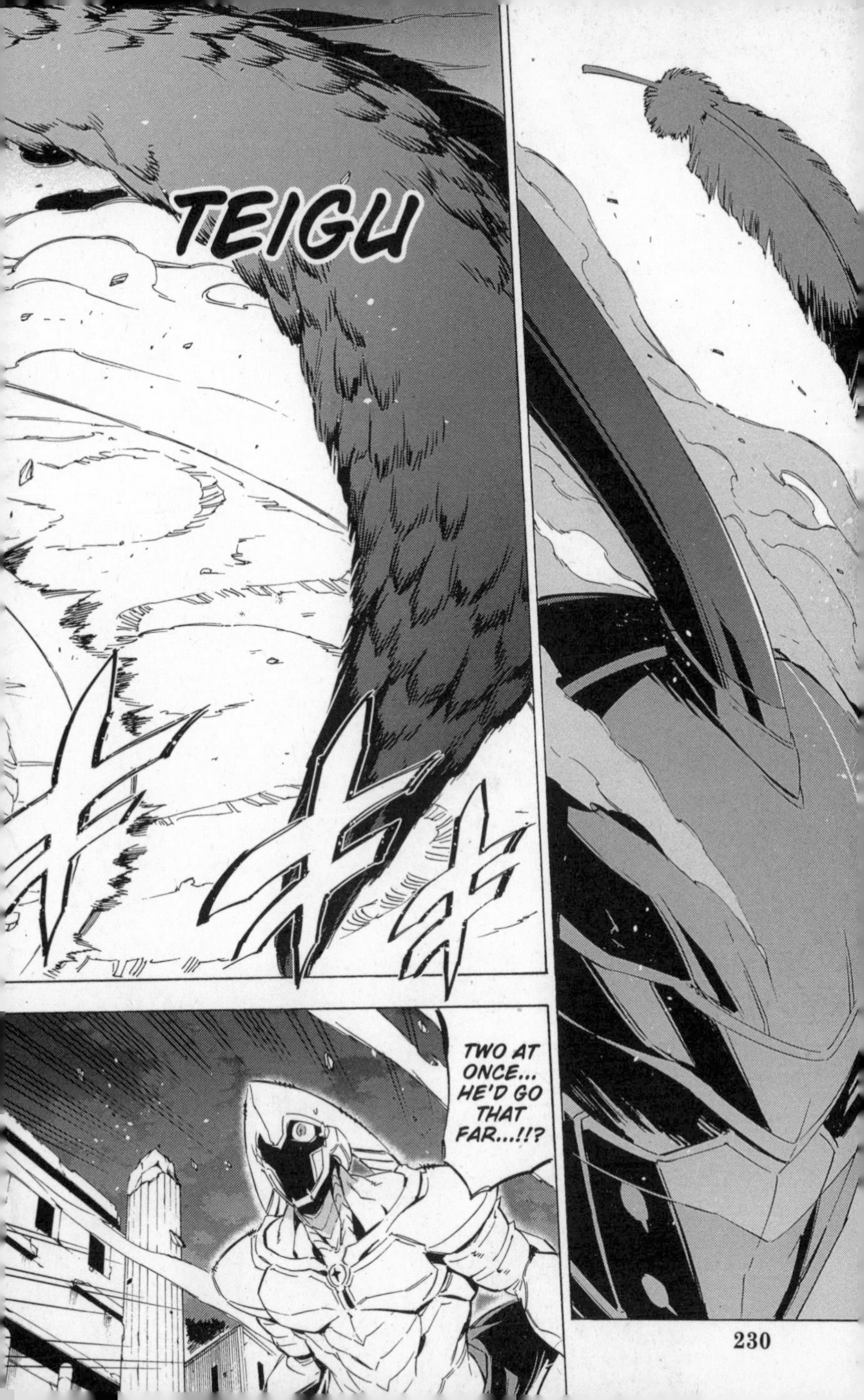
TEIGU
TWO AT ONCE... HE'D GO THAT FAR...!!?

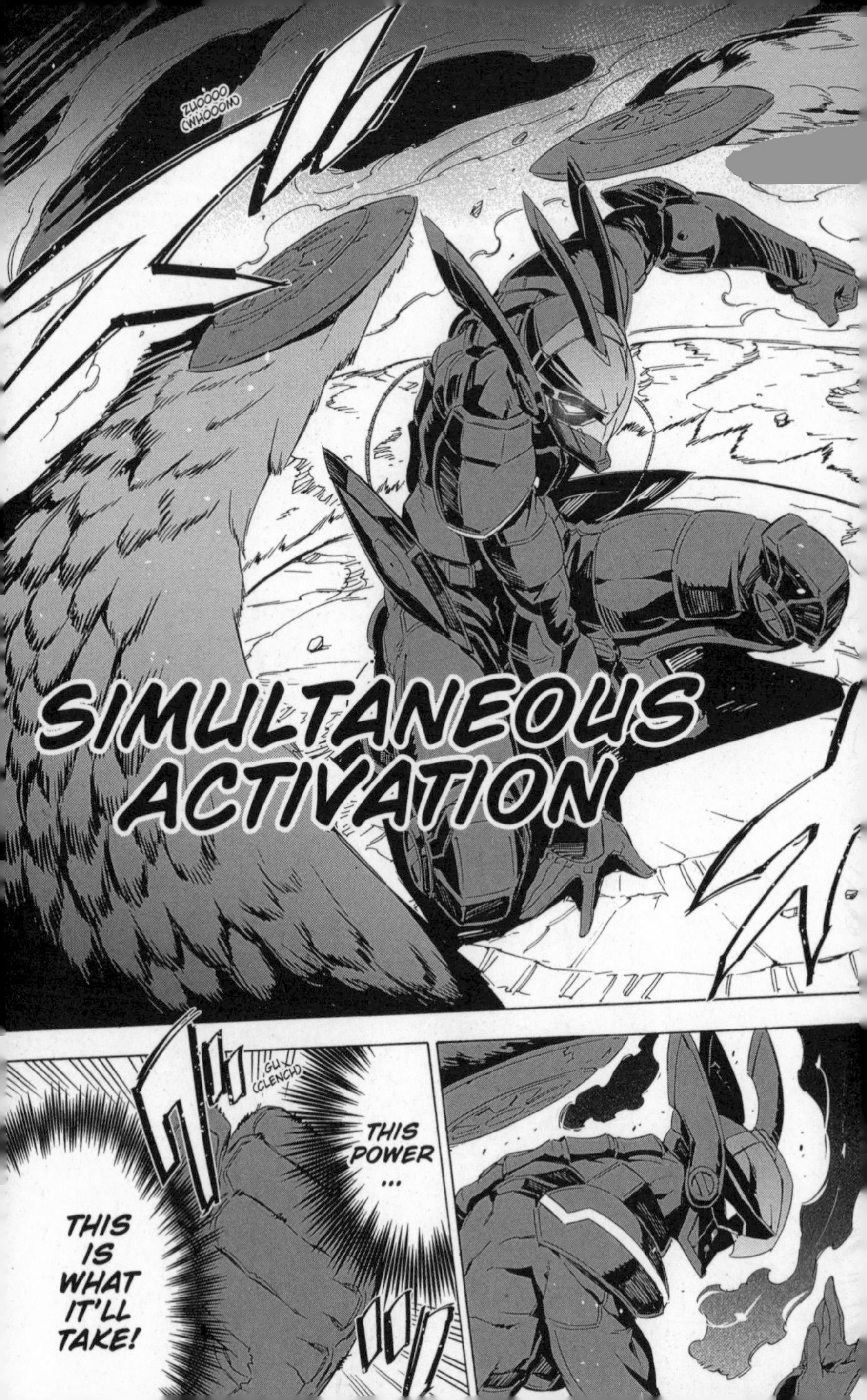
ZUOOOO
(WHOOOM)
SIMULTANEOUS ACTIVATION
GU
(CLENCH)
THIS POWER...
THIS IS WHAT IT'LL TAKE!

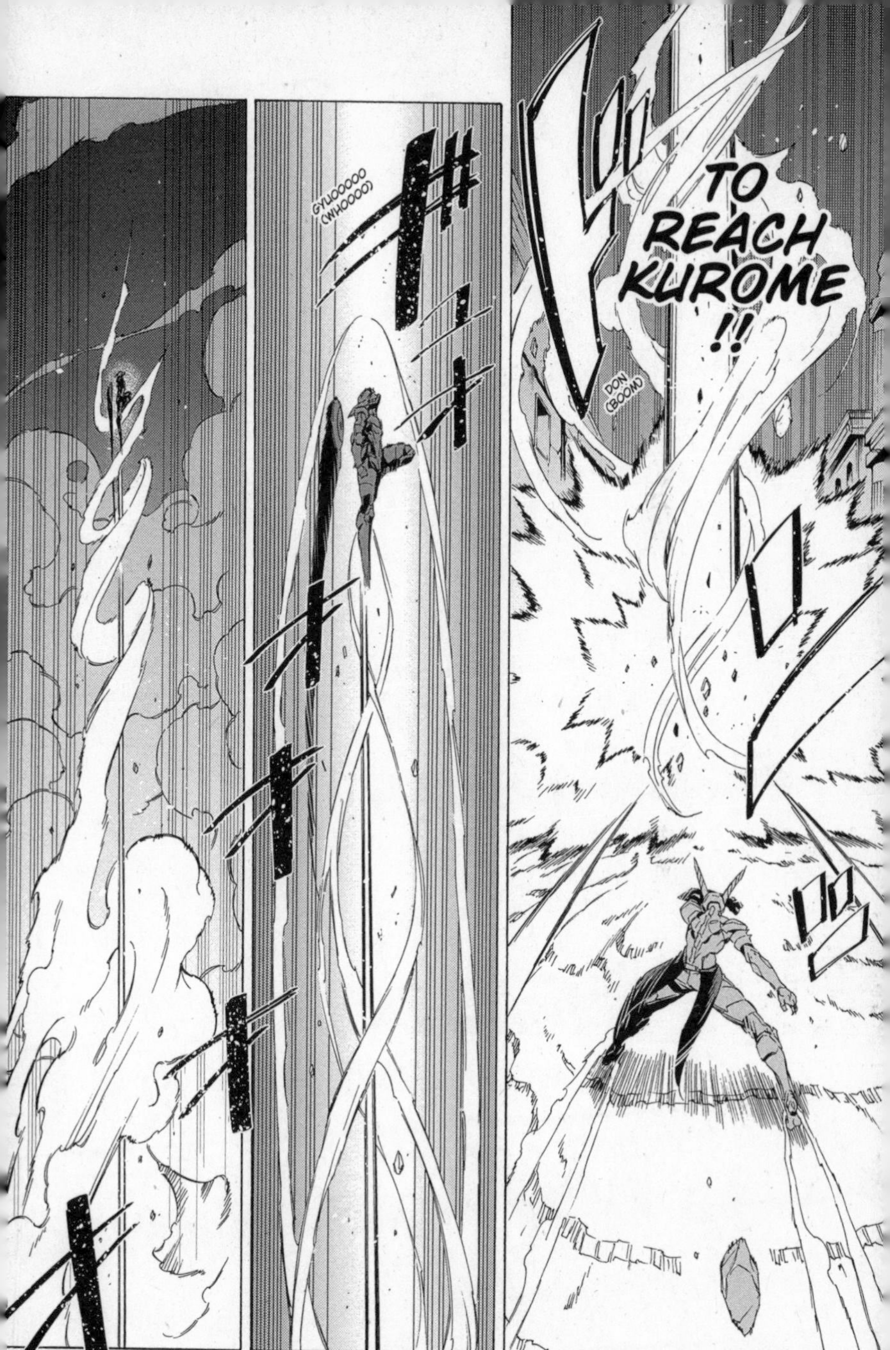
TO REACH KUROME!!
DON (BOOM)
GYUOOOOO (WHOOOO)

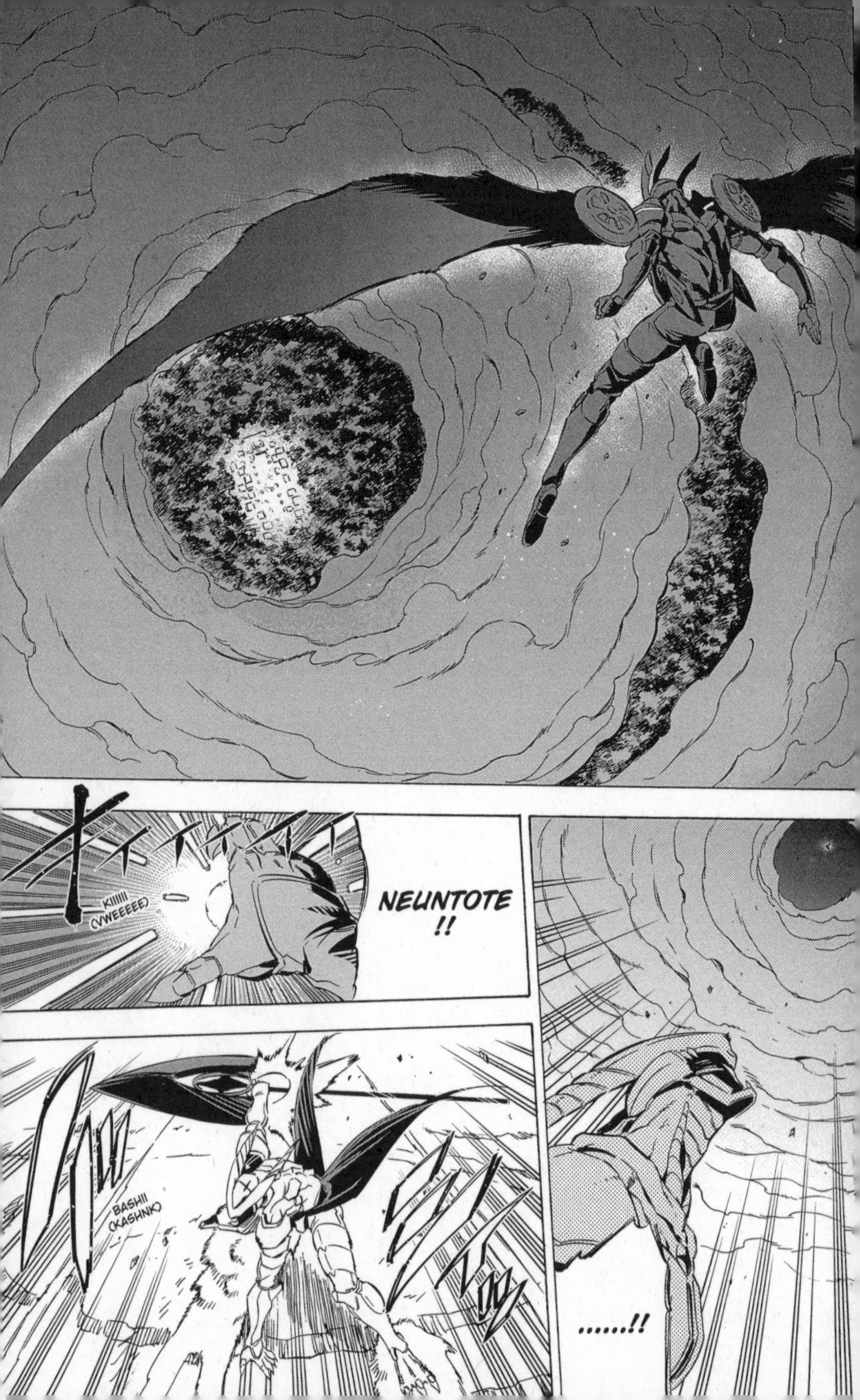
......!!
NEUNTOTE !!
KIIIIII (VWEEEEE)
BASHII (KASHNK)

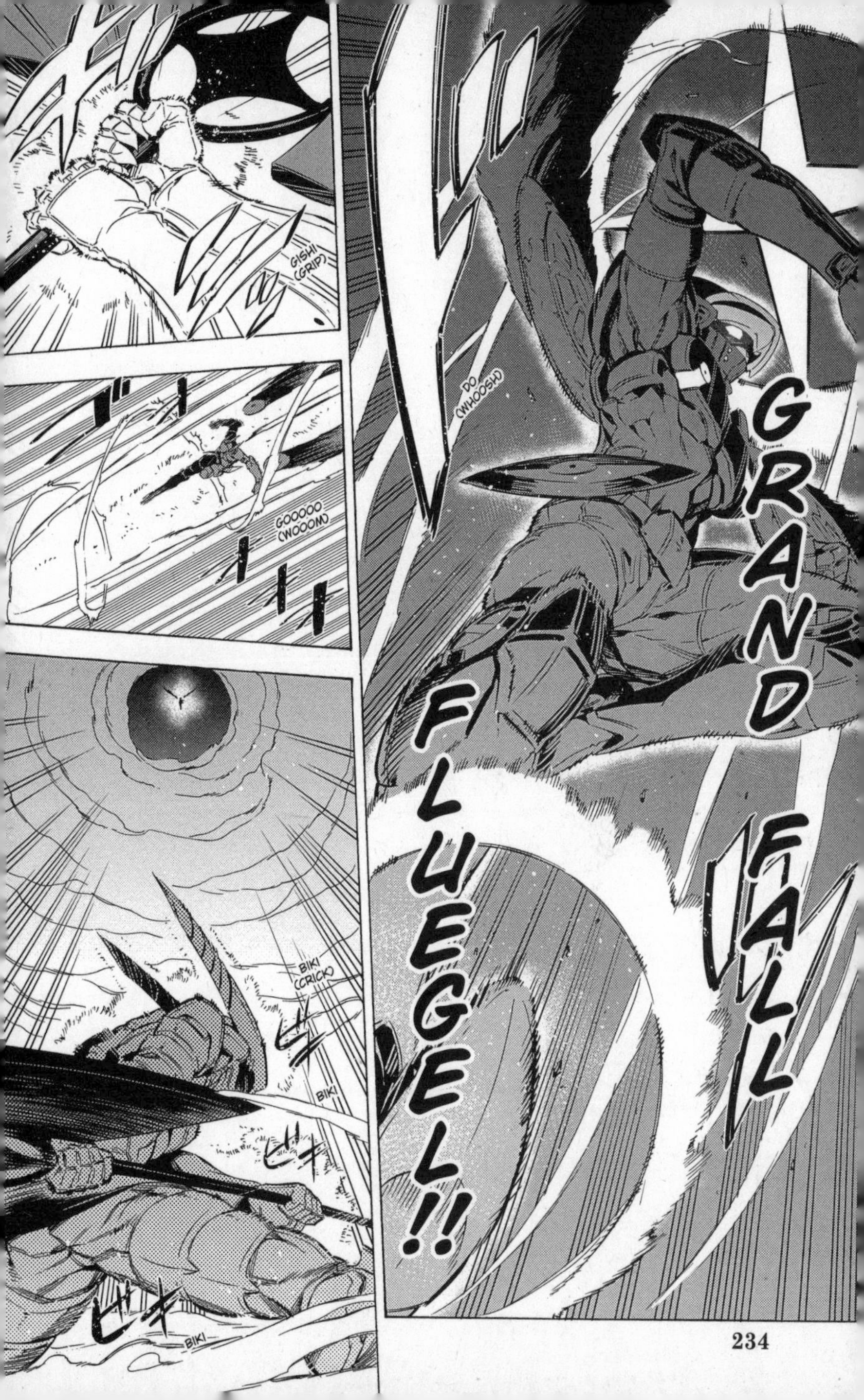
DO (WHOOSH)
GRAND FALL FLUEGEL!!
GISHI (GRIP)
GOOOOO (WOOOM)
BIKI (CRICK)
BIKI
BIKI

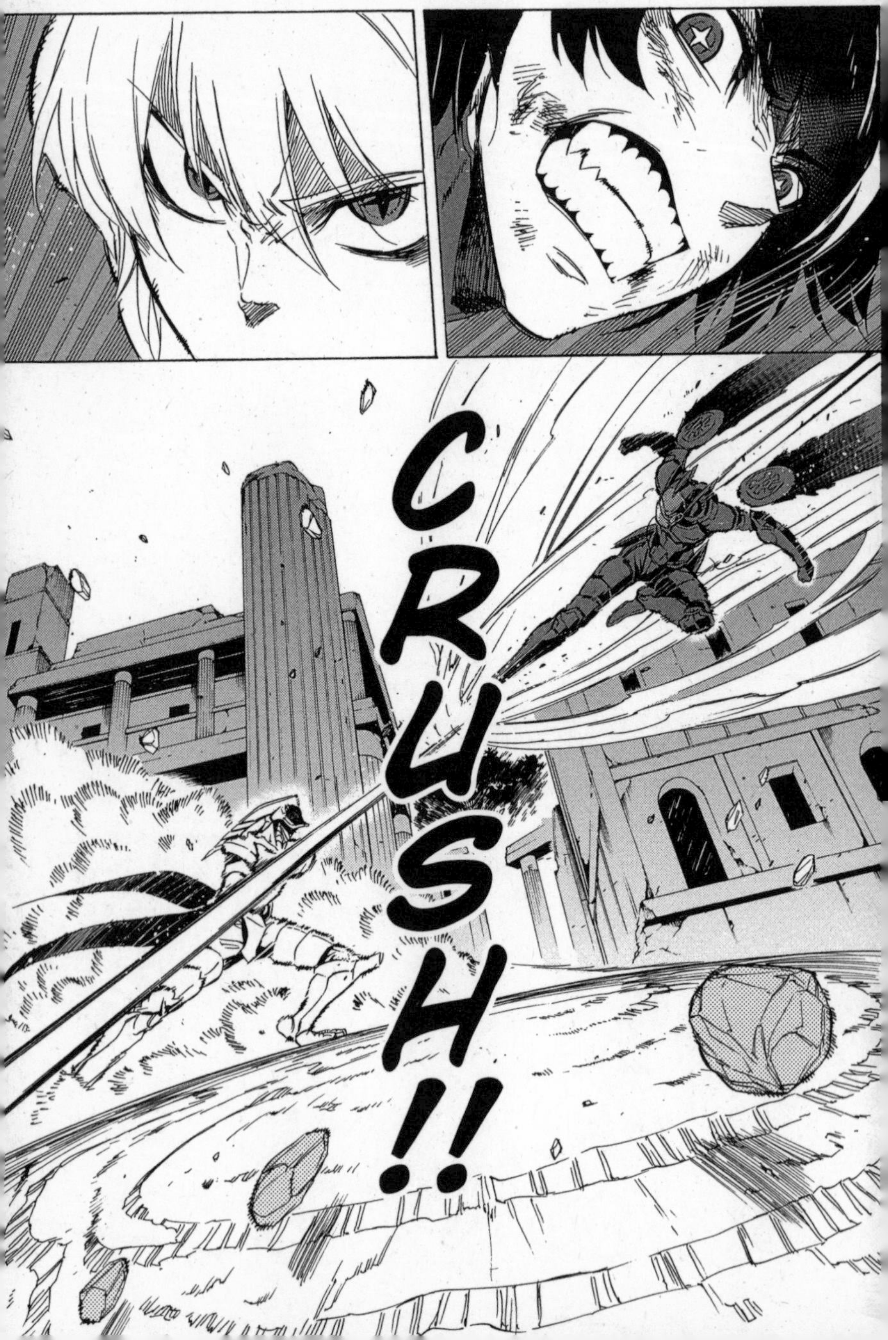
CRUSH!!

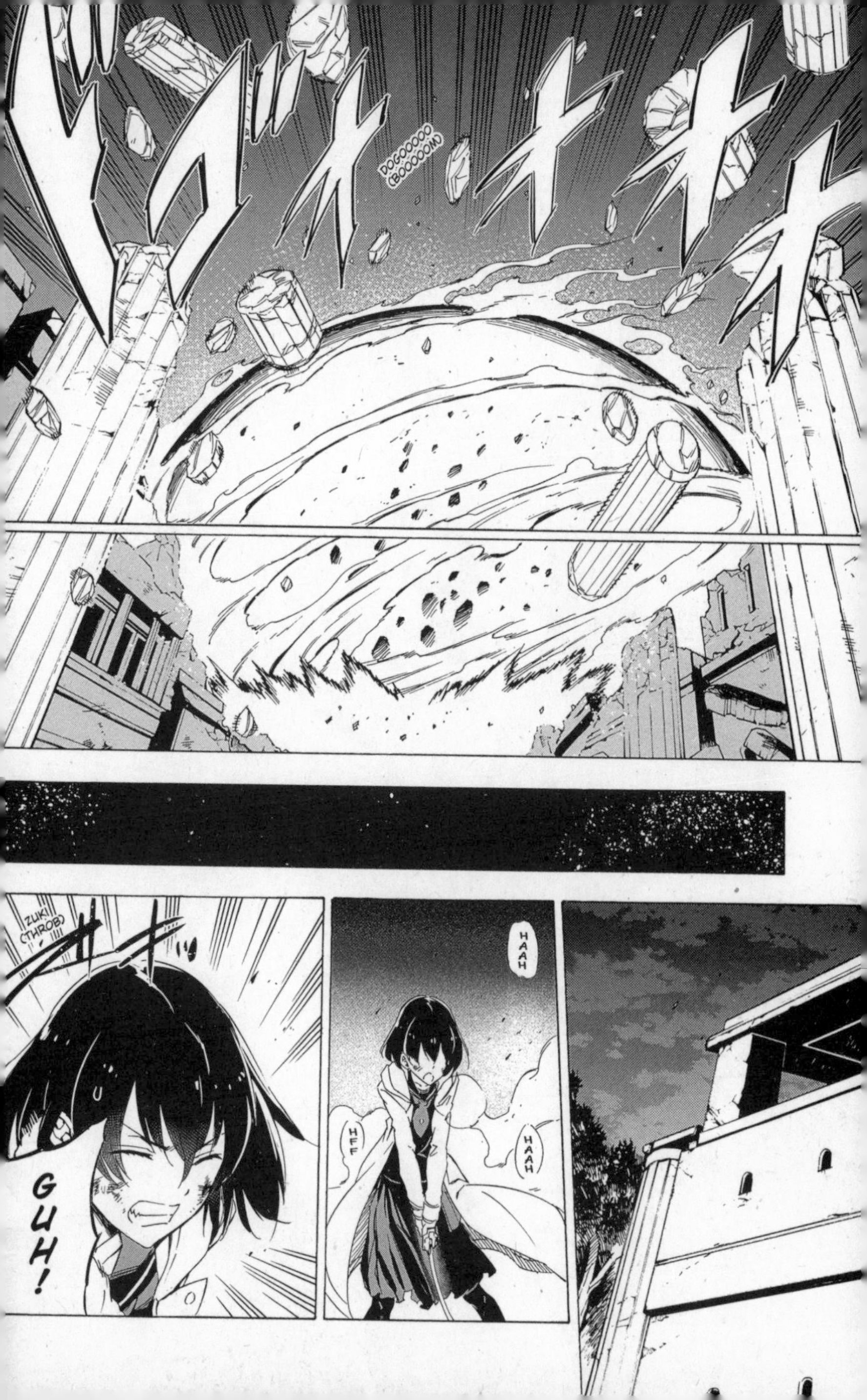
DOGOOOOO (BOOOOOM)
HAAH
HAAH
HFF
ZUKI (THROB)
GUH!

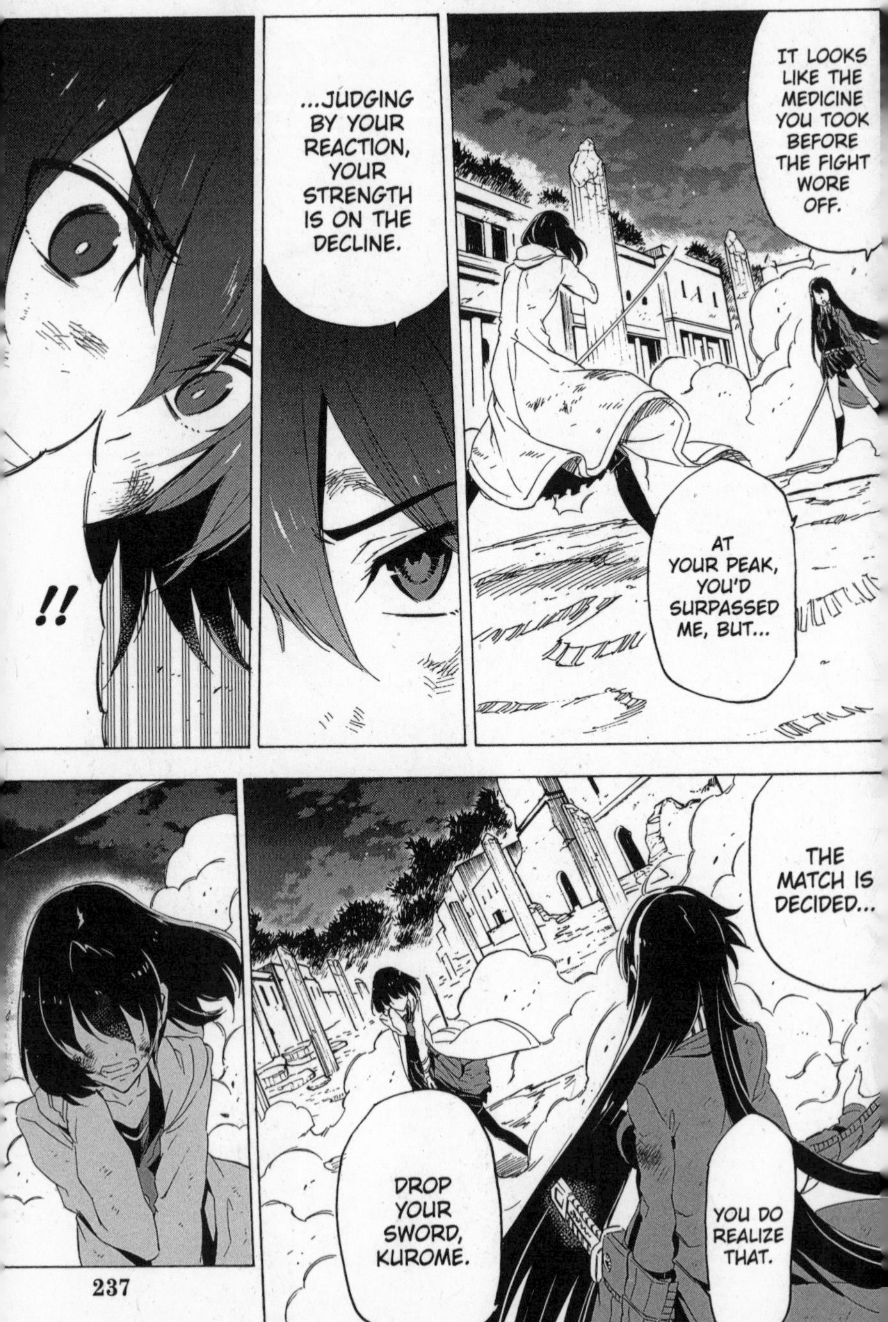
IT LOOKS LIKE THE MEDICINE YOU TOOK BEFORE THE FIGHT WORE OFF.
AT YOUR PEAK, YOU'D SURPASSED ME, BUT...
...JUDGING BY YOUR REACTION, YOUR STRENGTH IS ON THE DECLINE.
!!
THE MATCH IS DECIDED...
YOU DO REALIZE THAT.
DROP YOUR SWORD, KUROME.

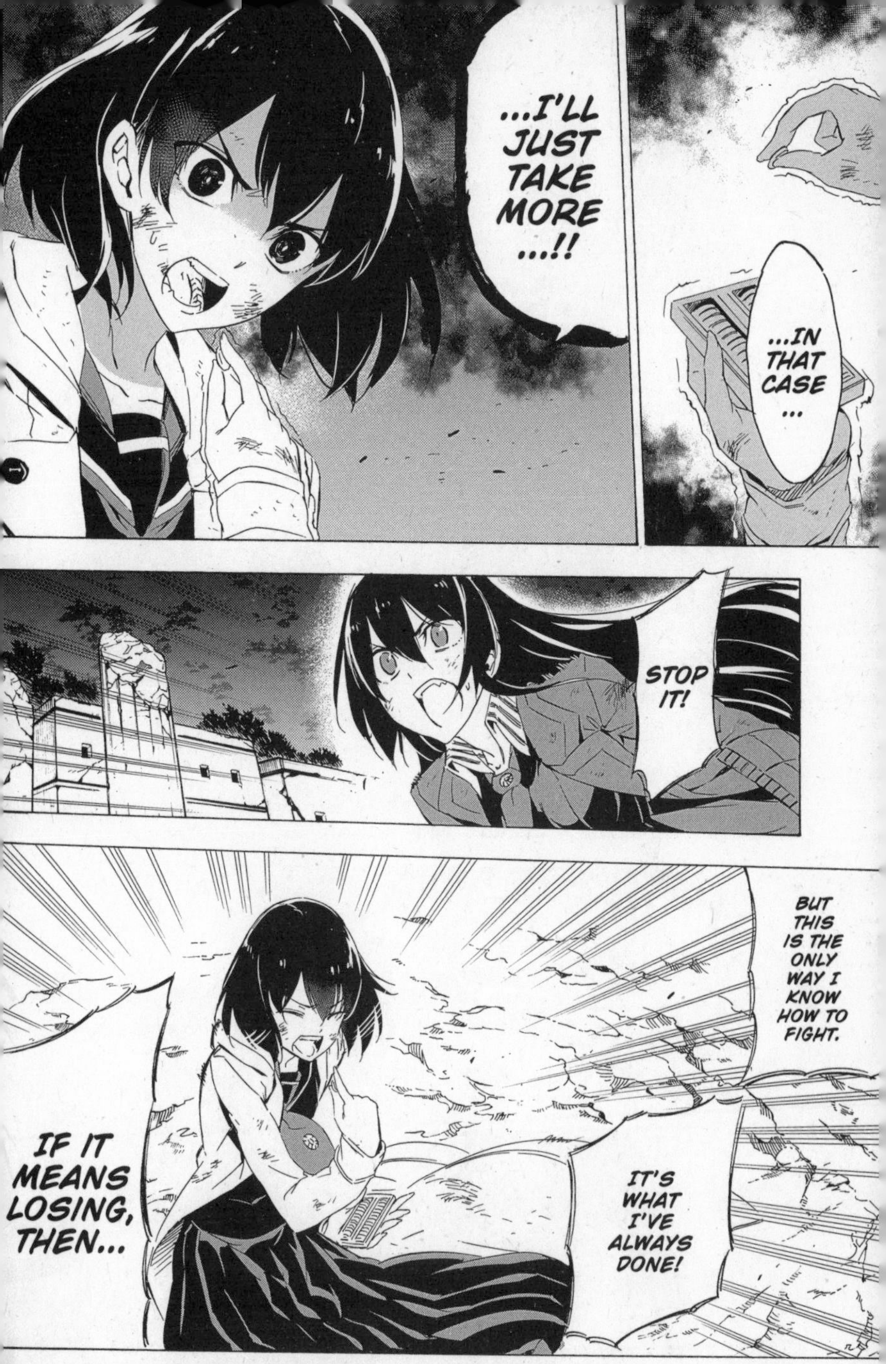
...IN THAT CASE...
...I'LL JUST TAKE MORE...!!
STOP IT!
BUT THIS IS THE ONLY WAY I KNOW HOW TO FIGHT.
IT'S WHAT I'VE ALWAYS DONE!
IF IT MEANS LOSING, THEN...

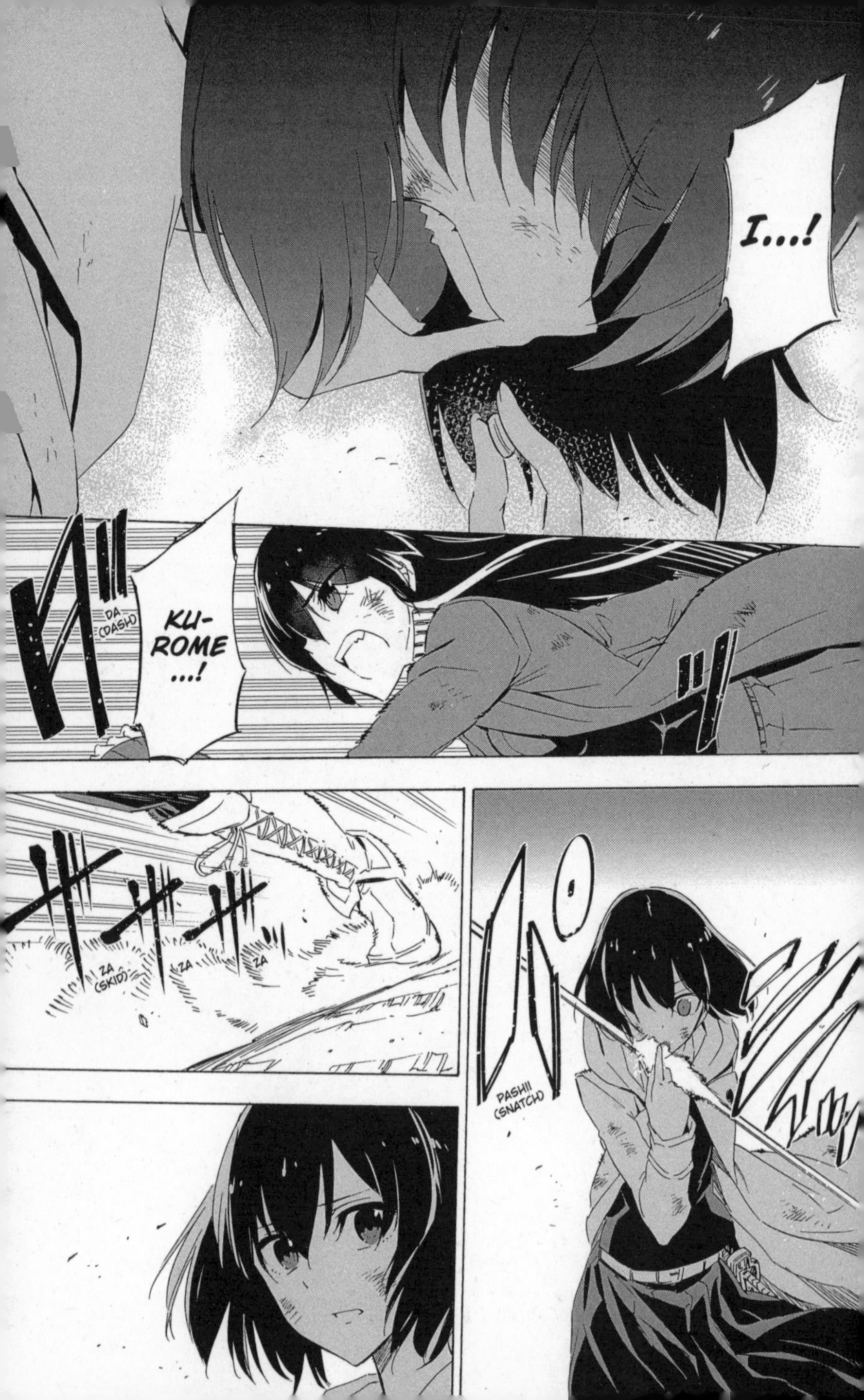
I...!
KU-ROME ...!
DA (DASH)
PASHII (SNATCH)
ZA (SKID)
ZA
ZA

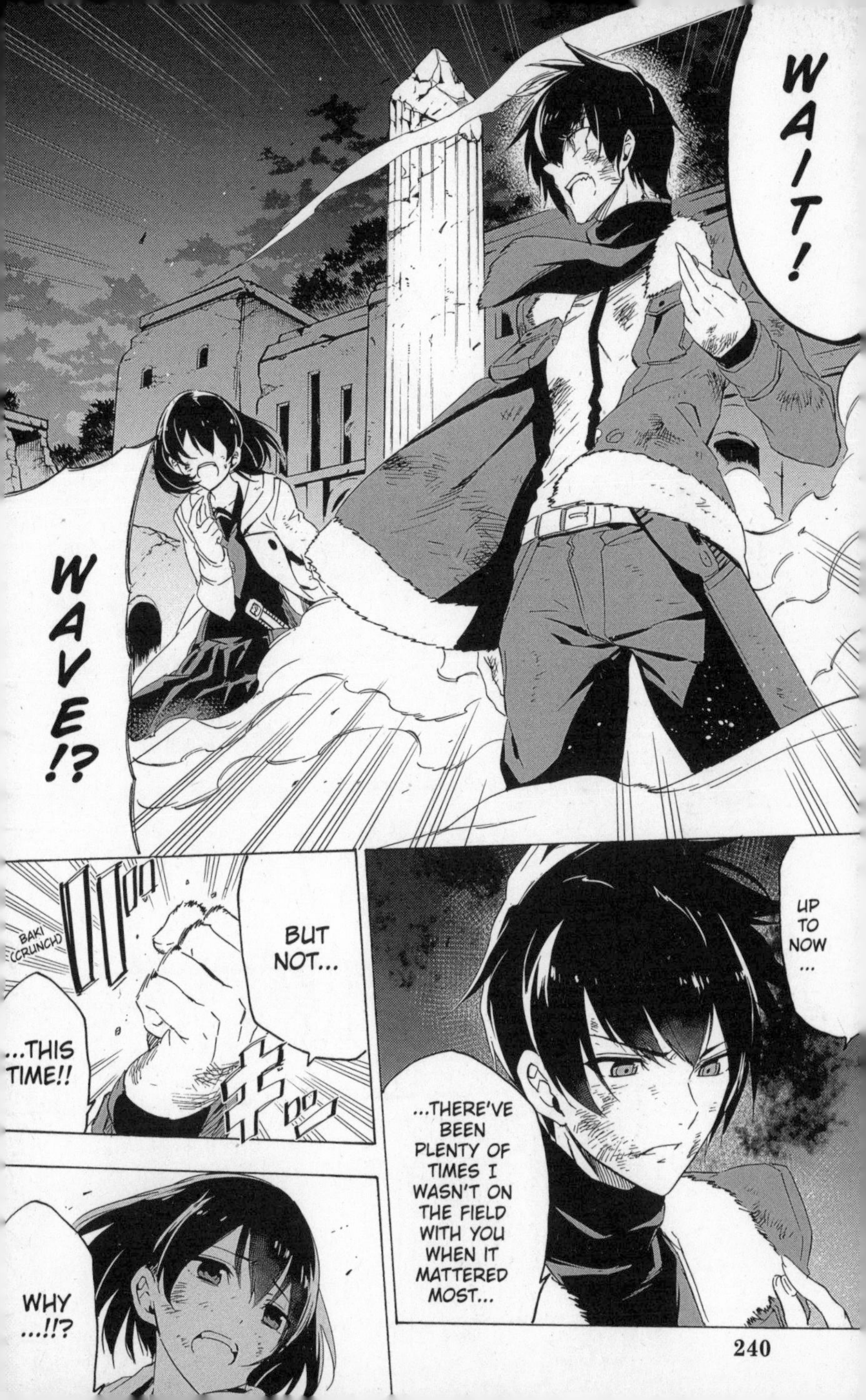

WAIT!
WAVE!?
UP TO NOW ...
...THERE'VE BEEN PLENTY OF TIMES I WASN'T ON THE FIELD WITH YOU WHEN IT MATTERED MOST...
BUT NOT...
BAKI (CRUNCH)
...THIS TIME!!
WHY ...!!?

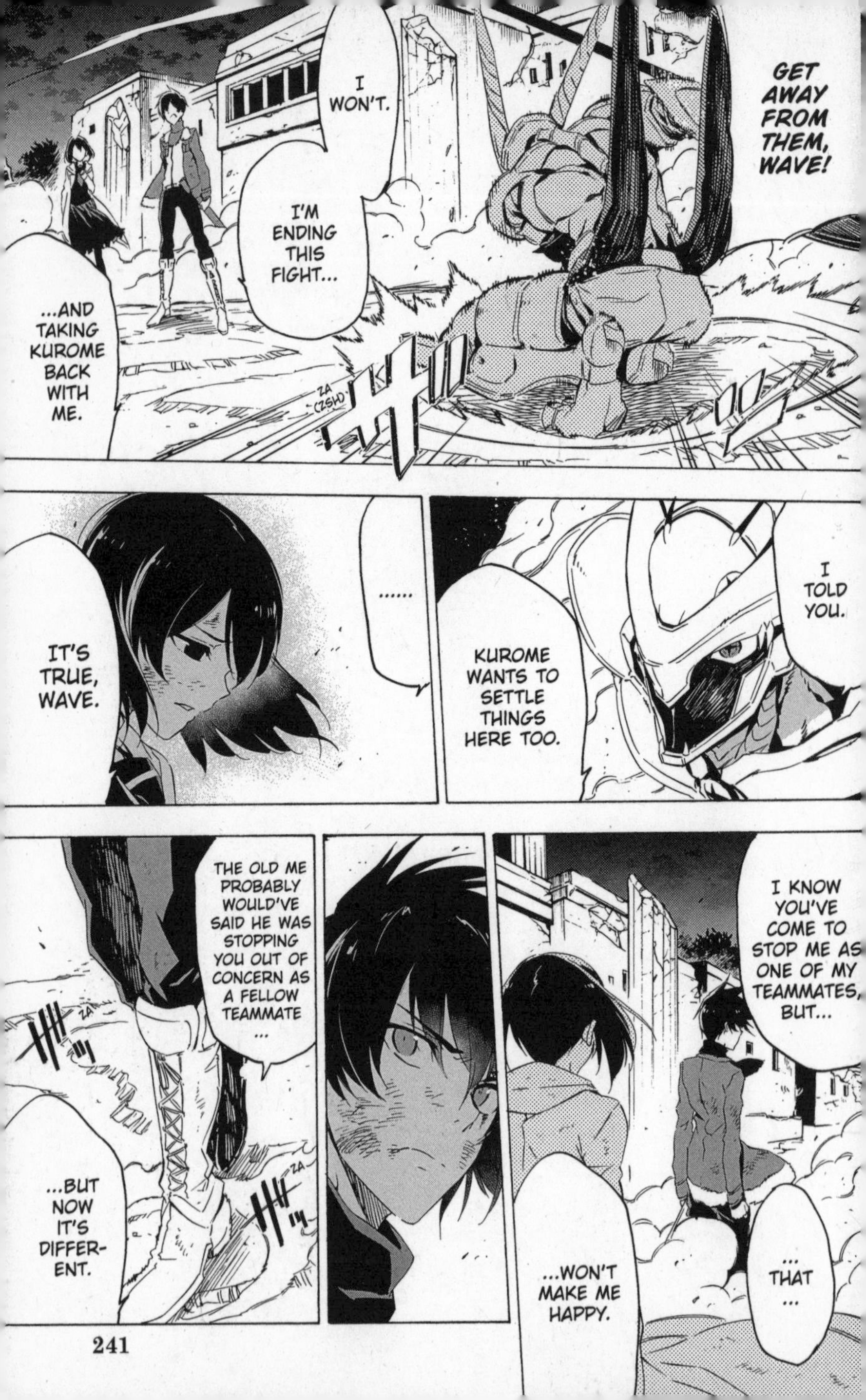
GET AWAY FROM THEM, WAVE!
I WON'T.
I'M ENDING THIS FIGHT...
...AND TAKING KUROME BACK WITH ME.
ZA (ZSH)
I TOLD YOU.
KUROME WANTS TO SETTLE THINGS HERE TOO.
......
IT'S TRUE, WAVE.
I KNOW YOU'VE COME TO STOP ME AS ONE OF MY TEAMMATES, BUT...
...THAT...
...WON'T MAKE ME HAPPY.
THE OLD ME PROBABLY WOULD'VE SAID HE WAS STOPPING YOU OUT OF CONCERN AS A FELLOW TEAMMATE...
ZA
...BUT NOW IT'S DIFFER-ENT.
ZA

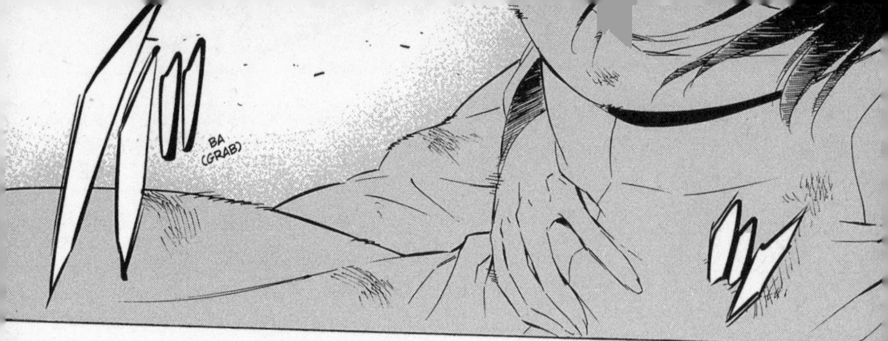
BA
(GRAB)
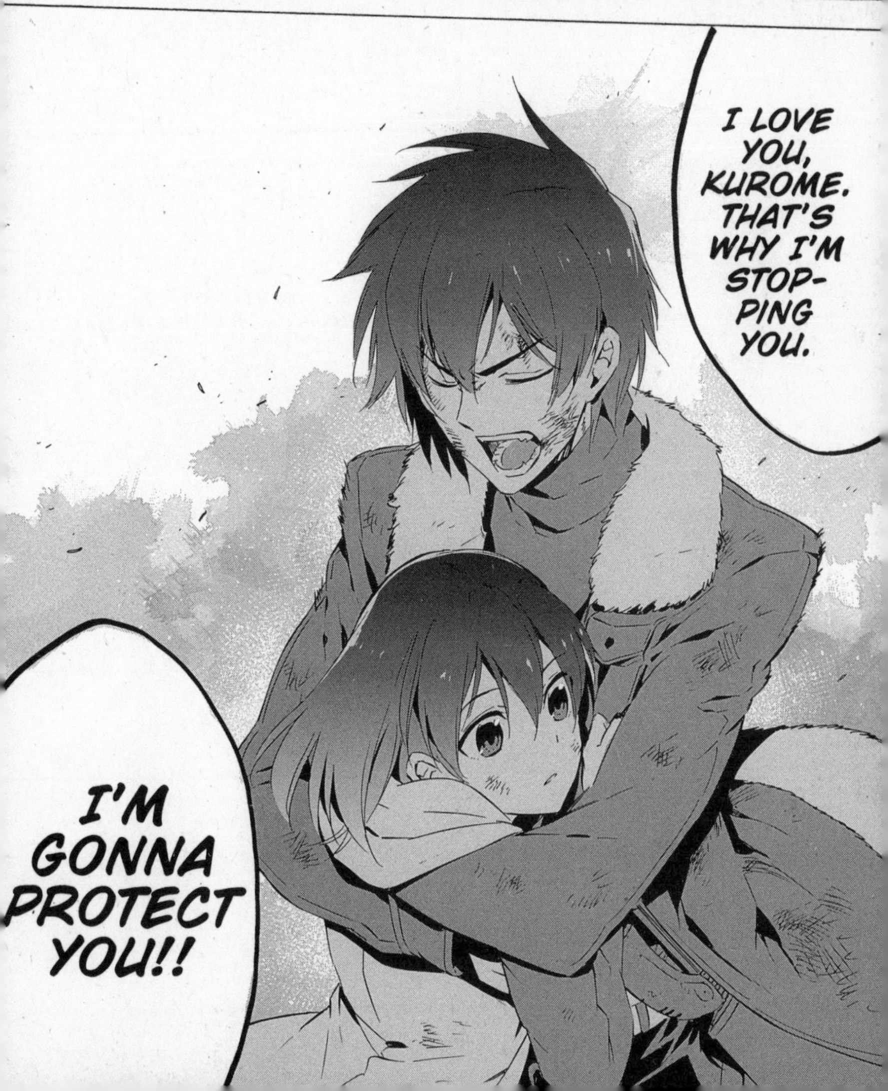
I LOVE YOU, KUROME. THAT'S WHY I'M STOP-PING YOU.
I'M GONNA PROTECT YOU!!

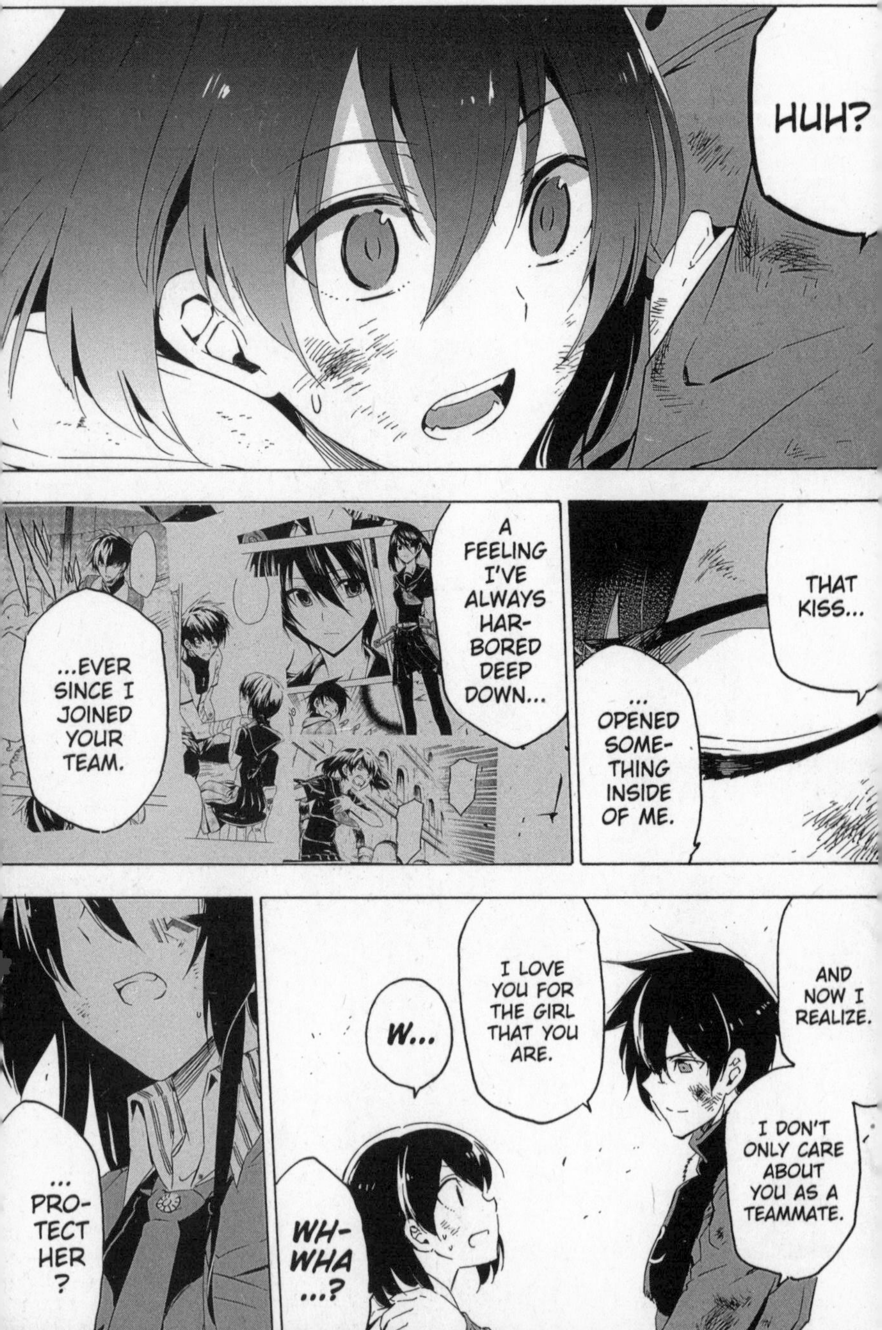
HUH?
THAT KISS...
...OPENED SOMETHING INSIDE OF ME.
A FEELING I'VE ALWAYS HARBORED DEEP DOWN...
...EVER SINCE I JOINED YOUR TEAM.
AND NOW I REALIZE.
I DON'T ONLY CARE ABOUT YOU AS A TEAMMATE.
I LOVE YOU FOR THE GIRL THAT YOU ARE.
W...
WH-WHA...?
...PROTECT HER?

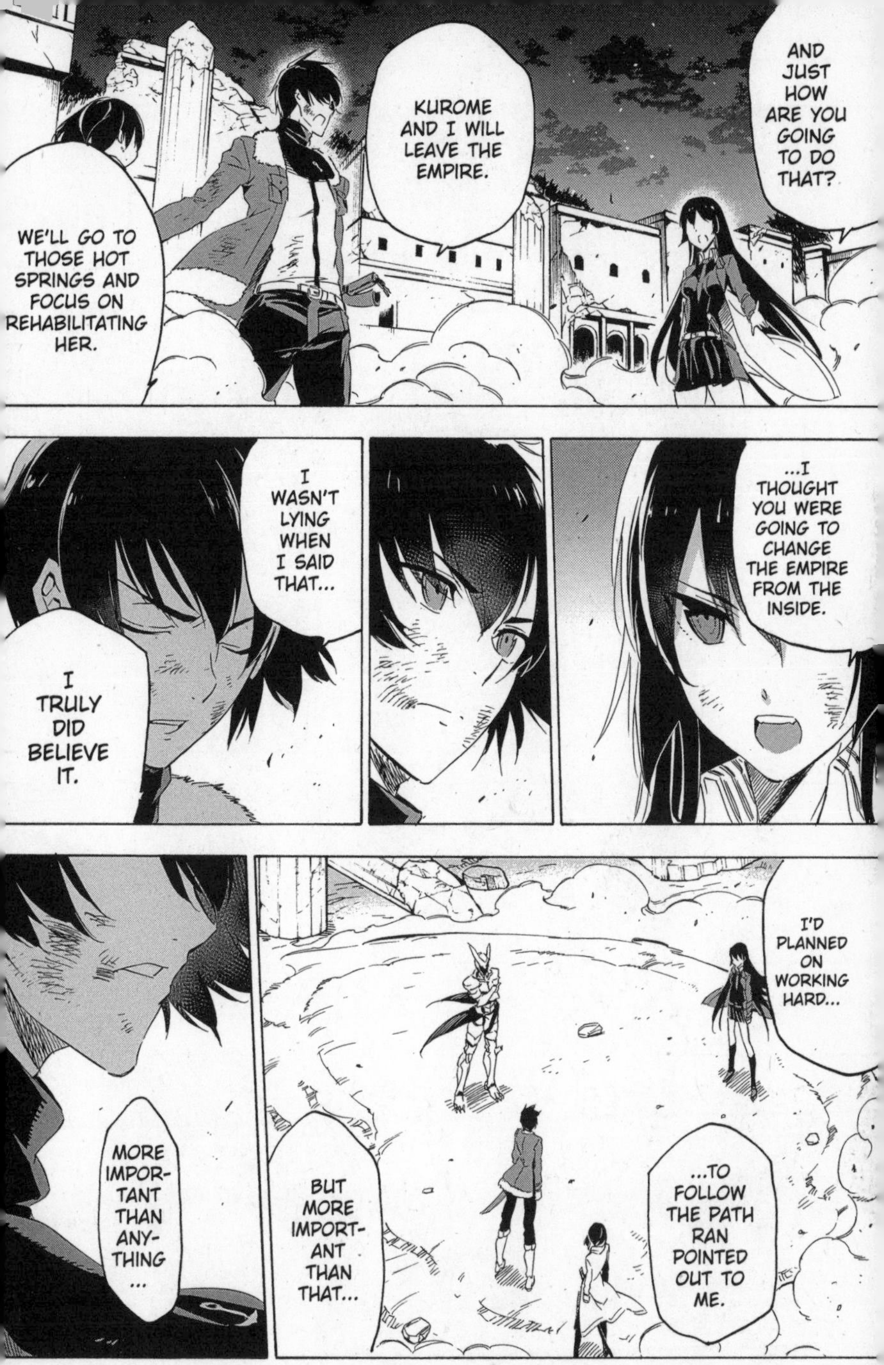
AND JUST HOW ARE YOU GOING TO DO THAT?
KUROME AND I WILL LEAVE THE EMPIRE.
WE'LL GO TO THOSE HOT SPRINGS AND FOCUS ON REHABILITATING HER.
...I THOUGHT YOU WERE GOING TO CHANGE THE EMPIRE FROM THE INSIDE.
I WASN'T LYING WHEN I SAID THAT...
I TRULY DID BELIEVE IT.
I'D PLANNED ON WORKING HARD...
...TO FOLLOW THE PATH RAN POINTED OUT TO ME.
BUT MORE IMPORT-ANT THAN THAT...
MORE IMPOR-TANT THAN ANY-THING ...

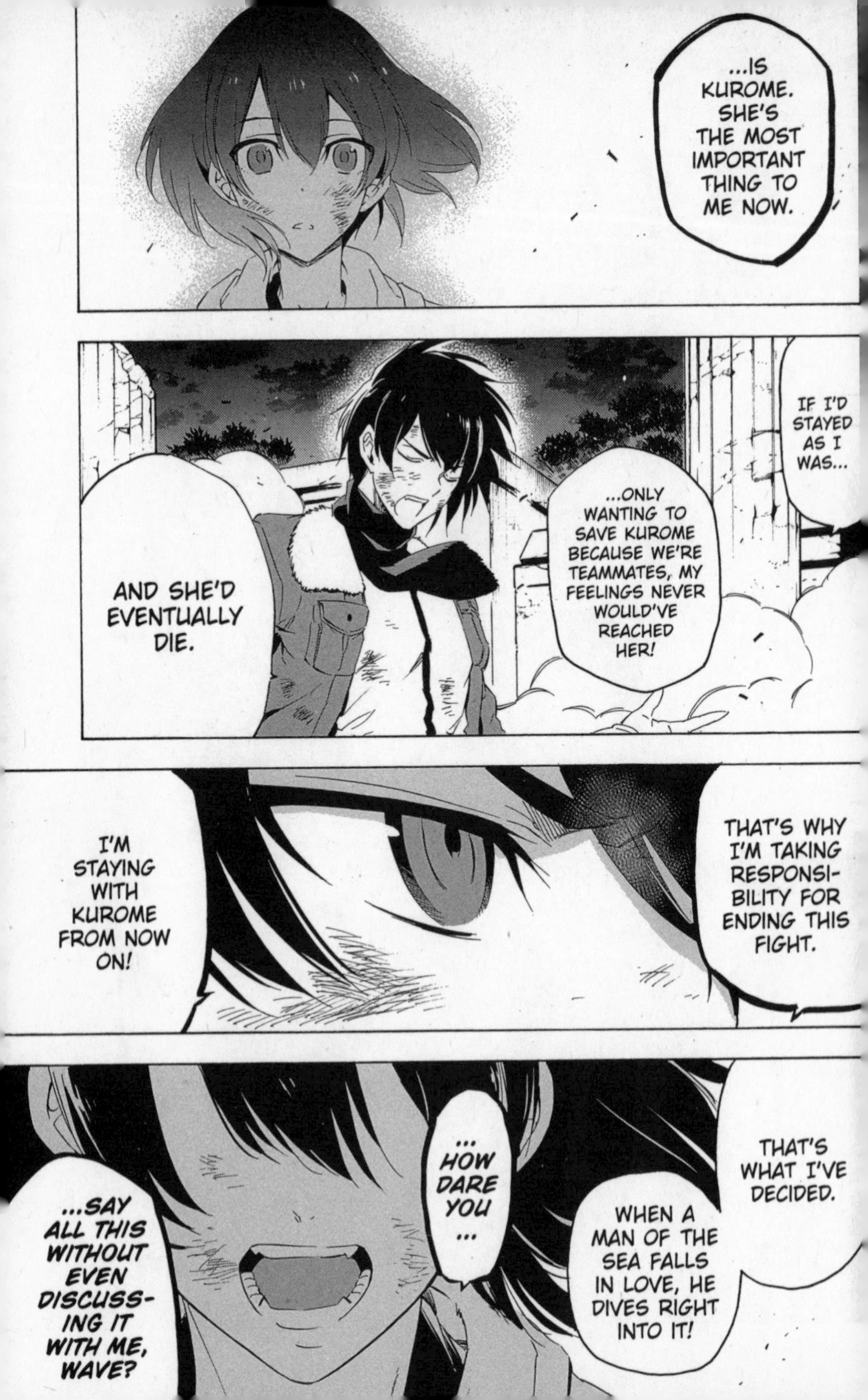
...IS KUROME. SHE'S THE MOST IMPORTANT THING TO ME NOW.
IF I'D STAYED AS I WAS...
...ONLY WANTING TO SAVE KUROME BECAUSE WE'RE TEAMMATES, MY FEELINGS NEVER WOULD'VE REACHED HER!
AND SHE'D EVENTUALLY DIE.
THAT'S WHY I'M TAKING RESPONSIBILITY FOR ENDING THIS FIGHT.
I'M STAYING WITH KUROME FROM NOW ON!
THAT'S WHAT I'VE DECIDED.
WHEN A MAN OF THE SEA FALLS IN LOVE, HE DIVES RIGHT INTO IT!
...HOW DARE YOU...
...SAY ALL THIS WITHOUT EVEN DISCUSSING IT WITH ME, WAVE?

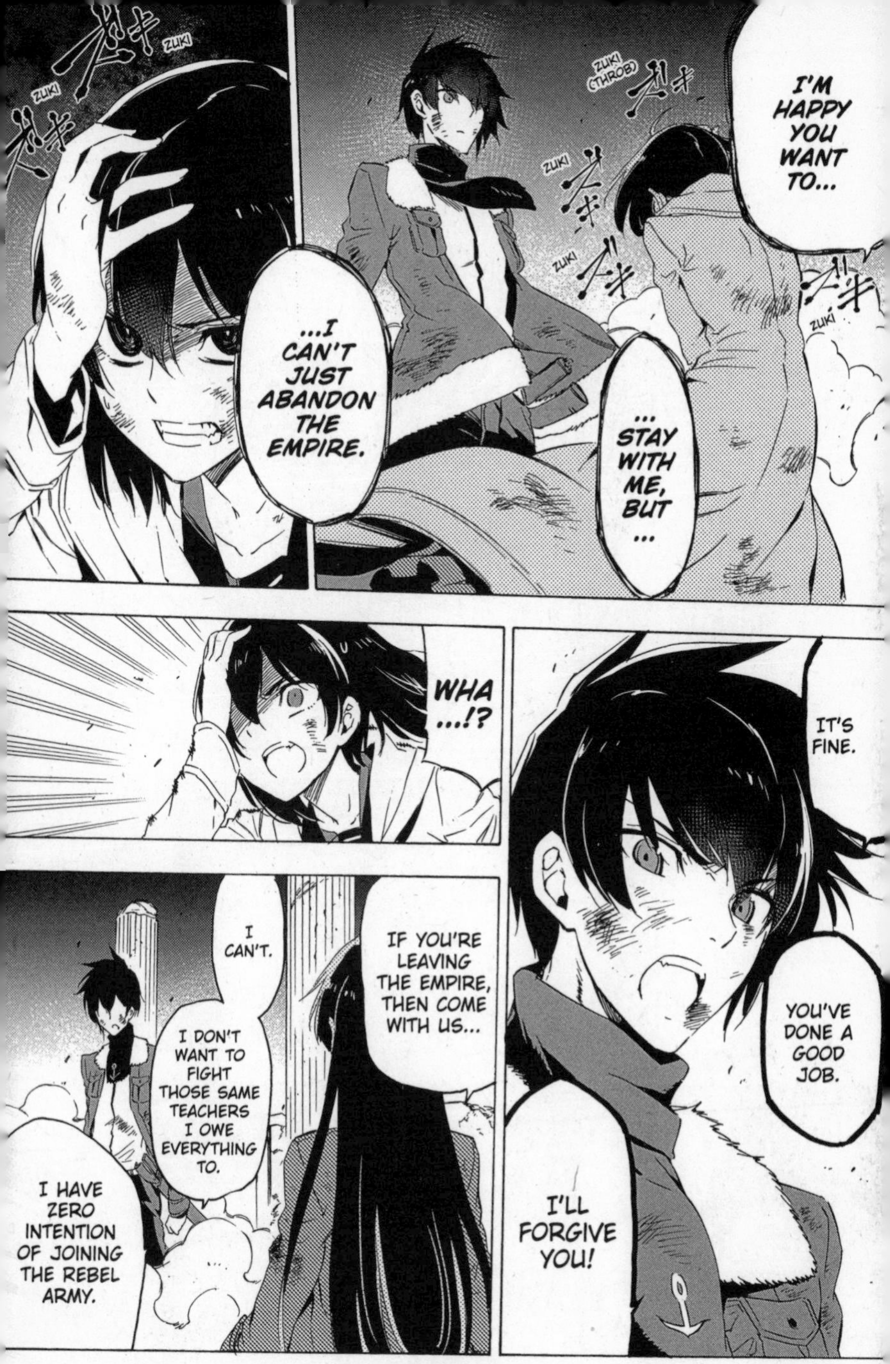
ZUKI (THROB)
I'M HAPPY YOU WANT TO...
ZUKI
ZUKI
ZUKI
...STAY WITH ME, BUT...
...I CAN'T JUST ABANDON THE EMPIRE.
ZUKI
ZUKI
...
IT'S FINE.
YOU'VE DONE A GOOD JOB.
I'LL FORGIVE YOU!
WHA...!?
IF YOU'RE LEAVING THE EMPIRE, THEN COME WITH US...
I CAN'T.
I DON'T WANT TO FIGHT THOSE SAME TEACHERS I OWE EVERYTHING TO.
I HAVE ZERO INTENTION OF JOINING THE REBEL ARMY.
...

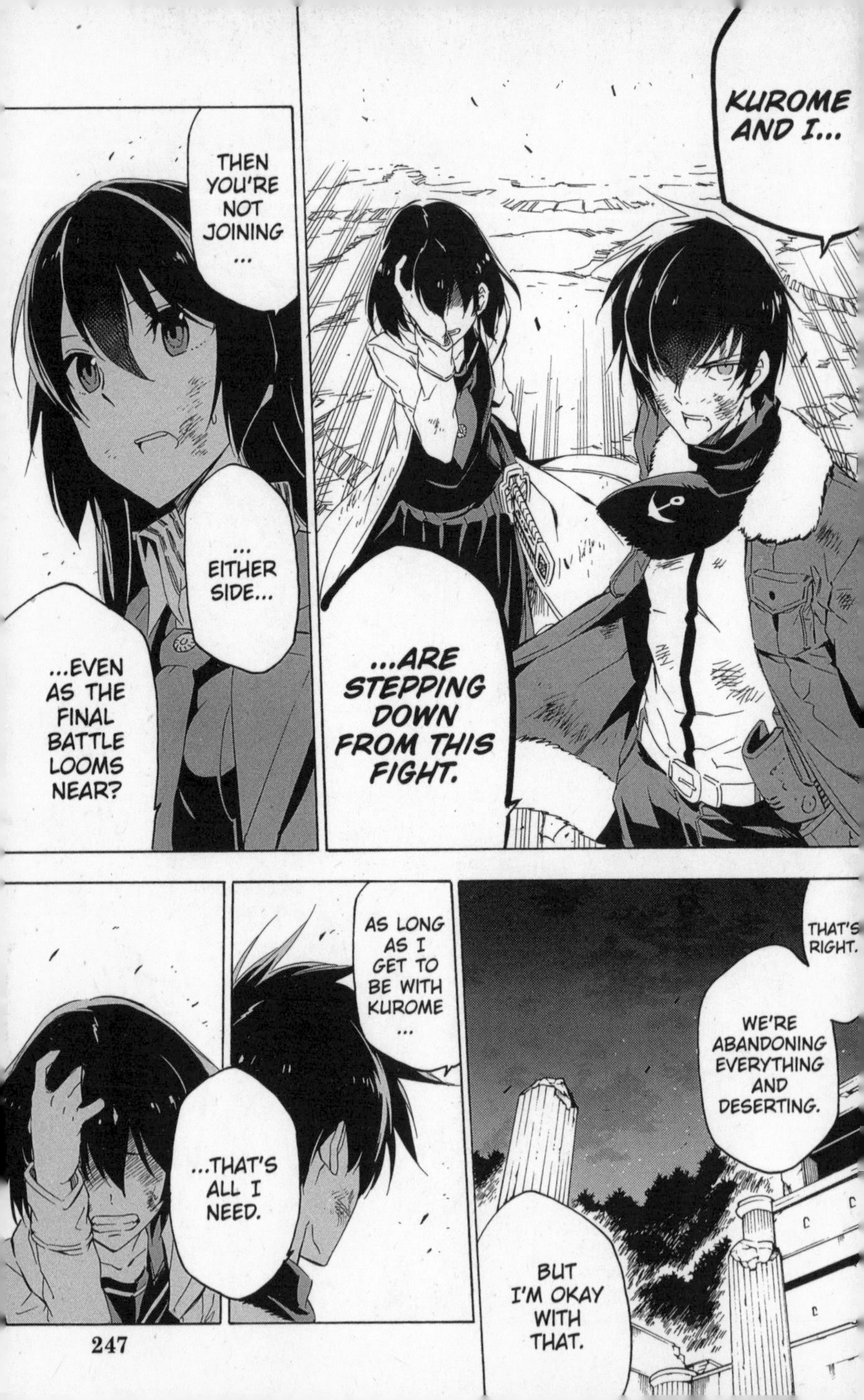
KUROME AND I...
...ARE STEPPING DOWN FROM THIS FIGHT.
THEN YOU'RE NOT JOINING ...
... EITHER SIDE...
...EVEN AS THE FINAL BATTLE LOOMS NEAR?
THAT'S RIGHT.
WE'RE ABANDONING EVERYTHING AND DESERTING.
BUT I'M OKAY WITH THAT.
AS LONG AS I GET TO BE WITH KUROME ...
...THAT'S ALL I NEED.

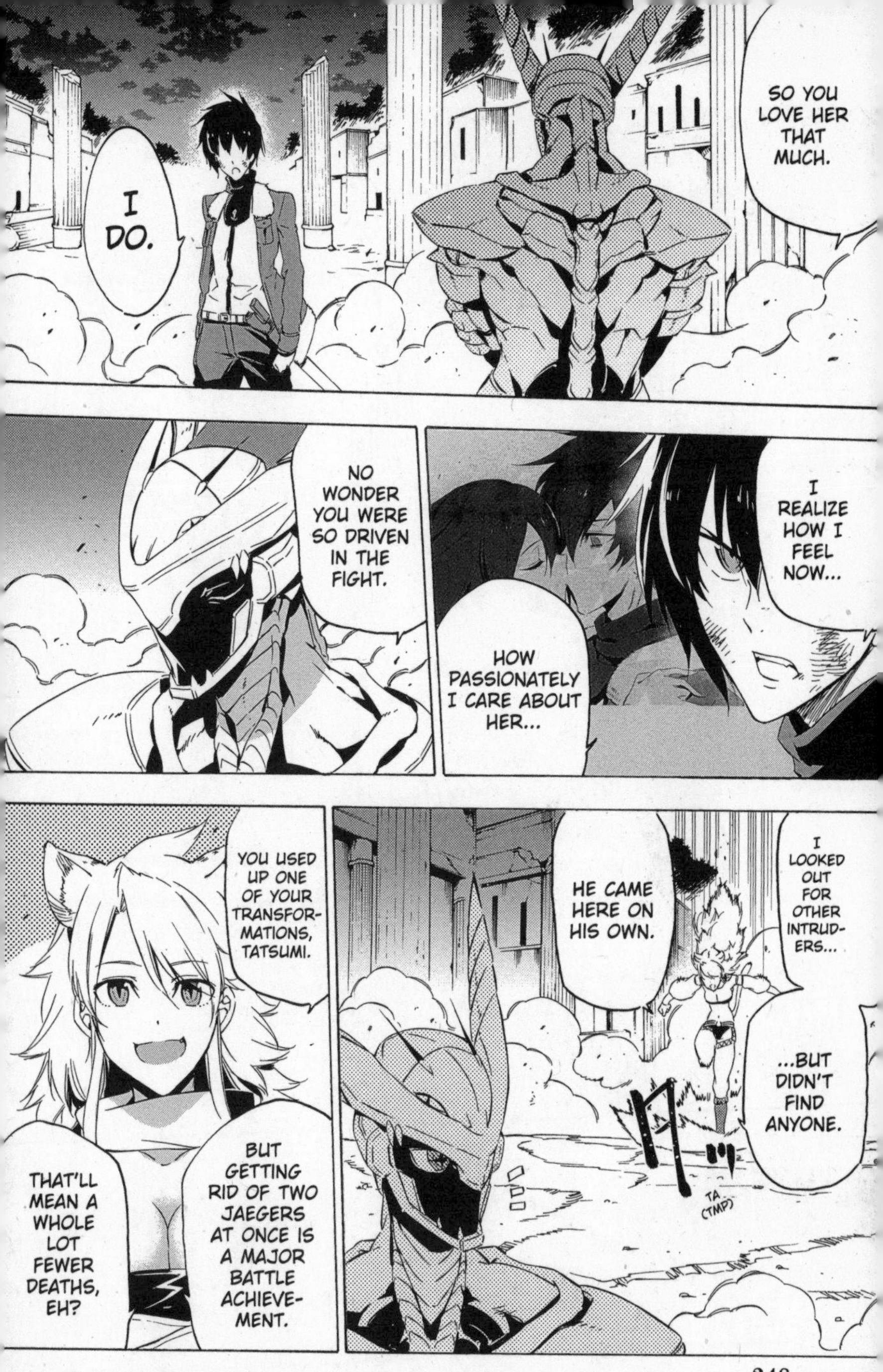
SO YOU LOVE HER THAT MUCH.
I DO.
I REALIZE HOW I FEEL NOW...
HOW PASSIONATELY I CARE ABOUT HER...
NO WONDER YOU WERE SO DRIVEN IN THE FIGHT.
I LOOKED OUT FOR OTHER INTRUDERS...
...BUT DIDN'T FIND ANYONE.
TA (TMP)
HE CAME HERE ON HIS OWN.
YOU USED UP ONE OF YOUR TRANSFORMATIONS, TATSUMI.
BUT GETTING RID OF TWO JAEGERS AT ONCE IS A MAJOR BATTLE ACHIEVEMENT.
THAT'LL MEAN A WHOLE LOT FEWER DEATHS, EH?

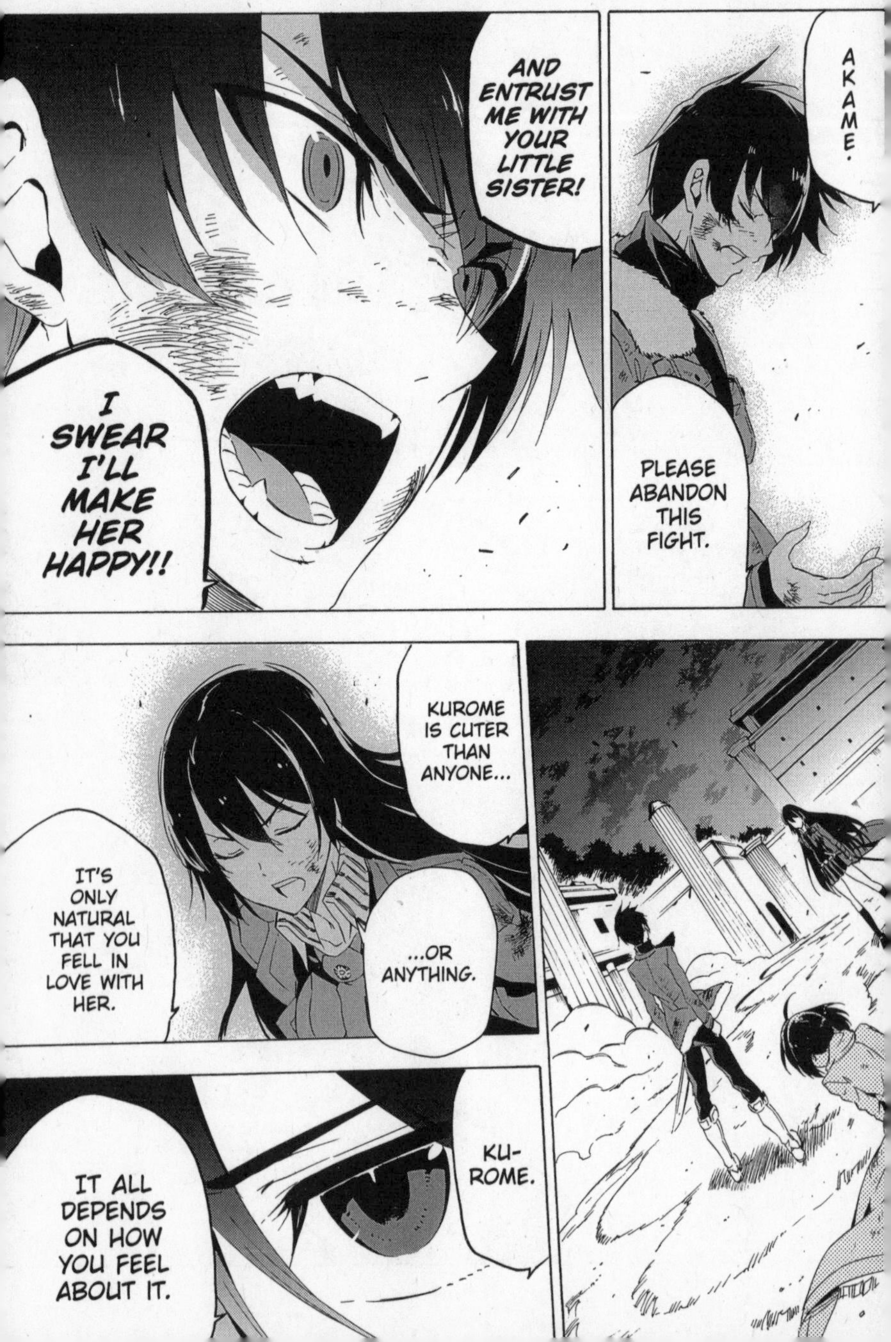
AKAME.
PLEASE ABANDON THIS FIGHT.
AND ENTRUST ME WITH YOUR LITTLE SISTER!
I SWEAR I'LL MAKE HER HAPPY!!
KUROME IS CUTER THAN ANYONE...
...OR ANYTHING.
IT'S ONLY NATURAL THAT YOU FELL IN LOVE WITH HER.
KU-ROME.
IT ALL DEPENDS ON HOW YOU FEEL ABOUT IT.

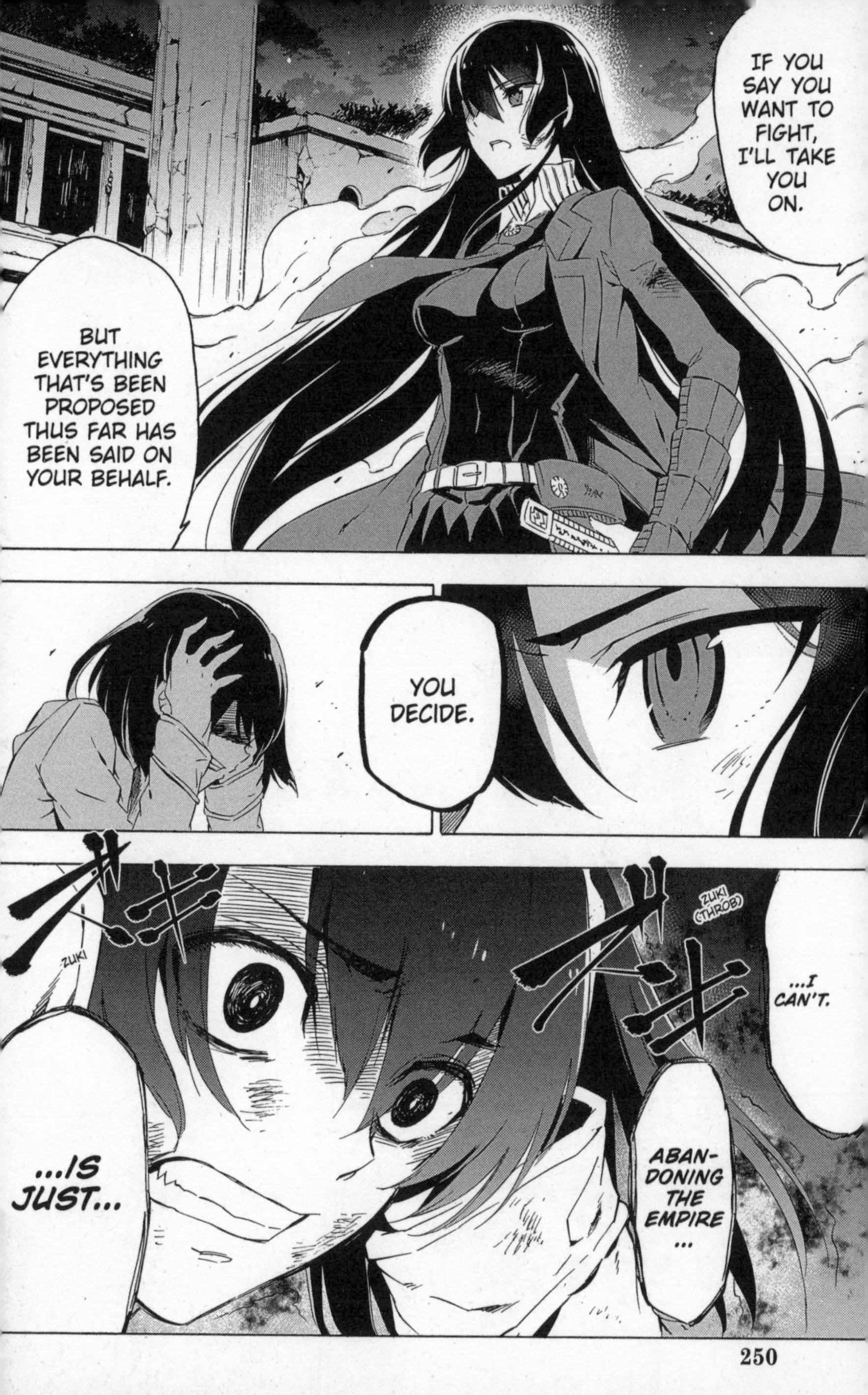
IF YOU SAY YOU WANT TO FIGHT, I'LL TAKE YOU ON.
BUT EVERYTHING THAT'S BEEN PROPOSED THUS FAR HAS BEEN SAID ON YOUR BEHALF.
YOU DECIDE.
ZUKI (THROB)
...I CAN'T.
ABAN-DONING THE EMPIRE ...
ZUKI
...IS JUST...

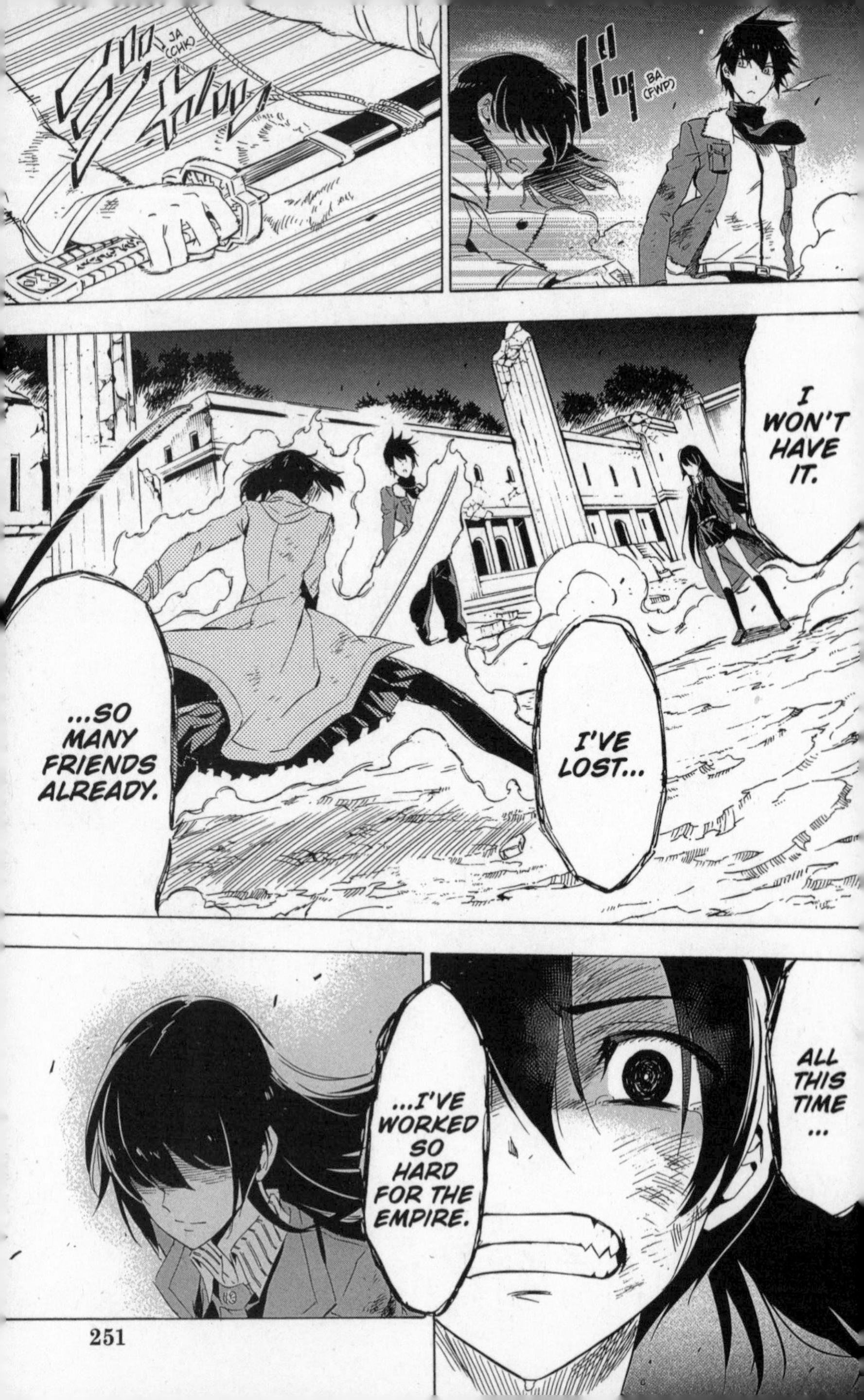
BA (FWD)
JA (CHK)
I WON'T HAVE IT.
I'VE LOST...
...SO MANY FRIENDS ALREADY.
ALL THIS TIME...
...I'VE WORKED SO HARD FOR THE EMPIRE.

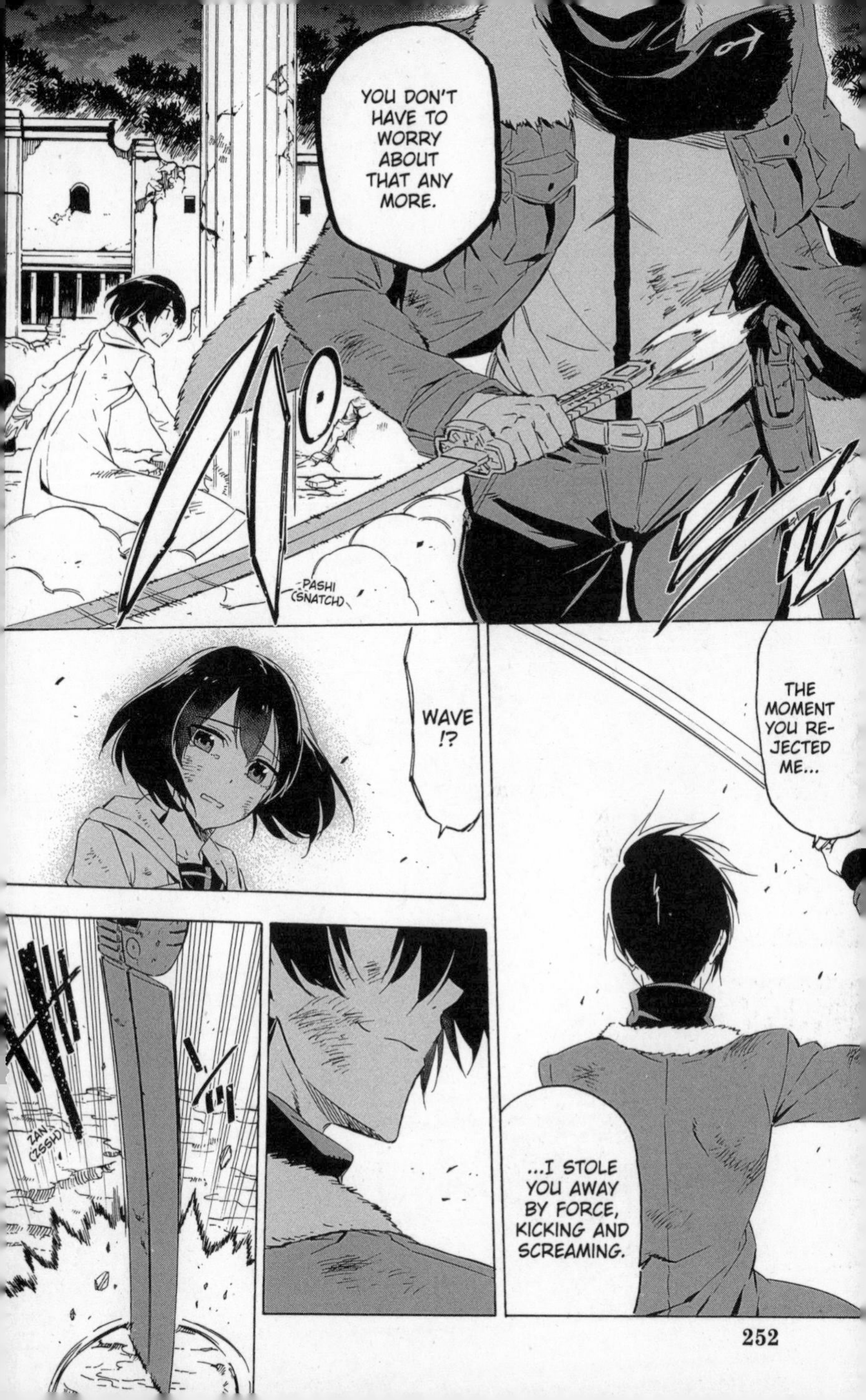
YOU DON'T HAVE TO WORRY ABOUT THAT ANY MORE.
PASHI (SNATCH)
THE MOMENT YOU RE-JECTED ME...
...I STOLE YOU AWAY BY FORCE, KICKING AND SCREAMING.
WAVE !?
ZAN (ZSSSH)

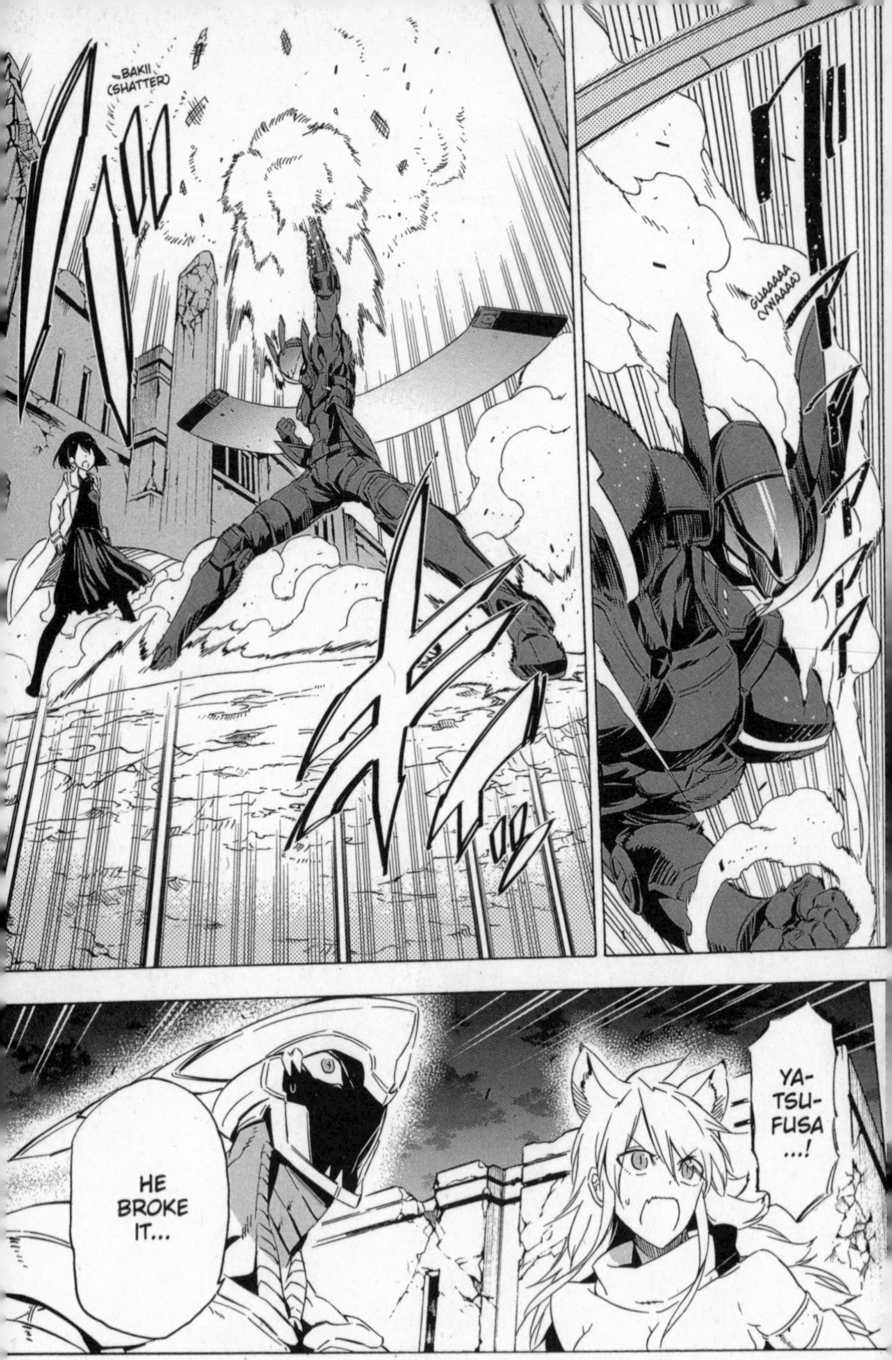
GUAAAAA (VWAAAA)
BAKII (SHATTER)
YA-TSU-FUSA ...!
HE BROKE IT...

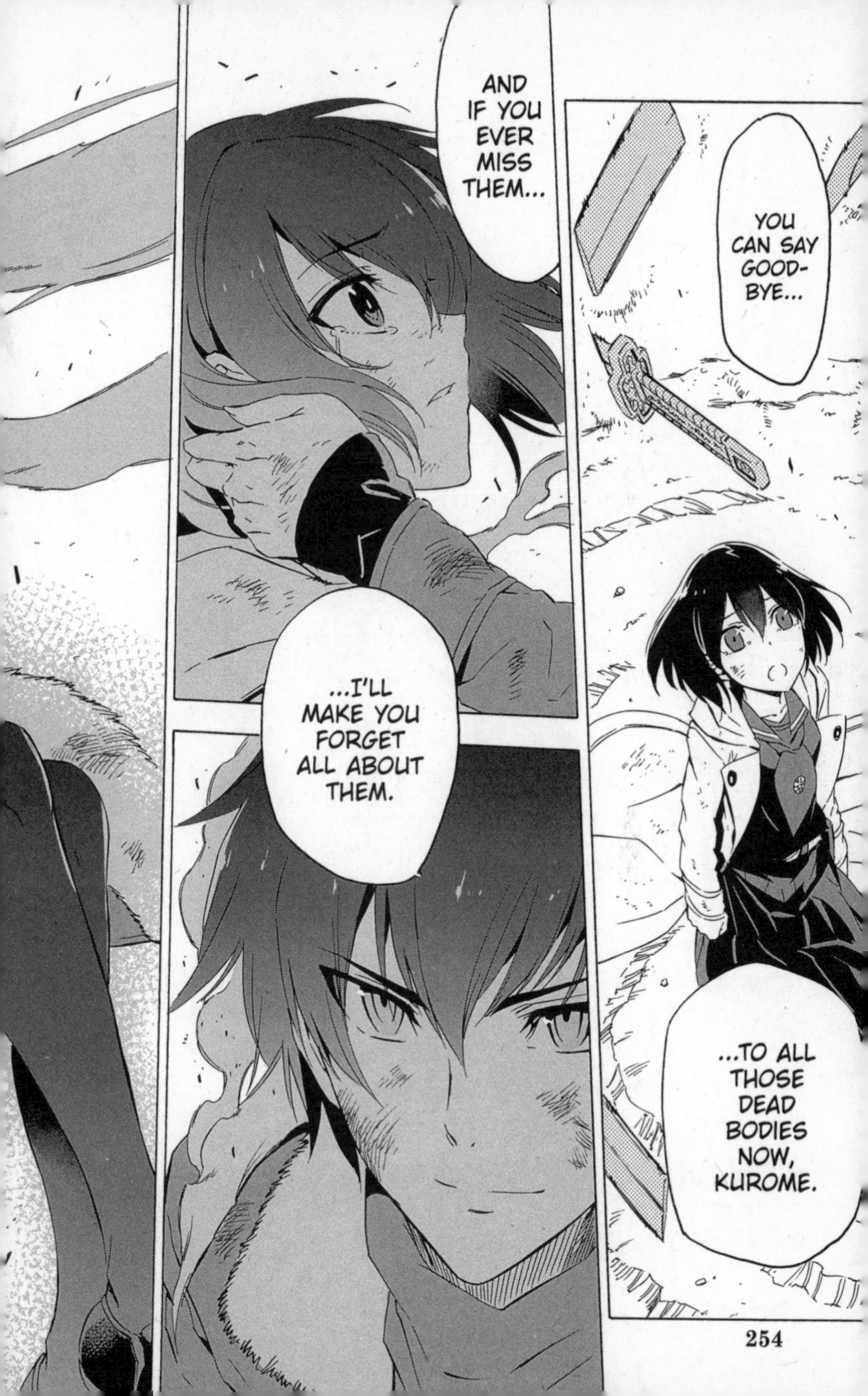
YOU CAN SAY GOOD-BYE...
...TO ALL THOSE DEAD BODIES NOW, KUROME.
AND IF YOU EVER MISS THEM...
...I'LL MAKE YOU FORGET ALL ABOUT THEM.

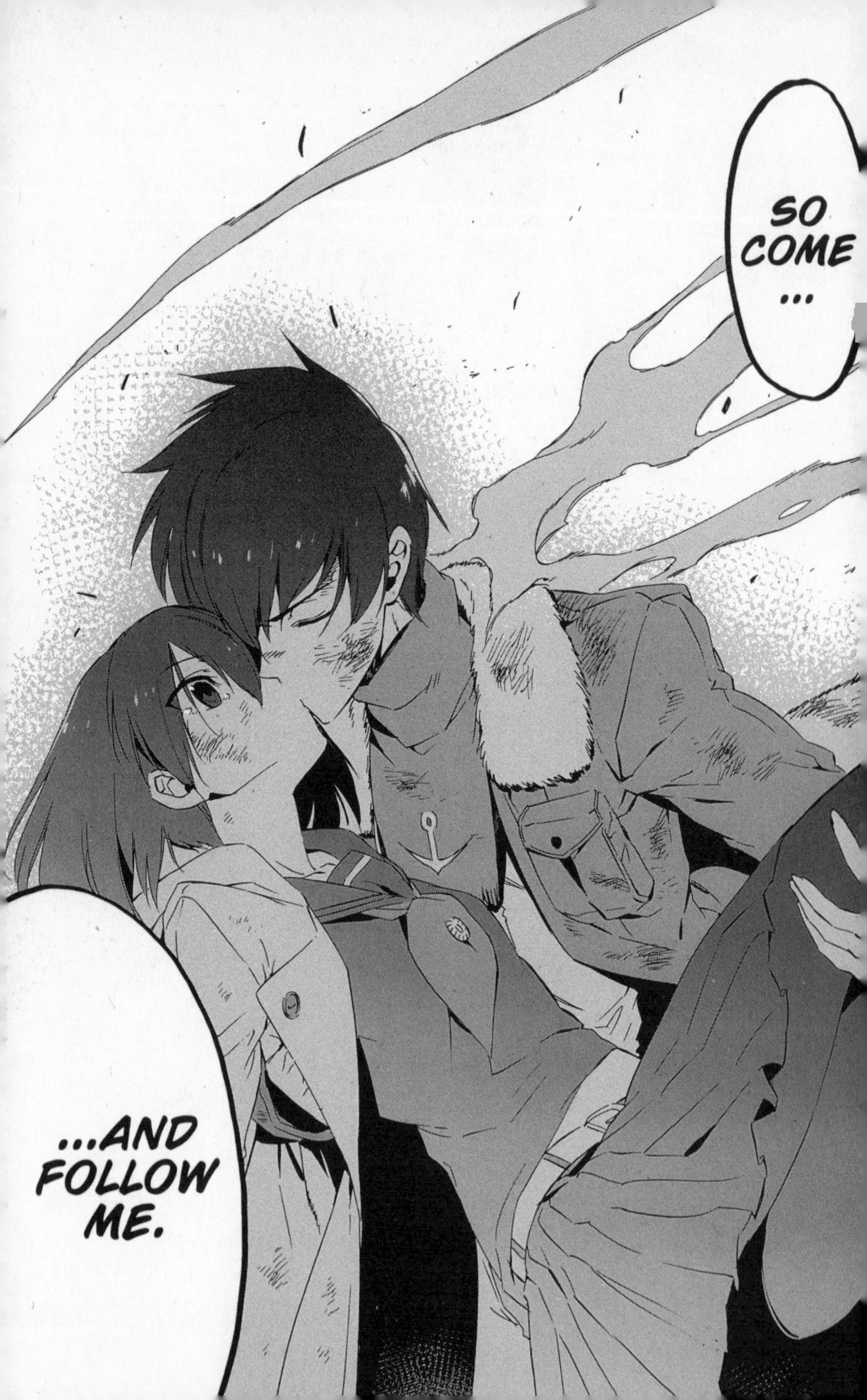
SO COME ...
...AND FOLLOW ME.

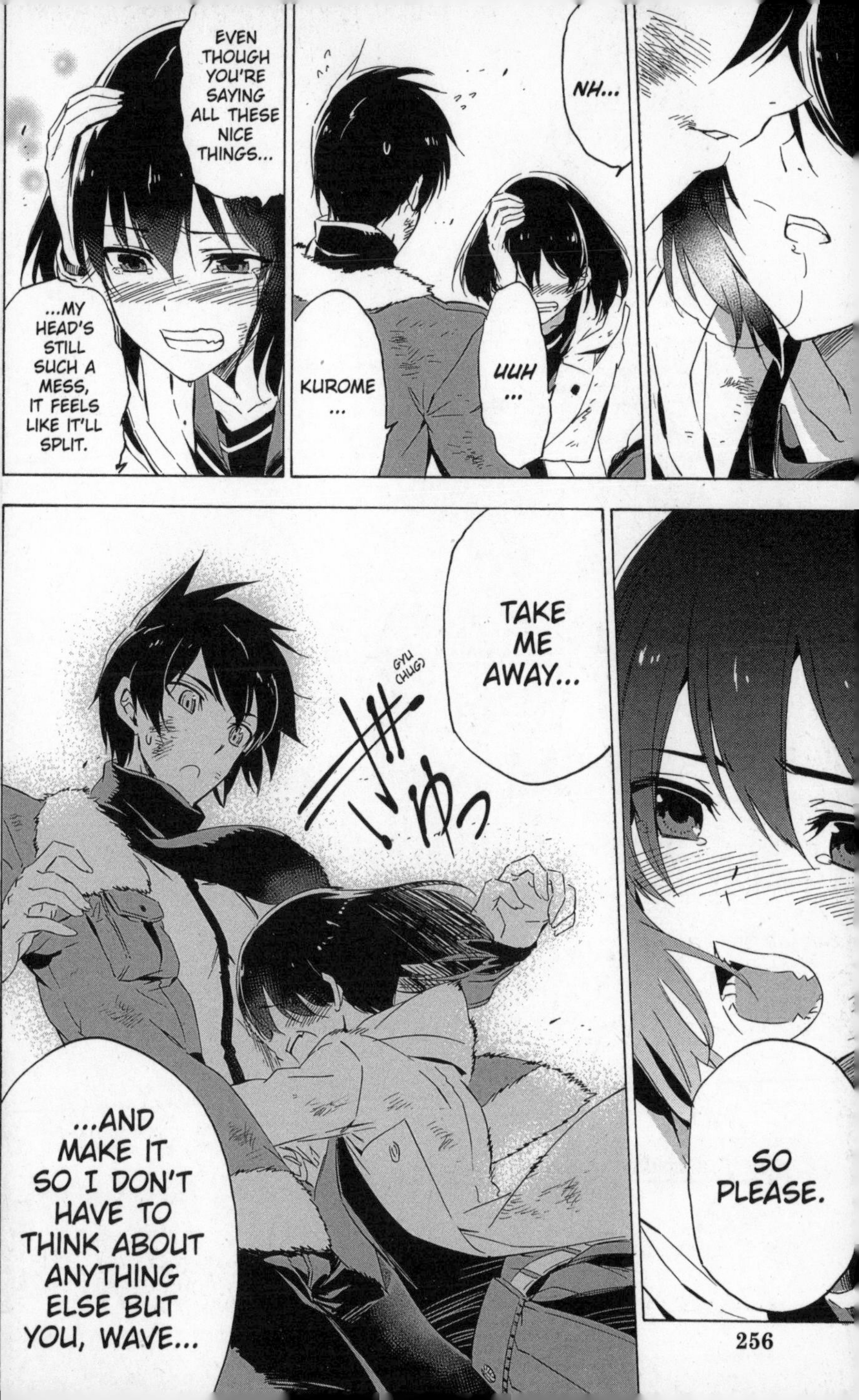
NH...
UUH ...
KUROME ...
EVEN THOUGH YOU'RE SAYING ALL THESE NICE THINGS...
...MY HEAD'S STILL SUCH A MESS, IT FEELS LIKE IT'LL SPLIT.
SO PLEASE.
TAKE ME AWAY...
GYU (HUG)
...AND MAKE IT SO I DON'T HAVE TO THINK ABOUT ANYTHING ELSE BUT YOU, WAVE...

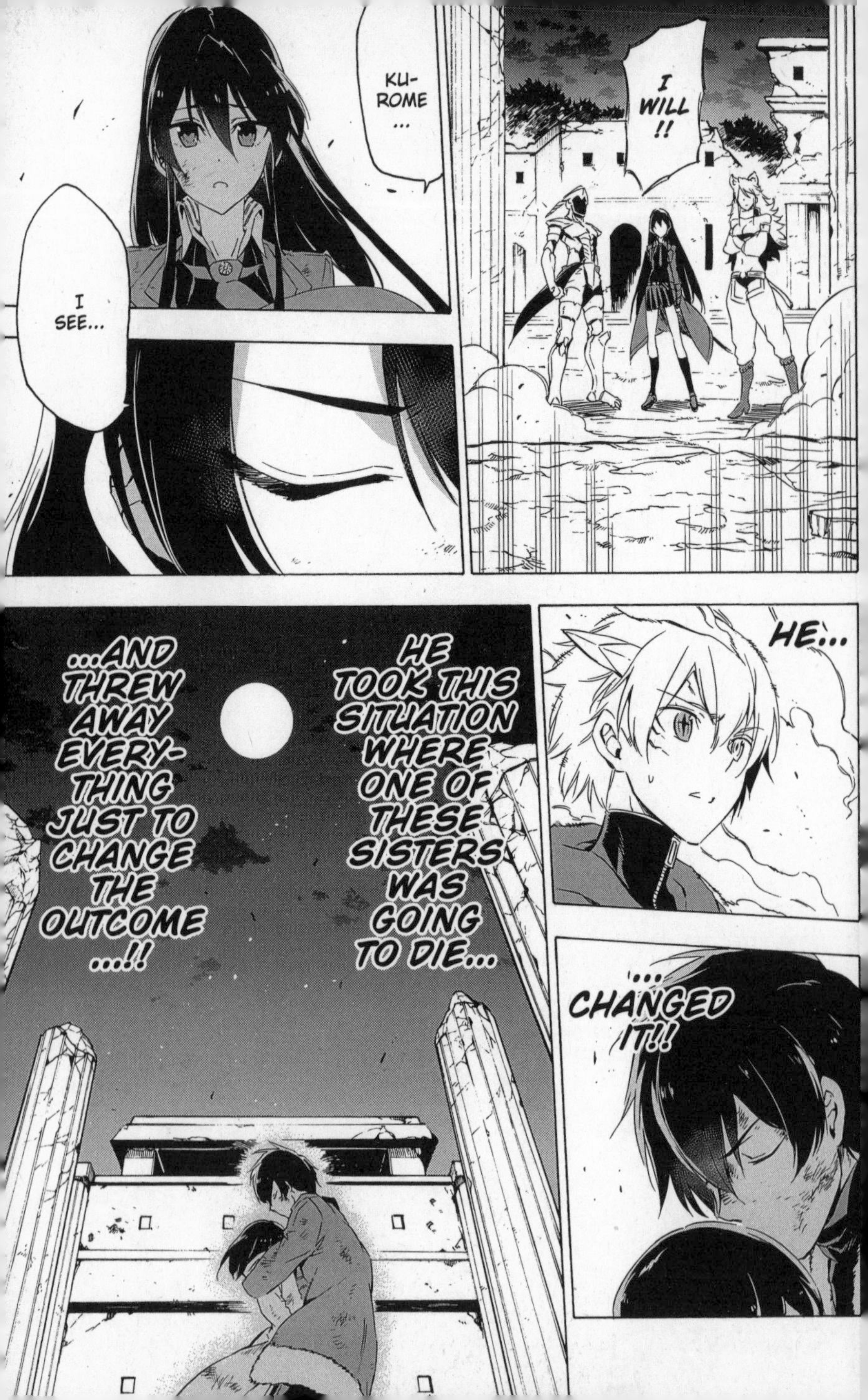

I WILL!!
KU-ROME...
I SEE...
HE...
...CHANGED IT!!
HE TOOK THIS SITUATION WHERE ONE OF THESE SISTERS WAS GOING TO DIE...
...AND THREW AWAY EVERY-THING JUST TO CHANGE THE OUTCOME...!!

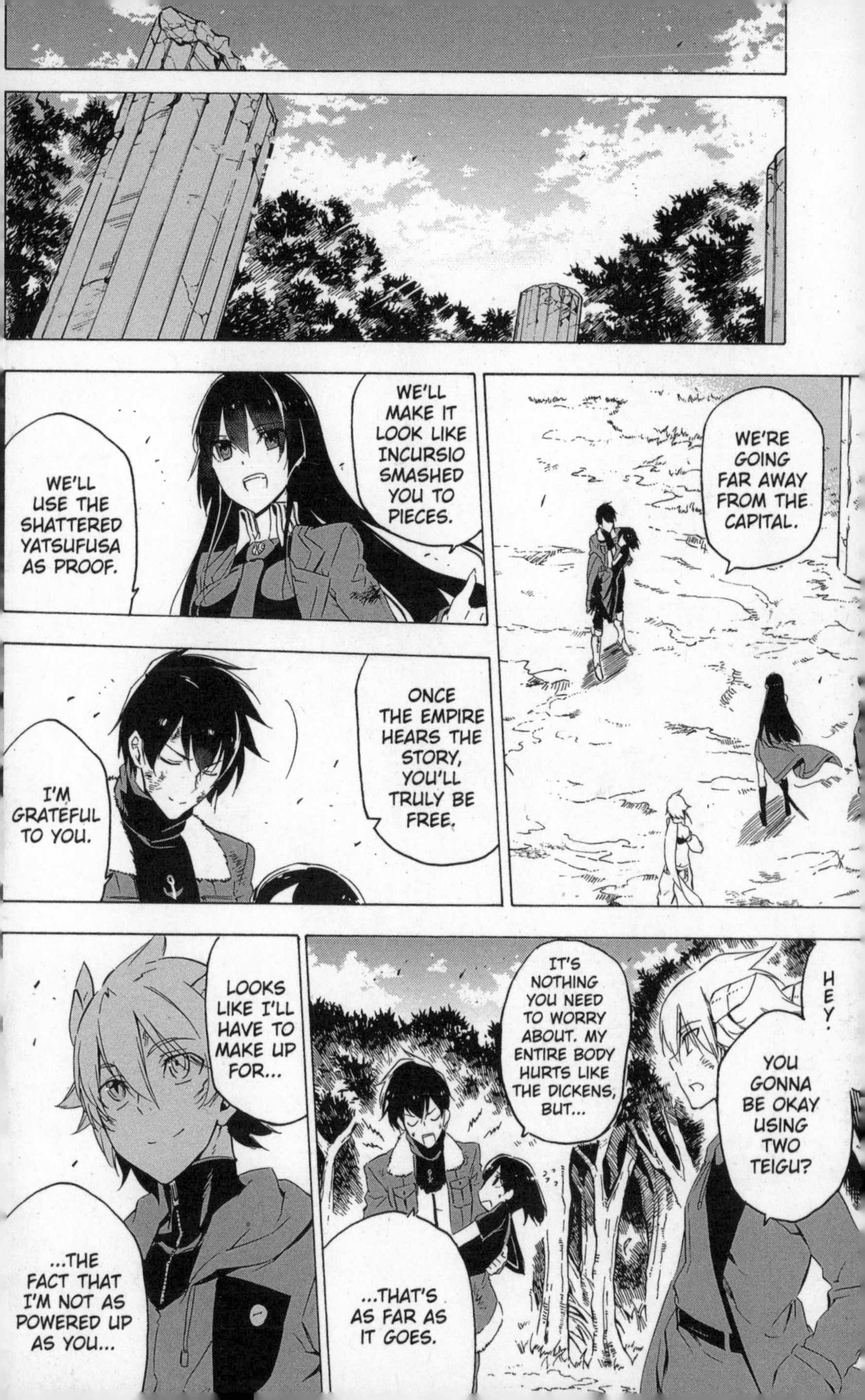
WE'RE GOING FAR AWAY FROM THE CAPITAL.
WE'LL MAKE IT LOOK LIKE INCURSIO SMASHED YOU TO PIECES.
WE'LL USE THE SHATTERED YATSUFUSA AS PROOF.
ONCE THE EMPIRE HEARS THE STORY, YOU'LL TRULY BE FREE.
I'M GRATEFUL TO YOU.
HEY.
YOU GONNA BE OKAY USING TWO TEIGU?
IT'S NOTHING YOU NEED TO WORRY ABOUT. MY ENTIRE BODY HURTS LIKE THE DICKENS, BUT...
...THAT'S AS FAR AS IT GOES.
LOOKS LIKE I'LL HAVE TO MAKE UP FOR...
...THE FACT THAT I'M NOT AS POWERED UP AS YOU...

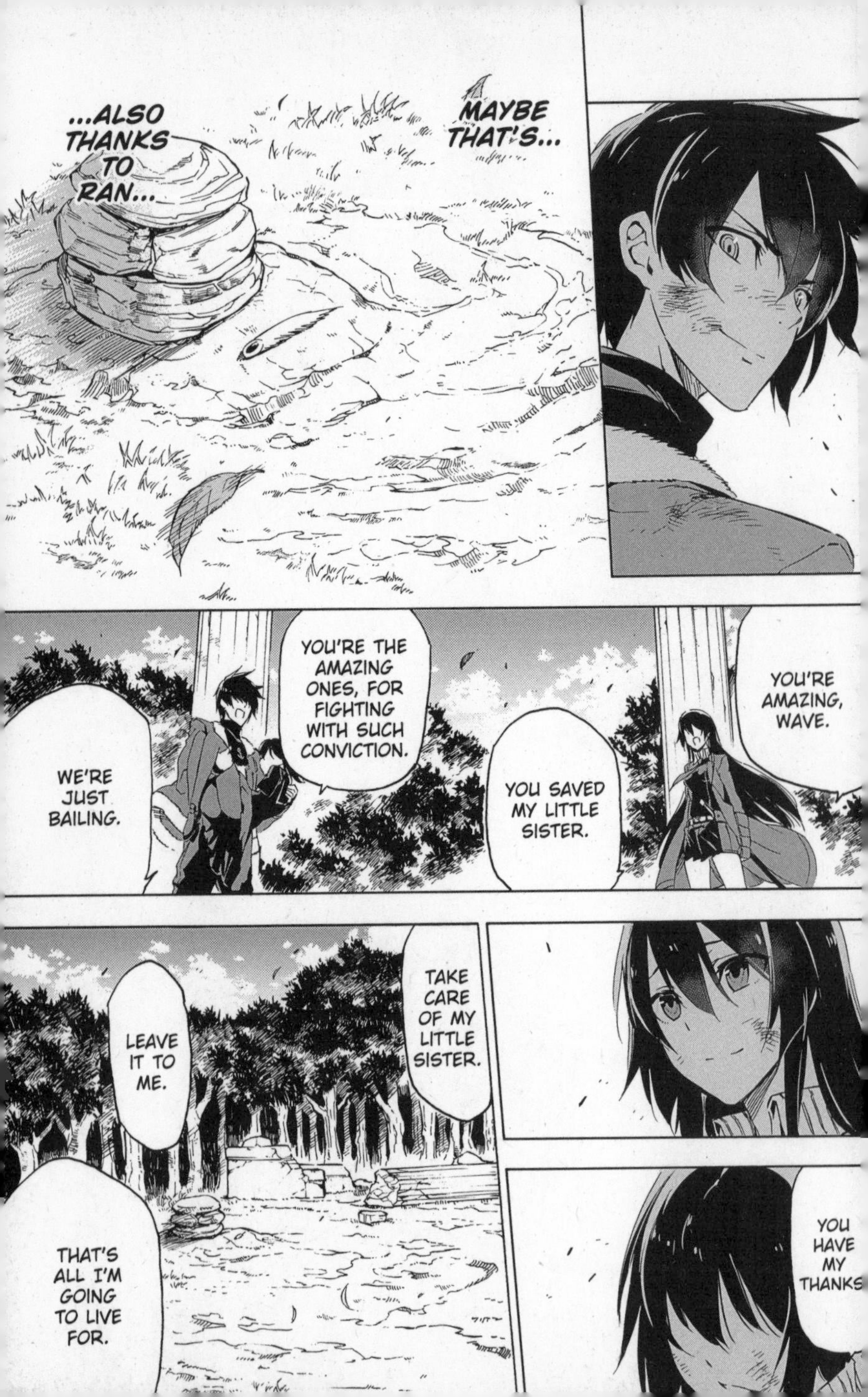
MAYBE THAT'S...
...ALSO THANKS TO RAN...
YOU'RE AMAZING, WAVE.
YOU SAVED MY LITTLE SISTER.
YOU'RE THE AMAZING ONES, FOR FIGHTING WITH SUCH CONVICTION.
WE'RE JUST BAILING.
YOU HAVE MY THANKS
TAKE CARE OF MY LITTLE SISTER.
LEAVE IT TO ME.
THAT'S ALL I'M GOING TO LIVE FOR.

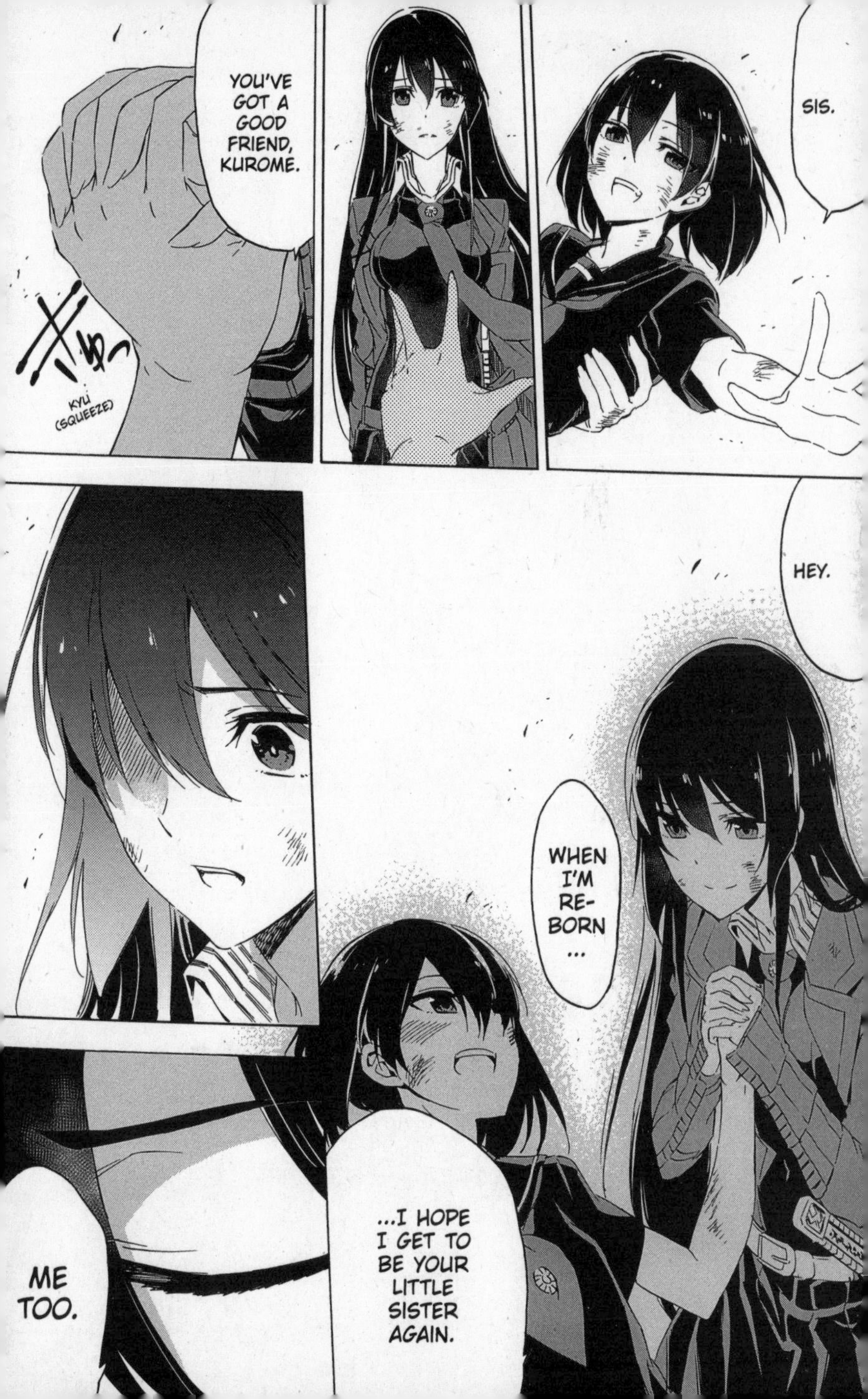
SIS.
YOU'VE GOT A GOOD FRIEND, KUROME.
KYU (SQUEEZE)
HEY.
WHEN I'M RE-BORN...
...I HOPE I GET TO BE YOUR LITTLE SISTER AGAIN.
ME TOO.

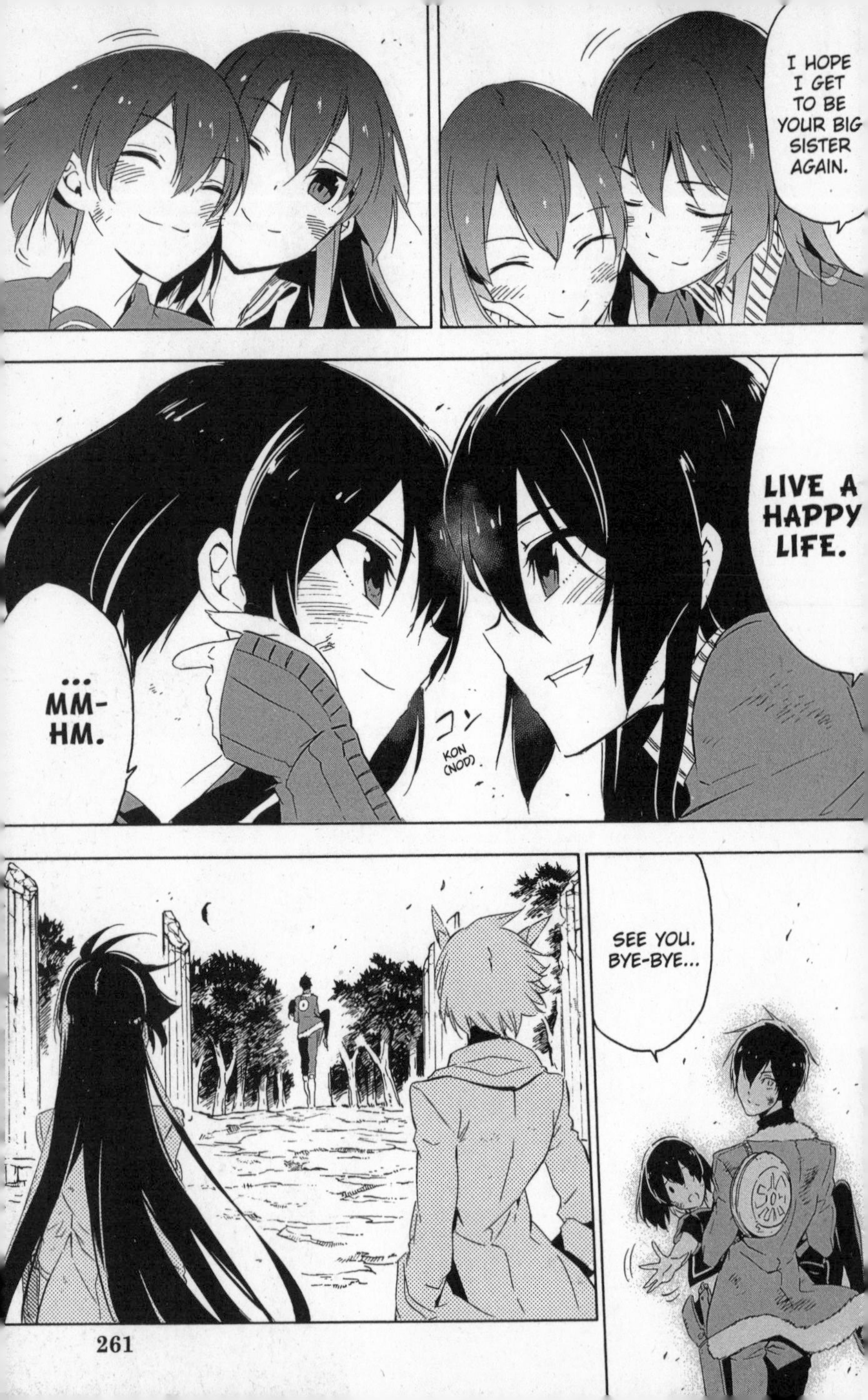
I HOPE I GET TO BE YOUR BIG SISTER AGAIN.
LIVE A HAPPY LIFE.
...MM-HM.
コン
KON (NOD)
SEE YOU. BYE-BYE...

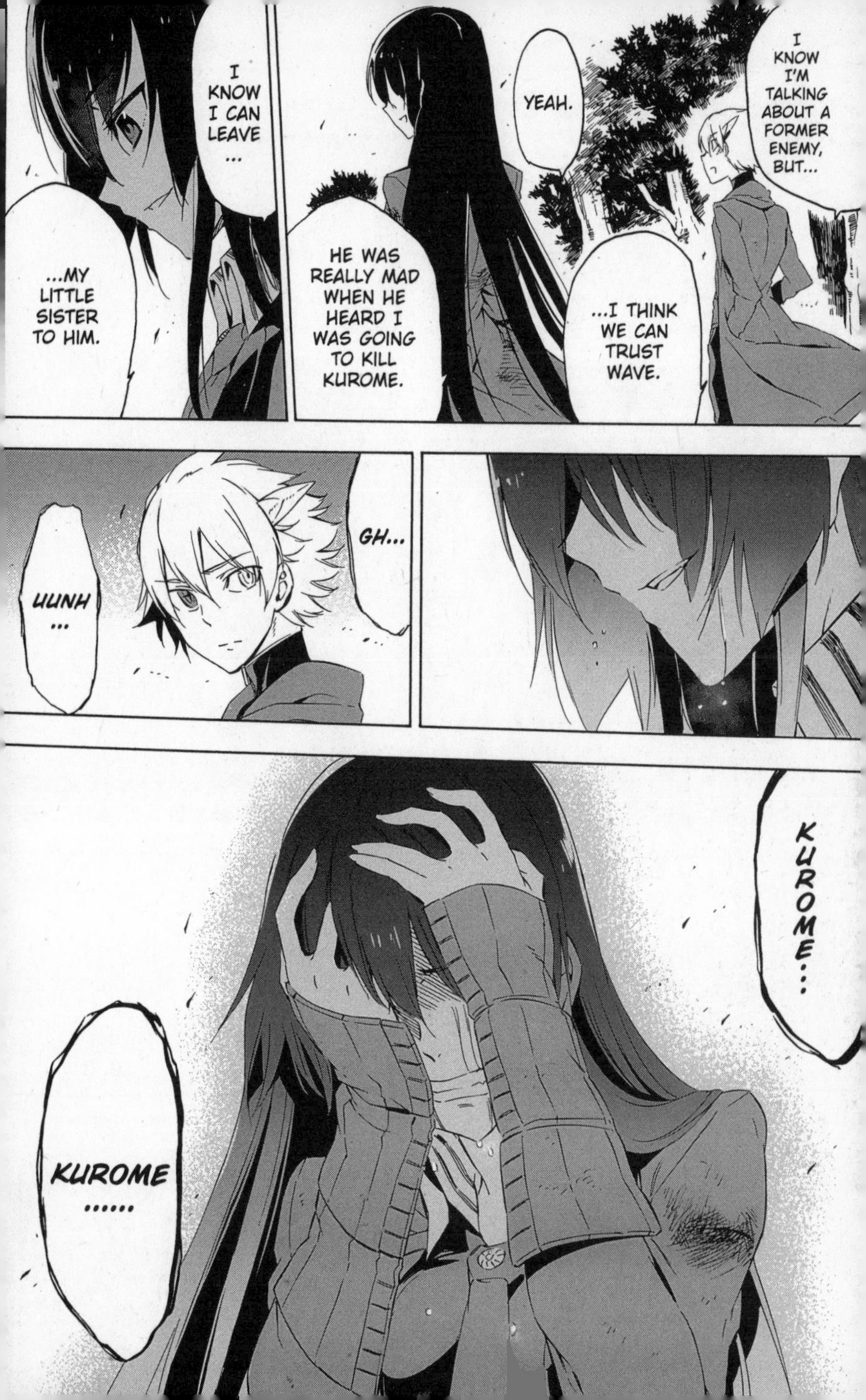
I KNOW I'M TALKING ABOUT A FORMER ENEMY, BUT...
...I THINK WE CAN TRUST WAVE.
YEAH.
HE WAS REALLY MAD WHEN HE HEARD I WAS GOING TO KILL KUROME.
I KNOW I CAN LEAVE...
...MY LITTLE SISTER TO HIM.
GH...
UUNH...
KUROME...
KUROME......

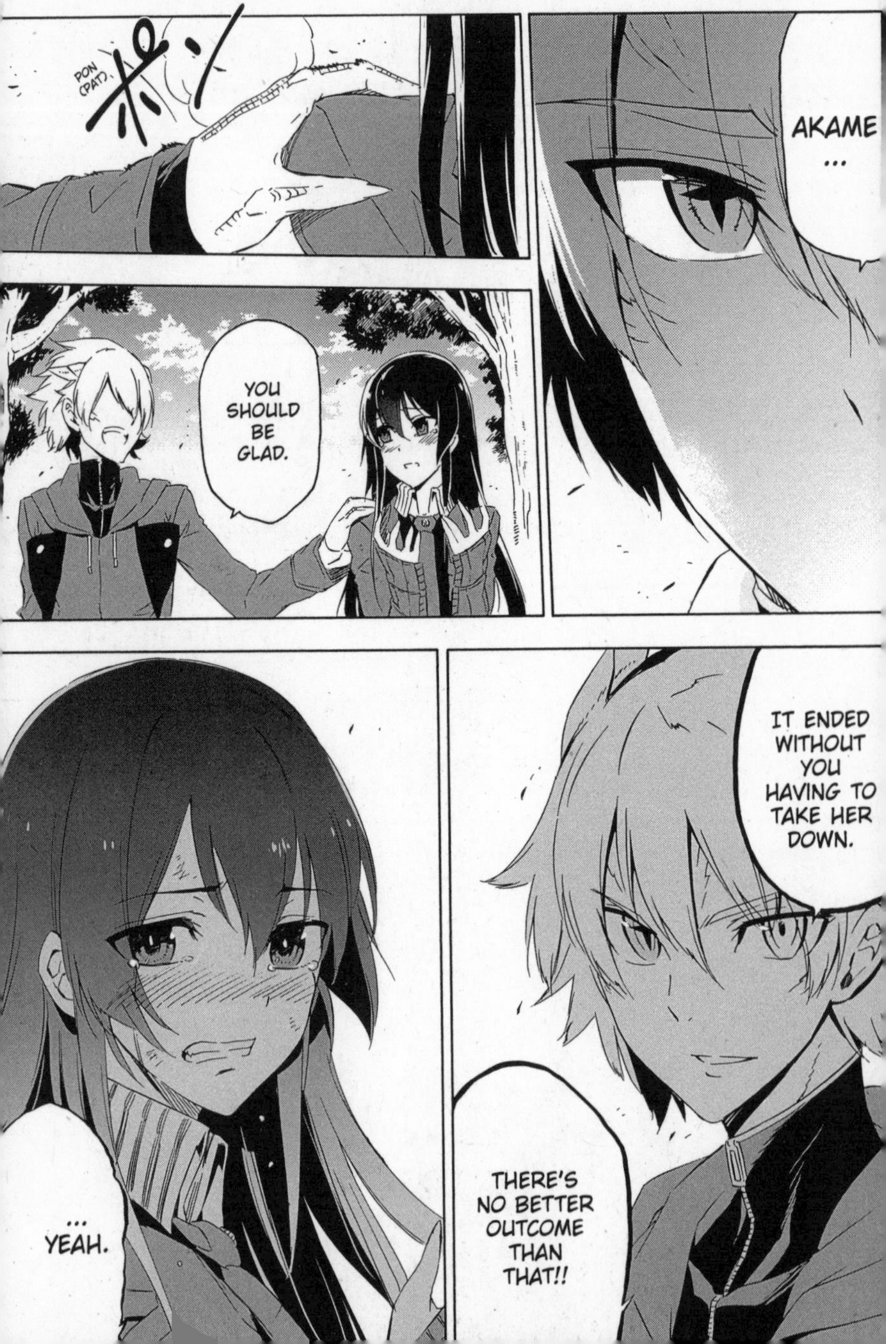
AKAME ...
PON (PAT)
YOU SHOULD BE GLAD.
IT ENDED WITHOUT YOU HAVING TO TAKE HER DOWN.
THERE'S NO BETTER OUTCOME THAN THAT!!
... YEAH.

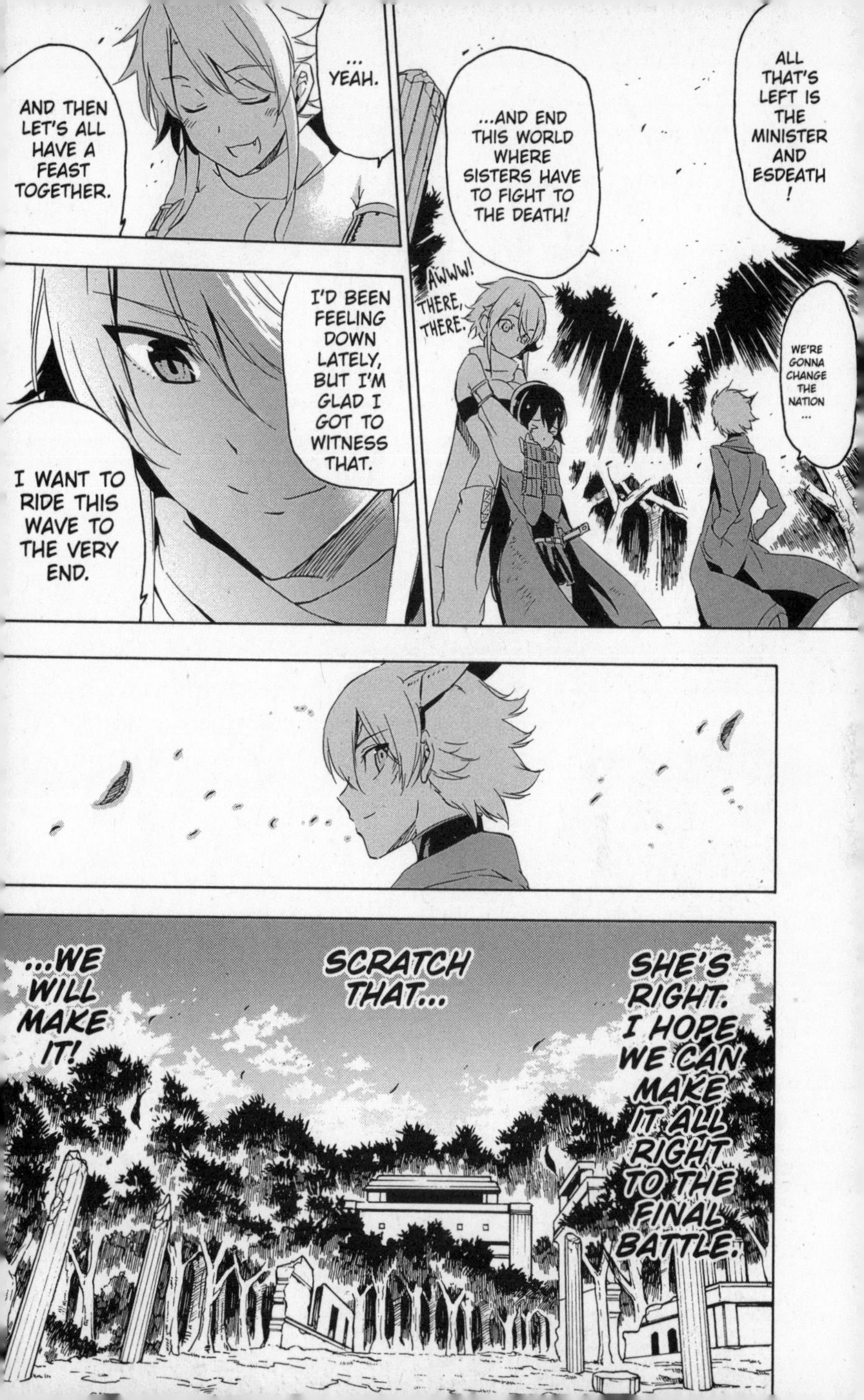
ALL THAT'S LEFT IS THE MINISTER AND ESDEATH!
...AND END THIS WORLD WHERE SISTERS HAVE TO FIGHT TO THE DEATH!
WE'RE GONNA CHANGE THE NATION...
AWWW! THERE, THERE.
...YEAH.
AND THEN LET'S ALL HAVE A FEAST TOGETHER.
I'D BEEN FEELING DOWN LATELY, BUT I'M GLAD I GOT TO WITNESS THAT.
I WANT TO RIDE THIS WAVE TO THE VERY END.
SHE'S RIGHT. I HOPE WE CAN MAKE IT ALL RIGHT TO THE FINAL BATTLE.
SCRATCH THAT...
...WE WILL MAKE IT!

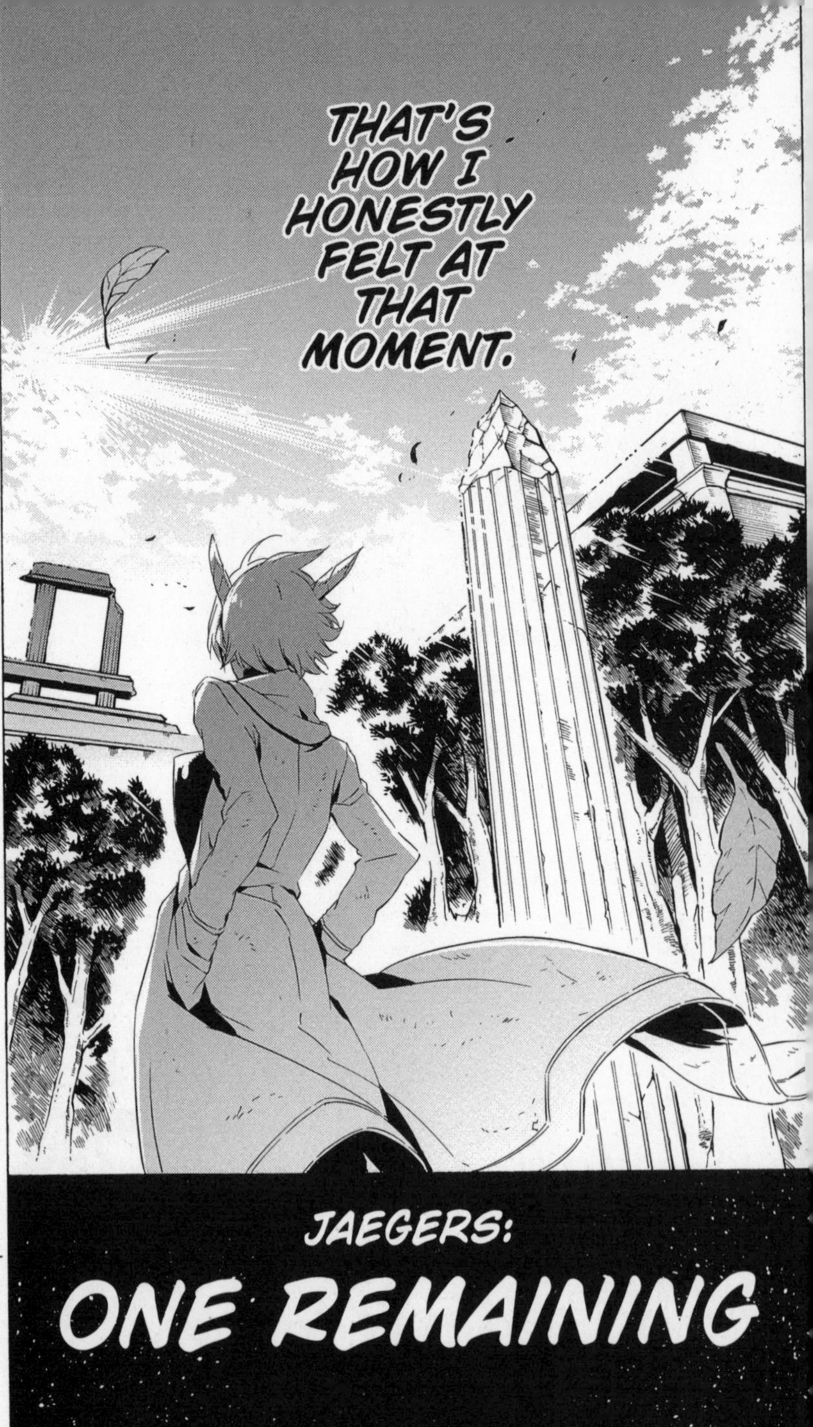
THAT'S HOW I HONESTLY FELT AT THAT MOMENT.
JAEGERS:
ONE REMAINING

AKAME GA KILL! 13 THE END

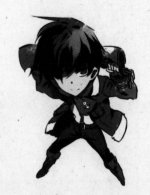

Akame ga KILL!

TAKAHIRO's POSTSCRIPT

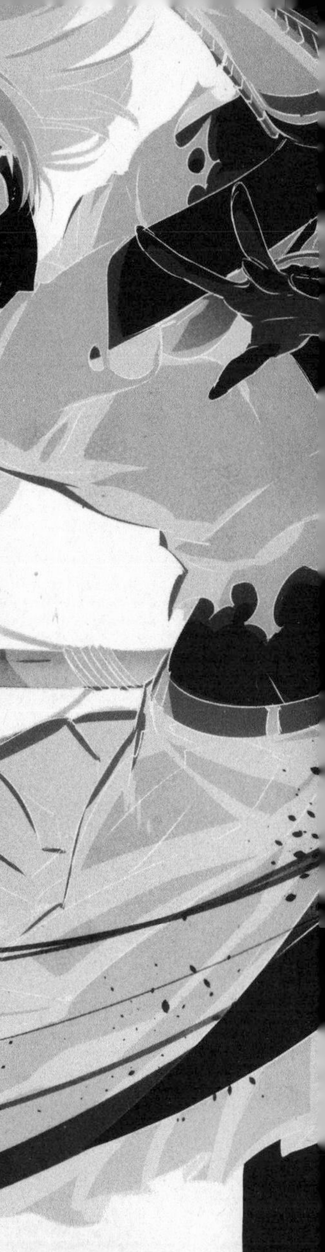

Hello, everyone.
This is Takahiro from Minato Soft.
Thank you for sticking around for the long ride. As always, I'd like to take a moment to give some extra commentary on things from this volume.

●Kurome
She has the makings of a princess, the way her parting kiss with the seaman lit a fire within him. Kurome and Wave's relationship deepened after the incident with Wild Hunt and its leader, Syura, and that has set them on a new pathway toward their destiny.

●Wave
He's the type who gets like this when he becomes impassioned about something. The Empire sees him as a dirty deserter. Kurome sees him as her prince. Witnessing the corruption of the Empire, all the feelings that had been building inside of him exploded. He laid down a hard "NO" to the idea of sisters spilling each other's blood.

●Akame
The "Rest in Pieces" switch was already explained in *Akame Zero*, but as I suspect there are some readers who aren't familiar with *Zero*, I made sure to include it here too. She now has a brother-in-law.

●Esdeath
Sharing the spoils of the hunt with all the other hunters is a way of life for the Partas tribe. Having come from the Partas tribe, she also lives by that culinary custom and often invites her subordinates to join her for a meal and shares her table with them. When she's in a good mood, she'll grill up some meat or cook a pot of stew. (She's a pretty good cook since cooking is a part of being at war.)

●Kairi
Part of the same unit raised on enhancement drugs, as Kurome was. He used to think he'd like to join the Elite Seven, but that never ended up happening. He's a familiar face to the sisters.

Akame ga Kill! 13

Main staff

HIRAIWA-KUN
ITOU-CHAN
FUJINO-SAN
IMAI-SAN

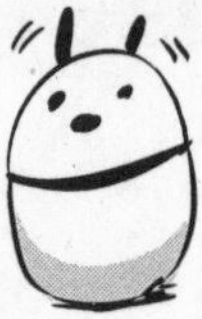

Main Partner

THE AUTHOR
TAKAHIRO-SAN

EDITOR
KOIZUMI-SAN & KIUCHI-SAN

Comment

Is everyone enjoying Monster Hunter? I'm sort of late to the party myself, but hey, it's me, Tashiro.

In October 2015, I got to participate in the Salon del Manga, a convention held in Spain. I'm ever grateful to the event staff and *Akame ga KILL!* fans there.

I'm going to keep working hard in Japan too! So thank you for your support.

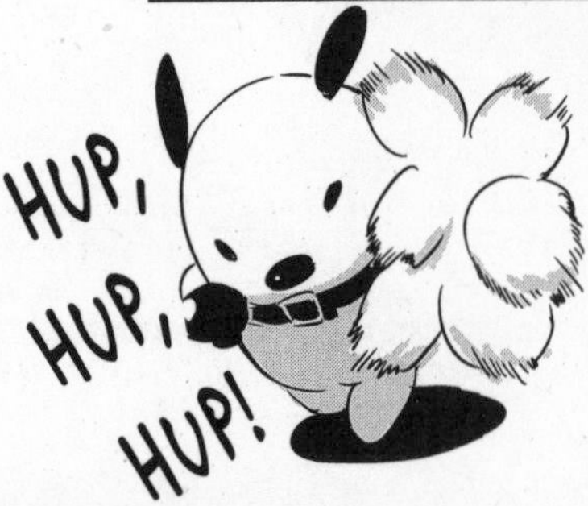
HUP, HUP, HUP!

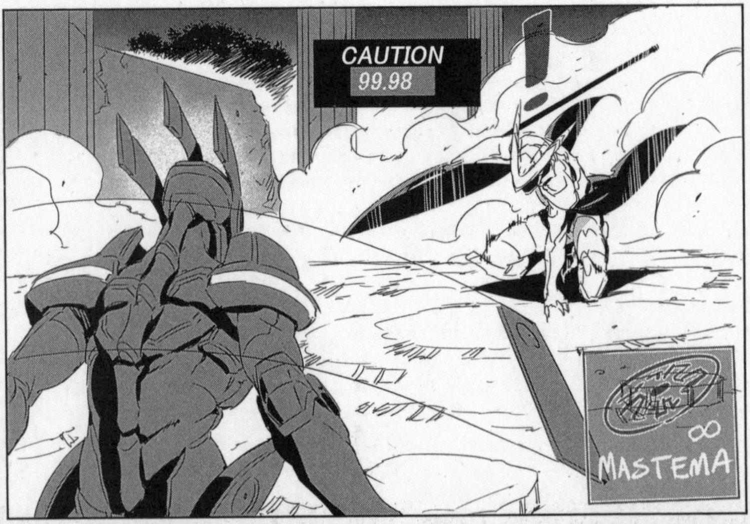
CAUTION
99.98
∞
MASTEMA

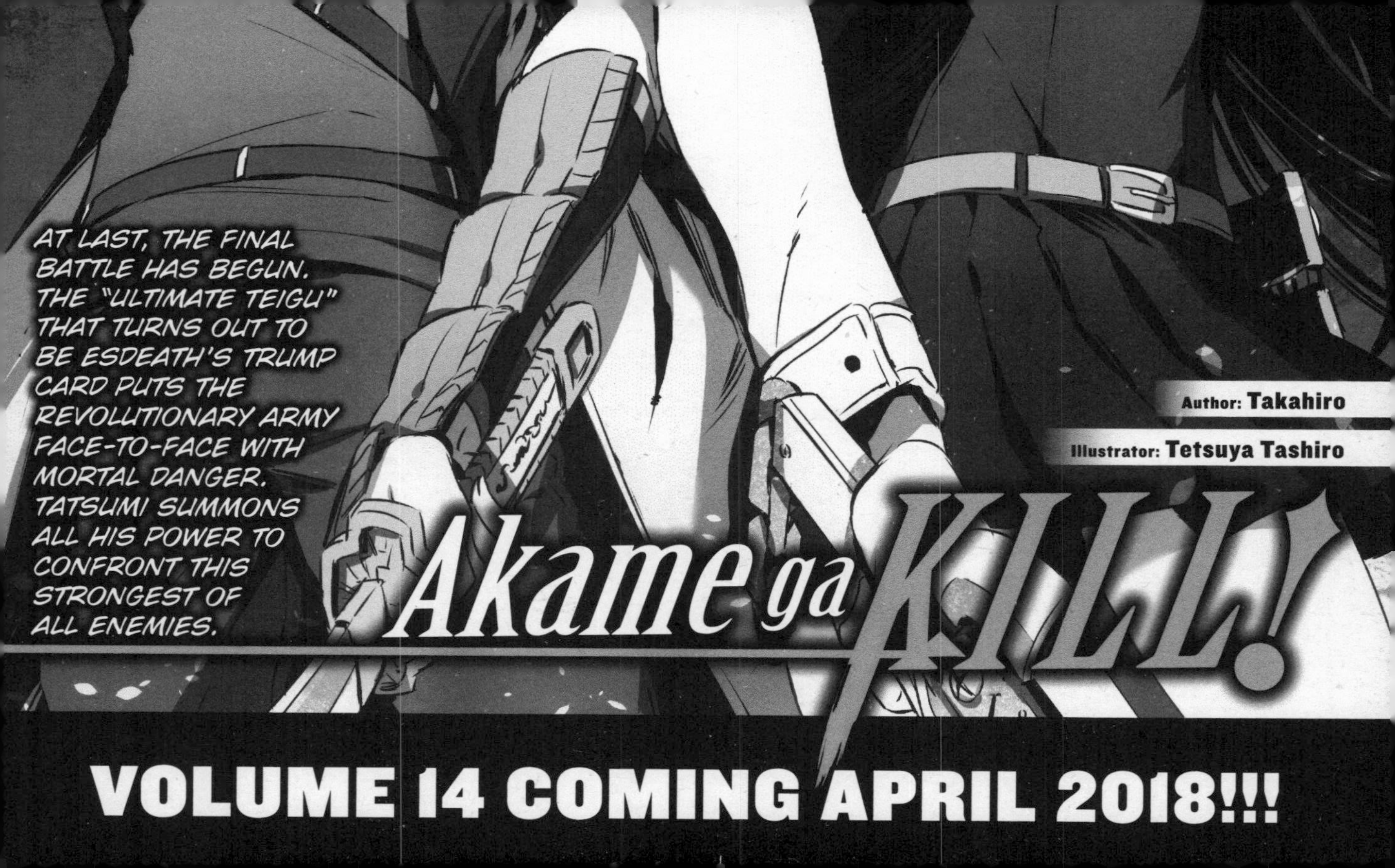
AT LAST, THE FINAL BATTLE HAS BEGUN. THE "ULTIMATE TEIGU" THAT TURNS OUT TO BE ESDEATH'S TRUMP CARD PUTS THE REVOLUTIONARY ARMY FACE-TO-FACE WITH MORTAL DANGER. TATSUMI SUMMONS ALL HIS POWER TO CONFRONT THIS STRONGEST OF ALL ENEMIES.
Author: Takahiro
Illustrator: Tetsuya Tashiro
Akame ga KILL!
VOLUME 14 COMING APRIL 2018!!!

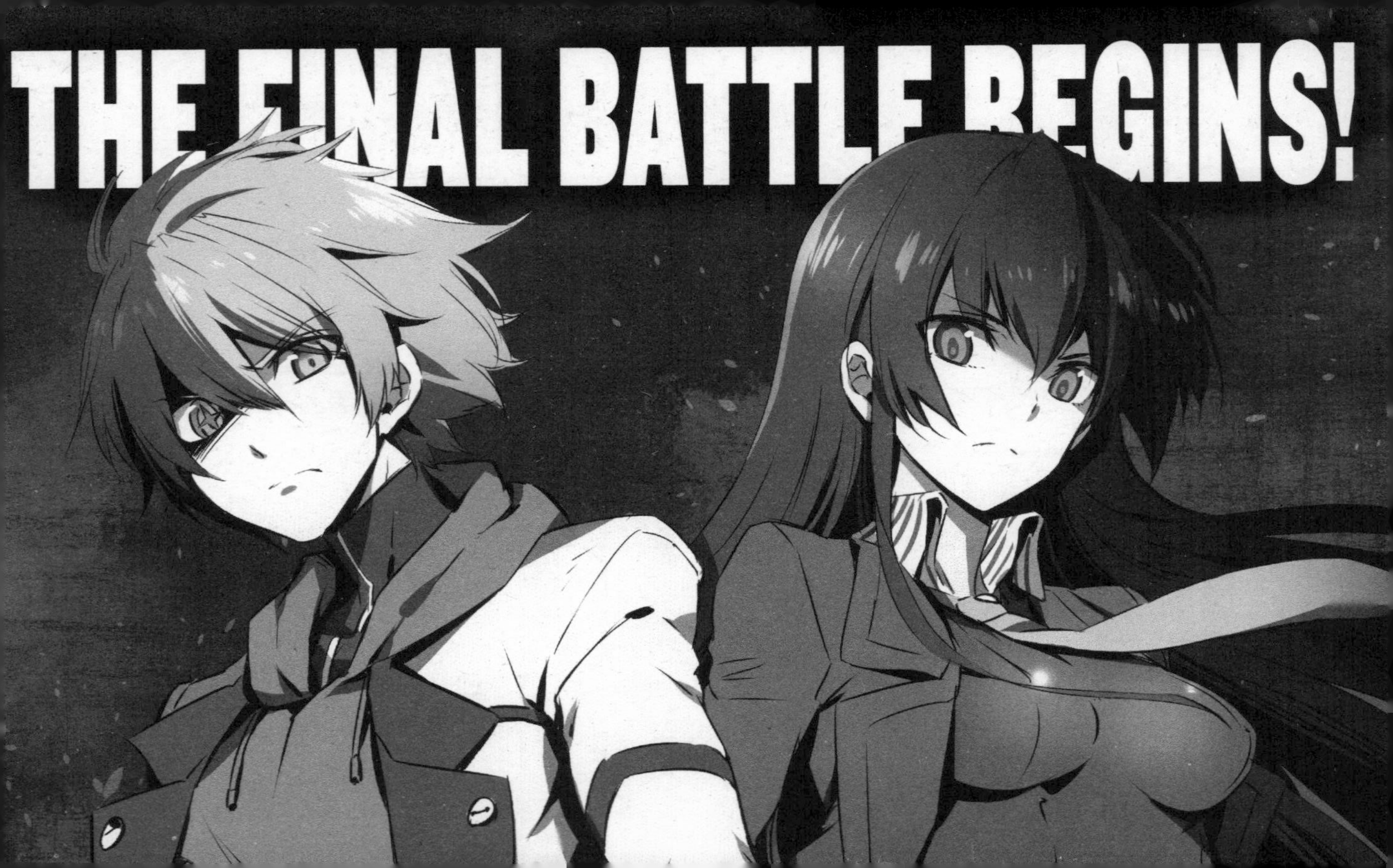
THE FINAL BATTLE BEGINS!

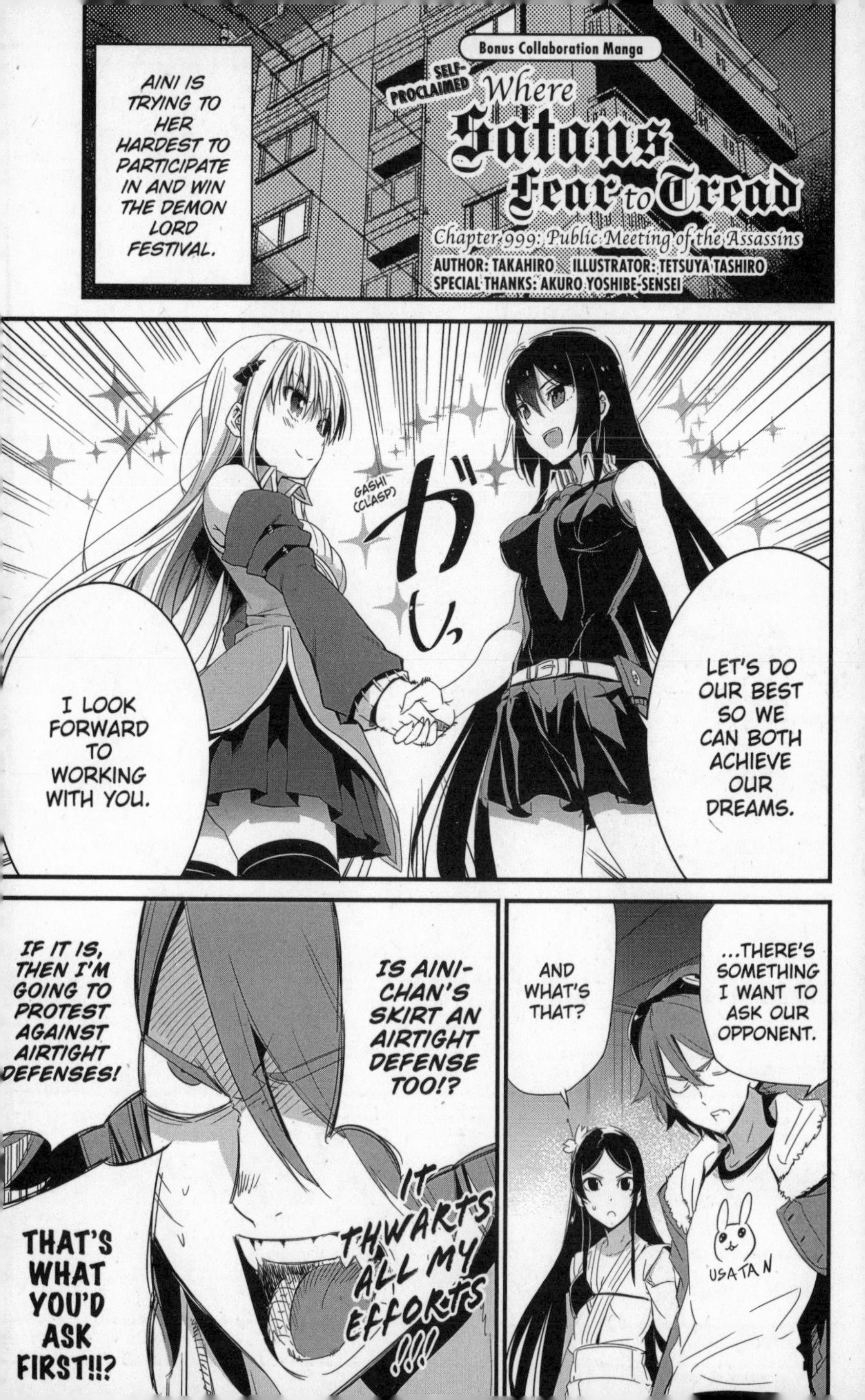
Bonus Collaboration Manga
SELF-PROCLAIMED Where Satans Fear to Tread
Chapter 999: Public Meeting of the Assassins
AUTHOR: TAKAHIRO ILLUSTRATOR: TETSUYA TASHIRO
SPECIAL THANKS: AKURO YOSHIBE-SENSEI
AINI IS TRYING TO HER HARDEST TO PARTICIPATE IN AND WIN THE DEMON LORD FESTIVAL.
LET'S DO OUR BEST SO WE CAN BOTH ACHIEVE OUR DREAMS.
GASHI (CLASP)
I LOOK FORWARD TO WORKING WITH YOU.
...THERE'S SOMETHING I WANT TO ASK OUR OPPONENT.
AND WHAT'S THAT?
USATAN
IS AINI-CHAN'S SKIRT AN AIRTIGHT DEFENSE TOO!?
IF IT IS, THEN I'M GOING TO PROTEST AGAINST AIRTIGHT DEFENSES!
IT THWARTS ALL MY EFFORTS!!!
THAT'S WHAT YOU'D ASK FIRST!!?

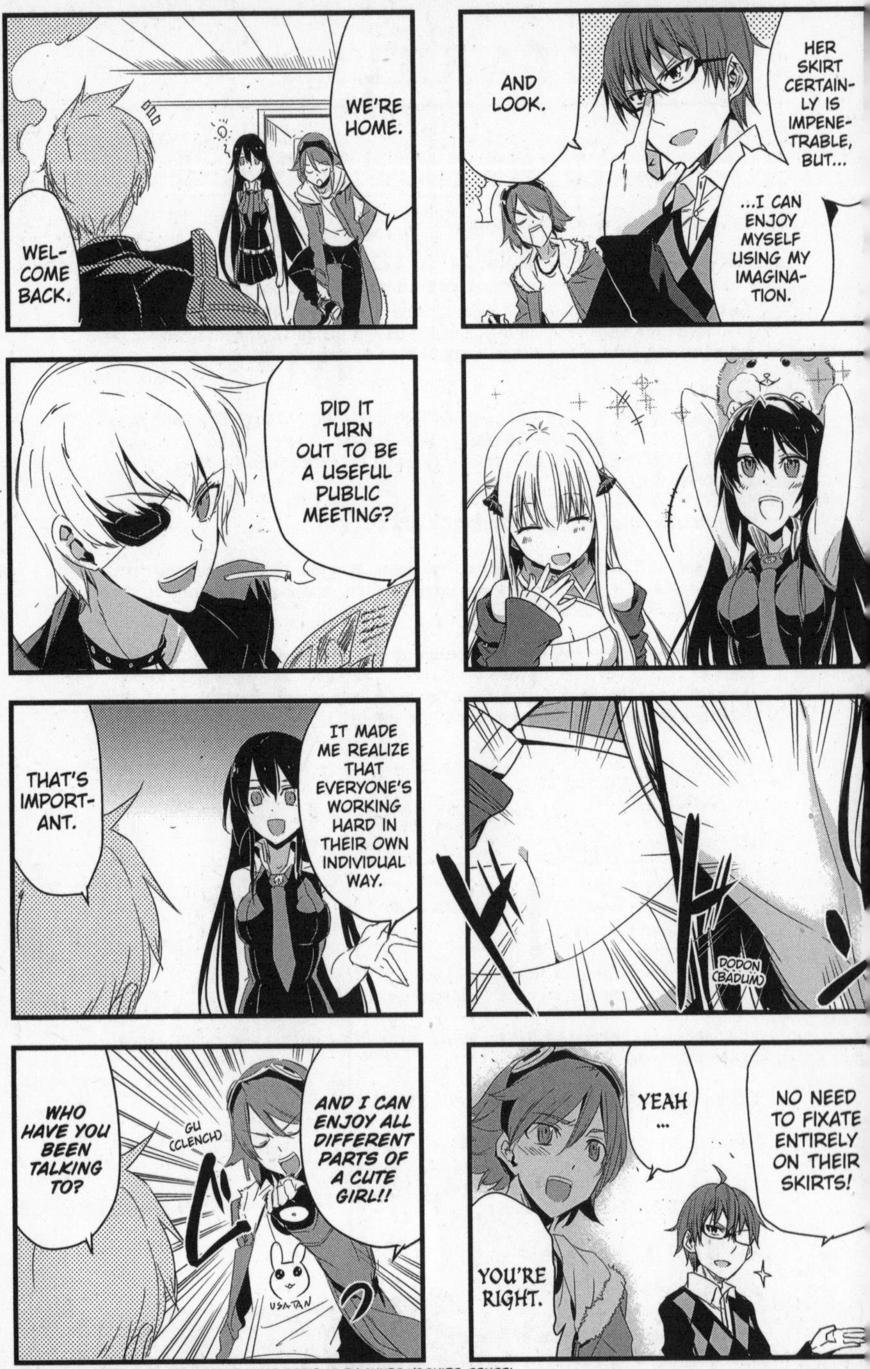
WE'RE HOME.
WEL-COME BACK.
DID IT TURN OUT TO BE A USEFUL PUBLIC MEETING?
IT MADE ME REALIZE THAT EVERYONE'S WORKING HARD IN THEIR OWN INDIVIDUAL WAY.
THAT'S IMPORT-ANT.
AND I CAN ENJOY ALL DIFFERENT PARTS OF A CUTE GIRL!!
GU (CLENCH)
WHO HAVE YOU BEEN TALKING TO?
USATAN
HER SKIRT CERTAIN-LY IS IMPENE-TRABLE, BUT...
AND LOOK.
...I CAN ENJOY MYSELF USING MY IMAGINA-TION.
DODON (BADUM)
NO NEED TO FIXATE ENTIRELY ON THEIR SKIRTS!
YEAH ...
YOU'RE RIGHT.

WHERE SATANS FEAR TO TREAD *CHARACTER DESIGNS BY AKURO YOSHIBE-SENSEI*

AKAME GA KILL! 13

Takahiro
Tetsuya Tashiro

Translation: Christine Dashiell
Lettering: Xian Michele Lee

AKAME GA KILL! Vol. 13
© 2016 Takahiro, Tetsuya Tashiro / SQUARE ENIX CO., LTD. First published in Japan in 2016 by SQUARE ENIX CO., LTD. English translation rights arranged with SQUARE ENIX CO., LTD. and Yen Press, LLC through Tuttle-Mori Agency, Inc., Tokyo.

English translation © 2018 by SQUARE ENIX CO., LTD.

Yen Press
1290 Avenue of the Americas
New York, NY 10104

Visit us at yenpress.com
facebook.com/yenpress
twitter.com/yenpress
yenpress.tumblr.com
instagram.com/yenpress

Yen Press is an imprint of Yen Press, LLC.
The Yen Press name and logo are trademarks of Yen Press, LLC.

The publisher is not responsible for websites (or their content) that are not owned by the publisher.

Library of Congress Control Number: 2015373812

First Yen Press Edition: January 2018

ISBNs: 978-0-316-47335-4 (paperback)
978-0-316-47336-1 (ebook)

10 9 8 7 6 5 4 3 2 1

BVG

Printed in the United States of America

W9-CLN-849